"With the help of attention paid to numerology and the *nomina sacra* the point is the sacredness of the New Testament was not so much an invention of the likes of Origen, Jerome, and Augustine, but much more part of the formation of canonical text as early as the witness of the earliest manuscripts. Even if it seems to the modern mindset something without graspable meaning, the symbolic power of a Christ-focused and aesthetic sense was revealed in the sacredness of his name to the earliest New Testament readers and the likes of Clement of Rome. Picking up on the insights of C.H. Roberts, B. S. Childs, and Theodore Zahn, among others, this is original, important, and edifying work, including a convincing rebuttal of the Sundberg Scripture/canon thesis."

MARK W. ELLIOTT, professorial fellow, Wycliffe College, Toronto, Canada;
professor of biblical and historical theology,
Highland Theological College, Scotland

"The topic of canon continues to be at the forefront of scholarly discussions today. But sometimes it seems we are rehashing the same topics over and over. Tomas Bokedal's new volume is different. It presses these canonical discussions in new and fresh directions. Creative and well-researched, this will be an important volume for anyone interested in the origins of the New Testament."

MICHAEL J. KRUGER, president and Samuel C. Patterson professor
of New Testament and early Christianity,
Reformed Theological Seminary Charlotte

"That the Scriptures are also a material artifact, embodying particular scribal practices, has become a subject of increasing interest. Tomas Bokedal offers us a truly fascinating exploration of the way in which the canon, the rule of faith, and the use of nomina sacra provided the hermeneutical principles for reading the Scriptures. By exploring the familiar (and unfamiliar) material from the first four centuries, Tomas Bokedal offers original and illuminating insights, opening up further dimensions in our exploration of the Scriptures."

JOHN BEHR, Regius Chair of Humanity, University of Aberdeen

Christ the Center

How the Rule of Faith, the *Nomina Sacra*, and Numerical Patterns Shape the Canon

Christ the Center

How the Rule of Faith,
the *Nomina Sacra*, and
Numerical Patterns
Shape the Canon

Tomas Bokedal

LEXHAM
ACADEMIC

Christ the Center: How the Rule of Faith, the Nomina Sacra, *and Numerical Patterns Shape the Canon*

Copyright 2023 Tomas Bokedal

Lexham Academic, an imprint of Lexham Press
1313 Commercial St., Bellingham, WA 98225
LexhamPress.com

The Sylvanus Greek font is used with permission from Accordance Bible Software.

Print ISBN 9781683596301
Digital ISBN 9781683596318
Library of Congress Control Number 2023930857

Lexham Editorial: Derek R. Brown, Mandi Newell, Katy Smith, Abigail Stocker, John Barach, Jessi Strong
Cover Design: Joshua Hunt
Typesetting: ProjectLuz.com

To dearest Anna

CONTENTS

PREFACE

The present volume on canonical shaping and the interconnectedness of scriptural canon, Rule of Faith, and *nomina sacra* highlights Christ and the divine name as the textual and theological center. In the literal sense, the book title *Christ the Center* may refer to the midpoint of the canonical text. For example, the middle paragraph of the Gospel of Matthew contains Matt 16:16, that is, Peter's confession: "You are the CHRIST, the SON of the living GOD," CY ɛI O X̅C̅ O Y̅C̅ TOY Θ̅Y̅ TOY ZⲰNTOC (the 203rd out of Matthew's 405 paragraphs, as per the ancient paragraph division, adopted by *The Greek New Testament, Producted at Tyndale House;* hereafter THGNT). Likewise, the approximate textual midpoint of Mark's Gospel, Mark 9:7, identifies Jesus the Christ by word of God: "This is my beloved SON; listen to him!" (*nomina sacra,* "sacred names," as in Codex Sinaiticus, here in small caps). As we shall see in this book, however, Christ is the center in more than one way.

This book's focus is mainly on first- to fourth-century textual shaping and interpretation. Theologically and hermeneutically, the study engages patterns of textual parts and textual wholes pertaining to Christology, scriptural canon, *regula fidei,* and the early editorial *nomina sacra* practice. Phrasings like "Christ the center" or "the heart of the matter is Christ" well summarize commonalities in all these phenomena: From Luke 24:27 and Ignatius's comment in his *Epistle to the Philadelphians,* "But, for me the Scriptures are JESUS CHRIST," to the second-century canon formation process for which the Rule-of-Faith pattern (*regula fidei*) becomes decisive. It is argued that similar hermeneutical principles—involving the person of Christ at the center of Triune faith—are coming to expression whether we are dealing with the *regula fidei* or with "proof from prophecy," holy writ, and the canon formation process. The second-article Christ concentration of the emerging Rule of Faith, Jesus as the most important *nomen sacrum*, or the Christ-centered Triune exegesis in Irenaeus are all examples of such christological hermeneutics. What in chapter 11 will be labeled "The Rule-of-Faith Pattern as Emergent Biblical Theology" will throughout the thirteen book chapters be closely linked to the *nomina sacra*. These textual demarcations of sacred names such as GOD ($\overline{\Theta C}$), JESUS ($\overline{IC}$) and SPIRIT ($\overline{\Pi N \Lambda}$), found on more or less every page of Greek New Testament manuscripts, may perhaps be best described as an early narrative creedal configuration engrafted into the canonical text(s). Beyond their sheer visibility on the page, these textual highlighters seem to be closely linked also to a new way of viewing biblical canonicity in terms of arithmetic patterns, associated with the Tetragrammaton, that will be presented in the book.

I want to thank Dr. Derek Brown, Dr. Todd Hains, Jesse Myers, Katy Smith, Mandi Newell, Lindsay John Kennedy, and the team at Lexham Press for approval of the manuscript and for helpful guidance and support during the editing process. I am grateful to Daniel Funke and NLA University College for support with indexing and proofreading of the present book. I extend my thanks also to the following institutions and persons for their support, in various capacities, as the included chapters were authored and revised for the present volume: NLA University College, Bergen, Norway, and King's College, University of Aberdeen, United Kingdom; the New Testament Research Seminars at University of Aberdeen and NLA University College; statistician Dr. Stein Andreas Bethuelsen for his input on statistical calculations pertaining to numerology; my doctoral students Zachary C. Bradley, Daniel Funke, Michael Hedrick, Rex J. Howe, Su Young Lee, Sung Min Park, and Dr. Michael Straus; my colleagues and friends Prof. John Webster (RIP), Prof. Larry W. Hurtado (RIP), Dr. Donald Wood, Dr. Nicolai Techow, Dr. Mark Nixon, Rev. Dr. Rune Imberg, Dr. Gunnar Johnstad, and his wife Ingrid Johnstad; Shachar Jacobson; Docent Per Garmannslund; Prof. Gunhild Hagesæter; my friend Per Holmer; my daughters Johanna, Naomi, and

Benedikta Bokedal; and my wife and colleague Anna Bokedal. The anthology is dedicated to my ever supportive and loving wife Anna.

Tomas Bokedal
Aberdeen, Scotland, April 2022

PERMISSIONS

Chapters written specifically for the present volume include chapters 1, 5, 7–10, and 13 as well as the appendix. The following material—republished here with permission and in slightly modified form (chs. 2–4, 6, 11–12)— previously appeared as follows:

Chapter 2: "Scripture in the Second Century," in *The Sacred Text: Excavating the Texts, Exploring the Interpretations, and Engaging the Theologies of the Christian Scriptures*, ed. Michael Bird and Michael Pahl (Piscataway, NJ: Gorgias, 2010), 43–61.

Chapter 3: "Canon/Scripture," in *The Dictionary of the Bible and Ancient Media*, ed. Tom Thatcher, Chris Keith, Raymond F. Person Jr., and Elsie R. Stern (London: Bloomsbury T&T Clark, 2017), 46–48.

Chapter 4: "Canon Formation and Interpretation—Problems and Possibilities," *CCTS Journal* 4 (2013): 9–75.

Chapter 6: "Triune Arithmetical Configurations in the New Testament," in *Names and Numbers: Nomina Sacra and Numerological Editorial Practice in Christian Scripture* (forthcoming).

Chapter 11: "The Rule-of-Faith Pattern as Emergent Biblical Theology," *Theofilos Supplement* 7 (2015): 57–75.

Chapter 12: "Notes on the *Nomina Sacra* and Biblical Interpretation," in *Beyond Biblical Theologies*, ed. Heinrich Assel, Stefan Beyerle and Christfried Böttrich, WUNT 295 (Tübingen: Mohr Siebeck, 2012), 263–95.

ABBREVIATIONS

א	Codex Sinaiticus
A	Codex Alexandrinus
AB	Anchor (Yale) Bible
ABRL	Anchor (Yale) Bible Reference Library
acc.	accusative
ACW	Ancient Christian Writers
ANF	*The Ante-Nicene Fathers: Translations of the Writings of the Fathers Down to A.D. 325.* Edited by Alexander Roberts and James Donaldson. 10 vols. 1885–1887.
Ant.	Josephus, *Jewish Antiquities*
1 Apol.	Justin Martyr, *Apologia i*
B	Codex Vaticanus
Barn.	Barnabas
BHS	*Biblia Hebraica Stuttgartensia*
BIS	Biblical Interpretation Series
C	Codex Ephraemi Rescriptus
Carm.	Gregory of Nazianzus, *Carmines*
Catech.	Augustine, *De catechizandis rudibus*
ch(s).	chapter(s)
1 Clem.	1 Clement
Comm. Jo.	Origen, *Commentarium in evangelium Joannis*
dat.	dative
DBW	Dietrich Bonhoeffer Werke
Dial.	Justin, *Dialogus cum Tryphone*
Did.	Didache

Doctr. chr.	Augustine, *De doctrina christiana*
Ep. fest.	Athanasius, *Epistulae festales*
Epid.	Irenaeus, *Epideixis tou apostolikou kērygmatos*
Eph.	Ignatius, *To the Ephesians*
ex(s).	example(s)
gen.	genitive
Haer.	Irenaeus, *Adversus haereses*
Hist. eccl.	Eusebius, *Historia ecclesiastica*
ICC	International Critical Commentary
Instr. Ps.	Hilary, *Instructio Psalmorum*
JBL	*Journal of Biblical Literature*
JHS	*Journal of Hellenic Studies*
JTS	*Journal of Theological Studies*
KAV	Kommentar zu den Apostolischen Vätern
Leg.	Athenagoras, *Legatio pro Christianis*
LXX	Septuagint Göttingen
LXXG	Göttingen: Vandenhoeck & Ruprecht, 1931–2006
LXXR	Rahlfs, Alfred, and Robert Hanhart. *Septuaginta: Id est Vetus Testamentum graece iuxta LXX interpretes.* 2nd ed. Stuttgart: Deutsche Bibelgesellschaft, 2006.
Migne	Migne, Jacques-Paul, ed. Patrologia graeca. 161 vols. Paris: Migne: 1857–1886.
MnSup	Mnemosyne Supplementum
MT	Masoretic Text
NA28	*Novum Testamentum Graece*, Nestle-Aland, 28th ed.
N.B.	*nota bene*, "note carefully"
Neot	*Neotestamentica*
nom.	nominative
NPNF	*A Select Library of Nicene and Post-Nicene Fathers of the Christian Church.* Edited by Philip Schaff and Henry Wace. 28 vols. in 2 series. 1886–1889. Repr., Peadody, MA: Hendrickson, 1996.
NrN	*Name-related Numerals*
NrNr	The numerals 23/32, 10, 13, 14, and 18

NS	*nomina sacra*
Pan.	Epiphanius, *Panarion* (*Adversus haereses*)
par.	parallel(s)
Phld.	Ignatius, *To the Philadelphians*
Praescr.	Tertullian, *De praescriptione haereticorum*
Prax.	Tertullian, *Adversus Praxean*
RSPT	*Revue des Sciences philosophiques et théologiques*
SBLDS	Society of Biblical Literature Dissertation Series
sg.	singular
Smyrn.	Ignatius, *To the Smyrnaeans*
ST	*Studia Theologica*
Strom.	Clement of Alexandria, *Stromateis*
Symb.	Augustine, *De symbolo ad catechumenos*
TENTS	Text and Editions for New Testament Study
TF	text family
THGNT	Jongkind, Dirk, Peter J. Williams, Peter M. Head, and Patrick James. *The Greek New Testament, Produced at Tyndale House*. Wheaton, IL: Crossway; Cambridge: Cambridge University Press, 2017.
TR	Textus Receptus
Trall.	Ignatius, *To the Trallians*
VCSup	Vigiliae Christianae Supplements
Vit. Const.	Eusebius, *Vita Constantini*
W	Codex Washingtonianus
WA.DB	Luther, Martin. *Werke: Kritische Gesamtausgabe; Deutsche Bibel*. Weimar: Böhlau, 1929–.
WUNT	Wissenschaftliche Untersuchungen zum Neuen Testament
YSH	Yale Studies in Hermeneutics

INTRODUCTION

The leading church father of the second century, Irenaeus of Lyons (ca. AD 125–202), gives us a vivid description of the interplay between the parts and the whole in biblical interpretation. In his apologetical work *Adversus haereses*, he likens the activity of biblical hermeneutics to the artistic crafting of a mosaic, where the scriptural bits and pieces making up the mosaic's whole need to be properly interlinked. To the extent that the hermeneutical artistry is well carried out, with individual passages attaining their proper place within the biblical whole, the result will be "a beautiful image of a king, carefully made out of precious stones" (*Haer.* 1.8.1). Failure in interpretation, on the other hand, says Irenaeus, occurs with arbitrary rearrangement of the biblical material and disorderly scriptural exposition, as performed by the gnostics and others. The esoteric, nonapostolic approach to the biblical texts embraced by the gnostic Valentinians thus results in a quite different outcome, with the whole instead appearing as a very different mosaic, in the distorted shape of a dog or fox.

As we think along with Irenaeus and reflect on his artwork of stones making up a meaningful whole, we may wish to continue exploring the important theme of biblical textuality and interpretation. In the present book, we will set out to do this in two ways. First, we shall presume a biblical text made up of scriptural parts also composing a scriptural whole. Continuous reflection on the canon, especially in chapters 3–10, will, for example, address the issues involved in the scriptural canon formation process and the ensuing unified conception of the Scriptures, which at the time of Irenaeus, Clement, and Tertullian appeared in the form of an Old and a New Testament. Second, we shall continue to reflect on

1

Scripture in the early church through Irenaeus's kingly imagery also in
a related way, namely by closely linking the emerging creedal matrix of
royal christological and Triune structures with scriptural interpretation
(ch. 11) and potential innerbiblical canonical shaping (chs. 5–10, and 13).
The Lyons bishop refers to this textual and doctrinal-canonical pattern
by the expression Rule of Truth (*regula veritatis*) or Rule of Faith (*regula
fidei*), or simply the Faith. Since the key words used to formulate the Rule
of Faith—GOD the FATHER, the SON LORD JESUS CHRIST, and the Holy
SPIRIT—are identical to the key terms also of another group of words,
commonly referred to by scholars as *nomina sacra* ("sacred names," ch.
12), that is, specially highlighted terms in Old and New Testament manuscripts (and beyond), the present book also seeks to relate these two
early Christian phenomena: *regula fidei* and *nomina sacra*.

The title of this book, *Christ the Center: How the Rule of Faith, the
Nomina Sacra, and Numerical Patterns Shape the Canon*, closely relates
to the concerns addressed by Irenaeus's kingly imagery in *Adversus haereses*—how the parts, constituting the total, together may form a both
meaningful and beautiful whole. As a property of the Scriptures, the
Scripture canon may here represent the textual whole made up of textual
parts at the canonical subunit levels; and—as will be argued below—this
canon is shaped, to a considerable degree, by the Triune Rule of Faith
and the affiliated scriptural-editorial system of *nomina sacra*. These textual
demarcations of GOD, JESUS, SPIRIT, and some additional "sacred words"
tend to occur in the text according to arithmetical patterns linked to the
divine name and alphabetical fullness configurations (discussed in chs.
5–10 below). A simple illustration of the latter involves the Hebrew alphabetical fullness numbers twenty-two and twenty-seven (the number of
consonants in the Hebrew alphabet, either excluding or including the five
end-letter forms—*kaph, mem, nun, pe*, and *tsade*), multiples of which were
reflected in the number of books in the Jewish and Christian Bible canons,
and apparently also in certain scriptural word-frequencies. Accordingly,
the early church fathers were aware of a link between the number of
books in the Jewish Bible canon and the twenty-two radicals of the
Hebrew alphabet, where twenty-two served as an alpha-numeric symbol
indicating canonical completion. The twenty-two books of the Syrian

Peshitta and the twenty-seven books of Athanasius's New Testament, too, were likewise arguably associated with such "alphabetical completeness." Analogously, the christological *nomen sacrum* υἱός (Υ̅Ϲ̅), "Son," features 22 times in 1 John and 27 times in the Catholic Epistles (where 1 John is included; THGNT, NA28), the key New Testament term λόγος, "word; speech; reason," appears 22 times in the Catholic Epistles and 330 times [15 × 22] in the twenty-seven-book New Testament (THGNT, NA28) and the *nomen sacrum* combination JESUS CHRIST (Ι̅Ϲ̅ Χ̅Ϲ̅) 44 times [2 × 22] in the Praxapostolos (Acts + Catholic Epistles) and 135 times [5 × 27] in the twenty-seven-book New Testament (NA28).

At the canonical subunit level, we may further note what looks like a series of deliberate *inclusios* (or ring compositions) built around this most frequently occurring *nomen sacrum* combination, namely JESUS CHRIST, such as the genitive form of JESUS CHRIST (Ι̅Υ̅ Χ̅Υ̅). Based on THGNT (in the following identical to NA28, except in Rom 1:1), we thus find the expression JESUS CHRIST (Ι̅Υ̅ Χ̅Υ̅) as a potential *inclusio* involving Gal 1:1 and 6:18 as well as 2 Pet 1:1 and 3:18, that is, the first and final verse of Galatians and 2 Peter, respectively. At the next canonical subunit level, JESUS CHRIST (Ι̅Υ̅ Χ̅Υ̅) as a potential compositional/editorial *inclusio*, involves (1) the first and last verse of the four Gospels and Acts—Matt 1:1 and Acts 28:31 (THGNT, NA28, B, TR; potentially demarcating the four-fold Gospel and Acts as a canonical subunit), (2) the first and last verse of the seven Catholic Epistles—Jas 1:1 and Jude 25 (THGNT, NA28, ℵ, B, A; potentially demarcating the Catholic Epistles as a canonical subunit), and (3) the first and last verse of Pauline Corpus—Rom 1:1 and Phlm 25 (ℵ, A; potentially demarcating the Pauline Corpus as a canonical subunit).[1]

In terms of numerological alphabetical structuring (involving the Hebrew alphabetical numerals 22/27 and the Hellenistic Greek alphabetical numeral 24), similar to that which we find in Ps 119 (with its 22 paragraphs and 24 occurrences of the Tetragrammaton) and other

---

1. The corresponding *inclusio* in NA28 has Χ̅Υ̅ Ι̅Υ̅ in Rom 1:1 and Ι̅Υ̅ Χ̅Υ̅ in Phlm 25. In Codex Sinaiticus Ι̅Υ̅ Χ̅Υ̅ appears as follows: The full New Testament 120 times [5 × 24], the Catholic Epistles 27 times, 1–2 Peter 17 times, Romans 17 times, and Pauline Corpus 78 times [3 × 26]; and Ἰησοῦς Χριστός (all case forms) as follows: The Catholic Epistles 34 times [2 × 17] (see 5.1 below for potential significance of the numbers 17, 24, and 26).

acrostic poetry, we may note, again, that the central New Testament *nomen sacrum* combination Jesus Christ (ι̅ϲ̅ χ̅ϲ̅) features—as a 22-multiple—44 times [2 × 22] in the Praxapostolos (Acts + Catholic Epistles) (NA28, THGNT), 88 times [4 × 22]—again, as a 22-multiple—in the Pauline Corpus (THGNT), and 135 times [5 × 27]—as a 27-multiple—in the twenty-seven-book New Testament corpus (NA28; potentially highlighting, innertextually, these respective texts as complete canonical subunits, for which Jesus as the Christ (ι̅ϲ̅ χ̅ϲ̅) makes up the major theme).[2]

BIBLIOGRAPHY

Lim, Timothy H. *The Formation of the Jewish Canon*. ABRL. New Haven: Yale University Press, 2013.

---

2. We may here note that the numerals 22, 24, and 27, in a Hebrew context, are numbers related to the Hebrew Bible canon, as the following quotation from Timothy H. Lim (*The Formation of the Jewish Canon*, ABRL [New Haven: Yale University Press, 2013], 40–41) indicates: "Jerome considered the twenty-two-book canon to be the count of the majority ('by most people'); the twenty-four-book enumeration is a variant enumerated by 'some.' He also seems to know a twenty-seven-book count when he states that there are five letters of the Hebrew alphabet that are 'double letters' ... that change shape depending on whether they are written at the beginning and in the middle (medial) or at the end (final)."

1

WHAT THIS BOOK IS ABOUT

As a foretaste of the discussion to follow, this first chapter will further appraise the hermeneutical project intrinsic in Irenaeus's imagery mentioned in the introduction by briefly focusing on the dynamics of Christian "Scripture-theology hermeneutics" of the parts and the whole. First, by attending to the structure of biblical and early Christian discourse by means of kerygmatic summary accounts, or faith summaries, made up of *nomina sacra*, pertaining to the interpretative whole (§1.1). Second, by paying special attention to Christ, Triune faith, and the scriptural whole (§1.2). Third, by taking a closer look at the interplay between Scripture and theology in the early Christian period (§1.3). Fourth, by brief reflection on the "biblical Christ" (§1.4). Fifth, by noting some basic aspects of the canon formation process, Triune faith, and *nomina sacra*, and their mutual relation (§1.5). And sixth, by providing a comment on the hermeneutical approach, scope, and outline of the present book (§1.6).

1.1 KERYGMATIC FAITH SUMMARIES
MADE UP OF *NOMINA SACRA*

From early on, Christianity found ways of expressing its faith and identity by means of symbols and summaries of the faith. A noted example is the staurogram (⳨), the ligature of the two Greek letters *tau* and *rho*—signifying the cross—used in early Bible manuscripts as a symbol of Christian faith (e.g., ⲥⲧⲟⲩ in John 19:19; P⁶⁶), and probably also by

5

Emperor Constantine I at his victory in AD 312 at the Milvian Bridge.[1] We recall the classic phrasing, said to have been revealed to the emperor and reviewed by Eusebius: "In this sign thou shalt conquer" (Greek: ἐν τούτῳ νίκα; Latin: *in hoc signo vinces*; *Vit. Const.* 1.28).

An equally famous example of the combined symbol and summary is the expression "JESUS CHRIST, SON of GOD, SAVIOR," conveyed by the secret Christian sign of the fish, and the forceful acronym ICHTHYS (ΙΧΘΥΣ)—the Greek word for "fish"—with its five letters representing the words "Jesus" ('Ιησοῦς), "Christ" (Χριστός), "God's" (Θεοῦ), "Son" (Υἱός) and "Savior" (Σωτήρ).[2] These five words, which are part of the so-called *nomina sacra* ("sacred names") word-group, were from early on specially highlighted terms in Christian Bible manuscripts. With these largely neglected standard text demarcations in mind, the opening verse of 2 Peter (2 Pet 1:1) thus may be rendered as follows (*nomina sacra* with overbars, as in Codex Alexandrinus; English renderings in small caps):

Simeon Peter, a servant and apostle of JESUS CHRIST [I̅Υ̅ X̅Υ̅], To those who have received a faith as precious as ours through the righteousness of our GOD [Θ̅Υ̅] and SAVIOR JESUS CHRIST [c̅p̅c I̅Υ̅ X̅Υ̅].[3]

---

1. For the centrality of the cross in early Christian discourse, see, e.g., 1 Cor 1:17–18 and Phil 3:18. See also the *nomina sacra* abbreviations of σταυρός, "cross," containing the *tau-rho*, in John 19:19, 25, 31 (c̅τ̅ο̅Υ̅; identified by Kurt Aland in P⁶⁶, as noted by Larry W. Hurtado, *The Earliest Christian Artifacts: Manuscripts and Christian Origins* [Grand Rapids: Eerdmans, 2006], 140n22). Cf. also Barn. 9:7–9, where the Greek letter *tau* signifies the cross. On the relationship between the *tau* and the *tau-rho*, Hurtado comments (*Earliest Christian Artifacts*, 147–48): "The Greek letter *tau* was viewed by Christians in the second century CE as a visual symbol of the cross of Jesus. Indeed, Justin Martyr (*1 Apol.* 55) indicates that second-century Christians could see visual allusions to Jesus' cross in practically any object with even the remote shape of a T (e.g., a sailing mast with crossbeam, a plow or other tools with a crosspiece of any kind, the erect human form with arms extended …). … So it seems most reasonable to regard the Christian appropriation of the *tau-rho* ligature as connected to, and likely prompted by this strong *visual* association of the Greek letter *tau* with Jesus' cross. This certainly also fits with the fact that the earliest known Christian uses of the *tau-rho* device are in the special *nomina sacra* writing of the words for 'cross' and 'crucify.' "

2. Cf. also the subtle visual allusion to the ancient Christian symbol of the fish in Caravaggio's *The Supper at Emmaus* (the snag in a wicker basket; see further Kelly Grovier, "The Supper at Emmaus: A Coded Symbol Hidden in a Masterpiece," BBC Culture 18 June 2021; https://www.bbc.com/culture/article/20210617-the-supper-at-emmaus-a-coded-symbol-hidden-in-a-masterpiece).

3. NRSV modified. The following twenty-three opening verses in the New Testament each contain one to six words (or more) from the *nomina sacra* (NS) word-group (i.e., any of the terms: JESUS, CHRIST, LORD, GOD, SPIRIT/SPIRITUAL, CROSS/CRUCIFY, FATHER, MAN/HUMAN BEING, SON,

A form of devotional, kerygmatic textual configuration, embodied by *nomina sacra* demarcations, here bring biblical text and kerygmatic-creedal material in direct contact by graphically highlighting the Greek rendering of the Name (θ͞υ), Jesus as the Messiah (ι͞υ χ͞υ), and a dyadic soteriologial reference, involving God's δικαιοσύνη ("the righteousness of our GOD [θ͞υ] and SAVIOR JESUS CHRIST [c͞p͞c ι͞υ χ͞υ]").

In terms of alphabetical fullness figures (i.e., multiples of 22/27 and 24, as discussed in the introduction above), we may note the following "alphabetical" (*alpha–omega/aleph–tav*; cf. Rev 1:8; 21:6; 22:13) appearances of the aforementioned *nomina sacra* in the canonical twenty-seven-book New Testament—with each of these *nomina sacra* appearances potentially signifying (an aspect of) textual completeness: Twenty-seven occurrences of CROSS (THGNT, NA28), 912 [38 × 24] of JESUS (THGNT), 135 [5 × 27] of JESUS CHRIST (NA28), 378 [14 × 27] of SON (THGNT), 27 of THE SON OF GOD (THGNT, NA28), and 24 of SAVIOR (THGNT, NA28).[4]

1.2 ATTENDING TO CHRIST, TRIUNE FAITH, AND THE SCRIPTURAL-CANONICAL WHOLE

Divine name and christological textual emphases by means of *nomina sacra* demarcations encounter the reader of Greek Old and New Testament manuscripts from the first and second century onward, and the sum appearance of these highlighted words in Christian Scripture has been aptly described by the renowned British papyrologist C. H. Roberts

---

ISRAEL, JERUSALEM, HEAVEN, SAVIOR, DAVID and MOTHER): Matt 1:1 (three NS), Mark 1:1 (four NS), John 1:1 (two NS), Acts 1:1 (one NS), Rom 1:1 (three NS), 1 Cor 1:1 (three NS), 2 Cor 1:1 (four NS), Gal 1:1 (four NS), Eph 1:1 (five NS), Phil 1:1 (four NS), Col 1:1 (three NS), 1 Thess 1:1 (five NS), 2 Thess 1:1 (five NS), 1 Tim 1:1 (six NS), 2 Tim 1:1 (five NS), Tit 1:1 (four NS), Phlm 1 (two NS), Heb 1:1 (one NS), Jas 1:1 (four NS), 1 Pet 1:1 (two NS), 2 Pet 1:1 (six NS), Jude 1 (six NS), Rev 1:1 (three NS).

4. The genitive form of the *nomen sacrum* combination JESUS CHRIST (ι͞υ χ͞υ) features altogether 120 times [5 × 24] in the New Testament of Codex Sinaiticus. The expression υἱὸς τοῦ θεοῦ, containing two *nomina sacra*, further occurs 17 times in the New Testament, and ὁ θεός appears 986 times [58 × 17] (for potential numerological significance of the number 17, affiliated with the Tegragrammaton, see table 5.1, ch. 5 below). If these alphabetical structures in the New Testament—listed in the main text above—are just randomly appearing (ch. 5 below argues to the contrary), the probability that these word-frequency multiples will appear in each case (for numbers between one and five hundred) is ca. 11 percent (or ca. one in nine random occurrences).

as "the embryonic creed of the first Church."[5] The German theologian
Dietrich Bonhoeffer (1906–1945), reflecting on this hermeneutically interesting aspect of the Christian manuscript tradition, memorably comments
on the basic *nomen sacrum* JESUS (I͞C, I͞H, I͞H͞C): "It is good, now and then,
to remind oneself of the times of the handwritten and illustrated Bibles,
in which the name of Jesus was rendered with special reverence and
beauty."[6] Prominent representations of the *nomen sacrum* CHRIST (X͞C, X͞P,
X͞P͞C) may also be noticed, as in the Book of Kells (ca. AD 800), where
the meticulously decorated *chi-rho* abbreviation (X͞P), signifying Christ,
may fill up a whole page.[7]

   Related scriptural christological emphases are variously and widely
conveyed in the early Christian centuries, for example, in the writings
of Clement of Alexandria (ca. AD 150–215), who relates Christ the Lord
to the Scriptures in the following words: "We have the Lord as the first
principle of our teaching, leading us to knowledge, from beginning to end,
in many and various ways through the Prophets, through the Gospel and
through the blessed Apostles" (*Strom.* 7.16.95).[8] Similarly Origen (ca. AD
185–254), Clement's student, as he comments on the christological unity
of the Scriptures: "All the Scriptures are one book because all the teaching [λόγον] that has come to us about Christ is recapitulated in one single
whole" (*Comm. Jo.* 5.6).[9]

---

5. C. H. Roberts, *Manuscript, Society and Belief in Early Christian Egypt*, Schweich Lectures 1977 (Oxford: Oxford University Press, 1979), 46.

6. Dietrich Bonhoeffer, *Illegale Theologenausbildung: Finkenwalde 1935–1937*, DBW 14 (Gütersloh: Gütersloher Verlagshaus, 1996), 510 (author's translation).

7. See https://www.bbc.com/culture/article/20160425-the-book-of-kells-medieval-europes-greatest-treasure.

8. The expression ὁ κύριος, the LORD, occurs altogether 351 times [13 × 27 = 3 × 3 × 39; cf. table 5.1 in ch. 5 below, for potential significance of 39] in the New Testament (THGNT; the corresponding figure in the Byzantine Greek New Testament [TF 35] is 364 [14 × 26]; cf. table 5.1, ch. 5 below, for potential significance of 26).

9. In terms of alphabetical completeness figures (i.e., multiples of 22/27 and 24, as discussed in the introduction above), we may note the 540 occurrences [20 × 27] in the New Testament, the 396 [18 × 22] in Pauline Corpus, and the 48 [2 × 24] in 2 Corinthians of words beginning with the three Greek letters χρι* (as in the words χρῖσμα, "anointing, anointment,," Χριστιανός, "Christian," Χριστός, "Christ, Messiah," and χρίω, "to anoint"); see also alphabetical word-frequencies for Ἰησοῦς χριστός, JESUS CHRIST, above, with 135 [5 × 27] appearances in the twenty-seven-book New Testament (NA28), 88 [4 × 22] in Pauline Corpus (THGNT), and 44 [2 × 22] in the Praxapostolos (THGNT, NA28).

Similar to the christological Scripture reading of Irenaeus, Clement, and Augustine (AD 354–430), the christological program of the Bible translator and expositor Martin Luther (ca. 1483–1546) analogously places Christ at the heart of the exegetical project. Christ is held to be the *scopus* of Scripture, the central figure and point of view. Christ, and the righteousness brought by him, become the beginning and end of scriptural interpretation. On a general hermeneutical note, the German philosopher Hans-Georg Gadamer (1900–2002) quotes Luther in this connection: "Whoever does not understand the subject matter, cannot elicit the sense from the words" (*Qui non intelligit res, non potest ex verbis sensum elicere*).[10] Luther variously portrays Christ as the heart of Scripture, stating that "Holy Scripture is that which 'urges Christ.'"[11] "The whole Scripture is about Christ alone everywhere, if we look to its inner meaning, though superficially it may sound different." Christ is "the sun and truth in Scripture." He is the geometrical center of the Bible. He is the point from which the whole circle is drawn.[12] Said differently—as phrased by Michael Straus, a contemporary American Bible translator—"the essence of the divine communication in *both* Testaments is Jesus Christ as their common subject matter (*die Sache*)—with the Bible's 'twofoldness' reflecting 'a mutually constitutive relationship' in that revelation."[13] Hence, whoever wants

10. Hans-Georg Gadamer, *Truth and Method*, trans. Joel Weinsheimer and Donald Marshall, 2nd ed. (New York: Continuum, 1989), 171.

11. Martin Hengel with Roland Deines, *The Septuagint as Christian Scripture: Its Prehistory and the Problem of Its Canon* (London: T&T Clark, 2002), 54, translating Luther's dictum, *ob sie Christum treibet*; WA.DB 7:384.

12. Luther citations taken from A. Skevington Wood, *Luther's Principles of Biblical Interpretation* (London: Tyndale Press, 1960); https://biblicalstudies.org.uk/pdf/tp/luther_wood.pdf.

13. Michael Straus ("The Word as Word: A Canonical-Hermeneutical Approach to Translation with Paul's Letter to the Colossians as a Test Case" [PhD diss., University of Aberdeen, 2021], 42), with reference to Francis Watson (*Text and Truth: Redefining Biblical Theology* [Edinburgh: T&T Clark; Grand Rapids: Eerdmans, 1997], 187) and Constantine R. Campbell and Jonathan T. Pennington (*Reading the New Testament as Christian Scripture* [Grand Rapids: Baker Academic, 2020], 3), who write: "we embrace the biblical canon as twofold, Old and New Testaments together ... both parts of the Christian canon mutually inform each other. At the same time, the New Testament claims to provide the ultimate revelation of God himself in Christ. This Logos, the Son, who is ever with the Father and has been incarnated at a time in history in Jesus, together with the indwelling Spirit, witnesses to the mystery of the Trinity. This is no small matter. This means that because of the fullness of revelation now given in the new covenant, all of the Bible should be read with the knowledge of the Triune God at hand, even though the Hebrew Scriptures do not explicitly speak in this way. This reading backward of the whole Bible is an important element in what it means to read Christianly."

to understand a biblical, or any other, text appropriately, Luther and Gadamer remind us, must "ask for its principal intention, the central point of view, i.e. its *scopus*."[14] In Gadamer's phrasing: "The grasp of the *scopus* forms the basis for the endless nuancing work involved in understanding."[15]

In modern biblical scholarship, this classic hermeneutical approach, pertaining to textual centeredness, has been adopted, in part, by scholars such as Brevard Childs, Peter Stuhlmacher, and Ulrich Luz.[16] In his distinguished Hermeneia series commentary on Matthew's Gospel, reflecting on method in New Testament studies, Luz thus can write:

One does not have to read the Bible in this way, but one must do so in order to read it as Christian Scripture." Similarly, Watson, *Text and Truth*, 179–80. For different scholarly approaches in this regard, see, e.g., Watson, *Text and Truth*, 181; and John Goldingay, *Do We Need the New Testament? Letting the Old Testament Speak for Itself* (Downers Grove, IL: IVP Academic, 2015).

14. Hans-Georg Gadamer, *Gadamer in Conversation: Reflections and Commentary*, ed. and trans. Richard E. Palmer, YSH (New Haven: Yale University Press, 2001), 52; and Tomas Bokedal, *The Formation and Significance of the Christian Biblical Canon: A Study in Text, Ritual and Interpretation* (London: Bloomsbury T&T Clark, 2014), 231–34.

15. Gadamer, *Gadamer in Conversation*, 52.

16. Brevard S. Childs, *Biblical Theology of the Old and New Testaments: Theological Reflection on the Christian Bible* (London: SCM, 1992); Childs, *Biblical Theology: A Proposal*, Facets (Minneapolis: Fortress, 2002). Cf. Stuhlmacher's (*Biblical Theology of the New Testament*, translated and edited by Daniel P. Bailey with the collaboration of Jostein Ådna [Grand Rapids, Eerdmans, 2018], 7, 815–18) comparison of Childs's independent treatment of the Old and New Testaments with Charles H. H. Scobie's unified approach to biblical theology (*The Ways of Our God: An Approach to Biblical Theology* [Grand Rapids: Eerdmans, 2003]). Regarding Childs's methodological approach, Stuhlmacher (*Biblical Theology of the New Testament*, 773) comments: "[Childs] stresses that the independent witness of the Hebrew Bible must not be prematurely fused with the likewise independent witness of the New Testament, but that both parts of the Christian canon must first be properly understood and appreciated in their own right. In this connection Childs also points to the fundamental importance of three factors: Yahweh's self-revelation in his name, his gracious self-disclosure to Israel in the covenant (cf. Exod 34), and his 'unity and uniqueness (Deut 6.4f.) which calls for utter devotion—heart, soul, and might.'" Stuhlmacher, *Biblical Theology of the New Testament*, 772: "New Testament exegesis does well to bring its results into a working relationship with dogmatics. Exegesis cannot and will not be denied its own dogmatic judgments, but the exegetical enterprise will end only in dilettantism if it thinks it is able to do the work of dogmatics on its own or to make it superfluous. This applies also to the difficult and still explosive theological question about the center of Scripture. When this question is raised, biblical exegesis can do no better than to discuss the debated facts and texts with all the methods at its disposal. But exegesis must also respect the fact that it does not solely or conclusively make the decision about the Scripture and its center. The search for the center of Scripture raises a whole set of debated problems: How are the Old and New Testaments related? Is it possible to comprehend the various New Testament traditions under a single theological perspective, or are they so different that they disallow any such panoramic view? How should we evaluate the ancient church's efforts to summarize the entire faith tradition in the so-called 'rule of faith' and the two-part biblical canon?"

The interpretations of the ancient church, the Middle Ages, and the early modern period before the Enlightenment are of abiding importance, because they always connect an individual biblical text to the entirety and the center of faith, whether that be the two-natures doctrine, the *regula fidei*, gnostic enlightenment, church dogma, or the Reformation's justification by faith. By contrast, historical-critical scholarship distances the text to be interpreted not only from the interpreters, their faith convictions, and the church's belief; it also, by emphasizing its distinctiveness, distances the text from the entirety of the biblical witness.[17]

In the modern period, informed precritical exegesis of the kind Luz here refers to surfaces as well in the neo-orthodox theologian Karl Barth (1886–1968). Kathryn Greene-McCreight describes the latter's overall christocentric, theological approach to Scripture with a reference to the *regula fidei*: "As did those from the earliest Christian tradition up until the dawning of the Enlightenment, Karl Barth shares with them a reading of Scripture that attends a canonical Rule, or the Rule of Faith."[18] The Rule of Faith, or *regula fidei*, brings Christology in contact with the wider Triune faith, structured around the three divine figures Father, Son, and Holy Spirit (cf. Matt 28:19; Did. 7.1, 3; Justin, *1 Apol.* 61; Irenaeus, *Epid.* 6; Tertullian, *Prax.* 2).

Now, if, for a moment, we broaden our interpretative scope and choose to endorse the theological approach of Robert Jenson as outlined in his *Systematic Theology*, we may note that name and narrative within the *regula fidei* matrix may indeed merge into one. Jenson writes:

> Thus the phrase "Father, Son, and Holy Spirit" is simultaneously a very compressed telling of the total narrative by which Scripture identifies God and a personal name for the God so specified; in it, name and narrative description not only appear together, as at the beginning of the Ten Commandments, but are identical. By virtue

---

17. Ulrich Luz, *Matthew 1–7: A Commentary*, rev. ed., Hermeneia (Minneapolis: Fortress, 2007), 64.

18. Greene-McCreight, "'A Type of the One to Come': Leviticus 14 and 16 in Barth's *Church Dogmatics*," in *Thy Word is Truth: Barth on Scripture*, ed. George Hunsinger (Grand Rapids: Eerdmans, 2012), 68.

of this logic, the triune phrase offers itself as a unique name for the
Christian God, and is then dogmatically mandated for that function by its constitutive place in the rite that establishes Christian
identity [in the words of Basil the Great, here referred to by Jenson:
"We must be baptized as we have received the command, and confess as we have been baptized, and worship as we have confessed:
Father and Son and Holy Spirit"].[19]

Jenson points to the Triune structure of Christian faith, embracing the
essential scriptural component of divine name and narrative, with particular attention directed to the notion of a scriptural whole. We may
already have noted, for example, the creedal features potentially associated with terms included among the editorial *nomina sacra* demarcations ("sacred names," including renderings of the Name) found in Old
Testament and New Testament manuscripts, such as the textual *nomina
sacra* emphases GOD ($\overline{\theta c}$), LORD ($\overline{\kappa c}$), FATHER ($\overline{\pi \eta \rho}$), SON ($\overline{\gamma c}$), JESUS
($\overline{\iota c}$), CHRIST ($\overline{\chi c}$), MAN/HUMAN BEING ($\overline{\lambda noc}$), CROSS/CRUCIFY ($\overline{c\tau poc}$),
and Holy SPIRIT ($\overline{\pi n \lambda}$). Together, these, and some six additional, spe-
cially highlighted, words make up a textually engrafted creedal-devotional
pattern throughout the Christian Scriptures (see further the following
second- to fifth-century manuscripts: P[45], P[46], P[66], P[75], Codex Sinaiticus,
Codex Alexandrinus; and other Greek Old Testament and New Testament
manuscripts).

1.3 SCRIPTURE AND THEOLOGY

A topic that has remained with the church from the first century onward—
including in academic theology—is the classic question of Scripture's
relation to theology, and vice versa. What are the mechanisms that so
smoothly—though sometimes with noted difficulties—seem to connect
the two, the biblical canonical (Old and New Testaments) with the theological and devotional discourse? For example, how is early baptismal
practice in the Triune name connected with Matt 28:19 or eucharistic
church practice linked to Matt 26:26–28?

---

19. Robert W. Jenson, *The Triune God*, vol. 1 of *Systematic Theology* (New York: Oxford University
Press, 1997), 46–47.

A first observation is that Scripture, and the New Testament in particular, is replete with devotional and applied theological language—such as the Great Commission in Matthew 28, the doxology in 2 Cor 1:3 or the Triune benediction later in the epistle (13:13). Another thing to note is the christological "proof-from-prophecy" hermeneutic—or Christology "according to the Scriptures"—that we find in Justin Martyr (ca. AD 100–165) and in one of the Rule-of-Faith formularies in Irenaeus, as the bishop of Lyons treats most of the christological material under the third article of faith about the Spirit of prophecy (*Haer.* 1.10.1). A third provisional remark to our question could be that doctrinal and liturgical formulations, endorsed by the faith communities, were immersed in biblical idioms from the beginning. The church, for example, tended to have a "more or less raw experience of its use of the Scriptures in the liturgy"; and Christian literature of the two first centuries may arguably be described as "one single large commentary on the Scriptures."[20] Within this scriptural universe, a particular quality to notice is the scriptural property of biblical canonicity (cf. ch. 3) and its immediate implications for theological and devotional ecclesial discourse. The present study will pay particular attention to this last point—the issues involved in the early canon formation process—but also to the former three points pertaining to the relationship between Scripture and emerging doctrinal structures as these can be noted through the theological and exegetical Rule-of-Faith pattern, which was present in the faith communities from the early stages of Christian identity formation onward.[21]

---

20. First quotation from Geoffrey Wainwright, *Doxology: The Praise of God in Worship, Doctrine and Life* (London: Epworth, 1980), 149–50. Second quotation from Oskar Skarsaune, "The Development of Scriptural Interpretation in the Second and Third Centuries—Except Clement and Origen," in *Hebrew Bible/Old Testament: The History of Its Interpretation*, ed. Magne Saebø (Göttingen: Vandenhoeck & Ruprecht, 1996), 1.1:375.

21. Regarding Christian dogma in the early church—being integrated in *regula fidei* phrasings and elsewhere—we can note, with Wolfhart Pannenberg (*Systematic Theology*, 3 vols. [Grand Rapids: Eerdmans, 1991], 1:9–10), the following: "The Greek word *dogma* can denote both a subjective opinion as distinct from certain knowledge and also a legally binding opinion or 'judgment.' ... If, on the one hand, Christian dogma was viewed analogously to philosophical teachings, on the other hand it was set in antithesis to the competing theories, since it did not come from humans but was 'spoken and taught by God' (Athenagoras, *Leg.* 11.1). As the Epistle to Diognetus puts it, the Christian faith does not rest on human teaching (5.3). Origen can thus describe Christian doctrines as *dogmata theou* (*In Matt.* 12.23). In this way the truth claim of Christian doctrine is formulated but at the same time

1.4 THE BIBLICAL CHRIST

The chapters of the present book present Christ as the focal point of most devotional, exegetical, and theological activity in the earliest Christian centuries. Irenaeus of Lyons, in the second century, can thus write: "For if anyone reads the [Jewish] Scriptures with attention, they will find in them an account of Christ" (*Haer.* 4.26.1); and, in Anthony Thiselton's phrasing: "Luke 24:27 and 45 uses the Old Testament as a frame of reference for understanding Christ, and Christ as an interpretive key for understanding the Old Testament."²² Correspondingly, a core element of the scripturally related Rule of Faith was the attentiveness to "the wholeness of Scripture" (Irenaeus, *Haer.* 1.8.1; 2.28.3; Augustine, *Catech.* 4.8; *Doctr. chr.* 1.16.40; 40.44), and the understanding that Christ and the Spirit were the "constitutive bond" between Old and New Testaments.²³ On a related note, Martin Kähler and Roland Deines even thematize the Jesus of history in such scriptural terms, which the following quotation from Deines reveals:

> The historical reductionism of the canonical Gospels (which Kähler sees in line with the paucity of Jesus narratives in the Pauline corpus) is actually their greatest achievement. By stripping off the

a decision is already made regarding it. If the dogmas of Christians are true, they are no longer the opinions of a human school. They are divine revelation. Nevertheless, they are still formulated and proclaimed by humans, by the church and its ministers. Hence the question can and must be raised whether they are more than human opinions, whether they are not merely human inventions and traditions but an expression of divine revelation. ... The usage that has established itself since Eusebius of Caesarea, who speaks of 'ecclesiastical dogmas' (*Hist. eccl.* 5.23.2; cf. 6.43.2), does not reject the claim of Origen and other early fathers that these dogmas are divine truth. It simply describes them in terms of the human bearer of the claim, i.e., the fellowship of Christians. It does not abandon the truth claim. It simply leaves it open to the extent, at least, that the church comes forward as the bearer of the claim and not its guarantor. This is the case with Eusebius when he thinks of dogmas essentially in terms of conciliar decrees and other common doctrines of the faith, e.g., the resurrection of the dead (*Hist. eccl.* 3.26.4). The church and empire took a momentous step beyond this stage when they made a codification of dogmas legally binding, thus not merely presupposing their truth but establishing it. This kind of codification terminated and silenced the process of reception relative to official doctrinal promulgation."

22. Anthony C. Thiselton, *New Horizons in Hermeneutics: The Theory and Practice of Transforming Biblical Reading* (Grand Rapids: Zondervan, 1992), 150.

23. For attentiveness to "the wholeness of Scripture," see Straus, "Word as Word," 13–14; and Thiselton, *New Horizons in Hermeneutics*, 154. "Constitutive bond" is from Peter Stuhlmacher, *Historical Criticism and Theological Interpretation of Scripture: Toward a Hermeneutics of Consent* (London: SPCK, 1977), 27; Straus, "Word as Word," 13.

merely historical, they allowed their readers to meet and to experience what he [Kähler] called the biblical or the real Christ.[24]

Kähler's basic christological thesis (as reviewed by Deines) is of particular interest for the present study. In Kähler's view, faith "in the living Christ" came into being not as the result of later projection on Jesus "but because he himself invokes such faith from us." What happens with his first followers and the evangelists repeats itself through the centuries: Jesus is experienced as a compelling and living counterpart through the Gospels and the other New Testament witnesses "to which we are indebted for our knowledge of historical revelation. Even today these books offer to every receptive heart that knowledge of the living God and of his acts through which it has pleased him continually to create trust in himself in the hearts of men."[25]

1.5 BIBLE CANON, TRIUNE FAITH, AND *NOMINA SACRA*

The apostolic canon formation process—one of this book's focal points—was from the beginning related to the historical as well as the scriptural Jesus/Lord Jesus Christ, whose words and deeds received their due authoritative place on a par with the Scriptures of Judaism. "The Scriptures and the Lord," "the Scriptures, the Lord, and the apostles," "the Lord and the apostles," and similar phrasings soon became standard designations to which the church referred "in all matters of faith and practice."[26]

As for the New Testament material in the nascent church, and its critical involvement in the canonical process, Bruce Metzger here provides a helpful account:

---

24. Roland Deines, "Jesus and the Jewish Traditions of His Time," *Early Christianity* 1 (2010): 362; Martin Kähler, *The So-Called Historical Jesus and the Historic Biblical Christ*, ed. and trans. Carl E. Braaten (Philadelphia: Fortress, 1964).

25. Martin Kähler, "Do Christians Value the Bible Because It Contains Historical Documents?," in *So-Called Historical Jesus*, 128; cited from Deines, "Jesus and the Jewish Traditions," 356–57. For a critical treatment of Kähler's classic lecture "The So-Called Historical Jesus and the Historic, Biblical Christ," see further Peter Stuhlmacher, *Jesus of Nazareth—Christ of Faith*, trans. Siegfried Schatzmann (Peabody, MA: Hendrickson, 1993), 1–38.

26. Bruce M. Metzger, *The Canon of the New Testament: Its Origin, Development, and Significance* (Oxford: Clarendon, 1987), 6.

the remembered and transmitted words of Jesus were treasured
and used, taking their place beside the Law and the Prophets and
being regarded as of equal or superior authority to them. ... At first
Jesus' teachings circulated orally from hearer to hearer, becoming,
so to speak, the nucleus of the new Christian canon. Then narratives were compiled recording the remembered words, along with
recollections of his deeds of mercy and healing.[27]

Narratives about Jesus, the "Son of God" (Matt 3:17, Mark 1:1, 11)—
embracing the periods prior to, and after, the Easter event—were further
directly connected with God, the sender of his Son (Matt 10:40; 15:24;
John 3:17; Heb 1:1–2), and the Spirit (Matt 3:16; Mark 1:8–12; Acts 2:38;
1 Cor 6:11). And Triune patterns began to emerge already within the New
Testament (Matt 28:19; 2 Cor 13:13). The word constellation "God," "Jesus
Christ," and "Spirit," accordingly, appear in eight passages/verses in the
New Testament (Rom 1:4; 15:30; 1 Cor 6:11; 2 Cor 13:13; Eph 1:17; 1 Thess
5:23; 1 Pet 1:2; 1 John 4:2)—with the included three words/expressions
θεός ($\overline{\theta\varsigma}$), Ἰησοῦς χριστός ($\overline{\iota\varsigma}$ $\overline{\chi\varsigma}$), and πνεῦμα ($\overline{\pi\nu\alpha}$) altogether featuring
twenty-six times in these eight verses (N.B.: the terms θεός and πνεῦμα
both appear twice in 1 John 4:2; the division of the NT text into verses
as we know it today was introduced by Robert Stephanus in the sixteenth
century).

A telling example of the way in which first-century phrasings brought
together Triune faith, Christology, and monotheistic theology proper with
the text of Scripture—drawing on the New Testament—can be found in

---

27. Metzger, *Canon of the New Testament*, 3. On the question of the historical character and
reliability of key portions of the synoptic tradition, cf. Joachim Jeremias, *New Testament Theology*
(London: SCM, 1971), 162: "The absence of Christological titles in the synoptic sayings about faith,
indeed simply the express mention of its reference to Jesus, is an indication of age of the first rank,
and a pointer to the origin of at least the nucleus of the synoptic statements of faith from the period
before Easter"; and Jeremias, *New Testament Theology*, 8: "The discovery that the sayings of Jesus are
to be set against an Aramaic background is of great significance for the question of the reliability of
the gospel tradition. This linguistic evidence takes us back into the realm of Aramaic oral tradition";
similarly Bart D. Ehrman, *Did Jesus Exist? The Historical Argument for Jesus of Nazareth* (New York:
HarperOne, 2012), 88: "There is very little dispute that some of the Gospel stories originated in
Aramaic and that therefore they go back to the earliest stages of the Christian movement in Palestine."

1 Clem. 46.6 (ca. AD 95/96).[28] Building on 1 Cor 8:6 and Eph 4:5, this largely neglected passage, embracing an early form of Triune monotheism, interestingly refers to "one GOD [ϵΝΑ ΘΝ] and one CHRIST [ϵΝΑ ΧΝ] and one SPIRIT [ϵΝ ΠΝΑ] of grace having been poured out upon us" (1 Clem. 46.6; *nomina sacra*, as in Codex Alexandrinus, in small caps).[29] Also in Paul's Epistle to the Romans (examples from the Greek New Testament [NA28]), similar Triune renderings surface, for example, in Rom 15:30 and elsewhere in Romans (1:4; 8:9; and 15:16, 19)—involving altogether seventeen appearances in these five verses/passages of the three terms "God," "Christ," and "Spirit"; and similarly in the Pauline Corpus, with altogether twenty-six occurrences of the three words "God," "Lord" and "Spirit," when appearing together in one and the same verse/passage (including Rom 1:4; 15:30; 1 Cor 6:11; 12:3; 2 Cor 13:13; Eph 1:17; 1 Thess 5:23; and 2 Thess 2:13). We may here recall Rom 15:30, involved in all three of the above Pauline examples, which reads: "I appeal to you, brothers and sisters, by our LORD JESUS CHRIST and by the love of the SPIRIT, to strive together with me in your prayers to GOD on my behalf" (for the figures seventeen and twenty-six, in these triadic name constellations,

---

28. Cf. Richard Bauckham (*Jesus and the God of Israel: God Crucified and Other Studies on the New Testament's Christology of Divine Identity* [Grand Rapids: Eerdmans, 2008], 57), who summarizes his two key points "about the relationship between monotheism and Christology in the New Testament: (1) New Testament writers clearly and deliberately include Jesus in the unique identity of the God of Israel; (2) The inclusion of the human life and shameful death, as well as the exaltation of Jesus, in the divine identity reveals the divine identity—who God is—in a new way." An alternative view on the emergence of Christology in the church, which Bauckham convincingly argues against (*Jesus and the God of Israel*, 58), "supposes that a Christology which attributed true divinity to Jesus could not have originated within a context of Jewish monotheism. On this view, divine Christology is the result of a transition from Jewish to Hellenistic religious and, subsequently, Hellenistic philosophical, categories. Nicaea represents the triumph of Greek philosophy in Christian doctrine. This way of reading the history seems to me to be virtually the opposite of the truth. In other words, it was actually not Jewish but Greek philosophical categories which made it difficult to attribute true and full divinity to Jesus. A Jewish understanding of divine identity was open to the inclusion of Jesus in the divine identity. But Greek and Platonic understanding of the relationship of God to the world made it extremely difficult to see Jesus as more than a semi-divine being, neither truly God nor truly human. In the context of the Arian controversies, Nicene theology was essentially an attempt to resist the implications of Greek philosophical understandings of divinity and to re-appropriate, in a new conceptual context, the New Testament's inclusion of Jesus in the unique divine identity."

29. See further L. Choppin, "La Trinité dans l'épître de Saint Clément 95–98," *RSPT* 13 (1924): 477–88; and Horacio E. Lona, *Der erste Clemensbrief*, KAV 2 (Göttingen: Vandenhoeck & Ruprecht, 1998), 493–94.

being potential references to the numerical values associated with the Tetragrammaton, see chs. 5–10 below).[30]

1.6 HERMENEUTICAL APPROACH, SCOPE, AND OUTLINE OF THE BOOK

This book begins with the story of the Christian Bible's formation, function, and interpretation in the late-first and second century AD. Why include the second century, we may ask? Why not just the Apostolic Age (ca. 30–70/100)? Why not the earliest apostolic period, prior to, and during, the time when the textual foundation for the Christian church was laid through oral proclamation of the gospel and the composition of Pauline letters and the Synoptic Gospels? A first historical response to this important question is the fact that much of the literary production that was to emerge as the final canonical text form(s) of the New Testament seems to have begun in the latter part of the first century, around the time when key apostles and primary witnesses to the Jesus event were passing; Peter and Paul in Rome in the mid-sixties, and James, the Lord's brother, in AD 62 (Josephus Ant. 20.200). Accordingly, both Irenaeus and Clement of Alexandria (ca. AD 150–215) tell us about Mark compiling his Gospel— linked to the preaching of Simon Peter—while Peter was in Rome and still alive (Clement), or when he had just passed (Irenaeus; Anti-Marcionite Prologues). Irenaeus further tells us of John writing toward the end of the century. Modern scholarship, too, commonly dates John's Gospel to the late first century AD. Similarly, the Apocalypse, which arguably was authored in the 90s. Some additional New Testament writings may also have been composed or redacted around this time. It therefore seems reasonable—as preferred here—to begin the study of the corpus of New Testament writings, their canonization and interpretation, and the emergence of a developed Christian scriptural theology from the turn of the

---

30. Romans 15:30 is involved in the following three Triune word constellations: θεός, Ἰησοῦς χριστός, and πνεῦμα featuring in eight verses in the New Testament, altogether twenty-six times, when each word/ expression is counted separately (search in Accordance on the form: θεός <AND> Ἰησοῦς χριστός <AND> πνεῦμα); textual scope: verse; the corresponding figure for θεός, κύριος, and πνεῦμα, featuring in eight Pauline verses, is twenty-six appearances in Pauline Corpus (search in Accordance on the form: θεός <AND> κύριος <AND> πνεῦμα); and for θεός, χριστός, and πνεῦμα, featuring in five verses in Romans, seventeen occurrences in Romans (search in Accordance on the form: θεός <AND> χριστός <AND> πνεῦμα).

century onward, when a discernible corpus of early Christian literature was emerging.

The biblical canon formation, pertaining to the new apostolic literature, became crucial for the regular communal Scripture reading more clearly only from the late first century on; and major canonical subunits, such as the fourfold Gospel, the thirteen- or fourteen-letter Pauline corpus, and the New Testament conceived as a literary whole, all probably emerged in the late-first/second century AD. The Apostolic Age, however, is still of importance and may—as we shall see—also be accessed through what we could call the "final canonical form(s)" of the New Testament text, emerging between the first and fourth centuries. This text—which eventually came to include twenty-seven writings—can be accessed, not least, through the early to mid-fourth-century megacodices Vaticanus and Sinaiticus and second- to third-century New Testament papyri, such as P[46] (Pauline Corpus), P[45] (Gospels and Acts), P[66] (John), and P[75] (Luke and John).

As with historical understanding in general, it is true also when applied to the early church and its principal texts, that time can actually help us perceive the object of study more clearly. Gadamer expresses this thought in the following words:

> In historical studies ... objective knowledge can be achieved only if there has been a certain historical distance. It is true that what a thing has to say, its intrinsic content, first appears only after it is divorced from the fleeting circumstances that gave rise to it. The positive conditions of historical understanding include the relative closure of a historical event, which allows us to view it as a whole, and its distance from contemporary opinions concerning its import.[31]

This emphasis on time as an element in the process of understanding that is fundamentally positive, and not negative—as it often appears to be in historical-critical analysis—is part of the basic hermeneutical approach

---

31. Gadamer, *Truth and Method*, 298.

of the studies included in this book (cf. John 12:16; Irenaeus *Haer.* 3.1.1).[32] Early Christian textual and literary composition, pertaining to the emerging New Testament, is taken into account throughout the following chapters as events of textual preservation, with a view also toward addressing future readers and to the universal features of the texts being preserved and received. As a matter of fact, the New Testament texts seem to have been designed for public reading in the faith communities (and beyond) from the outset.[33] This appears to be the case with respect to the Pauline letters (1 Thess 5:27; Col 4:16; 1 Cor 1:2; 2 Pet 3:16), and also regarding the Gospels, which "were written in the first place for worship."[34]

In addition to liturgical or devotional aspects, the chapters below addressing the biblical canon formation process (chs. 2–10) also elaborate on the relation between the biblical canon and the Rule of Faith (ch. 11) and the interaction between canon, Rule of Faith, and *nomina sacra* (specially highlighted "sacred names" in the biblical texts and elsewhere; chs. 4–12). Broader interpretative issues, bringing together the different threads of our discussion, were addressed above (ch. 1; specifically addressed also in ch. 13) and will be further ventilated in the six parts that make up the present volume (parts A–F), focusing on the following: Early Scripturality (part A), The Shaping of the Scriptural Canon (part B), A Numerological Approach to Biblical Canonicity (part C), *Regula Fidei* and Scriptural Theology (part D), *Nomina Sacra* and Biblical Interpretation (part E), and Concluding Reflections (part F, with a final

---

32. John 12:16: "His disciples did not understand these things at first, but when JESUS was glorified, then they remembered that these things had been written about him and had been done to him" (ESV; modified); Irenaeus, *Haer.* 3.1.1: "For we have known the 'economy' for our salvation [*dispositionem salutis nostrae*] only through those through whom the gospel came to us; and what they then first preached they later, by GOD's will, transmitted to us in the Scriptures so that would be the future foundation and pillar of our faith [*fundamentum et columnam fidei nostrae futurum*]" (trans. Robert Grant, *Irenaeus of Lyons*, Early Church Fathers [London: Routledge, 1997], 123–24, modified).

33. Martin Hengel, *The Four Gospels and the One Gospel of Jesus Christ* (London: SCM, 2000), 116; Bokedal, *Formation and Significance of the Christian Biblical Canon*, 254–56, 266–67. See also Richard Bauckham, "For Whom Were Gospels Written?," in *The Gospels for All Christians: Rethinking the Gospel Audiences*, ed. Richard Bauckham (Grand Rapids: Eerdmans, 1998), 9–48; and David A. Smith, *The Epistles for All Christians: Epistolary Literature, Circulation, and the Gospels for All Christians*, BIS 186 (Leiden: Brill, 2020).

34. Martin Hengel, "Eye-Witness Memory and the Writing of the Gospels," in *The Written Gospel*, ed. Marcus Bockmuehl and Donald A. Hagner (Cambridge: Cambridge University Press, 2005), 92.

chapter titled "Christological Textual Structuring of the New Testament Canon: Hermeneutical Reflection on the Parts and the Whole").

Overall, it is argued that the four interrelated focal points of the study— Jesus Christ and the divine name as center in (1) the canon formation process, (2) the Rule of Faith, (3) the triadic system of *nomina sacra*, and (4) numerical patterns involved in the shaping of canonical subunits— provide a christological foundation for scriptural theology, from the late first century onward.

BIBLIOGRAPHY

Bauckham, Richard. "For Whom Were Gospels Written?" Pages 9–48 in *The Gospels for All Christians: Rethinking the Gospel Audiences*. Edited by Richard Bauckham. Grand Rapids: Eerdmans, 1998.

———. *Jesus and the God of Israel: God Crucified and Other Studies on the New Testament's Christology of Divine Identity*. Grand Rapids: Eerdmans, 2009.

Bokedal, Tomas. *The Formation and Significance of the Christian Biblical Canon: A Study in Text, Ritual and Interpretation*. London: Bloomsbury T&T Clark, 2014.

Bonhoeffer, Dietrich. *Illegale Theologenausbildung: Finkenwalde 1935– 1937*. DBW 14. Gütersloh: Gütersloher Verlagshaus, 1996.

Bruner, Jerome S. *The Process of Education*. Cambridge: Harvard University Press, 1960.

Campbell, Constantine R., and Jonathan T. Pennington. *Reading the New Testament as Christian Scripture: A Literary, Canonical, and Theological Survey*. Reading Christian Scripture. Grand Rapids: Baker Academic, 2020.

Childs, Brevard S. *Biblical Theology: A Proposal*. Facets. Minneapolis: Fortress, 2002.

———. *Biblical Theology of the Old and New Testaments: Theological Reflection on the Christian Bible*. London: SCM, 1992.

Choppin, L. "La Trinité dans l'épître de Saint Clément 95–98." *RSPT* 13 (1924): 477–88.

Deines, Roland. "Jesus and Scripture: Scripture and the Self-Understanding of Jesus." Pages 39–70, 225–34 in *All That the Prophets Have Declared: The Appropriation of Scripture in the Emergence of Christianity*. Edited by Matthew R. Malcolm. Milton Keynes: Paternoster, 2015.

———. "Jesus and the Jewish Traditions of His Time." *Early Christianity* 1 (2010): 344–71.

Ehrman, Bart D. *Did Jesus Exist? The Historical Argument for Jesus of Nazareth*. New York: HarperOne, 2012.

Gadamer, Hans-Georg. *Gadamer in Conversation: Reflections and Commentary*. Edited and translated by Richard E. Palmer. YSH. New Haven: Yale University Press, 2001.

———. *Truth and Method*. Translated by Joel Weinsheimer and Donald Marshall. 2nd ed. New York: Continuum, 1989.

Goldingay, John. *Do We Need the New Testament? Letting the Old Testament Speak for Itself*. Downers Grove, IL: IVP Academic, 2015.

Grant, Robert M. *Irenaeus of Lyons*. Early Church Fathers. London: Routledge, 1997.

Greene-McCreight, Kathryn. "'A Type of the One to Come': Leviticus 14 and 16 in Barth's *Church Dogmatics*." Pages 67–85 in *Thy Word Is Truth: Barth on Scripture*. Edited by George Hunsinger. Grand Rapids: Eerdmans, 2012.

Grovier, Kelly. "The Supper at Emmaus: A Coded Symbol Hidden in a Masterpiece." *BBC Culture* 18 June 2021. https://www.bbc.com/culture/article/20210617-the-supper-at-emmaus-a-coded-symbol-hidden-in-a-masterpiece.

Hengel, Martin. "Eye-Witness Memory and the Writing of the Gospels." Pages 70–96 in *The Written Gospel*. Edited by Marcus Bockmuehl and Donald A. Hagner. Cambridge: Cambridge University Press, 2005.

———. *The Four Gospels and the One Gospel of Jesus Christ: An Investigation of the Collection and Origin of the Canonical Gospels*. Translated by John Bowden. London: SCM, 2000.

Hengel, Martin, with Roland Deines. *The Septuagint as Christian Scripture: Its Prehistory and the Problem of Its Canon.* London: T&T Clark, 2002.

Hurtado, Larry W. *The Earliest Christian Artifacts: Manuscripts and Christian Origins.* Grand Rapids: Eerdmans, 2006.

Jenson, Robert W. *The Triune God.* Vol. 1 of *Systematic Theology.* New York: Oxford University Press, 1997.

Jeremias, Joachim. *New Testament Theology.* London: SCM, 1971.

Kähler, Martin. "Do Christians Value the Bible Because It Contains Historical Documents?" Pages 100–148 in *The So-Called Historical Jesus and the Historic Biblical Christ.* Edited and translated by Carl E. Braaten. Philadelphia: Fortress, 1964.

———. *The So-Called Historical Jesus and the Historic Biblical Christ.* Edited and translated by Carl E. Braaten. Philadelphia: Fortress, 1964.

Lona, Horacio E. *Der erste Clemensbrief.* KAV 2. Göttingen: Vandenhoeck & Ruprecht, 1998.

Luz, Ulrich. *Matthew 1–7: A Commentary.* Rev. ed. Hermeneia. Minneapolis: Fortress, 2007.

Metzger, Bruce M. *The Canon of the New Testament: Its Origin, Development, and Significance.* Oxford: Clarendon, 1987.

Pannenberg, Wolfhart. *Systematic Theology.* Vol. 1. Grand Rapids: Eerdmans, 1991.

Roberts, C. H. *Manuscript, Society and Belief in Early Christian Egypt.* Schweich Lectures 1977. Oxford: Oxford University Press, 1979.

Scobie, Charles H. H. *The Ways of Our God: An Approach to Biblical Theology.* Grand Rapids: Eerdmans, 2003.

Skarsaune, Oskar. "The Development of Scriptural Interpretation in the Second and Third Centuries—Except Clement and Origen." Pages 373–442 in vol. 1, part 1 of *Hebrew Bible/Old Testament: The History of Its Interpretation.* Edited by Magne Saebø. Göttingen: Vandenhoeck & Ruprecht, 1996.

Skevington Wood, A. *Luther's Principles of Biblical Interpretation.* London: Tyndale Press, 1960. https://biblicalstudies.org.uk/pdf/ tp/luther_wood.pdf.

Smith, David A. *The Epistles for All Christians: Epistolary Literature, Circulation, and the Gospels for All Christians.* BIS 186. Leiden: Brill, 2020.

Straus, Michael. "The Word as Word: A Canonical-Hermeneutical Approach to Translation with Paul's Letter to the Colossians as a Test Case." PhD diss., University of Aberdeen, 2021.

Stuhlmacher, Peter. *Biblical Theology of the New Testament.* Translated and edited by Daniel P. Bailey with the collaboration of Jostein Ådna. Grand Rapids: Eerdmans, 2018.

———. *Historical Criticism and Theological Interpretation of Scripture: Toward a Hermeneutics of Consent.* London: SPCK, 1977.

———. *Jesus of Nazareth—Christ of Faith.* Translated by Siegfried Schatzmann. Peabody, MA: Hendrickson, 1993.

Thiselton, Anthony C. *New Horizons in Hermeneutics: The Theory and Practice of Transforming Biblical Reading.* Grand Rapids: Zondervan, 1992.

Wainwright, Geoffrey. *Doxology: The Praise of God in Worship, Doctrine and Life.* London: Epworth, 1980.

Watson, Francis. *Text and Truth: Redefining Biblical Theology.* Edinburgh: T&T Clark; Grand Rapids: Eerdmans, 1997.

PART A

CHRIST THE CENTER:
EARLY SCRIPTURALITY

2

SCRIPTURE IN THE
SECOND CENTURY

"Scripture in the Second Century" is a dynamic field of research. It may be difficult to pinpoint exactly what the topic includes, even if we stay within a Christian context. Is this referring to Jewish Scriptures, Christianized Jewish Scriptures, Gospel writings, Old and New Testament Scriptures, sacred writings, or simply preserved or lost religious texts from the second century C.E.? Whichever is preferred, "Scripture in the Second Century" has become an increasingly important area of research in biblical studies, patristic exegesis, and dogmatic theology alike.[1]

One reason for this, of course, is that, in the patristic scholar Oskar Skarsaune's wording, "in many respects, Christian literature of the period 30–250 C.E. may be said to be one single large commentary on the Scriptures."[2] Also, due to the formation of a core New Testament (NT) canon alongside the Jewish Scriptures during this time, and for other reasons, the second century certainly is "one of the most significant

---

1. Areas in particular that deal with our topic are studies on the canon, the 'parting of the ways' and early Christian reception of Old and New Testament writings.

2. Oskar Skarsaune, "The Development of Scriptural Interpretation in the Second and Third Centuries—except Clement and Origen," in Sæbø, M. (ed.), *Hebrew Bible/Old Testament: The History of Its Interpretation*, vol. 1, *From the Beginnings to the Middle Ages (until 1300)*, Part i, *Antiquity* (Göttingen: Vandenhoeck & Ruprecht, 1996), 375, here referring to the Jewish Scriptures.

periods in the history of the Christian Bible and its interpretation."[3] Thus, our topic has significance not only for understanding early Christian scriptural interpretation, but also for the development of Christian apologetics and the broader notion of Christian identity vis-à-vis Judaism and its Scriptures.

By the early second century, as Christianity began to reflect more on its own identity and also sought to mark out its own particular characteristics over against Judaism, and later in polemical encounters vis-à-vis Marcionism, Paganism and Gnosticism, various dimensions of the Scriptures were brought into focus. In order to analyze this second century situation I shall here single out the four properties of *usage, interpretation, text* and *canon* of Scripture. With special attention to these properties, this chapter shall consider the second century notion of Christian Scripture against the backdrop of the transference from Jewish to Christian Scripture from the mid-first century on. I will proceed thematically rather than historically, discussing scriptural usage in Justin and the Apostolic Fathers, and the pathway towards Christian Scripture. The subsequent section on interpretation will treat Christ-centered exegesis. In the final section I will discuss *nomina sacra* in *Barnabas* 9.7–9 and the relation between the Scriptures and the Rule of Faith, followed by a few notes on the formation of the Christian canon. The discussion will be limited mainly to some Christian "(proto-)orthodox" writers. First, however, a word on the meaning of our topic.

2.1 CHRISTIAN SCRIPTURE IN THE SECOND CENTURY

The notion of Scripture in the first Christian communities functioned both in continuity and discontinuity with its various pre-Christian and contemporary Jewish settings (the same prioritized text and canonical scope, but with different interpretations).[4] Judaism and Christianity thus formally shared the same Hebrew Bible, for second century Christianity

---

3. James Carleton Paget, "The Interpretation of the Bible in the Second Century," in *The New Cambridge History of the Bible*, ed. Joachim Schaper and James Carleton Paget (Cambridge: Cambridge University Press, 2013).

4. B. S. Childs, *Introduction to the Old Testament as Scripture* (London: SCM, 1979), 659–71.

often in Greek translation. With regard to interpretation, however, they differed. This was largely due to the widespread devotion to Jesus which affected scriptural interpretation (1 Cor 1:2), and the emergence of regulatory Jesus traditions (his words and deeds) within earliest Christianity, for which the final authority was Jesus himself (Matt 28:18; Ign. *Phld.* 8.2f.).[5] Thus, by comparing the diverse approaches to Scripture found in writers like Ignatius of Antioch (d. ca. 107/8 C.E.), the author of the *Epistle of Barnabas* (ca. 70–135 C.E.) and Justin Martyr (d. ca. 165 C.E.), it is not even always clear what is meant by statements of "final" authority, such as "Scripture says" or even the very word "Scripture." This ambiguity is tied up with christological re-readings and the formation of a unique Christian canon resulting in a two-testament Bible (i.e., "Scripture" is not complete without the Gospel and its interpretive center: the teaching, life, death and resurrection of Jesus the Messiah-Christ).[6] Already by the late first century C.E. the writings that began to form the NT were read in worship and attained other functions as well that had previously been exclusive to the Jewish Scriptures. It thus appears that the gospel tradition and the emerging NT text in their memorized oral, written and re-oralized forms had an immediate authority for the primitive church similar to that of the Jewish Scriptures.[7] Linking Christian scripturality to *usage, interpretation, text* and *canon* highlights what is happening in this process and makes us better equipped to understand the dynamic second century notion of Scripture.

2.2 USAGE OF JEWISH AND
EMERGING CHRISTIAN SCRIPTURES

The Apostolic Fathers (ca. 70–150 C.E.), except for the *Epistle of Barnabas* and *1 Clement,* refer to the oral or written NT tradition much more

---

5. Cf. Bruce M. Metzger, *The Canon of the New Testament: Its Origin, Development, and Significance* (Oxford: Clarendon, 1987), 2–8.

6. Clement of Alexandria and Tertullian and possibly Melito of Sardis are the first writers to label the Christian Bible "Old" and "New Testament".

7. On the term "re-oralisation", see Samuel Byrskog, *Jesus the Only Teacher: Didactic Authority and Transmission in Ancient Israel, Ancient Judaism and the Matthean Community* (Stockholm: Almqvist & Wiksell, 1994), 339.

frequently than to the Jewish Scriptures (some five to fifty times as often).[8] This is a strong indication of the high status these Christian texts held from early on. That there is a close connection here between usage of a writing and its canonicity, though often disputed among scholars, is nicely phrased by von Harnack: "The question *in what sense* the collection of writings known as the New Testament was regarded as a *Canon* of religion is not decided by saying that it was regarded as canonical, but can only be answered by finding out what use was actually made of this collection."[9] This is not to say that usage is the one and only dimension of canonicity, but it certainly seems to be a crucial aspect. Both the collection of the Pauline epistles into a corpus between roughly 60 and 120 C.E.,[10] and the formation of the Four-Gospel canon in the mid-second century,[11] or slightly earlier, involved usage. We can add to this that many of the NT writings, in particular the Gospels, seem to have been composed for such usage, to be read out aloud within the Christian worship setting (as Martin Hengel and others have argued). Some of these texts may even have been designed with the intention to establishing new Scripture, as Moody Smith has recently indicated: "Strangely, or not so strangely, the first and last books of the NT present themselves as scripture ... It attests the existence of the idea of distinctively Christian scriptures before the end of the first century."[12]

2.2.1 GOSPEL AND PROOF FROM PROPHECY IN JUSTIN MARTYR

Some decades after the composition of the NT Gospels, in Justin around 150 C.E., we come across an account of early Christian Sunday worship, in which, for the first time, the liturgical function of the Gospels is clearly

---

8. Franz Stuhlhofer, *Der Gebrauch der Bibel von Jesus bis Euseb: Eine statistische Untersuchung zur Kanonsgeschichte* (Wuppertal: Brockhaus, 1988), 67.

9. Adolf von Harnack, *Bible Reading in the Early Church* (London and New York, 1912), v; cited from John Barton, *The Spirit and the Letter* (London: SPCK, 1997), 32f.

10. For a comprehensive discussion, including Paul, Luke and/or Timothy as possible instigators of the collection process, see Stanley Porter, ed., *The Pauline Canon*, Pauline Studies 1 (Leiden: Brill, 2004).

11. Graham Stanton dates the formation of the fourfold Gospel shortly before 150 C.E., *Jesus and Gospel* (Cambridge: Cambridge University Press, 2004), 85.

12. D. Moody Smith, "When Did the Gospels Become Scripture?," *JBL* 119 (2000): 15.

a reality, turning out to be central for community life, and, to be noted, also for determining these writings' status vis-à-vis the Jewish Scriptures:

> On the day called Sunday all [believers] who live in cities or in the countryside gather together at one place, and the memoirs of the Apostles or the writings of the Prophets are read, as long as time permits. Then, when the reader has finished, the president of the assembly in a speech admonishes and invites all to imitate such examples of virtue. Then we all rise together and pray ... (1 Apol. 67).[13]

We notice here that the congregation each Sunday usually read from the Gospel ("the memoirs of the Apostles") "as long as time permits,"[14] that is, a so-called continuous reading (the texts read in order, the reader picking up where the assembly left off the Sunday before). Then they arguably proceed with readings from the prophetical writings, just as in the synagogue (Torah reading followed by a suitable reading from the Prophets, the *haftarah*, to supplement the Torah passage of the day), but with the important difference that the Torah reading here seems to have been exchanged for the Gospel reading.[15] Nevertheless, to our knowledge Justin never quotes a NT text as Scripture,[16] whereas his use of the Jewish Scriptures *as Scriptures* is overwhelming. As Skarsaune has argued in great detail, Justin continuously sets out to prove from Scripture that:

> 1) Jesus is the Messiah, Son of God; 2) the Law has a different position after Christ; 3) the community of believers in Jesus rather than the Jewish people is now the people of God. The scriptural proof can be said to have three foci: *de Christo, de lege, de ecclesia.*[17]

Other second century representatives of this major exegetical tradition, usually referred to as the "proof from prophecy," include the author of the

---

13. ANF 1:186.

14. cf. 1 Apol. 66.3 and Dial. 10.2.

15. For a critical discussion and references, see Oskar Skarsaune, In the Shadow of the Temple: Jewish Influences on Early Christianity (Downers Grove: InterVarsity, 2002), 384ff.

16. Skarsaune, In the Shadow of the Temple: Jewish Influences on Early Christianity, 280.

17. Skarsaune, "The Development of Scriptural Interpretation," 390–1.

Epistle of Barnabas, Melito of Sardis, Irenaeus and Tertullian.[18] The "Old Testament" is also strongly focused in the polemics of Justin, Irenaeus and Tertullian against Marcion (b. ca. 100 C.E.) and his rejection and negative treatment of everything Jewish, including the Scriptures. "Marcion emphatically did not cause the Church to have a New Testament; he did cause it to have an 'Old Testament', that is, to correlate the old Scriptures with its (already more or less formed) collection of Christian books."[19]

2.2.2 NEW TESTAMENT TEXTS IN THE APOSTOLIC FATHERS

Tracing the reception history of the Gospel and other NT writings to the time even before Justin, we are again back to the group of writings called the Apostolic Fathers, in which both orality and literacy are characteristic marks of Christian tradition transmission. The Apostolic Fathers as well as other early writers commonly refer to the emerging New Testament writings by rather free allusions.

1 Clement (ca. 70–100 C.E.) knows of several texts from the emerging NT, at least 1 Corinthians and most likely Romans and Hebrews.[20] However, in his important 1973 study on *1 Clement* Donald Hagner argues that the author alludes to a majority of the epistles making up the Pauline Corpus, and not only to a few. In addition to 1 Corinthians and Romans, that are most clearly alluded to, there seem to be allusions to Ephesians and Colossians, as well as probable knowledge of 2 Corinthians, Galatians, Philippians and the Pastorals.[21] There may also be allusions to Acts, 1 Peter and James. Hagner further directs our attention to the free use of Synoptic material found not only in *1 Clement*, but in the other Apostolic Fathers as well. In the *Didache* (ca. 50–150 C.E.) knowledge of the Synoptic tradition can be demonstrated, in particular dependency on Matthew, but

---

18. Skarsaune, "The Development of Scriptural Interpretation," 376.

19. Barton, *The Spirit and the Letter*, 58.

20. Andrew F. Gregory, "1 Clement and the Writings that Later Formed the New Testament," in *The Reception of the New Testament in the Apostolic Fathers* (ed. Andrew F. Gregory and Christopher M. Tuckett; Oxford: Oxford University Press, 2005), 154–5.

21. Donald A. Hagner, *The Use of the Old and New Testaments in Clement of Rome* (Leiden: Brill, 1973), 278ff. On memory quotation in the Apostolic Fathers, Hagner, *The Use of the Old and New Testaments in Clement of Rome*, 290ff.

arguably also on Luke.[22] Ignatius of Antioch is acquainted with at least some of Paul's letters, especially 1 Corinthians, which he "must have known ... almost by heart,"[23] Ephesians and 1 and 2 Timothy. He also most probably makes use of Matthew's Gospel and possibly Luke and John.[24] In his *Letter to the Philippians* (ca. 110–130 C.E.) the great bishop and martyr Polycarp of Smyrna seems to be familiar with 1 Corinthians, Ephesians and 1 Peter. There is also probable usage of 1 and 2 Timothy, 1 John, and perhaps Romans, Galatians and Philippians. It is also possible that Polycarp made use of one or more of the Gospels of Matthew, Mark, and/or Luke.[25] Regarding the *Epistle of Barnabas*, Carleton Paget thinks it is difficult to *demonstrate* that the author knew of any individual NT book, even if a general knowledge of Synoptic passion traditions can be shown; and perhaps, as Carleton Paget points out, something close to a quote of Matt 22 in *Barnabas* 4.14. Since Matt 22:14 is the only known parallel on offer, *Barnabas* 4.14 is quite possibly one of our earliest quotes (William Horbury dates the epistle to the late first century) of a Gospel writing as Scripture: "let us be on guard lest we should be found to be, as it is written, 'many called, but few chosen.' "[26]

From our brief analysis of some selected texts from the Apostolic Fathers we can conclude that there is great familiarity with letters of Paul in *1 Clement* and in Ignatius' and Polycarp's letters. In addition to Paul's influence, the influence of the Synoptic tradition can be noticed, in particular the Gospel of Matthew in the *Didache*, Ignatius' letters and the *Epistle of Barnabas*. Regarding the Johannine literature, based primarily

---

22. Christopher M. Tuckett, "The Didache and the Writings that Later Formed the New Testament," in Gregory and Tuckett, *The Reception of the New Testament in the Apostolic Fathers*, 126–7.

23. W. R. Inge, "Ignatius," in *The New Testament in the Apostolic Fathers* (Oxford: Clarendon Press, 1905), 61; Foster, in *The Reception of the New Testament in the Apostolic Fathers*, 185.

24. Foster, *The Reception of the New Testament in the Apostolic Fathers*, 185.

25. Michael W. Holmes, "Polycarp's Letter to the Philippians," in *The Reception of the New Testament*, 197, 226.

26. So Rhodes and Köhler. J. N. Rhodes, *The Epistle of Barnabas and the Deuteronomic Tradition* (WUNT II 188; Tübingen: Mohr-Siebeck, 2004), 153ff. Wolf-Dietrich Köhler thinks that dependence on Matthew is quite possible for *Barn.* 4.14; 5.8f and 7.9b; see his *Die Rezeption des Matthäusevangeliums in der Zeit vor Irenäus* (WUNT 2/24; Tübingen: Mohr-Siebeck, 1987). Metzger, *The Canon of the New Testament*, 57, does not convince to the contrary.

on the accounts of Irenaeus (ca. 130–202 C.E.), but also of Polycarp (ca. 69–155 C.E.) and Papias (ca. 60–130 C.E.), Charles Hill argues forcefully for the continuous use of the Fourth Gospel, the First Epistle and the Revelation among the "apostolic" churches "from a time very early in the second century on through to Irenaeus' day."[27]

2.2.3 ON THE WAY TO CHRISTIAN SCRIPTURE

Papias of Hierapolis assists us with a helpful comment on early Christian orality *versus* literacy. To him the oral gospel, "that which came from a living and abiding voice," was thought to be even more authoritative than the already appropriated written Gospel.[28] Whereas the function of the gospel tradition and the newly written Christian writings immediately became very significant to the Christian communities, the Jewish Scriptures, on the other hand, were in many cases not used extensively, or were not even present in their entirety.[29] Justin, teaching in Rome, for example, favors only a few OT books (Genesis, Isaiah and Psalms), while other books may not be quoted at all or only scarcely.[30] In this connection the Austrian statistician Franz Stuhlhofer notes that: "the early Church cited the Old Testament as 'Scripture,' but to begin with tended to possess it only in a fragmentary form. The New Testament, on the other hand, was widely available and was used much more heavily, but it was not yet cited as 'Scripture.' "[31] John Barton similarly concludes:

> The central importance of most of the writings that would come to form the New Testament is already established in the early second century, by the time of the Apostolic Fathers, and all but a very few Old Testament books (such as Isaiah or the Psalms)

---

27. Charles E. Hill, *The Johannine Corpus in the Early Church* (Oxford: Oxford University Press, 2004), 111.

28. Eusebius, *Ecclesiastical History* III.39, in *The Apostolic Fathers* (ed. Bart D. Ehrman; 2 vols.; LCL 25; Cambridge, Mass.: Harvard University Press, 2003), 2:99.

29. Only from the mid-second century on Christians began to more systematically produce their own Septuagint copies.

30. See Oskar Skarsaune, "Justin and His Bible," in *Justin Martyr and His Worlds* (ed. Sara Parvis and Paul Foster (eds.), Minneapolis: Fortress, 2007), 57–8.

31. Stuhlhofer, *Der Gebrauch der Bibel von Jesus bis Euseb*, 68. Cited in Barton, *The Spirit and the Letter*, 65.

already play second fiddle to the Christians' own writings. Indeed, it is not until the third century that citations begin to level out as between the two Testaments. All the indications are that the New Testament became almost instantly more important than the Old for the nascent Church ...[32]

Even given these observations, based largely on the French Biblia Patristica project, it is still of some significance for the formation of the Christian Bible that what is called "the words of the Lord," "the gospel" or "the apostle" in the early second century, a few decades later is explicitly referred to as "Scripture" on a par with the Old Testament (OT). While in the NT the term "Scripture" (graphē, occurring some 50 times) most often refers to the Jewish Scriptures—however not exclusively so, as 2 Pet 3:16 indicates—from the late first to the late second century Christian writers begin explicitly to include NT texts as well in their notion of Scripture. The earliest undisputed examples are Tatian in his anti-Hellenic writing Oration to the Greeks (13.1; ca. 170–75 C.E.), quoting John 1:5, and Theophilus of Antioch around 180 C.E. in his Ad Autolychum (iii.2), where he talks about the Evangelists as not less inspired by the Holy Spirit than the OT prophets.[33] However, beside Barnabas 4.14 (see above), already 2 Clement 2.4 (mid-second century) is arguably an example of NT text being reckoned as scriptural: "And another Scripture says, 'I came not to call the righteous, but sinners,' " referring either to Matt 9:13 or Mark 2:17.[34] In other words, we see here an important development within the early communities: the emergence of a specifically Christian notion of Scripture containing the Scriptures of old (the OT) side by side with a new body of regulatory writings from the apostolic and sub-apostolic age (the NT).

In this process Christian reading patterns are derived from, but also imposed on, the old Scriptures; parallel with such readings of Scripture, specifically Christian writings begin to form the NT. The core of these texts was received as authoritative to be read in worship alongside the Jewish Scriptures from roughly the mid- or late first to the early third

---

32. Barton, The Spirit and the Letter, 64.
33. Metzger, The Canon of the New Testament, 118.
34. See also Polycarp's Phil. 12.1, which seems to refer to Eph 4:26 as Scripture.

century, as witnessed, for example, by the Pauline writings (Col 4:16; cf.
2 Pet 3:16) and by Justin (1 *Apol.* 67). It is here striking, as Barton emphasizes, that "the Gospels were received as, in practice, even more important
than the Jewish Scriptures *before* they were old enough to have a natural
aura of sacred antiquity."[35] However, as we have seen above, there are
some noteworthy early, even first century, indications of the new apostolic writings already being conceived of as Scripture.

2.3 INTERPRETATION: CHRIST AS MID-POINT

The teaching of and about Christ—the gospel—whether in oral, written
or re-oralized form, was often prioritized, it seems, even over against
the Jewish Scriptures, which were now believed to be fulfilled. Christian
Judaists in the early second century, however, could still tend to regard
Jewish Scripture as the ultimate authority. Ignatius of Antioch tells us
about such different expectations of authority associated with the old
Scriptures in his *Letter to the Philadelphians* (8.2):[36]

> But I urge you to do nothing in a contentious way, but in accor-
> dance with the teaching of Christ. For I heard some saying: "If
> I do not find it in the ancient records [Gr. *Archaiois*=the Jewish
> Scriptures], I do not believe in the Gospel." And when I said to
> them, "It is written," they replied to me, "That is just the question."
> But for me, Jesus Christ is the ancient records; the sacred ancient
> records are his cross and death, and his resurrection, and the faith
> that comes through him—by which things I long to be made righ-
> teous by your prayer.[37]

It is natural to take Ignatius' use of the Greek *archaios*, "ancient record," and
his phrasing "it is written" in this quote to refer to the Jewish Scriptures.[38]
However, the point he seems to be making implies a broader meaning,

---

35. Barton, *The Spirit and the Letter*, 67.

36. On the difficulty of identifying Ignatius' opponents, see T. A. Robinson, *Ignatius of Antioch and the Parting of the Ways* (Peabody, Mass.: Hendrickson, 2009), 113–26.

37. Ehrman, *The Apostolic Fathers*, LCL 24, 1:291–92 (modified).

38. For the unparalleled use of *archaios* referring to the Jewish Scriptures, and to similar passages in Josephus and Philo, see W. R. Schoedel, "Ignatius and the Archives," *HTR* 71 (1978): 97–106.

which involves an overall textual conception embracing both the Jewish
Scriptures and their christological interpretation. Or should we rather say
that Ignatius and his Judaizing Christian dialogue partners are exhibiting
a problem: whether the old Scriptures and the Gospel are communicating the same Christian message, or whether the credibility of Christian
claims necessarily has to be grounded in the Jewish Scriptures? As the
Antiochian bishop on his journey under armed guard to martyrdom in
Rome sees things, the old Scriptures and the Gospel (in oral or written
form) speak of Jesus Christ, "his cross and death and his resurrection and
the faith which comes through him."[39] Ignatius here appears to emphasize his understanding of a creedal-like center of the Scriptures, consisting of a Christian narrative reading embracing this set of keywords.
Jesus Christ, his cross, death and resurrection are identified with the
very text of Ignatius' Scriptures. It is interesting to note that the reverentially abbreviated *nomina sacra* (some five to fifteen specially demarcated
sacred names) introduced universally in the Christian biblical manuscript tradition from around the late first century on, such as the Greek
words for Jesus, Christ and (the less consistently demarcated) cross could
quite possibly have had this creedal function that Ignatius here addresses.
Along these lines, in an often cited passage, the British papyrologist C. H.
Roberts has described the system of *nomina sacra* in the biblical manuscripts (including also the Greek words for Lord, God, Spirit and often
Father and Son) as "the embryonic creed of the first Church."[40] As we shall
see below, in the contemporary *Epistle of Barnabas* such use of *nomina
sacra* seem to be hermeneutically important by drawing attention to the
name of Jesus and his cross.

  Christ-centered reading as the point of convergence in much second
century Christian exegesis continues in the prolific church writer Origen
(ca. 185–254 C.E.), who makes a claim very similar to that of Ignatius
when in his *Commentary on John* (V.6) he writes that "all the Scriptures
are one book because all the teaching that has come to us about Christ is

---

39. Cf. *Phld.* 5.2 and 6.1.
40. Colin H. Roberts, *Manuscript, Society and Belief in Early Christian Egypt* (Oxford: Oxford
University Press, 1979), 46.

recapitulated in one single whole." Likewise Irenaeus (ca. 125–202 C.E.), for whom Christ makes up the *scopus*, the principle of the harmony of all Scripture, states:

> For if anyone reads the Scriptures with attention, he will find in them an account of Christ ... for Christ is the treasure which was hid in the field ... And, for this reason, indeed, when at this present time the law is read to the Jews, it is like a fable; for they do not possess the explanation of all things pertaining to the advent of the Son of God, which took place in human nature; but when it is read by the Christians, it is a treasure, hid indeed in a field, but brought to light by the cross of Christ ...[41]

Irenaeus here hints at the recurring scriptural interpretive pattern among some early church teachers, referred to above as the "proof from prophecy" tradition, often containing one or more of the three focal points *de Christo* (on Christ), *de lege* (on the Law) and *de ecclesia* (on the church).[42] On another level, here as frequently elsewhere, the bishop of Lyons gives voice to the patristic "dogma" of the unity of the Scriptures, Christ as the first principle of interpretation combined as well with what we could perhaps call a form of anti-Rabbinic reading. Taken together, these concerns of his and some of his predecessors open up to a hermeneutic movement from the Jewish law to the Messiah-Christ as the centre of Scripture, for the expansion of the Jewish Scriptures to include new Christian writings, as well as for the pertinence of some textual issues related to christology.

2.4 TEXT, INTERPRETATION, CANON

2.4.1 FINDING JESUS AND HIS CROSS IN GENESIS 14:14

The connection between text and interpretation is sometimes very close. An example of this is the rendering of Gen 14:14 of the number 318 in parts of the Christian manuscript tradition. This may even be our oldest

---

41. *Against Heresies* IV.26.1, ANF 1.
42. See "§2.2.1 Gospel and Proof from Prophecy" above.

known witness of *nomina sacra*,[43] the earliest exposition of which is found in the *Epistle of Barnabas*.[44] In *Barnabas* 9.7–9 the author presents an allegorical reading of the circumcision of Abraham's household by elaborating on the number 318, in the source rendered by the Greek letters TJE, instanced also in other contemporary early Christian manuscripts.[45] This indicates that the author of *Barnabas* had a Christian copy before him of Gen 14:14. The interesting text in *Barnabas* focusing on the name of Jesus and the dogma of grace signified by the cross reads:

> For Abraham, the first to perform circumcision, was looking ahead in the Spirit to Jesus when he circumcised. For he received the firm teachings of the three letters. For it says, "Abraham circumcised eighteen and three hundred men from his household." What knowledge, then, was given to him? Notice that first he mentions the eighteen and then, after a pause, the three hundred. The number eighteen [in Greek] consists of an Iota [J], 10, and an Eta [E], 8. There you have Jesus. And because the cross was about to have grace in the letter Tau [T], he next gives the three hundred, Tau. And so he shows the name Jesus by the first two letters, and the cross by the other. For the one who has placed the implanted gift of his covenant in us knew these things. No one has learned a more reliable lesson from me. But I know that you are worthy.[46]

Here a reference to the *nomen sacrum* for Jesus (JE=18) stands alongside the symbol of the cross (T=300). The cross, said to signify grace, is further treated in *Barnabas* 11 and 12, there in connection with Christian baptism and the serpent raised by Moses in the desert. That the symbolic representation of the number 318 was known in Christian circles is further confirmed by Clement of Alexandria (ca. 150–215 C.E.) in his reading of

---

43. See also "§2.3 Interpretation: Christ as Mid-Point" above, and "§2.4.3 Prioritized Texts and Canons" below.

44. Reidar Hvalvik, *The Struggle for Scripture and Covenant: The Purpose of the Epistle of Barnabas and Jewish-Christian Competition in the Second Century* (WUNT 2/82; Tübingen: Mohr-Siebeck, 1996), 23.

45. For references, see Larry W. Hurtado, *The Earliest Christian Artifacts: Manuscripts and Christian Origins* (Grand Rapids: Eerdmans, 2006), 146–7.

46. Ehrman, *The Apostolic Fathers*, 2:45–47.

Gen 14:14. However, for Clement this form of Christian gematria seems to
be past tradition rather than part of his own exegetical practice. Clement
comments: "For it is said that the character for 300 is by its shape a symbol
of the cross of the Lord."[47] On the whole, second century readings of the
Scriptures abound in references to the sign of the cross, not least in the
writings of Justin Martyr.

2.4.2 THE SCRIPTURES AND THE RULE OF FAITH

The second century church made wide use of creedal summaries. Taking
their point of departure in the NT (1 Cor 15:3ff; Acts 10:36–43; Rom 8:34;
2 Tim 2:8; 1 Pet 3:18ff),[48] and in oral tradition, these variously formulated
kerygmatic summaries occur, for example, in 1 Clement, Ignatius, Justin,
Irenaeus, Clement of Alexandria and Tertullian. In Ignatius, we find one-
limbed formulations (focusing on Christ), such as:

> Be deaf when anyone speaks to you apart from Jesus Christ, who
> was of the stock of David, who was from Mary, who was truly
> born, ate and drank, was truly persecuted under Pontius Pilate,
> was truly crucified and died in the sight of beings heavenly, earthly
> and under the earth, who also was truly raised from the dead, His
> Father raising him … (Trall. 9)[49]

Interestingly, in Ignatius (Smyrn. 1.1–2) both Jewish and Gentile believers
seem to embrace the same christological creed.[50]

From the late second century two- or three-limbed (i.e. dyadic or
triadic) summaries of the faith are referred to as the Rule of Faith, the
Rule of Truth, the Ecclesiastical Rule, or simply the Kerygma, or the
Faith. When presenting the four Evangelists and their written accounts
in Against Heresies, Irenaeus, for example, summarizes their teaching in
the Gospels by referring to this Rule: "These have all declared to us that
there is one God, Creator of heaven and earth, announced by the law and

---

47. Stromateis VI.2.84, 3–4, ANF 2.
48. See J. N. D. Kelly, Early Christian Creeds (3d rev. ed.; London; New York: Continuum, 1972; repr., 2006).
49. Kelly, Early Christian Creeds. (Translation modified)
50. Oskar Skarsaune, Jewish Believers in Jesus (Peabody, Mass.: Hendrickson, 2007), 509.

the prophets; and one Christ, the Son of God" (III.1.2). What he seems to
be saying is that the Rule of Faith is closely related to, or even equivalent
to, the narrative presentation in the written Gospel. To him, the Rule of
Faith—or the Rule of Truth as Irenaeus prefers to call it—is closely associated with the Gospels and the Scriptures as a whole. Thus, in Paul Blowers'
wording, when Irenaeus (or Tertullian) defends the church against the
Gnostics, the Rule of Faith is identified with Scripture's own intrinsic story-line "in order to avoid the Gnostics' double-talk, their propagating of
one myth on the philosophical level while still trying, on another level, to
communicate it with pieces of scriptural narrative."[51] This intimate connection between the biblical text and the particular reading pattern signified
by the church's Rule of Faith is also found in Clement of Alexandria. To
him the "Canon of the Church"—the phrase Clement often uses—is really
what keeps the Scriptures together as a unified whole: "The Canon of the
Church is the agreement and unity of the Law and the Prophets with the
Testament delivered at the coming of the Lord."[52]

2.4.3 PRIORITIZED TEXTS AND CANONS
IN JUDAISM AND CHRISTIANITY

A most important *textual property* of the Jewish Scriptures in the
Hellenistic setting was their translatability into the *lingua franca* of their
day, Koine Greek. The first and second century Christian choice of the
Greek Septuagint as the primary authoritative Bible translation for church
use was crucial. In Rabbinical Judaism it was paralleled by the emergence
of new Jewish translations into Greek of the Hebrew Scriptures, such as
that of Aquila (early second century C.E.), Theodotion (mid-second century C.E.) and Symmachus (ca. 150–250 C.E.). Also, while in the second
century large parts of Christianity kept to the Greek Bible (still, of course,
largely based on the Hebrew text), Rabbinic Judaism continued to use the
Hebrew (Tiberian) Masoretic text as its normative text.[53] Such variations

---

51. Paul M. Blowers, "The *Regula Fidei* and the Narrative Character of Early Christian Faith,"
Pro Ecclesia 6 (1997): 212.

52. *Stromateis* VI.125.2.

53. See John Eldwolde, "Language and Translation of the Old Testament," in J. W. Rogerson and
J. M. Lieu, eds. *The Oxford Handbook of Biblical Studies* (Oxford: Oxford University Press, 2006), 138f.

regarding translation and textual preference between Jews and Christians, however, were only the starting point for further differences.

The textual formats preferred also differed. Instead of the classic scroll format used by both Jews and Gentiles, Christian literature from the earliest second-century papyrus discoveries onwards was written almost exclusively on codices, the early equivalent to the modern book format. Yet another typical feature, already mentioned above, which set Christian Scripture apart from other literature, was the use of *nomina sacra* (sacred words), as distinct from the Jewish Tetragrammaton, in the manuscripts. That is, the textual demarcation of the five primary *nomina sacra* Jesus, Christ, Lord, God and Spirit (e.g., in extant second/third century OT and NT papyri, and in the fourth century Codex Sinaiticus), as well as of a few other words, made the Christian Scriptures editorially unique.[54] Moreover, there seems to have been a common Christian practice (although this is disputed among scholars) to collect testimonies of scriptural citations, arranged thematically, probably with brief Christian interpretations added. Such "testimony sources" appear to have been used by Justin and other Christian writers to demonstrate the fulfillment of scriptural prophecy.[55] These sources are perhaps best described as Greek "targumizing" of the standard Septuagint text.[56] As Justin believes he has the authentic Septuagint text in his source, he accuses the Jews of having interpolated and even removed certain passages from the Scriptures. In his *Dialogue* (71–73) he claims that Messianic prophesies have been undercut in Jewish copies of the Septuagint, for example when treating Ps 96:10. Justin mistakenly accuses the Jews of having cut out the words "from the tree" from the Septuagint text, by Justin supposed to be following after the phrase: "Say among the nations 'the Lord reigned.' " However, the Apologist seems unaware of the fact that here, as elsewhere, it is a matter of Christian interpolation in his own testimony source.

---

54. Cf. Martin Hengel, *The Four Gospels and the One Gospel of Jesus Christ: An Investigation of the Collection and Origin of the Canonical Gospels* (Harrisburg: Trinity, 2000), 118.

55. For use of the term "testimony sources," see Skarsaune, "Justin and His Bible," 56.

56. Skarsaune, "Justin and His Bible," 59.

Considering the use of the codex format,[57] *nomina sacra*, a preference of the Septuagint text, and a different ordering of the OT books[58] (as well as the probable usage of testimony sources), we can see that the Christian OT was easily recognizable and distinguishable from the Jewish Bible.

By the late second century when the bipartite Christian Bible was conceived of as sacred text made up of the "Old" and the "New Testament," an important step had been taken in terms of textuality, mirroring changes in scriptural use and interpretation that had emerged throughout the first and second centuries.[59]

Turning to the NT texts, based on the NT manuscript tradition, David Trobisch forcefully argues for the publication of a full 27 books edition of the NT with typical Christian features, such as the codex format, *nomina sacra* and the "canonical ordering" of the NT books, already in the second century.[60]

On the potential inclusion of so-called apocryphal NT writings in the Christian canon, such as the Gospels of Thomas and Peter, the church historian Eusebius' (ca. 260–339 C.E.) negative judgment largely applies also to the second century situation, as witnessed by Irenaeus and others: "Not a single one of these have been considered worth mentioning by any of the teachers standing in the ecclesiastical tradition" (*Ecclesiastical History* III.25).[61]

Regarding the canon of the OT it can be noted that Christianity from the beginning never was without a Bible, but shared its Scriptures with Judaism.[62] This is probably the reason why the so-called OT Apocrypha (from which many text allusions in the NT can be derived) surprisingly are never quoted as Scripture in the NT. The same tendency can be seen

---

57. However, cf. Skarsaune, "Justin and His Bible," 57.

58. See Childs, *Introduction to the Old Testament as Scripture*, 667.

59. Tomas Bokedal, "The Scriptures and the LORD: Formation and Significance of the Christian Biblical Canon. A Study in Text, Ritual and Interpretation" (PhD Diss., Lund University, 2005).

60. David Trobisch, *The First Edition of the New Testament* (New York: Oxford University Press, 2000). See also D. C. Parker's important critical review in *JTS* 53 (2002) 298–305.

61. Regarding the canonical status of the Gospel and Apocalypse of Peter and the Gospels of the Hebrews and the Egyptians, see Metzger, *The Canon of the New Testament*, 165–89.

62. See esp. Roger T. Beckwith, *The Old Testament Canon of the New Testament Church and its Background in Early Judaism* (Grand Rapids: Eerdmans, 1985).

in the Jewish historian Josephus, writing in the 90s C.E., who delimits
the Jewish canon to 22 books (arguably equal to the Christian 39 books
canon), "for which every Jew is willing to die" (*Against Apion* 1.38–41).[63]
Although there was a certain ambiguity or inconsistency in the early
church regarding the OT canon, when bishops and theologians like Melito
of Sardis (d. ca. 180 C.E.) and Origen (ca. 185–254 C.E.) produced lists of
the OT canon "they almost invariably reproduced a list of the books in
the Jewish Bible, and of these books only."[64] The Greek-speaking church
kept to this Jewish canon for some centuries to come.[65]

BIBLIOGRAPHY

Barton, John. *The Spirit and the Letter: Studies in the Biblical Canon*,
    London: SPCK, 1997.

Beckwith, Roger T. *The Old Testament Canon of the New Testament
    Church and its Background in Early Judaism*. Grand Rapids:
    Eerdmans, 1985.

Blowers, Paul. "The *Regula Fidei* and the Narrative Character of Early
    Christian Faith." *Pro Ecclesia* 6 (1997): 199–228.

Bokedal, Tomas. *The Scriptures and the* LORD: *Formation and Significance
    of the Christian Biblical Canon. A Study in Text, Ritual and
    Interpretation*. PhD Diss., Lund University, 2005.

Byrskog, Samuel. *Jesus the Only Teacher: Didactic Authority and
    Transmission in Ancient Israel, Ancient Judaism and the Matthean
    Community*. Stockholm: Almqvist & Wiksell, 1994.

Childs, Brevard S. *Introduction to the Old Testament as Scripture*.
    London: SCM, 1979.

Ehrman, Bart D. *The Apostolic Fathers*. Vol. 2, LCL 25. Cambridge, MA:
    Harvard University Press, 2003.

---

63. Beckwith, *The Old Testament Canon of the New Testament Church and its Background in Early Judaism*, 235ff., 119ff.

64. Skarsaune, *In the Shadow of the Temple*, 291, also discussing the early church's use of a wider OT canon.

65. including Athanasius of Alexandria, Cyril of Jerusalem, Epiphanius, Gregory of Nazianzus, but also the Latin Church Father Jerome.

* Special thanks to Dr Donald Wood and my wife Anna Bokedal for reading and commenting on an earlier draft of the present chapter.

Eldwolde, John. "Language and Translation of the Old Testament." Pages 135–58 in *The Oxford Handbook of Biblical Studies*. Edited by J. W. Rogerson and J. M. Lieu Oxford: Oxford University, 2006.

Foster, Paul. "The Epistles of Ignatius of Antioch and the Writings that Later Formed the New Testament." Pages 159–85 in *The Reception of the New Testament in the Apostolic Fathers*. Edited by A. F. Gregory and C. M. Tuckett. Oxford: OUP, 2005.

Gamble, Harry Y. *Books and Readers in the Early Church: A History of Early Christian Texts*. New Haven: Yale University Press, 1995.

Gregory, A. F. "1 Clement and the Writings that Later Formed the New Testament." Pages 129–58 in *The Reception of the New Testament in the Apostolic Fathers*. Edited by A. F. Gregory and C. M. Tuckett. Oxford: OUP, 2005.

Hagner, Donald A. *The Use of the Old and New Testaments in Clement of Rome*. Leiden: Brill, 1973.

Harnack, Adolf von. *Bible Reading in the Early Church*. London and New York, 1912.

Hengel, Martin. *The Four Gospels and the One Gospel of Jesus Christ: An Investigation of the Collection and Origin of the Canonical Gospels*. London: SCM, 2000.

Hill, Charles E. *The Johannine Corpus in the Early Church*. Oxford: OUP, 2004.

Hurtado, Larry W. *The Earliest Christian Artifacts: Manuscripts and Christian Origins*. Grand Rapids: Eerdmans, 2006.

Hvalvik, Reidar. *The Struggle for Scripture and Covenant: The Purpose of the Epistle of Barnabas and Jewish-Christian Competition in the Second Century*. Tübingen: Mohr-Siebeck, 1996.

Inge, W. R. "Ignatius." Pages 63–83 in *The New Testament in the Apostolic Fathers*. Oxford: Clarendon Press, 1905.

Kelly, J. N. D. *Early Christian Creeds*. Third revised edition. New York: Continuum, 1972; Repr., 2006.

Köhler, W.-D. *Die Rezeption des Matthäusevangeliums in der Zeit vor Irenäus*. WUNT 2/24. Tübingen: Mohr-Siebeck, 1987.

Metzger, Bruce M. *The Canon of the New Testament: Its Origin, Development, and Significance.* Oxford: Clarendon, 1987.

Paget, James Carleton. "The Interpretation of the Bible in the Second Century." In *The New Cambridge History of the Bible.* Edited by Joachim Schaper and James Carleton Paget. Cambridge: Cambridge University Press, 2013.

Parvis, Sarah and Paul Foster, eds. *Justin Martyr and His Worlds.* Minneapolis: Fortress, 2007.

Porter, Stanley E. ed. *The Pauline Canon,* Pauline Studies 1. Leiden: Brill, 2004.

Rhodes, J. N. *The Epistle of Barnabas and the Deuteronomic Tradition.* WUNT 2/188. Tübingen: Mohr-Siebeck, 2004.

Roberts, C. H. *Manuscript, Society and Belief in Early Christian Egypt.* Oxford: OUP, 1979.

Robinson, T. A. *Ignatius of Antioch and the Parting of the Ways.* Peabody: Hendrickson, 2009.

Schoedel, William R. "Ignatius and the Archives." HTR 71 (1978): 97–106.

Skarsaune, Oskar. "The Development of Scriptural Interpretation in the Second and Third Centuries – except Clement and Origen." Pages 373–450 in *Hebrew Bible/Old Testament: The History of Its Interpretation,* vol. 1, *From the Beginnings to the Middle Ages (until 1300),* Part I, *Antiquity.* Edited by Sæbø, M. Göttingen: Vandenhoeck & Ruprecht, 1996.

———. *In the Shadow of the Temple: Jewish Influences on Early Christianity.* Downers Grove: InterVarsity, 2002.

———. *Jewish Believers in Jesus.* Peabody, MA: Hendrickson, 2007.

Smith, D. Moody. "When Did the Gospels Become Scripture?" *JBL* 119 (2000): 3–20.

Stanton, Graham. *Jesus and Gospel.* Cambridge: Cambridge University, 2004.

Stuhlhofer, Franz. *Der Gebrauch der Bibel von Jesus bis Euseb: Eine statistische Untersuching zur Kanonsgeschichte.* Wuppertal: Brockhaus, 1988.

Tuckett, C. M. "The Didache and the Writings that Later Formed
    the New Testament." Pages 83–127 in *The Reception of the New
    Testament in the Apostolic Fathers*. Edited by A. F. Gregory and C.
    M. Tuckett. Oxford: OUP, 2005.

PART B

CHRIST THE CENTER: THE SHAPING OF THE SCRIPTURAL CANON

3

CANON/SCRIPTURE

The word "canon" (Greek κανών) originally meant a device that kept other things straight, a measuring stick, or a norm or rule (Gal 6:16), but it could also denote a normative list or a catalogue. When the early church applied the term to the Scriptures, they appealed to the normative aspect of the term as well as the understanding of "canon" as an authoritative collection, or delimited list, of regulative writings. In the latter sense(s), the word "canon" and its cognates were used by fourth-century church teachers onwards and have commonly been employed by scholars to describe the formation of the Jewish and the Christian Bible. While the "Sacred Books" (1 Macc. 12.9) or "Scripture(s)" (Rom 1:2; 1 Clem. 53.1; Greek γραφή) could have a similar or overlapping denotation, on a basic level, "Scripture" signifies authoritative written revelation of divine origin, whereas "canon" may be understood as a property of Sacred Scripture— designating its literary arrangement and delimitation, as well as normative address, as a corpus of Holy Writ.

Although the Jewish and Christian notions of "Scripture" and "canon" share some commonalities with other religious and secular "canons," several distinctive features within the Jewish-Christian textual tradition set its scriptural canon(s) apart as a unique literary formation. Whereas the literary canons of revered writers of classical Greece (and later literary canons providing benchmarks of excellence in their respective field) are largely priority lists that are in principle open or arbitrary and with little indications of censorship,[1] the Jewish and Christian scriptural canons often stress the grouping and ordering of the texts and tend to draw a sharp distinction between books being included and books excluded from the collection of Sacred Scriptures. Characteristically these Scriptures—made up of various literary genres and composed by numerous authors over a long period of time—are perceived as sacrosanct (Josephus C. *Apionem* 1.37–43; *m. Yad.* 4.6) or "God-breathed" (1 Tim 3:16; cf. Origen *De Principiis*, Pref. 8).

Beginning in ancient Israel, crucial moments in the transmission of the biblical material are the points of transition from mainly oral communication to written text. While in its oral phases the material is largely mediated through religious experts, when codified as writing, the written text tends to become "a source of authority by itself."[2] Already in the First Temple period the copying of such authoritative texts was carried out by highly skilled scribes, affiliated with the temple and/or, less likely, the royal palace.[3] The orally and textually transmitted traditions that gradually took shape as the text and canon of the Jewish Scriptures, were here closely associated with the Israelite-Judaean scribal culture. Characteristic of both Jewish and, later on, Christian transmission of central portions of the biblical material was the mutual interaction between oral and written textual means of transmission in which also memorization played a decisive role.[4] Even if earlier oral and written stages of the biblical text receive continual scholarly attention, in recent years, and in connection with a desire to apply a more holistic approach to the biblical literature, scholarship has shown renewed interest in the final form of the text, which the Jewish and Christian communities received and canonized as their authoritative text.[5]

Pre-Christian designations of the Jewish Scriptures that indicate an emerging two- or three-fold textual structuring include "the Law and the Prophets" (2 *Macc.* 15.9), "the Law and the Prophets and the other

---

1. Hägg 2010:109.
2. Van der Toorn 2007:206–7, 232.
3. Van der Toorn 2007:82–89.
4. Carr 2011, e.g. 25–34, as applied to the Book of Proverbs; Kelber and Byrskog 2009.
5. Barton 2007:185–91.

ancestral Books" (variously repeated thrice in the Prologue of *Ben Sira*; cf. Philo *De Vit. Cont.* 25). To this we may add later first-century references, such as "the Law and the Prophets" (Matt 22:40; Luke 16:16; John 1:45; Rom 3:21), "the Law of Moses and the Prophets and Psalms" (Luke 24:44), and Josephus' famous account in *Against Apion* 1.37–43 of the twenty-two divinely inspired Books claimed to be embraced by "every Jew," and underlined by the canonical formula ("no one has ventured to add to or to take away from them or to alter them"). Of the twenty-two Scriptures—Josephus, however, does not enumerate individual writings—five books of Moses, thirteen Prophets (cf. *Ant.* 10.35), and four remaining Books are mentioned. Arguably these twenty-two books are the same as the ones embraced by the twenty-four-book canon lists in the contemporary *4 Ezra* 14.45–48 and the rabbinic enumeration in *b. Baba Batra* 14b–15b, in which case Judges and Ruth, on the one hand, and Jeremiah and Lamentations, on the other, are counted separately. In addition to twenty-two—the number of letters of the Hebrew alphabet—or twenty-four, Jerome indicates that the Jewish Scriptures can be numbered also as twenty-seven (the five Hebrew "double letters" counted separately and linked to five books reckoned as double; *Prologue to the Books of Samuel and Kings*). As to the "closing" of the Jewish canon, scholarship is divided between those who hold that a delimited canon was formed in the Persian or Maccabean period and those who think that it remained "open" well into the first centuries of the Common Era.[6]

Interestingly, the shape of the Jewish twenty-two-book canon, in sections of five books (Moses), thirteen books (Prophets), and four books (Writings; cf. nn. 60–61, 69 and 73, ch. 4, below), as presented by Josephus in the late first century CE, appears to have left traces in the textual arrangement of the Christian Scriptures as well. Several early church teachers adhere, in theory, to a twenty-two-book Old Testament (e.g. Origen, Athanasius and Jerome), and a three-fold division is found in Luke 24:44. We may also notice some parallels in the structuring of the emergent New Testament. For example, our earliest extant Four-Gospel codex, P45 (early 3rd century), contains five books—Gospels and Acts—and an

6. Lim 2013:17.

early appearing arrangement of the Pauline letter corpus includes thirteen writings (excluding Hebrews; e.g. *Canon Muratori*, Tertullian and Gaius). The Jewish-Christian twenty-two-book structure seems to resonate again in Eusebius' enumeration of twenty-two New Testament writings among the Recognized Books (ἐν ὁμολογουμένοις): Four Gospels, Acts, fourteen Pauline epistles, 1 Peter, 1 John and Revelation (*HE* 3.25; cf. 3.3). The New Testament of the Syriac Peshitta, and most likely John Chrysostom's NT, represent twenty-two-book corpora similar to that enlisted by Eusebius (preceding his list of five Disputed Books).

From the first and second century on, the codex format—which was the characteristic Christian medium for the Scriptures—beside liturgical practice and theological reflection, helped organizing the church's New Testament as a two-fold Gospel–Apostle configuration;[7] and, before long, as four literary part-volumes that became the ecclesial standard up till the present.[8] In early canonical ordering, these comprised: The fourfold Gospel (cf. Irenaeus' emphasis on the number "four", *Haer.* 3.11.8), the eight books of Acts and seven Catholic Epistles, the Pauline fourteen-letter corpus ("twice seven Epistles", Amphilochius of Iconium *Iambics for Seleucus*), and the Book of Revelation (which also includes seven Epistles, Rev 2–3). As part of this NT canon, embracing twenty-seven writings (= 3 x 3 x 3), which bishop Athanasius in AD 367 (*Thirty-Ninth Festal Letter*) combined with a twenty-two-book OT canon (22 + 27 = 7 x 7), a form of numerology seems to have played a role associated with the number of letters in the Hebrew alphabet (twenty-two/twenty-seven)[9] and the notion of completion.[10] In this connection it is worth noting that to date we have no manuscripts in which "apocryphal" Gospels have been bound together with any of the canonical four.[11]

---

7. Cf. Bovon 2002.

8. Trobisch 2000:24–29, 103.

9. Lim 2013:41.

10. As to the significance commonly attached to the numbers three, four and seven, see Labuschagne 2000:1–19, 69–70; and Bokedal 2014:318–20.

11. Elliott 1996:107, 110.

By ca. 150–250 CE,[12] or arguably considerably earlier,[13] the numera-
tion of books in the canon of most Jews had become fixed as twenty-two,
or, as twenty-four: The tripartite Tanak—the Law, the Prophets and the
Writings—made up of twenty-four Sacred Books (*b. Baba Batra* 14b–15a;
a number known also to the author of *Gos. Thom.* 52, Victorinus, and
Jerome, and perhaps alluded to in Rev 4:4, 10).

When we consider the reception history of the Jewish and Christian
canon formations it appears that the Jewish twenty-four-book corpus
(corresponding to thirty-nine books of most Protestants), the wider
Christian OT canon including Apocrypha or Deuterocanonical books
(embraced e.g. by Augustine and the Roman Catholic Church), and a
Christian New Testament comprising twenty-seven books have crystal-
lized as the widely accepted canonical shaping within these respective
community contexts.

Integral to the canon formation process, some unique textual and ritual
qualities may be noticed. Perhaps the most conspicuous feature contributing to the textual sacredness in Second Temple Judaism, and onwards,
relates to the divine Name, the Tetragrammaton, which Jewish scribes
marked off reverentially in written forms.[14] When the early Christians
began producing their own Greek Scriptures this scribal practice was
modified and expressed in the so-called *nomina sacra*, specially sacred
words such as God, Jesus and Spirit written in contracted form in Old
and New Testament manuscripts. Selections from the Jewish Scriptures,
not in scroll, but in codex, format, supplied with *nomina sacra*, obtained
a particular Christian identity (cf. *Barn.* 9.7–9; P. Yale 1)[15] and were in this
way put side by side with the new Christian Scriptures for liturgical (Justin
1 Apol. 67)[16] and other usage roughly from the time of the composition of
the four Gospels, or a little later. In Theodor Zahn's phrasing: "What was
later named 'canonical,' was originally called 'read in corporate worship.' "[17]

---

12. Lim 2013:180.
13. Beckwith 1985:165.
14. Barton 1997:106–21.
15. Hengel 2000:118–19.
16. Hengel 2000:96.
17. Bokedal 2014:243.

BIBLIOGRAPHY

Barton, John. *The Old Testament: Canon, Literature and Theology: Collected Essays of John Barton.* Society for Old Testament Study Series. Ed. Margaret Barker. Aldershot, Hampshire: Ashgate, 2007.

———. *The Spirit and the Letter: Studies in the Biblical Canon.* London: SPCK, 1997.

Beckwith, Roger. *The Old Testament Canon of the New Testament Church and Its Background in Early Judaism.* Grand Rapids, MI: Eerdmans, 1985.

Bokedal, Tomas. *The Formation and Significance of the Christian Biblical Canon. A Study in Text, Ritual and Interpretation.* London: Bloomsbury: T&T Clark, 2014.

Bovon, François. "The Canonical Structure of Gospel and Apostle". Pages 516–27 in *The Canon Debate.* Edited by McDonald, Lee Martin, and James A. Sanders. Peabody, MA: Hendrickson, 2002.

Carr, David M. *The Formation of the Hebrew Bible: A New Reconstruction.* Oxford: Oxford University Press, 2011

Elliott, Keith J. "Manuscripts, the Codex and the Canon". *JSNT* 63 (1996): 105–23.

Hägg, Tomas. "Canon Formation in Greek Literary Culture." Pages 109–28 in *Canon and Canonicity: The Formation and Use of Scripture.* Edited by Einar Thomassen. Copenhagen, Denmark: Museum Tusculanum Press, University of Copenhagen, 2010.

Hengel, Martin. *The Four Gospels and the One Gospel of Jesus Christ: An Investigation of the Collection and Origin of the Canonical Gospels.* London: SCM Press, 2000.

Kelber, Werner H. and Samuel Byrskog, eds. *Jesus in Memory: Traditions in Oral and Scribal Perspectives.* Waco, TX: Baylor University Press, 2011.

Labuschagne, Casper J. *Numerical Secrets of the Bible: Rediscovering the Bible Codes.* North Richland Hills, TX: Bibal Press, 2000.

Lim, Timothy H. *The Formation of the Jewish Canon*. The Anchor Yale Bible Reference Library. New Haven: Yale University Press, 2013.

Trobisch, David. *The First Edition of the New Testament*. Oxford: Oxford University Press, 2000.

Van der Toorn, Karel. *Scribal Culture and the Making of the Hebrew Bible*. Cambridge, Massachusetts and London, England: Harvard University Press, 2007.

4

CANON FORMATION AND INTERPRETATION—PROBLEMS AND POSSIBILITIES

T hree major theorists—Theodor Zahn, Adolf von Harnack and Albert C. Sundberg, Jr.—have continued to shape the scholarly discussion on the Christian canon formation, Zahn and Harnack for more than a century. This chapter deals with problematic as well as promising trajectories in this lively debate. Our theorists suggest varying dates for the historical formation of a New Testament canon—ca. A.D. 100 (Zahn), ca. 200 (Harnack), and ca. 300–400 (Sundberg). While noting advantages in all three positions, I criticize at some length Sundberg's sharp distinction between the notions of "Scripture" and "canon," and place emphasis on the canon formation as a process involving a complex of components. Along these lines I also scrutinize Sundberg's sequential approach in which he perceives three main phases in the formation of the NT, namely, the rise of Christian literature to the status of Scripture (*step 1*), the conscious grouping of Christian writings into closed collections (*step 2*), and the formation of a NT list, which he describes as "canonization proper" (*step 3*). Paying rather close attention to Sundberg's analysis, I choose to place more stress on various dimensions, rather than sequential "steps" (Sundberg), in the process of canonization. However, akin to Zahn, Harnack and Sundberg, in focusing attention on the early

canonical process (Sundberg's *steps 1* and *2*), I still engage with chronological aspects of the process. Throughout the chapter, but especially in the
final section, I offer some constructive comments on the early canonical
process. Josephus's account of the Jewish scriptural canon in *Against Apion*
1.37–43 is discussed, as well as the canonical process in Irenaeus (with
potential parallels found in Josephus), the NT around A.D. 200, and the
mechanisms involved when the new Christian writings were associated
with the Jewish Scriptures, and *vice versa*. In my discussion I claim that
the canonization needs to be seen as a process beginning already in the
NT writings themselves with a New Testament canon clearly present in
the late second/early third century. Important stages in this process, such
as the formation of a delimited Pauline corpus and the fourfold Gospel
appear to have taken place no later than the second century.

All three hermeneutical emphases in our theorists are important for
a comprehensive understanding of Scripture, canon, and the canonical
process: Sundberg's communal–legal–conciliary, Harnack's apologetical–
communal, and Zahn's doxological–communal emphases. However, following on my focus on aspects of the early process, I indicate that Zahn's
account is undervalued. Through his approach we are drawn into the
early church's recognition of these Scriptures as divinely authorised in
the sphere of Christian worship, and as recognized as an integral part of
the life of the apostolic and sub-apostolic church.

Three major theories of the history of the New Testament canon
have now been discussed in biblical scholarship for almost fifty years.[1]
In Theodor Zahn's model a New Testament canon was present by A.D.
100, in Adolf von Harnack's by A.D. 200, and in Albert C. Sundberg's by
A.D. 400. With such diverse dating, what does this imply for the notion
of a scriptural canon?

According to Zahn an emerging NT canon appears as soon as a corpus
of new writings is used side by side with the Jewish Scriptures in the

---

1. John Barton, *The Spirit and the Letter: Studies in the Biblical Canon* (London: SPCK, 1997), 1–14;
Harry Y. Gamble, "The New Testament Canon: Recent Research and the Status Quaestionis," in
The Canon Debate, eds. Lee Martin McDonald and James A. Sanders (Peabody, Mass.: Hendrickson,
2002), 267–73.

context of worship.[2] A spontaneous development to this effect had taken place in the communities by A.D. 80–110.[3]

Von Harnack, who objected to this account of the new writings, emphatically claimed that we only have a New Testament canon, a collection of authoritative Christian writings, when the included texts are regarded as fully set on a par with the Jewish Scriptures, which only took place as part of an apologetic reaction on the part of the mainstream church. Consequently, Harnack and his equally influential pupil Hans von Campenhausen could argue that the formation of a New Testament canon was a reaction to a crisis,[4] ensuing in an anti-heretical "creation" that occurred towards the end of the second century as the status of the Christian writings indisputably attained an authority similar to that of the Jewish Scriptures. The title "New Testament" here becomes a seal and demonstration of the new scriptures being included among the Scriptures, that is, the Old and the emerging New Testament Scriptures.[5]

With an appeal to the ecclesial fourth-century employment of the term "canon" meaning "list, catalogue," Sundberg's position, by contrast, entails that a New Testament canon is in place only when a definite cataloguing

---

2. For Zahn the history of the New Testament canon concerns the question as to how the books of which the New Testament is made up form a unified whole (*Geschichte des Neutestamentlichen Kanons*, vol. 1 [Erlangen: Verlag von Andreas Deichert, 1888], 1). In his own words, it "gilt die Frage, wie die Bücher, aus welchen das Neue Testament aller sich christlich nennenden Kirchen seit mehr als einem Jahrtausend besteht, sich zu einem einheitlichen Ganzen von gleichartiger Bedeutung zusammengefunden haben."

3. Theodor Zahn, *Grundriss der Geschichte des Neutestamentlichen Kanons: Eine Ergänzung zu der Einleitung in das Neue Testament* (Leipzig: A. Deichert'sche Verlagsbuchh. Nachf. [Georg Böhme], 1901), 40: "[A]ls sicher darf gelten, daß um die Jahre 80–110 sowohl das 'vierfaltige' Ev als das Corpus der 13 Briefe des Paulus entstanden und in den gottesdienstlichen Gebrauch der heidenchristlichen Gemeinden auf der ganzen Linie von Antiochien bis Rom eingeführt worden sind, und daß diese beiden Sammlungen, welche den Grundstock des NT's bilden, von Anfang an im gottesdienstlichen Gebrauch und in der Vorstellung der Gemeinden von einem bald weiteren, bald engeren Kreis christlicher Schriften umgeben waren, welche in ähnlichem Maße, wie jene zwei Sammlungen, geeignet schienen, als gottesdienstliche Lesebücher der Erbauung und Belehrung der Gemeinden zu dienen." Justin Martyr is an early witness (ca. A.D. 150) to the Gospel (the memoirs of the Apostles) being read at the worship service together with the prophets (*1 Apol.* 67).

4. Christoph Markschies, "The Canon of the New Testament in Antiquity," in *Homer, the Bible, and Beyond: Literary and Religious Canons in the Ancient World*, eds. M. Finkelberg and G. G. Stroumsa (JSRC 2; Leiden: Brill), 176.

5. As the present chapter seeks to demonstrate, this process, in fact, looks very different than Harnack suggested: Old and New are linked much earlier, and in a variety of ways.

of the books to be included is present in a closed so-called canon list. Sundberg refers to the emergence of such catalogues or lists from the fourth and fifth centuries onward as "canonization proper."

Thus, depending on how we choose to define canonicity in regard to the new Christian scriptures, the notion of a canon may emerge spontaneously[6] from the life[7] of the apostolic and sub-apostolic church (Zahn), it may be defined as an anti-heretical device created by the late second-century church (Harnack/Campenhausen), or as a rather late ecclesiastical event, finally settled and defined by means of cataloguing the exact number of books to be included in the New Testament (Sundberg). According to the latter option, it is clear, as Sundberg maintains, that "the recognition that canonization proper is the definition of a New Testament list to which nothing can be added, nothing subtracted, removes canonization from the tacit implication that somehow canonization adheres to apostles, apostolic men, and the hearers of apostolic men and leaves the formation of a closed New Testament list as unequivocally the decision of the church."[8]

From this rough draft of three major players in the field, each representing a different approach, I shall address some terminological and interpretative problems (section 4.2 below) and possibilities (sections 4.3 and 4.4) involved in understanding the Christian canon formation process.

---

6. Cf. Brooke Foss Westcott, *The Bible in the Church* (London and New York: Macmillan, 1905): "the formation of the canon was among the first instinctive acts of the Christian society, resting upon the general confession of the Churches and not upon independent opinions of its members. The canon was not the result of a series of contests; rather, canonical books were separated from others by the intuitive insight of the Church." Cf. Barton, *The Spirit and the Letter*, 3; and Bruce M. Metzger, *The Canon of the New Testament: Its Origin, Development, and Significance* (Oxford: Clarendon, 1987), 21.

7. Especially ecclesial life pertaining to the Christian cult; Zahn, *Geschichte*, 83.

8. Sundberg, ("Towards a Revised History of the New Testament Canon," in *Studia Evangelica* [ed. F. L. Cross; Berlin: Akademie-Verlag, 1968], 461). As to a related point in regard to "apostolicity," in particular claims to apostolic authorship for writings included in the NT, see James D. G. Dunn, *Unity and Diversity in the New Testament* (London: SCM and Philadelphia: Trinity Press International, 1977, 2nd ed.), 386. For the impossibility of the church playing a dominating role in the canon formation process as outlined by Sundberg and others, see John Webster, *Holy Scripture: A Dogmatic Sketch* (Cambridge: Cambridge University, 2003), 63.

4.1 DATING OF THE FORMATION OF THE
NT CANON A KEY IN SUNDBERG'S MODEL

In the 1960s Albert C. Sundberg, Jr. worked on various projects related to both the Old and the New Testament canons.[9] In 1968 he published his important essay "Towards a Revised History of the New Testament Canon" in which he sets out to re-evaluate the scholarly criteria involved in an informed account of the canon formation in the early church. Quite rightly, Sundberg indicates that a thorough re-examination of the criteria, on which the early history of the canon has been based since before Harnack, has not been undertaken. Sundberg also recalls that Kurt Aland in a lecture on the canon to the New Testament Congress in the early 1960s, as a matter of course "assumed the same criteria as Harnack." The main outlines of the new corpus of writings, Sundberg points out, have only been slightly refined since then, with renewed emphasis on either Montanism or Marcionism spurring the collection of a New Testament, or emphasis on the publication of Acts prompting the formation of the Pauline letters.[10] Since Harnack, the longstanding consensus view was the assumption that a core New Testament canon was at hand around A.D. 200.[11] Having criticized this scholarly position in some detail, both in his 1968 article and in his essay "The Making of the New Testament Canon"

---

9. Albert C. Sundberg, *The Old Testament of the Early Church* (Cambridge: Harvard University, 1964); idem, "The Old Testament of the Early Church (A Study in Canon)," *HThR* 51 (1958): 205–26; idem, "Revised History."

10. Cf. Harnack's classical phrasing of the constitutive role of the Acts of the Apostles (*The Origin of the New Testament and the Most Important Consequences of the New Creation*, transl. J. R. Wilkinson (London: Williams & Norgate, 1925), 67: "The Acts is in a certain way the key to the understanding of the idea of the New Testament of the Church, and has given it the organic structure in which it stands before us. By taking its place at the head of the 'Apostolus' the Acts first made possible the division of the Canon into two parts and justified the combination of the Pauline Epistles with the Gospels." Cf. Jens Schröter, "Die Apostelgeschichte und die Entstehung des neutestamentlichen Kanons. Beobachtungen zur Kanonisierung der Apostelgeschichte und ihrer Bedeutung als kanonischer Schrift," in *The Biblical Canons*, eds. J.-M. Auwers and H. J. de Jonge (Leuven: Leuven University and Peeters, 2003), 395–429.

11. Harnack, *The Origin of the New Testament*, 113; cf. Brevard S. Childs, *The New Testament as Canon: An Introduction* (London: SCM, 1984), 18.

that appeared three years later,[12] Sundberg instead suggests a description of the history of the NT canon divided into three main steps:[13]

- *step* 1: the rise of Christian literature to the status of Scripture, to be treated as in some sense authoritative, a development for which there appear to have been no criteria other than circulation and authority parallel to that of the OT;

- *step* 2: the conscious grouping of Christian writings into closed collections such as the fourfold Gospel, and the Catholic epistles;

- *step* 3: "canonization proper, wherein the concern is not simply the acceptability of particular books but the formation of a NT list, a closed canon."

I shall use Sundberg's three-step model as a starting point for an introductory discussion of the terminology involved, in particular his use of "Scripture," "canon" and "canonization proper."

4.1.1 DATING INVOLVED IN SUNDBERG'S THREE PHASES

4.1.1.1 Having demonstrated that the so-called Alexandrian canon hypothesis is not only unprovable but erroneous,[14] Sundberg suggests that the first- and second-century church did not take over a "canon," a defined collection of exclusively authoritative writings from Judaism, but only

---

12. Abert C. Sundberg, "The Making of the New Testament Canon," in *The Interpreter's One-Volume Commentary on the Bible*, ed. Charles M. Laymon (New York: Abingdon, 1971), 1217.

13. Sundberg, "The Making of the New Testament Canon," 1217. Cf. Sundberg, "Revised History," 452; and "Canon of the NT," in *Interpreter's Dictionary of the Bible: Supplementary Volume*, ed. Keith Crim (Nashville: Abingdon, 1976), 137.

14. Albert C. Sundberg, "The Old Testament of the Early Church (A Study in Canon)," 205. The so-called Alexandrian canon hypothesis was formulated for the first time in the late 17th century and was embraced by subsequent scholarship (Semler, Ryle et al.). The hypothesis suggests the existence of a larger Jewish Alexandrian/diaspora biblical canon as compared to the narrower Palestinian. The New Testament writers and the early church are thought to have taken over this wider scriptural canon, which includes so-called Apocrypha, rather than the rabbinic 24 (or 22) book canon. Sundberg and others following him have convincingly shown that the hypothesis is without foundation. See esp. Sundberg, *Old Testament of the Early Church*. For further evidence, see Joachim Schaper, "The Rabbinic Canon and the Old Testament of the Early Church: A Social-Historical View," in *Canonization and Decanonization: Papers Presented to the International Conference of the Leiden Institute for the Study of Religions (LISOR), Held at Leiden 9–10 January 1997*, eds. A. van der Kooij and K. van der Toorn (Leiden: Brill, 1998), 93–95.

the "Scripture," that is "writings which are held in some sense as authoritative for religion."[15] In his understanding of both "Scripture" and "canon" a sharp distinction is presumed between the two. As *termini technici* in the history of the canon, Sundberg underlines the necessity of carefully distinguishing between the terms "canon"[16] and "scripture." The former refers to "a defined collection that is held to be exclusively, i.e. with respect to all other books, authoritative," whereas the latter signifies authoritative writings.[17] As the Christian Scriptures *in toto* are not catalogued in a canon list as exclusively authoritative in relation to other literature before the time of Eusebius, Athanasius and Jerome, Christianity does not possess a literary canon prior to the fourth and fifth centuries. In practice this also means that the church did not receive an OT canon from Judaism, "but rather scripture on the way to canonization."[18] Consequently, in Sundberg's model, "the comparison of the citations of Christian literature with Old Testament citations cannot establish canonicity for Christian writings" as Harnack had suggested.[19]

4.1.1.2 Sundberg's analysis of the second phase (*step 2* above), the conscious grouping of Christian writings into closed collections, begins with Marcion, who is thought to have initiated this phase.[20] However, over against von Harnack, John Knox and others,[21] Sundberg chooses not to lay too much emphasis on Marcion's role in the canon formation process. He rightly points out that the late-second-century stress on the fourfold

---

15. Sundberg, "The Making of the New Testament Canon," 1216. For criticism of Sundberg's position in this regard, see, e.g., D. N. Freedman, "Canon of the OT," in *Interpreter's Dictionary of the Bible: Supplementary Volume*, ed. Keith Crim (Nashville: Abingdon, 1976), 135. Sundberg's characterization of Scripture as "writings which are held *in some sense* as authoritative" (my italics) does not seem to correspond to many early/rabbinic Jewish and early Christian accounts of "Scripture," such as the one provided by Josephus in *Against Apion* 1.37–43 (see 2.2 below).

16. including its cognates "canonical" and "canonization."

17. Sundberg, "Revised History," 453.

18. Sundberg, "Revised History," 453.

19. Sundberg, "Revised History," 453. Sundberg, "Canon of the NT," 136.

20. Sundberg, "Revised History," 459.

21. Adolf von Harnack, *Marcion: das Evangelium vom fremden Gott: Eine Monographie zur Geschichte der Grundlegung der katholischen Kirche* (Darmstadt: Wissenschaftliche Buchgesellschaft, 1924, 2nd ed.); John Knox, *Marcion and the New Testament: An Essay in the Early History of the Canon* (Chicago: University of Chicago, 1942).

Gospel by the church, as testified to by Irenaeus, Tertullian and Origen, does not seem to be particularly dependent on Marcion.[22] In Sundberg's scheme the second phase in the history of the "canonical history" of the New Testament continues with discussions about the Pauline letter corpus, involving disagreements as to the inclusion of Hebrews, and the Catholic epistles.

4.1.1.3 Only in the third phase (*step 3* above), according to Sundberg's model, can we speak of canonization proper, "wherein the concern is not simply the concern over the acceptability of particular books, but with the formation of the New Testament list, the New Testament canon."[23] Somewhat surprisingly, Eusebius (in the East) is made the first representative of this third step in the history of the NT canon formation, soon to be followed by Jerome (in the West). Definitive events are, of course, the NT canon catalogues of Athanasius (Easter letter of 367), and the Western councils of Hippo (A.D. 393) and Carthage (A.D. 397 and 419), all of which issued a 27-book NT list paralleling our current New Testament canon. However, the Council of Laodicea (ca. A.D. 363)[24] only lists 26 NT books, excluding the Book of Revelation, and, as Sundberg indicates, Egypt had a larger NT and the Syriac-speaking church a much smaller one.[25] In Sherman Johnson's phrasing, commenting on Sundberg: "Thus more than 300 years after the Crucifixion ... the NT can[not] be defined with absolute precision."[26] As is well known, no conciliar decision on the scope of the NT canon that pertained to the church as a whole was

---

22. Sundberg, "Revised History," 459. For a very clear argumentation to this effect, see John Barton, "Marcion Revisited," in *The Canon Debate*, eds. L. M. McDonald and J. A. Sanders (Peabody, MA: Hendrickson, 2002), 341–54.

23. Sundberg, "Revised History," 460.

24. Canon 60 of the Council of Laodicea, which lists the books of the Old and New Testaments, appears to be added to Canon 59 (which reads: "Let no private psalms nor any uncanonical books be read in church, but only the canonical ones of the New and Old Testament") some time after the actual council that was held around A.D. 363. Accordingly, Canon 60 is not included in several Greek, Latin, and Syriac manuscripts (Metzger, *Canon*, 210, 312).

25. Sundberg, "The Making of the New Testament Canon," 1216–24. Cf. Sherman E. Johnson, "The New Testament and the Christian Community," in *The Interpreter's One-Volume Commentary on the Bible*, ed. Charles M. Laymon (New York: Abingdon, 1971), 1116.

26. Johnson, "The New Testament and the Christian Community," 1116. Cf. the different emphasis by Lee Martin McDonald, *Forgotten Scriptures: The Selection and Rejection of Early Religious Writings*

ever made in the Patristic period.[27] Against this background Sundberg's repeated stress on "canonization proper," i.e. the formation of NT lists, beginning in the fourth century, may appear puzzling if not perceived in a restricted sense.

4.2 PROBLEMS EMERGING FROM SUNDBERG'S CANON MODEL

4.2.1 SCRIPTURE AND CANON

Precisely for the sake of bringing terminological "clarity" to the discussion, Sundberg's distinction between "Scripture" and "canon" has become commonplace in biblical scholarship.[28] By emphasizing that early Christianity did not receive a "canon" from Judaism, only "scriptures" ("religious writings that were in some sense regarded as authoritative")[29] and that no significant effect of the Jewish biblical canon was "felt until Origen (253),"[30] Sundberg's definition of the terminology involved has deeply influenced the discussion.[31] Making reference to Sundberg, Michael W. Holmes, e.g., in a recent essay emphasizes that the two terms, "Scripture" and "canon," are not synonymous. However, when "canon" is defined as a "list" or "catalogue" of writings considered to be Scripture, it is still obvious that

---

(Louisville, Kent.: Westminster John Knox Press, 2009), 22: "Sundberg concluded that the notion and actual origins of a fixed New Testament canon are fourth-century developments."

27. This is emphasized by a range of scholars, such as Theodor Zahn, Harry Y. Gamble, Jens Schröter and Michael Kruger.

28. Sundberg, "Revised History," 453: "a clear technical differentiation between 'scripture' and 'canon' becomes essential to a clear and accurate history of the New Testament canon." Related to his three phases in the history of the NT canon, Sundberg's distinction between Scripture and canon, on the one hand, and between closed sub-collections and canon, on the other, are at the heart of his argument.

29. Sundberg, "Canon of the NT," 137.

30. Sundberg, "Canon of the NT," 137.

31. See, e.g., Gerald T. Sheppard, "Canon", in *The Encyclopedia of Religion*, ed. M. Eliade (New York: Macmillan, 1987), 62–69; Lee Martin McDonald, *The Biblical Canon: Its Origin, Transmission, and Authority* (Peabody, Mass., Hendrickson, 2007), 54–55, 285–322; and Michael W. Holmes, "The Biblical Canon," in *The Oxford Handbook of Early Christian Studies*, eds. S. Ashbrook Harvey and D. G. Hunter (Oxford: Oxford University, 2008), 406–408.

canon cannot be understood without Scripture. As Holmes points out, "'canon' presumes the existence of 'scripture.' "[32]

The relationship between the ecclesial notions of "Scripture" and "canon" can be seen also in other ways. If the "writings considered to be Scripture"[33] are said to make up a canon, or canon list, it is, of course, clear that canonicity must be a matter of list-making, but also of scriptural status—which seems to be the primary concern—for the writings so listed.[34] In his attempt to clearly separate the two notions, Sundberg therefore has to make the distinction between "Scripture" and "canon" unnaturally sharp.[35] In the end, however, his endeavour seems to be somewhat problematic. After all, Sundberg, too—as others before and after him—talks in terms of a "process of New Testament canonization,"[36] in which the history of the NT canon is viewed in three stages. Though it is not quite clear to me which of these that ought to be stressed when the question of the canon is brought to the table, or even which part of this process that is more appropriately described as "canonization proper" as compared to other stages in the process.[37] Why emphasize the third phase (Sundberg) over against the first and second (Harnack), or still earlier phases/dimensions (see section 4.4 below)? Childs, thus, rightly comments: "to conceive

32. Holmes, "The Biblical Canon," 406.

33. Holmes, "The Biblical Canon," 406.

34. This is not so clear, however, in Holmes's phrasing ("The Biblical Canon," 407): "Canonicity is a matter of list-making, not scriptural status." Cf. in this connection Timothy Lim's argument for an implied notion of canon in Second Temple Judaism clearly associated with the sacred Scriptures ("A Theory of the Majority Canon," *Expository Times* 124 (2013): 367.

35. For criticism of Sundberg's distinction, see S. J. P. K. Riekert, "Critical Research and the One Christian Canon Comprising Two Testaments," *Neotestamentica*, 14 (1981): 21–41; and Charles J. Scalise, *From Scripture to Theology: A Canonical Journey into Hermeneutics* (Downers Grove, IL: InterVarsity, 1996), 45.

36. Sundberg, "Revised History," 459. This process does not seem to be "closed" even in Sundberg's third stage (see section 4.1 above), which sets out to emphasize the "closed" character of "canonization proper." Cf. also Sherman Johnson's comment above. By "closed canon list" Sundberg appears to refer to a local or regional church decision regarding which books should and which should not be regarded scriptural. Thus, even if it is not his intention, in Sundberg's model the "closed collection," such as the fourfold Gospel (*step 2*) may even be regarded as more closed, delimited and definite than the "closed canon" (*step 3*).

37. In my view, the listing and delimitation of the writings included in the fourfold Gospel in Irenaeus as perhaps the most well-known example of what I would label "canonization" seems hermeneutically more significant than the inclusion of 3 John or the exclusion or inclusion of the *Shepherd* of Hermas in the fourth- and fifth-century communities.

of canon mainly as a dogmatic decision regarding the scope of the literature is to overestimate one feature within the process which is, by no means, constitutive of canon."[38]

Even in Sundberg's model "canonization proper" in the fourth-century church setting arguably does not make sense without his two prior phases, namely, respectively, the emergence of Christian *Scripture*, and the formation of closed collections of *Scriptures*, such as the fourfold Gospel. Canon here is not just about list-making, but is, more precisely, a matter of enlisting authoritatively[39] the entire corpus of already authoritative[40] Scriptures. As Hermann Wolfgang Beyer, and before him Adolf Jülicher, emphasized, "What really counted was the concept of norm inherent in the term."[41] Especially on Latin ground, it therefore soon became part of the Christian adoption of the fourth-century Greek term "canon" (κανών) and its derivatives to use it also as a designation of the Scriptures themselves, which were said to have "canonical authority" (*canonica auctoritas*), and which by the Latins were labelled "the canonical Scriptures" (*scripturae canonicae*) or "books" (*libri canonici*).[42] Even if it is not the case that "the distinction between Scripture and canon is untenable,"[43] as indicated by some scholars, we do need to keep in mind the intimate relation—and at times almost synonymity—between the two concepts when presenting the emergence of the NT canon.

So if the notion of Scripture is sharply distinguished from that of canon, as in Sundberg's model,[44] it may even be difficult to talk of a canonical

---

38. Though here pertaining to the OT canon, Childs's comment applies equally well to the New Testament canon formation (Brevard S. Childs, "The exegetical significance of Canon for the study of the Old Testament," in *International Organization for the Study of the Old Testament*, congress volume [Göttingen: Brill, 66–80]); cited from Riekert, "Critical Research," 31.

39. Cf. the Latin tag *norma normata*.

40. Cf. the Latin tag *norma normans*; see Metzger, *Canon*, 283.

41. Hermann Wolfgang Beyer, "Kanon," in *Theologisches Wörterbuch zum Neuen Testament*, vol. 3, ed. G. Kittel (Grand Rapids: Eerdmans, 1965), 601; Adolf Jülicher and Erich Fascher, *Einleitung in das Neue Testament* (Tübingen: Mohr Siebeck, 1931; 7ᵗʰ ed.), 555. See also Tomas Bokedal, *The Formation and Significance of the Christian Biblical Canon: A Study in Text, Ritual and Interpretation* (London: Bloomsbury T&T Clark, 2014).

42. For further examples, see Heinz Ohme, *Kanon ekklesiastikos* (Berlin: Walter de Gruyter, 1998), 478.

43. So Riekert, "Critical Research," 21–41; cited from Metzger, *Canon*, 30.

44. Cf. Sundberg ("Revised History," 453–54, 459), who nevertheless assumes a canonical process.

process at all, as Sundberg himself sets out to do (cf. 4.1.1 above), and as Brevard Childs and others would consider necessary in order to capture the profound significance of biblical canonicity.[45] Furthermore, if a fourth-century act of list-making is singled out as the most crucial component for the notion of an Old and New Testament canon,[46] does that not imply that the category of Scripture in all its aspects[47]—taken by itself—is less clear or less relevant for understanding the authoritative claim pertaining to the Christian or Jewish corpora of sacred texts?[48] In the end, is the notion of canon here primarily a conciliar expression of fourth-century dogma, or a formal *de iure* manifestation of the early post-Constantinian church with no lasting significance?[49]

4.2.2 OPEN OR CLOSED JEWISH CANON IN THE FIRST CENTURY?

A good deal of his impetus for distinguishing the notion of "Scripture" from that of "canon" is Sundberg's view of the scope of the Jewish Bible as partially fluid during the first century A.D. Thus, "[i]t is no longer satisfactory to use the terms 'scripture' and 'canon' synonymously. The church received 'scriptures,' ... from Judaism; but the church did not receive a canon, i.e., a closed collection of scripture to which nothing could be added, nothing subtracted."[50] The first thing to notice in this connection is that Sundberg does not appear to be talking of canon *as list*, but reverts to the common way of describing canon as "a closed collection of scripture,"[51] thereby depicting an aspect of the Scriptures as such. Canon can here be appropriately understood as a property of Sacred Scripture (see below).

Again, focusing on the scriptural books as such, along the lines of Sundberg, Lee Martin McDonald suggests that "'the Bible' in our modern

---

45. See Childs, *The New Testament as Canon*, 16–47.

46. So, e.g., Holmes, "The Biblical Canon," 407. See fnn. 34 and 37 above.

47. Cf. Harnack's canon model above, which places the category of Scripture at the centre, as does the canon model of Lim (see fn. 34 above), within a Pharisaic–Rabbinic setting.

48. Cf. section 4.2.2 below on Josephus's scriptural "canon." See further Sundberg, "Revised History"; and Scalise, *From Scripture to Theology*, 45.

49. Cf. Wofhart Pannenberg, *Systematic Theology*, vol. 1 (Grand Rapids: Eerdmans, 1991), 10 (cited in n. 21, ch. 1 above); and Sundberg, "Revised History," 461; cited in the introductory section above.

50. Sundberg, "Canon of the NT," 137.

51. Sundberg, "Canon of the NT," 137.

sense ... of a complete, fixed, and closed collection of books of Scripture [did not exist] as such in the Second Temple period. There is sufficient and sufficiently broad reference to 'the Scriptures' or 'the Law and the Prophets' to ensure that there were certainly sacred scriptures at the end of the Second Temple period, but the point would have to be demonstrated that 'the Bible' as such was an identifiable reality at that time."[52] It is therefore "strange ... and even anachronistic," according to McDonald, to argue "that Jesus or his apostles endorsed any biblical canon."[53]

However, critical voices of Sundberg's model have not been lacking. Since I am here seeking to problematize Sundberg's repeated disapproval of the traditional view that the early church could in some sense have received a canon of Scriptures from Judaism, some of these critics will be referred to below.

Already David N. Freedman mounted criticism in this regard, not least towards Sundberg's dependency on the presumed closing of the "Jewish canon" at Jamnia,[54] or around A.D. 90.[55] More systematically, Brevard Childs countered Sundberg's claim that "the highly flexible use of the Old Testament by the Christian church affords strong evidence for an open Jewish canon."[56] Over against Sundberg, Childs remarks that the Jewish canon was not necessarily unstable just because the "Christian church's

---

52. McDonald, *Forgotten Scriptures*, 71.

53. McDonald, *Forgotten Scriptures*, 123; cf. also McDonald, *Forgotten Scriptures*, 38.

54. Freedman, "Canon of the OT." The defining article in this regard was written already in 1964 by Jack P. Lewis, "What Do We Mean by Jabneh?," *Journal of Bible and Religion* 32 (1964):125–32. Lewis demonstrated that the so-called discussions of certain books at Jabneh or Jamnia were as a matter of fact "discussions between post-destruction rabbis about discussions of their intellectual predecessors more than a century earlier. The sources available to us neither refer to voting nor do they intimate that the status of books was at stake. The only books mentioned were books whose significant status was acknowledged beforehand." (Z. Zevit, "The Second–Third Century Canonization of the Hebrew Bible and Its Influence on Christian Canonizing," in *Canonization and Decanonization: Papers Presented to the International Conference of the Leiden Institute for the Study of Religions (LISOR), held at Leiden 9–10 January 1997*, eds A. van der Kooij and K. van der Toorn [Leiden: Brill, 1998], 139). Cf. also Emanuel Tov, *Textual Criticism of the Hebrew Bible* (Minneapolis: Fortress, 2012; 3rd rev. ed.), 177.

55. Cf. Sundberg, "The Making of the New Testament Canon," 1216.

56. Brevard S. Childs, *Biblical Theology of the Old and New Testaments: Theological Reflection on the Christian Bible* (London: SCM, 1992), 59. For a concise summary of some of the issues at stake, see Sid Z. Leiman's comments on Sundberg, *The Canonization of Hebrew Scripture: The Talmudic and Midrashic Evidence* (Hamden, Conn.: Archon Books, 1976), 203f. fn. 670.

use of it reflected a great degree of flexibility."[57] He further mentions scholars such as T. N. Swanson, Sid. Z. Leiman, and Roger T. Beckwith who have argued at length for a significant textual stability within certain circles of Judaism.[58] In four points Childs[59] then lists indirect evidence for the existence of a more stable Jewish canon at a considerably earlier date than that suggested by Sundberg: 1) Josephus's treatise *Against Apion* (1.37–43), written around A.D. 93, establishes the fixed number of the books of the Jewish Bible at twenty-two; as Josephus's account concerns traditions long held by Jews, Childs suggests that Josephus here reflects Pharisaic tradition from the mid-first century A.D. 2) The three sections of the Hebrew Bible may not have developed in a sequential, historical order; the Writings, or Hagiographa, may therefore, as Beckwith proposed,[60] have been a subsequent division within the Prophets.[61] 3) Childs then points to the lack of citation from "the Apocrypha" in Philo, Josephus, and the New Testament; "[s]imilarly, Ben Sira, the authors of the Maccabees, Hillel, Shammai and all the first-century Tannaim never cite the apocryphal literature as scripture."[62] 4) The final piece of evidence mentioned by Childs is, in his view, also the strongest, namely the connection between the evidence for a fixed Hebrew canon and the history of the stabilization of the Masoretic text.[63] Manuscripts from Qumran and adjacent caves indicate that the Masoretic text, including as well the books of Daniel, Ruth, and Lamentations, "had assumed a high level of stabilization by AD 70."[64] Implied here is the strong likelihood that

---

57. Childs, *Biblical Theology*, 59.

58. Childs, *Biblical Theology*, 59.

59. For a somewhat similar more recent treatment, see Arie van der Kooij, "Canonization of Ancient Hebrew Books and Hasmonean Politics," in *The Biblical Canons*, eds. J.-M. Auwers and H. J. de Jonge (Leuven: Leuven University and Peeters, 2003), 27–38.

60. Roger Beckwith, *The Old Testament Canon of the New Testament Church and its Background in Early Judaism* (Grand Rapids: Eerdmans, 1985), 142ff.

61. Childs, *Biblical Theology*, 60.

62. Childs here refers to Leiman, *The Canonization of Hebrew Scripture*, 39.

63. For a handy overview of the development and stabilization of the Masoretic Text, see Tov, *Textual Criticism of the Hebrew Bible*, 27–36; 174–76; cf. also 174–80 for a distinction between the development and stabilization of the consonantal Masoretic Text and the "possibility of a standardization process for the biblical text as a whole" (Tov, *Textual Criticism of the Hebrew Bible*, 27).

64. Childs, *Biblical Theology*, 60. Cf. also, Frank Moore Cross, *From Epic to Canon* (Baltimore, Maryland: John Hopkins University, 1998), 217.

a book's text "would not have been corrected and stabilized if the book had not already received some sort of canonical status."[65] At this juncture, where canon and textual criticism meet, we find support for the kind of approach to biblical canonicity propagated by Brevard Childs. In his own phrasing: "Only when the formation of the literature had reached a final stage of development within the canonical process did concern for the text of the literature emerge."[66] A similar concern, though with a different emphasis, is expressed by Frank Moore Cross, to which Hillel is a central figure for the emergence of both text and canon: "The fixation of the text and the fixation of the canon were thus two aspects of a single if complex endeavor."[67] Similarly, *mutatis mutandis*, for the New Testament we can note the significance of the late second century, both with regard to the appearance of a substantial NT canon (see 4.4.1 and 4.4.2 below), and the New Testament text. Only around this time quotations of the NT text amongst the early fathers "were no longer pure paraphrases or adaptations of the original text; instead, extensive literal citations from what was recognized as a New Testament became the rule." Barbara Aland talks in this connection of an evolving "text consciousness."[68]

In what follows, I will elaborate further on Childs's first point above, namely the implication and impact of Josephus's 22-book canon as reported in *Against Apion* 1.38–40:

we do not possess myriads of inconsistent books, conflicting with each other. Our books, those which are justly accredited, are but

65. Cross, *From Epic to Canon*, 217. For a more recent account of the fixation of the text of the Hebrew Bible, placing emphasis on the role of Hillel, see, e.g., Cross, *From Epic to Canon*, 205–18. Cf. also Bruce K. Waltke, "How We Got the Hebrew Bible: The Text and Canon of the Old Testament," in *The Bible at Qumran: Text, Shape, and Interpretation*, ed. P. W. Flint (Grand Rapids: Eerdmans, 2001), 27–50.

66. Brevard S. Childs, *Introduction to the Old Testament as Scripture* (London: SCM, 1979), 94.

67. Cross, *From Epic to Canon*, 223. As to the "uniform acceptance" of this canon in Pharisaic circles, Cross suggests the period between the two Jewish revolts against Rome, A.D. 70–132.

68. Barbara Aland, "The Significance of the Chester Beatty Papyri," in *The Earliest Gospels: The Origins and Transmission of the Earliest Christian Gospels—The Contribution of the Chester Beatty Gospel Codex P45*, ed. C. Horton, Journal for the Study of the New Testament Supplement Series 258 (London: T&T Clark, 2004), 117.

two and twenty, and contain the record of all time [i.e., five books of Moses, thirteen of the prophets, and four remaining books].[69]

Josephus here addresses our theme, whether the canon was closed or still open in the late first century.[70] Steve Mason has dealt with this, for our question, central passage (*Against Apion* 1.37–43). Though Mason is modest in his claims that have direct bearing on the canon discussion,[71] he nonetheless underlines clearer than many others one of Josephus's emphases in this passage:[72]

> Josephus claims his positions are held in common by all Judeans—women, children, prisoners of war—and he would presumably be vulnerable to refutation if he were making this up or presenting idiosyncratic views. It would accordingly be hard to argue from Josephus for an open canon or for one that had been recently settled—at Yavneh in the 70s and 80s, for example.[73]

Mason's conclusion in this regard is shared by some canon specialists (e.g., Childs and Beckwith). Though many scholars following Sundberg, and others of similar leanings, consider the Jewish canon as still in flux after Josephus's time,[74] I shall argue in the following that the doctrine of

---

69. LCL 186:179. *Against Apion* 1.39–40 reads: "Of these, five are the books of Moses, ... the prophets ... in thirteen books. The remaining four books contain hymns to God and precepts for the conduct of human life."

70. Steve Mason, "Josephus and His Twenty-Two Book Canon," in *The Canon Debate*, eds. L. M. McDonald and J. A. Sanders (Peabody, Mass.: Hendrickson, 2002), 111.

71. Mason, "Josephus and His Twenty-Two Book Canon," 111. Cf. esp. Mason's emphasis on "genres" rather than "divisions within the first-century canon" being specified in *Against Apion* 1.37–43. For a different interpretation, see Kooij, "Canonization of Ancient Hebrew Books," 29.

72. Cf., however, the section titled "The 'canon' of Josephus merits closer examination" in Cross, *From Epic to Canon*, 220–25; and Kooij, "Canonization of Ancient Hebrew Books."

73. Mason, "Josephus and His Twenty-Two Book Canon," 126. With reference to Albert C. Sundberg, the quote continues: "Those who are convinced by other evidence of the fluidity of scriptural boundaries in the first century do better, perhaps, to isolate Josephus as idiosyncratic, in spite of his claim to speak on behalf of Judeans, than to try to enlist his statements in support."

74. See, e.g., James A. Sanders, "The Issue of Closure in the Canonical Process," in *The Canon Debate*, eds. L. M. McDonald and J. A. Sanders (Peabody, Mass.: Hendrickson, 2002), 252–62; and Cross, *From Epic to Canon*, 219–29, esp. 228. Lim ("Majority Canon," 373) estimates that the Jewish canon "closed" roughly between A.D. 150 and 250.

"canon"[75] found in Josephus resurfaces in the early Christian conception of both an OT and, to some extent, also a NT canon. From the account of the Jewish 22-book Bible in *Against Apion* 1.37–43, we notice in particular the following eight features of the scriptural "canon":

1. it is *de facto* **closed**—it is delimited to 22 divinely inspired writings ("through the inspiration which they owed to God");

2. it consists of three rather **well-defined subunits**—five books of the Law, thirteen of the Prophets, and four remaining books,

3. **two of which are particularly emphasized** (namely, the Law and the Prophets);

4. it is **in principle closed** (i.e., the included books are thought to be written during the period of prophetic inspiration between the time of Moses and that of Artaxerxes I; 1.39–41);

5. it presents the included books as **conceived together**,

6. and as read as **a single "record"** (ἀναγραφή);[76]

7. it is embraced by **the canonical formula** (1.42: "no one has dared either to add anything or to take away from them or to alter them");

8. and finally, as the "decrees of God" it **functions as the basis for religious and everyday life** (1.42: "it is an instinct with every Jew, from the day of his birth, to regard them as the decrees of God, to abide by them, and, if need be, cheerfully to die for them.")

Josephus's account may have been representative of a broader notion of Scripture/canon[77] that arguably influenced the Christian canon forma-

---

75. Cf. Frank Cross, fn. 78 below.

76. Cf. Mason, "Josephus and His Twenty-Two Book Canon," 113.

77. Cf. Lim, "Majority Canon," 367: "there was indeed a notion of 'canon' in the Second Temple period, even if ancient Jews did not have a term for it."

tion at an early stage.[78] In the discussion that follows, I shall point out some (potential) parallels between this scriptural "canon" as outlined by Josephus in Rome around A.D. 93, and the emerging Christian "canon."[79]

4.2.3 SUNDBERG'S SECOND AND THIRD PHASES

As with Sundberg's conception of the first stage (*step 1*), focusing on scripturality,[80] a couple of problems arise also in regard to the second and third phases (*steps 2 and 3*). To begin with, Marcion cannot any longer easily be thought of as initiating the second phase.[81] In terms of chronology, we should also notice Sundberg's and Hahneman's still controversial dating of the important Muratorian canon to the fourth century (the Muratorian fragment hence belongs to Sundberg's *step 3*).[82] However, scholars are still confidently adhering to the traditional Western origin of the Muratorian canon in the late second century. Still crucial for the question of dating is the fragment's reference to Hermas, who is said to have written the *Shepherd* in the city of Rome "very recently, in our times, ... while bishop Pius was occupying the [Episcopal] chair of the church of the city of Rome" (*nuperrime temporibus nostris ... sedente cathedra urbis Romae ecclesiae Pio*).[83]

---

78. See further, e.g., Beckwith, *Old Testament Canon of the New Testament Church*. Cf. Cross, *From Epic to Canon*, 221: "Thinly concealed behind Josephus's Greek apologetics is a clear and coherent theological doctrine of canon ... Josephus is not alone in his testimony." For some critical remarks relating to Cross's account, see Beckwith, *Old Testament Canon of the New Testament Church*, 188.

79. On the reception of Josephus among early church teachers, see, e.g., Michael E. Hardwick, *Josephus as an Historical Source in Patristic Literature through Eusebius*, Brown Judaic Studies 128 (Atlanta, Ga.: Scholars Press), 1989.

80. We argued above that it is far from easy, along the lines of Sundberg's lines of reasoning, to clearly distinguish and separate from one another the notions of "Scripture" and "canon," as handed down by early Christianity (section 4.2.1); we also saw that it is not very clear that the early church only received a notion of "Scripture"—and not of "canon"—from Early and Rabbinic Judaism (section 4.2.2). The problems pointed to in sections 4.2.1 and 4.2.2 involve all three phases in Sundberg's model, his *step 1*, *step 2* and *step 3*. Thus, aspects from Sundberg's first phase (*step 1*) with its focus on scripturality cannot be as clearly distinguished as suggested from his *steps 2 and 3*.

81. See, e.g., Barton, "Marcion Revisited," 341–54. However, as seen above, Sundberg chooses not to put much emphasis on the role of Marcion for the late second-century canon development.

82. Albert C. Sundberg, "Canon Muratori: A Fourth-Century List," *Harvard Theological Review* 66 (1973):1–41; Geoffrey Mark Hahneman, *The Muratorian Fragment and the Development of the Canon* (Oxford: Clarendon, 1992).

83. Trans. Metzger, *Canon*, 307.

Bruce Metzger,[84] among others, and, more recently, Joseph Verheyden,[85] in a finely argued essay, arrive at the same conclusion: The few scholars who have opted for a later date than the late second/early third century have not won the day.[86] Thus, with the array of historians promoting the earlier dating, Sundberg and other proponents of a fourth-century Eastern provenance are challenged by a strong consensus over the last 150 years. Two observations can here be made. With the Muratorian canon located in the late second century, the old traditions about the Pauline corpus—said to contain letters only to seven churches—mentioned in the fragment have the potential of bringing the chronological component of Sundberg's *step 2*, the grouping of Christian writings into closed collections, back to Sundberg's *step 1*: that is, a time well before Marcion,[87] and perhaps also before the composition of the Apocalypse (cf. Rev 2–3) and the Ignatian letter corpus.[88] In the fragment, we thus come across what looks like a closed Corpus Paulinum (though not including Hebrews)[89] with the letters numbered—being addressed to seven churches, all in all thirteen letters, four of which are to individuals. As we will see below, the conception of a fourfold Gospel may also be located at a time prior to Marcion. Moreover, we already noticed the presence of a list of numbered books—twenty-two Scriptures (five + thirteen + four)—in Josephus in

---

84. Metzger, *Canon*, 193: "The arguments used recently by Sundberg to prove the list to be of eastern provenance (Syria–Palestine) and from the mid-fourth century have been sufficiently refuted (not to say demolished!) by Ferguson." Brevard Childs thinks Sundberg's dating is "tendentious and unproven" (*The New Testament as Canon*, 238).

85. Verheyden, "The Canon Muratori: A Matter of Dispute," in *The Biblical Canons*, eds. J.-M. Auwers and H. J. de Jonge (Leuven: Leuven University and Peeters, 2003), 487–556.

86. Verheyden, "The Canon Muratori: A Matter of Dispute," 487–556, e.g., 491 and 556. Already in the 19th century the two options were being discussed. With a reference to K. A. Credner, B. F. Westcott (*Canon*, 213 fn. 3), e.g., writes: "The opinions of those who assign it to the fourth century, or doubt its authenticity altogether, scarcely deserve mention." Quoted from Verheyden, "The Canon Muratori: A Matter of Dispute," 491 fn. 16.

87. Gamble, *Books and Readers in the Early Church: A History of Early Christian Texts* (New Haven: Yale University, 1995), 61: "the edition used by Marcion has every appearance of being a modified form of an older edition, an edition shaped by the idea that Paul wrote to precisely seven churches and in which the letters were arranged in a sequence of decreasing length."

88. Gamble, *Books and Readers in the Early Church: A History of Early Christian Texts*, 61. The seven letters in Rev 2:1–3:22 and the compilation by Polycarp of Ignatius's letters, also associated with the Asia Minor area, may both "well reflect an early edition of the Pauline letters presented as a collection of letters to seven churches."

89. As regards the inclusion of thirteen Pauline letters, the Muratorian fragment is similar to other contemporary Western corpora, such as Gaius's and probably also Irenaeus's.

the late first century. In terms of definiteness or closure, this may express
the phenomenon of scriptural canonicity in an even more final way than
is done in Eusebius of Caesarea or other fourth-century representatives,
such as Amphilochius of Iconium, both of whom take into consideration in
their lists—as Origen and the Muratorian Fragmentist before them[90]—the
notions of non-disputed and disputed Scripture.[91] In other words, some
of the fourth-century canon lists are not as final as sometimes thought.

4.3 INTERPRETATIVE CONSIDERATIONS

4.3.1 A POINT OF DEPARTURE FOR INTERPRETATION

In the foregoing, I have chosen to apply the noun "canon" and the adjective "canonical" to "collections of texts considered defining, essential, con-
stitutional, and/or foundational."[92] An important presupposition for my
argument has been the assumed strong connection between the Jewish
and the Christian scriptural corpora. Over against Sundberg, however,
I find connections not only between Jewish and Christian *Scripture*, but
also between *aspects of canonicity* in the two communities, *canonicity
viewed as a property of Scripture*.[93] The formation of the New Testament
is therefore, in a sense, viewed as "secondary," and arguably "linked by
dialectical relationships" to the prior collection of Jewish Scriptures in
a new canonical process.[94] This can be seen, in the broad parallel function of the new Christian writings with that of the Jewish Scriptures. As
indicated above, I will assume a canonical process with more emphasis
on the earlier stages of that process (in this respect following Zahn and
Harnack rather than Sundberg).

---

90. So Hermann von Lips, *Der neutestamentliche Kanon: Seine Geschichte und Bedeutung* (Zürich: Theologischer Verlag, 2004), 76.

91. See Metzger, *Canon*, 309–10, 313–14.

92. Z. Zevit, "The Second-Third Century Canonization of the Hebrew Bible," 133.

93. To this effect Emanuel Tov appropriately describes "canonization" in regard to the Hebrew Bible, on the one hand, as "acceptance of books as authoritative writings" and, on the other, as "referring to Scripture as a whole." (Tov, *Textual Criticism of the Hebrew Bible*, 20, 417). Cf. also Lim, "Majority Canon," 367; and Kooij, "Canonization of Ancient Hebrew Books," 29.

94. So Finkelberg and Stroumsa, "Introduction: Before the Western Canon" (Leiden: Brill, 2003), in *Homer, the Bible, and Beyond: Literary and Religious Canons in the Ancient World*, eds. M. Finkelberg and G. G. Stroumsa (Leiden: Brill, 2003), 3f.; cf. Barton, *The Spirit and the Letter*, 1.

Since I am interested in locating the roots of the notion of a Christian scriptural canon earlier than some scholars, I shall say a word as well of how I conceive of the "beginning" of that process. Focusing on the first two Christian centuries, my approach to the "beginning" of the canon or the canonical process is twofold: on the one hand historical-temporal, and on the other, reflexive, taking into account also a certain end or goal of the process (e.g., as expressed by Josephus in *Against Apion*, by Athanasius in his Thirty-Ninth Festal Letter, or by one of the more recent conciliar statements on the church's biblical canon).[95] The approach one takes towards the overall goal, character, or end of the canon formation process—or if one does not regard it as a process at all—necessarily affects one's view of the beginnings of biblical canonicity (cf. 4.3.2 below).[96]

In my sketch below of aspects of the early canonical process (section 4.4), I will be particularly attentive to aspects of the description of canonical Scripture found as well in Josephus's *Against Apion* 1.37–43, namely: its being *de facto* closed (1), made up of well-defined subunits, where the exact number of writings matters (2), with particular emphasis on two of the subunits (Law and Prophets, Gospel and Apostle) (3), its being in principle closed (4), presenting the individual books as conceived together as a unity (5), read as a single record (6), embraced by the canonical formula (7), and functioning as the basis for everyday and religious life (8). I take the fourth point above to be canon understood as *Scripture* (inspired by God) and the fifth as canon conceived within a particular framework (e.g., Torah centered).

In search for these aspects of "canonicity" I will take onboard John Barton's advice to consider all three of the models above, Zahn's, Harnack's and Sundberg's, as useful, each accounting for important aspects of the complex phenomenon of biblical canonicity.[97] However, I will differ from Sundberg by putting less emphasis on the distinction between Scripture

---

95. Cf. Hans-Georg Gadamer, *The Beginning of Philosophy* (New York: Continuum, 2001), 9–20; and Holmes, "The Biblical Canon," 415–21.

96. For the role of the element of effective history in historical work, see, e.g., Hans-Georg Gadamer, *Truth and Method*, translation revised by J. Weinsheimer and D. G. Marshall (New York: Continuum, 2nd rev. ed., 1993), 300–307.

97. Barton, *The Spirit and the Letter*, 1–16.

and canon, and from Harnack and Campenhausen by placing more emphasis on what Campenhausen (incorrectly in my view) calls the "pre-history" of the New Testament canon.[98]

Following on some additional comments below on our three main theorists (section 4.3.2), the rest of our discussion will focus attention on various dimensions of the early canonical process (sections 4.3.3 and 4.4), roughly corresponding to Sundberg's two first phases (*steps 1 and 2*), however with quite a different emphasis on the chronology of the phases/dimensions involved, as compared to Sundberg's model of a development in three sequential steps.

4.3.2 TWO WORDS ON SCHOLARLY PREFERENCES: ZAHN, HARNACK, SUNDBERG

At this point in our discussion, before dealing more directly with the early canon formation process (section 4.4), I shall briefly project our problem on the more subjective plane, namely the level of scholarly and personal preferences always involved in research. Clearly, the notion of canon takes on quite different meanings in our theorists. At face value, it may seem as if the three models endorsed, respectively, by Zahn, Harnack and Sundberg tend to imply different hermeneutical predispositions. Zahn certainly understood the Christian Scriptures and the collection of them as reflecting their fundamental "apostolic" character, especially as these were rooted in the context of worship and the life of the church from the earliest period. A key theme here is continuity with the beginnings of the Christian movement, as well as between the two main portions of Scripture, OT and NT. Harnack's and Campenhausen's canon concept, on the other hand, emphasizes that a writing must be explicitly referred to as "Scripture"—thus paralleling the church's attitude towards the OT Scriptures—before it can be considered canonical. Canonization for them is a rather suddenly appearing apologetic development in the church. Thus, if the New Testament canon is an "anti-Marcionite creation on

---

98. Hans von Campenhausen, *The Formation of the Christian Bible*, trans. J. A. Baker (Philadelphia: Fortress, 1972), 103.

Marcionite basis," as von Harnack suggested,[99] then the church's sudden creativity in this regard could for Harnack, as he elaborated his over-all theory, also lead to suggesting, along the lines of Marcion, the total removal of the Old Testament. Since the Jewish Scriptures are not a necessarily integrated part of Christian discourse they should not be seen as canonical and binding on the same level as the New Testament.[100] As Harnack—for whom canonical date is crucial[101]—sees it, the act of canonizing here helps creating a distance between earliest charismatic Christianity and the more institutionalized late second-century church.[102] The hermeneutical implications of his canon model are, of course, vast. Sundberg's definition, too, to some degree fits into the discontinuity model: being a decision of the church, "canonization proper" removes canonization from the apostolic age.[103]

While the main contours of these three positions—Zahn's, Harnack's and Sundberg's—are well known to biblical scholarship, the implied hermeneutics involved in each of the three models requires further discussion.[104]

Sundberg's, and to some extent Harnack's, model fit well with William Wrede's approach a century ago. Wrede famously maintains that "canon" is a dogmatic concept: "[N]o New Testament writing was born with the predicate 'canonical' attached." Anyone who treats these writings as such in historical work places him- or herself under the authority of the bishops and theologians of the second to fourth centuries.[105] Along these lines of thought, James Barr, too, maintains that "[c]anonization was done under

99. Harnack, *Marcion*, 357; cited from John Barton, *The Old Testament: Canon, Literature and Theology*, Society for Old Testament Study Monographs (Aldershot: Ashgate, 2007), 68.

100. Harnack, *Marcion*.

101. Similarly von Campenhausen, *Formation*, 103–104.

102. Adolf von Harnack, *Lehrbuch der Dogmengeschichte*, vol. 1 (Tübingen: Mohr Siebeck, 1909), §1.

103. Sundberg, "Revised History," 461. For a related point in regard to "apostolicity," in particular claims to apostolic authorship for writings included in the NT, see Dunn, *Unity and Diversity*, 386. As for the impossibility of the church playing a dominating role in the canon formation process as outlined by Sundberg and others, see Webster, *Holy Scripture*, 63.

104. Cf. Barton, *The Spirit and the Letter*, 1–14; and Gamble, "Recent Research," 267–94.

105. Cited from Heikki Räisänen, *Beyond New Testament Theology* (2nd ed; London: SCM, 2000), 21; see William Wrede, "The Task and Methods of 'New Testament Theology,'" in Robert Morgan, ed., *The Nature of New Testament Theology* (London: SCM, 1973), 70–71.

a faith structure very different from that of the biblical community."[106] In
Barr, as in Wrede and Heikki Räisänen, canonization is a theological and
political act belonging to the late fourth century. As they conceive it, this
act is accomplished largely in isolation from other textual–interpretative
properties of the early history of the NT canon.[107]

4.3.3 DIMENSIONS OF CANON/CANONICITY

As an alternative to Sundberg's outline of a development in three strictly
sequential phases—which as we saw (section 4.2 above) turns out to
be problematic at some points—I shall suggest that we instead view
Sundberg's three "steps" as dimensions of the canon formation process.
One advantage this gives us is that it solves the chronological impasse in
Sundberg's scheme, while at the same time making use of his three char-
acterizations. I therefore suggest the following dimensions of canonicity as a more effective way of conceiving the canon formation: canon *as
list* (corresponding to Sundberg's *step 3*), canon *as closed sub-collection of
Scriptures* (corresponding to Sundberg's *step 2*) and canon *as Scripture*
(corresponding to Sundberg's *step 1*). The main advantage that these three
(as well as other) dimensions provide when compared to Sundberg's three
phases, is the greater flexibility for analyzing the canon formation. Since
the three phases in Sundberg's model are not chronologically as distinguishable as he thought,[108] it seems more appropriate for the task before
us to emphasize the continuum between the three phases/dimension: e.g.,
to understand canon *as list* consisting of *closed sub-collections*, which in
their turn are constituted by *Scripture*. This also makes the dating associated with the various steps or stages in the process less important. To
this we can add a note of commonsensical nature, namely the fact that "a
history of the canon cannot take its point of departure in the concept of
'canon' since this concept is only demonstrable in the mid-fourth century

---

106. James Barr, *Holy Scripture: Canon, Authority, Criticism* (Oxford: Clarendon, 1983), 66.

107. Differently Peter Stuhlmacher (*How To Do Biblical Theology* [Eugene, Ore.: Pickwick
Publications, 1995], 57), who places more emphasis on the canonical process as a whole: "Traces of
this new canonical process can be seen as early as the middle of the first century."

108. Cf., e.g., Sundberg, "The Making of the New Testament Canon," 1223: "Through Origen we
are still in the period of scripture rather than canon."

(Canon 59 of Laodicea; Athanasius, Easter letter of 367) as signification of the Christian Bible."[109]

4.4 THE EARLY CANONICAL PROCESS— OLD AND NEW POSSIBILITIES OF VIEWING SCRIPTURE AS A WHOLE

4.4.1 SCRIPTURE, CANON, AND INTERPRETATION: THE CANONICAL PROCESS IN IRENAEUS

Irenaeus says in his Second Book *Against Heresies* that he is "most properly assured that the Scriptures are indeed perfect, since they were spoken by the Word of God and His Spirit"[110] (*Haer.* II, 28.2). To Irenaeus, the Scriptures contain the prophets, the Gospels and the apostles (II, 27.2; III, 8.1), that is, the Jewish Scriptures and most writings that were to be included in the New Testament.[111] According to Hans-Jochen Jaschke, "practically the whole New Testament as well as the Old Testament belong to the 'canon' of Irenaeus."[112] We may here notice, as Charles Hill does in a recent essay, that Irenaeus (or his scribe) most likely marked scriptural citations in his own apologetic work *Against Heresies* by using so called *diplai*—wedge-shaped marks (">")—in the book margins.[113] The late second-century papyrus P.Oxy. 405, which contains parts of *Against Heresies* (III, 9.3), makes use of such *diplai* to highlight a quote from

---

109. Wilhelm Schneemelcher, "Bibel III: Die Entstehung des Kanons des Neuen Testaments und der christlichen Bibel", in *Theologische Realenzyklopädie*, 6, eds. G. Krause and G. Müller (Berlin and New York: Walter de Gruyter, 1980), 25. The strong emphasis on the fourth-century notion of canon and the notion of "canonization proper" tends to go in the direction here dismissed by Schneemelcher.

110. ANF 1:399.

111. For the writings included in Irenaeus's NT, see fnn. 112 and 139 below.

112. Hans-Jochen Jaschke, "Irenäus von Lyon," TRE, vol. 16 (1987), 258–268, 261. Irenaeus never refers or alludes to Philemon, Jude and 3 John. According to Bernhard Mutschler (*Irenäus als johannischer Theologe: Studien zur Schriftauslegung bei Irenäus von Lyon* [Studien und Texte zu Antike und Christentum 21; Tübingen: Mohr Siebeck, 2004], 61), James and perhaps 2 Peter are alluded to. Mutschler in his detailed analysis concludes that of the 27 books of the NT Irenaeus cites 16, and of the remaining eleven eight are arguably alluded to or used, that is all in all 24 books. See further fn. 139 below. As for OT and NT use in Irenaeus, see Mutschler, *Irenäus als johannischer Theologe: Studien zur Schriftauslegung bei Irenäus von Lyon*, 61–117.

113. Charles E. Hill, "Irenaeus, the Scribes, and the Scriptures: Papyrological and Theological Observations from P.Oxy. 405," in *Irenaeus: Life, Scripture, Legacy*, eds. P. Foster and S. Parvis, (Minneapolis: Fortress, 2012), 119–130.

Matt 3:16–17.[114] As to the scribal use of these marks, Hill here refers to
the seventh-century archbishop Isidore of Seville, who comments that
"our scribes place this [diplai] in books of churchmen to separate or to
make clear the citations of Sacred Scriptures."[115] Interestingly, Irenaeus,
who is writing in the last quarter of the second century, here as elsewhere
treats New Testament texts on a par with the Old Testament.[116] Together
they make up "the entire Scriptures" (universae scripturae; II, 27.2; cf.
Josephus's canon features 5 and 6 under 4.2.2 above).[117] Since canon in
this regard (universae scripturae)[118] is best understood as a property of
sacred Scripture,[119] the close association of the old Scriptures with the
new apostolic scriptures, and vice versa,[120] here provides a key not only

---

114. C. H. Roberts dated P.Oxy. 405 to the late second century (Manuscript, Society and Belief in
Early Christian Egypt, The Schweich Lectures of the British Academy 1977 [Oxford: Oxford University,
1979], 23). In Roberts's words (Manuscript, Society and Belief in Early Christian Egypt, 53), this early
manuscript "reached Oxyrhynchus not long after the ink was dry on the author's manuscript." Cf.
Hill, "Irenaeus," 120, 237 fn. 12.

115. Hill, "Irenaeus," 127.

116. This is especially the case in his Adversus haereses and less so in his catechetical work Epideixis,
which is based on traditional "Proof-from-Prophecy" material drawn from the Jewish Scriptures. Cf.
Brooke Foss Westcott, The Bible in the Church (London and New York: Macmillan, 1905), 122. We
note, however, that Irenaeus's catechetical piece, Demonstration of the Apostolic Preaching, largely is
an exposition of Old Testament texts and themes. For this type of OT exegesis, see Campenhausen,
Formation, 183–85; and Oskar Skarsaune, "The Development of Scriptural Interpretation in the
Second and Third Centuries—except Clement and Origen," in Hebrew Bible/Old Testament: The
History of Its Interpretation, vol. 1, ed. M. Sæbø, (Göttingen: Vandenhoeck & Ruprecht, 1996).

117. Although Irenaeus very much emphasizes the gospel, proclaimed first in oral and later in
written form, and "handed down to us in the Scriptures, so that would be the foundation and pillar
of our faith" (Haer. III, 1.1; trans. Robert Grant, Irenaeus of Lyons [New York: Routledge, 1997; mod-
ified], 123–24), he nonetheless clearly places the written Gospel as part of a larger corpus of writings
made up of prophets and Gospel (II, 27.2), or prophets and apostles (III, 8.1). Campenhausen's claim
(Formation, 176), that "the first catholic canon was originally conceived as 'unicellular,' having one
section only" therefore has little to support it, or should at least not be taken too literally.

118. Cf. the quotes above (fn. 93) from Emanuel Tov, who takes canon/canonization as "referring
to Scripture as a whole."

119. See, e.g., my "The Scriptures and the LORD: Formation and Significance of the Christian
Biblical Canon. A Study in Text, Ritual and Interpretation" (PhD Diss., Lund University, 2005), 13–93,
esp. 79–85. If "canon" is mainly a fourth- or fifth-century category, which this chapter suggests it is
not, it does not necessarily need to be understood as a property of sacred Scripture.

120. As will be argued below, such association between the texts belonging to the old and the
new Scripture corpora takes place before the time of Irenaeus, e.g., in 2 Pet 3:15–16 and elsewhere.

to canonical date,[121] but also to the textual,[122] performative (public reading in churches)[123] and dogmatic–interpretative location of the canon (e.g., christological monotheism, and prophecy–fulfillment, framework).[124] The employment of the canonical formula in Book Four of *Adversus haereses* (33.8)[125]—neither to add to nor subtract from the Scriptures (cf. Josephus's canon feature 8 above)—gives further support to the seemingly close connection between the emergence of an expanded, and eventually rather fixed, second-century scriptural canon[126] and, complying with this, a Christian pattern of biblical interpretation. This, in turn, is partly due to the Christian first- and second-century modifications of the scope of the Scriptures[127] and the thereby implied change of interplay between textual part and textual whole (cf. Iren. *Haer.* II, 28.3; I, 8.1; 9.4; and Clem. *Strom.* VII, 16.95).[128]

In Irenaeus, canonical[129] delimitation with implications for interpretation is thematized also with regard to those who make unauthorized additions to the Scriptures, such as the Valentinians with their Gospel

---

121. *Pace* Sundberg ("Revised History," 453), who argues that "the church did not receive an Old Testament canon from Judaism, but rather scripture on the way to canonization."

122. E.g., common editorial features, such as *nomina sacra*, in OT and NT texts. Cf. David Trobisch's notes on the Greek "Old" and "New Testaments" sharing the same final redaction, for which these main titles have a literarily unifying and theologically binding function, *The First Edition of the New Testament* (Oxford: Oxford University, 2000), 103–104.

123. Cf. Eusebius's comment (*Hist. eccl.* II, 15) on Peter's approval of Mark's Gospel for public reading (or prayer) in the churches (τὸν ἀπόστολον ... κυρῶσαι τε τὴν γραφὴν εἰς ἔντευξιν ταῖς ἐκκλησίαις).

124. Cf. John Webster's article, "The Dogmatic Location of the Canon," *Neue Zeitschrift für systematische Theologie und Religionsphilosophie* 43 (2001), 17–43; and Tomas Bokedal, "The Scriptures and the LORD: Formation and Significance of the Christian Biblical Canon. A Study in Text, Ritual and Interpretation" (PhD Diss., Lund University, 2005), 28–34; and idem, "The Rule of Faith—Tracing its Origins," *Journal of Theological Interpretation* 7.2 (2013): 233–55

125. Cf. fn. below.

126. "Canon" can here be defined as "an authoritative collection of authoritative Scriptures"; cf. Metzger, *Canon*, 282–88.

127. The Scriptures, of course, always include the Jewish Scriptures/Old Testament.

128. In this connection Irenaeus mentions "the unfeigned preservation [*custoditio*], coming down to us, of the scriptures, with a complete collection allowing for neither addition nor subtraction" (*Haer.* IV, 33.8). Trans. Robert Grant, *Irenaeus of Lyons*, 161; cited from Hill, "Irenaeus," 120.

129. Although the term "canon" or "canonical" is not used until the fourth century to describe the scope of the biblical writings, aspects of the same or similar processes aimed at delimiting or preserving a precise group or number of writings can be seen earlier, which this article seeks to demonstrate.

of Truth (*Haer.* III, 11.9), the followers of Ptolemaeus who read what is unwritten (ἐξ ἄγραφον καὶ ἀναγινόσκοντες; I, 8.1), and the Marcosians who use apocryphal and false writings (ἀποκρύφων καὶ νόθων γραφῶν; I, 20.1).[130] Systematic reflection on delimitation—on what does and what does not belong to Scripture—also characterizes the criticism directed towards Marcion for dismissing the Jewish Scriptures (*Haer.* I, 27.2; Tert. *Marc.* I, 19.4), and for demolishing the fourfold form of the Gospel by only accepting a mutilated version of Luke (*Haer.* III, 11.9; 12.12).[131] The Ebionites are likewise corrected for exclusively holding on to the Gospel of Matthew and for rejecting the Pauline epistles (I, 26.2; III, 15.1). Disapproval is expressed also in regard to those who discard the Gospel of John (III, 11.9) or the Acts of the Apostles (III, 14.3–4; 15.1).[132] As to Irenaeus's concerns for scriptural scope, he is not alone but in good company. By the late second century, he emphasizes the necessity of acknowledging the complete number of Scriptures (cf. esp. III, 14.3–4),[133] as does his contemporaries in Carthage and Alexandria, Tertullian (*Marc.* V, 21; cf. *Praescr.* 38.7) and Clement (*Strom.* VII, 16.96). Exegesis and theology are naturally pursued with this scriptural whole in mind, as are the universal, and particular Christian, rules for scriptural interpretation. Together various such rules can be said to constitute an early "canonical approach" with emphasis given to the order (τάξις) and connection/sequence (εἱρμός) of the Scriptures, the hermeneutical play between textual parts and textual whole, the grasp of the *scopus* (the central point of view when seeking to understand a work appropriately), the "apostolic" and ecumenical[134] Rule-of-Faith pattern of scriptural interpretation (*Haer.*, I, 8.1–10.2; III,

---

130. See further my *Scriptures*, 283.

131. Irenaeus's famous defense of the fourfold Gospel in *Against Heresies* (III, 11.7–9) also belongs to his varied reflection on scriptural scope. For the probable existence of the fourfold Gospel already at the time of Marcion, see section 4.4.2 below.

132. Bokedal, *Scriptures*, 283. Tertullian similarly criticizes Marcion for not including the Pastoral Epistles among the Pauline letters (*Marc.* V, 21).

133. Or Scriptures belonging to a particular sub-group, such as the four Gospels, the two Lukan writings or the Pauline epistles.

134. Or universal; cf. Iren. *Haer.* I, 10.1–2.

1.2),[135] the cross of Christ as key to reading prophecies (*Haer.*, V, 26.1), and Scripture's self-sufficiency (Clem. *Strom.* VII, 16.96; Iren. *Haer.* II, 28.2).[136] The scriptural organization and scope—here referred to as the entire, or complete, number of Scriptures in their regulative function vis-à-vis the church (*Haer.* II, 27.2),[137] i.e., the scriptural canon—has a direct impact on all these second-century interpretative strategies, and *vice versa*.[138]

4.4.2 THE NEW TESTAMENT AROUND A.D. 200

In the strict sense, however—even if Irenaeus's "New Testament" may have embraced some 22 (or 24) books,[139] in shape similar to that described in the second-century Muratorian Fragment[140]—the bishop of Lyons may not actually have known or used the phrase "New Testament" as a label designating the Gospels and the other specifically Christian Scriptures.[141] The title "New Testament" is, however, familiar to Irenaeus's contemporaries, Clement of Alexandria (*Strom.* I, 5; V, 85) and Tertullian (*Marc.* IV, 1.1).

---

135. Tomas Bokedal, "The Rule of Faith: Tracing Its Origins," *Journal of Theological Interpretation* 7.2 (2013): 233–55.

136. *Strom.* VII, 16.96 "We obtain from the Scriptures themselves a perfect demonstration concerning the Scriptures."

137. Cf. the similar reference to the "entire Instrument" (*integrum instrumentum*) with regard to the New Testament in Tertullian (*Praescr.* 38.7).

138. For the mutual relationship between Scripture and Rule of Faith, see Johannes Kunze, *Glaubensregel, Heilige Schrift und Taufbekenntnis: Untersuchungen über die dogmatische Autorität, ihr Werden und ihre Geschichte, vornehmlich in der alten Kirche* (Leipzig: Dörffling & Franke, 1899); and Bokedal, "The Rule of Faith."

139. Irenaeus's New Testament writings mentioned by Eusebius, *Hist. Eccl.* 5, 8.1–8, include: the four Gospels, Paul (individual epistles not listed), 1–2 John, 1 Peter, Revelation, (and possibly in addition Hermas's *The Shepherd* and *Wisdom*); Eusebius further notes that Irenaeus quotes Hebrews and Wisdom in "a little book of various discourses" (*Hist. Eccl.* V, 26). To this should be added the Book of Acts, and perhaps also James and 2 Peter (as argued by Mutschler; see fn. 112 above). All in all, ca. 22 or 24 NT writings (23, according to Mutschler [*Irenäus als johanneischer Theologe*, 79]; however, if James, which is only weakly testified to, is excluded, we arrive at 22), if *The Shepherd* and *Wisdom* are excluded. When comparing the "New Testament" of Irenaeus with the Peshitta (containing 22 NT books), we notice that the latter differs from Irenaeus's NT by excluding Revelation, and by including James (which Irenaeus, according to Mutschler, may have had access to); it also includes Hebrews which Irenaeus may, but probably does not, count among the Scriptures.

140. For a late second-century dating of the Muratorian Fragment, see section 4.2.3 above; the Muratorian canon contains Gospels (probably four) of which Luke and John are mentioned, Acts, 13 epistles of Paul, Jude, two Epistles of John (1 and 2 John; or 2 and 3 John as well as 1 John), Revelation and Wisdom; it does not mention James, Hebrews or 2 Peter.

141. Cf., however, Trobisch, *First Edition*, 44, 106, who argues that Irenaeus did "refer to the second part of the Canonical Edition" by the "term *New Testament*."

The central function of the title can easily be seen up until and including the time of Athanasius in the middle of the fourth century,[142] when "the concepts 'canon' and 'testament' (or 'covenant') still marched side by side,"[143] although probably in the sense that "canon" was used as a designation for the whole Bible, i.e. for the collection of the sacred Scriptures recognized by the church, and that the two parts of the Bible were at the same time described by "testament."[144] For our present purposes, addressing as well some interpretative issues involved in the canon formation, the standard label for the second portion of the bipartite Scriptures, ἡ καινὴ διαθήκη ("the New Testament/Covenant"), is well suited, not least due to its theological orientation,[145] as is the derivative adjective, ἐνδιάθηκος ("testamented," indicating belonging to the scriptural canon, with particular emphasis on canonical scope/delimitation). These terms basically designated what the later term κανών (canon as list) was meant to denote (by cataloguing the writings to be included among the "divine Scriptures"), which can be seen, e.g., from the function of the derivative term ἐνδιάθηκος in Origen and Eusebius.[146]

However, even if none of the above terms were used in this sense by Irenaeus, the period at which he is active is still crucial for finding in our Patristic sources a more or less definite form of the New Testament.[147] It is here significant that Tertullian (ca. 160–220) around this time explicitly

---

142. And, of course, from the fourth century onwards until the present.

143. Wilhelm Schneemelcher, "General Introduction," in *New Testament Apocrypha*, vol. 1: *Gospels and Related Writings* (ed. W. Schneemelcher; Cambridge: James Clarke & Co. Ltd and Louisville: Westminster John Knox Press, 1991; 2nd ed.), 10.

144. Cf. Schneemelcher, "General Introduction," 10.

145. Cf. Schneemelcher, "General Introduction," 13. Through the labels "Old" and "New Covenant/Testament," each of the two collections of Scriptures becomes textually, hermeneutically and theologically related to the other. On the theological significance of these terms, Schneemelcher (p. 13) writes: "Behind the name for the documents of the divine will to salvation stands the theology of Irenaeus and his forefathers in Asia minor, 'who in their turn drew upon the ancient prophets and Paul.' In other words, the history of the term is only correctly understood when it is set in the context of the history of theology."

146. Differently Sundberg ("Revised History," 460), who argues that Origen "does not have a New Testament list or reflect the concept of a New Testament canon."

147. On the scope of Irenaeus's New Testament, see fnn. 112 and 139 above. As to the text of the New Testament, it is only with Irenaeus that "signs of an established text appear" (K. and B. Aland); Irenaeus is further "the earliest surviving writer of the Christian era who quotes the New Testament both extensively and accurately" (Souter). Cited from Hill, "Irenaeus," 120.

makes reference to "the entire Instrument" (*integro instrumento*), that is, what he considered to be all the New Testament Scriptures,[148] used not only by himself, but also by the Gnostic leader Valentinus (*Praescr.* 38.7).[149] The particular importance of the years around A.D. 200 for the emergence of the NT canon is indicated as well by Eusebius of Caesarea (ca. 263–339), who maintains that Irenaeus's contemporary, Clement of Alexandria (ca. 150–215/21), wrote concise comments on all the canonical Scriptures (πάσης τῆς ἐνδιαθήκου γραφῆς),[150] "not passing over even the disputed books"—i.e., "the Epistle of Jude and the other Catholic Epistles, the Epistle of Barnabas, and the Apocalypse known as Peter's" (*Hist. eccl.* VI, 14. 1). From the viewpoint of Eusebius, scriptural interpretation/commentary here goes hand in hand with the issue of canonicity. With his particular attention to the NT canon at this period, Eusebius also refers to Origen (ca. 185–254), who, at age 18 in A.D. 203, became the leader of the Catechetical School in Alexandria. Origen had access to all New Testament writings. Eusebius tells us that he distinguished between disputed and undisputed NT books.[151] Origen appears to have treated 23 books as undisputed, generally acknowledged writings (ὁμολογούμενα) and four as disputed (ἀμφιβαλλόμενα) among the Christian communities (James, 2 Peter, and 2 and 3 John),[152] whereas Eusebius mentions five of the New Testament books in his category of disputed writings

---

148. Tertullian uses *testamentum* (Testament) synonymously with *instrumentum* (Instrument) to designate the corpus of NT writings.

149. Cf. F. F. Bruce, "Thoughts on the Beginning of the New Testament Canon," *Bulletin of the John Rylands University Library of Manchester* 65 (1983): 37–60.

150. Literally, "all the testament-ed Scripture." Due to the natural connection between the title "New Testament" and the delimitation of the collection of writings thus titled, the concept of "testament-ed Scriptures" seems in some ways more appropriate than the later notion of canon used to signify the canonical Scriptures or the authoritative enumeration of these Scriptures. Cf. Zahn's remark below, fn. 178.

151. Metzger, *Canon*, 135–41. Cf. Sundberg ("Revised History," 460), who maintains that "canonization proper" is not simply the concern over the acceptability of particular books, or *de facto* variations in canonical scope, "but with the formation of the New Testament list, the New Testament canon."

152. Metzger, *Canon*, 141. Origen also counts Hermas's the *Shepherd* among the disputed writings. Like Eusebius he places books forged by heretics, such as the *Gospel of the Egyptians* in a category of rejected writings (ψευδῆ).

(ἀντιλεγόμενα),[153] viz., James, Jude, 2 Peter, 2 and 3 John (and in addition Hebrews, said not to be acknowledged by some).[154] Apparently these are disputed by some Christian communities, leaders, and theologians. As for the Revelation to John, however—in case of which interpretative matters (millenarianism) became crucial—discussions regarding its scriptural/canonical status do not seem to have occurred prior to the late second/early third century (the Alogi; Gaius).[155]

A quite recent suggestion as to the significance of the period under discussion is offered in David Trobisch's monographs on the NT canon.[156] Trobisch has suggested the publication of a complete New Testament already by the mid- to late second century.[157] With particular attention to the Greek NT manuscript tradition as a whole and to the ordering of the NT books, especially in the large Bible codices (fourth century onwards),[158] he concludes that the earliest edition of such a "New Testament," the *editio princeps*—which subsequently became the standard New Testament with the books placed in "canonical order"—must have been published some-time in the second century. Trobisch even conjectures that Polycarp (ca. 69–165) may have been the individual behind this archetypal first edition

---

153. *Hist. eccl.* III, 25: "disputed books, which are nevertheless familiar to most people of the church" (τῶν δ' ἀντιλεγομένων, γνωρίμων δ' οὖν ὅμως τοῖς πολλοῖς).

154. Eusebius himself seems to have accepted the view of Clement of Alexandria, that Hebrews was a work by Paul written in Hebrew, which was later translated into Greek by either Luke or Clement of Rome. Cf. Metzger, *Canon*, 203.

155. Revelation as an undisputed book among all Greek-speaking churches throughout the second century is stressed by Theodor Zahn, *Die bleibende Bedeutung des neutestamentlichen Kanons für die Kirche* (Leipzig: U. Dichert'sche Verlagsbuchh. Nachf., 1898), 8–9. Cf, however, Iren. *Haer.* III, 11.9, referred to above. Eusebius (*Hist. eccl.* III, 25) does not include Revelation among the disputed books, but somewhat inconsistently, in the same paragraph, places it both among the acknowledged (ὁμολογούμενα) and the spurious writings (νόθα). As to the third-century canon criticism involving the Book of Revelation, see Metzger, *Canon*, 104–105, 204–205, 212, 236, 240–47, and 273. Some valuable biographical notes addressing three different stages in Eusebius's thoughts on the canonical status of the Apocalypse are provided by Robert Grant, *Eusebius as Church Historian* (Eugene, Oreg.: Wipf & Stock, 1980), 126–27.

156. See, e.g., Trobisch, *First Edition*; and idem, *Paul's Letter Collection: Tracing the Origins* (Bolivar, Missouri: Quiet Waters Publications, 2001).

157. For partial appreciation of Trobisch's theory, see David C. Parker's review of Trobisch's theory in *JTS* 53 (2002): 298–305; and Larry Hurtado, "The New Testament in the Second Century: Text, Collections and Canon," in *Transmission and Reception: New Testament Text-critical and Exegetical Studies* (eds. J. W. Childers and D. C. Parker; Piscataway, N.J.: Gorgias, 2006), 21–22.

158. Trobisch, *First Edition*, 21–38.

of the canonical New Testament (*Die Kanonische Ausgabe*),[159] and that typi-cal editorial features included codex form (OT and NT texts are in this way put on a par), *nomina sacra* (highlighting the key figures of Christian faith in OT and NT texts)[160] and book titles (assigning the included writings to one of the NT part-volumes),[161] all with implications for scriptural inter-pretation through the forming of larger and modified textual wholes: The Gospel of John read with 1 John (titles indicating same author/authorial circle), and as part of the fourfold Gospel (sharing the phrasing "Gospel according to"),[162] Ephesians read with 1 Corinthians, 1 and 2 Timothy and other Pauline epistles (containing similar titles to addressees, and soon forming a sub-group of 13–14 letters within the emerging NT; cf. Ignatius and Polycarp),[163] Pauline letters read with the Gospel (cf. Ignatius),[164]

---

159. David Trobisch, "Who Published the New Testament?," *Free Inquiry*, 28.1 (Amherst, NY: Council of Secular Humanism, 2007/2008), 30–33.

160. On codex form and *nomina sacra*, see further below.

161. The four standard groups or volumes are a) the Gospels (titles indicating genre and apostle/associate to an apostle: [Εὐαγγέλιον] κατὰ Μαθθαίον κτλ., b) the Pauline epistles (Acts+Catholic Epistles; titles indicating addressees), c) the Apocalypse (title indicating genre and apostolic author), and, arguably appearing a little later as a complete part-volume, d) the so-called Prax-apostolos (titles indicating apostolic sender or, in the case of Acts, genre and protagonists). For further details, see Trobisch, *First Edition*; and for the somewhat more comlex picture of the division into groups of writings included in a single codex, see Eldon Jay Epp, "Issues in the Interrelation of New Testament Textual Criticism and Canon," in *The Canon Debate* (eds. L. M. McDonald and J. A. Sanders; Peabody, Mass.: Hendrickson, 2002), 487; further details on the Pauline letter corpus can be found in Benjamin Laird, "Early Titles of the Pauline Letters and the Formation of the Pauline Corpus," *BN* 175 (2017): 55–81.

162. This is implied by the title κατὰ Ἰοάννην and the early formation of the fourfold Gospel (cf. below). See also D. Moody Smith, *The Fourth Gospel in Four Dimensions: Judaism and Jesus, the Gospels and Scripture* (Columbia, SC: The University of South Carolina, 2008), 194: The traditional answer to the question of the originative relationship between John and the Synoptics posed as early as the second century, "is that John knew and approved of the other Gospels, and presumed knowledge of them as he wrote. Thus he wrote to supplement, mildly correct, or interpret the others."

163. Cf. Ign. *Eph.* 12.2. For use of NT books in Ignatius and Polycarp, see, e.g., Andrew Gregory and Christopher Tuckett, eds., *The Reception of the New Testament in the Apostolic Fathers* (Oxford: Oxford University, 2005); Metzger, *Canon*, 43–49, 59–63; and Paul Foster, "The Epistles of Ignatius of Antioch," in Paul Foster (ed.), *The Writings of the Apostolic Fathers* (London: T&T Clark, 2007), 103–7. Also the titles designating addressees set the Pauline letters apart as a distinctive group of writings from very early on, arguably sometime A.D. 60–120. For a Pauline corpus circulating before Marcion, see Ulrich Schmid, *Marcion und sein Apostolus: Rekonstruktion und historische Einordnung der marcionitischen Paulusbriefausgabe* (Berlin: Walter de Gruyter, 1995). Cf. Gamble, *Books and Readers*, 61, quoted in fn. 88 above.

164. Gamble, *Books and Readers*, 107: "It can ... be determined with certainty that he [Ignatius of Antioch] knew the Gospel of Matthew and four Pauline epistles: 1 Corinthians, Ephesians and 1 and 2 Timothy." "Gospel and Apostle" was an early way of referring to the NT material at a time

and the Old Testament typically not read without (indicated knowledge of) the New.[165] These and other "canonical reading patterns"[166] were part of Christian scriptural interpretation from very early on. Canonical or scriptural scope here already is—or implies—scriptural interpretation (cf. 2 Pet 3:16; 1 Tim 3:16; Iren. *Haer.* III, 1.2; Clem. *Strom.* VII, 16.95–96).[167]

We may here recall that Harnack and Campenhausen, as part of their historical analyses, also date the formation of the New Testament canon to roughly this period, that is, the late second century, or around the year A.D. 200.[168] Harnack interestingly maintains that "[t]he Canon of twenty-seven books, as we still have it to-day, is the Canon of the Alexandrian Church of the third century, but its nucleus is the New Testament as it was created about A.D. 200 in Rome."[169]

From this quick glance at both some ancient writers like Irenaeus, Clement, Origen and Eusebius, and modern scholars like Harnack, Campenhausen and Trobisch, we can apprehend that the late second and early third century are crucial for seeing more clearly in our sources a regionally completed New Testament (cf. *integrum instrumentum*, Tert. *Praescr.* 38), with a view towards a common scriptural canon for the

---

when Matthew and Pauline epistles became widespread in many Christian communities (already some of the Apostolic Fathers). For the influence of Paul on Mark, and a partial revision of Martin Werner's classic assertion "that the agreements between Mark and Paul reflect general early Christian viewpoints," see, e.g., Joel Marcus, "Mark—Interpreter of Paul," NTS 46 (2000): 473–87.

165. For various early Patristic models of scriptural (OT) interpretation, see, e.g., Skarsaune, "Development of Scriptural Interpretation."

166. From a hermeneutical vantage point, the category of either "canon" or "covenant" seems to be serviceable in this connection, in addition to "Scripture," since a rather significant modification of the text and reading of the Jewish Scriptures here are taking place. The big shift in this regard occurs in the first and second centuries involving as well awareness and reflection on scriptural scope, similar to the discussions on canonical delimitation in the fourth and fifth centuries A.D.

167. Cf. Clem. *Strom.* VII, 16.95: "For we have the Lord as the first principle of our teaching, leading us to knowledge, from beginning to end, in many and various ways through the Prophets, through the Gospel and through the blessed Apostles"); and *Strom.* VII, 16.96: "We obtain from the Scriptures themselves a perfect demonstration concerning the Scriptures"; Cf. also Kunze, *Glaubensregel, Heilige Schrift und Taufbekenntnis,* 147–52.

168. Adolf von Harnack, *Das Neue Testament um das Jahr 200: Theodor Zahns Geschichte des Neutestamentlichen Kanons (erster Band, erste Hälfte) geprüft* (Freiburg: Mohr Siebeck, 1989); Campenhausen, *Formation.*

169. Harnack, *The Origin of the New Testament,* 113.

church universal.[170] Two questions pertaining to the early canon formation process may here be raised:

First, how and when did the "New Testament" title emerge?

Second, in what ways did (allegedly) apostolic writings become associated with the Scriptures, and *vice versa*, so as to form a new enlarged body of sacred Scriptures?

In what follows, these two related questions with their respective implications for canonical date and interpretation will be discussed.

4.4.3 HOW AND WHEN DID THE "NEW TESTAMENT" TITLE EMERGE?

We find the label "New Testament" as a designation for the corpus of apostolic writings around the turn of the third century (A.D. 200) in Tertullian and in Clement of Alexandria.[171] The two titles, "Old Testament" and "New Testament," which are employed in parallel, here presuppose one another, which is particularly clear in Clement of Alexandria (*Strom.* II, 29.2).[172] The designation "Old Testament" (παλαιὰ διαθήκη), apparently used already by Melito of Sardis around A.D. 175 (Euseb. *Hist. eccl.* IV, 26.12–14), is worth noting. First of all, it arguably presumes the use of the corresponding title "New Testament" already in the late second century;[173] more noteworthy still, in terms of number (lit. "how many they are in number, and what is their order"; Euseb. *Hist. eccl.* IV, 26.12–14), it appears to assume a Jewish scriptural canon.[174] The "old," as understood by Melito, seems to be the Scriptures accepted by the synagogue as authoritative, or more correctly probably, by the Christians in Palestine; that is, this "Old Testament"—as in Melito's own canonical list of some 22–25 books[175]

---

170. So, e.g., Origen and Eusebius, but also Irenaeus (see above).

171. Tert. *Pud.* 1, *Prax.* 15; Clem. *Strom.* II, 29.2–3.

172. Cf. Campenhausen, *Formation*, 266.

173. Cf. Metzger, *Canon*, 123; and Trobisch, *First Edition*, 44. Differently Campenhausen, *Formation*, 265.

174. For the relation between the books numbered 22 and 24, and perhaps 25 in Melito, see Beckwith, *Old Testament Canon of the New Testament Church*, 183–85; 235–56, esp. 250–56.

175. Beckwith, *The Canon of the Old Testament of the New Testament Church*, 183–85. Some scholars argue that Melito, in terms of numbering, embraced a 22- or 24-book Bible; Beckwith, however, demonstrates that his count is partly non-Jewish, arriving at the odd number 25. A 22-book Bible is,

received from Palestine (*N.B.*, not from the large Jewish community in Sardis)—does not appear to have included apocryphal writings.[176] (A few decades later Origen sets the common [Eastern] Christian standard in terms of number of OT books at 22.) So, from a Christian vantage point, the term "old" in "Old Testament" does seem to designate what was held to be the scriptural corpus of the "old," or preceding, Jewish "covenant" (cf. 4.2.2 above).

The introduction of the titles "Old" and "New Testament" thus have a couple of significant hermeneutical implications: First, the presumption of a rather delimited, and in principle closed (cf. Josephus's canon feature 4; 4.2.2 above), corpus of sacred writings included in each Testament (Melito's "Old Testament" probably includes the books of the Jewish canon,[177] except Esther);[178] second, the chronological (old *vs.* new)[179] and interpretative (e.g., prophecy-fulfillment) distinction between the two text corpora. Sensibility towards such an ecclesial distinction seems to be largely lacking, for example, in the treatment of Scripture and covenant in the *Epistle of Barnabas* (commonly dated A.D. 70–135).[180] Thus the (implicit) need for textual–theological clarity in this regard. The new

---

of course, endorsed already by Josephus (*Against Apion* 1:37–41) and by others. See Mason, "Josephus and His Twenty-Two Book Canon," 110–27; Beckwith, *Old Testament Canon of the New Testament Church*, 235–40; and Skarsaune, *In the Shadow of the Temple: Jewish Influences on Early Christianity* (Downers Grove, Ill.: Intervarsity, 2002), 291–92.

176. Cf. F. F. Bruce, *The Canon of Scripture* (Downers Grove, Ill.: InterVarsity, 1988), 71–72: "Melito's list probably includes all the books of the Hebrew Bible except Esther."

177. See Beckwith, *Old Testament Canon of the New Testament Church*, 390.

178. Cf. von Harnack, *The Origin of the New Testament*, 34: "a collection of fundamental documents has already *the tendency to become final*, and certainly a collection of fundamental documents of a *Covenant* carries in itself the idea of complete finality." Similarly Theodor Zahn, *Grundriss*, 11: "Die Vorstellung einer *abgeschlossenen Sammlung von Offenbarungsurkunden* ist früher durch παλαιά und καινὴ διαθήκη ausgedrückt worden, und die Zugehörigkeit zu dieser seit Origenes durch ἐνδιάθηκος." Cf. also the discussions above on canonical scope pertaining to Irenaeus, Tertullian and Eusebius.

179. For various interpretations of the relationship between "old" and "new" in this connection, see Trobisch, *First Edition*, 62; R. A. Harrisville, "The Concept of Newness in the New Testament," *JBL* 74 (1955): 79: "Four distinctive features are found to be inherent in the concept of newness: the elements of contrast, continuity, dynamic, and finality"; quoted from Trobisch, *First Edition*, 137 fn. 49; cf. also Mogens Müller, "The Hidden Context: Some Observations to the Concept of the New Covenant in the New Testament," in *Texts and Contexts: Biblical Texts in Their Textual and Situational Contexts* (eds. T. Fornberg and D. Hellholm; Oslo/Copenhagen/Stockholm/Boston: Scandinavian University Press, 1995), 649–58.

180. We can also notice Marcion in this connection, who rejected the Jewish Scriptures altogether.

titles, distinguishing the two main text corpora, effectively solve this hermeneutical impasse,[181] while at the same time making Christianity more confidently appear as a covenant of the book, the bipartite Christian Scriptures.[182] In this way each of the main parts of the Scriptures has acquired a new name, which "simultaneously unites the two and distinguishes between them."[183]

Nevertheless, as to the relative significance of the title "New Testament," Theodor Zahn argued a little more than a century ago:

Now, as the name "New Testament" unambiguously expressed and doubtlessly presupposed the full equality between the apostolic Scriptures and the Old Testament, not only in function, but also in the church's perception, we may say that one can only talk of a "New Testament" with full historical right where the attribute "sacredness" has been awarded to the therein unified writings. Thereby, however, we have already said that with some historical right one can also talk about a New Testament with respect to the time during which the name "New Testament" was not common.[184]

Even if "sacredness" is a necessary attribute for these writings in their capacity as New Testament writings—as von Harnack suggested—we must nonetheless conclude with Zahn that "with some historical right one can also talk about a New Testament with respect to the time during which the name 'New Testament' was not common."[185] In other words, the first- and second-century canon formation process—which includes

181. As for the title καινὴ διαθήκη occurring in the manuscript tradition, see Table of Contents in Codex Alexandrinus. See further Trobisch, First Edition, 25 and 42 (supplied with an image of the New Testament book title from Codex Alexandrinus).

182. Pace Campenhausen, Formation, 267; and Trobisch, First Edition. Cf., however, the association of "testament" and "book" in Sir 24:23; 1 Macc 1:56 (βιβλίον διαθήκης); and Exod 24:7 (τὸ βιβλίον τῆς διαθήκης); referred to in Campenhausen, Formation, 136–37 fn. 48. Cf. also Müller, "Hidden Context."

183. Schneemelcher, "General Introduction", 13.

184. Theodor Zahn, Einige Bemerkungen zu Adolf Harnack's Prüfung der Geschichte des neutestamentlichen Kanons, vol. 1.1 (Erlangen and Leipzig: A. Deichert'sche Verlagshandlung Nachf. [Georg Böhme], 1889), 16–18.

185. As discussed above, Zahn's early dating of a canon of Christian Scriptures to about the end of the first century was forcibly disputed by Adolf von Harnack (see above, introduction, and section 4.1). On Zahn, see Gamble, "Recent Research," 267–69.

several of the most important components in the formation of the New Testament canon—is earlier than the labels "New Testament" and "canon" employed to signify the new Scriptures and their scope. A New Testament (or a core New Testament) as seen, e.g., in Irenaeus and some of his predecessors, was present in the Christian communities before the title "New Testament" was introduced as a designation for these writings.

4.4.4 IN WHAT WAYS DID APOSTOLIC WRITINGS BECOME ASSOCIATED WITH THE SCRIPTURES, AND VICE VERSA, SO AS TO FORM A NEW ENLARGED BODY OF SACRED SCRIPTURES?

Already in the New Testament writings we find well-known examples of Christian scriptural hermeneutics that closely associate the Scriptures with the apostolic message: the opening genealogy and the Fulfillment Quotations in Matthew;[186] the prophecy–fulfillment pattern found throughout the New Testament; Luke's paradigmatic "Beginning with Moses and all the Prophets" (Luke 24:25); Jesus's authoritative interpretation, "You have heard that it was said … But I tell you" (Matt 5);[187] Jesus's message seemingly put on a par with Scripture in John (18:8–9 and 18:32; cf. 3:14; 21:24–25);[188] and 2 Pet 3:16 placing letters of Paul ("all his letters") on a par with "the other Scriptures."

Commenting on the opening verses of Hebrews, Peter Stuhlmacher writes: "The saving word of God is only fully heard when the γραφαὶ ἅγιαι are understood in the light of the appearance of Jesus Christ and read together with the witness of the apostles."[189] And, relating to the canon formation process, Harnack in 1914 interestingly argues:

---

186. See further, e.g., Joel Kennedy, *The Recapitulation of Israel: Use of Israel's History in Matthew 1:1–4:11* (WUNT 2.257; Tübingen: Mohr Siebeck, 2008).

187. For various interpretations, see R. T. France, *The Gospel of Matthew*, NICNT (Grand Rapids, Eerdmans, 2007), 191ff.; and W. D. Davies and Dale C. Allison, *A Critical and Exegetical Commentary on the Gospel according to Saint Matthew*, ICC, vol. 1 (London: T&T Clark, 1988), 505ff.

188. See, e.g., Peter Stuhlmacher, *Biblische Theologie des Neuen Testaments: Von der Paulusschule bis zur Johannesoffenbarung*, vol. 2 (Göttingen: Vandenhoeck & Ruprecht, 1999), 281–82.

189. Stuhlmacher, *How To Do Biblical Theology*, 54.

The earliest motive force [leading to the creation of the New Testament], one that had been at work from the beginning of the Apostolic Age, was the supreme reverence in which the words and teaching of Christ Jesus were held. ... Thus side by side with the writings of the Old Testament appeared the Word of "the Lord," and not only so, but in the formula αἱ γραφαὶ καὶ ὁ κύριος the two terms were not only of equal authority, but the second unwritten term received a stronger accent than the first that had literary form. We may therefore say that *in this formula we have the nucleus of the New Testament.*[190]

However, as it turned out, various widely received accounts of "the Lord" were put into writing already in the second half of the first century (Luke 1:1–4). And "the Scriptures and the Lord" (cf., e.g., Paul's appeal to ὁ κύριος in 1 Cor 9:14, 11:23–25, and 1 Thess 4:15)[191] soon became "the Scriptures and the Gospel" (cf., e.g., 2 *Clem.* 2:4 and 8:5; *Did.* 11:3, 15:3; cf. Josephus's canon feature 5 [see section 4.3.1]). As part of this development, the character of the Gospel as a text that stands written appears to have been perceived by the author of the *Epistle of Barnabas* (4.14),[192] Papias (*Hist. eccl.* III, 39.3–4), the author of 2 *Clement* (2.4); Justin (*Dial.* 100.1; 103.6,8; 104.1; 105.6; 106.3; 107.1),[193] and others.[194] In light of its close relation to and endorsement of John's Gospel,[195] the repeated emphasis on what is written also in 1 John (cf. 1 John 1:4; 2:1; 2:7; 2:8; 2:12–14; 2:21, 2:26; 5:13) may be a move in this direction.

---

190. Von Harnack, *The Origin of the New Testament*, 7f.

191. For a brief treatment of the authority of "the Lord," see Jens Schröter, "Jesus and the Canon: The Early Jesus Traditions in the Context of the Origins of the New Testament Canon," in *Performing the Gospel: Orality, Memory, and Mark*, eds. R. Horsley et al. (Minneapolis: Fortress, 2006), 108–10.

192. Quoting as Scripture Matt 22:18: "let us be on guard lest we should be found to be, as it is written, 'many called, but few chosen' "; cf. J. N. Rhodes, *The Epistle of Barnabas and the Deuteronomic Tradition* (WUNT, 2. Reihe, 188; Tübingen: Mohr Siebeck, 2004), 154.

193. Cf. Peter Head, *How the New Testament Came Together* (Grove Biblical Series B51; Cambridge: Grove Books, 2009), 15.

194. It seems as if Papias's words of the "living and abiding voice" early in the second century are not so much about preference for oral tradition, but, as Larry Hurtado and others point out, instead "reflect the *literary* conventions of his time, in which one sought authority for one's *written* reports through claiming that they rested on authentic witnesses" (Hurtado, "Second Century," 3–27).

195. See 4.4.1 below.

4.4.4.1 NT Writings Presenting Themselves as Scripture

A rather unexpected approach towards the early development of specifically Christian Scriptures was aired a few years ago by D. Moody Smith in his 1999 Society of Biblical Literature presidential address, in which he maintained:

> Strangely, or not so strangely, the first and last books of the NT present themselves as scripture. ... [I]t attests the existence of the idea of distinctively Christian scriptures before the end of the first century.[196]

A handful of scholars have tended to agree with Smith on these indications towards scripturality,[197] found not only in Matthew and Revelation, but in other NT writings as well. These scholars have noticed that to discern what is, and what is not, specifically Christian Scripture appears to a considerable degree to be an issue addressed already within the NT texts themselves.[198] In fact, it accords well with what we know of their literary character and of their reception in the faith communities, using biblical-style language[199] and being designed for liturgical reading on a par with the other Scriptures (which is arguably part of their particular textuality or character as texts).[200] Reception to this effect may have been immediate in the case of Matthew's Gospel.[201] Commenting on Justin

---

196. D. Moody Smith, "When Did the Gospels Become Scripture?," *JBL* 119 (2000): 15. Cf. John Ashton, *Understanding the Fourth Gospel* (Oxford: Oxford University, 2nd ed., 2007), 344.

197. See Roland Deines, "Writing Scripture in the First Century", *EJT* 22 (2013): 101–109.

198. As pointed out above, it is important to recall that "the Lord" and "the Gospel" very soon (or immediately) have equal authority with "Scripture."

199. See, e.g., Georg Walser, *The Greek of the Ancient Synagogue: An Investigation on the Greek of the Septuagint, Pseudepigrapha and the New Testament* (Stockholm: Almqvist & Wiksell International, 2001); and R. T. France, *Matthew: Evangelist and Teacher* (Exeter: Paternoster, 1989), 64, 96–97, 128.

200. Our earliest direct witness is Justin, but the wide influence on Christian discourse affected by the Gospel of Matthew, as indicated by Édouard Massaux (*The Influence of the Gospel of Saint Matthew on Christian Literature Before Saint Irenaeus* (edited and with an introduction and addenda by A. J. Bellinzoni; Macon, GA: Mercer University and Leuven, Belgium: Peeters, 1990–93), points to both a liturgical and non-liturgical usage of the writing on a regular basis. Moreover, liturgical usage of emerging NT texts seems to be presupposed already in 2 Pet 3:16 and may have been a reason for writing down Mark and Matthew. On *Barn.* 4.14, see footnote 209 below.

201. Cf. Martin Hengel (*The Four Gospels and the One Gospel of Jesus Christ* (London: SCM, 2000), 116–17) on liturgical reading for which the four Gospels were primarily written; as to the reception

Martyr's reference to weekly liturgical readings of the Gospels side by side with the Prophets (*1 Apol.* 67, written soon after AD 150), Martin Hengel writes that the

> Christians certainly did not take over this Jewish form of the liturgy of the word later, decades after the separation from the synagogue, but basically merely continued the traditional Jewish form in the new eschatological community of salvation. In Rome it [public reading of Christian writings beside the Jewish Scriptures] could go back to the beginnings of the community which was first founded there, and which had a marked Jewish-Christian stamp, especially as the Gentile-Christians too were predominantly former godfearers.[202]

In terms of literary design and intention, Davies and Allison maintain that Matthew probably saw "his gospel as a continuation of the biblical history—and also, perhaps, that he conceived of his work as belonging to the same literary category as the scriptural cycles treating of OT figures."[203] Moreover, βίβλος γενέσεως is the author's deliberate evocation of the Genesis narrative, to which he intends to offer a counterpart (cf. Josephus's canon features 5 and 6 above).[204] Craig Evans makes a similar claim for Luke: "Luke sees his writings as a continuation of the scriptural story. ... The Lukan evangelist is a writer of Scripture, a hagiographer who is proclaiming what 'God has accomplished among us.' "[205] As regards the Gospel of John, Moody Smith points out that 1 John, by presupposing the Gospel of John, indicates that "some form of the Gospel of John

---

of Matthew as a written literary account no later than the early second century and probably earlier, see Graham Stanton, *Jesus and Gospel* (Cambridge: Cambridge University, 2004), 55; Head, *How the New Testament Came Together* 14; and Massaux, *Influence.*

202. Hengel, *Four Gospels*, 117.

203. W. D. Davies and Dale C. Allison, *A Critical and Exegetical Commentary on the Gospel According to Saint Matthew*, vol. 1 (ICC; London: T&T Clark, 1988), 187; quoted from Smith, "Gospels," 8.

204. Smith, "Gospels," 8.

205. Craig A. Evans, "Luke and the Rewritten Bible: Aspects of Lukan Hagiography", in *The Pseudepigrapha and Early Biblical Interpretation* (ed. James H. Charlesworth and C. A. Evans; Sheffield: JSOT Press, 1993), 200–201; cited from Smith, "Gospels," 9.

was, for certain circles, already functioning as scripture."[206] We may also note, with Smith,

> that the early Christian claim that the narrative and prophecies of old are fulfilled and continued in Jesus and the church prefigures, perhaps even demands, the production of more scripture, which will explain how this happened. Such scripture is required to explain this not first of all to outsiders but rather to Christians themselves. It becomes an essential part of their identity and self-understanding.[207]

Here Christian scriptural interpretation, expressed in the early prophecy-fulfillment claim, "prefigures, perhaps even demands, the production of more scripture." In other words: scriptural, or canonical, date "prefigured" as an implication of the earliest Christian pattern of scriptural interpretation.[208]

Having been received as written accounts (see above), the reception of the Gospels as Scripture is arguably seen in 2 *Clement* (2.4) and the *Epistle of Barnabas* (4.14) when Words of Jesus are quoted as Scripture.[209]

In Justin's account of the liturgical reading in the service of worship (1 *Apol.* 67), "the Memoirs of the Apostles" (i.e., the Gospels) are mentioned alongside and even prior to "the writings of the Prophets." The public reading of the Gospels may here have taken the place of the Torah reading in Christian worship, as Oskar Skarsaune and others point out (cf. 4.3.1 above, on the organizing function of the Torah for scriptural unity).[210]

---

206. Smith, "Gospels," 12. Cf. in this regard also 2 Pet 3:15–16 and 2 Tim 3:16 (which may not exclusively be a reference to the Jewish Scriptures).

207. Smith, "Gospels," 12. Cf. Deut 29:29, and John 14:18–26. See also the similar view in Peter Balla, "Challenges to Biblical Theology," in *New Dictionary of Biblical* Theology (eds. T. D. Alexander and B. S. Rosner; Leicester, England: InterVarsity, 2000), 23–24.

208. Balla, "Challenges to Biblical Theology," 23–24.

209. For *Barn.* 4:14, see J.N. Rhodes, *The Epistle of Barnabas and the Deuteronomic Tradition* (WUNT, 2. Reihe, 188; Tübingen: Mohr Siebeck, 2004), 153ff; and W.-D. Köhler, who thinks that dependence on Matthew is quite possible for *Barn.* 4.14; 5.8f and 7.9b, *Die Rezeption des Matthäusevangeliums in der Zeit vor Irenäus* (WUNT, 2:e Reihe 22; Tübingen: Mohr Siebeck, 1987). Pace Metzger, *Canon*, 57.

210. Skarsaune, *Temple*, 385. Skarsaune, *Temple*, 282: Whereas the conception of Scripture as a unity in the Jewish community centers upon the Torah, the Christian notion of Scripture differs in two important respects: The Christian Old Testament tends "to end with the three or four major

A couple of decades later, the first Christian writers who very explicitly treat the Gospels fully on a par with the books of the (Jewish) Scriptures are Tatian (A.D. 170–175) and Irenaeus (ca. A.D. 180).[211]

With a view to this dynamic first- and second-century history of reception, we may here recall Brevard Childs who emphasizes that canon consciousness arose at the inception of the Christian church and lies deep within the New Testament literature itself.[212] This, of course, points to a canonical process having its most critical moment at an early date—already indicated perhaps by the early reception of the written Gospel, which was placed side by side with, or viewed as part of, the Scriptures.

4.4.4.2 When Did the Term Euangelion Come to Designate a Written Rather Than an Oral Account?

Campenhausen's and Helmut Koester's traditional answer to this question is that Marcion was the first to think of the term "gospel" as referring to a written gospel in the early 140s. The author of 2 Clement (8.5; "the Lord says in the Gospel") and Justin Martyr, a few years later, are the first main stream Christians to use the term in this sense.

James Kelhoffer and Graham Stanton (following R. McL. Wilson and others),[213] however, have recently argued for an earlier date for the term "gospel" signifying a written account. Stanton points to one clear reference in 2 Clement (8.5) and four in the Didache (8.2; 11.3; 15.3–4f.). The word "gospel," a word with a clearly oral flavour is being used deliberately, it seems, in the Didache at the turn of the century (A.D. 100) to refer to a written Gospel. Most scholars tend to think that the Didache is composed after Matthew was written and therefore take it to refer to that Gospel as "the Gospel," e.g., in Did. 8.2: "pray like this, just as the Lord commanded in his Gospel" (ὡς ἐκέλευσεν ὁ κύριος ἐν τῷ εὐαγγελίῳ αὐτοῦ), and in 15:3: "Furthermore, correct one another not in anger but in peace, as you find

---

(longer) prophetical books," thus emphasizing the prophetical dimension; in addition, the Gospel is given a hermeneutically central role, as seen in Justin's account (1 Apol 67).

211. For Irenaeus's approach to the Gospels in this regard, cf. the balanced judgment by Stanton, *Jesus and Gospel*, 106.

212. Childs, *The New Testament as Canon*, 21.

213. For references, see Stanton, *Jesus and Gospel*, 9–62.

in the Gospel," and a few lines down regarding all your actions: "do them all just as you find it in the Gospel of our Lord" (*Did.* 15.4; ὡς ἔχετε ἐν τῷ εὐαγγελίῳ τοῦ κυρίου ἡμῶν). If we date the *Didache* to around A.D. 100, Stanton, rightly in my view, dates the meaning of the term "gospel" as occasionally referring to a written document even earlier, namely to the time when Matthew composes his Gospel. Even if Matthew (4:23; 9:35; 24:14; 26:13) seems to have removed four of Mark's eight uses of the term "gospel" (1:1, 14, 15; 8:35; 10:29; 13:10; 14:9; 16:15), he elaborates in an interesting way on the two that he keeps, to the extent that many scholars, including Kingsbury and Allison, are sympathetic to the view that the phrase in Matt 24:14 is Matthew's "capsule summary" of his work.[214] The verse reads: "And this gospel of the kingdom will be proclaimed throughout the whole world, as a testimony to all the nations, and then the end will come." In Matt 26:13, again, similar to the account of the anointing at Bethany in Mark, the emphasized phrase τὸ εὐαγγέλιον τοῦτο, with an added demonstrative pronoun τοῦτο to the Markan parallel (Mark 14:9), suggests that Matthew here thinks of "the gospel" as his own written account: "Truly, I say to you, wherever *this gospel* is proclaimed in the whole world, what she has done will also be told, in memory of her." If it is the case that Matthew tends towards this new use of the Pauline–Markan term εὐαγγέλιον, some sections in the Apostolic Fathers, such as those already referred to in the *Didache*, and further passages in the epistles of Ignatius, can more easily be interpreted along the same lines, as Stanton has suggested. In the epistle to the *Smyrnaeans* (5.1), Ignatius notes that "neither the prophecies, nor the law of Moses, nor ... τὸ εὐαγγέλιον" have persuaded his opponents. Stanton comments: "The juxtaposition of τὸ εὐαγγέλιον with Scriptural writings strongly suggests that, in this letter at least, Ignatius is referring to a writing—most probably Matthew's Gospel."[215]

As for the time between Matthew's composition and Justin's writings, we can conclude with Stanton, that there was a gradual transition of the way the term εὐαγγέλιον was used, from primarily referring to oral

---

214. See Stanton, *Jesus and Gospel*, 57, for references.
215. Stanton, *Jesus and Gospel*, 55.

proclamation (εὐαγγέλιον) to occasionally signifying a written "Gospel," probably already in Matthew and the *Didache*.

4.4.4.3 *Early Canonical Delimitation*

As indicated by the Muratorian fragment,[216] Irenaeus, Clement, and others, the fourfold Gospel had been received by large portions of the church by the late second century.[217] T. C. Skeat has pointed out that Irenaeus bases his account of the mystical significance of the number four on an earlier source dated to perhaps A.D. 170. And Larry Hurtado observes that "several recent studies agree in pushing back the likely origin of a fourfold Gospels collection to the earliest years of the second century":[218] Charles Hill, e.g., has argued that Papias knew the four canonical Gospels as a collection sometime ca. A.D. 125–135; Theo Heckel places a fourfold Gospel collection sometime around A.D. 120; Martin Hengel defends a similarly early date for the fourfold Gospel; and Graham Stanton, "[w]orking chronologically backwards from Irenaeus,"[219] concludes that a fourfold Gospels collection was being promoted from sometime shortly after A.D. 100, "though it took time to win its well-known supremacy."[220]

As mentioned above, also with regard to the Pauline corpus, a certain number is associated with it from very early on. The Muratorian fragment—alluding to what is probably a first-century tradition—says that Paul wrote to seven churches, and the number seven, possibly in association with the Pauline letters, also occurs in the Book of Revelation and in Ignatius's seven letters. The early 13-letter corpus apparently emerges in association with this tradition (letters sent to seven churches, and in addition to individuals). The likely "doubling" of the early Pauline letter corpus, addressed to seven churches, later seems to have resulted in a

---

216. On dating, see fnn. 84–86 above.

217. See Charles Hill, "The Four Gospel Canon in the Second Century" [http://youngadults. ccphilly.org/wp-content/uploads/2012/11/Four-Gospel-Canon-.pdf; accessed 04/02/13].

218. Hurtado, "Second Century," 20.

219. Hurtado, "Second Century," 20.

220. Hurtado, "Second Century," 20.

14-letter corpus (for potential numerological significance of seven, 13 and 14, see ch. 5, table 5.1 below).[221]

As to the number of books included in the OT canon, the early Church Fathers, especially in the East, in theory adhered to the Jewish canon—usually of 22 books (Justin, Melito [cf. 4.4.3 above], Origen, Cyril of Jerusalem, Athanasius, the Fathers of the Council of Laodicea, Gregorius of Nazianzus, Amphilochius of Iconium, Epiphanius of Salamis, Jerome, living in the East, and others; cf. 4.2.2 above).[222] The one who breaks with this tradition (to what seems to come close to a Jewish Rabbinic and Christian consensus) is Hilary of Poitiers (ca. 300–368), by making one small alteration in the old canon list of Origen. Where Origen explicitly excludes the two books of Maccabees,[223] Hilary instead adds the books of Tobit and Judith.[224] Thereby he deliberately chooses to break with what appears to be the general concern and consensus among the leading (Eastern) theologians of the early church—to stand in continuity with the synagogue on this particular issue.[225] In the wake of this new neglect of the Jewish background, Ambrose, who writes the first Christian commentary on an Apocryphal book (Tobit), and Augustine, with his strong argumentation against Jerome's learned remarks on OT Apocrypha, brought a new

---

221. Theologically significant, the number "two" figures as well, e.g., through the two major ways of interpreting Scripture: law and gospel, alongside the early apostolic and sub-apostolic teaching of the Two Ways, the early binitarian structure of the kerygma, and the First and the Second Coming of Christ. For problems involved in the various number of letters included in the early stages of formation of the Pauline Corpus, see Porter, "When and How was the Pauline Canon Compiled? An Assessment of Theories," Stanley E. Porter, ed., *The Pauline Canon* (Leiden: Brill, 2004), 95–127. The number "two" also figures in the basic division of OT and NT into Law and Prophets, and Gospel and Apostle (cf. Josephus's canon feature 3 [4.2.2 and 4.3.1 above]).

222. Ralph Hennings, "Der Briefwechsel zwischen Augustinus und Hieronymus und ihr Streit um den Kanon des Alten Testaments und die Auslegung von Gal 2,11–14," in J. den Boeft et al. (eds.), *Suppl. Vigiliae Christinae (Formerly Philosophia Patrum): Texts and Studies of Early Christian Life and Language*, vol. XXI (Leiden: Brill, 1994), 146ff.

223. This is the only explicit exclusion of books from the Old Testament canon made by Origen, who despite his apparent insistence on the 22-book canon, had a very generous attitude towards those other books (apocrypha) from the Septuagint group that were used for worship.

224. Beckwith, *Old Testament Canon of the New Testament Church*, 339–42.

225. Hennings, "Der Briefwechsel zwischen Augustinus und Hieronymus und ihr Streit um den Kanon des Alten Testaments und die Auslegung von Gal 2,11–14," 184–86.

agenda to the canon debate. This comes to the fore in several of the local synods held in the late fourth and the fifth century.[226]

Interestingly, the number 22—which was an important "canonical" number (together with the number 24),[227] the number of letters in the Hebrew alphabet (i.e., 22, or alternatively 27 when including final-form letters; cf. ch. 5, fn. 4 below)—was carried over also to the New Testament canon. Eusebius, having undertaken historical research on the first three Christian centuries with particular attention to the issue of the New Testament canon, says that NT books that are universally acknowledged (ὁμολογούμενα) are 22 in number: the "holy quaternion" of the Gospels, the Acts of the Apostles, the 14 Pauline Epistles, 1 Peter, 1 John and "if it really seems proper," the Apocalypse of John (*Hist. eccl.* III, 3.4). Also the Syrian Church's version of the Bible, the so-called Peshitta (beginning of the fifth century, or a little earlier) contained 22 New Testament books which are the same as those enlisted by Eusebius, however with James included instead of the Apocalypse. Possibly in Irenaeus, too, we may have, as far as we can see from extant writings, another example of a 22-book New Testament (22 books, and in addition perhaps the *Shepherd* of Hermas, and possibly *Wisdom*).

Together with the Greek translation of *Book of Jubilees* 2, Josephus, too, as discussed above (4.2.2),[228] may have been an important source of inspiration for the early church in emphasizing a 22-book canon: five books of Moses, the prophets in thirteen books, and four books containing hymns to God (*Against Apion* 1.39–40).

---

226. See further Beckwith (*Old Testament Canon of the New Testament Church*) for a thorough treatment of the early uncertainty among Christian communities concerning the scope of their Old Testament.

227. The only standard Jewish counts of the canonical books were 22 and 24. Cf. Beckwith, *Old Testament Canon of the New Testament Church*, 250–52. As a parallel to Josephus's canon features (4.2.2 above), we can also note the perception of the Old Testament (or the prophets) as closed ("the prophets, whose number is complete") in the Muratorian fragment when the *Shepherd of Hermas* is discussed.

228. For a critical discussion on the important but somewhat controversial reference in *Jubilees* 2, to "22 Hebrew books" or "22 books among the Hebrews," see Beckwith, *Old Testament Canon of the New Testament Church*, 235–40 (240).

Interestingly, our earliest preserved Four-Gospel codex, P[45] (early 3rd century), contains five books—Gospels and Acts[229]—as does the important fifth-century Codex Bezae Cantabrigiensis;[230] and an early Pauline letter corpus, like the one used by Hippolytus,[231] Irenaeus, Tertullian (and by others in the West),[232] arguably contained 13 letters.[233] That many of the regional bibles (e.g., that of Irenaeus, Tertullian, and the Peshitta) seem to have embraced 22 (or thereabout) NT books does not appear to be a coincidence, as Eusebius also seems to emphasize (*Hist. eccl.* III, 3.4; see above; cf. Josephus's canon features 1–4 above, 4.2.2 and 4.3.1).

In any case, the 22-book canon arranged in sub-groups, mentioned by Josephus and testified to, in one form or another, by several early Eastern Church Fathers,[234] appear to have been a source of inspiration for at least some segments of the Church, which largely seem to have adopted a similar basic structure for the early New Testament (some focus on the number 22, as indicated, e.g., by Eusebius; direct linkage through the titles "Old" and "New Testament"; often 2–4 sub-groups included in each Testament;[235] the first five NT books mirroring the OT position of the five books of the Pentateuch [i.e., prior to Acts being grouped together with the Catholic Epistles], and 13 Pauline letters possibly reflecting 13 books of the Prophets, according to Josephus's count; cf. Josephus's canon feature 2 above, 4.2.2).

---

229. Likewise, the third-century P[53], containing Matt 26:29–40 and Acts 9:33–10:1, arguably embraced the fourfold Gospel and Acts, or otherwise perhaps just Matthew and Acts. Regarding further early association between Gospels and Acts, we also notice that literary dependence on Matthew, Luke, John and Acts may be demonstrated for Mark 16:9–20; cf. James A. Kelhoffer, *Miracle and Mission: The Authentication of Missionaries and Their Message in the Longer Ending of Mark* (WUNT 2.112; Tübingen: Mohr Siebeck, 2000), 137–56.

230. Codex Bezae also includes a fragment from 3 John.

231. Metzger, *Canon*, 150.

232. Cf. Zahn, *Die bleibende Bedeutung*, 8.

233. Similarly the third century (A.D. 200–250) Syrian NT, which, according to Julius A. Bewer (*The History of the New Testament Canon in the Syrian Church* [Chicago: University of Chicago, 1900], 65) contained four Gospels, Acts and 13 Pauline epistles.

234. Cf. 4.4.4.3 at fn. 222 above.

235. Cf. Tov, *Textual Criticism of the Hebrew Bible*, 130. In addition to the early division into, and emphasis on, Law and Prophets, we can note that "[t]he Greek canon may be conceived of as consisting of three, four, or five divisions."

4.4.4.4 *The Codex Format*

Arguably, the very act of putting the authoritative gospel message into writing is significant. The early Christian scribes and/or NT authors appear to have chosen a new format both for the New Testament and the Old Testament texts, namely the codex form. As far back as we can see from our manuscripts—that is, roughly the mid-second century—the codex form, and not the scroll, appears as the standard book format for Christian Scripture. As for the Christian treatment of the Jewish Scriptures, C. H. Roberts tellingly writes: "the transference of the Law from its sacrosanct form to a format of no antiquity and little regard … must have seemed to the Jew an act of sacrilege."[236] Commenting on Roberts, Frances Young remarks: "the use of the codex has dramatic implications for the reception and appropriation of the Jewish books. They were physically 'taken over'—not just re-read but re-formed."[237] In addition to the new scriptural format, the introduction of *nomina sacra* (contraction or suspension supplied with a horizontal overbar of some five to fifteen Greek words, such as "God," "Lord," "Jesus," "Spirit" etc.) in the Greek Jewish Scriptures appears to have made a similar change in terms of perception and understanding of the writings, placing the old and the new Christian Scriptures on a par in this regard. We see a "Christianisation" of the Jewish Scriptures both when the codex is employed as the new book format and when the *nomina sacra* convention is introduced.[238] The *Epistle of Barnabas* 9.7–9, of course, is a well-known example of how *nomina sacra*—Jesus's name and the symbol of the cross—may affect scriptural interpretation (see further 2.4.1, 11.5.1 and 12.6.4).

4.5 CONCLUDING REMARKS

In my discussion above I have sought to emphasize the New Testament canon formation as a process involving first-, second-, and third- to

---

236. C. H. Roberts, "Books in the Greco-Roman World," 61; cited from Frances Young, *Biblical Exegesis and the Formation of Christian Culture* (Cambridge: Cambridge University, 1997), 13.

237. Young, *Biblical Exegesis*, 14.

238. An example of this is when *nomina sacra* such as "Spirit" and "Jesus"—arguably first marked off in the New Testament—are introduced into the Jewish Scriptures as well (attaining also potentially non-sacral meanings; e.g., when referring to Joshua). Cf. Young, *Biblical Exegesis*, 123f.

fourth-century developments. Since canon here is understood as a property of sacred Scripture, pertaining to the reading of Scripture as a whole, I criticize Sundberg's sharp distinction between the notions of "Scripture" and "canon." Due to my emphasis on the canonical process *qua* process, I also critique Sundberg's account of "canonization proper." Even if Zahn's model of a NT canon emerging around A.D. 80–110 is somewhat favoured in my argument, emphasis is also placed on dimensions of the New Testament canon formation becoming visible in the late second/ early third century—as seen in ancient church teachers such as Irenaeus, Tertullian and Origen, and stressed by modern scholars such as Harnack, Campenhausen and Trobisch. By emphasizing the association in various ways between the old and the new Scriptures, I point to an early emerging pattern for Christian scripturality, embracing as well various dimensions of canonicity. By stressing the formation of the New Testament as a continuous process, beginning already in the New Testament writings, a particular aim is to avoid portraying the canon formation in terms of stark discontinuities, along the lines of Sundberg and Campenhausen. I will let two quotes, with which I strongly disagree, from these authors— both published in 1968—close our discussion:

> [T]he recognition that canonization proper is the definition of a New Testament list to which nothing can be added, nothing subtracted, removes canonization from the tacit implication that somehow canonization adheres to apostles, apostolic men, and the hearers of apostolic men and leaves the formation of a closed New Testament list as unequivocally the decision of the church.[239]

> The dominant opinion is that the beginnings of the New Testament can be traced back into the first century or at least into the first decades of the second. It is customary to talk of a "canon of the Four Gospels," a "canon" of the Pauline Epistles, and an "apocalyptic canon," even before the time of Marcion. Our sources certainly do nothing to justify such ideas. But the situation is further confused by the fact that there is no one agreed definition of the

239. Sundberg, "Revised History," 461.

concept of the canon ... The fact that a work which later became a "New Testament" book is occasionally echoed or utilised or alluded to is not "canonisation"; indeed, taken for what it is and no more, it is not even a move in that direction[.][240] [241]

BIBLIOGRAPHY

Aland, Barbara Aland. "The Significance of the Chester Beatty Papyri." Pages 108–21 in *The Earliest Gospels: The Origins and Transmission of the Earliest Christian Gospels – The Contribution of the Chester Beatty Gospel Codex P⁴⁵*. Edited by C. Horton. Journal for the Study of the New Testament Supplement Series 258. London: T&T Clark, 2004.

Ashton, John. *Understanding the Fourth Gospel*. Second Edition. Oxford: Oxford University, 2007.

Balla, Peter. "Challenges to Biblical Theology." In *New Dictionary of Biblical Theology*. Edited by T. D. Alexander and B. S. Rosner. Leicester, England: InterVarsity, 2000.

Barr, James. *Holy Scripture: Canon, Authority, Criticism*. Oxford: Clarendon, 1983.

Barton, John. "Marcion Revisited." Page 341–54 in *The Canon Debate*. Edited by L. M. McDonald and J. A. Sanders. Peabody, MA: Hendrickson, 2002.

———. *The Old Testament: Canon, Literature and Theology*. Society for Old Testament Study Monographs. Aldershot: Ashgate, 2007.

———. *The Spirit and the Letter: Studies in the Biblical Canon*. London: SPCK, 1997.

Beckwith, Roger. *The Old Testament Canon of the New Testament Church and its Background in Early Judaism*. Grand Rapids: Eerdmans, 1985.

Bewer, Julius A. *The History of the New Testament Canon in the Syrian Church*. Chicago: University of Chicago, 1900.

---

240. Campenhausen, *Formation*, 103.

241. I want to express my thanks to my colleague Dr Donald Wood for commenting on an earlier draft of the present chapter.

Beyer, Hermann Wolfgang. "Kanon." Pages 600–06 in *Theologisches Wörterbuch zum Neuen Testament*. Vol. 3. Edited by G. Kittel. Grand Rapids: Eerdmans, 1965.

Bokedal, Tomas. *Formation and Significance of the Christian Biblical Canon: A Study in Text Ritual and Interpretation*. London: Bloomsbury T&T Clark, 2014.

———. "The Rule of Faith: Tracing Its Origins." *Journal of Theological Interpretation* 7.2 (2013): 233–55.

———. "The Scriptures and the Lord: Formation and Significance of the Christian Biblical Canon. A Study in Text, Ritual and Interpretation." PhD Diss., Lund University, 2005.

Bruce, F. F. *The Canon of Scripture*. Downers Grove: IVP, 1988.

———. "Thoughts on the Beginning of the New Testament Canon." *Bulletin of the John Rylands University Library of Manchester* 65 (1983): 37–60.

Campenhausen, Hans von. *The Formation of the Christian Bible*. Translated by J. A. Baker. Philadelphia: Fortress, 1972.

Childs, Brevard S. *Biblical Theology of the Old and New Testaments: Theological Reflection on the Christian Bible*. London: SCM, 1992.

———. "The exegetical significance of Canon for the study of the Old Testament." Paged 66–80 in *International Organization for the Study of the Old Testament*. Göttingen: Brill.

———. *Introduction to the Old Testament as Scripture*. London: SCM, 1979.

———. *The New Testament as Canon: An Introduction*. London: SCM, 1984.

Cross, Frank Moore. *From Epic to Canon*. Baltimore, MD: John Hopkins University, 1998.

Davies, W. D. and Dale C. Allison. *A Critical and Exegetical Commentary on the Gospel according to Saint Matthew*. ICC, Vol. 1. London: T&T Clark, 1988.

Deines, Roland. "Writing Scripture in the First Century." *EJT* 22 (2013): 101–109.

Dunn, James D. G. *Unity and Diversity in the New Testament*. 2nd
    edition. London: SCM and Philadelphia: Trinity Press
    International, 1977.

Epp, Eldon Jay. "Issues in the Interrelation of New Testament Textual
    Criticism and Canon." Pages 485–515 in *The Canon Debate*.
    Edited by L. M. McDonald and J. A. Sanders; Peabody, MA:
    Hendrickson, 2002.

Evans, Craig A. "Luke and the Rewritten Bible: Aspects of Lukan
    Hagiography." Pages 170–201 in *The Pseudepigrapha and Early
    Biblical Interpretation*. Edited by James H. Charlesworth and C.
    A. Evans. Sheffield: JSOT Press, 1993.

Finkelberg, M. and G. G. Stroumsa. "Introduction: Before the Western
    Canon." Page 3f in *Homer, the Bible, and Beyond: Literary and
    Religious Canons in the Ancient World*. Edited by M. Finkelberg
    and G. G. Stroumsa. Leiden: Brill, 2003.

Foster, Paul. "The Epistles of Ignatius of Antioch." Pages 159–85 in
    *The Writings of the Apostolic Fathers, The Reception of the New
    Testament in the Apostolic Fathers*. Edited by Paul Foster. London:
    T&T Clark, 2007.

France, R. T. *The Gospel of Matthew*. NICNT. Grand Rapids: Eerdmans,
    2007.

———. *Matthew: Evangelist and Teacher*. Exeter: Paternoster, 1989.

Freedman, D. N. "Canon of the OT." Pages 130–36 in *Interpreter's
    Dictionary of the Bible: Supplementary Volume*. Edited by Keith
    Crim. Nashville: Abingdon, 1976.

Gadamer, Hans-Georg. *The Beginning of Philosophy*. New York:
    Continuum, 2001.

———. *Truth and Method*. Translation revised by J. Weinsheimer and D.
    G. Marshall. New York: Continuum, 2nd rev. ed., 1993.

Gamble, Harry Y. *Books and Readers in the Early Church: A History of
    Early Christian Texts*. New Haven: Yale University, 1995.

———. "The New Testament Canon: Recent Research and the Status
    Quaestionis." Pages 267–73 in *The Canon Debate*. Edited by

Lee Martin McDonald and James A. Sanders. Peabody, Mass.: Hendrickson, 2002.

Grant, Robert. *Eusebius as Church Historian*. Eugene, OR: Wipf & Stock, 1980.

———. *Irenaeus of Lyons*. New York: Routledge, 1997.

Gregory, Andrew, and Christopher Tuckett, eds. *The Reception of the New Testament in the Apostolic Fathers*. Oxford: Oxford University, 2005.

Hahneman, Geoffrey Mark. *The Muratorian Fragment and the Development of the Canon*. Oxford: Clarendon, 1992.

Hardwick, Michael E. *Josephus as an Historical Source in Patristic Literature through Eusebius*. Brown Judaic Studies 128. Atlanta, GA: Scholars Press, 1989.

Harnack, Adolf von. *Das Neue Testament um das Jahr 200: Theodor Zahn's Geschichte des Neutestamentlichen Kanons (erster Band, erste Hälfte) geprüft*. Freiburg: Mohr Siebeck, 1989.

———. *Lehrbuch der Dogmengeschichte*, Vol. 1. Tübingen: Mohr Siebeck, 1909.

———. *Marcion: das Evangelium vom fremden Gott: Eine Monographie zur Geschichte der Grundlegung der katholischen Kirche*. Second Edition. Darmstadt: Wissenschaftliche Buchgesellschaft, 1924.

———. *The Origin of the New Testament and the Most Important Consequences of the New Creation*. Translated by J. R. Wilkinson. London: Williams & Norgate, 1925.

Harrisville, R. A. "The Concept of Newness in the New Testament." *JBL* 74 (1955): 69–79.

Head, Peter. *How the New Testament Came Together*. Grove Biblical Series B51. Cambridge: Grove Books, 2009.

Hengel, Martin. *The Four Gospels and the One Gospel of Jesus Christ*. London: SCM, 2000.

Hennings, Ralph. "Der Briefwechsel zwischen Augustinus und Hieronymus und ihr Streit um den Kanon des Alten Testaments und die Auslegung von Gal. 2,11–14." In *Suppl. Vigiliae Christinae (Formerly Philosophia Patrum): Texts and Studies of Early*

Christian Life and Language, vol. XXI. Edited by J. den Boef.
Leiden: Brill, 1994.

Hill, Charles. "The Four Gospel Canon in the Second Century,"
http://youngadults.ccphilly.org/wp-content/uploads/2012/11/
Four-Gospel-Canon-.pdf; accessed 04/02/13.

———. "Irenaeus, the Scribes, and the Scriptures: Papyrological and
Theological Observations from P.Oxy. 405." Pages 119–30 in
Irenaeus: Life, Scripture, Legacy. Edited by P. Foster and S. Parvis.
Minneapolis: Fortress, 2012.

Holmes, Michael W. "The Biblical Canon." Pages 406–26 in *The Oxford
Handbook of Early Christian Studies*. Edited by S. Ashbrook
Harvey and D. G. Hunter. Oxford: Oxford University, 2008.

Hurtado, Larry W. "The New Testament in the Second Century:
Text, Collections and Canon." Pages 3–27 in *Transmission and
Reception: New Testament Text-critical and Exegetical Studies*.
Edited by J. W. Childers and D. C. Parker. Piscataway, N.J.:
Gorgias, 2006.

Jaschke, Hans-Jochen. "Irenäus von Lyon." *TRE*, vol. 16 (1987): 258–68.

Johnson, Sherman E. "The New Testament and the Christian
Community." Page 1116 in *The Interpreter's One-Volume
Commentary on the Bible*. Edited by Charles M. Laymon. New
York: Abingdon, 1971.

Jülicher, Adolf and Erich Fascher. *Einleitung in das Neue Testament*.
Seventh Edition. Tübingen: Mohr Siebeck, 1931.

Kelhoffer, James A. *Miracle and Mission: The Authentication of
Missionaries and Their Message in the Longer Ending of Mark*.
WUNT 2.112. Tübingen: Mohr Siebeck, 2000.

Kennedy, Joel. *The Recapitulation of Israel: Use of Israel's History in
Matthew 1:1-4:11*. WUNT 2.257. Tübingen: Mohr Siebeck, 2008.

Knox, John. *Marcion and the New Testament: An Essay in the Early
History of the Canon*. Chicago: University of Chicago, 1942.

Köhler, W.-D. *Die Rezeption des Matthäusevangeliums in der Zeit vor
Irenäus*. WUNT, 2:e Reihe 22; Tübingen: Mohr Siebeck, 1987.

Kooij, Arie van der. "Canonization of Ancient Hebrew Books and
    Hasmonean Politics." Pages 27–28 in *The Biblical Canons*. Edited
    by J.-M. Auwers and H. J. de Jonge. Leuven: Leuven University
    and Peeters, 2003.

Kruger, Michael J. *Canon Revisited: Establishing the Origins and
    Authority of the New Testament Books*. Wheaton, IL: Crossway,
    2012.

Kunze, Johannes. *Glaubensregel, Heilige Schrift und Taufbekenntnis:
    Untersuchungen über die dogmatische Autorität, ihr Werden und
    ihre Geschichte, vornehmlich in der alten Kirche*. Leipzig: Dörffling
    & Franke, 1899.

Laird, Benjamin. "Early Titles of the Pauline Letters and the Formation
    of the Pauline Corpus." *BN* 175 (2017): 55–81.

Leiman, Sid Z. *The Canonization of Hebrew Scripture: The Talmudic and
    Midrashic Evidence*. Hamden, CT: Archon Books, 1976.

Lewis, Jack P. "What Do We Mean by Jabneh?" *Journal of Bible and
    Religion* 32 (1964): 125–32.

Lim, Timothy. "A Theory of the Majority Canon." *Expository Times* 124
    (2013): 365–73.

Lips, Hermann von. *Der neutestamentliche Kanon: Seine Geschichte und
    Bedeutung*. Zürich: Theologischer Verlag, 2004.

Marcus, Joel. "Mark – Interpreter of Paul." *NTS* 46 (2000): 473–87.

Markschies, Christoph. "The Canon of the New Testament in
    Antiquity." In *Homer, the Bible, and Beyond: Literary and Religious
    Canons in the Ancient World*. Edited by M. Finkelberg and G. G.
    Stroumsa. JSRC 2; Leiden: Brill.

Mason, Steve. "Josephus and His Twenty-Two Book Canon." Pages
    110–27 in *The Canon Debate*. Edited by L. M. McDonald and J. A.
    Sanders. Peabody, MA: Hendrickson, 2002.

Massaux, Édouard. *The Influence of the Gospel of Saint Matthew
    on Christian Literature Before Saint Irenaeus*. Edited by A.
    J. Bellinzoni. Macon, GA: Mercer University and Leuven,
    Belgium: Peeters, 1990–93.

McDonald, Lee Martin. *The Biblical Canon: Its Origin, Transmission, and Authority.* Peabody, MA, Hendrickson, 2007.

——. *Forgotten Scriptures: The Selection and Rejection of Early Religious Writings.* Louisville, KY: Westminster John Knox Press, 2009.

Metzger, Bruce M. *The Canon of the New Testament: Its Origin, Development, and Significance.* Oxford: Clarendon, 1987.

Müller, Mogens. "The Hidden Context: Some Observations to the Concept of the New Covenant in the New Testament." Pages 649–58 in *Texts and Contexts: Biblical Texts in Their Textual and Situational Contexts.* Edited by T. Fornberg and D. Hellholm. Oslo/Copenhagen/Stockholm/Boston: Scandinavian University Press, 1995.

Mutschler, Bernhard. *Irenäus als johannischer Theologe: Studien zur Schriftauslegung bei Irenäus von Lyon.* Studien und Texte zu Antike und Christentum 21; Tübingen: Mohr Siebeck, 2004.

Ohme, Heinz. *Kanon ekklesiastikos.* Berlin: Walter de Gruyter, 1998.

Pannenberg, Wofhart. *Systematic Theology.* Vol. 1. Grand Rapids: Eerdmans, 1991.

Parker, David C. "Review of David Trobisch, *The First Edition of the New Testament.*" *JTS* 53 (2002): 298–305.

Porter, Stanley E. "When and How was the Pauline Canon Compiled? An Assessment of Theories." Pages 95–127 in *The Pauline Canon.* Edited by Stanley E. Porter. Leiden: Brill, 2004.

Räisänen, Heikki. *Beyond New Testament Theology.* Second Edition. London: SCM, 2000.

Rhodes, J. N. *The Epistle of Barnabas and the Deuteronomic Tradition.* WUNT, 2. Reihe, 188. Tübingen: Mohr Siebeck, 2004.

Riekert, S. J. P. K. "Critical Research and the One Christian Canon Comprising Two Testaments." *Neotestamentica,* 14 (1981): 21–41.

Roberts, C. H. *Manuscript, Society and Belief in Early Christian Egypt.* The Schweich Lectures of the British Academy 1977. Oxford: Oxford University, 1979.

Sanders, James A. "The Issue of Closure in the Canonical Process."
    Pages 252–62 in *The Canon Debate*. Edited by L. M. McDonald
    and J. A. Sanders. Peabody, Mass.: Hendrickson, 2002.

Scalise, Charles J. *From Scripture to Theology: A Canonical Journey into
    Hermeneutics*. Downers Grove: InterVarsity, 1996.

Schaper, Joachim. "The Rabbinic Canon and the Old Testament of
    the Early Church: A Social-Historical View". Pages 93–106
    in *Canonization and Decanonization*: Papers Presented to the
    International Conference of the Leiden Institute for the Study of
    Religions (LISOR), Held at Leiden 9–10 January 1997. Edited by
    A. van der Kooij and K van der Toorn. Leiden: Brill, 1998.

Schmid, Ulrich. *Marcion und sein Apostolus: Rekonstruktion und
    historische Einordnung der marcionitischen Paulusbriefausgabe*.
    Berlin: Walter de Gruyter, 1995.

———. "Bibel III: Die Entstehung des Kanons des Neuen Testaments
    und der christlichen Bibel." Pages 22–48 in *Theologische
    Realenzyklopädie*, 6. Edited by G. Krause and G. Müller. Berlin
    and New York: Walter de Gruyter, 1980.

Schneemelcher, Wilhelm. "General Introduction." Pages 9–76 in *New
    Testament Apocrypha*, Vol. 1: Gospels and Related Writings.
    Second edition. Edited by. W. Schneemelcher. Louisville:
    Westminster John Knox Press, 1991.

Schröter, Jens. "Die Apostelgeschichte und die Entstehung des
    neutestamentlichen Kanons. Beobachtungen zur Kanonisierung
    der Apostelgeschichte und ihrer Bedeutung als kanonischer
    Schrift." Pages 395–429 in *The Biblical Canons*. Edited by J.-M.
    Auwers and H. J. de Jonge. Leuven: Leuven University and
    Peeters, 2003.

———. "Jesus and the Canon: The Early Jesus Traditions in the
    Context of the Origins of the New Testament Canon." Pages
    104–22 in *Performing the Gospel: Orality, Memory, and Mark*.
    Edited by R. Horsley et al. Minneapolis: Fortress, 2006.

Sheppard, Gerald T. "Canon." Pages 62–69 in *The Encyclopedia of
    Religion*. Edited by M. Eliade. New York: Macmillan, 1987.

Skarsaune, Oskar. *In the Shadow of the Temple: Jewish Influences on Early Christianity*. Downers Grove: Intervarsity, 2002.

———. "The Development of Scriptural Interpretation in the Second and Third Centuries – except Clement and Origen." In *Hebrew Bible/Old Testament: The History of Its Interpretation*. Vol. 1 Edited by M. Sæbø. Göttingen: Vandenhoeck & Ruprecht, 1996.

Smith, D. Moody. *The Fourth Gospel in Four Dimensions: Judaism and Jesus, the Gospels and Scripture*. Columbia, SC: The University of South Carolina, 2008.

———. "When Did the Gospels Become Scripture?" *JBL* 119 (2000): 3–20.

Stanton, Graham. *Jesus and Gospel*. Cambridge: Cambridge University, 2004.

Stuhlmacher, Peter. *Biblische Theologie des Neuen Testaments: Von der Paulusschule bis zur Johannesoffenbarung*. Vol. 2. Göttingen: Vandenhoeck & Ruprecht, 1999.

———. *How To Do Biblical Theology*. Eugene, OR: Pickwick Publications, 1995.

Sundberg, Albert C. "Canon Muratori: A Fourth-Century List." *Harvard Theological Review* 66 (1973): 1–41.

———. "Canon of the NT." Pages 136–40 in *Interpreter's Dictionary of the Bible: Supplementary Volume*. Edited by Keith Crim. Nashville: Abingdon, 1976.

———. "The Making of the New Testament Canon." Pages 1216–24 in *The Interpreter's One-Volume Commentary on the Bible*. Edited by Charles M. Laymon. New York: Abingdon, 1971.

———. *The Old Testament of the Early Church*. Cambridge: Harvard University, 1964.

———. "Towards a Revised History of the New Testament Canon." In *Studia Evangelica*. Edited by F. L. Cross; Berlin: Akademie-Verlag, 1968.

———. "The Old Testament of the Early Church (A Study in Canon)." *HTR* 51 (1958): 205–26.

Tov, Emanuel. *Textual Criticism of the Hebrew Bible*. Third Revised
    Edition. Minneapolis: Fortress, 2012.

Trobisch, David. *The First Edition of the New Testament*. Oxford: Oxford
    University, 2000.

———. *Paul's Letter Collection: Tracing the Origins*. Bolivar, Missouri:
    Quiet Waters Publications, 2001.

———. "Who Published the New Testament?" Free Inquiry, 28.1.
    Amherst, NY: Council of Secular Humanism (2007/2008):
    30–33.

Verheyden, Joseph. "The Canon Muratori: A Matter of Dispute." Pages
    487–556 in *The Biblical Canons*. Edited by J.-M. Auwers and H. J.
    de Jonge. Leuven: Leuven University and Peeters, 2003.

Walser, Georg. *The Greek of the Ancient Synagogue: An Investigation on
    the Greek of the Septuagint, Pseudepigrapha and the New Testament*.
    Stockholm: Almqvist & Wiksell International, 2001.

Waltke, Bruce K. "How We Got the Hebrew Bible: The Text and
    Canon of the Old Testament." Pages 27–50 in *The Bible at
    Qumran: Text, Shape, and Interpretation*. Edited P. W. Flint.
    Grand Rapids: Eerdmans, 2001.

Webster, John. "The Dogmatic Location of the Canon." *Neue Zeitschrift
    für systematische Theologie und Religionsphilosophie* 43 (2001):
    17–43.

———. *Holy Scripture: A Dogmatic Sketch*. Cambridge: Cambridge
    University, 2003.

Westcott, Brooke Foss. *The Bible in the Church*. London and New York:
    Macmillan, 1905.

Wrede, William. "The Task and Methods of 'New Testament
    Theology.' " Pages 68–116 in Robert Morgan, *The Nature of New
    Testament Theology*. London: SCM, 1973.

Young, Frances M. *Biblical Exegesis and the Formation of Christian
    Culture*. Cambridge: Cambridge University, 1997.

Zahn, Theodor. *Die bleibende Bedeutung des neutestamentlichen Kanons
    für die Kirche*. Leipzig: U. Dichert'sche Verlagsbuchh. Nachf.,
    1898.

———. *Einige Bemerkungen zu Adolf Harnack's Prüfung der Geschichte des neutestamentlichen Kanons.* Vol. 1.1. Erlangen and Leipzig: A. Deichert'sche Verlagshandlung Nachf. Georg Böhme 1889.

———. *Geschichte des Neutestamentlichen Kanons.* Vol. 1. Erlangen: Verlag von Andreas Deichert, 1888.

———. *Grundriss der Geschichte des Neutestamentlichen Kanons: Eine Ergänzung zu der Einleitung in das Neue Testament.* Leipzig: A. Deichert'sche Verlagsbuch. Nachf. Georg Böhme, 1901.

Zevit, Z. "The Second–Third Century Canonization of the Hebrew Bible and Its Influence on Christian Canonizing." Pages 133–60 in *Canonization and Decanonization: Papers Presented to the International Conference of the Leiden Institute for the Study of Religions* (LISOR), Held at Leiden 9–10 January 1997. Edited by A. van der Kooij and K. van der Toorn. Leiden: Brill, 1998.

PART C

YHWH THE CENTER:
A NUMEROLOGICAL APPROACH
TO BIBLICAL CANONICITY

5

TEXTUAL ARITHMETIC
PATTERNING

5.1 INTRODUCTION

Numerical structuring is often associated with the shaping of biblical texts. Irenaeus famously argues that the Gospels must be four (*Haer.* 3.11.8). Other church fathers link the number seven with key canonical subunits (Pauline Corpus, Catholic Epistles);[1] and the more than fifty occurrences of the number seven are central to the structure of the book of Revelation (e.g., Rev 6:1–8:1; 8:2–11:19; 15:1–19:21). Moreover, just as the acrostic Psalms 34, 111, and 112 are all alphabetically arranged with twenty-two sections, paralleling the number of letters in the Hebrew alphabet, alphabetical structuring characterizes, as well, Psalm 119 with its twenty-two paragraphs, each of which contains eight strophes and

---

1. Bruce M. Metzger's (*The Canon of the New Testament: Its Origin, Development, and Significance* [Oxford: Clarendon, 1987], 154–55) translation of Irenaeus reads: "It is not possible that the Gospels can be either more or fewer in number than they are, since there are four directions of the world in which we are, and four principal winds. ... The four living creatures [of Rev 4:9] symbolize the four Gospels. ... And there were four principal covenants made with humanity, through Noah, Abraham, Moses, and Christ (*Adv. Haer.* III. xi. 8)." Metzger comments: "Thus for Irenaeus the Gospel canon is closed and its text is holy." The Muratorian Canon (ca. AD 200), further, notes that Paul wrote "by name to only seven churches" and Amphilochius of Iconium (ca. 340–395), who comments on the fourteen Pauline epistles (including Hebrews), says that these are "twice seven epistles," and with regard to the Catholic Epistles he observes that "some say we must receive seven"; quoted from Metzger, *Canon of the New Testament*, 306, 314. Cf. also the letters to the seven churches in Rev 2–3.

with each strophe beginning with the same letter.[2] Numerical features thus appear to be embedded in various layers of the biblical material.

HEBREW AND GREEK ALPHABETICAL NUMERALS

At the macrocanonical level, Josephus and early church teachers, such as Origen and Athanasius, count the number of books contained in the Jewish Scriptures at twenty-two (see further chs. 3 and 4 above).[3] In Athanasius, the alphabetical-completeness pattern may arguably apply as well to his New Testament twenty-seven-book corpus, since the number of consonants in the Hebrew alphabet can be counted either as twenty-two or as twenty-seven (the five end-letter forms counted separately).[4] Protestant Bibles—possibly adhering to a similar alphabetical inclination—usually include altogether sixty-six canonical books [3 × 22].[5] By analogy, canonical shaping of the number of New Testament writings in the early church could sometimes be identical to that of the Jewish Scriptures,

---

2. In addition to these, acrostics are found elsewhere in the Psalter (Pss 9–10; 25; 37; and 145) and the Jewish Scriptures, e.g., in Lam 1–4; and Prov 31:10–31.

3. Origen, in Eusebius, *Hist. eccl.* 6.25; Athanasius, *Ep. fest.* 39; Epiphanius, *Pan.* 8.6.1–4; Gregory of Nazianzus, *Carm.* 1.12; Hilary, *Instr. Ps.* 15; Jerome, *Prologus Galeatus*. References from Edmon Gallagher, *Hebrew Scripture in Patristic Biblical Theory: Canon, Language, Text*, VCSup 114 (Leiden: Brill, 2012), 86n68. Josephus does not explicitly connect the number twenty-two as many of the early church teachers do. See Edmon L. Gallagher and John D. Meade, eds., *The Biblical Canon Lists from Early Christianity: Texts and Analysis* (Oxford: Oxford University Press, 2017), 60n12. However, Roger Beckwith (*The Old Testament Canon of the New Testament Church and Its Background in Early Judaism* [Grand Rapids: Eerdmans, 1985], 250) points out that the link between the twenty-two canonical books and the twenty-two letters of the Hebrew alphabet is referred to in Jubilees, Origen, Jerome, and Epiphanius, and "it is too self-evident not to have been obvious to Josephus as well."

4. Cf. Timothy H. Lim, *The Formation of the Jewish Canon*. ABRL (New Haven: Yale University Press, 2013), 40–41: "Jerome considered the twenty-two-book canon to be the count of the majority ('by most people'); the twenty-four-book enumeration is a variant enumerated by 'some.' He also seems to know a twenty-seven-book count when he states that there are five letters of the Hebrew alphabet that are 'double letters' (*kaph, mem, nun, peh,* and *tsadeh)* that change shape depending on whether they are written at the beginning and in the middle (medial) or at the end (final). The canonical implication is that Samuel, Kings, Chronicles, Ezra, and Jeremiah with Kinoth (or Lamentations) are reckoned as double, thus increasing the total to twenty-seven." However, as Beckwith underscores (*Old Testament Canon*, 252), the standard counts of the canonical books of the Hebrew Bible were twenty-two and twenty-four. Athanasius's count may have been inspired also by the fact that the sum of twenty-two and twenty-seven is forty-nine, which equals seven times seven, another numerical structure signifying completeness.

5. Cf. ch. 3 above (repr. of Tomas Bokedal, "Canon/Scripture," in *The Dictionary of the Bible and Ancient Media*, ed. Tom Thatcher et al. [London: Bloomsbury T&T Clark, 2017], 46–48). For potential numeric significance for the count of the Old Testament writings as thirty-nine, see table 5.1 below.

when set at twenty-two; for example, Eusebius's twenty-two undisputed New Testament books, the twenty-two books of the Syrian Peshitta, and probably also John Chrysostom's New Testament.[6] Augustine's wider Old Testament canon, delimited to forty-four writings [2 × 22], may also deliberately have connected to the Hebrew alphabetical number.[7]

It is possible, as well, that the medieval and modern division of the biblical material into chapters may have connected to this type of alphabetical arrangement, with Isaiah's 66 chapters [3 × 22] and Revelation's 22. There is also the possibility that this alphabetical patterning applies, in part, even to the ancient paragraph division in the biblical manuscripts, now endorsed by the Tyndale House Greek New Testament (hereafter THGNT) with its 54 paragraphs [2 × 27] for 2 Corinthians, 405 [15 × 27] for Matthew, and 1458 [2 × 27 × 27] for Gospels + Acts.[8] Interestingly, the textual midpoint in THGNT of Matthew's altogether 405 paragraphs

---

6. Cf. Introduction, note 2 above. Gallagher summarizes the early Christian consensus view regarding the alphabetical twenty-two as follows: "The delimitation of the OT by the 22 books 'according to the Hebrews' extends through (nearly) all of the Greek canon lists of the first four centuries, whether the number was mentioned or not. Fewer Latin authors acknowledge the number 22, but Hilary, Jerome, and Rufinus may all be cited. ... The reason the number 22 was so important can only be that patristic authors desired to maintain the connection with the Hebrew alphabet, even when they do not make this connection explicit"; Gallagher, *Hebrew Scripture*, 92. Cf. Metzger, *Canon of the New Testament*, 214–15.

7. Augustine's Old Testament canon corresponds to the contemporary list approved at Hippo and the canon list issued by Innocent I. This Old Testament canon list was later approved by the Council of Trent in 1546. Cf. Gallagher and Meade, *Biblical Canon Lists*, 225. We may compare Augustine's possible deliberate inclusion of the multiple twenty-two into his delimitation of the Old Testament canon to forty-four [2 × 22] with the seven-church tradition concerning Pauline Corpus, which, by Amphilocius of Iconium (*Iambics for Seleucus*) is referred to as Paul writing "twice seven epistles" to the churches.

8. The paragraph count here includes superscripts and subscripts (book titles). In the THGNT the paragraphing of the ancient manuscripts is embraced according to the following principles laid out in the introduction: "Paragraphs are informed by manuscripts, in particular by those from the fifth century or earlier. We have not included every paragraph mark from these early manuscripts: we have included only divisions that occur in two such manuscripts (except in the Apocalypse where, due to more limited attestation, we have only required one). These paragraph marks often differ from those most widely followed today, but we have found that those that at first glance appear eccentric often display an inner logic when studied more closely" (THGNT, 512). Parallel to Matthew's 405 paragraphs [15 × 27] with potential allusion to the alphabetical number 27, Mark's Gospel has 192 paragraphs [8 × 24], for which the Greek alphabetical number 24 may have played a role. Philippians and 1 Thessalonians, too, are divided into 24 paragraphs, and Revelation into 120 [5 × 25]. Cf. also the sixth-century Archbishop Andrew of Caesarea's division of the Book of Revelation into 24 discourses and 72 chapters [3 × 24] (Bruce M. Metzger and Bart D. Ehrman, *The Text of the New Testament: Its Transmission, Corruption, and Restoration*, 4th ed. [Oxford: Oxford University Press, 2005], 36.).

is Peter's confession, "You are the CHRIST, the SON of the living GOD," in Matt 16:16 (Matt 16:16 makes up the middle paragraph, the 203rd, in Matthew's Gospel).

Further interesting data can be provided for the number of columns used for the four Gospels in Codex Sinaiticus, which is 484 [22 × 22], and the number of pages allocated to the fourfold Gospel in Codex Washingtonianus, which is 374 [17 × 22].[9] In both cases a reference to the Hebrew alphabetical fullness number 22 may be intended (for further similar examples, see appendix below).[10] Moreover, both on Greek and Jewish grounds, the Hellenistic Greek alphabetical (and Hebrew canonical) number 24 is significant as a canonical signal, for example, in the Homeric works, both of which—apparently for no other reason than that of signaling alphabetical all-comprehensiveness—were divided into 24 books, and in the rabbinic scriptural twenty-four-book canon.[11]

NUMERALS PERTAINING TO THE DIVINE NAME

A less-known model for structuring the biblical material is around the numerical value associated with the Tetragrammaton, יהוה (and a

---

9. Moreover, the number of columns in Sinaiticus used for John's Gospel is 108 [4 × 27]. Two particularly interesting numerals—one alphabetically aligned, and the other numerically linked to the divine name—encounters the reader of Sinaiticus which has 484 columns [22 × 22] for the Gospels and 578 columns [2 × 17 × 17] for the rest of the New Testament (where 17 may be a numerical reference to the Tetragrammaton; see footnote 12 below and table 5.1).

10. The number of lines per column and the number of columns used for the four Gospels in Codex Sinaiticus (London, British Library, fourth century majuscule) being 48 [2 × 24] and 484 [22 × 22], respectively (http://www.codex-sinaiticus.net/en/manuscript.aspx); similar alphabetical figures feature for the four Gospels in GA260; the number of lines per column and the number of leaves in the Gospels codex GA1443 (eleventh century minuscule; dated to 1047) being 22 and 308 [14 × 22], respectively; similar alphabetical figures feature as well for the Gospels codices GA534; GA1443; and GA2252; Codex Mosquensis GA 018; and the Gospels lectionary GA Lect 1627. (For the above figures, see http://www.csntm.org/Manuscript.)

11. The standard number of lines per column, e.g., in Codex Sinaiticus is 48 [2 × 24]; the number of letters in the Hellenistic Greek alphabet is 24. Gallagher (*Hebrew Scripture*, 87) helpfully quotes Michael Haslam in connection to Homer (Haslam, "Homeric Papyri and Transmission of the Text," in *A New Companion to Homer*, ed. Ian Morris and Barry B. Powell, MnSup 163 [Leiden: Brill, 1997], 58): "According to Michael Haslam, the scholars who divided Homer's two epics into 24 books each did so despite interrupting traditional episodic divisions and limiting the size of a book to much less than a scroll could actually contain. This they did specifically because they were concerned with the alphabet. 'It is not a numerical system but an alphabetical one, and the α–ω partitioning must have been devised for its symbolism, advertising Homer's all-comprehensiveness.'" See also Bruce Heiden, "The Placement of 'Book Divisions' in the Iliad," *JHS* 118 (1998): 68.

conjectural archaic form of the word, אהוה), which is either 26 (10 = י) or
17 (1 = א ;0 + 1 = י).¹² Psalm 23 seems to be shaped with such a model in
mind, according to a simple ABA pattern, with 26 words in the first half
of the psalm (A), arguably representing divine presence, followed by the
three central words כי־אתה עמדי, "for you are with me" (B), and finally
the 26 closing words (A'), again representing divine presence.¹³ In terms
of word count, we can further note that the Septuagint arrangement of
Psalm 23 (LXX Ps 22) similarly connects with the sacred number 26, with
the Davidic psalm made up of altogether 104 words [4 × 26].¹⁴

---

12. Y (= 10) + H (= 5) + W (= 6) + (H= 5)= 26. Regarding 17, in Casper J. Labuschagne's
phrasing: "[As for the] divine name number 17, … it is … possible that 17 is the numerical value of a
conjectured *ahweh*, אהוה, which is to *'ehyeh*, אהיה, 'I am' (Ex. 3:14), as *yahweh*, יהוה, is to *yihyeh*, יהיה,
'he is': 17 = ' h w h, 1+5+6+5 = אהוה"; Labuschagne, "General Introduction to Logotechnical Analysis
(Rev.)," University of Groningen, 2016, 4; http://www.labuschagne.nl/aspects.pdf (emphasis original).
As Labuschagne points out, the numbers 17 and 26 also both happen to be the numerical value of
kabod, or *kabôd*, "glory." Cf. also Carlos del Valle, "Abraham Ibn Ezra's Mathematical Speculations
on the Divine Name," in *Mystics of the Book: Themes, Topics, and Typologies*, ed. by Robert A. Herrera
(New York: Peter Lang, 1993) 161: "According to Ibn Ezra, there are three proper names (Shem-ha-
'esem) of God: Yah, Ehyeh, and YHWH. 'The prophets,' he declares, 'established the name of the
two letters [Yah], that of the four letters [YHWH], and the name Ehyeh [as] the proper names of the
Most High. … The remainder of the divine names found in the Bible are adjectives [shemot ha-to'ar].'
In the commentary on Ex 3:15 he expressly states, 'These three names are proper names.' Ibn Ezra
attributes the same derivation to the three proper divine names: Yah, Ehyeh, and YHWH. Obviously
he is thinking of the root hayah ('to be,' 'to exist') as the ultimate root from which the three names
are derived." I am grateful to Jamie Grant for directing me to del Valle's article.
    In the Pentateuch YHWH occurs 1,820 times, which can be penned with the divisors 7 or 70 or
26, as 7 × 10 × 26, or as 70 × 26. In the book of Jonah, similarly, YHWH is repeated 26 times and in
2 Samuel the Tetragrammaton interestingly occurs 153 times, which corresponds to 9 × 17 or 3² × 17
(where 17 is the numerical value of YHWH when *yod* (or a conjectured aleph) counts as 1 (instead
of 10); cf. also potential allusion to the Name in John 21:11 (153 = 9 × 17 = 1 + 2 + 3 + 4 … + 16 + 17).
    13. Casper J. Labuschagne, *Numerical Secrets of the Bible: Introduction to Biblical Arithmology*
(Eugene, OR: Wipf & Stock, 2016), 11. See also Crispin Fletcher-Louis, *Jesus Monotheism*, vol. 1:
Christological Origins: The Emerging Consensus and Beyond (Eugene, OR: Cascade, 2015), 39–49. We
may also note that the *nomen sacrum* πατήρ, "Father," occurs 22 times in the Psalms (Rahlfs), and
ὁ ἄνθρωπος—another *nomen sacrum*—26 times, while words in the *nomina sacra* word-group com-
mencing with ἀνθρωπ* and σωτηρ* feature, respectively, 108 [4 × 27] and 78 times [3 × 26] in the
Psalms. Moreover, the word σωτηρία is found 34 times [2 × 17] in the Psalms, 54 times [2 × 27] in
the Historical Books, and 27 times in the Prophets; and σωτήριον 17 times in the Historical Books
(Rahlfs), 24 times in the Prophets (Rahlfs), and 136 times [8 × 17] in the full Rahlfs. For potential
significance of the numbers 24 and 27, see table 5.1 below. On another count, where terms connected
with *maqqep* are counted as one word in the Masoretic Text, the number of words in Ps 23 is 52 [2
× 26], which is a multiple of 26.
    14. Alternatively, if the introductory three words of the psalm—Ψαλμὸς τῷ Δαυιδ—are excluded,
the psalm contains all in all 101 words (101 is the 26th prime number). The word-count for Ps 23
in the Vulgate is 85 Latin words [5 × 17], which is another multiple of one of the numerical values
associated with the divine name. I want to extend my thanks to my wife Anna Bokedal for pointing

As for the numeral 26 at a macrocanonical level, we may recall the common Eastern exclusion of the book of Revelation from the New Testament, which, as a result, was to contain all in all twenty-six books in many Eastern churches.[15] Perhaps similar thinking—with potential deliberate numerical reference to the Tetragrammaton—lies behind as well the twelfth- to thirteenth-century and modern structuring of the full New Testament corpus into altogether 260 chapters [10 × 26]?[16] If that is the case, it would align nicely also with another scriptural 26-multiple, namely the 2600 occurrences [10 × 10 × 26] of the key Hebrew term *Elohim*, אלהים, "God; god," in the MT (*BHS*; i.e., the twenty-four-book Old Testament).[17]

In other words—and in line with the above examples—various numerical structures in the biblical texts appear to be arithmetically associated with the divine name, either through alphabetical connotation (multiples

to the Vulgate in this connection. For further structuring of the biblical material around the numerals 26 and 17, see, e.g., Labuschagne, *Numerical Secrets of the Bible*, 75–104.

15. In the Greek New Testament manuscript tradition, the entire New Testament of twenty-seven books is extant in ca. 60 manuscripts, whereas the twenty-six-book New Testament (excluding Revelation) is extant in ca. 150 manuscripts. Cf. Eldon Jay Epp, "Issues in the Interrelation of New Testament Textual Criticism and Canon," in *The Canon Debate: On the Origins and Formation of the Bible*, ed. Lee Martin McDonald and James A. Sanders (Peabody, MA: Hendrickson, 2002), 487.

16. Alternatively, 238 chapters [14 × 17] for the twenty-six-book New Testament (excluding Revelation; cf. table 5.1 below for potential significance of the numbers 14 and 17). Cf. Scot McKendrick, "Introduction," in *Bible Manuscripts: 1400 Years of Scribes and Scripture*, ed. Scot McKendrick and Kathleen Doyle (London: British Library, 2007), 11: "Only in the early 13th century did teachers and students of the university of Paris begin to use the standardized system of chapter numbering that we now use. Often ascribed to Stephen Langton (d. 1228), Archbishop of Canterbury, this means of referencing biblical text remained the principal one until the introduction of verse numbers by Robert Estienne for his edition of the Bible in French, printed at Geneva in 1553." However, as Franciscus van Liere points out, it is likely that the division into chapters, close to the one known today, predates Stephen Langton "and was invented sometime in the twelfth century, most likely in England"; van Liere, *An Introduction to the Medieval Bible* (Cambridge: Cambridge University Press, 2014), 43. Division of the New Testament into 260 [10 × 26] chapters, with potential allusion to the numerical value of the Tetragrammaton (which is either 26 or 17) may be compared to the division of the Pentateuch into 187 chapters [11 × 17], or that of Jeremiah and Luke-Acts into 52 chapters [2 × 26], the Synoptic Gospels into 68 chapters [4 × 17], and the four Gospels + Acts into 117 chapters [3 × 39; cf. table 5.1 below for potential significance of the number 39]. We may also note the number of chapters with possible alphabetical reference, such as Leviticus (27 chs.), Joshua (24 chs.), 2 Samuel (24 chs.), 1 Kings (22 chs.), Isaiah (66 chs. [3 × 22]), Ezekiel (48 chs. [2 × 24]), Luke (24 chs.), and Revelation (22 chs.).

17. אלהים further appears (figures from *BHS*) 374 times [17 × 22] in Deuteronomy, 26 times in Hosea, 17 times in Job, 507 times [3 × 13² = 13 × 39] in the Former Prophets, 27 times in Numbers, 54 times [2 × 27] in 2 Samuel, 154 times [7 × 22] in 1–2 Samuel, 204 times [12 × 17] in 1–2 Kings, and 22 times in Daniel (see table 5.1 below for potential significance of 13 and 39).

of 22, 24, or 27; cf. Rev 1:8) or by direct association with the numerical values linked to the Tetragrammaton (multiples of 17 or 26). Accordingly, *Elohim*, אלהים, "God; god," appears in Daniel 22 times and in Hosea 26 times.

5.2 ALPHABETICAL (22, 24, 27)
AND DIVINE NAME MULTIPLES (17, 26):
GOD, MESSIAH, SPIRIT

As we observe frequencies of the Hebrew term *Elohim*, אלהים, "God; god; gods," which appear in the MT as multiples linked to the divine name (26 times in Hosea) and alphabetical numerals (22 times in Daniel), we may not be surprised to see similar figures also for the Tetragrammaton, YHWH, יהוה (*BHS*).[18] Examples include the following figures for YHWH, יהוה (in boldface below): the Pentateuch **1820 occurrences** [70 × 26], Numbers **396 occurrences** [18 × 22], and Deuteronomy **550 occurrences** [5 × 5 × 22]. For the term משיח, "anointed; messiah," we may further note the **17 occurrences** of the term in 1–2 Samuel/the Former Prophets; and for the word רוּחַ, "s/Spirit; wind," **51 occurrences** [3 × 17] in Isaiah, **52 occurrences** [2 × 26] in Ezekiel, **154 occurrences** [7 × 22] in the Latter Prophets, **24 occurrences** in Ecclesiastes, and **378 occurrences** [14 × 27= 14 × 3 × 3 × 3] in the full MT (cf. the **378 occurrences** [14 × 27] of πνεῦμα in the 27-book NT of Codex Sinaiticus [א]); and the unpointed רוח featuring **44 times** [2 × 22] in the Pentateuch and **154 times** [7 × 22] in the Writings.[19] Similar numerical patterns appear as well when the unpointed ברך "bless; kneel; knee" and יהוה, "YHWH," appear together in the same verse (cf., e.g., Gen 24:27).[20]

---

18. E.g., אלהים occurs 26 times in Hosea, 17 times in Job, and 2600 times [10 × 10 × 26] in the full MT. Further, אלהים occurs 27 times in Numbers, 54 times [2 × 27] in 2 Samuel, 154 times [7 × 22] in 1–2 Samuel, and 22 times in Daniel; cf. note 17 above and ch. 7, note 21 below. Moreover, the letter constellation האלהים appears 135 times [5 × 27] in the Prophets, 24 times in 1 Samuel, 44 times [2 × 22] in 1–2 Samuel, 26 times in 1 Kings, and 187 times [11 × 17] in the Writings.

19. Moreover, in the MT (*BHS*) דוד, "David," appears as follows: 1–2 Samuel 576 times [24 × 24], 1 Kings 78 times [3 × 26], 1–2 Kings 96 times [4 × 24], the Former Prophets 672 times [2 × 14 × 24; cf. table 5.1 below for potential significance of 14]; and in Rahlfs, Δαυίδ, "David," occurs 550 times [5 × 5 × 22] in 1–2 Samuel, 85 times [5 × 17] in 1 Kings, and 110 times [5 × 22] in the Poetical Books (excluding Odes and Psalms of Solomon. The 378 occurrences of πνεῦμα in the NT of א were also noted in a previous private conversation with Rex J. Howe.).

20. According to Emanuel Tov (Textual Criticism of the Hebrew Bible, 3rd rev. ed. [Minneapolis, MN: Fortress Press, 2012], 49), "[t]he concept of a verse (pasuq) is known from the Talmud, and

The New Testament, too, embraces similar figures of divine-name multiples and alphabetical multiples pertaining to the Name (NA28), such as θεός, "God," occurring **54 times** [2 × 27] in 1–2 Thessalonians, χριστός, "anointed; messiah," featuring **54 times** [2 × 27] in the four Gospels, and πνεῦμα, "Spirit; spirit; wind," occurring **54 times** [2 × 27] in 1–2 Thessalonians.[21] Πνεῦμα further appears **24 times** both in Revelation (cf. Rev 1:8) and John's Gospel, **102 times** [6 × 17] in the four Gospels, **78 times** [3 × 26] in the Synoptic Gospels, **34 times** [2 × 17] in Romans, and **17 times** in 2 Corinthians; moreover, πνεῦμα ἅγιον occurs **17 times** in Acts and **24 times** in Luke-Acts; and θεός features **96 times** [4 × 24] in Revelation, **51 times** [3 × 17] in Matthew, **289 times** [17 × 17] in Luke-Acts, **153 times** [9 × 17] in Romans, **22 times** in 1 Timothy, **68 times** [4 × 17] in Hebrews, and **616 times** [4 × 7 × 22] in Pauline Corpus.[22]

In the next chapter (ch. 6) we shall examine further some triadic/Triune arithmetical patterns pertaining to the Name (e.g., word-frequency patterns associated with "God," "Christ," and "Spirit"). First, however, to be better equipped for this numerological exploration, we shall provide an outline in table form of the basic numerals involved (table 5.1 below).

---

the rabbis were used to a fixed division of the biblical text into verses." The following search in Accordance ברך <AND> יהוה gives these results (occurrences of the two words counted separately): the Pentateuch 108 times [4 × 27], 1 Chronicles 22 times, and the full MT 360 times [15 × 24].

21. Moreover, the *nomen sacrum* Δαυίδ, "David," occurs 17 times in Matthew and 24 times in Luke-Acts.

22. As for πνεῦμα and θεός, or related letter constellations, occurring in the same verse/passage, we may note the following figures (the modern division of the NT text into verses were introduced in the 16th century; search in Accordance; each term/letter constellation counted separately): for πνεῦμα <AND> θεός: Catholic Epistles **26 times**; for πνευμα* <AND> θεός: Pauline Corpus 105 times [7 × 15], 1–2 Peter 15 times, Praxapostolos 45 times [3 × 15] (for potential numerical significance of 15, see table 5.1 below), New Testament **187 times** [11 × 17]; for πν* <AND> θε*: Gospels 44 times [2 × 22], Gospels + Acts 68 times [4 × 17], Acts **24 times**, Praxapostolos 54 times [2 × 27], Catholic Epistles 30 times [2 × 15; see table 5.1 below for potential significance of the number 15], New Testament 242 times [11 × 22]; and for πνε* <AND> θε*: Acts 22 times, Praxapostolos 52 times [2 × 26], New Testament 240 times [10 × 24]. Correspondingly for πνευμα* <AND> κύριος we may note the following figures: Synoptic Gospels/four Gospels 17 times, Acts/Praxapostolos 24 times, New Testament 102 times [6 × 17]; for πνεῦμα <AND> κυρι*: New Testament 96 times [4 × 24]; for πνευμα* <AND> κυρι*: New Testament 104 times [4 × 26]; for πνευμα* <AND> κυ*: Acts/Praxapostolos 26 times, Gospels + Acts 45 times [3 × 15; for potential significance of 15, see table 5.1 below], and New Testament 110 times [5 × 22]. If the above figures for the fourfold Gospels (102 [6 × 17]) and the Synoptics (78 [3 × 26]) are deliberate on the part of authors/editors/scribes, this may have implications also for their literary interdependency (John and the Synoptics; the Synoptic Problem). πνεῦμα ἅγιος + ἅγιος πνεῦμα further occurs 24 times in Acts. ὁ θεός, moreover, occurs 153 times [9 × 17] in Acts and 260 times [10 × 26] in Luke-Acts (NA28).

5.3 SIGNIFICANT JEWISH AND
BIBLICAL SYMBOLICAL NUMBERS

For potentially symbolic numbers used in part C (chs. 5-10), including the two groups of numerals referred to above, I have provided a list in table 5.1, supplied with brief comments regarding their symbolical meaning.[23]

Table 5.1. Significant Jewish and biblical symbolic numbers.

Jewish/Biblical Symbolic Numbers	Basic Symbolic Meaning
3	One of the most significant of all sacred or symbolical numbers, God's own number (Rev 1:4), representing divine fullness, and the vertical dimension of the world.
4	Representing the horizontal dimension of the world, including the four cardinal directions (Rev 7:1).
7 [3 + 4]	The frequently occurring number of fullness, abundance, and completeness, representing cosmic order (the number ἑπτά occurs 24 times in the Gospels and 88 times [4 × 22] in the New Testament [NA28]).[24]
8 [7 + 1]	Symbolizing resurrection and new creation in early Christianity (ὀκτώ occurs 8 times in the New Testament).
10	A mnemotechnical perfect number that represents fullness/totality (Clem. *Strom.* 6.11).
11 [4 + 7]	The sum of 4 as the number of extensiveness and 7 as the number of fullness, 11 seems to have developed in the course of time a separate status as a number expressing fulfilment.[25]

---

23. A modified version of table 5.1 can be found in Tomas Bokedal, "'But for Me, the Scriptures are Jesus Christ' (IC XC; Ign. *Phld.* 8:2): Creedal Text-Coding and the Early Scribal System of Nomina Sacra," in *Studies on the Paratextual Features of Early New Testament Manuscripts*, ed. Stanley E. Porter, David I. Yoon, and Chris S. Stevens, TENTS (Leiden: Brill, forthcoming 2023).

24. Labuschagne, *Numerical Secrets of the Bible*, 26–31. For the numbers 3, 4, 7, 12, 24, and other significant numbers in the book of Revelation and elsewhere, see Michael J. Gorman, *Reading Revelation Responsibly: Uncivil Worship and Witness; Following the Lamb into the New Creation* (Eugene, OR: Cascade Books, 2011), 18–19; I'm grateful to Sverre Bøe for directing me to this volume by Gorman.

25. Labuschagne, *Numerical Secrets of the Bible*, 70–73.

Jewish/Biblical Symbolic Numbers	Basic Symbolic Meaning
12 [3 × 4]	Signifying completeness, perfection (of the kingdom of God), and totality (the product of 3 and 4, representing God and the world, or the vertical and the horizontal dimensions of the world, respectively).[26]
14 [2 × 7]	The numerical value of the Hebrew name "David," דוד, *Dawid* (*dalet* [= 4] + *vav* [= 6] + *dalet* [= 4]).
18	The numerical value of the Hebrew word for *life*, *khai*, חי, (*khet* [= 8] + *yod* [= 10]). 18 is also the numerical value of the early *nomen sacrum* for Jesus, ιη̄ (= 18, iota= 10 +eta= 8). Cf. Barn. 9.
17	Representing one of the numerical values associated with the divine name YHWH/AHWH: *yod* (= 1[0])/*aleph* (= 1) + *he* (= 5) + *vav* (= 6) + *he* (= 5) = 17 (which is the seventh prime number).[27]
26	Representing the numerical value of the divine name YHWH, the Tetragrammaton: *yod* (= 10) + *he* (= 5) + *vav* (= 6) + *he* (= 5) = 26 = 15 (YH) + 11 (WH). Both 17 and 26 (and 15)
15	represent, each in its own way, the presence of God through his name YHWH.[28] Both also represent the Hebrew word *kabod*, כבוד
23	/כבד, "glory" (*kbd* = 17 or 26; or, when spelled *kbwd* = 23 or 32).
32	*Kabod* symbolism in the Bible means that God and his glory are "regarded as belonging inextricably together" (cf. Exod 33:17–23; and Barn. 12.7: "the glory of Jesus").[29] We may add here as well the
13	numerical value for God as one (Hebrew: *ekhad*, אחד), which is 13;
39	thus, YHWH (= 26) + *ekhad* (= 13), "The LORD is one" = 39.

26. Labuschagne, *Numerical Secrets of the Bible*, 24.

27. Cf. Labuschagne's phrasing ("General Introduction to Logotechnical Analysis (Rev.)," 4): "it is ... possible that 17 is the numerical value of a conjectured *'ahweh*, אהוה, which is to *'ehyeh*, אהיה, 'I am' (Ex. 3:14), as *yahweh*, יהוה, is to *yihyeh*, יהיה, 'he is': 17 = ' h w h, 1+5+6+5 = יהוה." See also note 12, ch. 5 above.

28. Labuschagne, *Numerical Secrets of the Bible*, 89–90.

29. On Exod 33:17–23, see Labuschagne, *Numerical Secrets of the Bible*, 90. See also Fletcher-Louis, *Jesus Monotheism*, 39–49; and Richard Bauckham, "Confessing the Cosmic Christ (1 Corinthians 8:6 and Colossians 1:15–20)," in *Monotheism and Christology in Greco-Roman Antiquity*. Edited by Matthew V. Novenson. Supplements to Novum Testamentum (Leiden: Brill, 2020), 141–43.

Jewish/Biblical Symbolic Numbers	Basic Symbolic Meaning
22 [2 × 11] 24 [2 × 12] 27 [3 × 3 × 3]	The number of letters in the Hellenistic Greek (24) and Hebrew alphabets (22, or 27, when including the 5 end consonant forms), representing completeness and totality.

BIBLIOGRAPHY

Bauckham, Richard. "Confessing the Cosmic Christ (1 Corinthians 8:6 and Colossians 1:15–20)." Pages 139–71 in *Monotheism and Christology in Greco-Roman Antiquity*. Edited by Matthew V. Novenson. Supplements to Novum Testamentum. Leiden: Brill, 2020.

Beckwith, Roger. *The Old Testament Canon of the New Testament Church and Its Background in Early Judaism*. Grand Rapids: Eerdmans, 1985.

Bokedal, Tomas. "'But for Me, the Scriptures Are Jesus Christ' ($\overline{\text{IC}}$ $\overline{\text{XC}}$; Ign. *Phld.* 8:2): Creedal Text-Coding and the Early Scribal System of Nomina Sacra." In *Studies on the Paratextual Features of Early New Testament Manuscripts*. Edited by Stanley E. Porter, David I. Yoon, and Chris S. Stevens. TENTS. Leiden: Brill, forthcoming 2023.

―――. "Canon/Scripture." Pages 46–48 in *The Dictionary of the Bible and Ancient Media*. Edited by Tom Thatcher, Chris Keith, Raymond F. Person Jr., and Elsie R. Stern. London: Bloomsbury T&T Clark, 2017. Repr. as chapter 3 in this volume.

del Valle, Carlos. "Abraham Ibn Ezra's Mathematical Speculations on the Divine Name." Pages 159–76 in *Mystics of the Book: Themes, Topics, and Typologies*. Edited by Robert A. Herrera. New York: Peter Lang, 1993.

Epp, Eldon Jay. "Issues in the Interrelation of New Testament Textual Criticism and Canon." Pages 485–515 in *The Canon Debate: On*

the Origins and Formation of the Bible. Edited by Lee Martin
　　McDonald and James A. Sanders. Peabody, MA: Hendrickson,
　　2002.

Fletcher-Louis, Crispin. *Jesus Monotheism*, vol. 1: *Christological Origins:
　　The Emerging Consensus and Beyond*. Eugene, OR: Cascade
　　Books, 2015.

Gallagher, Edmon. *Hebrew Scripture in Patristic Biblical Theory: Canon,
　　Language, Text*. VCSup 114. Leiden: Brill, 2012.

Gallagher, Edmon, and John D. Meade, eds. *The Biblical Canon Lists
　　from Early Christianity: Texts and Analysis*. Oxford: Oxford
　　University Press, 2017.

Gorman, Michael J. *Reading Revelation Responsibly: Uncivil Worship and
　　Witness: Following the Lamb into the New Creation*. Eugene, OR:
　　Cascade, 2011.

Haslam, Michael. "Homeric Papyri and Transmission of the Text."
　　Pages 55–100 in *A New Companion to Homer*. Edited by Ian
　　Morris and Barry B. Powell. MnSup 163. Leiden: Brill, 1997.

Heiden, Bruce. "The Placement of 'Book Divisions' in the Iliad." *JHS*
　　118 (1998): 68–81.

Labuschagne, Casper J. "General Introduction to Logotechnical
　　Analysis (Rev.)." University of Groningen, 2016. http://www.
　　labuschagne.nl/aspects.pdf.

———. *Numerical Secrets of the Bible: Introduction to Biblical Arithmology*.
　　Eugene, OR: Wipf & Stock, 2016.

Lim, Timothy H. *The Formation of the Jewish Canon*. ABRL. New
　　Haven: Yale University Press, 2013.

McKendrick, Scot. "Introduction." Pages 6–11 in *Bible Manuscripts:
　　1400 Years of Scribes and Scripture*. Edited by Scot McKendrick
　　and Kathleen Doyle. London: British Library, 2007.

Metzger, Bruce M. *The Canon of the New Testament: Its Origin,
　　Development, and Significance*. Oxford: Clarendon, 1987.

Metzger, Bruce M. and Bart D. Ehrman, *The Text of the New Testament: Its Transmission, Corruption, and Restoration*, 4th ed. Oxford: Oxford University Press, 2005.

Tov, Emanuel. *Textual Criticism of the Hebrew Bible*, 3rd rev. ed. Minneapolis, MN: Fortress Press, 2012.

Van Liere, Franciscus. *An Introduction to the Medieval Bible*. Cambridge: Cambridge University Press, 2014.

6

TRIUNE ARITHMETICAL CONFIGURATIONS IN THE NEW TESTAMENT

Having observed some significant numerical patterns in Chapter 5 associated with the alphabet and the divine and related names—such as God, messiah and Spirit—we shall now explore some further Triune arithmetical structures in the New Testament (6.1 and 6.2) and briefly also in early patristic literature (6.3). Again, our focus will be on two groups of numerals, on the one hand multiples of Hebrew and Greek alphabetical numbers, indirectly related to the Name (22-/27- and 24-multiples; cf. Rev 1:8) and, on the other, multiples directly related to the Name (17- and 26-multiples). I shall refer to these two groups of numbers as *Name-related Numeral(s)* (hereafter NrN).

Based on these NrN, in order to detect potentially Triune arithmetical configurations, two methods will be employed. On the one hand, the method used in 1.5 above, where each of the words making up a particular Triune structure is present in each of the verses included in the count (6.1 below; e.g., the altogether **17 occurrences** of the three words θεός, χριστός and πνεῦμα present in Rom 1:4, 8:9; 15:16, 19, 30); and, on the other hand, an additional method based on simple addition in a text of the three words/expressions included in the Triune structure (6.2 below;

e.g., the addition in 1 Thessalonians of θεός 36 occurrences + χριστός 10 occurrences + πνεῦμα 5 occurrences = **51 occurrences** [3 x 17] of the three words).

6.1 TRIUNE CONFIGURATIONS NUMERICALLY RELATED TO THE DIVINE NAME IN 34 NT VERSES[1]

As we saw in the Introduction above (1.5), based on verse-by-verse occurrences, the NT text seems to embrace a number of Triune *NrN* configurations, such as the altogether **26 occurrences** in the full NT—allocated to eight NT passages[2]—of the three words θεός, υἱός and πνεῦμα, when appearing together in the same verse (each word counted separately; search in Accordance 13 on the form: θεός <AND> υἱός <AND> πνεῦμα (THGNT, NA28, ℵ, TR, TF35). The corresponding figure for Corpus Paulinum is **17 occurrences** (textual scope: verse; THGNT, NA28, ℵ, TR, TF35; NB: the modern division of the NT text into verses was made in the sixteenth century; alternative figure when instead THGNT paragraph is used as textual scope: **132 [6 x 22] occurrences**). Corresponding Triune NT configurations, embracing eight verses,[3] include, as well, θεός <AND> Ἰησοῦς χριστός <AND> πνεῦμα, featuring altogether **26 times** in the full New Testament (or **34 times** [2 x 17] if Ἰησοῦς and χριστός are counted separately; textual scope: verse; each word/expression counted separately; THGNT, NA28, ℵ; alternative figure when THGNT paragraph is used as textual scope: **182 occurrences** [7 x 26] in the full New Testament). Triune *NrN* configurations further include θεός <AND> κύριος <AND> πνεῦμα, embracing eight verses,[4] which appear all in all **26 times** in Corpus Paulinum (each word counted separately; THGNT, NA28, ℵ, TR, TF35), and the three terms θεός <AND> χριστός <AND> πνεῦμα—occurring

---

1. The following 20 NT verses are discussed in the first five examples below: Mark 3:11; Luke 1:35; Acts 2:17; Rom 1:4; 1:9; 8:9; 8:14; 15:16; 15:19; 15:30; 1 Cor 6:11; 12.3; 2 Cor 13:13; Gal 4:6; Eph 1:17; 1 Thess 5:23; 2 Thess 2:13; Heb 10:29; 1 Pet 1:2; 1 John 4:2. An additional 14 NT verses appear in the two final examples, namely Luke 8:29; Acts 10:38; 16:18; 1 Cor 10:4; 2 Cor 3:3; Eph 1:3; Phil 2:1; 3:3; Col 3:16; Heb 9:14; 1 Pet 1:11; 2:5; 3:18; and 4:14.

2. Mark 3:11; Luke 1:35; Acts 2:17; Rom 1:4; 1:9; 8:14; Gal 4:6; and Heb 10:29.

3. Rom 1:4; 15:30; 1 Cor 6:11; 2 Cor 13:13; Eph 1:17; 1 Thess 5:23; 1 Pet 1:2; and 1 John 4:2.

4. Rom 1:4; 15:30; 1 Cor 6:11; 12:3; 2 Cor 13:13; Eph 1:17; 1 Thess 5:23; and 2 Thess 2:13. For the potential significance of the number eight, see table 5.1. ch 5 above.

together in five verses—which feature altogether **17 times** in Romans (each word counted separately; THGNT, NA28, ℵ, TR, TF35; textual scope: verse; alternative figure for θεός <and> κύριος <and> πνεῦμα when THGNT paragraph is used as textual scope: **170 times [10 x 17]**).[5]

We may also note the following similar *NrN* searches that include Triune word/letter constellations in Accordance 13: θεο* <AND> χρι* <AND> πνε*: Romans **17 occurrences** (THGNT, NA28, ℵ, TR), the full New Testament **68 occurrences [4 x 17]** (THGNT, NA28; textual scope: verse); and πα* <AND> χρ* <AND> πν*: the full New Testament **52 occurrences [2 x 26]** (THGNT, NA28; textual scope: verse; alternative figure when THGNT paragraph is used as textual scope: **676 occurrences [26 x 26]**).

In summation, the aforementioned Triune *NrN* structures all embrace three terms/expressions/letter constellations, the respective sum of which equals multiples of one of the two numerical values associated with the Tetragrammaton, YHWH (17- or 26-multiples).

6.2 STANDARD TRIUNE NRN CONFIGURATIONS BASED ON ADDITION OF NT WORD-FREQUENCIES

An alternative way, and methodologically more reliable, that editors, scribes and authors may have used to structure these forms of arithmetical Triune NT configurations, it seems, is by simple addition of word-frequencies in a text; for example—based on the Triune structure in Matt 28:19—the addition in various canonical sub-units of the respective occurrences of the terms "f/Father," "s/Son" and "holy Spirit," πατήρ, υἱός and ἅγιος πνεῦμα (ἅγιον πνεῦμα/ἁγίου πνεύματος), and corresponding addition of related Triune word constellations. The following seventeen results containing *NrN* emerge (i–xvii; divine Name (17- and 26-multiples) and alphabetical numerals (22-, 24- and 27-multiples) in boldface below; figures from the Accordance 13 digital version of Tyndale House Greek New Testament, Crossway and Cambridge University, 2017):

---

5. Rom 1:4; 8:9; 15:16; 15:19; and 15:30. Corresponding results for θεός <and> χριστός <and> πνεῦμα for Corpus Paulinum is 39 occurences and for Praxapostolos 14 occurrences (textual scope: verse; see table 5.1, ch. 5 for potential numerological significance of 39 and 14).

i) for πατήρ + υἱός + ἅγιος πνεῦμα (cf. Matt 28:19):

- Matthew: πατήρ 63x + υἱός 89x + ἅγιος πνεῦμα 1x = **153x** [9 x 17]⁶

- Luke: πατήρ 56x + υἱός 77x + ἅγιος πνεῦμα 2x = **135x** [7 x 27]

- Luke-Acts: πατήρ 91x + υἱός 98x + ἅγιος πνεῦμα 9x = **198x** [9 x 22]

- Luke-Acts: πατήρ 91x + υἱός 98x = **189x** [7 x 27]

- 1–2 Cor: πατήρ 11x + υἱός 6x = **17x**

ii) for πατήρ + υἱός + ἅγιος πνεῦμα (singular forms; cf. Matt 28:19):
- Matthew: πατήρ 61x + υἱός 73x + ἅγιος πνεῦμα 1x = **135x** [5 x 27]

- Four Gospels: πατήρ 259x + υἱός 224x + ἅγιος πνεῦμα 3x = **486x** [18 x 27]

- Pauline Corpus: πατήρ 61x + υἱός 41x + ἅγιος πνεῦμα 2x = **104x** [4 x 26]

- Pauline Corpus: πατήρ 61x + υἱός 41x = **102x** [6 x 17]

- NT: πατήρ 361x + υἱός 307x + ἅγιος πνεῦμα 12x = **680x** [40 x 17]

iii) for πατήρ + υἱός + πνεῦμα ἅγιος:
- Matthew: πατήρ 63x + υἱός 89x + πνεῦμα ἅγιος 2x = **154x** [7 x 22]

- Mark: πατήρ 18x + υἱός 35x + πνεῦμα ἅγιος 1x = **54x** [7 x 27]

- Gospels+Acts: πατήρ **308x** + υἱός **278x** + πνεῦμα ἅγιος 30x = **616x** [28 x 22]

---

6. 63x = 63 times; 89x = 89 times; 1x = 1 time; and 153x = 153 times.

iv) for πατήρ + υἱός + πνεῦμα ἅγιος (singular forms):
- Matthew: πατήρ 61x + υἱός 73x + πνεῦμα ἅγιος 2x = **136x** [8 x 17]

- Synoptics: πατήρ 128x + υἱός **170x** + πνεῦμα ἅγιος 10x = **308x** [14 x 22]

v) for ὄνομα + πατήρ + υἱός + ἅγιος πνεῦμα (cf. Matt 28:19):
- Matthew: ὄνομα 23x + πατήρ 63x + υἱός 89x + ἅγιος πνεῦμα 1x = **176x** [8 x 22][7]

Comment 1: In these first five examples (i–v) we can note the consistency with which Matthew's Gospel reappears, arithmetically highlighting the varying Triune *NrN* constellations connected to Matt 28:19 (NB: if these *NrN* are just randomly occurring—contrary to the argument of the present chapter—the likelihood for them to occur is ca. one in five appearances, i.e., 20 percent probability *in each case* for these Name-related multiples (multiples of 17 and 26, and 22, 24 and 27)):

- Matthew: πατήρ + υἱός + ἅγιος πνεῦμα = **153 occurrences** [9 x 17]

- Matthew: πατήρ + υἱός + ἅγιος πνεῦμα (singular forms) = **135 occurrences** [5 x 27]

- Matthew: πατήρ + υἱός + πνεῦμα ἅγιος = **154 occurrences** [7 x 22]

- Matthew: πατήρ + υἱός + πνεῦμα ἅγιος (singular forms) = **136 occurrences** [8 x 17]

- Matthew: ὄνομα + πατήρ + υἱός + ἅγιος πνεῦμα = **176 occurrences** [8 x 22]

---

7. In addition, Luke: ὄνομα **34x** [2 x 17] + πατήρ 56x [4 x 14] + υἱός 77x [7 x 11] +ἅγιος πνεῦμα 2x = 169x [13 x 13] (THGNT)/**170x** [10 x 17] (NA28). See Table 5.1 for potential significance of 13.

Comment 2: By using a different way of counting (used in 6.1 above), we may also note the following *NrN* in the full New Testament—based on the Triune configuration present in Matt 28:19—for the letter constellations πα* <AND> υἱ* <AND> πν* (textual scope: verse; appearing in Matt 1:20; 28:19; Luke 12:10; Acts 2:17; Rom 8:15 and Gal 4:6):

- NT: πα* <AND> υἱ* <AND> πν* = **22 occurrences**

- NT: πα* <AND> υιο* <AND> πνεῦμα = **22 occurrences**

- NT: πα* <AND> υἱός <AND> πνεῦμα = **17 occurrences**

vi) for ὄνομα (sg. nom./acc.) + πατρός + υἱοῦ + ἁγίου πνεύματος (cf. Matt 28:19):
- Matthew: ὄνομα (sg. nom./acc.) 11x + πατρός 21x + υἱοῦ 9x + ἁγίου πνεύματος 1x = **42x** [3 x 14] (cf. table 5.1 for potential numerological significance of 14)

- Four Gospels: ὄνομα (sg. nom./acc.) **44x** + πατρός 58x + υἱοῦ **17x** + ἁγίου πνεύματος 1x = **120x** [5 x 24]

vii) for ὄνομα (sg. nom./acc.) + πατρός + υἱοῦ + πνεύματος (cf. Matt 28:19):
- Luke: ὄνομα (sg. nom./acc.) 16x + πατρός 8x + υἱοῦ 4x + πνεύματος 6x = **34x** [2 x 17]

- Four Gospels: ὄνομα (sg. nom./acc.) **44x** + πατρός 58x + υἱοῦ **17x** + πνεύματος 16x = **135x** [5 x 27]

- NT: ὄνομα (sg. nom./acc.) 106x + πατρός 101x + υἱοῦ 36x + πνεύματος 95x = **338x** [13 x 26] (cf. table 5.1 above for potential numerological significance of 13)

viii) for πατήρ + υἱός + πνεῦμα (singular forms; cf. Matt 28:19):
- Mark: πατήρ 18x + υἱός 31x + πνεῦμα 19x = **68x** [4 x 17]

- 1–3 John: πατήρ 16x + υἱός **24x** + πνεῦμα 11x = **51x** [3 x 17]

- Praxapostolos: πατήρ 36x + υἱός 37x + πνεῦμα 89x = **162x** **[6 x 27 = 6 x 3 x 3 x 3]**

- 1–2 Cor: πατήρ 9x + υἱός 3x + πνεῦμα **54x** = **66x** [3 x 22]

- Rev: πατήρ 5x + υἱός 5x + πνεῦμα **17x** = 27x [3 x 3 x 3]

ix) for ὄνομα + πατήρ + υἱός + πνεῦμα (cf. Matt 28:19):
- Four Gospels: ὄνομα 97x + πατήρ 273x + υἱός 257x + πνεῦμα **102x** = **729x** [27 x 27 = (3 x 3 x 3) x (3 x 3 x 3)]

- 1–2 Thess: ὄνομα 2x + πατήρ 8x + υἱός 4x + πνεῦμα 8x = **22x**[8]

x) for ὄνομα[9] + πατήρ + υἱός + πνεῦμα (singular forms; cf. Matt 28:19):
- John: ὄνομα 25x + πατήρ 131x + υἱός 54x + πνεῦμα **24x** = **234x** [3 x 3 x 26]

- Luke-Acts: ὄνομα 91x + πατήρ 60x + υἱός 76x + πνεῦμα **96x** = **323x** [19 x 17]

---

8. In addition, Gospels+Acts: ὄνομα 157x + πατήρ **308x** [14 x 22] + υἱός 278x + πνεῦμα 172x = **915** [61 x 15]; Catholic Epistles: ὄνομα 10x + πατήρ 28x + υἱός **27x** + πνεῦμα 25x = **90x** [6 x 15]; and Revelation: ὄνομα 38x + πατήρ 5x + υἱός 8x + πνεῦμα **24x** = 75x [5 x 15]. See table 5.1 for potential significance of 15.

9. We may note as well the following word combinations, involving ὄνομα (search in Accordance 13; each of the included items occurs together in each included verse, and each word is counted separately; textual scope:verse): ὁ <AND> ὄνομα <AND> αὐτός (cf. Matt 1:21, 23; 12:21): Mark **34** occurrences [2 x 17], Luke **110** occurrences [5 x 22], four Gospels **286 occurrences** [13 x 22 = 11 x 26], 1 Cor **17** occurrences, Pauline Corpus **72** occurrences [3 x 24]; ὁ <AND> ὄνομα <AND> αὐτός <AND> Ἰησοῦς (cf. Matt 1:21, 25; Luke 1:31; 2:21): Synoptic Gospels **51 occurrences** [3 x 17], four Gospels 65 occurrences/**66 occurrences** [3 x 22] in NA28, Acts **52** occurrences [2 x 26], Gospels+Acts 117 occurrences [3 x 39] (see Table 5.1 for potential numerical significance of 39), and NT **156** occurrences [6 x 26]; ὁ <AND> ὄνομα <AND> αὐτός <AND> Ἰησοῦς Χριστός: Acts 24 occurrences, Pauline Corpus **26** occurrences; ὁ <AND> ὄνομα <AND> οὗτος (cf. Luke 1:61; Acts 4:17; 5:28; 9:21 and 1 Pet 4:16): Acts **81** occurrences [3 x 27], Pauline Corpus **34 occurrences** [2 x 17], Praxapostolos **96** occurrences [4 x 24], Catholic Epistles 15 occurrences (cf. table 5.1 for potential numerical significance of 15); ὁ <AND> ὄνομα <AND> αὐτός <AND> λόγος (cf. Rev 19:13): NT **27** occurrences; ὁ <AND> ὄνομα <AND> αὐτός <AND> θεός (cf. Matt 1:23): John **22** occurrences, Pauline Corpus **51** occurrences [3 x 17]; ὄνομα <AND> κύριος (cf. Matt 21:9): Synoptic Gospels 17 occurrences, Praxapostolos **34 occurrences** [2 x 17], Pauline Corpus 23 occurrences/**24 occurrences** in Codex Sinaiticus (ℵ), NT **81** occurrences [3 x 27]/**85 occurrences** [5 x 17] in Codex Sinaiticus (ℵ); ὄνομα <AND> Ἰησοῦς (cf. Acts 26:9 and Phil 2:10): NT **78** occurrences [3 x 26]; and ὄνομα <AND> Ἰησοῦς <AND> Χριστός (cf. Acts 2:38; 3:6; 4:10; 8:12; 10:48; 16:18): Gospels+Acts 24 occurrences, Praxapostolos 24 occurrences, NT **52** occurrences [2 x 26].

- Catholic Epistles: ὄνομα 10x + πατήρ 25x + υἱός **27x** + πνεῦμα 23x = **85x** [5 x 17]

- NT: ὄνομα 219x + πατήρ 361x + υἱός 307x + πνεῦμα 345x = **1232x** [4 x 14 x 22]

Comment 3: In addition to Matthew's Gospel (*Comment 1* above), the following canonical sub-units—related to the Triune formulation in Matt 28:19—are also richly represented in the above examples of *NrN* (i–x, including *Comment 2*):

The four Gospels (for which 27 [3 x 3 x 3] may be a reference to the Triune Name, and for which the squared numeral, 27—**729 occurrences** [27 x 27]—may signify "holiness," in line with acknowledged OT symbolism):[10]

- Four Gospels: πατήρ + υἱός + ἅγιος πνεῦμα = **486x** [18 x 27] = 18 x 3 x 3 x 3] (for potential significance of 18, see table 5.1)

- Four Gospels: ὄνομα (sg. nom./acc.) + πατρός + υἱοῦ + ἁγίου πνεύματος = **120x** [5 x 24]

- Four Gospels: ὄνομα (sg. nom./acc.) + πατρός + υἱοῦ + πνεύματος = **135x** [5 x 27 = 5 x 3 x 3 x 3]

- Four Gospels: ὄνομα + πατήρ + υἱός + πνεῦμα = **729x** [27 x 27 = (3 x 3 x 3) x (3 x 3 x 3)]

The full New Testament:

- NT: πατήρ + υἱός + ἅγιος πνεῦμα = **680x** [40 x 17]

- NT: ὄνομα (sg. nom./acc.) + πατρός + υἱοῦ + πνεύματος = **338x** [13 x 26]

---

10. On the symbolic significance of the square in the Hebrew thought world, Kalinda Rose Stevenson (*The Vision of Transformation: The Territorial Rhetoric of Ezekiel 40–48* (SBLDS 154, Atlanta: Scholars Press, 1996), 34–5, 42, 47–58) notes that in association with the Temple the square functions as a material representation of a theology of holiness. Thus, a perfect square in Ezekiel is the "shape" of pure holiness.

- NT: ὄνομα + πατήρ + υἱός + πνεῦμα = 232x [4 x 14 x 22]

- NT: πα* <AND> υιο* <AND> πνεῦμα = 22x

- NT: πα* <AND> υἱός <AND> πνεῦμα = 17x

Seventeen canonical sub-units that include one or both of the Lukan writings:
- Luke: πατήρ + υἱός + ἅγιος πνεῦμα = 135x [7 x 27 = 7 x 3 x 3 x 3]

- Luke-Acts: πατήρ + υἱός + ἅγιος πνεῦμα = 198x [3 x 3 x 22]

- Luke-Acts: πατήρ + υἱός = 189x [7 x 27 = 7 x 3 x 3 x 3]

- Four Gospels: πατήρ + υἱός + ἅγιος πνεῦμα (sg.) = 486x [18 x 27 = 18 x 3 x 3 x 3]

- NT: πατήρ + υἱός + ἅγιος πνεῦμα (sg.) = 680x [40 x 17]

- Gospels+Acts: πατήρ + υἱός + πνεῦμα ἅγιος = 616x [2 x 14 x 22]

- Synoptics: πατήρ + υἱός + πνεῦμα ἅγιος (sg.) = 308x [14 x 22]

- NT: πα* <AND> υιο* <AND> πνεῦμα = 22x

- NT: πα* <AND> υἱός <AND> πνεῦμα = 17x

- Four Gospels: ὄνομα (sg. nom./acc.) + πατρός + υἱοῦ + ἁγίου πνεύματος = 120x [5 x 24]

- Luke: ὄνομα (sg. nom./acc.) + πατρός + υἱοῦ + πνεύματος = 34x [2 x 17]

- Four Gospels: ὄνομα (sg. nom./acc) + πατρός + υἱοῦ + πνεύματος = 135x [5 x 27 = 5 x 3 x 3 x 3]

- NT: ὄνομα (sg. nom./acc.) + πατρός + υἱοῦ + πνεύματος = **338x** [13 x 26]

- Praxapostolos: πατήρ + υἱός + πνεῦμα (sg.) = **162x** [6 x 27 = 6 x 3 x 3 x 3]

- Four Gospels: ὄνομα + πατήρ + υἱός + πνεῦμα = **729x** [27 x 27 = (3 x 3 x 3) x (3 x 3 x 3)]

- Luke-Acts: ὄνομα + πατήρ + υἱός + πνεῦμα (sg.) = **323x** [19 x 17]

- NT: ὄνομα + πατήρ + υἱός + πνεῦμα (sg.) = **1232x** [4 x 14 x 22]

xi) for θεός + χριστός + πνεῦμα (cf. 2 Cor 13:13 and 1 *Clem.* 46.6):[11]
- Luke: θεός 122x + χριστός 12x + πνεῦμα 36x = **170x** [10 x 17]

- Acts: θεός 165x + χριστός 25x + πνεῦμα 70x = **260x** [10 x 26]

- Synoptics: θεός 223x + χριστός 35x + πνεῦμα 78x = **336x** [14 x 24]

- Gospels+Acts: θεός 469x + χριστός 79x + πνεῦμα 172x = **720x** [2 x 15 x 24 = 3 x 10 x 24]

- 1–2 Pet: θεός 46x + χριστός 30x + πνεῦμα 9x = **85x** [5 x 17]

- 1–2 Cor: θεός 184x + χριστός 111x + πνεῦμα 57x = **352x** [4 x 4 x 22]

- Col: θεός 21x + χριστός 25x + πνεῦμα 2x = **48x** [2 x 24]

- 1 Thess: θεός 36x + χριστός 10x + πνεῦμα 5x = **51x** [3 x 17]

- 1–2 Tim: θεός 34x + χριστός 28x + πνεῦμα 6x = **68x** [4 x 17]

---

11. 1 Clem. 46.6 reads: "Do we not have one GOD and one CHRIST and one SPIRIT of grace having been poured out upon us" (1 Clem. 46.6; trans. Michael Holmes, modified; *nomina sacra*—as in Codex Alexandrinus—in small caps).

- Pauline Corpus: θεός 614x + χριστός 394x + πνεῦμα 158x = 1166x [53 x 22][12]

Comment 4: Regarding the NrN figures that exclusively or inclusively involve Luke and/or Acts above (xi), we may note *the potential significance of all factors* involved, that is, 10, 17, 24 and 26. The beautiful numerical constellation for Luke and Acts, **170 [10 x 17]** and **260 [10 x 26] occurrences**, respectively—alluding to the two numerical values associated with the Tetragrammaton—is here of special interest (for potential numerical function of 10, see table 5.1 above).[13] Similarly the figures for the Synoptics and Gospels+Acts, which involve multiples of 14 and 15 (see table 5.1 above for potential significance of these numerals: 10, 14 and 15):

- Luke: θεός + χριστός + πνεῦμα = **170x [10 x 17]**

- Acts: θεός + χριστός + πνεῦμα = **260x [10 x 26]**

- Synoptics: θεός + χριστός + πνεῦμα = **336x [14 x 24]**

- Gospels+Acts: θεός + χριστός + πνεῦμα = **720x [2 x 15 x 24]**

Comment 5: For numbers between 1 and 500, 101 numbers are NrN, containing multiples of 22, 24, 27, 17 and 26, that is 20.2 percent, or one in five. That is, if the above figures (listed under xi) have not been deliberately

---

12. In addition, 1–3 John: θεός 67x + χριστός 11x + πνεῦμα 12x = **90x [6 x 15]**; and the 27-book NT: θεός 1312x + χριστός 529x + πνεῦμα 379x = **2220x [148 x 15]**. See table 5.1 for potential significance of 15.

13. Cf. the similar NrN frequencies in NA28 for "God," ὁ θεός, in Acts and Luke-Acts: Acts 153 occurrences [9 x 17] and Luke-Acts 260 occurrences [10 x 26]; and for θεός in Luke-Acts in Codex Sinaiticus (א): 288 occurrences [12 x 24]; and for the *nomen sacrum* "God" in the genitive in א: ΘΝ in Luke-Acts: 136 occurrences [8 x 17]; and for the *nomen sacrum* "God" in the accusative in א: ΘΝ in Luke: 26 occurrences; moreover for the *nomen sacrum* "Lord" in the nominative in א: ΚϹ in Acts: 22 occurrences, and in Luke-Acts: 54 occurrences [2 x 27]; further, in the genitive, dative and accusative in א: ΚΥ 27 occurrences in Luke (including genitive forms of κύριος, a few other words, and the letter combination κυ at the end of a line); κω in Luke-Acts (including dative forms of κύριος, a few other words, and the letter combination κω at the end of a line): 26 occurrences; ΚΝ in Luke-Acts: 22 occurrences in Luke-Acts; and κε in Luke (including vocative forms of κύριος, a few other words, and the letter combination κε at the end of a line): 27 occurrences (and 45 occurrences [3 x 15] in Luke-Acts; 44 occurrences [2 x 22] in Matthew–Mark; 102 occurrences [6 x 17] in the fourfold Gospel; 120 occurrences [5 x 24] in the four Gospels+Acts; 17 occurrences in Corpus Paulinum; 14 in Revelation (for potential significance of 14, see table 5.1 above); and 153 occurrences [9 x 17] in the full NT).

introduced into the text as part of the NT, but are appearing randomly (contrary to the argument of the present chapter), ca. 20 percent of the above figures, or one in five, *in each case*, would be such a Name-related Numeral (NrN). That means that we get an unexpectedly high presence of NrN for the following canonical sub-units:

a) Luke and Acts (two NrN (Luke, Acts) out of two possibilities (Luke, Acts), that is 100 percent; alternatively, 67 percent if Luke-Acts as a canonical sub-unit is counted seaparately);

b) Gospels and Acts (four NrN (Luke, Acts, Synoptics, Gospels+Acts) out of eight possibilities (Matt, Mark, Luke, John, Synoptics, Luke-Acts, Four Gospels, Gospels+Acts, that is 50 percent); and

c) Corpus Paulinum (five NrN (1–2 Cor, Col, 1 Thess, 1–2 Tim, the Pauline Corpus) out of 18 possibilities (the fourteen Pauline letters counted individually, 1–2 Cor, 1–2 Thess, 1–2 Tim and the Pauline Corpus), that is 28 percent).

xii) for θεός + χριστός + πνεῦμα (singular forms; cf. 2 Cor 13:13 and 1 *Clem.* 46.6):

- 1 Pet: θεός 39x + χριστός **22x** + πνεῦμα 7x = **68x** [4 x 17]

- 1 John: θεός 62x + χριστός 8x + πνεῦμα 11x = **81x** [3 x 27 = 3 x 3 x 3 x 3]

- 1 Cor: θεός 103x + χριστός 64x + πνεῦμα 37x = **204x** [12 x 17]

- Heb: θεός **68x** + χριστός 12x + πνεῦμα 8x = **88x** [4 x 22]

- NT: θεός 1304x + χριστός 529x + πνεῦμα 345x = **2178x** [99 x 22]

Comment 6: As for the items listed in xi–xii above, we may especially note the NrN for the Petrine letters (67 percent NrN), the two Pauline epistles to the Corinthians (67 percent NrN) and the seven items involving the Pauline Corpus (1 Cor, 1–2 Cor, Col, 1 Thess, 1–2 Tim, Heb, Corpus Paulinum; 39 percent NrN), which, again, may indicate that these NrN are not just randomly occurring:

- 1–2 Pet: θεός + χριστός + πνεῦμα = 85x [5 x 17]

- 1 Pet: θεός + χριστός + πνεῦμα (sg.) = 68x [4 x 17]

- 1–2 Cor: θεός + χριστός + πνεῦμα = 352x [4 x 4 x 22]

- 1 Cor: θεός + χριστός + πνεῦμα (sg.) = 204x [3 x 4 x 17]

- Pauline Corpus: θεός + χριστός + πνεῦμα = 1166x [53 x 22]

xiii) for θεός + κύριος + πνεῦμα (cf. Rom 1:4):
- Four Gospels: θεός 304x + κύριος 254x + πνεῦμα 102x = **660x** [2 x 15 x 22 = 3 x 10 x 22]

- Gospels+Acts: θεός 469x + κύριος 362x + πνεῦμα 172x = **1003x** [59 x 17][14]

- 1–2 Thess: θεός **54x** + κύριος 46x + πνεῦμα 8x = **108x** [4 x 27 = 4 x 3 x 3 x 3][15]

xiv) for θεός + κύριος + πνεῦμα (singular forms; cf. Rom 1:4):
- 1 Pet: θεός 39x + κύριος 8x + πνεῦμα 7x = **54x** [2 x 27 = 2 x 3 x 3 x 3]

- 2 Pet: θεός 7x + κύριος 14x + πνεῦμα 1x = **22x**

- Catholic Epistles: θεός 133x + κύριος 42x + πνεῦμα 23x = **198x** [9 x 22 = 3 x 3 x 22]

- Gal: θεός 30x + κύριος 6x + πνεῦμα 18x = **54x** [2 x 27 = 2 x 3 x 3 x 3]

- 1–2 Thess: θεός **54x** + κύριος 46x + πνεῦμα 8x = **108x** [4 x 27 = 4 x 3 x 3 x 3] (same as in xiii above)

---

14. 59 is the 17th prime number.

15. In addition, Mark: θεός 49x + κύριος 18x + πνεῦμα 23x = **90x** [6 x 15]. See table 5.1 for potential significance of 15. Numerologically, 4 x 3 x 3 x 3 may signify the Triune Name (3 x 3 x 3) for all people (4; cf. table 5.1).

Comment 7: In xiv above, we may note the high presence of *NrN* for 1 and 2 Peter (67 percent *NrN*) and the Catholic Epistles (50 percent *NrN*). Since the Johannine epistles lack the word κύριος, for the Catholic Epistles we are here dealing with altogether six canonical sub-units that contain all three words, θεός, κύριος and πνεῦμα (Jam, 1 Pet, 2 Pet, 1–2 Pet, Jude and the seven-letter Catholic Epistles collection). Of these six sub-units we encounter *NrN* in three cases, namely for 1 Pet (**54 occurrences [2 x 27]**), 2 Pet (**22 occurrences**), and the Catholic Epistles (**198 occurrences [9 x 22]**), that is, in 50 percent of the possible cases.

xv) θεός + Ἰησοῦς χριστός + πνεῦμα (cf. Rom 15:30)

- 1–2 Pet: θεός 46x + Ἰησοῦς χριστός **17x** + πνεῦμα 9x = **72x** [3 x 24 = 3 x 3 x 8]

- 2 Cor: θεός 79x + Ἰησοῦς χριστός 6x + πνεῦμα **17x** = **102x** [6 x 17 = 2 x 3 x 17]

- 1–2 Cor: θεός 184x + Ἰησοῦς χριστός 19x + πνεῦμα 57x = **260x** [10 x 26]

- Col: θεός 21x + Ἰησοῦς χριστός 1x + πνεῦμα 2x = **24x** [3 x 8]

- 2 Tim: θεός 12x + Ἰησοῦς χριστός 2x + πνεῦμα 3x = **17x**

- Tit: θεός 13x + Ἰησοῦς χριστός 3x + πνεῦμα 1x = **17x**[16]

xvi) θεός + Ἰησοῦς χριστός + πνεῦμα (singular forms; cf. Rom 15:30)

- Luke-Acts: θεός 284x + Ἰησοῦς χριστός 11x + πνεῦμα **96x** = **391x** [23 x 17]

- Four Gospels: θεός 302x + Ἰησοῦς χριστός 5x + πνεῦμα 89x = **396x** [18 x 22 = 2 x 3 x 3 x 22]

---

16. The Triune structure θεός + χριστός Ἰησοῦς + πνεῦμα gives the following results for Corpus Paulinum: θεός 614x + χριστός Ἰησοῦς 83x + πνεῦμα 158x = 855x [57 x 15] (for potential significance of the number 15, see table 5.1, ch. 5 below).

- Catholic Epistles: θεός 133x + Ἰησοῦς χριστός 33x + πνεῦμα 23x = **189x** [7 x 27 = 7 x 3 x 3 x 3]

- 1 Cor: θεός 103x + Ἰησοῦς χριστός 13x + πνεῦμα 37x = **153x** [**9 x 17** = 3 x 3 x 17]

- 2 Cor: θεός 79x + Ἰησοῦς χριστός 6x + πνεῦμα **17x** = **102x** [6 x 17 = **2 x 3 x 17**] (same as in xv above)

- 1–2 Cor: θεός **182x** + Ἰησοῦς χριστός 19x + πνεῦμα **54x** = **255x** [**15 x 17** = 3 x 5 x 17]

- 2 Tim: θεός 12x + Ἰησοῦς χριστός 2x + πνεῦμα 3x = **17x** (same as in xv above)

- Tit: θεός 13x + Ἰησοῦς χριστός 3x + πνεῦμα 1x = **17x** (same as in xv above)

Comment 8: In xv and xvi above, we may particularly notice the presence of *NrN* in the Catholic Epistles, for 1–2 Pet (xv) and for the seven-letter collection (xvi): 1–2 Pet: θεός + Ἰησοῦς χριστός + πνεῦμα = **72 occurrences** [3 x 24] and the seven Catholic Epistles (forms in the singular): θεός + Ἰησοῦς χριστός + πνεῦμα = **189 occurrences** [7 x 27]. A very high representation of *NrN* is further found in the Corinthian epistles (67 percent in xv; 100 percent in xiv; and 83 percent in xv+xvi); similarly in the Pastoral Epistles (50 percent *NrN* in xv and xvi; alternatively 75 percent, if 1–2 Tim **45 occurrences** [3 x 15] is included as a *NrN*, as in the next Chapter (Chapter 7), where we will count also 15-multiples among the *NrN*):

- 2 Cor: θεός + Ἰησοῦς χριστός + πνεῦμα = **102x** [6 x 17]

- 1–2 Cor: θεός + Ἰησοῦς χριστός + πνεῦμα = **260x** [10 x 26]

- 1 Cor: θεός + Ἰησοῦς χριστός + πνεῦμα (sg.) = **153x** [9 x 17]

- 2 Cor: θεός + Ἰησοῦς χριστός + πνεῦμα (sg.) = **102x** [6 x 17]

- 1–2 Cor: θεός + Ἰησοῦς χριστός + πνεῦμα (sg.) = 255x [15 x 17]

- 2 Tim: θεός + Ἰησοῦς χριστός + πνεῦμα = 17x

- Tit: θεός + Ἰησοῦς χριστός + πνεῦμα = 17x

xvii) θεός + υἱός + πνεῦμα (cf. Gal 4:6)
- Four Gospels: θεός 304x + υἱός 257x + πνεῦμα 102x = 663x [3 x 13 x 17 = 17 x 39] (see table 5.1 for potential significance of 39)

  - 1 Pet: θεός 39x + υἱός 1x + πνεῦμα 8x = 48x [2 x 24]

  - 1 John: θεός 62x + υἱός 22x + πνεῦμα 12x = 96x [4 x 24]

  - 1 Thess: θεός 36x + υἱός 3x + πνεῦμα 5x = 44x [2 x 22]

  - 2 Thess: θεός 18x + υἱός 1x + πνεῦμα 3x = 22x

  - 1–2 Thess: θεός 54x + υἱός 4x + πνεῦμα 8x = 66x [3 x 22]

  - Heb: θεός 68x + υἱός 24x + πνεῦμα 12x = 104x [4 x 26]

  - Pauline Corpus: θεός 614x + υἱός 65x + πνεῦμα 158x = 837x [31 x 27 = 31 x 3 x 3 x 3]

xviii) θεός + υἱός + πνεῦμα (singular forms; cf. Gal 4:6)
- Acts: θεός 162x + υἱός 10x + πνεῦμα 66x = 238x [14 x 17]

  - 1–3 John: θεός 67x + υἱός 24x + πνεῦμα 11x = 102x [6 x 17]

  - Rom: θεός 153x + υἱός 8x + πνεῦμα 34x = 195x [13 x 15 = 5 x 39] (cf. table 5.1 ch.5 above for potential significance of 15 and 39)

  - Col: θεός 21x + υἱός 1x + πνεῦμα 2x = 24x

  - 2 Thess: θεός 18x + υἱός 1x + πνεῦμα 3x = 22x

Comment 9: The Pauline Epistles appear in these two final examples (xvii and xviii) of Triune structures with high representation of NrN. Since the term "son," υἱός, only occurs in altogether twelve Pauline canonical sub-units (Rom, 1 Cor, 2 Cor, 1–2 Cor, Gal, Eph, Col, 1 Thess, 2 Thess, 1–2 Thess, Heb and the 14-letter Pauline Corpus; excluding Phil, 1 Tim, 2 Tim, 1–2 Tim, Tit and Phlm), the five Triune Pauline sub-unit structures in xvii above that embrace NrN (namely 1 Thess, 2 Thess, 1–2 Thess, Heb and the full Pauline Corpus) make up 42 percent of the total number of Pauline canonical sub-units containing this particular Triune structure, θεός + υἱός + πνεῦμα. Of these five units the Thessalonian epistles exhibit 100 percent NrN (1 Thess, 2 Thess, and 1–2 Thess), all of which are 22-multiples:

- 1 Thess: θεός + υἱός + πνεῦμα = **44x** [**2 x 22**]

- 2 Thess: θεός + υἱός + πνεῦμα = **22x**

- 1–2 Thess: θεός + υἱός + πνεῦμα = **66x** [**3 x 22**]

- Heb: θεός + υἱός + πνεῦμα = **104x** [**4 x 26**]

- Pauline Corpus: θεός + υἱός + πνεῦμα = **837x** [**31 x 27 = 31 x 3 x 3 x 3**]

Comment 10: Pertaining to the varying Triune NrN structures above, we noted in particular the high NrN representation in Matthew (five different Triune matrices related to the Triune pattern in Matt 28:19; *Comment 1*); the fourfold Gospel, involving an alphabetical squared number potentially signifying special holiness (**729** [**27 x 27**]; *Comment 3*); the Lukan writings (*Comment 3*); the perfect figures involving Triune patterns in Luke and Acts (**170** [**10 x 17**] and **260** [**10 x 26**]), relating to the Tetragrammaton (*Comment 4*); the Petrine and Corinthian epistles (*Comment 6*); Paul's letters to the Corinthians (*Comment 8*); and the Pauline Epistles (*Comment 9*). In addition, we may note the overall high representation in these examples (i-xviii) of NrN in the four Gospels, 1 and 2 Peter, Corpus Paulinum and the full New Testament (cf. Matt 28:19, Rom 1:4 and 2 Cor 13:13):

Four Gospels:

- Four Gospels: πατήρ + υἱός + ἅγιος πνεῦμα (singular forms) = 486x [18 x 27]

- Four Gospels: ὄνομα (sg. nom./acc.) + πατρός + υἱοῦ + ἁγίου πνεύματος = 120x [5 x 24]

- Four Gospels: ὄνομα (sg. nom./acc.) + πατρός + υἱοῦ + πνεύματος = 135x [5 x 27]

- Four Gospels: ὄνομα + πατήρ + υἱός + πνεῦμα = 729x [27 x 27]

- Four Gospels: θεός + κύριος + πνεῦμα = 660x [2 x 15 x 22]

Comment 11: Regarding the fourfold Gospel, the following observations may be made: a) the five NrN above are all alphabetical multiples, one of which is a square number, namely 729 [27²], which may indicate special holiness (see Comment 3 above); b) altogether four different Triune configurations are involved in the above five NrN, namely: πατήρ + υἱός + ἅγιος πνεῦμα, ὄνομα + πατήρ + υἱός + ἅγιος πνεῦμα, ὄνομα + πατήρ + υἱός + πνεῦμα, and θεός + κύριος + πνεῦμα; c) of the four Triune NrN configurations involved, one occurs twice (ὄνομα + πατήρ + υἱός + πνεῦμα) and contains a squared alphabetical numeral, namely, again, 729 [27²]; and d) three of the five NrN above contain two factors of potential numerological significance, noted in table 5.1 above—namely 486x [18 x 27], 729x [27 x 27] and 660x [2 x 15 x 22] (i.e., the factors 18 and 27; 27 and 27; and 15 and 22). Taken together, observations a–d indicate that these NrN may have been intended on the part of editors, scribes and authors prior to and during the editing of the final canonical text-form.

1 and 2 Peter:

- 1–2 Pet: θεός + χριστός + πνεῦμα = 85x [5 x 17]

- 1 Pet: θεός + χριστός + πνεῦμα (sg.) = 68x [4 x 17]

- 1 Pet: θεός + κύριος + πνεῦμα = 54x [2 x 27]

- 2 Pet: θεός + κύριος + πνεῦμα = **22x**

- 1–2 Pet: θεός + Ἰησοῦς χριστός + πνεῦμα = **72x** [3 x 24]

- 1 Pet: θεός + υἱός + πνεῦμα = **48x** [2 x 24]

Comment 12: Several Triune NrN structures are included as well in the texts of 1 and 2 Peter. The pattern θεός + χριστός + πνεῦμα, which we find in 1 Pet (θεός + χριστός + πνεῦμα (forms in the singular) **68 occurrences** [4 x 17]), occurs as a triadic structure also in other early Christian texts (e.g., 2 Cor 13:13 and 1 *Clem.* 46.6). I tend to think that this is an early layer also in the Petrine literature, occurring as a 17-multiple in 1 Pet (17-multiples for the same Triune structure is also found in other portions of the NT (1 Cor, 1 Thess)). Among the Petrine letters, 1 Pet is worth noting with its three NrN linked to three different Triune configurations: θεός + χριστός + πνεῦμα **68 occurrences** [4 x 17], θεός + κύριος + πνεῦμα **54 occurrences** [2 x 27], and θεός + υἱός + πνεῦμα **48 occurrences** [2 x 24]. Moreover, in 1–2 Pet two Triune structures are linked to NrN, namely θεός + χριστός + πνεῦμα **85 occurrences** [5 x 17] and θεός + Ἰησοῦς χριστός + πνεῦμα **72 occurrences** [3 x 24].

Corpus Paulinum:

- Pauline Corpus: πατήρ + υἱός + ἅγιος πνεῦμα = **104x** [4 x 26]

- Pauline Corpus: πατήρ + υἱός = **102x** [6 x 17]

- Pauline Corpus: θεός + χριστός + πνεῦμα = **1166x** [53 x 22]

- Pauline Corpus: θεός + υἱός + πνεῦμα = **837x** [31 x 27]

Comment 13: As in the case with the fourfold Gospel, the above Triune NrN configurations in Corpus Paulinum demonstrate the presence of a variety of Triune structures also in the Pauline epistles, namely the following three, arguably recognized and intended by the editors of the 14-letter corpus: πατήρ + υἱός + ἅγιος πνεῦμα, θεός + χριστός + πνεῦμα, and θεός + υἱός + πνεῦμα. We may further note that of our five categories of NrN (multiples of 17 and 26, on the one hand, and of 22/27 and 24, on

the other), the editors of the Pauline Corpus have included only multiples
of the main Hebrew numerals (17 and 26, on the one hand, and 22 and
27, on the other; excluding the Greek alphabetical numeral 24). Another
detail to notice, with regard to NrN, is the Triune structure πατήρ + υἱός
+ ἅγιος πνεῦμα 104x [4 x 26], which is at the same time a dyadic structure,
πατήρ + υἱός 102x [6 x 17]. The corresponding NrN for 1–2 Cor is πατήρ
+ υἱός 17 occurrences (see below; cf. the later Eastern creedal Triune
structures, emphasizing the oneness of Father and Son, according to the
pattern outlined in 1 Cor 8:6; see further 11.2–11.6 below).

1 and 2 Corinthians:

- 1–2 Cor: πατήρ + υἱός = 17x

- 1–2 Cor: πατήρ + υἱός + πνεῦμα (sg.) = 66x [3 x 22]

- 1–2 Cor: θεός + χριστός + πνεῦμα = 352x [4 x 4 x 22]

- 1 Cor: θεός + χριστός + πνεῦμα (sg.) = 204x [3 x 4 x 17]

- 2 Cor: θεός + Ἰησοῦς χριστός + πνεῦμα = 102x [2 x 3 x 17]

- 1–2 Cor: θεός + Ἰησοῦς χριστός + πνεῦμα = 260x [10 x 26]

- 1 Cor: θεός + Ἰησοῦς χριστός + πνεῦμα (sg.) = 153x [3 x 3 x 17]

- 2 Cor: θεός + Ἰησοῦς χριστός + πνεῦμα (sg.) = 102x [2 x 3 x 17]

- 1–2 Cor: θεός + Ἰησοῦς χριστός + πνεῦμα (sg.) = 255x [3 x 5 x 17]

Comment 14: The above Triune arithmetical results for the two Corinthian
letters, involving three canonical sub-units (1 Cor, 2 Cor and 1–2 Cor)
demonstrate an impressive array of nine NrN (eight different figures, since
two of the items are identical). If we assume that the Triune configurations
in 1 Cor contain an earlier textual layer, as compared to that of 2 Cor and
1–2 Cor, a) we may note two early Triune structures in 1 Cor, namely the
altogether 204 occurrences [3 x 4 x 17] for θεός + χριστός + πνεῦμα (sg.)
and the 153 [3 x 3 x 17] for θεός + Ἰησοῦς χριστός + πνεῦμα (sg.)— both of
which are 17-multiples (we may also notice that these two Triune NrN

stuctures, together with that of 2 Cor, all contain the factor "three," once as a squared number: 3 x 3); b) the key Triune arithmetical structure for 1 Cor here seems to be forms in the singular of θεός + χριστός (alternatively Ἰησοῦς χριστός) + πνεῦμα, which is the same early Triune structure that we find as well, e.g., in 2 Cor 13:13 and in 1 *Clem.* 46.6.

1 and 2 Thessalonians:

- 1–2 Thess: ὄνομα + πατήρ + υἱός + πνεῦμα = **22x**

- 1 Thess: θεός + χριστός + πνεῦμα = **51x** [**3 x 17**]

- 1–2 Thess: θεός + κύριος + πνεῦμα = **108x** [**4 x 27**]

- 1–2 Thess: θεός + κύριος + πνεῦμα (sg.)= **108x** [**4 x 27**]

- 1 Thess: θεός + υἱός + πνεῦμα **44x** = [**2 x 22**]

- 2 Thess: θεός + υἱός + πνεῦμα = **22x**

- 1–2 Thess: θεός + υἱός + πνεῦμα = **66x** [**3 x 22**]

- 2 Thess: θεός + υἱός + πνεῦμα (sg.) = **22x**

Comment 15: As in the case with 1 Cor above (*Comment 14*), we may presume also in the case of the Thessalonian letters that textual–Triune configurations in 1 Thess may be the earliest when compared with those in 2 Thess and 1–2 Thess. For 1 Thess, too, a 17-multiple appears for the arguably early Triune structure θεός + χριστός + πνεῦμα = **51 occurrences** [**3 x 17**]. Triune figures displaying alphabetical multiples may have been introduced slightly later into the texts,[17] as exemplified by the rest of the items above, involving 2 Thess and 1–2 Thess, and the following Triune patterns: ὄνομα + πατήρ + υἱός + πνεῦμα (1–2 Thess), θεός + κύριος + πνεῦμα (1–2 Thess), and θεός + υἱός + πνεῦμα (2 Thess, 1–2 Thess). Overall, two Triune *NrN* structures are noted for 1 Thess (θεός + χριστός + πνεῦμα 51 [**3 x 17**] and θεός + υἱός + πνεῦμα **44x** [**2 x 22**]), one additional

---

17. As for the question of dating early Christian use of *NrN* (*NrN* pertaining to the divine Name being slightly earlier than alphabetical *NrN* in the Pauline writings) see also Bokedal, "'But for Me, the Scriptures are Jesus Christ.'".

NrN for 2 Thess (θεός + υἱός + πνεῦμα 22x) and, finally, three NrN for
1–2 Thess (ὄνομα + πατήρ + υἱός + πνεῦμα 22x, θεός + κύριος + πνεῦμα
108x [4 x 27] and θεός + υἱός + πνεῦμα 66x [3 x 22]). As we saw examples of above (*Comment 14*), the factor "three" is present also as part of
the following triadic/Triune NrN pertaining to 1 Thess and 1–2 Thess:
1 Thess: **51 occurrences** [3 x 17]; 1–2 Thess: **108 occurrences** [4 x 27 =
4 x 3 x 3 x 3]; and 1–2 Thess: **66 occurrences** [3 x 22].

The full New Testament:

- NT: πατήρ + υἱός + ἅγιος πνεῦμα = **680 occurrences** [4 x
  10 x 17]

- NT: ὁ πατήρ + ὁ υἱός + ὁ πνεῦμα = **726 occurrences** [3 x
  11 x 22]

- NT: ὁ πατήρ + ὁ υἱός = **550 occurrences** [5 x 5 x 22]

- NT: ὄνομα (sg. nom./acc.) + πατρός + υἱοῦ + πνεύματος =
  338 occurrences [13 x 26]

- NT: ὄνομα +πατήρ + υἱός + πνεῦμα (sg.) = **1232 occurrences**
  [4 x 14 x 22]

- NT: πα* <AND> υιο* <AND> πνεῦμα = **22 occurrences**

- NT: πα* <AND> υιος <AND> πνεῦμα = **17 occurrences**

- NT: θεός + χριστός + πνεῦμα (sg.) = **2178 occurrences** [3 x
  3 x 11 x 22]

Comment 16: Two basic Triune structures are represented in this list of
NrN that involves the full New Testament, namely the following: a) πατήρ
+ υἱός + πνεῦμα (rendered in seven various forms in the list above) and b)
θεός + χριστός + πνεῦμα. In the following two examples of triadic/Triune
NrN above, representing structures a and b, the factor "three" is present:
NT: ὁ πατήρ + ὁ υἱός + ὁ πνεῦμα = **726 occurrences** [3 x 11 x 22] (structure a); and NT: θεός + χριστός + πνεῦμα (sg.) = **2178 occurrences** [3 x

3 x 11 x 22] (structure b; including the number three squared, 3 x 3; for potential numerological significance of 11, see table 5.1 above).

As for the two Triune structures above in the full New Testament that include the term ὄνομα we may note the inclusion of the numeral 13, on the one hand (with possible reference to the oneness of God; see further table 5.1 above), and the number 14, on the other (with possible reference to the Davidic Messiah; see further table 5.1 above): NT: ὄνομα (sg. nom./ acc.) + πατρός + υἱοῦ + πνεύματος **338 occurrences** [13 x 26]; and NT: ὄνομα + πατήρ + υἱός + πνεῦμα **1232 occurrences** [4 x 14 x 22].

The two basic Triune NrN patterns above (a and b) attained a central place in the development of Triune theology from early on (Matt 28:19; Did. 7.1, 3; 2 Cor 13:13; 1 *Clem.* 46.6 and 58.2). When, in the next section, we take a brief look also at similar Triune configurations in three Greek church fathers, we shall see that the same basic NrN patterns (a) πατήρ + υἱός + πνεῦμα and b) θεός + χριστός / Ἰησοῦς χριστός + πνεῦμα) are represented in each of these theologians: Basil the Great, Athanasius and Eusebius.

6.3 TRIUNE TEXTUAL PATTERNS
IN EARLY CHURCH FATHERS

Similar Triune textual patterns, as those discussed above, are common as well in some early church fathers, such as Basil the Great (ca. 330–379 AD), Athanasius (ca. 296–373 AD) and Eusebius (ca. 260–339 AD), in whom we find the following Trinitarian configurations, multiples of which are linked to alphabetical fullness (22, 24 and 27) or divine Name numerals (17 and 26):[18]

---

18. In the first two illustrations below (Basil the Great and Athanasius), arithmetically noted Triune word patterns are found for searches in Accordance 13 on the form θεός <AND> πατήρ <AND> υἱός <AND> πνεῦμα, where the constellation of included words appear in the same verse/passage. In the first example, 20 verses/passages in Basil's *On the Holy Spirit* are involved and the following figures are included in the count: θεός 32x + πατήρ 25x + υἱός **27x** + πνεῦμα 52x [2 x 26] = **136x** [8 x 17]. In the third illustration (Eusebius), arithmetically noted Triune and dyadic structures occur in Accordance 13 on the form πατήρ + υἱός, where the included words are counted separately before being added. In this particular example, the following figures appear for *Hist. Eccl.* vol. 7: πατήρ 12x + υἱός 5x = **17x.**

Basil the Great, On the Holy Spirit (*Migne, Accordance* 13; textual scope: verse)

- θεός <AND> πατήρ <AND> υἱός <AND> πνεῦμα **136x** [8 x 17]

- ὁ θεός <AND> ὁ πατήρ <AND> ὁ υἱός <AND> ὁ πνεῦμα **22x**

- θεός <AND> χριστός <AND> πνεῦμα **130x** [5 x 26]

- ὁ υἱός <AND> ὁ θεός **52x** [2 x 26]

- θεός (242x [11x22]) + υἱός (183x) = **425x** [5 x 5 x 17]

- πνεῦμα <AND> ἅγιος **312x** [13 x 24 = 12 x 26 = 3 x 4 x 26]

Athanasius, Arians and Serapion (*Migne, Accordance* 13; textual scope: verse)

- ὁ πατήρ <AND> ὁ υἱός <AND> ὁ πνεῦμα *Serapion* **675x** [5 x 5 x 27 = 5 x 5 x 3 x 3 x 3]

- ὁ ὄνομα <AND> ὁ πατήρ <AND> ὁ υἱός <AND> ὁ πνεῦμα *Serapion* **288x** [12 x 24 = 3 x 4 x 24]

- θεός <AND> κύριος <AND> πνεῦμα *Arians* **352x** [16 x 22 = 4 x 4 x 22]

- θεός <AND> Ἰησοῦς χριστός <AND> πνεῦμα *Arians* **54x** [2 x 27 = 2 x 3 x 3 x 3]

- θεός <AND> Ἰησοῦς χριστός <AND> πνεῦμα *Serapion* **308x** [14 x 22]

- ὁ θεός <AND> Ἰησοῦς χριστός <AND> ὁ πνεῦμα *Arians* + *Serapion* **240x** [10 x 24]

- ὁ υἱός <AND> ὁ θεός *Serapion* **378x** [14 x 27 = 14 x 3 x 3 x 3]

Eusebius, Ecclesiastical History (*Migne, Accordance 13*)

- πατήρ + υἱός *Hist. Eccl.* vols. 1–10 **170x [10 x 17]**, vol. 7 **17x**, vol. 10 **27x [3 x 3 x 3]** [19]

- ὄνομα + πατήρ + υἱός *Hist. Eccl.* vols. 1–10 **288x [12 x 24 = 3 x 4 x 24]**, vol. 7 **27x [3 x 3 x 3]**

- ὄνομα + πατήρ + υἱός + πνεῦμα *Hist. Eccl.* vols. 1–10 **374x [22 x 17]**, vol. 5 **68x [4 x 17]**, vol. 10 **44x [2 x 22]**

- θεός + χριστός + πνεῦμα *Hist. Eccl.* vols. 1–10 **816x [2 x 24 x 17 = 3 x 4 x 4 x 17]**, vol. 4 **52x [2 x 26]**, vol. 10 **104x [4 x 26]**

- ὁ θεός + ὁ χριστός + ὁ πνεῦμα *Hist. Eccl.* vols. 1–10 **384x [16 x 24 = 4 x 4 x 24]**, vol. 2 **34x [2 x 17]**, vol. 4 **26x**, vol. 6 **24x**, vol. 9 **17x** [20]

The first thing to note regarding the above NrN patterns from three Greek church fathers is the varying methodology arguably embraced to detect NrN, namely the two different methods used above; on the one hand that employed in 6.1 (search in Accordance 13 on the form θεός <AND> χριστός <AND> πνεῦμα), and, on the other, the method used in 6.2 (search for number of occurrences in Accordance 13 for each of the included words separately, followed by addition of the emerging results: number of occurrences of θεός + number of occurrences of χριστός + number of occurrences of πνεῦμα). In the texts by Basil the Great and Athanasius the authors/editors appear to have employed the first of these methods (discussed in 6.1 above), whereas Eusebius in his *Ecclesiastical History* seems to have used the second (discussed in 6.2 above; for further similar examples, see also section 8.1 below on Ignatius of Antioch).

The next thing to notice is, again, the various Triune NrN patterns that are found in each of these texts. Three Triune NrN figures in Basil

---

19. πατήρ + υἱός *Hist. Eccl.* vols. 1–10 **170x [10 x 17]** (πατήρ 118x + υἱός 52x [2 x 26] = 170x [10 x 17]), vol. 7 **17x** (πατήρ 12x + υἱός 5x = 17x), vol. 10 **27x** (πατήρ 19x + υἱός 8x = 27x).

20. The corresponding Triune configuration for Acts is: ὁ θεός 151x + ὁ χριστός 10x + ὁ πνεῦμα 37x = **198x [9 x 22]**; and for Corpus Paulinum: ὁ θεός 28x + ὁ χριστός 92x + ὁ πνεῦμα 67x = **187x [11 x 17]**; and, again, for Corpus Paulinum, the dyadic arithmetical structure: ὁ θεός 28x + ὁ χριστός 92x = **120x [5 x 24]**; moreover, for Ephesians ὁ θεός 22x + ὁ χριστός 23x + ὁ πνεῦμα 7x = **52x [2 x 26]**; and for 1–2 Tim ὁ θεός 15x + ὁ χριστός 1x + ὁ πνεῦμα 1x = **17x**.

the Great *On the Holy Spirit*, namely the following: θεός <AND> πατήρ <AND> υἱός <AND> πνεῦμα **136 occurrences** [8 x 17]; ὁ θεός <AND> ὁ πατήρ <AND> ὁ υἱός <AND> ὁ πνεῦμα **22 occurrences**; and θεός <AND> χριστός <AND> πνεῦμα **130 occurrences** [5 x 26]. Similarly in Athanasius's *Letter to Serapion*, with the following three Triune *NrN* structures: ὁ πατήρ <AND> ὁ υἱός <AND> ὁ πνεῦμα **675 occurrences** [5 x 5 x 27]; ὁ ὄνομα <AND> ὁ πατήρ <AND> ὁ υἱός <AND> ὁ πνεῦμα **288 occurrences** [12 x 24]; and θεός <AND> Ἰησοῦς χριστός <AND> πνεῦμα **308 occurrences** [14 x 22]. In Eusebius's *Historia Ecclesiastica*, too, the following three Triune *NrN* structures may be noted: ὄνομα + πατήρ + υἱός + πνεῦμα vols. 1–10 **374 occurrences** [22 x 17], vol. 5 **68 occurrences** [4 x 17], vol. 10 **44 occurrences** [2 x 22]; θεός + χριστός + πνεῦμα vols. 1–10 **816 occurrences** [2 x 24 x 17], vol. 4 **52 occurrences** [2 x 26], vol. 10 **104 occurrences** [4 x 26]; and ὁ θεός + ὁ χριστός + ὁ πνεῦμα vols. 1–10 **384 occurrences** [16 x 24], vol. 2 **34 occurrences** [2 x 17], vol. 4 **26 occurrences**, vol. 6 **24 occurrences**, and vol. 9 **17 occurrences**.

6.4 CONCLUDING REMARKS

In this chapter we focused special attention on various triadic/Triune textual configurations in the New Testament (6.1 and 6.2)—some of which are already well known to biblical scholars, such as: "The grace of the LORD JESUS CHRIST, the love of GOD, and the communion of the Holy SPIRIT be with all of you" (2 Cor 13:13; NRSV, modified). By counting the number of occurrences of each of the items included in Triune structures appearing in one and the same verse/passage, we noted that these may occur with frequencies aligned with what I label *Name-related Numerals* (*NrN*), indirectly or directly pertaining to the divine Name (i.e., multiples of the three alphabetical numerals 22, 24 or 27, on the one hand, and 17 and 26, associated with the numerical value of the Tetragrammaton, on the other; *NrN* in boldface below).

One of the noted examples in the present chapter (based on search in Accordance 13) was the Triune pattern θεός <AND> Ἰησοῦς χριστός <AND> πνεῦμα present across eight NT verses (Rom 1:4; 15:30; 1 Cor 6:11; 2 Cor 13:13; Eph 1:17; 1 Thess 5:23; 1 Pet 1:2; and 1 John 4:2) with the three words/expressions appearing altogether **26 times** (or **34 times** [2 x 17] if Ἰησοῦς and χριστός are counted separately; each word/expression counted separately; THGNT, NA28, ℵ; textual scope: verse; alternative figure when THGNT paragraph is used as textual scope: **182 times** [7 x 26]).

Another, more reliable, method (which does not depend on division of the NT text into verses) used in the chapter to detect Triune *NrN* structures instead added the individual occurrences in a canonical sub-unit of each of the words included in a Triune structure, such as θεός 79x + Ἰησοῦς χριστός 6x + πνεῦμα 17x = **102 occurrences** [6 x 17] in 2 Cor, and θεός 184x + Ἰησοῦς χριστός 19x + πνεῦμα 57x = **260 occurrences** [10 x 26] in 1–2 Cor. Some of these *NrN* appeared with full (100 percent) consistence across some canonical sub-units, such as the singular forms in 1 Cor, 2 Cor and 1–2 Cor of θεός + Ἰησοῦς χριστός + πνεῦμα, resulting in **153 occurrences** [9 x 17] (1 Cor), **102 occurrences** [6 x 17] (2 Cor) and **255 occurrences** [15 x 17] (1–2 Cor). Another noteworthy series of examples that appear to be editorially designed were the five different *NrN* structures of the Triune configuration πατήρ + υἱός + (ἅγιος) πνεῦμα in Matt 28:19, which all feature in Matthew's Gospel (*Comment 1* above, involving the following *NrN*):

- πατήρ + υἱός + ἅγιος πνεῦμα = **153 occurrences** [9 x 17]

- πατήρ + υἱός + ἅγιος πνεῦμα (singular forms) = **135 occurrences** [5 x 27]

- πατήρ + υἱός + πνεῦμα ἅγιος = **154 occurrences** [7 x 22]

- πατήρ + υἱός + πνεῦμα ἅγιος (singular forms) = **136 occurrences** [8 x 17]

- ὄνομα + πατήρ + υἱός + ἅγιος πνεῦμα = **176 occurrences** [8 x 22]

In addition to these five Triune numerical configurations, we may also observe the fourteen-multiple in the following related configuration in Matthew (cf. table 5.1 and appendix for potential significance of the number 14): ὄνομα (sg. nom./acc.) 11x + πατρός 21x + υἱοῦ 9x + ἁγίου πνεύματος 1x/πνεύματος ἁγίου 1x = 42x [3 x 14]. As we are here engaging triadic/Triune textual arithmetical structures, we noted above, as well the presence of the factor "three" in several of these NrN: **204 occurrences** [3 x 4 x 17] (1 Cor), **102 occurrences** [2 x 3 x 17] (2 Cor) and **255 occurrences** [3 x 5 x 17] (1–2 Cor). This included as well Triune structures embracing the full New Testament, as in the following two examples: ὁ πατήρ + ὁ υἱός + ὁ πνεῦμα = **726 occurrences** [3 x 11 x 22], and singular forms of θεός + χριστός + πνεῦμα = **2178 occurrences** [3 x 3 x 11 x 22].

Similar textual patterns were found, as well, in some early Greek fathers (6.3), such as the following Triune NrN structures: Basil the Great, *On the Holy Spirit*: θεός <AND> χριστός <AND> πνεῦμα **130 occurrences** [5 x 26]; Athanasius, *Arians*: θεός <AND> Ἰησοῦς χριστός <AND> πνεῦμα **54 occurrences** [2 x 27 = 2 x 3 x 3 x 3]; and Eusebius, *Historia Ecclesiastica*: θεός + χριστός + πνεῦμα vols. 1–10 **816 occurrences** [2 x 24 x 17 = 3 x 4 x 4 x 17], vol. 4 **52 occurrences** [2 x 26], and vol. 10 **104 occurrences** [4 x 26].

BIBLIOGRAPHY

Bokedal, Tomas. "'But for Me, the Scriptures are Jesus Christ' (I̅C̅ X̅C̅; Ign. *Phld.* 8:2): Creedal Text-Coding and the Early Scribal System of Nomina Sacra." In *Studies on the Paratextual Features of Early New Testament Manuscripts.* Edited by Stanley E. Porter, David I. Yoon, and Chris S. Stevens. TENTS. Leiden: Brill, forthcoming 2023.

Stevenson, Kalinda Rose. *The Vision of Transformation: The Territorial Rhetoric of Ezekiel 40–48.* SBLDS 154. Atlanta: Scholars Press, 1996.

7

NAME-RELATED NUMERALS IN THE NEW TESTAMENT: INNERTEXTUAL CANONICAL SHAPING

In line with the scriptural and patristic word-frequency figures discussed above (ch. 6), the present chapter sets out to explore the potential significance of broader textual arithmetic structures in the biblical canon—in particular with respect to the New Testament. We shall now continue looking at multiples of our two groups of *Name-related Numerals* (*NrN*); on the one hand, twenty-two, twenty-seven, and twenty-four, which are the number of consonants in the Hebrew alphabet (twenty-two/twenty-seven consonants/consonant forms) and the Hellenistic Greek alphabet (twenty-four letters), and, on the other hand, the numerical values associated with the four letters that make up the divine name, that is, seventeen or twenty-six, alternatively fifteen for the short-form יה, "Yah."[1] We shall see that word- and phrase-frequencies involving multi-

---

1. The Hebrew alphabetical consonants, or consonantal forms, are twenty-two, or twenty-seven, if the five end-letter forms (*kaph, mem, nun, pe,* and *tsade*) are included. Cf. Timothy H. Lim, *The Formation of the Jewish Canon*, AYBRL (New Haven: Yale University Press, 2013), 41 (quoted in note 2, Introduction, and note 4, ch. 5 above). With regard to the number twenty-four, cf. n. 2, Introduction, above. Fifteen is my own addition to the numerals seventeen and twenty-six, based on the frequent occurrence of multiples of all three numbers in word-frequency pattern in the Hebrew Bible, LXX, and New Testament texts, as well as in other early Greek Christian texts.

ples of these six numbers—fifteen, seventeen, and twenty-six, on the one
hand, and twenty-two, twenty-four, and twenty-seven, on the other—may
have recurrent textual significance throughout the Greek New Testament
material. *Name-related Numeral(s) (NrN)* are marked in boldface below.[2]

In what follows, I shall make a cumulative argument based on word
frequencies—by a series of three observations (observations 1–3)—involving the above two groups of numerals, suggesting that word-frequency
multiples of these (and a few additional) numbers are consistently present in the various canonical subunits that make up the New Testament.

For each of the three observations (observations 1–3), I shall list the
canonical textual subunits involved. Tentative implications of these observations for the textual structuring of the biblical canon will be briefly discussed; below, I will reflect on the likelihood (for p-value, cf. n. 28, 8.3
below) that such word- and phrase-frequencies pertaining to the Name
were used as part of an inner-canonical shaping of the New Testament
material, by means of which the respective textual subunits were woven
into a whole.[3]

7.1 OBSERVATION 1: THE ΠΙΣΤΙΣ WORD-GROUP

As an initial illustration of NrN embedded in the New Testament text, I
note that πίστις, "faith, belief, trust, faithfulness" and the πίστις word-group
consistently occur with frequencies involving alphabetical (22/24/27) and
divine name (15/17/26) multiples, with πίστις featuring **24 times** in the
four Gospels/Synoptic Gospels (John does not contain the word πίστις),
15 times in Acts, **26 times** in Luke-Acts (39 times in Gospels + Acts; cf.
table 5.1 above for potential significance of 39), **26 times** in the Catholic
Epistles, **22 times** in Galatians, **27 times** in 1–2 Timothy, **243 times** [**9 ×**

---

2. Whereas in ch. 6 above we included five basic numbers among the NrN (twenty-two-, twen-
ty-four- and twenty-seven-multiples, on the one hand, and seventeen-, and twenty-six-multiples,
on the other), here in ch. 7 we will include altogether six numbers, i.e., alphabetical (twenty-two-,
twenty-four- and twenty-seven-multiples) and divine name numerals (fifteen-, seventeen-, and
twenty-six-multiples).

3. Unless indicated otherwise, the figures below are taken from the Accordance 13 digital versions
of the THGNT; the LXXG Septuagint; the Hebrew Bible (*BHS*); Michael Holmes, *Apostolic Fathers:
Greek Texts and English Translations of Their Writings*, 3rd ed. (Grand Rapids: Baker Academic, 2007);
and a few additional Accordance digital texts.

27] in the full New Testament; ἡ πίστις **17 times** in Romans and **17 times** in the Catholic Epistles; ἐκ πίστεως **22 times** in Pauline Corpus; πιστός **66 times** [3 × 22] in the twenty-seven-book New Testament; and πιστεύω **132 times** [6 × 22] in the four Gospels, **17 times** in the Catholic Epistles, **54 times** [2 × 27] in Praxapostolos (Acts and the Catholic Epistles), **242 times** [11 × 22] in the twenty-seven-book New Testament; πιστ* (words beginning with the four letters πιστ-) **24 times** in Matthew, **26 times** in Luke, **170 times** [10 × 17] in the four Gospels, **27 times** in Galatians, and **24 times** in 1–2 Thessalonians (figures from THGNT); and πισ* (words beginning with the three Greek letters πισ-) **17 times** in Mark, **24 times** in Luke, **132 times** [6 × 22] in the four Gospels, **44 times** [2 × 22] in the Catholic Epistles (see also n. 4 below), **85 times** [5 × 17] in Praxapostolos, **54 times** [2 × 27] in Romans, **17 times** in 1 Corinthians, **27 times** in 1–2 Corinthians, **24 times** in Galatians, and **476 times** [4 × 7 × 17] in the twenty-seven-book New Testament.[4]

In sum, the arithmetical *NrN* patterning noted above (observation 1; not including texts listed in footnote 4) involves the textual composition and/or editing of the following twelve canonical subunits (listed in the old canonical order, with Praxapostolos before the

---

4. Praxapostolos is a standard canonical text unit in the New Testament manuscript tradition, consisting of Acts (Greek: Πράξεις ἀποστόλων) and the seven Catholic Epistles. In addition to these figures we can note, as well, the following: ἡ πίστις (sg. nom.) **30 times** [2 × 15] in the New Testament, τῇ πίστει **22 times** in the New Testament, τὴν πίστιν **27 times** in the New Testament, *πιστ* **858 times** [39 × 22 = 33 × 26] in the New Testament, **375** [25 × 15] in Pauline Corpus (NA28; **376 times** in THGNT), and **51 times** [3 × 17] in Matthew, **πι* 289 times** [17 × 17] in Matthew, **52 times** [2 × 26] in 1 Peter, **26 times** in 2 Peter, **78 times** [3 × 26] in 1–2 Peter, **27 times** in 1–3 John, **85 times** [5 × 15] in 2 Corinthians, **52 times** [2 × 26] in Galatians, **34 times** [2 × 17] in 1 Thessalonians, **22 times** in 2 Thessalonians, **30 times** [2 × 15] in Titus, **120 times** [5 × 24] in Hebrews, and **850 times** [50 × 17] in Pauline Corpus (NA28; **851 times** in THGNT). The following similar results are found in the Ignatian letters: πίστις: the seven-letter Ignatian Corpus **27 times**; πιστ*: *Ephesians* **15 times**, the seven-letter Ignatian Corpus **51 times** [3 × 17]; π*: *Ephesians* **162 times** [6 × 27], *Trallians* **72 times** [3 × 27], *Romans* **66 times** [3 × 22], *Smyrneans* **104 times** [4 × 26], *Polycarp* **81 times** [3 × 27]. Corresponding New Testament figures for π* (number of words beginning with the letter π) are **880 times** [40 × 22] in Mark, **1768 times** [4 × 17 × 26] in Acts, 1 Peter **144 times** [6 × 24], 2 Peter **78 times** [3 × 26], 1 John **132 times** [6 × 22], 2 John **24 times**, 1–2 John **156 times** [6 × 26], 1–3 John **170 times** [10 × 17], Jude **44 times** [2 × 22], Philippians **136 times** [8 × 17], 1 Timothy **176 times** [8 × 22]; πι*: Matthew **75 times** [5 × 15], James **22 times**, Romans **68 times** [4 × 17], 1–2 Corinthians **51 times** [3 × 17], 1 Timothy **34 times** [2 × 17], Hebrews **44 times** [2 × 22], etc. If any of these *NrN* frequencies is intended on the part of editors, authors, or scribes as frequencies of the two suggested groups of multiples, the listed figures are of significance for the textual and canonical shaping of the respective text units.

Pauline epistles, as in THGNT): Matthew, Luke, the four Gospels, Luke-Acts, the Praxapostolos, the Catholic Epistles, Romans, Galatians, 1–2 Thessalonians, 1–2 Timothy, Pauline Corpus, and the twenty-seven-book New Testament.

In the present chapter, we are especially interested in the relationship between the presence of NrN in a given text and the subcanonical identity of the text in question. It is here also of relevance to note the inner-canonical relationship between various canonical subunits and their inclusion of NrN for a particular word (πίστις), letter constellation (πισ*), or phrase (ἐκ πίστεως). Thus, based on NrN for the πίστις word-group we can notice the inner-canonical relationship between the noun πίστις occurring **15 times** in Acts and **26 times** in the presumably related canonical subunit Luke-Acts. The frequency of the noun in Acts (**15 occurrences**) is here interdependent on the frequency of the term in the canonical subunit Luke-Acts (**26 occurrences**).

So, if this particular inner-canonical NrN relationship was in the mind of the editors, authors, and/or scribes who composed and edited the Lukan writings, we may be able to make a good case also for the parallel event of canon formation at this subcanonical level that is closely related to the wording of the respective texts. Text, canon, and inner-canonical textual weaving into a canonical whole here become concrete realities. Other similar NrN examples involving the πίστις word-group demonstrate the same textual relationship between text and subcanonical unit. For example, the verb πιστεύω occurring **132 times** [6 × 22] in the four Gospels and **242 times** [11 × 22] in the full New Testament. In this case, too, the two canonical subunits—the fourfold Gospel and the twenty-seven-book New Testament corpus—appear to be mutually linked to one another by means of NrN frequencies of this key New Testament verb, "to believe," πιστεύω. Yet another example, involving several subcanonical units, can be detected for the letter-constellation πισ* with the following four NrN results, involving the Lukan writings: Luke **24 occurrences**, the fourfold Gospel **132 occurrences** [6 × 22], Praxapostolos (Acts + Catholic Epistles) **85 occurrences** [5 × 17], and the full New Testament **476 occurrences** [2 × 14 × 17]. In this particular example, based on NrN, four seemingly interdependent canonical subunits assist in construing a thoroughly interdependent canonical text and canon. Given the high, consistent presence in the New Testament material of several of the above terms from the πίστις word-group (higher than expected if these words would occur just randomly; cf. n. 28, 8.3 below) we may here get a glimpse of some of the original reasoning behind the canon formation process: the relationship between text/wording and the formation of the various subcanonical text-units, and their mutual inner-canonical linking.

The argument of the present chapter is that for each new canonical subunit that was added to the already existing corpus of new Christian Scriptures (such as the adding of the completed Luke-Acts, presumably subsequent to the finalizing of the Synoptic Gospels), careful adjustment with regard to NrN was required. I suggest that we may be in a position to observe some of this logic by carefully noting the respective NrN. For example, the **24 occurrences** of the noun πίστις present in the completed Synoptic Gospels (Matthew 8 times, Mark 5 times, Luke 11 times), the **15 occurrences** in Acts and the **26 occurrences** in Luke-Acts, as well as the presumably related NrN constellation for πίστις also for the 39 occurrences of the term in the four Gospels + Acts (for potential numerological significance of the number 39, see table 5.1 above). These figures for πίστις are based on THGNT and NA28; however, even if we were to base our search for NrN on Codex Sinaiticus (‫א‬), Textus Receptus (TR), and text family (TF) 35/the Majority Text, similar NrN results would appear, with πίστις occurring as follows: four Gospels **24 occurrences**, Luke-Acts **27 occurrences**, Acts 16 occurrences, the four Gospels + Acts 40 occurrences [4 x 10], and Praxapostolos 42 occurrences [3 x 14] (‫א‬, TR, TF 35).

In terms of statistics for the verb πιστεύω in the Catholic Epistles–Praxapostolos–the twenty-seven-book New Testament (with NrN at three directly related canonical levels), we may note the three occurrences of NrN out of the four possible word-frequencies for figures above 9 (i.e., 75 percent NrN: Catholic Epistles **17 occurrences**, Acts 37 occurrences, Praxapostolos **54 occurrences** [2 × 27], New Testament **242 occurrences** [11 × 22]). The number of occurrences of πιστ* in the canonical Gospels is also worth noticing, with three NrN out of five word-frequencies for the fourfold Gospel (i.e., 60 percent NrN: Matthew **24 occurrences**, Mark 20 occurrences [2 × 10], Luke **26 occurrences**, John 100 occurrences

[10 × 10], the four Gospels **170 occurrences** [10 × 17]). The same proportion of NrN, that is, 60 percent NrN, appears as well for "πισ*" (search in Accordance on this form) in the four Gospels–twenty-seven-book New Testament (Matthew 20 occurrences [2 × 10], Mark **17 occurrences**, Luke **24 occurrences**, John 71 occurrences, the four Gospels **132 occurrences** [6 × 22], the full New Testament **476 occurrences** [4 × 7 × 17]; only these six items included in the count; cf. also the following corresponding NrN for "πισ*": Catholic Epistles **44x** [2 x 22] and Praxapostolos **85x** [5 x 17]).

A high proportion of NrN, namely, 100 percent, further appears in the full New Testament for the three words in the πίστις word-group: πίστις (**243 occurrences** [9 × 27]); πιστός (**66 occurrences** [3 × 22]) and πιστεύω (**242 occurrences** [11 × 22]).[5] The corresponding figure for the fourfold Gospel is 67 percent NrN, with πίστις and πιστεύω occurring **24** and **132 times** [6 × 22], respectively, in the four Gospels.

An unexpectedly high proportion of NrN—namely, 100 percent—further appears for the following searches in Accordance, involving the verb πιστεύω (proximity search involving the two [or more] included words based on verse units; each word counted separately):

- πιστεύω <AND> Ἰησοῦς (cf. John 12:11), for figures above 10 in individual New Testament books, John **51 occurrences** [3 × 17], that is, 100 percent NrN;[6]

- πιστεύω <AND> κύριος (cf. Acts 18:8), for figures above 11 in individual New Testament books, Acts **24 occurrences**, that is, 100 percent NrN;[7]

---

5. The noun πίστις occurs **243 times** [9 × 27] in THGNT and NA28. The verb πιστεύω features **242 times** [11 x 22] in THGNT, **238 times** [14 × 17] in Codex Sinaiticus (ℵ), and 241 times in NA28. The one difference between THGNT and NA28 regarding use of the verb πιστεύω and the adjective πιστός can be found in 1 Pet 1:21, where NA28 (here following Codex Vaticanus and Codex Alexandrinus) has πιστούς, instead of πιστεύοντας, as in THGNT (here following P⁷², Codex Sinaiticus, and TF 35/the Majority Text).

6. Cf. also the similar Accordance search πιστεύω <AND> εἰς <AND> Ἰησοῦς (cf. John 12:11): John **30 times** [2 × 15], i.e., 100 percent NrN for figures above four in individual New Testament books; and πιστεύω <AND> ὁ Ἰησοῦς Gospels + Acts 39 times (see table 5.1 above for potential numerological significance of 39).

7. Cf. also the similar Accordance search πιστεύω <AND> ἐπί <AND> κύριος (cf. Acts 18:8): twenty-seven-book New Testament **22 times**; πιστεύω <AND> ὁ κύριος New Testament **27 times**;

- πιστεύω <AND> ἐγώ (cf. Matt 18:6 and John 4:41), for figures above 14 in individual New Testament books, John **110
  occurrences** [5 × 22], that is, 100 percent *NrN;*

- πιστεύω <AND> σύ (cf. Matt 8:13 and John 6:30), for figures
  above 13 in individual New Testament books, John **78 occurrences** [3 × 26], that is, 100 percent *NrN;*[8]

- πιστεύω <AND> αὐτός (cf. Matt 21:32 and John 2:11; 8:31),
  for figures above 12 in individual New Testament-books,
  Matthew **17 occurrences**, Mark **17 occurrences**, Luke
  15 occurrences, John **144 occurrences** [6 × 24], Acts **52
  occurrences** [2 × 26], and Romans **17 occurrences**, that is,
  100 percent *NrN.*[9]

7.2 OBSERVATION 2: THE *NOMEN SACRUM*
ΥΙΟΣ AND OTHER *NOMINA SACRA*

Next, we turn to the *nomen sacrum* υἱός, "son," which occurs as a *NrN* **22
times** in 1 John, **24 times** in 1–3 John (the first canonical unit of which
1 John is part), and **27 times** in the Catholic Epistles (the second canonical unit of which 1 John is part), **48 times** [2 × 24] in the Praxapostolos
(Acts + Catholic Epistles; the third canonical unit of which 1 John is part),
and **378 times** [14 × 27] in the twenty-seven-book New Testament (the

---

and πιστεύω <AND> ὁ θεός (cf. John 14:1) John **22 times**, four Gospels **24 times**, and Catholic
Epistles **24 times**.

8. Cf. also the similar Accordance search πιστεύω <AND> γίνομαι <AND> σύ (cf. Matt 8:13): four
Gospels **17 times**, New Testament **34 times** [2 × 17].

9. Cf. also the similar Accordance search πιστεύω <AND> διά <AND> αὐτός (cf. John 1:7), with
100 percent *NrN* for figures above 11 in individual New Testament books: John **34 times** [2 × 17] (in
addition, the following figures: Gospels + Acts **54 times** [2 × 27], twenty-seven-book New Testament
68 times [4 × 17]); and the following results for πιστεύω <AND> ἐπί <AND> αὐτός (cf. Matt 27:42):
Gospels + Acts **22 times**, Praxapostolos **15 times**, New Testament **44 times** [2 × 22]. *Name-related
Numerals* and related numerals (such as multiples of 14; cf. table 5.1 above) are found also for πιστεύω
<AND> οὗτος: Synoptic Gospels 16 times (THGNT, NA28)/14 times (א), John **44 times** [2 × 22]
(א; 42 times [3 × 14] in THGNT, NA28), Gospels + Acts **66 times** [3 × 22], Praxapostolos 14
times (THGNT, NA28, א), Pauline Corpus **15 times** (THGNT, NA28, א), New Testament 87 times
(THGNT, NA28, א)/88 times [4 × 22] (TF 35). And cf. also the similar Accordance search πιστεύω
<AND> ἐκεῖνος: Gospels + Acts **27 times**, New Testament **34 times** [2 × 17].

fourth canonical unit of which 1 John is part).¹⁰ In all five cases, these respective word-frequencies contain multiples of alphabetical numbers, namely, in order, 22, 24, 27, 24, and 27. Again, the suggestion this chapter makes is that these NrN—involving the term υἱός (and other words)— were, or may have been, deliberate on the part of those engaged in the composition, editing and/or copying of the textual subunits that make up the New Testament.¹¹ Based on the above five NrN, these word-frequency figures may therefore serve as a means to determining the inner-canonical shaping of these respective textual units: 1 John, 1–2 John/1–3 John, the Catholic Epistles, the Praxapostolos, and the full New Testament.

Other examples of this numerological feature involving the *nomina sacra* word-group, in the full New Testament, include the following alphabetical NrN (22-, 24- and 27-multiples): **24 occurrences** of σωτήρ, "savior"; **27** of σταυρός, "cross"; **24** of κύριος ὁ θεός, "Lord God";¹² **27** of τὴν βασιλείαν τοῦ θεοῦ, "the kingdom of God"; **176 [8 × 22]** of τὸ πνεῦμα, "the Spirit"; **24** of κύριος Ἰησοῦς χριστός, "Lord Jesus Christ" (NA28); **48 [2 × 24]** of ἐν κυρίῳ, "in the Lord"; **135 [5 × 27]** of Ἰησοῦς χριστός (NA28), "Jesus Christ"; **24** of ὁ δὲ Ἰησοῦς λέγει, "but Jesus says"; **24** of αὐτὸς Ἰησοῦς; **550 [15 × 22]** of ἄνθρωπος, "human being"; **162 [6 × 27]** of ὁ ἄνθρωπος (forms in the sg.); **81 [3 × 27]** of υἱὸς τοῦ ἀνθρώπου (forms in the sg.), "Son of Man"; **44 [2 × 22]** of ἐν τῷ οὐρανῷ, "in heaven"; **24** of ἐν τῷ οὐρανῷ (forms in the sg.); **24** of θεός πατήρ, "God the Father;" **24** of πάτερ, "f/ Father"; **110 [5 × 22]** of πατήρ (sg. nom.); **24** of πατέρες; **108 [4 × 27]** of

---

10. Corresponding figures in NA28: 1 John **22 times**, 1–3 John **24 times**, Catholic Epistles **27 times**, Praxapostolos **48 times [2 × 24]**, New Testament 381 times; and in Codex Sinaiticus (ℵ): 1 John **22 times**, 1–3 John **24 times**, Catholic Epistles **27 times**, Praxapostolos 49 times [7 × 7], New Testament 371 times. For an introduction to *nomina sacra*, see Larry W. Hurtado, *The Earliest Christian Artifacts: Manuscripts and Christian Origins* (Grand Rapids: Eerdmans, 2006), 95–134; and, for a discussion of 15/17 standard *nomina sacra*— Ἰησοῦς, Χριστός, κύριος, θεός, πνεῦμα/πνευματικός, σταυρός/σταυρόω, πατήρ, ἄνθρωπος, υἱός, Ἰσραήλ, Ἰερουσαλήμ, οὐρανός, σωτήρ, Δαυείδ, and μήτηρ—see Tomas Bokedal, "Notes on the *Nomina Sacra* and Biblical Interpretation," in *Beyond Biblical Theologies*, ed. Heinrich Assel, Stefan Beyerle, and Christfried Böttrich, WUNT 295 (Tübingen: Mohr Siebeck, 2012), 263–95; repr. as chapter 12 in this volume.

11. See further Tomas Bokedal, "'But for Me, the Scriptures are Jesus Christ' (IC XC; Ign. Phld. 8:2): Creedal Text-Coding and the Early Scribal System of Nomina Sacra," in *Studies on the Paratextual Features of Early New Testament Manuscripts*, ed. Stanley E. Porter, David I. Yoon, and Chris S. Stevens, TENTS (Leiden: Brill, forthcoming).

12. In addition, **24** of δὲ θεός and **144 [6 × 24]** of θεός ὁ.

ὁ πατήρ (forms in the nom.), **24** of τῷ πατρί (forms in the dat.); and **72** [**3 × 24**] of τὸν πατέρα.[13] Again, these New Testament examples involving terms from the *nomina sacra* word-group (made up of 15 or 17 individual words such as GOD, JESUS, and SPIRIT) are all "alphabetical multiples," that is, they are representative figures of about half of our *NrN*, namely multiples of the three alphabetical numerals 22, 24, and 27.

In sum, the arithmetic patterning observed above of the *nomen sacrum* υἱός and some additional *nomina sacra* arrangements (observation 2) involves the textual composition of the following five canonical subunits: 1 John, 1–2 John/1–3 John, the Catholic Epistles, the Praxapostolos, and the twenty-seven-book New Testament.

Regarding the number of appearances of the *nomen sacrum* υἱός, in 1–3 John, for figures above 2 (1 John **22 times**, 2 John twice, 3 John 0 times, 1–3 John **24 times**), 100 percent are *NrN*; and in the Catholic Epistles (James once, 1 Peter once, 2 Peter once, 1–2 Peter twice, 1 John **22 times**, 2 John twice, 3 John 0 times, 1–3 John **24 times**, Jude 0 times), likewise, 100 percent of the occurrences are *NrN*; the corresponding figure for the Praxapostolos (Acts 21 times, James once, 1 Peter once, 2 Peter once, 1–2 Peter twice, 1 John **22 times**, 2 John twice, 3 John 0 times, 1–3 John **24 times**, Jude 0 times) is 67 percent *NrN*; and for the New Testament as a whole, for figures above 13 (Matthew 89 times, Mark 35 times, Luke 77 times [7 × 11], Synoptic Gospels 201 times, John 56 times [4 × 14], the four Gospels 257 times, Luke-Acts 98 times [7 × 14], Gospels + Acts 278 times, 1 John **22 times**, 1–3 John **24 times**, Praxapostolos **48 times** [**2 × 24**], Catholic Epistles **27 times**, Hebrews **24 times**, Pauline Corpus 65 times, the twenty-seven-book New Testament **378 times** [**14 × 27**]), 40 percent are *NrN* (i.e., six *NrN* out of fifteen possible word-frequencies). These figures, again, appear to be arithmetically designed. Again, we note that if this is not the case—contrary to the argument of this book—the

---

13. In the Pentateuch (LXXG), the following figures for πατήρ—exemplifying our two groups of multiples, 22/24/27 and 15/17/26—are found: πατήρ: Leviticus **24 times**, Numbers **30 times** [**2 × 15**]; ὁ πατήρ: Numbers **24 times**, Deuteronomy **68 times** [**4 × 17**]; πατήρ (sg. nom.): Genesis **48 times** [**2 × 24**], the Pentateuch **60 times** [**4 × 15**]; πατρός: Genesis **78 times** [**3 × 26**], Leviticus **17 times**, Numbers **15 times**; τοῦ πατρός: Pentateuch **102 times** [**6 × 17**]; πατρί: Genesis **27 times**; τῷ πατρί: Genesis **26 times**; τὸν πατέρα: Pentateuch **44 times** [**2 × 22**]; πατήρ (forms in the sg.): Numbers **22 times**; ὁ πατήρ (forms in the sg.): Numbers **17 times**, the Pentateuch **225 times** [**15 × 15**].

expected proportion for randomly appearing alphabetical NrN (multiples of 22, 24, and 27) would be, on average, around 11 percent for each individual NrN listed above.[14]

7.3 OBSERVATION 3: THE *NOMEN SACRUM* ΘΕΟΣ

In two early Pauline letters, Galatians and 1 Thessalonians, ὁ θεός, "God," appears **17** and **26 times** (THGNT), respectively, which happen to be the two numeric values associated with the Tetragrammaton, YHWH (cf. table 5.1 above).[15] The corresponding figure for the twenty-seven-book New Testament corpus is **986 times** [58 × 17], which is also a multiple of 17. Similarly, in Romans, both ὁ θεός (nom. sg.) and τῷ θεῷ (dat. sg.) occur **26 times**,[16] and in the Praxapostolos, as well, the frequency of ὁ θεός (nom. sg.) appears as a 26-multiple, with **78 occurrences** [3 × 26]; in Acts, moreover, τὸν θεόν (acc. sg.) appears **26 times**. In like manner, the word θεός (all cases) occurs **153 times** [9 × 17 = 3² × 17] in Romans, that is, as a multiple of 17, and, in 1–2 Timothy, θεός features **34 times** [2 × 17] and in Hebrews **68 times** [4 × 17], again as multiples of 17.[17] Other parts of the New Testament, too, demonstrate potential connection between word-frequency and the numerical values of the Name, for example, in Matthew's Gospel, with its **51** [3 × 17] (NA28 and B) or **52**

---

14. Fifty-seven numerals between 1 and 500 are alphabetical multiples ("alphabetical" NrN), i.e., the numbers 22, 24, 27, 44, 48, 54, etc., i.e., ca. 11 percent.

15. The corresponding figures in NA28 are: Galatians 18 times and 1 Thessalonians **27 times**; and in Codex Sinaiticus: Galatians 18 times and 1 Thessalonians 28 times. In NA28, for the individual letters in Pauline Corpus, ὁ θεός appears as a NrN in 5 out of 8 cases for figures above 12, that is, 62.5 percent are NrN.

16. Corresponding figures in NA28 are: ὁ θεός (nom. sg.) **26 times**, and τῷ θεῷ (dat. sg.) **26 times**; and in B (Codex Vaticanus): ὁ θς **26 times**, and τῷ θω **24 times**. We may note as well that for ὁ θεός in the individual Pauline letters in TF 35/Textus Receptus, for figures above 7, 100 percent are NrN (i.e., NrN in 4 out of 4 cases; Romans **26 times**, 1 Corinthians **24 times**, 2 Corinthians **15 times**, Hebrews **22 times**). The corresponding figure for THGNT/NA28 is 75 percent NrN (Romans **26 times**, 1 Corinthians **24 times**, 2 Corinthians **15 times**, Hebrews 21 times). In addition to this high figure for individual Pauline letters, in NA28, for the full Pauline Corpus ὁ θεός occurs 117 times [3 × 39; see table 5.1 above for potential significance of 39] (116 times in THGNT). The corresponding figure for ὁ θεός in NA28 is: Praxapostolos 80 times [8 × 10].

17. **153 times** [9 × 17] in Romans (THGNT; Textus Receptus, TF 35)/**150 times** [10 × 15] (B; ℵ). This is the same figure (**153 times**) that we find in Matthew for the total number of occurrences of πατήρ (63 times), υἱός (89 times), and ἅγιον πνεῦμα (once), when added: 63 + 89 + 1 = **153** [9 × 17] (cf. Matt 28:19). Corresponding figure for Hebrews in ℵ: **66 times** [3 × 22].

[2 × 26] **occurrences** of θεός (THGNT and א).[18] Further, in Luke-Acts (NA28), ὁ θεός features **260 times** [10 × 26] and θεός **289 times** [17 × 17 = 17²]. For Luke-Acts, we may also note the **17 appearances** of τῷ θεῷ (dat. sg.), and the **78** [3 × 26] of θεός (nom. sg.)—that is, three times the numerical value of the Name [3 × 26].[19]

From studying the Septuagint (LXXG), we are reminded of similar patterns, with **17 occurrences** of θεός in Jonah and **34** [2 × 17] in Hosea. Of arguable significance for all the above figures are the parallel features that surface in segments of the MT, where—as noted above—the number of occurrences of the Tetragrammaton, YHWH, appear as follows (*BHS*): **1820 times** [70 × 26] in the Pentateuch, **153** [9 × 17] in 2 Samuel, **26** in Jonah, **34** [2 × 17] in Zephaniah, and **17** in Nehemiah. Along similar textual "Name-structuring" lines of reasoning, Old Testament scholars such as Claus Schedl and Casper Labuschagne have set out to detect numerical structures in the MT of the Pentateuch, focusing on the numerals **17** and **26** and some other key numbers as their basis.[20]

In sum, the *NrN* patterning observed above involves the textual composition/editing/scribal adjustment of the following canonical subunits: Matthew, Luke-Acts, Romans, 1–2 Timothy, Hebrews, Acts, Praxapostolos, the twenty-seven-book New Testament; Jonah, Hosea, the Pentateuch, Zephaniah, and Nehemiah.

In terms of *NrN* statistics, we may note, again, that the Tetragrammaton in the Pentateuch appears as follows (*BHS*): the Pentateuch **1820 occurrences** [70 × 26], Genesis **165 occurrences** [11 × 15], Numbers **396 occurrences** [18 × 22], and Deuteronomy **550 occurrences** [5 × 5 × 22], that is, in four cases out of these six word-frequencies we encounter *NrN*, that is, **67 percent** *NrN* (Pentateuch **1820 occurrences**, Genesis

---

18. θεός in Matthew occurs **51 times** [3 × 17] in B (including one occurrence in Matt 6:8, not present in NA28) and in NA28 (including one occurrence in Matt 6:33 not present in B); and **52 times** [2 × 26] in the THGNT (including one occurrence in Matt 6:33 not present in א) and **52 times** [2 × 26] in א (including one occurrence in Matt 6:32 not present in THGNT). In W θεός features **54 times** [2 × 27].

19. The corresponding figure for 1–2 Corinthians is **51** [3 × 17].

20. See, e.g., Claus Schedl, *Baupläne des Wortes: Einführung in die biblische Logotechnik* (Vienna: Herder, 1974), and Casper J. Labuschagne, *Numerical Secrets of the Bible: Introduction to Biblical Arithmology* (Eugene, OR: Wipf & Stock, 2016). For Johannine emphasis on the number 17, see also Richard Bauckham, "The 153 Fish and the Unity of the Fourth Gospel," *Neot* 36 (2002): 82–85.

165 occurrences, Exodus 398 occurrences, Leviticus 311 occurrences, Numbers **396 occurrences**, Deuteronomy **550 occurrences**). The corresponding LXX result (for figures above 6) for κύριος ὁ θεός is 60 percent NrN (Pentateuch **476 occurrences** [4 × 7 × 17], Genesis 42 occurrences [3 × 14], Exodus **45 occurrences** [3 × 15], Leviticus **44 occurrences** [2 × 22], Numbers 6 occurrences, Deuteronomy 339 occurrences; LXXG).[21]

A high proportion of NrN is present as well in the New Testament corpus, as observable in the table below (table 7.1), which contains various constellations of the *nomen sacrum* θεός/θε*:

Table 7.1. New Testament NrN Pertaining to the Nomen Sacrum θεός.

Term	New Testament Text (THGNT, if not indicated otherwise)	Frequency (15-, 17- and 26- multiples)	Term	New Testament Text (THGNT, if not indicated otherwise)	Frequency (22-, 24- and 27-multiples)
θεός	Matthew	52 [2 × 26]	θεός	John	81 [3 × 27]
	Acts	165 [11 × 15]		1–2 Thessalonians	54 [2 × 27]
	Romans	153 [9 × 17]		1 Timothy	22
	1 Corinthians	105 [7 × 15]		Revelation	96 [4 × 24]
	1–2 Timothy	34 [2 × 17]			
	Hebrews	68 [4 × 17]			
ὁ θεός	Romans	105 [7 × 15]	ὁ θεός	Mark	44 [2 × 22]
	Galatians	17		Ephesians	22
	1 Thessalonians	26		Catholic Epistles	96 [4 × 24]
	1–2 Timothy	15			
	New Testament	986 [58 × 17]			
			θεοσ*	Romans	154 [7 × 22]
				Pauline Corpus	616 [2 × 14 × 22]

---

21. We may note, as well, some of the corresponding figures in the MT for יהוה אלהים: Exodus 39 times (cf. table 5.1 above), Leviticus **26 times**, Joshua **54 times** [2 × 27], 1 Kings **44 times** [2 × 22], 2 Kings **27 times**, the Prophets (Former + Latter Prophets) **297 times** [11 × 27], 2 Chronicles **85 times** [5 × 17], the twenty-four-book MT **891 times** [3 × 11 × 27]; as for NrN in individual books of the MT, for figures above 14, five out of thirteen are NrN, i.e., 38 percent.

Term	NT Text	Frequency	Term	NT Text	Frequency
θεο*	Gospels	306 [18 × 17]	θεο*	Romans	154 [7 × 22]
	Praxapostolos	300 [20 × 15]		Colossians	22
ὁ θεο*	1–3 John	30 [2 × 15]	ὁ θεο*	Mark	44 [2 × 22]
	Acts	153 [9 × 17]		1 John	27
	Gospels + Acts (NA28)	405 [27 × 15]		Gospels + Acts (NA28)	405 [15 × 27]
	Luke-Acts (NA28)	260 [10 × 26]		Catholic Epistles	96 [4 × 24]
	Romans	105 [7 × 15]		1 Corinthians (NA28)	66 [3 × 22]
	Galatians	17		Ephesians	22
	1 Thessalonians	26		Hebrews (NA28)	54 [2 × 27]
	1–2 Timothy	15			
θεο	Matthew	52 [2 × 26]	*θεο*	Gospels	308 [14 × 22]
	Praxapostolos	306 [18 × 17]		Gospels + Acts (NA28)	484 [22 × 22]
	2 Timothy	17		1 Corinthians	108 [4 × 27]
	1–2 Timothy	45 [3 × 15]		2 Corinthians	81 [3 × 27]
	Pauline Corpus	645 [43 × 15]		1 Timothy (NA28)	27
				Revelation	96 [4 × 24]
θε*	Synoptics	420 [2 × 14 × 15]	θε*	Matthew	135 [5 × 27]
	Gospels (NA28)	578 [2 × 17 × 17]		Acts (NA28)	220 [10 × 22]
	1 John	68 [4 × 17]		Romans	176 [8 × 22]
	Praxapostolos (NA28)	375 [25 × 15]		1 Thessalonians	44 [2 × 22]
	2 Corinthians	130 [5 × 26]		2 Thessalonians	22
	Galatians	45 [3 × 15]		1–2 Thessalonians	66 [3 × 22]
	1–2 Timothy	45 [3 × 15]		1 Timothy	27
	Pauline Corpus	748 [2 × 22 × 17]		Pauline Corpus	748 [2 × 17 × 22]

Term	NT Text	Frequency	Term	NT Text	Frequency
ὁ θε*	Luke	119 [7 × 17][22]	ὁ θε*	Praxapostolos	264 [12 × 22]
	1 John	60 [4 × 15]		Romans	110 [5 × 22]
	2 Corinthians	52 [2 × 26]		1 Corinthians	66 [3 × 22]
	1 Thessalonians	26[23]			
θε	1 Corinthians	180 [12 × 15]	*θε*	2 Corinthians	132 [6 × 22]
	Galatians	75 [7 × 15]		2 Thessalonians	27
θεός (sg. nom/ voc.)	Luke	15	θεός (sg. nom./ voc.)	Hebrews	24
	Gospels	52 [2 × 26][24]			
	1–2 Corinthians	51 [3 × 17]			
ὁ θεός (sg. nom/ voc.)	Gospels	45 [3 × 15]	θεός (sg. nom./ voc.)	1 Corinthians	24
	Praxapostolos	78 [3 × 26]			
	Romans	26			
	2 Corinthians	15[25]			
θεοῦ	Galatians	15	θεοῦ	Luke	72 [3 × 24]
	Colossians	15		1–2 Peter	27
	Gospels	180 [12 × 15]		1–2 Corinthians	96 [4 × 24]
	Luke-Acts (NA28)	130 [5 × 26]			
	New Testament	690 [2 × 23 × 15]			
τοῦ θεοῦ	John	34 [2 × 17]	τοῦ θεοῦ	Matthew	24
	1 John	34 [2 × 17]		Luke	66 [3 × 22]

---

22. Acts 161 times [7 × 23], Luke-Acts 280 times [20 × 14], Gospels + Acts 460 times [20 × 23].

23. 1 Thessalonians **27 times** (NA28), 1–2 Thessalonians 39 times (NA28).

24. Gospels + Acts 117 times [3 × 39] (NA28), 1 John 13 times, Catholic Epistles 23 times, Romans 32 times. Cf. table 5.1 above for 13, 23, 32 and 39.

25. 1–2 Corinthians 39 times.

Term	NT Text	Frequency	Term	NT Text	Frequency
	Pauline Corpus	180 [12 × 15][26]		Acts	54 [2 × 27]
				Luke-Acts	120 [5 × 24]
				Praxapostolos (NA28)	110 [5 × 22]
				Hebrews	22
θεῷ	Gospels + Acts	34 [2 × 17]	θεῷ	Luke-Acts	24
	1–2 Corinthians (NA28)	26		Praxapostolos	27
τῷ θεῷ	Romans	26	τῷ θεῷ	Gospels + Acts	24
θεόν	Acts	30 [2 × 15]	θεόν	Gospels	48 [2 × 24]
	Gospels + Acts	78 [3 × 26]		Pauline Corpus	44 [2 × 22]
	Praxapostolos	51 [3 × 17][27]			
	Romans	15			
τὸν θεόν	Acts	26[28]	τὸν θεόν	Luke	22
				Luke-Acts	48 [2 × 24]
				Gospels + Acts	66 [3 × 22]

In sum, the numeric patterning observed in table 7.1 above—listing 117 New Testament *NrN* pertaining to the *nomen sacrum* θεός/θε*—involves the textual composition/editing/scribal adjustment of the following canonical subunits: Matthew, Mark, Luke, the Synoptics, John, the four Gospels, Acts, Luke-Acts, Gospels + Acts, 1–2 Peter, 1 John, the Catholic Epistles, the Praxapostolos, Romans, 1 Corinthians, 2 Corinthians, 1–2 Corinthians, Galatians, Ephesians, Colossians, 1 Thessalonians, 2 Thessalonians, 1–2 Thessalonians, 1 Timothy, 2 Timothy, 1–2 Timothy, Hebrews, the Pauline Corpus, Revelation, the twenty-seven-book New Testament. That is, the figures concern altogether 30 canonical subunits pertaining to the New Testament, and their textual/innertextual shaping.

---

26. Corresponding figure for Pauline Corpus in NA28 is **182 times** [7 × 26].

27. θεόν: New Testament **150 times** [10 × 15] (TR; THGNT 148 times).

28. τὸν θεόν: Praxapostolos 39 times (cf. table 5.1 above); New Testament 112 times [8 × 14].

Of potential interest for further research in this regard is the relation-ship, based on NrN, between the four Gospels/the Synoptics, on the one hand, and the Lukan writings as part of the Gospels/Luke-Acts/Gospels + Acts/Praxapostolos, on the other (cf., e.g., θεός (sg. nom./voc.): Luke **15 occurrences** and the four Gospels **52 occurrences** [2 × 26]; τοῦ θεοῦ: Matthew **24 occurrences**, Luke **66 occurrences** [3 × 22], and John **34 occurrences** [2 × 17], Acts **54 occurrences** [2 × 27], and Luke-Acts **120 occurrences** [5 × 24]; θεῷ: Luke-Acts **24 occurrences**, Gospels + Acts **34 occurrences** [2 × 17], and Praxapostolos **27 occurrences**; θεόν: the four Gospels **48 occurrences** [2 × 24], Acts **30 occurrences** [2 × 15], Gospels + Acts **78 occurrences** [3 × 26], Praxapostolos **51 occurrences** [3 × 17]; and τὸν θεόν: Luke **22 occurrences**, Acts **26 occurrences**, Luke-Acts **48 occurrences** [2 × 24], and Gospels + Acts **66 occurrences** [3 × 22]).

Of the above NrN, the ones linked to Romans (and other Pauline letters) are particularly worth noting, as the following figures indicate (THGNT; for comparison, a few examples of NrN, involving θεός/θε*, from ℵ and LXXG are included as well):

θεός/θε* in Romans, 1 Corinthians, and 1–2 Thessalonians:
- θεός in Romans: θεός **153 times** [9 × 17]; ὁ θεός **105 times** [7 × 15]; θεοσ* **154 times** [7 × 22]; θε* **176 times** [8 × 22]; ὁ θε* **110 times** [5 × 22]; θ* **216 times** [8 × 27]; and ὁ θ* **130 times** [5 × 26]; in addition: ὁ θεός (sg. nom./voc.) **26 times**; τῷ θεῷ **26 times**; θεόν **15 times**; and θεός (sg. forms) **153** [9 × 17] (= θεός **153 times** [9 × 17], since Romans does not contain any plural forms of θεός).[29]

- θεός in 1 Corinthians: θεός **105 times** [7 × 15]; θε* **130 times** [5 × 26]; ὁ θε* **66 times** [3 × 22]; θ* **154 times** [7 × 22]; and ὁ θ* **78 times** [3 × 26]; in addition: ὁ θεός (sg. nom./voc.) **24 times**.[30]

---

29. θεός (nom. sg.) further appears 32 times in Romans (for potential numerological significance of 32, see table 5.1); and θεοῦ and τοῦ θεοῦ (gen. sg.) feature 77 times [7 × 11] and 42 times [3 × 14], respectively (for potential significance of the numbers 7, 11, and 14, see table 5.1 above).

30. θεοῦ (gen. sg.) further appears 56 times [4 × 14] in 1 Corinthians (see table 5.1 above for potential significance of 14) and **96 times** [4 × 24] in 1–2 Corinthians.

- θεός in 1 and 2 Thessalonians: θεός in 1–2 Thessalonians **54 times** [2 × 27]; ὁ θεός in 1 Thessalonians **26 times**; θε* in 1 Thessalonians **44 times** [2 × 22], 2 Thessalonians **22 times**, and 1–2 Thessalonians **66 times** [3 × 22]; ὁ θε* in 1 Thessalonians **26 times**; θ* in 1–2 Thessalonians **78 times** [3 × 26]; ὁ θ* in 1 Thessalonians **27 times**, and 2 Thessalonians **15 times**.

θεός in Codex Sinaiticus:

- θεός: Romans **150 times** [10 × 15], 1 Corinthians **104 times** [4 × 26], Philippians **24 times**, Hebrews **66 times** [3 × 22], Pauline Corpus **612 times** [2 × 18 × 17].

- ο θ͞ς : 1–2 Corinthians 39 times, Pauline Corpus 117 times [3 × 39] (cf. table 5.1 above for potential significance of 39).

- θ͞ω: 1–2 Corinthians **26 times**, Pauline Corpus **102 times** [6 × 17].

θεός/θε* in LXX Göttingen:

- θεός in the Twelve Prophets (LXXG): θεός Hosea **34 times** [2 × 17], Amos **22 times**, and Jonah **17 times**; ὁ θεός in Amos **22 times**; θε* in Twelve Prophets **168 times** [7 × 24], Micah **15 times**, Jonah **17 times**, and Zechariah **15 times**; θ* in Twelve Prophets **396 times** [18 × 22], Joel **34 times** [2 × 17], and Nahum **17 times**.

- θεός in Ezekiel (LXXG): θεός **48 times** [2 × 24]; ὁ θε* 39 times; θ* **384 times** [16 × 24]; and ὁ θ* **182 times** [7 × 26].

7.4 CONCLUDING REMARKS

In the present chapter we have discussed the relationship between *NrN* for a selection of word-, letter-constellation-, and phrase-frequencies, on the one hand, and the canonical subunits in which these appear, on the other hand. To the extent that there is a correlation between the two, we may have good reason to suspect that the respective canonical sub-units have been designed with such *NrN* patterns in mind, resulting in a close inner-canonical connection between text and canon, including as well varying innertextual connections between various canonical sub-units. Another focal point of the chapter was the continued accumulative argument (undertaken in chs. 5–10) for the likelihood of the presence of deliberately introduced *NrN* as part of the biblical, and especially the New Testament, text.

BIBLIOGRAPHY

Bauckham, Richard. "The 153 Fish and the Unity of the Fourth Gospel." *Neot* 36 (2002): 77–88.

Bokedal, Tomas. "'But for Me, the Scriptures Are Jesus Christ' ($\overline{\text{IC}}$ $\overline{\text{XC}}$; Ign. *Phld.* 8:2): Creedal Text-Coding and the Early Scribal System of Nomina Sacra." In *Studies on the Paratextual Features of Early New Testament Manuscripts*. Edited by Stanley E. Porter, David I. Yoon, and Chris S. Stevens. TENTS. Leiden: Brill, forthcoming.

———. "Notes on the *Nomina Sacra* and Biblical Interpretation." Pages 263–95 in *Beyond Biblical Theologies*. Edited by Heinrich Assel, Stefan Beyerle, and Christfried Böttrich. WUNT 295. Tübingen: Mohr Siebeck, 2012. Repr. as chapter 12 in this volume.

Holmes, Michael. *Apostolic Fathers: Greek Texts and English Translations of Their Writings*. 3rd ed. Grand Rapids: Baker Academic, 2007.

Hurtado, Larry W. *The Earliest Christian Artifacts: Manuscripts and Christian Origins*. Grand Rapids: Eerdmans, 2006.

Labuschagne, Casper J. *Numerical Secrets of the Bible: Introduction to Biblical Arithmology*. Eugene, OR: Wipf & Stock, 2016.

Lim, Timothy H. *The Formation of the Jewish Canon*. ABRL. New Haven: Yale University Press, 2013.

Schedl, Claus. *Baupläne des Wortes: Einführung in die biblische Logotechnik*. Vienna: Herder, 1974.

8

METHODOLOGY:
DETECTING *NAME-RELATED*
NUMERALS AT DIFFERENT
CANONICAL LEVELS

I n the three previous chapters (chs. 5–7) we explored arithmetical textual patterns based on two groups of numerals, namely alphabetical (22-, 24- and 27-multiples) and divine name multiples (15-, 17- and 26-multiples), referred to as *Name-related Numerals* (NrN; NrN are in boldface below).[1] We first observed some general arithmetical patterns involving NrN, such as the acrostic Psalm 119, the alphabetical **twenty-two-book delimitation** of the Hebrew Bible canon, the **484 columns** [**22 × 22**] allocated to the fourfold Gospel in Codex Sinaiticus, the **1820 appearances** [**70 × 26**] of the Tetragrammaton in the Pentateuch, the **260 New Testament chapters** [**10 × 26**], the textual structuring of both the Hebrew and Greek versions of Psalm 23 (Ps 22 LXX) based on the number 26—a number directly associated with the divine name (ch. 5). We then focused attention on Triune arithmetical configurations in the New Testament based on NrN. Examples included the altogether **170 occurrences** [**10 × 17**] in Luke and the **260** [**10 × 26**] in Acts of the sum of

---

1. The NrN referred to in chs. 5 and 6 above included multiples of 17 and 26, on the one hand, and 22, 24, and 27, on the other. NrN in ch. 7 included multiples of 15, 17, and 26, on the one hand, and 22, 24, and 27, on the other.

the words θεός, χριστός, and πνεῦμα (ch. 6). In line with a quite impressive series of results involving NrN, especially for the New Testament writings, we proceeded to explore also an important consequence of these findings, namely the potential innertextual canonical shaping of the New Testament material, such as the emergence of the *nomen sacrum* "Son" and, as will be discussed in this chapter, the nomen sacrum "Israel," according to NrN patterns at various canonical subunit levels. As for the latter term—explored in this chapter—the following results emerge, involving seven canonical subunits: "Israel," Ἰσραήλ, featuring **15 times** in Acts, **27 times** in Luke-Acts, **26 times** in the Synoptics, **30 times** [2 × 15] in the four Gospels, **45 times** [3 × 15] in Gospels + Acts, **15 times** in Praxapostolos, and **68 times** [4 × 17] in the twenty-seven-book New Testament (potentially affecting the inner-canonical shaping of altogether seven canonical subunits).

In the present chapter (ch. 8), we shall further reflect methodologically on our use of NrN and their inclusion in the biblical material as textual-arithmetical structuring devices (with a particularly strong probability case appearing at 8.3 n. 28 below). We shall begin our brief methodological excursion by first looking at the potential use of NrN in the seven Ignatian letters, followed by reflection on the logic behind the employment of NrN also in the biblical material.

8.1 OBSERVATION 4: *NOMINA SACRA* IN THE IGNATIAN LETTERS AND REFLECTION ON METHOD USED TO DETECT NRN

With the figures in table 5.1, chapter 5 above, in fresh memory, it may be of interest to apply these to the use of *nomina sacra* also beyond the biblical writings. The term πνεῦμα and other *nomina sacra*, for example, interestingly appear with high consistency as NrN in the Ignatian letter corpus (middle recension) as shown in table 8.1 below.[2] We can easily

---

2. *Nomina sacra* are specially written short forms for God (ΘΕΟC), Lord (ΚΥΡΙΟC), Jesus (ΙΗCΟΥC), Christ (ΧΡΙCΤΟC), Spirit (ΠΝΕΥΜΑ), and up to ten additional words present in Greek biblical manuscripts. The phenomenon involves the highlighting of central figures of the Christian faith. Usually written as contractions (first and final letter, sometimes including also middle letters), the standard appearance of these in Greek Bible manuscripts is as follows: Θ͞C, ͞Κ͞C, ͞Ι͞C, ͞Χ͞C, and ͞Π͞Ν͞Α. Ignatius of Antioch (or his scribe), ca. AD 110, arguably made use of *nomina sacra* contractions. A fifth-century papyrus containing Ignatius's letters includes the following contractions: ͞Θ͞C, ͞Θ͞Υ, ͞Θ͞Ω, ͞Θ͞Ν, ͞Ι͞C,

see that most numerals in table 8.1, from 3 and upward, turn out to be included also among the symbolical numbers included in table 5.1 above, such as the number of appearances in the seven Ignatian letters of the phrase Ἰησοῦς χριστός—namely 26 times, 18 times, 17 times, 15 times, 18 times, 11 times, 3 times, and 108 times [4 × 27], respectively:

Table 8.1. *Nomina sacra* word-group frequencies in the Ignatian letters (*NrN* in boldface).

NS Word-Group	Ephesians	Magnesians	Trallians	Romans	Philadelphians	Smyrnaeans	Polycarp	The Ignatian 7-Letter Corpus
1. Ἰησοῦς	33 [3 × 11]	**22** [**2 × 11**]	19	17	**22** [**2 × 11**]	12	3	128 [4 × 32][3]
2. χριστός	33 [3 × 11]	**22** [**2 × 11**]	19	18	21	14	3	**130** [**5 × 26**][4]
χρ*	39	**27**	**24**	23	**24**	15	4	**156** [**6 × 26**][5]
Ἰησοῦς χριστός	**26**	18	**17**	**15**	18	11	3	**108** [**4 × 27**][6]
3. κύριος	9	2	2	1	7	5	8	**34** [**2 × 17**][7]
4. θεός	43	23	13	**26**	**22**[8]	25	24	**176** [**8 × 22**]

ῙΥ, ΚΥ, ΚΩ, ΚΝ, ΠΡΙ, ΠΝΑ, ΧΣ, and ΧΥ (Ignatius *Smyrn.* 3.3–12.1; Kurt Aland, *Repertorium der griechischen christlichen Papyri, II: Kirchenväter–Papyri*, Teil 1: *Beschreibungen*, Patrische Texte und Studien 42 [Berlin: de Gruyter, 1995]).

3. Corresponding figure in the seven-letter Ignatian Corpus for Ἰησοῦ (sg. gen./dat.): **88 times** [**4 × 22**].

4. Corresponding figure in the seven-letter Ignatian Corpus for χριστόν (sg. acc.): **15 times**.

5. Corresponding figure in the seven-letter Ignatian Corpus for *χρ*: **170 times** [**10 × 17**] (*Trallians* **24 times** and *Romans* **27 times**).

6. Corresponding figure in the seven-letter Ignatian Corpus for Ἰησοῦς χριστός (sg. nom.): **22 times**.

7. Corresponding figures in the seven-letter Ignatian Corpus for κυ*: 39 times (cf. table 5.1); and for κ*: **697 times** [**41 × 17**] (*Trallians* **85 times** [**5 × 17**], *Philadelphians* **105** [**7 × 15**], *Polycarp* **72 times** [**3 × 24**]).

8. Following Latin and Armenian manuscripts, omitting θεός in *Phld.* 5.1.

NS Word-Group	Ephesians	Magnesians	Trallians	Romans	Philadelphians	Smyrnaeans	Polycarp	The Ignatian 7-Letter Corpus
ὁ θεός	8	1	3	8	3	4	3	30 [2 × 15][9]
θεο*	45 [3 × 15]	25	14	27	24	31	28	194
5. πνεῦμα	3	5	3	2	4	3	2	22
6. πατήρ	9	12	7	6	5	5	1	45 [3 × 15]
ὁ πατήρ	6	4	4	3	2	3	-	22
7. ἄνθρωπος	5	-	1	2	3	1	-	12
ἀνθρωπ*	7	-	1	3	4	2	-	17
8. υἱός	3	2	-	2	-	1	-	8

Table 8.1 reveals a largely hidden dimension of the Ignatian letter corpus, namely a potentially numeric aspect of the text—with particular word-frequency emphasis seemingly placed on NrN, that is, multiples of the numbers 15, 17, and 26, on the one hand, and 22, 24, and 27, on the other (marked in boldface in table 8.1, and below).[10] We may notice, in particular, the NrN pertaining to the full Ignatian letter corpus in the right column: Most of these figures are NrN. In addition we may here detect, as we did in chapter 6 above, a Triune pattern by means of the following word-frequency constellations: for the seven-letter corpus, θεός (**176 times**) + Ἰησοῦς χριστός (**108 times**) + πνεῦμα (**22 times**) = **306 occurrences** [18 × 17 = 2 × 3 × 3 × 17]; for To the Ephesians, θεός (43 times) + Ἰησοῦς χριστός (**26 times**) + πνεῦμα (3 times) = **72 occurrences** [3 × 24]; for To the Philadelphians, θεός (**22 times**) + Ἰησοῦς χριστός (18 times) + πνεῦμα (4 times) = **44 occurrences** [2 × 22]; for To the Smyrnaeans, θεός (25 times) + Ἰησοῦς χριστός (11 times) + πνεῦμα (3 times) = 39 occurrences (cf. table 5.1 above, for potential numerological significance of the number 39); for the seven-letter corpus, πατήρ (**45 times**) + υἱός (8 times) + πνεῦμα (**22**

---

9. Corresponding figure in the seven-letter Ignatian Corpus for τοῦ θεοῦ (sg. gen.) **17 times**.

10. Other recurring numerals/word-frequency multiples are 8, 11, 12, 13, 14, and 18.

times) = **75 occurrences** [5 × 15]; and for *To the Ephesians*, πατήρ (9 times) + υἱός (3 times) + πνεῦμα (3 times) = **15 occurrences** (i.e., two NrN—75 and 15—out of three possible candidates, for figures above 10, that is, 67 percent NrN in the Ignatian corpus for the sum of the number of occurrences of πατήρ + υἱός + πνεῦμα).

In terms of methodology, we may note the following (points 1–7 below) as we identify NrN in the Ignatian corpus, and similar numerical word-frequency patterns also in other early Christian and Jewish texts, such as the Septuagint, Josephus, the New Testament, and Eusebius's *Ecclesiastical History*.[11]

1. **The *nomina sacra* word-group:** All, or most, terms in the *nomina sacra* word-group present in the Ignatian corpus appear to be included in the apparently special arithmetic treatment of these words observable in table 8.1, that is, their treatment as NrN.[12] Also some other words in the Ignatian corpus receive a similar treatment, such as ζάω, "to live," ἀποθνήσκω, "to die," πίστις, "faith, belief, trust," and ὄνομα, "name," occurring **22, 15, 27,** and **24 times**, respectively;[13]

2. **NrN—two groups of numbers, and their multiples, pertaining to the divine name:** In our analysis of *nomina sacra*, multiples of two groups of numerals stand out in the Ignatian text, namely multiples of the alphabetical numbers 22/27 and 24, on the one hand, and multiples of the numerical values associated with the Tetragrammaton, 15, 17, and 26, on the other. Frequencies in table 8.1 of each of the words Ἰησοῦς (**17 times** and **22 times**) and χριστός (**22 times** and **26 times**), for example, include references to both alphabetical and divine

---

11. The scriptorium at Caesarea enabled Bishop Eusebius to supply Emperor Constantine with fifty copies of Scripture (*Vit. Const.* 4.34–7).

12. In addition to the eight *nomina sacra* listed in table 8.1, the Ignatian epistles include also the following words, which are sometimes demarcated as *nomina sacra* in contemporary or later manuscripts: σταυρόω (3 times), σταυρός (6 times), σταυρο* (9 times), Δαυίδ (5 times).

13. The terms included in the New Testament triad "faith, hope, love" seem to be presented in the seven-letter Ignatian corpus with NrN in mind: πίστις **27 times**, πιστ* **51 times** [3 × 17] (cf. observation 1 in ch. 7 above), ἐλπίς **11 times**, ἐλπι* **15 times**, ἀγάπη **45 times** [3 × 15], ἀγαπ* **72 times** [3 × 24].

name numbers, as do the number of appearances of θεός (**22 times**, **24 times**, and **26 times**).

3. **Textual collection/canonical framework:** Just as there seems to be an intertextual numerical connection between the Ignatian corpus and the biblical text (cf. observations 1, 2, and 3 in ch. 7 above, with regard to *NrN*), there also appears to be an arithmetic connection, by means of *NrN*, between word-frequencies in individual writings in various early Christian text corpora and numerical aspects of the respective corpora viewed as textual wholes, as in the following examples: Ἰησοῦς χριστός occurs **17 times** in the *Epistle to the Trallians* and **108 times** [4 × 27] in the Ignatian seven-letter corpus; similar potential numerical references to the divine name (17) and to Hebrew alphabetical fullness (22 or 27) also encounter the attentive reader of the New Testament, where Ἰησοῦς χριστός occurs **17 times** in 1–2 Peter, on the one hand, and **44** [2 × 22] and **88 times** [4 × 22], respectively, in Praxapostolos and Pauline Corpus, on the other. In the critical edition of the full twenty-seven-book New Testament corpus, Ἰησοῦς χριστός features either **135** [5 × 27] **times** (NA28) or 140 times [10 × 14] (THGNT).[14]

4. **Statistics:** In terms of word-frequency patterns, the probability that multiples of any of the numbers 15/17/26 or 22/24/27 will occur randomly in a text is around 26 to 28 percent (e.g., numbers between 15 and 250 included in the count, of which 65 numerals are *NrN*, gives 26 percent). Thus, the probability that a frequently recurring word or phrase like Ἰησοῦς χριστός, by chance will appear as an *NrN* in the *Letter to the Ephesians* (**26 times**), and, at the same time as an *NrN* in the letter-corpus as a whole (**108 times** [4 × 27]), is about 7.7 percent (cf.

---

14. Ἰησοῦς χριστός features 140 times [10 × 14] in the full twenty-seven-book New Testament corpus (THGNT), which may include a reference to the Davidic numeral 14 (cf. table 5.1 above and appendix below). The corresponding figure in NA28 is **135 times** [5 × 27], with 83 occurrences in Pauline Corpus instead of **88** [4 × 22], as in THGNT.

also n. 28 below).[15] Moreover, that we would end up with NrN for most of the terms in the *nomina sacra* word-group in the Ignatian letters seems unlikely, if these numerical patterns were not deliberate, either at the editorial–scribal or at the authorial–compositional level, or at both levels. Regarding statistical data, if we choose to include figures at 15 or above in the Ignatian letters (15 being the lowest of the NrN), we get the following results for the seven individual letters and the Ignatian corpus viewed as a whole (cf. table 8.1):

i.   50 percent NrN for Ἰησοῦς (33 times, **22 times**, 19 times, **17 times**, **22 times**, 128 times; three NrN out of, in total, six possibilities; numbers at 15 or above included in the count);

ii. 33 percent NrN for χριστός (33 times, **22 times**, 19 times, 18 times, 21 times, **130 times**; two NrN out of, in total, six possibilities; numbers at 15 or above included in the count);

iii. 71 percent NrN for χρ* (39 times, **27 times**, **24 times**, 23 times, **24 times**, **15 times**, **156 times**; five NrN out of, in total, seven possibilities; numbers at 15 or above included in the count);[16]

iv. 67 percent NrN for Ἰησοῦς χριστός (**26 times**, 18 times, **17 times**, **15 times**, 18 times, **108 times**; four NrN out of, in total, six possibilities; numbers at 15 or above included in the count);

---

15. 0.2766 × 0.2766 = 0.0765075 ≈ 7.7 percent (or lower, if we use instead the figures 0.26 x 0.26 ≈ 6.8 percent), that is, the probability—within a NrN framework—for this to occur is about 1 in 13. As for the appearances of Ἰησοῦς χριστός in the Ignatian corpus, for figures above 11, four out of six possible cases are NrN, that is, 67 percent of the figures are NrN (*To the Ephesians* **26 times**, *To the Magnesians* 18 times, *To the Trallians* **17 times**, *To the Romans* **15 times**, *To the Philadelphians* 18 times, the Ignatian seven-letter corpus **108 times** [4 × 27]; not included in the count: *To the Smyrnaeans* 11 times and *To Polycarp* 3 times; regarding 18 and 11 as potential additional significant numerals, see table 5.1 above).

16. As indicated in table 5.1 above, multiples of 39 could also potentially be included among the NrN.

v. 57 percent NrN for θεός (43 times, 23 times, **26 times, 22 times**, 25 times, **24 times, 176 times**; four NrN out of, in total, seven possibilities; numbers at 15 or above included in the count);

vi. 43 percent NrN for θεο* (**45 times**, 25 times, **27 times, 24 times**, 31 times, 28 times, 194 times; three NrN out of, in total, seven possibilities; numbers at 15 or above included in the count);

vii. 100 percent NrN for the following six *nomina sacra*: κύριος (**34 times**), ὁ θεός (**30 times**) πνεῦμα (**22 times**), πατήρ (**45 times**), ὁ πατήρ (**22 times**), and ἀνθρωπ* (**17 times**; one NrN out of, in total, one possibility for each of these six *nomina sacra*; numbers at 15 or above included in the count).

In sum, if we assume that these arithmetical NrN patterns have not been deliberately designed as such, all the aforementioned figures (i–vii) turn out to be above the expected outcome *in each case*, for randomly occurring NrN, which is 26 to 28 percent in each case. Thus, overall NrN figures at or above 40 percent (i, iii–vii), 50 percent (i, iii–v, vii), 60 percent (iii–iv, vii), 70 percent (iii, vii), and 100 percent (vii, including six terms) quite strongly indicate—to the contrary—that we are here not dealing with pure chance. In other words, NrN patterns in the Ignatian corpus appear to be the result of intended compositional, editorial, and/or scribal design strategies.

5. **Examples of various length/forms of a word (or words with a common stem) being double or triple frequency-coded (multiples of 15/17/26 or 22/24/26):** NrN word-frequencies for χριστός (and some additional words beginning with the letters χρ-) in Ignatius's *Epistle to the*

Magnesians occur as follows: χριστός **22 occurrences**, χρισ* **26 occurrences, and** χρ* **27 occurrences.** Similar patterns can be seen for the following words/letter constellations: θεός (*To the Romans* **26 times**, *To the Philadelphians* **22 times**), θεο* (*To the Romans* **27 times**, *To the Philadelphians* **24 times**), χριστός (*To the Magnesians* **22 times**, Ignatian corpus **130 times** [5 × 26]), χριστ* (*To the Magnesians* **26 times**), and χρ* (*To the Magnesians* **27 times**, Ignatian corpus **156 times** [6 × 26]).[17] A parallel illustration from the New Testament, in addition to the figures in observation 3 in chapter 7 above, is διδάσκαλος appearing **17 times** in Luke and **48 times** [2 × 24] in the four Gospels; διδασκ* **27 times** in Matthew, **34 times** [2 × 17] in Luke, and **17 times** in Acts; διδα* **30 times** [2 × 15] in Matthew and **120 times** [5 × 24] in the four Gospels; and διδ* **88 times** [4 × 22] in Matthew and **357 times** [3 × 7 × 17] in the four Gospels (NA28; THGNT, from which the above figures are taken has 355 occurrences for the four Gospels; corresponding figure in א is **352 occurrences** [16 × 22]).[18]

6. **Examples of NrN word-frequencies (multiples of 15/17/26 or 22/24/26) with the article (arthrous) and without (anarthrous):** πατήρ appearing **45 times** [3 × 15] in the Ignatian corpus, and ὁ πατήρ **22 times**; θεός appearing **176 times** [8 × 22] in the Ignatian corpus, and ὁ θεός **30 times** [2 × 15]. Parallels from the Septuagint and the New Testament to this phenomenon regarding the number of occurrences of κύριος and ὁ κύριος, respectively, look as follows (figures from Rahlfs and THGNT):

    i. Leviticus **340 times** [20 × 17] (κύριος) and **78 times** [3 × 26] (ὁ κύριος);

---

17. Another example from the Ignatian corpus is πίστις **27 times**, πιστ* **51 times** [3 × 17], *πισ* **136 times** [8 × 17], and *πιστευ* **108 times** [4 × 27].

18. We can also note that ὁ διδάσκαλος appears **17 times** in the Gospels/New Testament.

ii.   2 Samuel **221** times [13 × 17] (κύριος) and **66 times** [2 × 22] (ὁ κύριος);

iii.   2 Maccabees **45 times** [3 × 15] (κύριος) and **30 times** [2 × 15] (ὁ κύριος);

iv.   Historical Books **2655 times** [177 × 15] (κύριος) and **576** [24 × 24] (ὁ κύριος);

v.   Hosea **48 times** [2 × 24] (κύριος) and **15 times** (ὁ κύριος);

vi.   Luke **104 times** [4 × 27] (κύριος) and **45 times** [3 × 15] (ὁ κύριος);

vii.   John **52 times** [2 × 26] (κύριος) and **17 times** (ὁ κύριος);

viii. Acts **108 times** [4 × 27] (κύριος) and **68 times** [4 × 17] (ὁ κύριος), and, finally;

ix.   2 Thessalonians **22 times** (κύριος) and **15 times** (ὁ κύριος).

7.   **The terms κύριος and θεός in early Christian and Jewish texts as positive control group (see further appendix, ex. 3, for a more comprehensive *NrN* analysis of the appearances of κύριος in the Pentateuch and the New Testament):**

i.   In Eusebius's *Church History* (Migne, Accordance), made up of ten books, κύριος and θεός appear with the following frequencies:

a.   κύριος: Book 2 **17 times**, book 5 **30 times** [2 × 15], book 6 **24 times**, book 7 **17 times**, and book 10 **22 times;**[19]

---

19. In addition, ὁ θεός occurs with the following frequencies: book 3 **27 times**, book 5 **24 times**, book 6 **15 times**. See also note 20 below

b. θεός: Book 1 **75 times** [5 × 15], book 4 **26 times**, book 6 **27 times**, book 7 **44 times** [2 × 22], book 8 **24 times**, book 10 **72 times** [3 × 27].[20]

ii. In two of Bishop Athanasius's writings (Migne, Accordance) we find our specified word-frequency patterns for κύριος and ὁ θεός, allocated as follows:

a. *On the Incarnation:*

- κύριος **60 times** [4 × 15] and ὁ θεός **119 times** [7 × 17];

b. *Letter to Serapion*

- κύριος **108 times** [4 × 27] and ὁ θεός **182 times** [7 × 26].

iii. In the Jewish history writer Josephus's work *Antiquitates Judaicae* (1890 Niese edition, Accordance) κύριος is employed **27 times** and θεός **1606 times** [73 × 22]. In Josephus's *Collected Works* θεός occurs **1914 times** [87 × 22] and ὁ θεός **1455 times** [97 × 15].[21]

a. In 1 Clement (ca. AD 95/96; Holmes, *Apostolic Fathers*, Accordance), from about the same time as Josephus's *Antiquities*, the word κύριος is used **66 times** [3 × 22];[22]

b. In the Didache it appears **24 times**;

---

20. In addition, in books 1–10: κύριος (sg. nom.) **44 times** [2 × 22] (book 1 15 times), ὁ κύριος (sg. nom.) **15 times**, κυρίου **96 times** [4 × 24], κυρίῳ **15 times**, κυρι* **225 times** [15 × 15], ὁ κυρι* **130 times** [5 × 26] (book 5 26 times, book 6 15 times), κυρ* **234 times** [9 × 26 = 6 × 39; see table 5.1 above for potential significance of 39], ὁ κυ* **135 times** [5 × 27] (book 5 26 times, book 6 15 times, book 7 17 times), θεῷ **34 times** [2 × 17], τοῦ θεοῦ **108 times** [4 × 27] (book 1 22 times, book 7 15 times), *θεο* **704 times** [32 × 22]; see table 5.1 above for potential significance of 32] (book 2 45 times [3 × 15], book 6 51 times [3 × 17]).

21. In Josephus's *Against Apion*, θεός features **110 times** [5 × 22], and ὁ θεός features **45 times** [3 × 15].

22. Michael Holmes, *Apostolic Fathers: Greek Texts and English Translations of Their Writings*, 3rd ed. (Grand Rapids: Baker Academic, 2007).

c. In the seven Ignatian letters, κύριος is used altogether **34 times [2 × 17]**;[23] in some of the Old Testament pseudepigrapha such as Testament of Levi (*The Greek Pseudepigrapha* [electronic text prepared by Craig A. Evans, 2013, Accordance]) we find the same pattern, with κύριος appearing **51 times [3 × 17]**;

d. In the Protevangelium of James (*The Apocryphal Gospels* [electronic text prepared by Craig A. Evans, 2009, Accordance]), κύριος features **81 times [3 × 27]**.

In sum, in addition to the Ignatian letters and other patristic (e.g., 1 Clement, Eusebius, and Athanasius) and early Jewish literature (e.g., Josephus), the arithmetic NrN configurations observed above involve the textual composition and editing of the following canonical subunits: Leviticus, 2 Samuel, the Historical Books, Hosea, Matthew, Luke, John, the four Gospels, Acts, 2 Thessalonians, Pauline Corpus, 1–2 Peter, and the Praxapostolos.

In the next section (§8.2), we shall broaden our selection of *nomina sacra* to include samples of ten (Ἰσραήλ, υἱός, πνεῦμα, κύριος, θεός, πατήρ, μήτηρ, σταυρός, Δαυίδ, and σωτήρ) of the altogether fifteen *nomina sacra* (see further ch. 12 below) for the purpose of detecting additional NrN in various canonical subunits, associated with these "sacred," textually high-lighted, New Testament words. This is followed by further analysis, and listing, of NrN at various canonical subunit levels, involving a broader selection of words (§§8.3 and 8.4).

---

23. In another text among the Apostolic Fathers, the Epistle of Barnabas, κύριος occurs 107 times in Holmes's text edition. I have argued elsewhere (Tomas Bokedal, "'But for Me, the Scriptures Are Jesus Christ' [IC XC; Ign. *Phld.* 8:2]: Creedal Text-Coding and the Early Scribal System of Nomina Sacra," in *Studies on the Paratextual Features of Early New Testament Manuscripts*, ed. Stanley E. Porter, David I. Yoon, and Chris S. Stevens, TENTS [Leiden: Brill, forthcoming]) that this should rather be **108 times [4 × 27]**.

8.2 OBSERVATION 5:
NOMINA SACRA FEATURING AS *NRN*
AT DIFFERENT CANONICAL LEVELS

Listed below are examples of *nomina sacra* in the New Testament, appearing as *NrN* at different canonical levels (figures from the THGNT, unless otherwise indicated).[24]

Ἰσραήλ

- Ἰσραήλ occurring as *NrN* in seven canonical subunits, at five canonical levels: Acts **15 times**, Luke-Acts **27 times**, Synoptic Gospels **26 times**, four Gospels **30 times** [2 × 15], Gospels + Acts **45 times** [3 × 15], Praxapostolos **15 times**, twenty-seven-book New Testament **68 times** [4 × 17].

υἱός

- υἱός occurring as *NrN* in five canonical subunits, at five canonical levels (also mentioned above): **22 times** in 1 John, **24 times** in 1–3 John, **27 times** in the Catholic Epistles, **48 times** [2 × 24] in the Praxapostolos, and **243 times** [9 × 27] in the full New Testament.

πνεῦμα

- πνεῦμα ἅγιον (*NrN* at three to four canonical levels): (1) Acts **17 times**; (2) Luke-Acts **24 times**; (3) four Gospels + Acts **30 times** [2 × 15]; (4) twenty-seven-book New Testament **45 times** [3 × 15] (NA28; THGNT 46 times [2 × 23]).

- τὸ πνεῦμα (*NrN* at four canonical levels): (1) Mark **15 times**, John **15 times**; (2) four Gospels **51 times** [3 × 17]; (3) Gospels + Acts **88 times** [4 × 22]; (4) twenty-seven-book New Testament corpus **176 times** [8 × 22].

---

24. The below data, in modified form, also appear in Tomas Bokedal, *Names and Numbers: Nomina Sacra and Numerological Editorial Practice in Christian Scripture*, forthcoming.

- πνεῦμα (*NrN* at two to three canonical levels): (1) John **24 times**; (2) Synoptic Gospels **78 times** [3 × 26]; (3) four Gospels **102 times** [6 × 17].

- πνεῦμα (forms in the sg.; *NrN* at three canonical levels): (1) Luke **30 times** [2 × 15], John **24 times**; (2) Luke-Acts **96 times** [4 × 24]; (3) twenty-seven-book New Testament corpus **345 times** [23 × 15].

- πνεῦμα (forms in the sg.; *NrN* at four canonical levels): (1) Romans **34 times** [2 × 17], 2 Corinthians **17 times**; (2) 1–2 Corinthians **54 times** [2 × 27]; (3) Pauline Corpus **150 times** [10 × 15]; (4) twenty-seven-book New Testament corpus **345 times** [23 × 15].

- πνεύματος (*NrN* at one to two canonical levels; NA28): (1) Gospels + Acts 39 times; (2) twenty-seven-book New Testament **96 times** [4 × 24].

- πνεύματι (various *NrN* at two to three canonical levels): (1) four Gospels **24 times**; (2) Gospels + Acts **34 times** [2 × 17]; (3) Praxapostolos **15 times**; (twenty-seven-book New Testament 91 times [7 × 13]).

- πνεύματι (1) 1–2 Corinthians **17 times**; (2) Pauline Corpus **48 times** [2 × 24]; (twenty-seven-book New Testament 91 times [7 × 13]).

- *πνευ* (*NrN* at three canonical levels):[25] (1) John **24 times**, 2 Corinthians **17 times**, Ephesians **17 times**; (2) four Gospels **102 times** [6 × 17], Synoptic Gospels **78 times** [3 × 26], Catholic Epistles **27 times**, (Pauline Corpus 184 times [8 × 23]); (3) twenty-seven-book New Testament **408 times** [17 × 24].

---

25. For the Catholic Epistles (**27 times**), the following words, and their number of occurrences, are included in the count: πνεῦμα 25 times and πνευματικός twice.

- πνευματικός (NrN at three canonical levels): (1) 1 Corinthians **15 times** (THGNT, NA28); (2) Pauline Corpus **24 times**; (3) twenty-seven-book New Testament corpus **26 times**.

κύριος

- κύριος (sg. nom., NrN at three canonical levels): (1) 1–2 Corinthians **22 times** (THGNT, NA28); (2) Pauline Corpus **66 times** [3 × 22] (THGNT, NA28), four Gospels **68 times** [4 × 17] (NA28); (3) twenty-seven-book New Testament corpus **176 times** [8 × 22] (NA28). For κύριος (sg. forms; NA28) NrN occur at three canonical levels: Matthew **78 times** [3 x 26]; Synoptics **198 times** [9 x 22]; twenty-seven-book New Testament **702 times** [27 x 26 = 3 x 3 x 3 x 26].

- ὁ κύριος (sg. nom., NrN at three canonical levels; NA28): (1) Matthew **17 times**, Luke **24 times**; (2) Synoptic Gospels **45 times** [3 × 15]; (3) four Gospels **52 times** [2 × 26], Praxapostolos **17 times** (Gospels + Acts 64 times [2 × 32]).

- ὁ κύριος (sg. nom., NrN at three canonical levels; THGNT): (1) Matthew **17 times**, Luke **26 times**; (2) Synoptic Gospels **48 times** [2 × 24]; (four Gospels 56 times [4 × 14]); (3) twenty-seven-book New Testament **110 times** [5 × 22].

- ὁ κύριος (NrN at three to four canonical levels): (1) Matthew **26 times**, Luke **45 times** [3 × 15]; (2) Synoptic Gospels **78 times** [3 × 26] (THGNT; NA28 77 times); (3) Gospels + Acts **162 times** [6 × 27] (NA28; THGNT 163 times); (4) twenty-seven-book New Testament **351 times** [13 × 27].

- κυρίου (NrN at five canonical levels): (1) Matthew **15 times**, Luke **26 times**; (2) Synoptic Gospels **45 times** [3 × 15]; (3) four Gospels **51 times** [3 × 17]; (4) Gospels + Acts **96 times** [4 × 24]; (5) twenty-seven-book New Testament **240 times** [10 × 24].

- τοῦ κυρίου (*NrN* at two to three canonical levels; NA28):
  (1) Synoptic Gospels **15 times**; (four Gospels 18 times);
  (2) Gospels + Acts **51 times** [3 × 17]; (3) twenty-seven-book
  New Testament **150 times** [10 × 15].

- τοῦ κυρίου (1) Praxapostolos **51 times** [3 × 17] (= Acts 33
  times + Catholic Epistles 18 times); (2) twenty-seven-book
  New Testament **150 times** [10 × 15].

- τοῦ κυρίου (1) Pauline Corpus **78 times** [3 × 26]; (2) twenty-seven-book New Testament **150 times** [10 × 15].

- *κυρ* (*NrN* at two to three canonical levels):[26] (1) Luke **108
  times** [4 × 27], John **52 times** [2 × 26] (Luke-Acts 224 times
  [16 × 14]); (2) four Gospels **264 times** [12 × 22].

- *κυρ* (1) 2 Timothy **17 times**, 1 Corinthians **68 times** [4 ×
  17], Ephesians **27 times**, Philippians **15 times**, Colossians 17
  times, 1 Thessalonians **24 times**, 2 Thessalonians **22 times**,
  Hebrews **17 times**; (2) 1–2 Timothy **24 times**; (3) Pauline
  Corpus **306 times** [18 × 17].

θεός

- θεοῦ (*NrN* at three to four canonical levels): (1) Luke **72 times**
  [3 × 24]; (2) Luke-Acts **130 times** [5 × 26] (NA28; THGNT
  129 times); (3) four Gospels **180 times** [12 × 15]; (4) twenty-seven-book New Testament **690 times** [2 × 23 × 15].

- τοῦ θεοῦ (*NrN* at three to four canonical levels; NA28):
  (1) Matthew **24 times**, Luke **66 times** [3 × 22]; (2) Luke-Acts
  120 times [5 x 24] (THGNT); (3) four Gospels **153 times** [9
  × 17]; (4) Gospels + Acts **208 times** [8 × 26].

---

26. For Luke (**108 times** [4 × 27]), the following words, and their number of occurrences, are included in the count: Κυρηναῖος once, Κυρήνιος once, κυριεύω once, κύριος **104 times** [4 × 26], and συγκυρία once.

- ὁ θεός (NA28; NrN at three canonical levels): (1) Acts **153 times [9 × 17]**; (2) Luke-Acts **260 times [10 × 26]**; (3) Gospels + Acts **405 times [15 × 27]**.

- θεῷ (NrN at two to three canonical levels): (1) Luke-Acts **24 times**; (2) Gospels + Acts **34 times [2 × 17]**; (3) Praxapostolos **27 times**.

πατήρ
- πατήρ (sg. nom., NrN at three to four canonical levels): (1) John **51 times [3 × 17]**; (2) Synoptic Gospels 39 times; (3) four Gospels **90 times [6 × 15]** (Gospels + Acts 92 times [4 × 23]); (4) twenty-seven-book New Testament **110 times [5 × 22]**.

- πάτερ (NrN at one canonical level): (1) twenty-seven-book New Testament **24 times**.

μήτηρ
- μήτηρ (NrN at three canonical levels): (1) Matthew **26 times**, Mark **17 times**, Luke **17 times**; (2) Synoptic Gospels **60 times [4 × 15]**; (3) Gospels + Acts **75 times [5 × 15]**.

- μητέρα (NrN at one canonical level): (1) twenty-seven-book New Testament **26 times**.

- *μητ* (NrN at three canonical levels):[27] (1) Luke **26 times** (Luke-Acts 42 times [3 × 14]); (2) Synoptic Gospels **81 times [3 × 27]**; (3) twenty-seven-book New Testament **154 times [7 × 22]**.

σταυρός
- σταυρός (NrN at one canonical level): (1) twenty-seven-book New Testament **27 times**.

---

27. The following words, and their number of occurrences, are included in the count: μήτε 6 times, μήτηρ **17 times**, μήτι twice, and μήτρα once.

- σταυρ* (*NrN* at two canonical levels): (1) Matthew **15 times**, John **15 times**; (2) four Gospels **51 times** [3 × 17].

- στα* (*NrN* at two canonical levels): (1) Mark **17 times**, John **17 times**; (2) four Gospels **66 times** [3 × 22].

- στ* (*NrN* at two canonical levels): (1) Matthew **48 times** [2 × 24], Mark **30 times** [2 × 15], Romans **15 times**, 1 Corinthians **15 times**, Revelation **51 times** [3 × 17], Luke **54 times** [2 × 27]; (2) Synoptic Gospels **132 times** [6 × 22]; (2) Synoptic Gospels **132 times** [6 x 22], Praxapostolos **85 times** [5 x 17].

Δαυίδ
- Δαυίδ (*NrN* at two to three canonical levels): (1) Matthew **17 times**; (2) Luke-Acts **24 times**; (3) four Gospels 39 times.

- *Δα* (*NrN* at three canonical levels): (1) Matthew **165 times** [11 × 15]; (2) Synoptic Gospels **442 times** [17 × 26]; (3) four Gospels **660** [2 × 15 × 22].

- *Δα* (*NrN* at two to three canonical levels): (1) Acts **189 times** [7 × 27]; (2) 1–2 John **22 times**; (3) Catholic Epistles **54 times** [2 × 27], Praxapostolos **243 times** [9 × 27].

- *Δα* (*NrN* at one to three canonical levels): (1) 1 Thessalonians **17 times**; (2) 1–2 Corinthians **88 times** [4 × 22]; (3) Pauline Corpus 273 times [7 × 39].

σωτήρ
- σωτήρ (*NrN* at one canonical level): (1) twenty-seven-book New Testament **24 times**.

- σωτ* (*NrN* at three canonical levels): (1) Luke-Acts **17 times**; (2) Praxapostolos **22 times** (Catholic Epistles 13 times); (3) twenty-seven-book New Testament **75 times** [5 × 15].

8.3 OBSERVATION 6: ΕΓΩ, ΣΥ, ΛΟΓΟΣ

As we look beyond the *nomina sacra* word-group, toward some other frequently occurring New Testament terms, such as the pronouns ἐγώ and σύ, we may, in fact, continue to notice an unexpectedly high presence of NrN in the various canonical subunits. The following examples involving the pronoun ἐγώ seem to illustrate this (figures below from THGNT, unless otherwise indicated).

NrN of ἐγώ in the New Testament feature as follows:

ἐγώ (all forms): (1) Matthew **270 times** [10 × 27]; (2) Mark **130** [**5 × 26**] (NA28; THGNT 129 times); (3) Luke **288 times** [12 × 24]; (4) Acts **312 times** [12 × 26]; (5) Luke-Acts **600 times** [**25 × 24**]; (6) the four Gospels + Acts **1540 times** [**70 × 22**]; (7) 1–2 Peter **24 times**; (8) Praxapostolos **435 times** [**29 × 15**] (NA28; THGNT 438 times); (9) Romans **150 times** [10 × 15]; (10) 1–2 Corinthians **312 times** [12 × 26]; (11) Ephesians **45 times** [3 × 15] (NA28; THGNT 46 times [2 × 23]); (12) Philippians **60 times** [4 × 15]; (13) Colossians **24 times**; (14) 1 Thessalonians **51** times [3 × 17]; (15) 2 Thessalonians **26 times**; (16) 1 Timothy **15 times**; (17) Philemon **22 times**; (18) Hebrews **66 times** [3 × 22]; (19) Revelation **102 times** [6 × 17]. A high proportion of *NrN* can here be noted, not least, for the Lukan writings (THGNT): Luke **288 times** [12 × 24], Acts **312 times** [12 × 26 = 13 × 24], Luke-Acts **600 times** [40 × 15 = 5 × 5 × 24], "Gospels + Acts **1540 times** [70 x 22 = 5 x 14 x 22]. If we make a statistical calculation based on 12 successful *NrN* hits in THGNT, in 12 individual New Testament books (Matthew **270x**, Luke **288x**, Acts **312x**, Romans **150x**, Philippians **60x**, Colossians **24x**, 1 Thessalonians **51x**, 2 Thessalonians **26x**, 1 Timothy **15x**, Philemon **22x**, Hebrews **66x**, and Revelation **102x**) out of 23 possible cases (23 New Testament books included: 1 Peter 6x, 2 John 6x, 3 John 6x, and Jude 7x

excluded from the count, due to low numbers), the result is ca.
0.0138, or a probability of ca. one in a hundred.[28] In addition to
this figure, we may note the six forms of ἐγώ appearing as NrN
in the full New Testament listed below (THGNT), which makes
it even more unlikely that these NrN are not editorially intended.

Corresponding figures for the Catholic Epistles in Codex
Sinaiticus (‭א‬) look as follows: James **26 times**, 1–2 Peter **27
times**, 1 John **60 times** [4 × 15], 1–2 John **66 times** [3 × 22],
1–3 John **72 times** [3 × 24], Catholic Epistles **132 times** [6 ×
22]. That is, more or less all relevant figures for ἐγώ appear as
NrN in ‭א‬ (Catholic Epistles; corresponding figures in ‭א‬ for the
Synoptic Gospels and the fourfold Gospel are **682 times** [31 ×
22] and **1207 times** [71 × 17], respectively).

Corresponding figures for the twenty-seven-book New Testament
(THGNT, unless otherwise indicated; for items 1–19, see above):
(20) ἐγώ (sg. nom) **340 times** [20 × 17]; (21) New Testament μου
567 times [21 × 27]; (22) μοι **225 times** [15 × 15]; (23) ἐμοί **96 times**
[4 × 24]; (24) με **285 times** [19 × 15]; (25) ἐμέ **90 times** [6 × 15]
(NA28; THGNT 94 times); (26) ἐγώ (acc. forms) **550 times** [25

---

28. This calculation was pursued in close dialogue with statistician Dr. Stein Andreas Bethuelsen:
Assumption: We study n= 23 books; for each of these we expect 'success' in p= 0.284 of the cases.
No design would mean that p is equal for each of the books; additionally, for the computation, we
assume that they are independent. Then X= number of successes is binomially distributed with
parameters n= 23 and p= 0.284. Based on the above, we perform a hypothesis test:
Null hypothesis: Ho: p≤0.284
versus
Alternative hypothesis: Ha: p>0.284
The p-value, the probability of observing something at least as 'extreme' in favor of Ha as what
we observe, X=x (here x=12), given Ho is true, is then:

$$P(X \geq x|p = 0.284) = \sum_{m=x}^{23} P(X = m|p = 0.284)$$

$$P(X \geq x|p = 0.284) = \sum_{m=x}^{23} \left(\frac{23!}{m!}\right) 0.284^m (1 - 0.284)^{23-m}$$

$$P(X \geq x|p = 0.284) = 0.0138.$$

x 22]. We note that most appearances of ἐγώ—including nominative, genitive, dative, and accusative forms—feature as NrN in the twenty-seven-book New Testament corpus.

If we posit that these arithmetical figures are not deliberately introduced into the Christian Bible manuscripts, the probability that the aforementioned NrN are arbitrary (and not deliberate) is about 26 to 28 percent *in each case* for the figures presented above. Against this option, the present chapter makes an accumulative case arguing that the NrN presented throughout the chapter have been deliberately designed as NrN at the compositional and/or editorial-scribal level.

NrN of σύ in the New Testament feature as follows: σύ (all forms): (1) The four Gospels **1474 times** [67 × 22]; (2) Acts **264 times** [12 × 22]; (3) 1 John **34 times** [2 × 17]; (4) 1–3 John **52 times** [2 × 26]; (5) Romans **130 times** [5 × 26] (NA28; THGNT 129 times); (6) 1 Corinthians **153 times** [9 × 17] (THGNT)/**154 times** [7 × 22] (NA28); (7) 2 Corinthians **156 times** [6 × 26]; (8) Galatians **52 times** [2 × 26]; (9) Ephesians **48 times** [2 × 24] (NA28; THGNT 47 times); (10) Philippians **52 times** [2 × 26]; (11) 1 Timothy **15 times**; (12) Philemon **24 times**; (13) Hebrews **60 times** [4 × 15] (NA28; THGNT 61 times); (14) Pauline Corpus **901** [53 × 17] (NA28; THGNT 899 times); (15) the twenty-seven-book New Testament **2907 times** [3 × 57 × 17] (NA28; THGNT 2901 times; ℵ **2889 times** [107 x 27].”

Λόγος
In the twenty-seven-book New Testament various forms of the word λόγος further appear as follows:

λόγος **330 times** [15 × 22], λόγος **68 times** [4 × 17] (sg. nom.), λόγος (nom. forms) **78 times** [3 × 26], λόγου **27 times** (sg. gen.), λόγῳ **45 times** [3 × 15] (sg. dat.), λόγον **130 times** [5 × 26] (sg. acc.), λόγος (acc. forms) **153 times** [9 × 17], λόγος (sg. forms) **270 times** [10 × 27], λογ* **384 times** [16 × 24], *λογοσ* **338 times** [13 × 26]. That is, ten different forms of the word λόγος feature with potentially intended or deliberate word-frequency patterns (NrN).

In Pauline Corpus various forms of the word λόγος appear as follows:

λόγος **96 times** [4 x 24] (1 Corinthians **17 times**, 1–2 Corinthians **26 times**, 1–2 Timothy **15 times**), ὁ λόγος **48 times** [2 × 24], λόγος (sg. nom.)/λόγος (nom. forms) **30 times** [2 × 15], λόγον **27 times** (sg. acc.), λόγος (forms in the sg.) **85 times** [5 × 17] (1–2 Corinthians **22 times**), λογ* 140 times [10 × 14], ὁ λογ* 56 times [4 × 14], *λογ* 230 times [10 × 23], *λογοσ* 100 times [10 × 10]. That is, five to nine different forms of the word λόγος feature with potentially deliberate word-frequency (NrN) patterns.

In Luke-Acts various forms of the word λόγος appear as follows:

ὁ λόγος **72 times** [3 × 24] (Luke **22 times**), λόγος (dat. forms) **17 times**, λόγος (acc. forms) **48 times** [2 × 24], *λογ* **154 times** [7 × 22], λόγος 14 times (nom. sg.), λόγος (gen. forms) 14 times (see table 5.1 for potential significance of 14).

8.4 OBSERVATION 7: EXAMPLES OF NRN TERMS FROM THE WIDER CLASS OF BIBLICAL VOCABULARY

Table 8.2. 15/17/26/39-multiples from the wider class of potentially frequency-coded New Testament (THGNT) and LXX vocabulary (LXXG, unless otherwise indicated).

Term	Text	Frequency	Term	Text	Frequency
O ΑΓΑΘΟC[29]	New Testament	34 [2 × 17]	ΕΥΡΙCΚΩ	Four Gospels	102 [6 × 17]
ΑΓΙΟC	Ephesians	15	ΕCΧΑΤΟC	New Testament	52 [2 × 26]
	Revelation	26	ΖΗΤΕΩ	John	34 [2 × 17]
	2 Esdras	15		Psalms	30 [2 × 15]
	1 Maccabees	39	ΖΩΗ	Sirach	51 [3 × 17]
	Odes	17	O ΖΩΗ	Genesis	15
O ΑΓΙΟC	Acts	34 [2 × 17]		Pentateuch	30 [2 × 15]
	Exodus	39	HCAIAC	Isaiah	17
	Leviticus	45 [3 × 15]	ΘΑΝΑΤΟC	Psalms + Odes	30 [2 × 15]
	Numbers	45 [3 × 15]		Sirach	30 [2 × 15]
	Psalms + Odes	39	ΘΗCAYPOC	New Testament	17

29. O ΑΓΑΘΟC features **22 times** in 1–2 Samuel (Rahlfs), 39 times in the Poetical Books (Rahlfs; Psalms of Solomon excluded; 42 times [3 × 14] when Psalms of Solomon is included). ΑΓΑΘΟC appears in the four Gospels **22 times**, in the New Testament **102 times [6 × 17]** (NA28), in the Pentateuch (LXXG) 39 times; ΑΓΑΘΟC features also in 1 Clement **22 times**, Shepherd of Hermas 42 times [3 × 14], Eusebius *Hist. eccl.* books 1–10 **44 times [2 × 22]**, Athanasius *Contra gentes* **22 times** and *Orationes contra Arianos* **26 times.**

Term	Text	Frequency	Term	Text	Frequency
AIMA	Gospels + Acts	39	ΙΠΠΟC	New Testament	17
	Praxapostolos	17	ΙΠΠ*	New Testament	17
	Numbers	15	ΚΑΙΡΟC	Pauline Corpus	34 [2 × 17]
	Pentateuch	156 [6 × 26]		New Testament	85 [5 × 17]
ΑΙΩΝΙΟC	John	17		Twelve Prophets	15
	Four Gospels	30 [2 × 15]		Daniel (Rahlfs)	34 [2 × 17]
	Pentateuch	45 [3 × 15]	ΚΑΤΑΒΑΙΝΩ	John	17
ΑΙΡΩ	John	26		Four Gospels	45 [3 ×15]
	New Testament	102 [6 × 17]		Isaiah	17
	Numbers	15	ΚΕΛΕΥΩ	Acts	17
	Pentateuch	45 [3 × 15]	ΚΕΛΕΥ*	New Testament	26
	1 Maccabees	15	ΛΑΜΒΑΝΩ	Hebrews	17
	Psalms	17		Pauline Corpus	51 [3 × 17]
Η ΑΛΗΘΕΙΑ	Pauline Corpus	26		Deuteronomy	52 [2 × 26]
	Psalms	34 [2 × 17]	ΛΟΓΟC	1 Corinthians	17
ΑΜΑΡΤΙΑ	John	17		1-2 Corinthians	26
	1 John	17	Ο ΛΟΓΟC	Gospels + Acts	150 [10 × 15]
	Psalms + Odes	34 [2 × 15]		1 Maccabees	45 [3 × 15]
	Jeremiah + Baruch	17		Isaiah	26
	Ezekiel	26		Jeremiah	102 [6 × 17]

Term	Text	Frequency
ΑΠΟΚΑΛΥΠΤΩ	New Testament	26
ΑΠΟΚΑΛΥ*	Pauline Corpus	26
	1–2 Samuel (Rahlfs)	17
ΑΠΤΩ	Four Gospels	34 [2 × 17]
	Pentateuch	52 [2 × 26]
ΑΡΕΣΚΩ	New Testament	17
ΑΡΕΣ*	Pauline Corpus	15
ΑΡΤΟΣ	Psalms	17
	Isaiah	15
ΑΡΧΙΕΡΕΥΣ	Luke	15
	Hebrews	17
ΓΕΝΝΑΩ	Matthew	45 [3 × 15]
	Four Gospels	68 [4 × 17]
ΓΡΑΜΜΑ*	Pentateuch	15
	Genesis	78 [3 × 26]
ΓΡΑΦΩ	2 Chronicles	26
	1 Maccabees	30 [2 × 15]
ΓΡΑΦ*	1–2 Corinthians	30 [2 × 15]
	1 Esdras	26
Η ΓΥΝΗ	Luke	17

Term	Text	Frequency
ΜΑΚΑΡΙΟΣ	Luke	15
	Four Gospels	30 [2 × 15]
ΜΕΤΑΝΟΕΩ	New Testament	34 [2 × 17]
ΝΙΚΑΩ	Revelation	17
ΝΟΜΟΣ	Synoptic Gospels	17
	Acts	17
	Luke-Acts	26
Η ΟΔΟΣ	Deuteronomy	34 [2 × 17]
	Pentateuch	75 [5 × 15]
ΟΡΑΩ	John	68 [4 × 17]
	Deuteronomy	51 [3 × 17]
	Pentateuch	360 [24 × 15]
	Psalms	75 [5 × 15]
	Jeremiah	51 [3 × 17]
	Lamentation	17
ΠΑΙΣ	Ezekiel	75 [5 × 15]
	Deuteronomy	15
	2 Chronicles	39
ΠΑΡΑΔΙΔΩΜΙ	Luke	17
	John	15

Term	Text	Frequency	Term	Text	Frequency
	Four Gospels	51 [3 × 17]		Luke-Acts	30 [2 × 15]
	Revelation	15		New Testament	119 [7 × 17]
ΔΙΑΘΗΚΗ	Hebrews	17		Psalms + Odes	17
	Pauline Corpus	26	ΠΑΣΧΑ	Four Gospels	26
	Genesis	26	ΠΕΡΙΠΑΤΕΩ	John	17
	Pentateuch	85 [5 × 17]	ΠΙΝΩ	Four Gospels	51 [3 × 17]
	Twelve Prophets	15		Jeremiah	17
ΔΙΑΚΟΝΟΣ	New Testament	30 [2 × 15]	Η ΠΙΣΤΙΣ	Romans	17
ΔΙΔΑΣΚΑΛΟΣ	Luke	17	ΠΙΣΤ*	Four Gospels	170 [10 × 17]
Ο ΔΙΔΑΣΚΑΛΟΣ	Four Gospels	17		Psalms	17
ΔΙΔΑΣΚΩ	Mark	17	ΠΟΙΕΩ	Acts	68 [4 × 17]
	Luke	17		Genesis	165 [11 × 15]
ΔΙΔΑΣΚ*	Mark	30 [2 × 15]	ΠΟΙΜΗΝ	Four Gospels	15
	Luke	34 [2 × 17]		Ezekiel	17
	John	17 (based on Vaticanus)	ΠΟΙΜ*	New Testament	39
	Acts	17		Genesis	26
	Luke-Acts	51 [3 × 17]		Jeremiah + Baruch	34 [2 × 17]
	Pauline Corpus	45 [3 × 15]	Η ΠΡΟΣΕΥΧΗ	New Testament	26
ΔΙΚΑΙΟΣΥΝΗ	Romans	34 [2 × 17]	ΠΡΟΣΕΥΧΟΜΑΙ	Four Gospels	45 [3 × 15]

Term	Text	Frequency
Η ΔΙΚΑΙΟϹΥΝΗ	Isaiah	51 [3 × 17]
	Pauline Corpus	17
ΔΙΚΑΙΟ*	Luke	17
	Catholic Epistles	30 [2 × 15]
	Psalms + Odes	156 [6 × 26]
	Job	45 [3 × 15]
ΔΟΞΑ	Luke-Acts	17
	Revelation	17
	Exodus	15
	2 Chronicles	15
	Twelve Prophets	15
	Isaiah	68 [4 × 17]
Η ΔΟΞΑ	John	15
	Four Gospels	26
	1 Maccabees	15
ΕΙΡΗΝΗ	Ezekiel	15
Η ΕΙΡΗΝΗ	New Testament	17
	Rahlfs	17[30]

Term	Text	Frequency
ΠΡΟϹΕΥΧ*	Matthew	17
	Four Gospels	51 [3 × 17]
	Pauline Corpus	34 [2 × 17]
ΠΡΟΒΑΤΟΝ	Four Gospels	34 [2 × 17]
	John	15
ΤΟ ΠΡΟΒΑΤΟΝ	Deuteronomy	15
	Ezekiel	15
ΠΡΟΦΗΤΗϹ	Acts	30 [2 × 15]
	Praxapostolos	34 [2 × 17]
	Pentateuch	15
Ο ΠΡΟΦΗΤΗϹ	Matthew	26
	Luke	15
ΠΡΟΦΗΤ*	John	15
	Acts	34 [2 × 17]
	Ezekiel	52 [2 × 26]
ΡΑΒΒΙ	Four Gospels	15
ΡΑΒΒ*	Four Gospels	17
ΡΙΖΑ	New Testament	17

30. Distribution of Η ΕΙΡΗΝΗ in Rahlfs: Tobit once, 1 Maccabees twice, Psalms 3 times, Sirach once, Micah once, Zechariah once, Malachi once, Isaiah 3 times, Jeremiah 3 times, Baruch once (these figures from Rahlfs all agree with LXXG, except perhaps for Tobit once, which I have not yet had the opportunity to check).

Term	Text	Frequency
ΕΙΡΗΝ*	Pauline Corpus	52 [2 × 26]
ΕΙCΕΡΧΟΜΑΙ	Mark	30 [2 × 15]
	John	15
	Acts	34 (NA28; THGNT 32)
	Hebrews	17
	Exodus	34 [2 × 17]
	Leviticus	17
	Isaiah	17
Η ΕΚΚΛΗCΙΑ	1 Corinthians	15
	Pauline Corpus	45 [3 × 15]
	New Testament	78 [3 × 26]
	2 Chronicles	17
Η ΕΛΠΙC	New Testament	17
	Rahlfs	45 [3 × 15]
ΕΛΠΙ*	Romans	17
ΕΝΤΟΛΗ	Synoptic Gospels	17
	New Testament	68 [4 × 17]
ΕΞΟΥCΙΑ	New Testament	102 [6 × 17]
ΕΟΡΤΗ	John	17
	Pentateuch	34 [2 × 17]

Term	Text	Frequency
CΑΛΠ*	Revelation	17
	Pentateuch	30 [2 × 15]
COΦΙΑ	1 Corinthians	17
	New Testament	51 [3 × 17]
	Proverbs (Rahlfs)	45 [3 × 15]
	Wisdom (Rahlfs)	30 [2 × 15]
COΦ*	Pauline Corpus	45 [3 × 15]
	2 Chronicles	15
	Psalms + Odes	17
	Sirach (Rahlfs)	90 [6 × 15]
CΠΕΡΜΑ	Four Gospels	17
	Genesis	60 [4 × 15]
	Deuteronomy	15
	Isaiah	34 [2 × 17]
ΤΟ CΠΕΡΜΑ	New Testament	17
	Isaiah	15
CΤΡΕΦΩ	Four Gospels	17
CΩΖΩ	Luke	17
ΦΩΝΗ	Exodus	30 [2 × 15]
ΧΑΡΙC	Acts	17

Term	Text	Frequency	Term	Text	Frequency
ΕΠΑΓΓΕΛΙΑ	New Testament	52 [2 × 26]		Pentateuch	26
Η ΕΠΑΓΓΕΛΙΑ	New Testament	34 [2 × 17]	ΧΡΥΣ*	Revelation	26[31]
ΕΣΘΙΩ	Genesis	52 [2 × 26]		New Testament	45 [3 × 15]
	Exodus	39	ΨΥΧΗ	New Testament	102 [6 × 17]
	Deuteronomy	68 [4 × 17]		Exodus	17
ΕΥΑΓΓΕΛΙΟΝ	Pauline Corpus	60 [4 × 15]		Deuteronomy	34 [2 × 17]
ΕΥΑΓΓΕΛ*	Luke-Acts	30 [2 × 15]		Psalms	150 [10 × 15]
ΕΥΛΟΓ*	Four Gospels	26		Sirach	85 [5 × 17]
ΕΥΛΟΓ*	Pauline Corpus	30 [2 × 15]		Ezekiel	39
ΕΥΡΙΣΚΩ	Luke	45 [3 × 15]			

31. Cf. also other "color" words in Revelation: λευχ* (cf. λευκός, "white") Revelation **17 times** (New Testament **27 times**); μελ* (cf. μέλας, "black," and μέλλω, "be about to") Revelation **17 times**; and, in addition πυρ* (cf. πυρρός/πυρράζω, "red," and πῦρ, "fire") Matthew **17 times**, Gospels + Acts **45 times** [3 × 15], Praxapostolos **17 times**; πυ* four Gospels **51 times** [3 × 17], Acts **26 times**, Revelation **44 times** [2 × 22]; πορ* (cf. πορφυροῦς/πορφύρα, "purple") Praxapostolos **54 times** [2 × 27], Revelation **22 times**.

Table 8.3. 22/24/27-multiples from the wider class of potentially frequency-coded New Testament (THGNT) and LXX vocabulary (LXXG, unless otherwise indicated).

Term	Text	Frequency	Term	Text	Frequency
ΑΓΓΕΛΟΣ	Four Gospels	54 [2 × 27]	ΗΛΙΑΣ	Four Gospels	27
	Pauline Corpus	27	ΗΣΑΙΑΣ	New Testament	22
	Praxapostolos	27	ΘΑΝΑΤΟΣ	Romans	22
ΑΓΙΟΣ	Acts	54 [2 × 27]	ΘΕΑΟΜΑΙ	New Testament	22
	Praxapostolos	72 [3 × 24]	ΘΕΛΗΜΑ	Four Gospels	22
	2 Maccabees	22	ΘΕΡΙ]*	Four Gospels	24
	Isaiah	66 [3 × 22]	ΙΧΘΥ*	New Testament	22
Ο ΑΓΙΟΣ	Pentateuch	132 [6 × 22]	ΚΑΙΡΟΣ	Deuteronomy	22
ΑΙΜΑ	Exodus	27		Psalms + Odes	22
ΑΙΡΩ	Psalms + Odes	22	ΚΑΛΕΩ	Praxapostolos	27
ΑΙΩΝΙΟΣ	Pauline Corpus	27	ΚΑΛΟΣ	Four Gospels	48 [2 × 24]
	Isaiah	22	ΚΑΤΑΒΑΙΝΩ	Psalms + Odes	22
ΑΚΟΗ	New Testament	24		Ezekiel	22
ΑΚΟΥΩ	Mark	44 [2 × 22]	ΚΡΙΣΙΣ	Four Gospels	27
	Luke-Acts	154 [7 × 22]		Psalms	24
	Numbers	27		Jeremiah + Baruch + Lamentation	24
ΑΛΗΘΕΙΑ	Pauline Corpus	48 [2 × 24]	ΛΑΜΒΑΝΩ	Praxapostolos	44 [2 × 22]

Term	Text	Frequency
ΑΜΑΡΤΙΑ	Romans	48 [2 × 24]
	Psalms	27
ΑΠΟΚΑΛΥ*	Leviticus	27
ΑΡΕC*	New Testament	22
ΑΡΤΟC	John	24
	Four Gospels	81 [3 × 27]
	Genesis	22
ΑΡΧΙΕΡΕΥC	Mark	22
	Acts	22
ΒΑΠΤΙ*	Four Gospels	66 [3 × 22]
	Acts	27
	Luke-Acts	44 [2 × 22]
ΒΑCΙΛΕΙΑ	New Testament	162 [6 × 27]
ΒΑCΙΛ*	Pentateuch	132 [6 × 22]
ΓΡΑΜΜΑΤΕΥC	Matthew	22
ΓΡΑΜΜΑ*	Luke-Acts	22
ΓΡΑΦ*	New Testament	240 [10 × 24]
Η ΓΥΝΗ	Pauline Corpus	22
	Gospels + Acts	54 [2 × 27]

Term	Text	Frequency
	2 Chronicles	24
	1 Maccabees	48 [2 × 24]
	Isaiah	48 [2 × 24]
ΛΟΓΟC	Mark	24
	Pauline Corpus	96 [4 × 24]
	New Testament	330 [15 × 22]
	Jeremiah	168 [7 × 24]
Ο ΛΟΓΟC	Pauline Corpus	48 [2 × 24]
ΜΕΤΑΝΟΕΩ	Rahlfs	24
ΜΥCΤΗΡΙΟΝ	New Testament	27
ΝΟΜΟC	Gospels + Acts	48 [2 × 24]
	Pauline Corpus	135 [5 × 27]
	Praxapostolos	27
ΟΔΟC	Matthew	22
	Deuteronomy	48 [2 × 24]
	2 Chronicles	22
Η ΟΔΟC	Ezekiel	72 [3 × 24]
	Genesis	24
ΟΡΑΩ	Luke	81 [3 × 27]

Term	Text	Frequency	Term	Text	Frequency
ΔΙΑΚΟΝΟC	Pauline Corpus	22		Four Gospels (NA28; THGNT 269)	270 [10 × 27]
ΔΙΔΑCΚΑΛΟC	Four Gospels	48 [2 × 24]		Acts	66 [3 × 22]
ΔΙΔΑCΚΩ	New Testament	96 [4 × 24]		Pentateuch	360 [15 × 24]
	Psalms + Odes	27		Psalms + Odes	88 [4 × 22]
ΔΙΔΑCΚ*	Matthew	27		Twelve Prophets	44 [2 × 22]
	Four Gospels	108 [4 × 27] (based on B; THGNT 107)		Isaiah	72 [3 × 24]
	Psalms + Odes	27	ΠΑΙC	New Testament	24
ΔΙΚΑΙΟCΥΝΗ	Ezekiel	22	ΠΑΡΑΒΟΛΗ	Four Gospels	48 [2 × 24]
	Prophets (Rahlfs)	110 [5 × 22]	ΠΑΡΑΔΙΔΩΜΙ	Gospels + Acts	96 [4 × 24]
ΔΟΞΑ	Sirach	54 [2 × 27]		Deuteronomy	22
Η ΔΟΞΑ	Isaiah	48 [2 × 24]	ΠΑΡΟΥCΙΑ	New Testament	24
ΕΙΡΗΝΗ	Psalms	24	ΠΑCΧΑ	Gospels + Acts	27
	Jeremiah	24	ΠΙCΤΙC	New Testament	243 [9 × 27]
ΕΙΡΗΝ*	Four Gospels	27		Galatians	22
ΕΙCΕΡΧΟΜΑΙ	2 Chronicles	22	Η ΠΙCΤΙC	Praxapostolos	24
	Twelve Prophets	22	ΠΟΙΕΩ	Luke	88 [4 × 22]
	Jeremiah + Baruch + Lamentations	44 [2 × 22]	ΠΟΙΜΗΝ	Rahlfs	81 [3 × 27]
ΕΚΚΛΗCΙΑ	Praxapostolos	27	ΠΡΕCΒΥΤΕΡΟC	Four Gospels	24
	1 Corinthians	22	ΤΟ ΠΡΟΒΑΤΟΝ	New Testament	22

Term	Text	Frequency	Term	Text	Frequency
	2 Chronicles	24		Genesis	44 [2 × 22]
ΕΚΛΕΓΟΜΑΙ	New Testament	22		Pentateuch	88 [4 × 22][32]
ΕΚΛΕΚΤΟΣ	New Testament	22	ΠΡΟΣΕΥΧ*	Luke	22
ΕΝΤΟΛΗ	Four Gospels	27		Psalms + Odes	44 [2 × 22]
ΕΞΟΥΣΙΑ	Four Gospels	44 [2 × 22]	ΠΡΟΦΗΤΗΣ	New Testament	144 [6 × 24]
	Daniel	22	ΠΡΟΦΗΤ*	1 Corinthians	22
ΕΟΡΤΗ	Four Gospels	24	ΣΑΛΠ*	New Testament	24
Η ΕΠΑΓΓΕΛΙΑ	Pauline Corpus	27	ΣΗΜΕΙΟΝ	Four Gospels	48 [2 × 24]
ΕΣΘΙΩ	Matthew	24	ΦΑΝΕΡΟΩ	Pauline Corpus	24
	Mark	27	ΦΩΝΗ	Four Gospels	44 [2 × 22]
	1 Corinthians	27		Acts	27
ΕΥΑΓΓΕΛ*	Praxapostolos	22		Genesis	27
ΕΥΛΟΓΕΩ	Four Gospels	24	ΧΑΡΙΣ	Romans	24 (ΝΑ28; THGNT 23)
ΕΥΡΙΣΚΩ	Matthew	27		Pauline Corpus	108 [4 × 27] (ΝΑ28; THGNT 107)
	New Testament	176 [8 × 22]		New Testament	154 [7 × 22]
	Deuteronomy	22	ΨΥΧΗ	Four Gospels	48 [2 × 24]
	Sirach	48 [2 × 24]		Numbers	48 [2 × 24]
ΖΩΗ	New Testament	135 [5 × 27]		Jeremiah	54 [2 × 27]
	Ezekiel	22			

32. The total number of occurrences of ΤΟ ΠΡΟΒΑΤΟΝ in Rahlfs is 140 [10 × 14].

Table 8.4. The Way, the Truth, the Life

Term	Book	Word-frequency	Term	Book	Word-frequency
ζωή	Historia ecclesiastica	30 [2 × 15]	ἡ ὁδός	New Testament	78 [3 × 26]
	Shepherd of Hermas	54 [2 × 27]		Gospels + Acts	66 [3 × 22]
	Josephus, Antiquities	17		Matthews	17
	New Testament	135 [5 × 27]		Luke	15
	Four Gospels	52 [2 × 26]		Praxapostolos	22
	Gospels + Acts	60 [4 × 15]		Acts	17
	Praxapostolos	17		Pentateuch	75 [5 × 15]
	Pauline Corpus	39		Genesis	24
	Revelation	17		Deuteronomy	34
	Prophets	45 [3 × 15]		Judges	17
	Sirach	45		1–2 Samuel	30 [2 × 15]
	Ezekiel	22		Sirach	15
ἡ ζωή	New Testament	48 [2 × 24]	ἀλήθεια	Twelve Prophets	26
	Four Gospels	15		Hist. eccl., book 4	17
	Genesis	15		Hist. eccl., book 5	17
	Pentateuch	30 [2 × 15]		Shepherd of Hermas	22
ζάω	Historia ecclesiastica	45 [3 × 15]		Catholic Epistles	26

Term	Book	Word-frequency	Term	Book	Word-frequency
	Shepherd of Hermas	75 [5 × 15]		Pauline Corpus	48 [2 × 24]
	Ignatian letter corpus	22	ἡ ἀλήθεια	Josephus Antiquities	51 [3 × 17]
	Josephus, *War*	81 [3 × 27]		Josephus *War*	17
	New Testament	140 [10 × 14]		John	17
	John	17		Pauline Corpus	26
ὁδός	*Historia ecclesiastica*	30 [2 × 15]		Psalms (LXXG)	34 [2 × 17]
	Shepherd of Hermas	17	ἀληθής	Gospels + Acts	17
	Matthew	22		New Testament	26
	Genesis	30 [2 × 15]	ἀληθ*	*Historia ecclesiastica*	156 [6 × 26]
	Deuteronomy	48 [2 × 24]		*Hist. eccl.*, book 3	22
	1–2 Samuel	48		*Hist. eccl.*, book 4	26
	1 Kings	48		*Hist. eccl.*, book 5	27
	2 Chronicles	22		Josephus *Antiquities*	168 [7 × 24]
	Tobit	15		Four Gospels	75 [5 × 15]
	Jerermiah + Baruch	68 [4 × 17]		Pentateuch (LXXG)	24
	Ezekiel	72 [3 × 24]		Historical Books (Rahlfs)	72 [3 × 24]
	Genesis Rahlfs/LXXG	30 [2 × 15]		Prophets (Rahlfs)	51 [3 × 17]
	Deuteronoy Rahlfs/LXXG	48 [2 × 24]	ἡ ἀληθ*	Josephus *War*	26
ἡ ὁδός	Josephus *Works*	88 [4 × 22]		New Testament	75 [5 × 15]

BIBLIOGRAPHY

Aland, Kurt. *Repertorium der griechischen christlichen Papyri, II: Kirchenväter–Papyri. Teil 1: Beschreibungen.* Patristische Texte un Studien 42. Berlin: de Gruyter, 1995.

Bokedal, Tomas. "'But for Me, the Scriptures Are Jesus Christ' ($\overline{\text{IC}}$ $\overline{\text{XC}}$; Ign. *Phld.* 8:2): Creedal Text-Coding and the Early Scribal System of Nomina Sacra." In *Studies on the Paratextual Features of Early New Testament Manuscripts.* Edited by Stanley E. Porter, David I. Yoon, and Chris S. Stevens. TENTS. Leiden: Brill, forthcoming 2023.

—————. *Names and Numbers: Nomina Sacra and Numerological Editorial Practice in Christian Scripture.* Forthcoming.

Holmes, Michael. *Apostolic Fathers: Greek Texts and English Translations of Their Writings.* 3rd ed. Grand Rapids: Baker Academic, 2007.

9

NOMINA SACRA WORD-FREQUENCIES RELATED TO THE DIVINE NAME (SEVENTEEN- AND TWENTY-SIX-MULTIPLES)

W e shall now concentrate mainly on two of the *NrN* discussed above, namely multiples of twenty-six and seventeen, that is, the two numbers directly related to the Tetragrammaton (N.B. provided that arithmetical dimensions of the text addressed below are not deliberately designed on the part of the authors, editors and scribes—contrary to the argument of the present chapter—the likelihood that any word-frequency multiple of twenty-six or seventeen will occur in the text is ca. 8.7 percent *in each case*, that is less than one in eleven, for numbers between 1 and 200).[1] Since several of the *NrN* in the present chapter are based on the division of the biblical text into verses—but also other text units such as clauses and THGNT paragraphs—and since the versification of the

---

1. Several of the figures below are published as well in Tomas Bokedal, "The Rule-of-Faith Pattern and the Formation of Canonical Sub-Units," in *The New Testament Canon in Contemporary Research*, ed. Benjamin P. Laird and Stanley E. Porter, TENTS (Leiden: Brill, forthcoming). A modified list of the items below is also published in Tomas Bokedal, "The Bible Canon and Its Significance," in *Canon Formation: Tracing the Role of Sub-Collections in the Biblical Canon*, ed. W. Edward Glenny and Darian Lockett (London: Bloomsbury T&T Clark, forthcoming).

New Testament (placing verse-divisions in the text) occurred relatively recently, in the sixteenth century, this chapter is the most exploratory of the chapters in Part C. Yet, the sheer number of *nomina sacra* (hereafter NS) word-frequencies in the various text units listed below, involving primarily multiples of twenty-six and/or seventeen, is a further indication that these arithmetical dimensions of the biblical texts have been designed with these figures in view. This applies to the Hebrew Jewish as well as to the Greek Christian Scriptures.

Do Hebrew textual features involving arithmetic dimensions perhaps reflect scribal work in Jerusalem from around 120 BC and onward? Or are we dealing with yet earlier Jewish Hebrew and Greek text-compositional strategies? A recent article by Torleif Elgvin making the case for a royal (scribal) library in Jerusalem from John Hyrcanus's time may here open up for an initial clue, and perhaps even for the possibility of Hebrew arithmetical patterns being systematically incorporated into the biblical material in the late second century BC.[2]

9.1 *NOMINA SACRA* WORD-FREQUENCIES PERTAINING TO THE NAME (SEVENTEEN- AND TWENTY-SIX-MULTIPLES)

Most of the NrN below are multiples of either twenty-six or seventeen, that is, the two numbers related to the Tetragrammaton (these and other NrN are marked in boldface). Abbreviations used, in addition to THGNT (Tyndale House Greek New Testament), NA28 (Nestle-Aland 28th edition), BHS (*Biblia Hebraica Stuttgartensia*), Rahlfs, and LXXG (LXX Göttingen), are (Accordance 13 digital versions) TF 35 (Byzantine Greek New Testament, Majority Text, text family 35), TR (Textus Receptus), א (Codex Sinaiticus), W (Codex Washingtonianus):

---

2. See Torleif Elgvin, "Post-exilic History and Archaeology and the Formation of Biblical Literature," in *Epigraphy, Iconography, and the Bible*, ed. Meir Lubetski and Edith Lubetski, Hebrew Bible Monographs 98 (Sheffield: Sheffield Phoenix, 2022). See also Casper J. Labuschagne, "General Introduction to Logotechnical Analysis (Rev.)" (University of Groningen, 2016), http://www.labuschagne.nl/aspects.pdf.

1. ὄνομα (which is not *per se* a *nomen sacrum*) occurs in the Pauline Corpus **26 times** (THGNT, NA28, TF 35, TR, א).

2. θεός appears in Romans **153 times** [9 × 17] (THGNT, NA28, TF 35, TR), 1–2 Timothy **34 times** [2 × 17], Hebrews **68 times** [4 × 17] (THGNT, NA28);[3] Matthew **52 times** [2 × 26] (THGNT, א) and Luke-Acts **289 times** [17 × 17] (NA28);[4] corresponding figures for LXXG: Esther (O-text) **26 times**, Hosea **34 times** [2 × 17], Jonah **17 times**; corresponding figures for κύριος (sg. forms; NA28) Matthew **78 times** [3 x 26], Luke **102 times** [6 x 17], John **52 times** [2 × 26], Acts **104 times** [4 x 26], the twenty-seven-book New Testament **702 times** [27 x 26]; and for the Hebrew Bible: יהוה, "YHWH," Pentateuch **1820 times** [70 × 26], 2 Samuel **153 times** [9 × 17], Jonah **26 times**, Zephaniah **34 times** [2 × 17], Nehemiah **17 times**; and אלהים, "God; god, deity," 1–2 Kings **204 times** [12 × 17], Hosea **26 times**, Job **17 times**, the MT **2600 times** [10 × 10 × 26].

3. ὁ θεός (sg. nom.) Romans **26 times** (THGNT, NA28);[5] Praxapostolos **78 times** [3 × 26]; and in Rahlfs: Deuteronomy **208 times** [8 × 26], Esther **17 times**, Daniel + Susannah + Bel and the Dragon **26 times**, the Major Prophets (Isaiah + Jeremiah + Baruch + Ezekiel + Daniel + Susannah + Bel and the Dragon) **208 times** [8 x 26]; corresponding figures for ὁ κύριος Matthew **26 times**, Synoptic Gospels **78 times** [3 x 26], John **17 times**, Acts **68 times** [4 x 17], twenty-seven-book New Testament 351 times [3 x 3 x 39]; cf. table 5.1 for potential significance of 39].

---

3. Corresponding figure for Romans in א is **150 times** [10 × 15] (see table 5.1 above for potential numerical significance of 15). Corresponding figure for Hebrews in א is **66 times** [3 × 22] (see table 5.1 above for potential numerical significance for 22).

4. Corresponding figure in א is **288 times** [12 × 24] (see table 5.1 above for potential numerical significance of 24)

5. Corresponding figure for ὁ θεός in Pauline Corpus 116 times (THGNT)/117 times [3 × 39] (NA28 and א; see table 5.1 for potential numerical significance of 39).

4. πνεῦμα Romans **34 times** [2 × 17] (THGNT, NA28, א),
   2 Corinthians **17 times** (THGNT, NA28, TF 35, TR, א);
   Synoptic Gospels **78 times** [3 × 26] (THGNT, NA28),[6] four
   Gospels **102 times** [6 × 17] (THGNT, NA28)/**104 times** [4 ×
   26] (TF 35, TR, W); (corresponding figures for ὁ (τὸ) πνεῦμα
   Synoptic Gospels **30 times** [2 x 15], four Gospels **45 times** [3
   x 15], four Gospels + Acts **81 times** [3 x 27], Praxapostolos
   45 times [3 x 15], Pauline Corpus **66 times** [3 x 22]); and for
   the Hebrew Bible: רוּחַ, "spirit; wind," Isaiah **51 times** [3 × 17],
   and Ezekiel **52 times** [2 × 26].

5. ἄνθρωπος Pauline Corpus **136 times** [8 × 17] (THGNT,
   NA28);[7] corresponding figures in Rahlfs: 1–2 Samuel **34
   times** [2 × 17], 2 Kings **26 times**, Esther **17 times**, Historical
   Books **234 times** [9 × 26], Poetical Books (excluding Odes
   and Psalms of Solomon) **390 times** [10 × 39 = 15 × 26],
   Jeremiah + Baruch + Lamentations **85 times** [5 × 17]; and
   in the Hebrew Bible: the unpointed אדם Former Prophets
   34 times [2 × 17], 1–2 Chronicles **26 times,** and the Writings
   221 times [13 × 17]. Corresponding figures for ὁ ἄνθρωπος
   four Gospels **144 times** [6 x 24], twenty-seven-book New
   Testament **162 times** [6 x 27].

In addition to the above 17- and 26-multiples linked to NS frequencies in various canonical subunits—with potential numerical reference to the Tetragrammaton—we note, as well, configurations for combinations of NS (or letter combinations linked to NS). In the following we shall thus look at combinations of two or more words, occurring together in each OT or NT verse included in the count (search in Accordance on the form Word 1 <AND> Word 2); textual scope: verse, unless indicated otherwise (N.B.: division of the Jewish Scriptures into verses was known already by the rabbis; verses were introduced into the New Testament by Robertus

---

6. Corresponding figure in W is **81 times** [3 × 27] (see table 5.1 above for potential numerical significance of 27)

7. Corresponding figure in א* is 137 (א* includes three occurrences of ἄνθρωπος in Rom 5:18 as compared to two in THGNT and NA28)

Stephanus in the sixteenth century). Each word will be counted separately. For comparison, we shall include as well searches with alternative textual scope (such as clause; sentence; and THGNT paragraph; unless indicated otherwise, textual scope in the examples below, 6–8, is verse) and searches that are otherwise independent of the versification of the text — on the form Word 1 + Word 2 — that represent a broader range of NrN (figures below are from the Accordance digital version of THGNT, unless otherwise indicated):

Nomina Sacra *Configurations Involving* ὄνομα

6. ὄνομα <AND> Ἰησοῦς: New Testament **78 times** [3 × 26]; search in Accordance, THGNT, on the form: ὄνομα <AND> Ἰησοῦς result: ὄνομα (36 times)/τοὔνομα (once) and Ἰησοῦς (41 times), involving 37 New Testament verses, in which the two words appear together in each verse; the total number of occurrences of the two words in these verses is **78**.[8] ὄνομα + Ἰησοῦς: 1–2 Corinthians **51 times** [3 x 17] (ὄνομα 6 times + Ἰησοῦς **45 times**), Philippians **26 times** (ὄνομα 4 times + Ἰησοῦς **22 times**).

7. ὄνομα <AND> χριστός: Pauline Corpus **17 times** (ὄνομα Pauline Corpus **26 times**); corresponding figures for ὄνομα <AND> ὁ <AND> Χριστός: Acts **34 times** [2 × 17].[9] ὄνομα + χριστός: Pauline Corpus **420 times** [2 x 14 x 15].

8. ὄνομα <AND> υἱός: four Gospels **26 times**; corresponding figures for ὄνομα <AND> ὁ <AND> υἱός: Gospels + Acts **78 times** [3 × 26] (Matthew–Mark **34 times** [2 × 17] **34 times**

---

8. Corresponding figure for ὁ <AND> ὄνομα <AND> ὁ Ἰησοῦς: New Testament 39 times, Acts 22 times; and for ὁ <AND> ὄνομα <AND> ὁ κύριος: New Testament 118 times [THGNT]/117 times [3 × 39] (NA28); moreover, the following figures: ὄνομα <AND> Ἰησοῦς χριστός: New Testament **30 times** [2 × 15]; ὄνομα <AND> θεός: New Testament **72 times** [3 × 24], Gospels + Acts **22 times**; ὄνομα <AND> κύριος: New Testament **81 times** [3 × 27], Synoptic Gospels **17 times**, Acts **30 times** [2 × 15], Praxapostolos **34 times** [2 × 17]; ὄνομα <AND> ἐκεῖνος: New Testament **17 times**, Gospels + Acts **15 times**; ὄνομα <AND> αὐτός: four Gospels **144 times** [6 × 24], Matthew **27 times**, and Luke-Acts **132 times** [6 × 22].

9. Corresponding figures for Praxapostolos **45 times** [3 × 15], New Testament **105 times** [7 × 15].

[2 x 17]).[10] ὄνομα + υἱός: Gospels + Acts **435 times [29 x 15]**; ὄνομα + ὁ υἱός: four Gospels **272 times [4 x 4 x 17]** (Matthew–Mark **119 times [7 x 17]**). τὸ ὄνομα + ὁ υἱός: four Gospels **234 times [3 x 3 x 26]**.

9. ὄνομα <AND> κύριος: Synoptic Gospels **17 times**, Praxapostolos **34 times [2 × 17]**; corresponding figures for Rahlfs: Exodus **26 times**, 1–2 Chronicles **85 times [5 × 17]**, Sirach **17 times**, Zechariah **17 times**. ὄνομα + κύριος: Praxapostolos **220 times [10 x 22]**.

10. ὄνομα <AND> ὁ κύριος: Praxapostolos **26 times**; corresponding figure for ὄνομα <AND> ὁ <AND> κύριος: Acts **78 times [3 × 26]** (NA28),[11] New Testament **204 times [12 × 17]** (THGNT, NA28); ὄνομα + ὁ κύριος: Praxapostolos **162 times [6 x 27]**.

11. ὄνομα <AND> ὁ θεός: New Testament **68 times [4 × 17]**; corresponding figures for ὄνομα <AND> ὁ <AND> θεός: John **17 times**, Pauline Corpus **68 times [4 × 17]**;[12] and for ὄνομα <AND> ὁ <AND> θεός: in Rahlfs: Genesis **150 times [10 × 15]**, Leviticus **17 times**, Deuteronomy **221 times [13 × 17]**, Judges **17 times**. Corresponding figures for ὄνομα + ὁ θεός: twenty-seven-book New Testament **1224 times [3 x 24 x 17]** (NA28)/ **1207 times [71 x 17]** (א); and in Rahlfs: Genesis **357 times [3 x 7 x 17]**.

12. ὄνομα <AND> ὁ ἄνθρωπος: New Testament **17 times**; corresponding figures for ὄνομα <AND> ὁ <AND> ἄνθρωπος: Acts/ Praxapostolos **34 times [2 × 17]**, Revelation **26 times**.[13] Corresponding results for ὄνομα + ὁ ἄνθρωπος twenty-seven-book New Testament **484 times [22 x 22]** (THGNT)/ **435 times [29 x 15]** (א).

---

10. Corresponding figures for Luke **15 times** and John **24 times** (Luke–John 39 times).

11. Corresponding figure for the four Gospels **44 times [2 × 22]** (THGNT)/**45 times [3 × 15]** (NA28).

12. Corresponding figure for Praxapostolos is **44 [2 × 22]**.

13. Corresponding figure for the full New Testament: **88 times [4 × 22]**.

Triune Nomina Sacra *Configurations*

13. θεός <AND> υἱός <AND> πνεῦμα: Pauline Corpus (cf. Gal 4:6)
17 times (textual scope: verse; alternative result when THGNT
paragraph is used as textual scope: **132 times [6 x 22]**),[14] New
Testament **26 times**. Corresponding figures for θεός + υἱός +
πνεῦμα: Four Gospels **663 times [39 x 17]**, Hebrews **104 times**
[4 x 26], Pauline Corpus **837 times [31 x 27]**, New Testament
2069 times (THGNT)/ **2064 times [86 x 24]** (‎ℵ).[15]

14. "*θε*" <AND> "*υι*" <AND> "*πν*": Gospels + Acts **26 times**.
Corresponding figures for "*θε*" <and> "*υι*" <and> "*πν*":
2691 times [3 x 23 x 39] (THGNT)/ **2754 times [2 x 3 x 27**
x 17] (NA28)/ **2856 times [7 x 24 x 17]** (Byzantine Textform
2005); cf. table 5.1 for potential significance of 3 (the divine/
Triune number), 23 ("glory") and 39 ("God is one").

15. θεός <AND> χριστός <AND> πνεῦμα (cf. Rom 1:4 and 1 Pet
1:2): Romans **17 times** (cf. the Triune one GOD–one CHRIST–
one SPIRIT formulary in 1 Clem. 46.6).[16] Corresponding
figures for θεός + χριστός + πνεῦμα: Luke **170 times [10 x**
17], Acts **260 times [10 x 26]**, Synoptic Gospels **336 times**
[14 x 24], four Gospels + Acts **720 times [2 x 15 x 24]**, 1–2
Corinthians **352 times [16 x 22]**, Colossians **48 times [2 x**
24], 1 Thessalonians **51 times [3 x 17]**, 1–2 Timothy **68 times**
[4 x 17], Pauline Corpus **1166 times [53 x 22]**.

16. θεο* <AND> χρι* <AND> πνε*: Romans **17 times**, New
Testament **68 times [4 × 17]**.[17] Corresponding figures for

---

14. θεός 6 times, υἱός 6 times, πνεῦμα 5 times = **17 times** (search in Accordance on the form θεός
<AND> υἱός <AND> πνεῦμα; the three words occurring in each of the verses included in the count).

15. Corresponding figures for ὁ <AND> θεός <AND> υἱός <AND> πνεῦμα Luke-Acts **15 times**,
Gospels + Acts **22 times**.

16. Corresponding figures for Pauline Corpus 39 times, and Catholic Epistles 14 times (see table
5.1 above). Corresponding figure for θεός <AND> υἱός <AND> πνεῦμα in 1 Clement is **24 times** and
for θεο* <AND> χρι* <AND> πνε* **24 times**. Corresponding figure for ὁ <AND> θεός <AND> χριστός
<AND> πνεῦμα in the Pauline Corpus **75 times [5 × 15]**.

17. Corresponding figures for θεο* <AND> χρι* <AND> πνε* in Praxapostolos: **22 times**; and
for ὁ <AND> θεο* <AND> χρι* <AND> πνε* in Ephesians: **15 times**, and in the Pauline Corpus: **90**

θεο* + χρι* + πνε*: Romans 256 [8 x 32] (THGNT)/**1200**
[**8 x 10 x 15 = 50 x 24**] (NA28); twenty-seven-book New
Testament **2280 times** [**152 x 15**] (NA28).

17. θεός <AND> Ἰησοῦς χριστός <AND> πνεῦμα (cf. Rom 1:4, 1 Pet
1:2, and Rom 15:30): New Testament **26 times**[18] (textual
scope: verse: alternative result when THGNT paragraph is
used as textual scope: **182 times** [**7 x 26**]); cf. 6.2 *Comment*
8 above.

18. "*θε*" <AND> "*ιη*" <AND> "*χρ*" <AND> "*πν*" (search
on this form in Accordance): Romans **17 times**, 1 Peter **17
times**, New Testament **102 times** [**6 × 17**].[19]

19. θεός <AND> κύριος <AND> πνεῦμα (cf. Rom 15:30): Pauline
Corpus **26 times** (textual scope: verse; alternative result
when THGNT paragraph is used as textual scope: **170 times**
[**10 x 17**]);[20] corresponding figures for ὁ <AND> θεός <AND>
κύριος <AND> πνεῦμα: Pauline Corpus **52 times** [**2 × 26**]; cf.
6.2 above, ex. xiii and xiv.

20. "*θε*" <AND> "*κυ*" <AND> "*πν*": Synoptic Gospels **17
times**, Luke-Acts **26 times**, Pauline Corpus **52 times** [**2 ×
26**].[21] Corresponding figures for " "*θε*" + "*κυ*" + "*πν*":
Synoptic Gospels **1674** [**62 x 27**]; cf. 6.2 above, ex. xiii and xiv.

---

times [6 × 15].

18. Corresponding figure for ὁ <AND> θεός <AND> Ἰησοῦς χριστός <AND> πνεῦμα in the full New Testament: **54 times** [**2 × 27**].

19. Corresponding figures for 1 John **15 times** and Praxapostolos **48 times** [**2 × 24**].

20. Corresponding figures in Rahlfs (textual scope: verse): the Historical Books **15 times**, the Prophets **22 times**. Corresponding figure in the Hebrew Bible for יהוה <AND> אלהים <AND> רוח: **45 times** [**3 × 15**]. We can also note the following potentially Triune figure: πατήρ <AND> ἐγώ <AND> πνεῦμα (cf. John 14:26 and 15:26): New Testament **24 times**. I am grateful to Øystein Bru Schjelderup for pointing me to these Johannine passages.

21. Corresponding figures for Gospels + Acts **44 times** [**2 × 22**], 1-2 Corinthians **24 times**, and the full New Testament **110 times** [**5 × 22**].

21. *πα* <AND> *υι* <AND> *πν* (cf. Matt 28:19): Synoptic Gospels/four Gospels **17 times**. Corresponding figures for the twenty-seven-book New Testament **5170** [**5 x 47 x 22**]. [22]

22. εἷς/εἰς <AND> καί <AND> τρεῖς: Synoptic Gospels **34 times** [**2 × 17**], Revelation **17 times**, New Testament **78 times** [**3 × 26**];[23] corresponding figures for κύριος <AND> εἷς/εἰς (cf. Mark 12:29): 1–2 Thessalonians **26 times**, Gospels + Acts **153 times** [**9 × 17**];[24] and for ὁ <AND> κύριος <AND> εἷς/εἰς: 1–2 Corinthians **51 times** [**3 × 17**], 1 Thessalonians **34 times** [**2 × 17**], Pauline Corpus **182 times** [**7 × 26**] (THGNT, NA28, ℵ), 2 Peter **17 times**, Jude **17 times**.[25]

23. θεός <AND> κύριος <AND> Ἰησοῦς χριστός <AND> πνεῦμα: Pauline Corpus **24 times**; corresponding figures for θεός <AND> κύριος <AND> Ἰησοῦς <AND> χριστός <AND> πνεῦμα: Pauline Corpus **30 times** [**2 x 15**] (textual scope: verse; alternative result when THGNT paragraph is used as textual scope: **168 times** [**7 x 24**]). Corresponding figures for θεός + κύριος + Ἰησοῦς χριστός + πνεῦμα: twenty-seven-book New Testament **2184** [**6 x 14 x 26 = 7 x 13 x 24 = 4 x 14 x 39**].

---

22. Corresponding figure for Gospels + Acts **22 times**.

23. As for the New Testament configuration εἷς/εἰς <AND> καί <AND> τρεῖς (εἷς 13 times, εἰς 10 times, καί 37 times, τρεῖς **17 times**), the number 13 may be a numerological reference to the Hebrew word for one, *ekhad*, אֶחָד (occurring 13 times in Zechariah and 1 Chronicles, respectively), which has the numerical value 13 (*aleph*=1 + *khet*=8 + *dalet*= 4 = 13). By adding 13 (representing God's oneness) to **26** (representing God's Name) we get **39** ("God is one"), which may be numerologically indicated by the 39 Old Testament books, and by the following New Testament configurations: θεός <AND> χριστός <AND> πνεῦμα Romans **17 times**, Pauline Corpus **39 times**; and Ἰησοῦς <AND> χριστός <AND> υἱός <AND> θεός New Testament **39 times**. Corresponding figure for εἷς/εἰς <AND> ἐν <AND> τρεῖς: New Testament **15 times**.

24. Corresponding figures in Acts **60 times** [**4 × 15**], Matthew–Mark **44 times** [**2 × 22**], 2 Peter **15 times**, New Testament **288 times** [**12 × 24**].

25. Corresponding figures in Matthew **81 times** [**3 × 27**], Synoptic Gospels **192 times** [**8 × 24**], 1 Corinthians **24 times**, 2 Corinthians **27 times**, 2 Thessalonians **24 times**, 1–2 Peter **30 times** [**2 × 15**], Praxapostolos **195 times** [**13 × 15**](THGNT)/**189 times** [**7 × 27**] (ℵ).

Comment: One of the earliest Triune formulations that we find in 1 Clem. 46.6, involving the terms θεός, χριστός, and πνεῦμα, here, arithmetically, surfaces as well in Paul's epistle to the Romans (ex. 15 above; altogether **17 occurrences** of these words allocated to five verses in Romans when they appear together in each of the five verses). The corresponding figure in Pauline Corpus is 39 (which may be a numerical allusion to YHWH *ekhad*; cf. table 5.1). Romans 15:30 appears to be a key verse in this connection, since it is involved in all the following Triune configurations: θεός <AND> κύριος <AND> πνεῦμα: Pauline Corpus **26 times**; θεός <AND> Ἰησοῦς χριστός <AND> πνεῦμα: New Testament **26 times**; θεο* <AND> χρι* <AND> πνε*: Romans **17 times**, New Testament **68 times** [4 × 17]; and θεός <AND> χριστός <AND> πνεῦμα: Romans **17 times**, Pauline Corpus 39 times.

Dyadic/Christological Nomina Sacra *Configurations*

24. πα* <AND> υι*: Hebrews **34 times** [2 × 17], Pauline Corpus **68 times** [4 × 17] (πατήρ <AND> υἱός: 1–3 John **17 times**). Corresponding figure for πα* + υι*: Pauline Corpus **1026** [**38 x 27**].

25. υἱός <AND> θεός: Pauline Corpus **52 times** [2 × 26], John **34 times** [2 × 17], New Testament **204** [12 × 17] (Luke-Mark **34 times** [2 × 17]).[26]

26. Ἰησοῦς χριστός <AND> θεός: 1–2 Corinthians **26 times**, New Testament **153 times** [9 × 17] (THGNT)/**24 times** (NA28).[27] Corresponding figure for Ἰησοῦς χριστός + θεός: 1–2 Corinthians **204 times** [12 x 17] (NA28).

---

26. Corresponding figures in Matthew **24 times**, Gospels + Acts **108 times** [4 × 27], Romans **15 times**, Praxapostolos **54 times** [2 × 27]; corresponding figures for ὁ <AND> υἱός <AND> θεός: Luke **60 times** [4 × 15], John **105 times** [7 × 15], four Gospels **243 times** [9 × 27] (Matthew–Mark **78 times** [3 × 26], Luke–John **165 times** [11 × 15]), Acts **54 times** [2 × 27], Gospels + Acts **297 times** [11 × 27], 1–2 Corinthians **17 times**, Pauline Corpus **135 times** [5 × 27], 1 John **96 times** [4 × 24], Praxapostolos **168 times** [7 × 24].

27. Corresponding figure for Praxapostolos: **44 times** [2 × 22].

27. Ἰησοῦς χριστός <AND> ὁ θεός: New Testament **78 times** [3 × 26] (textual scope: verse; alternative result when THGNT paragraph is used as textual scope: **210 times** [14 x 15]).[28]

28. χριστὸς Ἰησοῦς <AND> κύριος: New Testament **26 times** (textual scope: verse;[29] alternative result when THGNT paragraph is used as textual scope: **90 times** [6 x 15])

Nomina Sacra *Configurations Involving* θεός, κύριος, *and* οὐρανός

29. θεός <AND> κύριος: 1 Corinthians **26 times**, Gospels + Acts **68 times** [4 × 17];[30] corresponding figures in the Hebrew Bible for יהוה <AND> אלהים: 2 Samuel **52 times** [2 × 26], Latter Prophets **546 times** [3 × 7 × 26], and Psalms **170 times** [10 × 17].

30. θεός <AND> πατήρ: Pauline Corpus **85 times** [5 × 17] (textual scope: verse; alternative result when THGNT paragraph is used as textual scope: **182 times** [7 x 26]), Luke-Acts **34 times** [2 × 17], Praxapostolos **52 times** [2 × 26] (textual scope: verse; alternative result when THGNT paragraph is used as textual scope: **136 times** [8 x 17]);[31] corresponding figure for LXXG: Pentateuch **187 times** [11 × 17]; and for אלהים <AND> אב: MT **425 times** [5 × 5 × 17] (the New Testament meaning of "f/Father" is often different compared to that in the LXX and the MT).

---

28. Corresponding figures for ὁ <AND> Ἰησοῦς χριστός <AND> θεός: Romans **66 times** [3 × 22], 1 Thessalonians **26 times**, 2 Thessalonians **15 times**, 1 Peter **17 times**, 1–2 Peter **22 times**, 1 John **15 times**, Catholic Epistles **66 times** [3 × 22], and New Testament 320 times [10 × 32].

29. Corresponding figure for the Pauline Corpus **24 times**.

30. Corresponding figures for the four Gospels 39 times (Matthew–Mark **15 times**, Luke–John **24 times**) and 1–2 Corinthians 39 times; and for ὁ <AND> θεός <AND> κύριος: Luke **48 times** [2 × 24], Luke-Acts **130 times** [5 × 26], Gospels + Acts **180 times** [12 × 15] (NA28), Romans **75 times** [5 × 15], 1 Thessalonians **60 times** [4 × 15], Hebrews **15 times**, and Praxapostolos **119 times** [7 × 17] (NA28).

31. Corresponding figures for the four Gospels **45 times** [3 × 15], Acts **30 times** [2 × 15], Gospels + Acts **75 times** [5 × 15], and Catholic Epistles **22 times**; and for ὁ <AND> θεός <AND> πατήρ: Matthew **30 times** [2 × 15], Synoptic Gospels 42 times [3 × 14], Acts **88 times** [4 × 22], Gospels + Acts **204 times** [12 × 17], 1–2 Corinthians **24 times**, Ephesians **22 times**, 1 Thessalonians **26 times**, Pauline Corpus **165 times** [11 × 15], 1–3 John **26 times**, and Praxapostolos **138 times** [6 × 23].

31. θεός <AND> ὑπάρχω: Acts **17 times** (textual scope: verse;[32]
alternative result when THGNT paragraph is used as textual
scope: 39 times). Corresponding figures for θεός + ὑπάρχω:
twenty-seven-book New Testament 1372 [7 x 14 x 14].

32. θεός <AND> οὐρανός: Acts **17 times**, Pauline Corpus **17 times**.
Corresponding figure for θεός + οὐρανός: Pauline Corpus **645**
[43 x 15].[33]

33. θεός <AND> λόγος (λόγος *per se* is not a *nomen sacrum*): four
Gospels **26 times** (א)/ **24 times** (THGNT;[34] textual scope:
verse; alternative result when THGNT paragraph is used as
textual scope: **88 times** [4 x 22]), New Testament **156 times**
[6 × 26] (we may note, in addition, that the expression λόγος
ὁ θεός (λόγος τοῦ θεοῦ; cf. Heb 4:12 and Rev 19:13) occurs **34
times** [2 × 17] in the New Testament).

34. κύριος <AND> κύριος: Synoptic Gospels **34 times** [2 × 17].[35]

35. οὐρανός <AND> οὐρανός: New Testament **34 times** [2 × 17]
(textual scope: verse; alternative result when THGNT paragraph is used as textual scope: **108 times** [4 x 27]).

36. οὐρανός <AND> βασιλε*: New Testament **78 times** [3 × 26].

Nomina Sacra *Configurations Involving* χριστός *and* Ἰησοῦς
37. χριστός <AND> κύριος: Ephesians **17 times**, 1–2 Peter **17
times**; corresponding figure in Rahlfs: 1 Samuel **34 times**

---

32. Corresponding figure for the full New Testament is **22 times** (see table 5.1 above for potential
significance of the number 22); and for ὁ <AND> θεός <AND> ὑπάρχω: New Testament **51 times** [3 × 17].

33. Corresponding figure for ὁ θεός <AND> οὐρανός: New Testament **72 times** [3 × 24]; and for
ὁ <AND> θεός <AND> οὐρανός: Matthew **22 times** (Luke–John **22 times**), John 14 times, Acts **48
times** [2 × 24], Luke-Acts 56 times [4 × 14], Pauline Corpus **30 times** [2 × 15], and Praxapostolos
60 times [4 × 15].

34. Corresponding figures for the four Gospels **24 times**, Luke-Acts **45 times** [3 × 15], Pauline
Corpus **66 times** [3 × 22]; corresponding figures for ὁ θεός <AND> λόγος: four Gospels **22 times**,
Luke-Acts **45 times** [3 × 15], Revelation **22 times**, and New Testament **132 times** [6 × 22].

35. Corresponding figures for 1–2 Corinthians **24 times**, Pauline Corpus **54 times** [2 × 27], and
New Testament 112 times [8 × 14].

[2 × 17];[36] corresponding figures for χριστός <AND> ὁ κύριος: 1–2 Corinthians **26 times**.[37] Corresponding figures for χριστός + κύριος: Ephesians **72 times** [3 x 24], 1–2 Peter **52 times** [2 x 26].

38. Ἰησοῦς <AND> χριστός: 2 Timothy **26 times** (textual scope: verse;[38] alternative/same result when THGNT paragraph is used as textual scope: **26 times**). Corresponding figure for Ἰησοῦς + χριστός: 2 Timothy **26 times**.

39. ιησ* <AND> χρι*: 2 Timothy **26 times** (textual scope: verse; alternative result when THGNT paragraph is used as textual scope: **26 times**). Corresponding figure for Ἰησοῦς + χριστός: 2 Timothy **26 times**, New Testament **493 times** [29 × 17]. Corresponding figures for ιησ* + χρι*: 2 Timothy **26 times**, twenty-seven-book New Testament **1452 times** [3 x 22 x 22].[39]

40. κύριος <AND> χριστὸς Ἰησοῦς: New Testament **26 times** (textual scope: verse;[40] alternative result when THGNT paragraph is used as textual scope: **90 times** [6 x 15]).

41. Ἰησοῦς <AND> Ἰησοῦς: New Testament **78 times** [3 × 26] (furthermore, Ἰησοῦ: Matthew **26 times**, four Gospels **78 times** [3 × 26], Luke-Acts **51 times** [3 × 17], four Gospels

---

36. Corresponding figures for Romans **24 times**, Ephesians **17 times**, Pauline Corpus **156 times** [6 × 26] (NA28), and the full New Testament **210 times** [14 × 15]; and for ὁ <AND> χριστός <AND> κύριος: Luke-Acts 42 times [3 × 14], 2 Corinthians **24 times**, Philippians **24 times**, 1 Thessalonians **34 times** [2 × 17], 2 Thessalonians **44 times** [2 × 22], 1–2 Thessalonians **78 times** [3 × 26], 1 Timothy **22 times**, Pauline Corpus **340 times** [20 × 17], 2 Peter **30 times** [2 × 15], Jude **22 times**, Catholic Epistles **75 times** [5 × 15], and Praxapostolos **112 times** [8 × 14].

37. Corresponding figures in Romans **22 times**, 1–2 Thessalonians **22 times**, Pauline Corpus **110 times** [5 × 22].

38. Corresponding figures in the four Gospels **22 times**, Romans **60 times** [4 × 15], 2 Timothy **26 times**, 1–2 Timothy **54 times** [2 × 27], Pauline Corpus **352 times** [16 × 22], and 1–2 Peter **34 times** [2 × 17].

39. Presumably based on John 20:31 and the NS Ἰησοῦς, χριστός, υἱός, and θεός, the Majority Text seems to have boosted these figures, featuring the following Accordance results for ι* <AND> χ* <AND> υ* <AND> θ*: New Testament **240 times** [10 × 24] (TF 35)/**234 times** [9 × 26] (Byzantine text form 2005)/**238 times** [14 × 17] (Ecumenical Patriarchal Text 1904/1912; cf. the acronym ΙΧΘΥΣ).

40. Corresponding figure for Pauline Corpus **24 times**. Corresponding figure for κύριος + χριστός Ἰησοῦς: **375 times** [5 x 5 x 15].

+ Acts **110 times** [5 x 22]; and Ἰησοῦς: New Testament **912 times** [38 x 24]).

42. χριστός <AND> υἱός: four Gospels **26 times**;[41] corresponding figures for ὁ <AND> χριστός <AND> υἱός: New Testament **156 times** [6 × 26].[42]

43. "*ιη*" <AND> "*χρ*" <AND> "*υι*" <AND> "*θε*" (search in Accordance on this form; cf. Mark 1:1 and John 20:31): four Gospels/Gospels + Acts **17 times**, New Testament **51 times** [3 × 17].

Nomina Sacra *Configurations Involving* πνεῦμα

44. πνεῦμα <AND> κύριος: Synoptic Gospels/Gospels **17 times**, Luke-Acts **34 times** [2 × 17];[43] corresponding figure for Rahlfs: Isaiah **26 times**; and in the Hebrew Bible for יהוה <AND> רוח: Twelve Prophets **34 times** [2 × 17]; and for אלהים <AND> רוח: Twelve Prophets **17 times**; corresponding figure for πνεῦμα <AND> Ἰησοῦς χριστός: Pauline Corpus **22 times**.

45. πνεῦμα <AND> ἅγιος (ἅγιος per se is not a *nomen sacrum*; however, *sanctus* together with *spiritus* is often highlighted as NS in Latin New Testament manuscripts): Pauline Corpus **52 times** [2 × 26], Acts **85 times** [5 × 17], Gospels + Acts **136 times** [8 × 17] (NA28). Corresponding figures for πνεῦμα <and> ἅγιος (based on clause rather than verse as textual scope): Acts **85 times** [5 × 17], Pauline Corpus **48 times** [2

---

41. Corresponding figure for Praxapostolos **15 times**.

42. Corresponding figure for 1–3 John 42 times [3 × 14] (Luke-Mark **24 times**, John **24 times** Corresponding figure for κύριος + χριστός Ἰησοῦς: **375 times** [5 x 5 x 15].).

43. Corresponding figure for Acts **24 times**; corresponding figure for πνεῦμα <AND> ὁ κύριος: New Testament **60 times** [4 × 15]; for τὸ πνεῦμα <AND> ὁ κύριος: Pauline Corpus **22 times**; and for ὁ <AND> πνεῦμα <AND> κύριος: Acts **68 times** [4 × 17] (NA28), Luke-Acts **90 times** [6 × 15], Gospels + Acts **96 times** [4 × 24] (NA28), 1 Corinthians 39 times, Pauline Corpus **132 times** [6 × 22], and Revelation **17 times**.

x 24], four Gospels **52 times** [2 x 26], twenty-seven-book New Testament **195 times** [13 x 15 = 5 x 39].[44]

Nomina Sacra *Configurations Involving* σωτήρ

46. σωτήρ <AND> θεός: New Testament **26 times**; corresponding figures for σωτήρ <AND> ὁ <AND> θεός: New Testament **52 times** [2 × 26].[45]

47. σωτήρ <AND> Ἰησοῦς: New Testament **26 times** (textual scope: verse; alternative result when THGNT paragraph is used as textual scope: 39 times);[46] corresponding figure for σωτήρ <AND> ὁ <AND> Ἰησοῦς: Catholic Epistles **26 times**.[47] Corresponding figure for σωτήρ <and> Ἰησοῦς (based on clause rather than verse as textual scope): New Testament **24 times**. Corresponding results for σωτήρ + Ἰησοῦς: New Testament **936 times** [2 x 18 x 26 = 24 x 39], Catholic Epistles **48 times** [2 x 24].

48. σωτήρ <AND> Ἰησοῦς <AND> χριστός: Praxapostolos/Catholic Epistles **17 times** (textual scope: verse; alternative/same result when THGNT paragraph is used as textual scope: **17 times**); corresponding figure for ὁ <AND> σωτήρ <AND> Ἰησοῦς <AND> χριστός: 2 Peter **26 times**. Corresponding figures for σωτήρ <and> Ἰησοῦς <and> χριστός (based on clause

---

44. Corresponding figures for Praxapostolos **90 times** [6 × 15] (NA28); for ὁ πνεῦμα <AND> ἅγιος: four Gospels **22 times**, Luke-Acts **44 times** [2 × 22], Pauline Corpus **17 times**, New Testament **75 times** [5 × 15]; for ὁ πνεῦμα <AND> ὁ ἅγιος: Acts/Praxapostolos **34 times** [2 × 17]; for ὁ <AND> πνεῦμα <AND> ἅγιος: four Gospels **130 times** [5 × 26] (NA28), Synoptic Gospels **117** [3 × 39] (NA28), Acts **220 times** [10 × 22], 1 Corinthians **17 times**, Ephesians **22 times**, Hebrews **27 times**, and New Testament **486 times** [18 × 27] (NA28); and for ὁ <AND> ὁ πνεῦμα <AND> ὁ ἅγιος: Synoptic Gospels **45 times** [3 × 15], four Gospels **52 times** [2 × 26], Acts **78 times** [3 × 26], Gospels + Acts **162 times** [6 × 27], Pauline Corpus **39 times**, Praxapostolos **110 times** [5 × 22] (NA28), and New Testament **210 times** [14 × 15].

45. Corresponding figures for σωτήρ <AND> ὁ <AND> θεός: Luke-Acts/Gospels + Acts **15 times**, Titus **22 times**.

46. Corresponding figure for σωτήρ <AND> κύριος <AND> Ἰησοῦς: New Testament **15 times** (for potential significance of the number 15, see table 5.1 above).

47. Corresponding figure for Pauline Corpus **24 times**.

rather than verse as textual scope): Praxapostolos/Catholic
Epistles 14 times (cf. table 5.1 for potential significance of
14), New Testament **34 times** [2 x 17]. Corresponding figures for σωτήρ + Ἰησοῦς + χριστός: Acts **96 times** [4 x 24],
2 Peter **22 times.**

Christ-Creed and Creed-Related Configurations

49. αὐτός <AND> γίνομαι <AND> ἄνθρωπος: New Testament **52
times** [2 × 26].[48]

50. αὐτός <AND> ἀποστέλλω <AND> Ἰησοῦς: New Testament **26
times.**[49]

51. Ἰησοῦς <AND> ἔρχομαι: Synoptic Gospels **78 times** [3 × 26]
(ὁ ἔρχομαι four Gospels **26 times**; ἐρχόμενος New Testament
26 times; ὁ ἐρχόμενος New Testament **17 times.**[50]

52. ὁ Ἰησοῦς <AND> ἔρχομαι: John **68 times** [4 × 17], Luke-Acts
17 times, New Testament **136 times** [8 × 17]; corresponding
figure for ὁ <AND> Ἰησοῦς <AND> ἔρχομαι: Praxapostolos
68 times [4 × 17], New Testament **561 times** [3 × 11 × 17].[51]

53. θεός <AND> ἔρχομαι: Synoptic Gospels **26 times**, New
Testament **85 times** [5 × 17].

---

48. We may note as well the following figures for αὐτός <AND> γίνομαι <AND> ἄνθρωπος: Luke
15 times, Matthew–Mark **17 times**, Gospels + Acts **44 times** [2 × 22] (see table 5.1 above for potential numerical significance for 15 and 22); corresponding figure for αὐτός <AND> γίνομαι <AND> ὁ
ἄνθρωπος: four Gospels **15 times**; and for αὐτός <AND> γίνομαι <AND> ὁ <AND> ἄνθρωπος: Matthew
17 times (א), Luke **30 times** [2 × 15], Synoptic Gospels **60 times** [4 × 15] (א), four Gospels **66
times** [3 × 22] (א), Acts **17 times** (א), Luke-Acts **48 times** [2 × 24] (א), Praxapostolos **24 times**
(א). Corresponding figures for γίνομαι <AND> ἄνθρωπος (cf. Phil 2:7): Luke **24 times**, four Gospels
45 times [3 × 15] (Matthew–Mark **17 times**), New Testament **81 times** [3 × 27]; and in Rahlfs:
Historical Books **66 times** [3 × 22], Poetical Books **45 times** [3 × 15] (including Psalms of Solomon).

49. Corresponding figure for αὐτός <AND> ἀποστέλλω <AND> ὁ Ἰησοῦς: New Testament 14 times
(cf. table 5.1 above for potential significance of 14).

50. We may also note the following alphabetical multiple: ἐρχόμενον: New Testament **17 times**;
ὁ <AND> ἐρχόμενος: New Testament **72 times** [3 × 24].

51. Corresponding figures for Luke **60 times** [4 × 15], Pauline Corpus **15 times**, and 1 John **22
times.**

54. ὁ θεός <AND> ἔρχομαι: Synoptic Gospels **26 times**, New Testament **78 times** [3 × 26].[52]

55. ἀκολουθέω <AND> ἐγώ (cf. Matt 8:22; 9:9): New Testament/ Gospels + Acts **78 times** [3 × 26].[53]

56. ἀκολούθει <AND> μοι (cf. Matt 8:22; 9:9): Synoptic Gospels **17 times**.

57. ἀκολουθέω <AND> αὐτός (cf. Matt 4:20, 22, 25): Mark **52 times** [2 × 26], Luke **34 times** [2 × 17].[54]

58. τίς <AND> ἐγώ <AND> λέγω <AND> εἰμί (cf. Matt 16:15; Mark 8:29, Luke 9:20: τίνα με λέγετε εἶναι): Synoptic Gospels **119 times** [7 × 17], New Testament **260 times** [10 × 26].

59. σύ <AND> τίς <AND> ἐγώ <AND> λέγω <AND> εἰμί (cf. Matt 16:15; Mark 8:29; Luke 9:20: ὑμεῖς δὲ τίνα με λέγετε εἶναι): Matthew **17 times**, Synoptic Gospels **52 times** [2 × 26], Pauline Corpus **17 times**.

60. σύ <AND> δέ <AND> τίς <AND> ἐγώ <AND> λέγω <AND> εἰμί (cf. Matt 16:15; Mark 8:29, Luke 9:20: ὑμεῖς δὲ τίνα με λέγετε εἶναι): Synoptic Gospels/ Gospels **26 times**.

61. σύ <AND> εἰμί <AND> ὁ χριστός (cf. Mark 8:29): four Gospels **51 times** [3 × 17], Luke-Acts **17 times**, New Testament **78 times** [3 × 26];[55] corresponding results for σύ <AND> εἰμί <AND> χριστός: Luke **17 times**, Synoptic Gospels **45 times** [3 × 15], Luke-Acts **26 times**, Romans **17 times**. Corresponding

---

52. Corresponding figure for Gospels + Acts **48 times** [2 × 24]; corresponding figures for ὁ <AND> θεός <AND> ἔρχομαι: Luke **27 times**, Pauline Corpus **51 times** [3 × 17], and New Testament **240 times** [10 × 24].

53. Corresponding figure for Mark **15 times**.

54. We may note as well the following figures for ἀκολουθέω <AND> αὐτός: New Testament **216 times** [8 × 27], Gospels + Acts **196 times** [14 × 14], Luke-Acts **42 times** [3 × 14] (see table 5.1 above for potential numerical significance of 27 and 14).

55. Corresponding results for σύ <AND> εἰμί <AND> ὁ <AND> χριστός (NA28): Luke **22 times**, (Matthew–Mark **51 times** [3 × 17]), Romans **15 times**, Colossians **44 times** [2 × 22], 1 Thessalonians **15 times**, Pauline Corpus **168 times** [7 × 24], New Testament **297 times** [11 × 27].

figures for σύ <and> εἰμί <and> χριστός (based on clause
rather than verse as textual scope): Synoptic Gospels **27
times**, four Gospels **39 times** (cf. 5.1 above for potential significance of **39**), Pauline Corpus **44 times** [**2 x 22**], New
Testament **95 times** (THGNT)/ **96 times** [**4 x 24**] (NA28).[56]

62. "σύ" <AND> "ει" <AND> "ὁ χριστός" (search in Accordance
on this form; cf. Mark 8:29): New Testament **34 times** [**2
× 17**]; corresponding figures for "σύ" <AND> "ει" <AND>
"ὁ" <AND> "χριστός" (search in Accordance on this form):
Synoptic Gospels **34 times** [**2 × 17**], John **17 times**, four
Gospels **51 times** [**3 × 17**].[57] Corresponding figure for "σύ"
<and> "ει" <and> "ὁ χριστός" (based on sentence rather than
verse as textual scope): New Testament **34 times** [**2 x 17**].

63. ἐγώ <AND> εἰμί <AND> ὁ χριστός (cf. Matt 24:5): Pauline
Corpus **26 times**.[58]

64. Ἰησοῦς <AND> ἀποθνῄσκω: Gospels + Acts **17 times**;[59] corresponding figures for ὁ <AND> Ἰησοῦς <AND> ἀποθνῄσκω:
John **34 times** [**2 × 17**].

---

56. Corresponding figures for σύ <AND> εἰμί <AND> ὁ <AND> χριστός in Codex Sinaiticus (א):
Four Gospels **105 times** [**7 × 15**], Mark **15 times**, Pauline Corpus **154 times** [**7 × 22**], 1–2 Corinthians
44 times [**2 × 22**], 1 Thessalonians **15 times**; in TF 35: New Testament **330 times** [**15 × 22**], four
Gospels **132 times** [**6 × 22**], Synoptic Gospels **85 times** [**5 × 17**], Luke **24 times**, Acts **15 times**, Luke-
Acts **39 times**, 1 Corinthians **54 times** [**2 × 27**], 1–2 Corinthians **66 times** [**3 × 22**], Colossians **44
times** [**2 × 22**]; and in NA28: New Testament **297 times** [**11 × 27**], Pauline Corpus **168 times** [**7 ×
24**], Romans **15 times**, Colossians **44 times** [**2 × 22**], 1 Thessalonians **15 times**.

57. Corresponding figure for the twenty-seven-book New Testament: 56 times [**4 × 14**].

58. Corresponding figure in Gospels + Acts **44 times** [**2 × 22**] (Luke–John **30 times** [**2 × 15**]).
Corresponding figures for ἐγώ <AND> εἰμί <AND> ὁ <AND> χριστός: Synoptic Gospels **44 times** [**2 ×
22**] (Matthew–Mark **26 times**, Luke-Mark **24 times**), four Gospels 84 times [**6 × 14**], 2 Corinthians
24 times, Ephesians **17 times**, Philippians **17 times**, Praxapostolos 42 times [**3 × 14**].

59. Corresponding figures in John **15 times**, New Testament **24 times**.

65. Ἰησοῦς <AND> αἷμα: New Testament **26 times**; corresponding figure for ὁ <AND> Ἰησοῦς <AND> αἷμα: 1 John/Praxapostolos **17 times.**[60]

66. χριστός <AND> αἷμα: New Testament **17 times.**

67. αἷμα <AND> μου (cf. Matt 26:28) four Gospels **17 times**; corresponding figure for ὁ (τὸ) αἷμα <AND> μου: New Testament **17 times;**[61]

68. αἷμα <AND> ἐγώ (cf. Matt 26:28): New Testament **52 times** [2 × 26];[62] ὁ <AND> αἷμα <AND> ἐγώ: Matthew **26 times**, Gospels + Acts **78 times** [3 × 26].[63]

69. αἷμα <AND> αὐτός (cf. Rom 3:25): Pauline Corpus **26 times;**[64] corresponding figures for ὁ <AND> αἷμα <AND> αὐτός: four Gospels **78 times** [3 × 26], Romans **17 times**, Hebrews **26 times.**[65]

70. θεός <AND> δικαιοσύνη (cf. Rom 1:17; 10:3): Pauline Corpus **51 times** [3 × 17].[66]

---

60. Corresponding figures in Hebrews **22 times**, Pauline Corpus **27 times**, New Testament **77** times [7 × 11].

61. Corresponding figures for μου <AND> ὁ <AND> αἷμα: Synoptic Gospels **24 times**, Gospels + Acts **42 times** [3 × 14] (Luke-John **26 times**).

62. Corresponding figures in the Synoptic Gospels **15 times**, four Gospels **27 times**; corresponding figures for ὁ αἷμα <AND> ἐγώ: Gospels + Acts **27 times** (Luke–John 14 times).

63. Corresponding figures in the Synoptic Gospels 39 times, the four Gospels **60 times** [4 × 15], Luke-Acts **24 times**, Praxapostolos **24 times.**

64. Corresponding figures in Gospels + Acts **44 times** [2 × 22], Praxapostolos **15 times**, New Testament **108 times** [4 × 27]. Corresponding figures for ὁ αἷμα <AND> αὐτός: Synoptic Gospels **15 times**, Luke-Acts **15 times**. Corresponding figures for ἐν <AND> αἷμα <AND> αὐτός (cf. Rom 10:3): four Gospels **26 times**, Pauline Corpus 23 times, Revelation **27 times**, New Testament **81 times** [3 × 27]; and for ἐν <AND> τὸ αἷμα <AND> αὐτός: four Gospels **17 times**, Pauline Corpus 14 times, Revelation **17 times.**

65. Corresponding figures for Matthew **22 times**, Luke **22 times**, John 23 times (Luke–John **45** times [3 × 15]), Acts 32 times, Luke-Acts **54 times** [2 × 27], Gospels + Acts **110 times** [5 × 22], Pauline Corpus 69 times [3 × 23], Praxapostolos 39 times, Revelation **90 times** [6 × 15], New Testament 276 [12 × 23] (see table 5.1 above for potential numerological significance of 23, 32, and 39).

66. Corresponding figure for Romans **27 times**. Corresponding figures for αὐτός <AND> δικαιοσύνη: Synoptic Gospels/four Gospels **17 times**, New Testament **88 times** [4 × 22], Gospels + Acts **24 times**, Romans **24 times** (as for the numerals 22 and 24, see table 5.1 above). Corresponding

71. Ἰησοῦς <AND> δικαιοσύνη: New Testament **17 times**.[67]

72. χριστός <AND> ἀνάστασις <AND> νεκρός (cf. Acts 26:23): New Testament **17 times** (textual scope: verse; alternatively, **34 times** [2 x 17], when textual scope is sentence.[68]

73. ἀνάστασις <AND> νεκρός (cf. Matt 22:31; Acts 17:32): New Testament **34 times** [2 × 17]; corresponding figures for ὁ <AND> ἀνάστασις <AND> νεκρός: Gospels + Acts **34 times** [2 × 17].[69]

74. χριστός <AND> ἀνάστασις: New Testament **17 times** (textual scope: verse; alternative result when THGNT paragraph is used as textual scope: **54 times** [2 x 27]); corresponding figure for ὁ <AND> χριστός <AND> ἀνάστασις: Praxapostolos **17 times**.[70]

75. αὐτός <AND> ἀνάστασις: New Testament **51 times** [3 × 17] (textual scope: verse;[71] alternative result when THGNT paragraph is used as textual scope: **136 times** [8 x 17]).

76. Ἰησοῦς <AND> ἐγείρω: Pauline Corpus **17 times** (textual scope: verse; alternative result when THGNT paragraph is used as textual scope: 39 times).[72]

---

figures for ὁ θεός <AND> δικαιοσύνη: Pauline Corpus (Romans 20 times, Galatians 6 times; excluding Hebrews 3 times) **26 times**. Corresponding figures for ὁ <AND> θεός <AND> δικαιοσύνη: Galatians 14 times, Pauline Corpus **108 times** [4 × 27], Pauline Corpus (excluding Hebrews 6 times) **102 times** [6 × 17].

67. Corresponding figure for ὁ <AND> Ἰησοῦς <AND> δικαιοσύνη: Romans **30 times** [2 × 15].

68. Corresponding figure for ὁ <AND> χριστός <AND> ἀνάστασις <AND> νεκρός (cf. Acts 26:23): Praxapostolos 14 times.

69. Corresponding figures for Acts **22 times**, and for the full New Testament **60 times** [4 × 15].

70. Corresponding figure for the full New Testament **30 times** [2 × 15].

71. Corresponding figures for the four Gospels 23 times, Acts 14 times, Luke-Acts **22 times**.

72. Corresponding figures for Ἰησοῦς <AND> ἐγείρω: New Testament **48 times** [2 × 24] (THGNT)/**52 times** [2 × 26] (NA28)/**51 times** [3 × 17] (ℵ, TF 35, TR), four Gospels **27 times** (NA28, ℵ; THGNT 25 times), Pauline Corpus 17 times (THGNT, TF 35, TR; NA28 19 times); and for αὐτός <AND> ἐγείρω: Matthew **54 times** [2 × 27] (THGNT; NA 28 57 times), Mark **30 times** [2 × 15] (THGNT, NA28), Synoptic Gospels **105 times** [7 × 15] (THGNT)/**108 times** [4 × 27] (NA28), Gospels + Acts **144 times** [6 × 24] (NA28; THGNT 141 times), Praxapostolos **27 times** (THGNT,

77. θεός <AND> ἐγείρω <AND> νεκρός: Luke-Acts **17 times**, New Testament **51 times** [3 × 17] (textual scope: verse;[73] alternative result when THGNT paragraph is used as textual scope: **150 times** [10 x 15]).

78. πίστις <AND> Ἰησοῦς <AND> χριστός: New Testament **78 times** [3 × 26] (textual scope: verse;[74] alternative result when THGNT paragraph is used as textual scope: **255 times** [15 x 17]); corresponding figure for πίστις <AND> Ἰησοῦς χριστός: Pauline Corpus **17 times**;[75] corresponding figure for ὁ <AND> πίστις <AND> Ἰησοῦς <AND> χριστός: Praxapostolos **26 times**.[76]

Nomina Sacra *Configurations Involving* ἄνθρωπος

79. Ἰησοῦς <AND> ἄνθρωπος: Pauline Corpus **17 times**, Gospels + Acts **68 times** [4 × 17]; corresponding figures for Ἰησοῦς <AND> ὁ ἄνθρωπος: Synoptic Gospels **26 times** (Matthew–Mark **17 times**);[77] corresponding figures for ὁ <AND> Ἰησοῦς <AND> ἄνθρωπος: Praxapostolos **17 times** (Matthew–Mark **85 times** [5 × 17]).[78]

80. χριστός <AND> ἄνθρωπος: Pauline Corpus **34 times** [2 × 17] (textual scope: verse; alternative result when THGNT

NA28), Pauline Corpus **30 times** [2 × 15] (THGNT; NA28 29 times), New Testament **180 times** [12 × 15] (THGNT)/**182 times** [7 × 26] (NA28).

73. Corresponding figures in Codex Sinaiticus (א): Pauline Corpus **27 times**, New Testament **54 times** [2 × 27]. Corresponding figure for ὁ θεός <AND> ἐγείρω <AND> νεκρός: New Testament 39 times. Corresponding figures for ὁ <AND> θεός <AND> ἐγείρω <AND> νεκρός: Gospels + Acts 42 times [3 × 14], Romans **15 times**, 1–2 Corinthians **17 times**, Pauline Corpus **48 times** [2 × 24].

74. Corresponding figures for Pauline Corpus 64 times [2 × 32], Praxapostolos 14 times (for potential significance of the numerals 32 and 14, see table 5.1 above). Corresponding figure for ὁ πίστις <AND> Ἰησοῦς <AND> χριστός: New Testament **27 times**.

75. Corresponding figure for the full New Testament **24 times**.

76. Corresponding figures for Romans **15 times**, 1 Timothy **22 times**, 1–2 Timothy 32 times, New Testament 126 times [7 × 18].

77. Corresponding figures for ὁ Ἰησοῦς <AND> ἄνθρωπος; four Gospels **48 times** [2 × 24] (Matthew–Mark **24 times**; Luke–John **24 times**).

78. Corresponding figures for ὁ <AND> Ἰησοῦς <AND> ἄνθρωπος: Mark **24 times**, Synoptic Gospels **120 times** [6 × 24], Luke-Acts **45 times** [3 × 15] (Luke–John **96 times** [4 × 24]).

paragraph is used as textual scope: **195 times** [13 x 15 = 5 x 39]).

81. θεός <AND> ἄνθρωπος: Synoptic Gospels **52 times** [2 × 26]; corresponding figure in Rahlfs: the Prophets **85 times** [5 × 17]; and in the Hebrew Bible for אדם <AND> אלהים: Latter Prophets **26 times**; corresponding figure for θεός <AND> ὁ ἄνθρωπος: Synoptic Gospels **26 times**, New Testament **85 times** [5 × 17].[79]

82. ἄνθρωπος <AND> ἄνθρωπος: Synoptic Gospels **51 times** [3 × 17] (textual scope: verse; alternative result when THGNT paragraph is used as textual scope: **130 times** [5 x 26]). ἄνθρωπος occurs **136 times** [8 x 17] in Pauline Corpus, **550 times** [5 x 5 x 22] in the New Testament. Corresponding figures for ἄνθρωπος <and> ἄνθρωπος (based on clause rather than verse as textual scope): Pauline Corpus **15 times**; and for ἄνθρωπος <and> ἄνθρωπος (based on sentence rather than verse as textual scope): Matthew 20 times (THGNT)/ **26 times** (NA28), Synoptic Gospels **54 times** [2 x 27], Praxapostolos **68 times** [4 x 17] (THGNT)/ **75 times** [5 x 15] (NA28), Pauline Corpus 39 times (NA28; see table 5.1 for potential significance of 39), New Testament **120 times** [5 x 24] (NA28).

83. "Son of Man," ὁ υἱός ὁ ἄνθρωπος: New Testament **78 times** [3 × 26].[80]

84. "Son of Man"

   i. σύ <AND> υἱός <AND> ἄνθρωπος: Luke **26 times**, four Gospels **78 times** [3 × 26]. Corresponding figures for σύ + υἱός + ἄνθρωπος: Matthew **660 times** [2 x 15 x 22], Mark **255 times** [15 x 17], Synoptic Gospels **1534 times**

---

79. Corresponding figures in Luke-Acts **24 times** and Praxapostolos **15 times**.
80. Corresponding figure in Luke **22 times**.

[59 x 26] (**59 is the 17th prime number**), Praxapostolos
560 times [4 x 10 x 14] (see 5.1 above for potential significance of 4, 10 and 14), Romans **168 times** [7 x 24], 2
Corinthians **168 times** [7 x 24], Ephesians **60 times** [4
x 15], Colossians **66 times** [3 x 22], 1–2 Thessalonians
135 times [5 x 27 = 3 x 3 x 15], 1–2 Timothy **51 times** [3
x 17], Philemon **24 times**, Pauline Corpus **1100 times**
[50 x 22].[81]

ii.   οὗτος \<AND\> υἱός \<AND\> ἄνθρωπος: New Testament **45
      times** [3 × 15]; for οὗτος \<and\> υἱός \<and\> ὁ ἄνθρωπος:
      New Testament **44 times** [2 x 22], Synoptic Gospels **30
      times** [2 x 15]; and for οὗτος \<and\> υἱός \<and\> εἰμί \<and\>
      ὁ ἄνθρωπος: four Gospels **22 times**, New Testament **27
      times**. Corresponding result for οὗτος \<and\> υἱός \<and\>
      ἄνθρωπος (based on clause rather than verse as textual
      scope): Luke **15 times**. Corresponding figures for οὗτος
      + υἱός + ἄνθρωπος: four Gospels **1224 times** [5 x 15 x 17].[82]

iii. Ἰησοῦς \<AND\> υἱός \<AND\> ἄνθρωπος: four Gospels/
      Gospels + Acts/New Testament **51 times** [3 × 17].

iv.   ὁ Ἰησοῦς \<AND\> ὁ υἱός \<AND\> ὁ ἄνθρωπος: New Testament
      26 times.

v.   Ἰησοῦς \<AND\> ὁ \<AND\> υἱός \<AND\> ὁ \<AND\> ἄνθρωπος:
      four Gospels/New Testament **130 times** [5 × 26].[83]

---

81. We can note as well the following alphabetical figure: σύ \<AND\> υἱός \<AND\> ἄνθρωπος: New
Testament **81 times** [3 × 27]; and for σύ \<AND\> εἰμί \<AND\> ὁ \<AND\> υἱός \<AND\> ὁ \<AND\> ἄνθρωπος:
Synoptic Gospels **24 times**.

82. We may also note the following alphabetical figure: Ἰησοῦς \<AND\> ὁ υἱός ὁ ἄνθρωπος: New
Testament **24 times**.

83. We may note as well the following alphabetical figures: Ἰησοῦς \<AND\> ὁ \<AND\> υἱός \<AND\>
ὁ \<AND\> ἄνθρωπος: Luke **22 times**; and for αὐτός \<AND\> ὁ \<AND\> υἱός \<AND\> ὁ \<AND\> ἄνθρωπος:
Mark **88 times** [4 × 22], Luke **72 times** [3 × 24], four Gospels **486 times** [18 × 27]. Corresponding
figures for Ἰησοῦς \<AND\> εἰμί \<AND\> ὁ \<AND\> υἱός \<AND\> ὁ \<AND\> ἄνθρωπος: New Testament/four
Gospels 39 times (see table 5.1 above; Matthew–Mark **22 times**, Luke–John **17 times**).

vi. θεός \<AND\> ὁ \<AND\> υἱός \<AND\> ὁ \<AND\> ἄνθρωπος: Luke **17 times**.[84]

vii. θεός \<AND\> υἱός \<AND\> ἄνθρωπος: New Testament **26 times**; corresponding figure for θεός \<AND\> υἱός \<AND\> ὁ \<AND\> ἄνθρωπος: Luke **17 times**.[85]

viii. ἐγώ \<AND\> ὁ υἱός ὁ ἄνθρωπος: four Gospels/New Testament **17 times**.

ix. οὗτος \<AND\> ὁ \<AND\> ἄνθρωπος: four Gospels **306 times** [**18 × 17**], Gospels + Acts **425 times** [**5 × 5 × 17**], Pauline Corpus **68 times** [**4 × 17**], Acts **119 times** [**7 × 17**].[86]

9.2 CONCLUDING NOTE

In this chapter we have continued to explore NrN configurations as a way of structuring the New Testament, the Septuagint, and the Hebrew biblical texts. The starting point for our analysis was the fifteen words in the *nomina sacra* word-group (GOD, LORD, JESUS, CHRIST, SPIRIT, CROSS/CRUCIFY, MAN/HUMAN BEING, F/FATHER, S/SON, ISRAEL, JERUSALEM, SAVIOR, DAVID, MOTHER, HEAVEN), which resulted in over eighty examples of various NrN configurations involving *nomina sacra* or related vocabulary.

---

84. We may also note the following alphabetical figures: θεός \<AND\> ὁ \<AND\> υἱός \<AND\> ὁ \<AND\> ἄνθρωπος: Luke-Acts **24 times**, New Testament **66 times** [**3 × 22**].

85. Corresponding figures for the four Gospels **48 times** [**2 × 24**] (Luke–John **42 times** [**3 × 14**]), Luke-Acts **24 times**, New Testament **66 times** [**3 × 22**]. Corresponding figures for the configuration υἱός \<AND\> ὁ ἄνθρωπος: Mark **34 times** [**2 × 17**], Synoptic Gospels **150 times** [**10 × 15**], John **26 times**, and four Gospels **176 times** [**8 × 22**].

86. Corresponding figures for the Synoptic Gospels **216 times** [**8 × 27**] (Matthew–Mark **132 times** [**6 × 22**]), Praxapostolos **135 times** [**5 × 27**]. I am grateful to Suyoung Lee for discussions about some of the above figures, arguably pertaining to the notion of the Son of Man.

10

NAME-RELATED NUMERALS: CONCLUDING REFLECTION

In part C, on arithmetical aspects of the biblical canon, I have introduced what I call *Name-related Numeral(s)* (*NrN*; marked in boldface below), that is, multiples of the three Hebrew and Hellenistic Greek alphabetical fullness numbers **22/27** and **24**, on the one hand (e.g., as used by, or in later editing of works by, Homer, Josephus, and Athanasius), and multiples of three numerical values associated with the Tetragrammaton, **15**, **17**, and **26**, on the other. *Name-related Numerals* in the biblical material seem to appear as part of an arithmetical pattern, providing textual structure—similar to that of the function of the *nomina sacra*—by linking the text to the divine name (cf. Isa 41:4; 44:6; 48:12; Rev 1:8; 21:6; 22:13) and textual completeness (cf. Rev 22:13). There are several examples of such *NrN* organization (figures based on the THGNT and *BHS*, unless otherwise indicated):

- At the macrocanonical level: the **22** or **24 books** included in the Jewish Scripture canon, the **27 books** of the widely received New Testament and the **66 books** [3 × 22] of standard Protestant Bibles;

- At the codicological level: in Codex Sinaiticus (similar arithmetical characteristics feature also in Vaticanus, Alexandrinus, and Washingtonianus; see appendix), the **48 lines** [2 × 24] used per page, the **484 columns** [22 × 22] devoted to the four Gospels and the altogether **578 columns** [2 × 17 × 17] to the remaining 23 New Testament books;

- At the level of paragraphing (the ancient paragraph division embraced by THGNT): Matthew **405 paragraphs** [15 × 27] (with Peter's confession, "You are the CHRIST," as the textual midpoint, with 202 paragraphs preceding and 202 following Matt 16:16), Mark **192** [8 × 24] **paragraphs**, and the four Gospels + Acts **1458 paragraphs** [2 × 27 × 27];

- At the chapter division level (introduced in medieval Bible manuscripts): Luke's **24 chapters**, Matthew–Mark's **44 chapters** [2 × 22], the Synoptic Gospels's **68 chapters** [4 × 17], Luke–John's **45 chapters** [3 × 15], Luke-Acts's **52 chapters** [2 × 26], Revelation's **22 chapters**, and the **260 chapters** [10 × 26] of the full New Testament; it is here worth noting as well the old chapter/*kephalaia* division, e.g., of the four Gospels into **221 chapters** [13 x 17] (including the introductions of the four Gospels that are not formally included among the numbered *kephalaia*) in Codex Alexandrinus;

- At the microcanonical level of Old Testament word-frequencies linked to NrN (and canonical subunits devised at the microcanonical level): the **2600 occurrences** [10 × 10 × 26] of the Hebrew term *Elohim*, אלהים, "God; god, deity," in the MT, the **204 appearances** [12 × 17] of the term in 1–2 Kings, the **26** in Hosea, and the **17** in Job; moreover, in the Pentateuch, the Tetragrammaton, יהוה, features altogether **1820 times** [70 × 26], **165 times** [11 × 15] in Genesis, **396** [18 × 22] in Numbers, and **550** [5 × 5 × 22] in Deuteronomy, that is, for the Pentateuch, four out of, in total, six word-frequency figures turn out to be NrN (i.e., ca. 67 percent NrN; cf. observation 3. ch. 7, above). The corresponding results for θεός (sg. forms) in LXXG show the same tendency: the Pentateuch **962 occurrences** [37 × 26], Exodus **165** [11 × 15], Leviticus **68** [4 × 17], that is, three out of, in total, six word-frequencies for θεός in the six subcanonical units that make up the Pentateuch are NrN (i.e., 50 percent NrN;

observation 3 above). Corresponding figures for θεός (sg. forms) in Rahlfs demonstrate the same inclination: the Pentateuch **969 occurrences** [57 × 17], Genesis **272 occurrences** [4 × 4 × 17], Leviticus **68 occurrences** [4 × 17], and Numbers **60 occurrences** [4 × 15], that is four out of, in total, six word-frequencies are *NrN* (i.e., 67 percent *NrN*); similar results feature as well for κύριος ὁ θεός, "Lord God," in LXXG: the Pentateuch **476 times** [4 × 7 × 17], Exodus **45 times** [3 × 15], and Leviticus **44 times** [2 × 22], that is, in three out of five possible cases we get *NrN* (i.e., 60 percent *NrN*; Numbers is excluded from the count, since the book only has six appearances of κύριος ὁ θεός);

- At the microcanonical level of Old Testament and New Testament word-frequencies linked to *NrN* (and canonical subunits devised at the microcanonical level): the *nomen sacrum* πνεῦμα (sg. forms): the Pentateuch **27 times** (i.e., 100 percent *NrN*; corresponding figure for רוח [unpointed] in the Pentateuch [MT] **44 times** [2 × 22], i.e., 100 percent *NrN*), the twenty-seven-book New Testament **345 times** [23 × 15], Luke **30 times** [2 × 15], John **24 times**, Luke–John **54 times** [2 × 27], Acts **66 times**, Luke-Acts **96 times** [4 × 24] (i.e., 100 percent *NrN* for the Lukan writings: Luke, Acts, and Luke-Acts), Pauline Corpus **150 times** [10 × 15], Romans **34 times** [2 × 17], 2 Corinthians **17 times**, 1–2 Corinthians **54 times** [2 × 27], and Revelation **17 times**; the *nomen sacrum* οὐρανός (LXXG and THGNT): the Pentateuch **105 times** [7 × 15], Genesis **44 times** [2 × 22], Exodus **15 times**, Deuteronomy **45 times** [3 × 15] (i.e., 100 percent *NrN* for figures above 1 in the Pentateuch); the Synoptic Gospels **135 times** [5 × 27], the four Gospels **153 times** [9 × 17], Acts **26 times**, and Revelation **52 times** [2 × 26]; the *nomen sacrum* υἱός (forms in the sg.; LXXG) Genesis **153 times** [9 × 17], Exodus **15 times**, Numbers **132 times** [6 × 22], and Deuteronomy **27**

times (for figures above eight, four out of, in total, five are NrN in the Pentateuch, i.e., 80 percent NrN).

- At the microcanonical level of New Testament word-frequencies linked to NrN (and canonical subunits devised at the micro-canonical level; figures from THGNT, unless otherwise indicated): the *nomen sacrum* Ἰσραήλ, **featuring 15 times** in Acts, **27 times** in Luke-Acts, **26 times** in the Synoptics, **30 times** [2 × 15] in the four Gospels, **45 times** [3 × 15] in Gospels + Acts, **15 times** in Praxapostolos, and **68 times** [4 × 17] in the twenty-seven-book New Testament (affecting the inner-ca-nonical shaping of altogether seven canonical subunits); the *nomen sacrum* υἱός, appearing **22 times** in 1 John, **24 times** in 1–3 John, **27 times** in the Catholic Epistles, **48 times** [2 × 24] in the Praxapostolos, and **243 times** [9 × 27] in the full New Testament (affecting the inner-canonical shaping of altogether five canonical subunits); the personal pronoun ἐγώ in the New Testament: Matthew **270 times** [10 × 27], Luke **288 times** [12 × 24], Acts **600 times** [5 × 5 × 24], four Gospels + Acts **1540 times** [70 × 22], Romans **150 times** [10 × 15], 1–2 Corinthians **312 times** [13 × 24 = 12 × 26], Philippians **60 times** [4 × 15], Colossians **24 times**, 1 Thessalonians **51 times** [3 × 17], 2 Thessalonians **26 times**, 1 Timothy **15 times**, Philemon **22 times**, Hebrews **66 times** [3 × 22], 1–2 Peter **24 times** (N.B. NrN for ἐγώ in the Catholic Epistles of Codex Sinaiticus [א]: James **26 times**, 1–2 Peter **27 times**, 1 John **60 times** [4 × 15], 1–2 John **66 times** [3 × 22], 1–3 John **72 times** [3 × 24], the seven Catholic Epistles **132 times** [6 × 22]), Revelation **102 times** [6 × 17] (cf. footnote 28 ch. 8 above); and for the full twenty-seven-book New Testament, the following five NrN for various forms of ἐγώ: ἐγώ **340 times** [20 × 17] (sg. nom.), μου **567 times** [21 × 27], μοι **225 times** [15 × 15], ἐμοί **96 times** [4 × 24], and με **285 times** [19 × 15] (the pronoun ἐγώ in the above examples affects the inner-canonical shaping of altogether twenty-one canonical subunits); related to the aforementioned figures are, as well, the expression ἐγώ εἰμι (including κἀγώ εἰμι in Acts 26:29; Rahlfs and THGNT) featuring **24 times** in Leviticus, **24 times** in John, and **48 times** [**2 × 24**] in the Pentateuch, the Historical Books, and the New Testament, respectively;

- At the microcanonical level of combined word-frequencies, linked to NrN, we can note

  - The Triune structure θεός + χριστός + πνεῦμα (similar Triune patterns were found as well for other parts of the New Testament and in Ignatius of Antioch, Eusebius, Athanasius, and Basil the Great):

    - Luke: θεός 122 times + χριστός 12 times + πνεῦμα 36 times = **170 times** [**10 × 17**];

    - Acts: θεός **165 times** + χριστός 25 times + πνεῦμα 70 times = **260 times** [**10 × 26**];

    - Synoptics: θεός 223 times + χριστός 35 times + πνεῦμα **78 times** = **336 times** [**14 × 24**];

    - Gospels + Acts: θεός 469 times + χριστός 79 times + πνεῦμα 172 times = **720 times** [**2 × 15 × 24**].

For subcanonical constellations involving Luke and Acts, regarding the sum θεός + χριστός + πνεῦμα, we here detect an outcome of four NrN, that is, 57 percent NrN (Luke, Acts, Synoptic Gospels, Gospels + Acts) out of, in total, seven possibilities (Luke, Synoptic Gospels, four Gospels, Acts, Gospels + Acts, Praxapostolos, the full New Testament; here excluding Luke-Acts);

  - And the following kerygmatic structures pertaining to Matt 16:15, Mark 8:29, and Luke 9:20 (NrN, multiples of 17 and 26 in the below examples):

    - τίς <AND> ἐγώ <AND> λέγω <AND> εἰμί (cf. Matt 16:15; Mark 8:29, Luke 9:20: τίνα με λέγετε εἶναι;): Synoptic Gospels **119 times** [**7 x 17**] (textual scope:

verse)/ **110 times** [**5 x 22**] (textual scope: sentence),
New Testament **260 times** [**10 x 26**] (textual scope:
verse)/ **255 times** [**15 x 17**] (textual scope: sentence).

- σύ <AND> τίς <AND> ἐγώ <AND> λέγω <AND> εἰμί
  (cf. Matt 16:15; Mark 8:29, Luke 9:20: ὑμεῖς δὲ τίνα
  με λέγετε εἶναι;): Matthew **17 times** (textual scope:
  verse)/ **17 times** (textual scope: sentence), Synoptic
  Gospels **52 times** [**2 x 26**] (textual scope: verse)/ 46
  [2 x 23] (textual scope: sentence), Pauline Corpus **17
  times** (textual scope: verse)/ 14 times (textual scope:
  sentence; see table 5.1 above for potential significance
  of 14 and 23).

- σύ <AND> δέ <AND> τίς <AND> ἐγώ <AND> λέγω
  <AND> εἰμί (cf. Matt 16:15; Mark 8:29, Luke 9:20:
  ὑμεῖς δὲ τίνα με λέγετε εἶναι;): Synoptic Gospels/four
  Gospels **26 times** (textual scope: verse)/ **27 times**
  (textual scope: sentence).

- σύ <AND> εἰμί <AND> ὁ χριστός (cf. Mark 8:29: σὺ εἶ ὁ
  χριστός): four Gospels **51 times** [**3 x 17**] (textual scope:
  verse)/ 49 times [7 x 7] (textual scope: sentence),
  Luke-Acts **17 times** (textual scope: verse)/ 19 times
  (textual scope: sentence), Gospels + Acts **54 times** [2
  x 27] (textual scope: verse)/ **52 times** [2 x 26] (textual scope: sentence), Pauline Corpus **24 times** (textual scope: verse)/ 111 times (textual scope: sentence),
  New Testament **78 times** [**3 x 26**] (textual scope:
  verse)/ 163 times (textual scope: sentence);[1] corresponding results for σύ <AND> εἰμί <AND> χριστός:
  Luke **17 times** (textual range: verse), Synoptic Gospels
  45 times [**3 x 15**] (textual range: verse), Luke-Acts **26**

---

1. Corresponding results for σύ <AND> εἰμί <AND> ὁ <AND> χριστός (NA28): Luke **22 times**,
(Matthew–Mark **51 times** [3 × 17]), Romans **15 times**, Colossians **44 times** [2 × 22], 1 Thessalonians
15 times, Pauline Corpus **168 times** [7 × 24], New Testament **297 times** [11 × 27].

times (textual range: verse), Romans **17 times** (textual range: verse).[2]

- σύ (sg. nom.) <AND> εἰ (εἶ/εἶ) <AND> ὁ χριστός (sg. nom.; cf. Mark 8:29): New Testament **34 times** [2 x 17] (textual scope: verse)/ **34 times** [2 x 17] (textual scope: sentence); corresponding figures for σύ (sg. nom.) <AND> εἰ <AND> ὁ (masc. sg. nom.) <AND> χριστός (sg. nom.): Synoptic Gospels **34 times** [2 x 17] (textual scope: verse)/ 32 times [textual scope: sentence] (cf. 5.1 above for potential significance of 32), John **17 times** (textual scope: verse)/ **17 times** (textual scope: sentence), four Gospels **51 times** [3 x 17] (textual scope: verse)/ 49 times [7 x 7] (textual scope: sentence).

- αὐτός <AND> εἰμί <AND> ὁ <AND> χριστός (cf. Matt 16:20): 1 John **26 times**.[3]

- οὗτος <AND> εἰμί <AND> ὁ <AND> χριστός (cf. Luke 23:35; John 4:29; 7:26; Acts 9:22): John **51 times** [3 × 17], 1 Corinthians **17 times**, Pauline Corpus **78 times** [3 × 26], Praxapostolos **78 times** [3 × 26].[4]

---

2. Corresponding figures for σύ <AND> εἰμί <AND> ὁ <AND> Χριστός in Codex Sinaiticus (ℵ): four Gospels **105 times** [7 × 15], Mark **15 times**, Pauline Corpus **154 times** [7 × 22], 1–2 Corinthians **44 times** [2 × 22], 1 Thessalonians **15 times**; in TF 35 (Majority Text): New Testament **330 times** [15 × 22], four Gospels **132 times** [6 × 22], Synoptic Gospels **85 times** [5 × 17], Luke **24 times**, Acts **15 times**, Luke-Acts 39 times (see table 5.1 above for potential significance of 39), 1 Corinthians **54 times** [2 × 27], 1–2 Corinthians **66 times** [3 × 22], Colossians **44 times** [2 × 22]; and in NA28: New Testament **297 times** [11 × 27], Pauline Corpus **168 times** [7 × 24], Romans **15 times**, Colossians **44 times** [2 × 22], 1 Thessalonians **15 times**.

3. Corresponding figures in Luke **44 times** [2 × 22], Gospels + Acts **162 times** [6 × 27], 1 Corinthians **27 times**, 1–2 Corinthians 39 times, Pauline Corpus **120 times** [6 × 24], and the full New Testament 318 times (cf. Barn. 9.8–9). Corresponding figures for αὐτός <AND> εἰμί <AND> ὁ χριστός: Luke **24 times**, John **24 times** (100 percent N*r*N for individual New Testament books, for figures above 10).

4. Corresponding figures in Acts **24 times** and 1 Corinthians: **24 times**. Corresponding figure for οὗτος εἰμί <AND> ὁ χριστός: New Testament **15 times**.

We will close our concluding reflection with three additional examples of unexpectedly high rates of NrN: (1) an example illustrating the wider employment of the NrN practice in texts also beyond the Old and New Testaments, (2) the *nomen sacrum* θεός/θε* *in Romans, and* (3) the words πίστις, πιστεύω, and πιστός in the New Testament and beyond:

1. The *nomen sacrum* κύριος and θεός appeared as NrN in a wider range of texts beyond the biblical writings, as the following results indicate (observation 4, ch. 8):

- In Eusebius's *Church History* (Migne, Accordance), made up of ten books, κύριος and θεός occurred with the following frequencies:

  - κύριος: book 2 **17 times**, book 5 **30 times** [2 × 15], book 6 **24 times**, book 7 **17 times**, and book 10 **22 times**; and

  - θεός: book 1 **75 times** [5 × 15], book 4 **26 times**, book 6 **27 times**, book 7 **44 times** [2 × 22], book 8 **24 times**, book 10 **72 times** [3 × 27];

- In two of Bishop Athanasius's writings (Migne, Accordance) we found our specified word-frequency patterns for κύριος and ὁ θεός allocated as follows:

  - *On the Incarnation*: κύριος: **60 times** [4 × 15] and ὁ θεός **119 times** [7 × 17];

  - *Letter to Serapion*: κύριος: **108 times** [4 × 27] and ὁ θεός **182 times** [7 × 26];

- In Josephus's *Jewish Antiquities* (1890 Niese edition, Accordance): κύριος: **27 times** and θεός **1606 times** [73 × 22];

- In 1 Clement: κύριος **66 times** [3 × 22];

- In the Didache: κύριος **24 times;**

- In the seven Ignatian Letters: κύριος **34 times** [2 × 17], θεός **176 times** [8 × 22], ὁ θεός **30 times** [2 × 15]; and

- In Protevangelium of James: κύριος **81 times** [3 × 27].

2. Moreover, the number of occurrences in Romans of the *nomen sacrum* θεός/θε* appeared to be aligned to the same numerological pattern, with the following NrN resulting from our search in THGNT: θεός **153 times** [9 × 17]; ὁ θεός **105 times** [7 × 15]; θεοσ* **154 times** [7 × 22]; θε* **176 times** [8 × 22]; ὁ θε* **110 times** [5 × 22]; θ* **216 times** [8 × 27]; and ὁ θ* **130 times** [5 × 26]; in addition: ὁ θεός (sg. nom.) **26 times**, τῷ θεῷ **26 times**, and θεόν **15 times**.

3. In our discussion of the words πίστις, πιστεύω, and πιστός (observation 1, ch. 7 above), we saw a high presence of NrN, for example, in the full twenty-seven-book New Testament, with the following eight NrN:

- πίστις **243 times** [3 × 3 × 3 × 3 × 3 = 3 × 3 × 27]

- πιστεύω **242 times** [2 × 11 × 11 = 11 × 22][5]

- πιστός **66 times** [3 × 22]

- πισ* **476** [4 × 7 × 17 = 2 × 14 × 17] (search in Accordance on this form)

- *πισ* **858 times** [3 × 11 × 26 = 22 × 39] (search in Accordance

- on this form)

- ἡ πίστις (sg. nom.) **30 times** [2 × 15]

- τῇ πίστει **22 times**

- τὴν πίστιν **27 times**

---

5. For text-critical comments pertaining to πιστεύω (THGNT; P⁷², ℵ, TF 35/Majority Text) and πιστός (NA28; B, A) in 1 Pet 1:21, see note 5 in ch. 7 above.

Corresponding *NrN* for the four Gospels:

- πίστις **24 times**

- πιστεύω **132 times** [6 × 22]

- πισ*/πιστ* **170 times** [10 × 17]

- *πισ* **270 times** [10 × 27]

Corresponding *NrN* for the Synoptic Gospels:

- πίστις **24 times**

- πιστεύω **34 times** [2 × 17]

Corresponding *NrN* for Luke-Acts:

- πίστις **26 times**

- *πιστ* **135 times** [7 × 27]

Corresponding *NrN* for the Catholic Epistles:

- πίστις **26 times**

- πιστεύω **17 times**

- *πισ* **75 times** [5 × 15]

Corresponding *NrN* for the Praxapostolos:

- πιστεύω **54 times** [2 × 27]

- πισ* **105 times** [7 × 15]

- *πισ* **187 times** [11 × 17]

Corresponding *NrN* for Galatians:

- πίστις **22 times**

- πισ*/πιστ* **27 times**

- *πι* **52 times** [2 × 26]

Corresponding *NrN* for 1–2 Timothy:
- πίστις **27 times**

Corresponding *NrN* for the Pentateuch (LXXG):
- πιστεύω **15 times**

- πι* **144 times** [6 × 24]

Corresponding *NrN* for the seven-letter Ignatian corpus:
- πίστις **27 times**

- πισ*/πιστ* **51 times** [3 × 17]

- *πισ* **136 times** [8 × 17]

Corresponding *NrN* for Eusebius's *Ecclesiastical History*, books 1–10:
- πίστις **104 times** [4 × 26]

- πισ* **198 times** [9 × 22]

Corresponding *NrN* for Basil the Great's *On the Holy Spirit*:
- πίστις **45 times** [3 × 15]

- πιστεύω **27 times**

- πισ*/πιστ* **81 times** [3 × 27]

- πι* **88 times** [4 × 22]

Corresponding *NrN* for word combinations containing πίστις and πιστεύω (textual scope: verse, unless indicated otherwise):
- πίστις <AND> Ἰησοῦς <AND> χριστός (cf. Act 24:24, and Gal 2:16: πίστεως Ἰησοῦ χριστοῦ): New Testament **78 times** [3 × 26];[6]

---

6. Corresponding figure for ὁ πίστις <AND> Ἰησοῦς <AND> χριστός: New Testament **27 times.**

- πίστις <AND> Ἰησοῦς χριστός (cf. Gal 2:16: πίστεως Ἰησοῦ χριστοῦ): Pauline Corpus **17 times**;[7]

- ὁ <AND> πίστις <AND> Ἰησοῦς <AND> χριστός (cf. Acts 24:24: τῆς εἰς χριστὸν Ἰησοῦν πίστεως): Praxapostolos **26 times** (textual scope: verse)[8]/ **26 times** (textual scope: clause);

- ὁ <AND> εἰς <AND> πίστις <AND> Ἰησοῦς <AND> χριστός (cf. Acts 24:24: τῆς εἰς χριστὸν Ἰησοῦν πίστεως): Praxapostolos **15 times** (textual scope: verse)/ **15 times** (textual scope: clause), New Testament **44 times** [2 × 22];

- πιστεύω <AND> Ἰησοῦς (cf. John 4:21; 12:11): John **51 times** [3 × 17] (textual scope: verse)/ **15 times** (textual scope: clause) (100 percent NrN for individual New Testament books, for figures above 10);[9]

- πιστεύω <AND> Ἰησοῦς <AND> χριστός: Pauline Corpus **15 times**;

- πιστεύω <AND> κύριος (cf. Acts 18:8; 100 percent NrN, for figures above 11 in individual New Testament books):[10] Acts **24 times**, Luke-Acts **26 times** (textual scope: verse)/ **22 times** (textual scope: clause), four Gospels **15 times**, Gospels + Acts 39 times (textual scope: verse)/ **22 times** (textual scope: clause; for potential numerological significance of 39, see table 5.1, ch. 5 above);[11]

---

7. Corresponding figure for the full New Testament **24 times**.

8. Corresponding figures for Romans **15 times**, and 1 Timothy **22 times**.

9. Cf. also the similar Accordance search πιστεύω <AND> εἰς <AND> Ἰησοῦς (cf. John 12:11): John **30 times** [2 × 15], i.e., 100 percent NrN for figures above four in individual New Testament books; and πιστεύω <AND> ὁ Ἰησοῦς: Gospels + Acts 39 times (see table 5.1 above for potential numerological significance of 39).

10. Cf. also the similar search πιστεύω <AND> ἐπί <AND> κύριος (cf. Acts 18:8): twenty-seven-book New Testament **22 times**; πιστεύω <AND> ὁ κύριος: New Testament **27 times**; and πιστεύω <AND> ὁ θεός (cf. John 14:1): John **22 times**, four Gospels **24 times**, and Catholic Epistles **24 times**.

11. Cf. also the similar search πιστεύω <AND> επι <AND> κύριος (cf. Acts 18:8): twenty-seven-book New Testament **22 times**; πιστεύω <AND> ὁ κύριος: New Testament **27 times**; and πιστεύω <AND> ὁ θεός (cf. John 14:1): John **22 times**, four Gospels **24 times** and Catholic Epistles **24 times**.

- πιστεύω <AND> ὁ κύριος: New Testament **27 times** (textual scope: verse)/ **22 times** (textual scope: clause)/ **51 times** [**3 x 17**] (textual scope: sentence); cf. also πιστεύω <and> ὁ χριστός: New Testament **17 times** (textual scope: verse)/ **26 times** (textual scope: sentence);

- πιστεύω <AND> ὁ <AND> κύριος: New Testament **108 times** [4 × 27], John **30 times** [2 × 15], four Gospels 39 times, Acts **52 times** [2 × 26] (textual scope: verse)/ 39 times (textual scope: clause; cf. table 5.1 above for potential significance of 39), Pauline Corpus **17 times**;

- πιστεύω <AND> ἐγώ (cf. Matt 18:6 and John 4:41; 100 percent *NrN*, for figures above 14 in individual New Testament-books): John **110 times** [5 × 22];

- πιστεύω <AND> σύ (cf. Matt 8:13 and John 6:30; 100 percent *NrN*, for figures above 13 in individual New Testament-books):[12] John **78 times** [3 × 26];

- πιστεύω <AND> αὐτός (cf. Matt 21:32; and John 2:11; 8:31; 100 percent *NrN*, for figures above 12 in individual New Testament-books):[13] Matthew **17 times**, Mark **17 times**, Luke **15 times**, John **144 times** [6 × 24], Acts **52 times** [2 × 26], Romans **17 times**.[14]

---

12. Cf. also the similar search πιστεύω <AND> γίνομαι <AND> σύ (cf. Matt 8:13): four Gospels **17 times**, New Testament **34 times** [2 × 17].

13. Cf. also the similar search πιστεύω <AND> διά <AND> αὐτός (cf. John 1:7), with 100 percent *NrN* for figures above 11 in individual New Testament books: John **34 times** [2 × 17] (in addition, the following figures: Gospels + Acts **54 times** [2 × 27], twenty-seven-book New Testament **68 times** [4 × 17]); and the following results for πιστεύω <AND> ἐπί <AND> αὐτός (cf. Matt 27:42): Gospels + Acts **22 times**, Praxapostolos **15 times**, New Testament **44 times** [2 × 22]. *NrN* and related numerals (such as multiples of 14; cf. table 5.1 above) are found also for πιστεύω <AND> οὗτος: Synoptic Gospels 16 times (THGNT, NA28)/14 times (ℵ), John **44 times** [2 × 22] (ℵ; THGNT, NA28 42 times [3 × 14]), Gospels + Acts **66 times** [3 × 22], Praxapostolos 14 times (THGNT, NA28, ℵ), Pauline Corpus **15 times** (THGNT, NA28, ℵ), New Testament 87 times (THGNT, NA28, ℵ)/**88 times** [4 × 22] (TF 35).

14. Cf. also the similar search πιστεύω <AND> ἐκεῖνος: Gospels + Acts **27 times**, New Testament **34 times** [2 × 17].

BIBLIOGRAPHY

Bauckham, Richard. "The 153 Fish and the Unity of the Fourth Gospel." *Neot* 36 (2002): 77–88.

Beckwith, Roger. *The Old Testament Canon of the New Testament Church and Its Background in Early Judaism.* Grand Rapids: Eerdmans, 1985.

Bokedal, Tomas. "'But for Me, the Scriptures Are Jesus Christ' ($\overline{\text{IC}}$ $\overline{\text{XC}}$; Ign. *Phld.* 8:2): Creedal Text-Coding and the Early Scribal System of Nomina Sacra." In *Studies on the Paratextual Features of Early New Testament Manuscripts.* Edited by Stanley E. Porter, David I. Yoon, and Chris S. Stevens. TENTS. Leiden: Brill, forthcoming 2023.

———. "Canon/Scripture." Pages 46–48 in *The Dictionary of the Bible and Ancient Media.* Edited by Tom Thatcher, Chris Keith, Raymond F. Person Jr., and Elsie R. Stern. London: Bloomsbury T&T Clark, 2017. Repr. as chapter 3 in this volume.

———. *Names and Numbers: Nomina Sacra and Numerological Editorial Practice in Christian Scripture.* Forthcoming.

———. "Notes on the *Nomina Sacra* and Biblical Interpretation." Pages 263–95 in *Beyond Biblical Theologies.* Edited by Heinrich Assel, Stefan Beyerle, and Christfried Böttrich. WUNT 295. Tübingen: Mohr Siebeck, 2012. Repr. as chapter 12 in this volume.

Epp, Eldon Jay. "Issues in the Interrelation of New Testament Textual Criticism and Canon." Pages 185–515 in *The Canon Debate: On the Origins and Formation of the Bible.* Edited by Lee Martin McDonald and James A. Sanders. Peabody, MA: Hendrickson, 2002.

Gallagher, Edmon. *Hebrew Scripture in Patristic Biblical Theory: Canon, Language, Text.* VCSup 114. Leiden: Brill, 2012.

Gallagher, Edmon L., and John D. Meade, eds. *The Biblical Canon Lists from Early Christianity: Texts and Analysis.* Oxford: Oxford University Press, 2017.

Gorman, Michael J. *Reading Revelation Responsibly: Uncivil Worship and Witness: Following the Lamb into the New Creation*. Eugene, OR: Cascade, 2011.

Haslam, Michael. "Homeric Papyri and Transmission of the Text." Pages 55–100 in *A New Companion to Homer*. Edited by Ian Morris and Barry B. Powell. MnSup 163. Leiden: Brill, 1997.

Heiden, Bruce. "The Placement of 'Book Divisions' in the Iliad." *JHS* 118 (1998): 68–81.

Hurtado, Larry W. *The Earliest Christian Artifacts: Manuscripts and Christian Origins*. Grand Rapids: Eerdmans, 2006.

Labuschagne, Casper J. "General Introduction to Logotechnical Analysis (Rev.)." University of Groningen, 2016. http://www.labuschagne.nl/aspects.pdf.

———. *Numerical Secrets of the Bible: Introduction to Biblical Arithmology*. Eugene, OR: Wipf & Stock, 2016.

Liere, Frans van. *An Introduction to the Medieval Bible*. Cambridge: Cambridge University Press, 2014.

Lim, Timothy H. *The Formation of the Jewish Canon*. ABRL. New Haven: Yale University Press, 2013.

McKendrick, Scot. "Introduction." Pages 6–11 in *Bible Manuscripts. 1400 Years of Scribes and Scripture*. Edited by Scot McKendrick and Kathleen Doyle. London: British Library, 2007.

Metzger, Bruce M. *The Canon of the New Testament: Its Origin, Development, and Significance*. Oxford: Clarendon, 1987.

Schedl, Claus. *Baupläne des Wortes: Einführung in die biblische Logotechnik*. Vienna: Herder, 1974.

Stevenson, Kalinda Rose. *The Vision of Transformation: The Territorial Rhetoric of Ezekiel 40–48*. SBLDS 154. Atlanta: Scholars Press, 1996.

APPENDIX:
BIBLE ARITHMETIC IN THE BIBLE
MANUSCRIPTS: ADDITIONAL EXAMPLES

INTRODUCTION

How did the texts of the New Testament emerge, how are they designed, and could it be the case that numerical signposts are built into the texts? In this appendix, I will further address the question of what role arithmetic or numerological aspects seem to have played in the creation of the Greek biblical text, with a focus on the New Testament. The appendix draws attention to the special emphasis in the manuscript tradition on seemingly frequency-coded words and textual structures. After a couple of introductory examples of arithmetic dimensions of the biblical text (exs. 1 and 2), I offer an illustration containing NrN (*Name-related Numerals*) for the *nomen sacrum* κύριος, "LORD; lord, master, Sir" in the Pentateuch and the New Testament (ex. 3). A final section presents early codicological data aligned to NrN (ex. 4).[15]

EXAMPLE 1: THE DAVIDIC NUMBER 14

The messianic name David has the numerical value 14 (Hebrew *Dawid*, "David" = 14, where the three included consonants have the following numerical values: *dalet* [= 4] + *vav* [= 6] + *dalet* [= 4] = 14). In other words, Hebrew consonants can function both as letters and as numbers. The genealogy of the Gospel of Matthew seems to allude to this, referring to 3 times 14 generations that are said to precede the birth of the Messiah (Matt 1:17).[16] Do we perhaps find this potential numerological allusion to

---

15. All figures in the present chapter regarding phrase- and word-frequency searches (Old Testament, New Testament, Apostolic Fathers, church fathers, various Bible manuscripts, etc.) are based mainly on searches made in digital versions of the respective texts in Accordance.

16. See, e.g., W. D. Davies and Dale C. Allison Jr. (*A Critical and Exegetical Commentary on the Gospel according to Saint Matthew*, vol. 1: *Introduction and Commentary on Matthew 1–7*, ICC [London: T&T Clark, 2004], 165), who opt for *gematria* linked to "David," and the name "David," as the key to interpreting Matt 1:1–17: "We suspect *gematria* because David's name has the value fourteen and because in Mt 1:2–16 there are 3 × 14 generations. But there is an additional observation to be made. David's name is fourteenth on the list. This is telling. In a genealogy of 3 × 14 generations, the one name with three consonants and a value of fourteen is also placed in the fourteenth spot. When one adds that this name is mentioned immediately before the genealogy (1:1) and twice at its conclusion

the number 14, and the significance of the name of David, also in other biblical settings? We may pose this question in regard to:

a. The 14 times the phrase ΥΙΟC ΔΑΥΙΔ, "son of David," is mentioned in the New Testament (THGNT, NA28, ℵ, TF 35, TR);[17]

b. The 14 times each of the following key phrases occur in Mark's Gospel: Η BACIΛΕΙΑ ΤΟΥ ΘΕΟΥ, "The kingdom of God," and Ο ΥΙΟC ΤΟΥ ΑΝΘΡΩΠΟΥ, "Son of Man" (THGNT, NA28);[18]

c. The 140 repetitions [10 × 14] of the word combination ΙΗCΟΥC ΧΡΙCΤΟC, "Jesus Christ," in the New Testament (THGNT), 14 of which are allocated to 1–2 Thessalonians (THGNT, NA28);

d. The 14 New Testament occurrences of the verb ΤΑΠΕΙΝΟΩ, "make low; humble" (THGNT, NA28, ℵ, TF 35, TR; cf. Phil 2:8);[19]

e. The 14 occurrences of the word TEKNON, "child," in Matthew as well as in Luke (THGNT, NA28);[20]

(1:17), and that it is honoured by the title, king, coincidence becomes effectively ruled out. The name, David, is the key to the pattern of Matthew's genealogy."

17. The capital letter form of the letter sigma can be written either as "Σ" or, as in early Bible manuscripts and in the following, as "C."

18. The phrase ΥΙΟC ΤΟΥ ΑΝΘΡΩΠΟΥ appears, in addition, 14 times in Luke, whereas ΥΙΟC ΤΟΥ ΑΝΘΡΩΠΟΥ (all forms) occurs 24 times in Luke (cf. table 5.1 above). We may note, as well, that the Hebrew term דוד, "David," e.g., features 98 times [7 × 14] in 1–2 Kings.

19. Words beginning with the five letters ΤΑΠΕΙ* appear 34 times [2 × 17] in the New Testament.

20. We may note in addition that the term ΝΗΠΙΟC, "young; infant; child," appears 14 times in the New Testament (THGNT, TF 35, TR). Moreover, ΤΟ TEKNON (all forms) occurs 14 times in the Synoptic Gospels, 15 times in the four Gospels, and 39 times in the New Testament (THGNT, NA28; see table 5.1 above for potential numerical significance of 15 and 39). Words beginning with the four letters ΤΕΚΝ* occur altogether 14 times in Matthew and Luke, respectively, 42 times [3 × 14] in Pauline Corpus, 24 times in Praxapostolos, and 110 times [5 × 22] in the New Testament.

f. The 14 instances in Jeremiah of BACIΛEIA, "kingship; king-dom," HΓEMΩN, "prince," and ΘPONOC, "throne," respectively (Rahlfs, LXXG);

g. The 14 appearances in Rahlfs of the messianically loaded H XPICIC, "the anointing";

h. The 14 times the central phrase O BACIΛEYC TΩN IOYΔAIΩN, "the king of the Jews," appears in the New Testament/four Gospels,[21] which can be compared with the 14 times in Rahlfs that we encounter the expression ΔAYIΔ O BACIΛEYC, "King David; David the King" (when we exclude one occurrence of the phrase in 4 Maccabees);[22] or the 28 times [2 × 14] that the expression OIKOC ΔAYIΔ, "House of David," is repeated, or the 42 times [3 × 14] BACIΛEYC ΔAYIΔ, "King David," are found in Rahlfs (cf. the 42 generations in Matt 1:17 to King David);[23]

i. The 14 occurrences of the name IHCOYC, "Jesus," in 1 Timothy, Hebrews, and Revelation, respectively.[24]

---

21. The phrase O BACIΛEYC TΩN IOYΔAIΩN (all forms) is found in Matt 27:11, 37; Mark 15:2, 9, 12, 26; Luke 23:3, 37, 38; and John 18:33, 39; 19:3, 19, 21. The phrase BACIΛEYC TΩN IOYΔAIΩN (all forms; without the initial article) occurs 17 times in the Gospels/New Testament (Matt 2:2 and 27:29, in addition to the references above; cf. table 5.1 above for possible significance of the number 17).

22. In Rahlfs the phrase ΔAYIΔ O BACIΛEYC is allocated to the following books: 1 Samuel (once), 1 Chronicles (6 times), 2 Chronicles (5 times), 1 Esdr. (once), Hosea (once), and 4 Macc (once). Cf. note 23 below.

23. We may note as well that the phrase (including the article) O OIKOC ΔAYIΔ, "House of David," occurs 17 times in Rahlfs. BACIΛEYC ΔAYIΔ is allocated to the following Septuagint books (Rahlfs): 2 Samuel (21 times), 1 Kings (8 times), 2 Kings (once), 1 Chronicles (11 times), and 2 Chronicles (once).

24. Other words that occur 14 times in Hebrews—potentially linking them numerologically to the Davidic messianic promise—include EΠAΓΓEΛIA, "promise"; IEPEYC, "priest"; and NOMOC "law; instruction"; other words that appear 14 times in Revelation include ACTHP, "star"; and ΔOYΛOC, "slave; servant."

EXAMPLE 2: SIGNIFICANT WORD-FREQUENCIES
OF SIGNIFICANT NUMERALS

Even a quick glance at the Septuagint and the New Testament seems to give
an indication of the emphasis on certain numerical values and frequencies,
such as the number 7, ΕΠΤΑ, which occurs 7 times in 1 Samuel, 2 Samuel,
and Nehemiah (Rahlfs), respectively;[25] the number 12, ΔΩΔΕΚΑ, which
is found 12 times in Luke and—in the form that begins with the letters
ΔΩΔΕΚΑ*—120 times [10 × 12] in Rahlfs; the number 8, ΟΚΤΩ—the
early Christian symbol for the resurrection and the new creation (cf. 1 Pet
3:20; Luke 9:28; and John 20:26; see also Justin *Dial.* 178 [*ANF* 1:138])—
that occurs 8 times in the New Testament— and the number 13, ΔΕΚΑ
ΤΡΕΙΣ (which is the numerical value of the Hebrew אחד [*ekhad*], "one"),
which appears 13 times in LXX Rahlfs (cf. Deut 6:4). In the MT, the
Hebrew אחד (*ekhad*), "one," also appears 13 times both in 1 Chronicles
and in Zechariah and 26 times [2 × 13] in Deuteronomy, with possible or
probable allusion to the numerical value of YHWH, Yahweh, which is 26.[26]

The symbolically important number 7, again, has a wide-ranging function in the Christian Scriptures and occurs, for example, 154 times [2 ×
77 = 14 × 11 = 7 × 22] in the Pentateuch (Rahlfs), 24 times in the four
Gospels (THGNT, NA28, TR35, TR), and 88 times [4 × 22] in the New
Testament as a whole (NA28; 81 times [3 × 27] in א)—on all three occasions with possible reference to the alphabetical completeness numbers
22/27 and 24 (= number of letters in the Hebrew and Hellenistic Greek

---

25. In the Pentateuch (Rahlfs) we encounter the number 7 altogether 154 times [7 × 22], i.e.,
the alphabetical fullness number 22 × 7; LXXG here, instead, has 155 occurrences of ΕΠΤΑ, with
15 appearances of the number in Exodus, instead of 14, as in Rahlfs. The Hebrew word for "seven,"
שבע, too, we encounter in the MT, 7 times in Isaiah, Zechariah, and Job, respectively.

26. In Luke 13:16 the number 8 is included as part of the number 18 (ΔΕΚΑ ΚΑΙ ΟΚΤΩ) and in
John 5:5 as part of the number 38 (ΤΡΙΑΚΟΝΤΑ ΚΑΙ ΟΚΤΩ). We may note, as well, that ΟΚΤΩ,
"eight" appears 8 times in 1 Chronicles. The corresponding Hebrew word שמנה, "eight," similarly, can
be found 8 times in Numbers, Ezra, and 1–2 Samuel, respectively. In Rahlfs, the number 13 (ΔΕΚΑ
ΤΡΕΙΣ) occurs 7 times: Gen 17:25; Josh 19:6; 21:4, 6, 19, 33; Ezek 40:11; 1 time (ΤΡΕΙΣ ΚΑΙ ΔΕΚΑ)
in LXX: Num 29:13; and 5 times (ΤΡΙΣΚΑΙΔΕΚΑ) in LXX: Num 29:14; 1 Kgs 7:38; 1 Chr 6:45, 47;
and 26:11. All in all 13 times. אחד (*ekhad*), "one," is made up of the three consonants *aleph, khet,* and
dalet, the numerical sum of which is 13: *aleph* (= 1) + *khet* (= 8) + *dalet* (= 4) = 13. For numerical
values associated with the Tetragrammaton (17 and 26, respectively), see table 5.1 above. In the
Pentateuch YHWH appears 1820 times [70 × 26]. In the book of Jonah, YHWH further occurs 26
times; and in 2 Samuel the Name features 153 times [9 × 17].

alphabets, respectively).[27] We can also note the number 4, TECCAPEC (cf. Matthew 24:31 par; John 11:17; Acts 10:11), which appears 27 times in the book of Revelation (THGNT; and 39 times in the twenty-seven-book New Testament, THGNT), that is, another potential alphabetical completeness reference.[28] Hints in the New Testament about the significance of alphabetical fullness, we see, as already mentioned, in several passages in the book of Revelation (1:8; 4:4, 10; 5:8; 11:16; 19:4; 21:6; 22:13).[29] Furthermore, the number of the short-form for the name of God, 15 (YH = 15) may be indirectly glimpsed in texts such as Acts 27:28 and Gal 1:18, or in the 15 occurrences of the number 15 in the Septuagint (excluding OT Apocrypha);[30] and the number arguably associated with the divine name, 17, in John 21:11, where the great catch of fish consists of 153 fish $[9 \times 17 = 3^2 \times 17]$, which is a multiple of 17 (see table 5.1 above).[31] One hundred fifty-three is a "perfect numeral" or, more precisely, a "triangular number," in biblical number symbolism.[32]

---

27. For potential significance of the numbers 7, 11, 14, and 22, see table 5.1 above. The number 7 occurs 88 times in NA28 as well as in TF 35/the Majority Text; 87 times in THGNT as well as in TR. Cf. Rev 1:8; 4:4, 10; 5:8; 11:16; 19:4; 21:6; and 22:13.

28. Twenty-seven is the number of letters in the Hebrew alphabet when the five end-consonant forms are included in the count. For potential significance of 39 $[3 \times 13]$, see table 5.1 above

29. The significance of some of these numerals is emphasized, not least, in the book of Revelation, with several examples of figures being multiples of 3, 4, 7, 8, 14, 15, 22, and 24 (e.g., Rev 1:4; 4:4, 6; 11:2; 12:6; 21:13, 14, 17).

30. *Yod*= 10, *he*= 5. We may note that יה occurs 49 times $[7 \times 7]$ in the MT and *יה occurs 1914 times $[87 \times 22]$ in the Pentateuch, 598 times $[23 \times 26]$ in 1–2 Samuel, 486 times $[18 \times 27]$ in Isaiah, 960 times $[40 \times 24]$ in Jeremiah, 450 times $[2 \times 15 \times 15]$ in Ezekiel, 85 times $[5 \times 17]$ in Amos, 26 times in Jonah, 44 times $[2 \times 22]$ in Micah, 60 times $[4 \times 15]$ in Nehemiah and 646 times $[38 \times 17]$ in 2 Chronicles. The number 15 features 15 times in Rahlfs (Old Testament Apocrypha excluded from this count) according the following allocation: ΔΕΚΑ ΠΕΝΤΕ (6 times: Gen 5:10; 7:20; 27:15; 2 Sam 19:18; 2 Chr 25:25; Isa 38:5), ΠΕΝΤΕΚΑΙΔΕΚΑ (7 times: Exod 27:14; 37:13; Lev 27:7; Judg 8:10; 2 Sam 9:10; 2 Kgs 14:17; Hos 3:2), ΠΕΝΤΕ ΚΑΙ ΔΕΚΑ (once: 2 Kgs 20:6), ΔΕΚΑ ΚΑΙ ΠΕΝΤΕ (once: 1 Kgs 7:40).

31. Cf. Casper J. Labuschagne, *Numerical Secrets of the Bible: Introduction to Biblical Arithmology* (Eugene, OR: Wipf & Stock, 2016), 75–104; and Richard Bauckham, "The 153 Fish and the Unity of the Fourth Gospel," *Neot* 36 (2002): 82–85.

32. One hundred fifty-three is the sum of the 17 numbers in the series 1–17, and in John 21:11, the number 153 symbolizes the all-comprehensive number of peoples (Raymond E. Brown, *The Gospel According to John*, Anchor Bible Commentary 29 [1974; repr., New Haven & London: Yale University Press, 2008], 1097), or all nations (Casper Labuschagne), which is "caught" through the apostolic mission and gathered into the kingdom of God. Cf. Labuschagne, *Numerical Secrets of the*

EXAMPLE 3: *NRN* ASSOCIATED WITH
THE *NOMINA SACRA* ΚΎΡΙΟΣ, ΘΕΟΣ, AND ΠΝΕΥΜΑ

In what follows, we shall place special emphasis on two word-frequency groups that seem to attain particular significance in the New Testament text. As discussed in some detail in chapters 5–10 above, these are, on the one hand, multiples of the Hebrew and Greek alphabetical integers 22/27 and 24, and, on the other hand, multiples of word frequencies aligned to the three numeric values associated with the Tetragrammaton, YHWH: 15, 17, and 26.[33] I label these *Name-related Numerals* (*NrN*).

Highlighted Numerals

Name-related Numerals as well as multiples of the number 39 in the examples below are marked in boldface; multiples of the numbers 10, 13, 14 and 18 as well as the two numbers 23 and 32, which are not categorized as *NrN*, are written in italics (cf. the list of numerals in table 5.1, ch. 5 above). Below, I shall refer to this latter group of six additional, but related, numerals as *NrNr* (23/32, 10, 13, 14, and 18).

Bible, 165n10: "Incidentally in the Easter-passage in Acts 2:5–13 exactly 17 peoples and lands are mentioned." See also Bauckham, "153 Fish," 82–85.

33. For the integers 22/27 and 24, see table 5.1, and ch. 5 above. For the numerical values 17, 26, and 15 of the Tetragrammaton, see table 5.1 above.

Table A.1. The Pentateuch (LXX Göttingen): NrN for κύριος. Figures at 15 or above included in the NrN percentage count.

LXX Göttingen	Genesis	Exodus	Leviticus	Numbers	Deuteronomy	Pentateuch	NrN (Name-related Numerals)
Lord (all forms; sg. forms)							
κύριος	221 [13 × 17]	393	338 [13 × 26]	395	553	1900 [19 × 10 × 10]	2/6 (33%) NrN
κύριος (sg.)	219	393	338 [13 × 26]	395	552 [23 × 24]	1897	2/6 (33%) NrN
ὁ κύριος	62	35	78 [3 × 26]	10	3	188	1/4 (25%) NrN
ὁ κύριος (sg.)	62	35	78 [3 × 26]	10	2	187 [11 × 17]	2/4 (50%) NrN
NrN	1/4 (25%) NrN	0/4 (0%) NrN	4/4 (100%) NrN	0/2 (0%) NrN	1/2 (50%) NrN	1/4 (25%) NrN	
Lord (various cases)							
κύριος	105 [7 × 15]	238 [14 × 17]	119 [7 × 17]	179	346	987 [47 × 21]	3/6 (50%) NrN
ὁ κύριος	13	11	0	3	1	28 [2 × 14]	0/1 (0%) NrN
κυρίου	54 [2 × 27]	56 [4 × 14]	105 [7 × 15]	120 [5 × 24]	123	458	3/6 (50%) NrN
τοῦ κυρίου	22	2	0	1	1	26	2/2 (100%) NrN
κυρίῳ	23	60 [4 × 15]	111	77	37	308 [14 × 22]	2/6 (33%) NrN
τῷ κυρίῳ	17	18	78 [3 × 26]	4	1	118	2/4 (50%) NrN
κύριον	17	27	3	13	38	98 [7 × 14]	2/4 (50%) NrN
τὸν κύριον	9	4	0	2	0	15	1/1 (100%) NrN
NrN	5/6 (83%) NrN	3/5 (60%) NrN	3/4 (75%) NrN	1/3 (33%) NrN	0/4 (0%) NrN	3/8 (37.5%) NrN	

LXX Göttingen	Genesis	Exodus	Leviticus	Numbers	Deuteronomy	Pentateuch	NrN (Name-related Numerals)
NrN Total 6/10 (60%) NrN	3/9 (33%) NrN	7/8 (87.5%) NrN	1/5 (20%) NrN	1/6 (17%) NrN	4/12 (33%) NrN		
χυρι* 227	394	338 [13 × 26]	397	553	1909 [83 × 23]		
χυρ* 228	394	340 [2 × 10 × 17]	397	553	1912		

Table A.2. The Pentateuch (LXX Göttingen): NrN for forms in the singular of κύριος, θεός, and πνεῦμα. Figures at 15 or above included in the NrN percentage count.

LXX Göttingen	Genesis	Exodus	Leviticus	Numbers	Deuteronomy	Pentateuch	NrN (Name-related Numerals)
κύριος (sg.)	219	393	338 [13 × 26]	395	552 [23 × 24]	1897	2/6 (33%) NrN
ὁ κύριος (sg.)	62	35	78 [3 × 26]	10	2	187 [11 × 17]	2/4 (50%) NrN
θεός (sg.)	275 [5 × 5 × 11]	165 [11 × 15]	68 [4 × 17]	61	393	962 [37 × 26]	3/6 (50%) NrN
ὁ θεός (sg.)	243 [9 × 27]	136 [8 × 17]	62	50 [5 × 10]	361	852	2/6 (33%) NrN
πνεῦμα (sg.)	7	5	0	13	2	27	1/1 (100%) NrN
τὸ πνεῦμα (sg.)	2	1	0	5	1	9	0/0 NrN
NrN	1/4 (25%) NrN	2/4 (50%) NrN	3/4 (75%) NrN	0/3 (0%) NrN	1/3 (33%) NrN	3/5 (60%) NrN	

Table A.3. Gospels, Luke-Acts, Gospels + Acts, Praxapostolos, the full New Testament: NrN for κύριος. Figures at 15 or above included in the NrN percentage count; columns and rows with NrN at 41–50 percent (light gray), 51–99 percent (medium gray), and 100 percent (dark gray) colored.

		Matthew	Mark	Matthew–Mark	Luke	Synoptics	John	Luke–John
Lord (all forms; sg. forms)	κύριος	80 [8 × 10]	18	98 [7 × 14]	104 [4 × 26]	202	52 [2 × 26]	156 [6 × 26]
	κύριος (sg.)	78 [3 × 26]	18	96 [4 × 24]	102 [6 × 17]	198 [9 × 22]	52 [2 × 26]	154 [7 × 22]
	ὁ κύριος	26	7	33	45 [3 × 15]	78 [3 × 26]	17	62
	ὁ κύριος (sg.)	25	7	32	44 [2 × 22]	76	17	61
	NrN	2/4 (50%) NrN	0/2 (0%) NrN	1/4 (25%) NrN	4/4 (100%) NrN	2/4 (50%) NrN	4/4 (100%) NrN	2/4 (50%) NrN
Lord (various cases)	κύριος	20 [2 × 10]	10	30 [2 × 15]	32	62	8	40 [4 × 10]
	ὁ κύριος	17	5	22	26	48 [2 × 24]	8	34 [2 × 17]
	κυρίου	15	4	19	26	45 [3 × 15]	6	32
	τοῦ κυρίου	4	1	5	8	13	3	11
	κυρίῳ	3	1	4	7	11	0	4
	τῷ κυρίῳ	3	1	4	6	10	0	6
	κύριον	6	2	8	10	18	6	16
	τὸν κύριον	1	0	1	4		6	10
	NrN	2/3 (67%) NrN	0/0 NrN	2/3 (67%) NrN	2/3 (67%) NrN	2/4 (50%) NrN	0/0 NrN	1/4 (25%) NrN
	NrN Total	4/7 (57%) NrN	0/2 (0%) NrN	3/7 (43%) NrN	6/7 (86%) NrN	4/8 (50%) NrN	4/4 (100%) NrN	3/8 (37.5%) NrN

Four Gospels	Acts	Luke-Acts	Gospels + Acts	Praxa- postolos	27-book NT	NrN
254	108 [4 × 27]	212	362	150 [10 × 15]	719	5/13 (38.5%) NrN
250 [5 × 5 × 10]	105 [7 × 15]	207	355	147	705 [47 × 15]	8/13 (61.5%) NrN
95	68 [4 × 17]	113	163	92 [4 × 23]	351 [13 × 27]	6/12 (50%) NrN
93	66 [3 × 22]	110 [5 × 22]	159	90 [6 × 15]	345 [23 × 15]	6/12 (50%) NrN
0/4 (0%) NrN	4/4 (100%) NrN	1/4 (25%) NrN	0/4 (0%) NrN	2/4 (50%) NrN	3/4 (75%) NrN	
70 [7 × 10]	22	54 [2 × 27]	92 [4 × 23]	31	178	3/11 (27%) NrN
56 [4 × 14]	11	37	67	16	110 [5 × 22]	6/10 (60%) NrN
51 [3 × 17]	45 [3 × 15]	71	96 [4 × 24]	71	240 [10 × 24]	7/11 (64%) NrN
16	33	41	49 [7 × 7]	50 [5 × 10]	147	0/6 (0%) NrN
11	11	18	22	13	100 [10 × 10]	1/3 (33%) NrN
10	11	17	21	11	42 [3 × 14]	1/3 (33%) NrN
24	12	22	36 [2 × 18]	17	69 [3 × 23]	3/7 (43%) NrN
11	11	15	22	13	46 [2 × 23]	2/3 (67%) NrN
2/4 (50%) NrN	2/3 (67%) NrN	4/8 (50%) NrN	3/8 (37.5%) NrN	1/5 (20%) NrN	2/8 (25%) NrN	
2/9 (22%) NrN	6/7 (86%) NrN	5/12 (42%) NrN	3/12 (25%) NrN	3/9 (33%) NrN	5/12 (42%) NrN	

Table A.4. Luke-Acts, Praxapostolos, New Testament: *NrN* for singular forms of θεός, κύριος, and πνεῦμα. Figures at 15 or above included in the *NrN* percentage count; columns and rows with *NrN* at 41–50 percent (light gray), 51–99 percent (medium gray), and 100 percent (dark gray) colored.

	Luke	Acts	Luke-Acts	Praxapostolos	27-book New Testament	NrN
God, Lord, S/spirit (sg. forms)						
θεός (sg.)	122	162	284	295	1304	1/5 (20%)
ὁ θεός (sg.)	107	150 [10 × 15]	257	246	985	1/5 (20%)
κύριος (sg.)	102 [6 × 17]	105 [7 × 15]	207	147	705 [47 × 15]	3/5 (60%)
ὁ κύριος (sg.)	44 [2 × 22]	66 [3 × 22]	110 [5 × 22]	90 [6 × 15]	345 [23 × 15]	5/5 (100%)
πνεῦμα (sg.)	30 [2 × 15]	66 [3 × 22]	96 [4 × 24]	89	345 [23 × 15]	4/5 (80%)
τὸ πνεῦμα (sg.)	11	36 [2 × 18]	47	45 [3 × 15]	166	1/4 (25%)
NrN	3/5 (60%)	5/6 (83%)	2/6 (33%)	2/6 (33%)	3/6 (50%)	

Table A.5. Catholic Epistles, Praxapostolos: *NrN* for singular forms of θεός, κύριος, and πνεῦμα. Figures at 15 or above included in the *NrN* percentage count; columns and rows with *NrN* at 41–50 percent (light gray), 51–99 percent (medium gray), and 100 percent (dark gray) colored.

	God, Lord, Pneuma (sg. forms)	θεός (sg.)	ὁ θεός (sg.)	κύριος (sg.)	ὁ κύριος (sg.)	πνεῦμα (sg.)	πνεῦμα (sg.; א)	πνεῦμα (sg.; TF 35)	τὸ πνεῦμα (sg.)
NrN		2/9 (22%)	2/8 (25%)	2/4 (50%)	3/3 (100%)	1/3 (33%)	3/3 (100%)	3/3 (100%)	1/2 (50%)
Praxapostolos		295	246	147	90 [6 × 15]	89	90 [6 × 15]	90 [6 × 15]	45 [3 × 15]
Acts		162 [6 × 27]	150 [10 × 15]	105 [7 × 15]	66 [3 × 22]	66 [3 × 22]	66 [3 × 22]	66 [3 × 22]	36 [2 × 18]
Catholic Epistles		133	96 [4 × 24]	42 [3 × 14]	24	23	24	24	9
Jude		4	1	6	3	2	2	2	0
1–3 John		67	61	0	0	11	12	11	8
1–2 John		64 [2 × 32]	58	0	0	11	12	11	8
3 John		3	3	0	0	0	0	0	0
2 John		2	0	0	0	0	0	0	0
1 John		62	58	0	0	11	12	11	8
1–2 Peter		46 [2 × 23]	25	22	12	8	8	9	0
2 Peter		7	5	14	9	1	1	1	0
1 Peter		39	20	8	3	7	7	8	0
James		16	9	14	9	2	2	2	1

Christ the Center

Table A.6. Catholic Epistles: NrN for κύριος. Figures at 15 or above included in the NrN percentage count; columns and rows with NrN at 50 percent (light gray), 51–99 percent (medium gray), and 100 percent (dark gray) colored.

	James	1 Peter	2 Peter	1–2 Peter
Lord (all forms; sg. forms)				
κύριος	14	8	14	0
κύριος (sg.)	14	8	14	0
ὁ κύριος	9	3	9	12
ὁ κύριος (sg.)	9	3	9	12
Lord (various cases)				
κύριος	3	1	3	4
ὁ κύριος	3	1	1	2
κυρίου	10	4	9	13
τοῦ κυρίου	5	1	8	9
κυρίῳ	0	0	2	2
τῷ κυρίῳ	0	0	0	0
κύριον	1	3	0	3
τὸν κύριον	1	1	0	1
NrN	0/0 (0%) NrN	0/0 (0%) NrN	0/0 (0%)	0/0 (0%)
κυρι*	14	8	**15**	23
κυρ*	14	8	**15**	23

1 John	2 John	3 John	1–2 John	1–3 John	Jude	Catholic Epistles
0	0	0	0	0	6	42 [3 × 14]
0	0	0	0	0	6	42 [3 × 14]
0	0	0	0	0	3	24
0	0	0	0	0	3	24

1 John	2 John	3 John	1–2 John	1–3 John	Jude	Catholic Epistles
0	0	0	0	0	2	9
0	0	0	0	0	0	5
0	0	0	0	0	3	26
0	0	0	0	0	3	17
0	0	0	0	0	0	2
0	0	0	0	0	0	0
0	0	0	0	0	1	5
0	0	0	0	0	0	2
0/0	0/0	0/0	0/0	0/0	0/0	4/6 (67%)

1 John	2 John	3 John	1–2 John	1–3 John	Jude	Catholic Epistles
0	2	0	2	2	7	46 [2 × 23]
0	2	0	2	2	7	46 [2 × 23]

Table A.7. Pauline Letters: NrN for κύριος. Figures at 15 or above included in the NrN percentage count; columns and rows with NrN at 40–49 percent (gray), 50 percent (light gray), 51–99 percent (medium gray), and 100 percent (dark gray) colored. This table moves across pages 272–73 and continues at the top of pages 274–75.

	Romans	1 Corinthians	2 Corinthians	1-2 Corinthians	Galatians	Ephesians	Philippians	Colossians	1 Thessalonians	2 Thessalonians
Lord (all forms; sg. forms)										
κύριος	43	67	29	96 [4 × 24]	6	26	15	16	24	22
κύριος (sg.)	43	66 [3 × 22]	29	95	6	24	15	14	24	22
ὁ κύριος	19	41	15	56 [4 × 14]	3	13	3	8	16	15
ὁ κύριος (sg.)	19	41	15	56 [4 × 14]	3	12	3	7	16	15

	Romans	1 Corinthians	2 Corinthians	1-2 Corinthians	Galatians	Ephesians	Philippians	Colossians	1 Thessalonians	2 Thessalonians
NrN	0/4 (0%) NrN	1/4 (25%) NrN	2/4 (50%) NrN	1/4 (25%) NrN	0/0	2/2 (100%) NrN	2/2 (100%) NrN	0/2 (0%) NrN	2/4 (50%) NrN	4/4 (100%) NrN

	Romans	1 Corinthians	2 Corinthians	1-2 Corinthians	Galatians	Ephesians	Philippians	Colossians	1 Thessalonians	2 Thessalonians
Lord (various cases)										
κύριος	7	16	6	22	1	2	2	1	4	6
ὁ κύριος	1	10	3	13	0	1	1	1	3	5
κυρίου	12	30 [2 × 15]	14	44 [2 × 22]	4	8	3	4	13	13
τοῦ κυρίου	9	20 [2 × 10]	8	28 [2 × 14]	3	4	2	2	11	10
κυρίῳ	18	14	3	17	1	13	9	6	5	3
τῷ κυρίῳ	6	5	1	6	0	6	0	2	0	0

1–2 Thessalonians	1 Timothy	2 Timothy	1–2 Timothy	Titus	Philemon	Hebrews	Pauline Corpus	27-book New Testament	NrN
46 [2 × 23]	6	17	23	0	5	16	292	719	6/15 (40%) NrN
46 [2 × 23]	6	17	23	0	5	16	287	705 [47 × 15]	7/14 (50%) NrN
31	5	12	17	0	2	6	158	351 [13 × 27]	4/10 (40%) NrN
31	5	12	17	0	2	6	156 [6 × 26]	345 [23 × 15]	5/10 (50%) NrN

| 0/4 (0%) NrN | 0/0 | 2/2 (100%) NrN | 2/4 (50%) NrN | 0/0 | 0/0 | 0/2 (0%) NrN | 1/4 (25%) NrN | 3/4 (75%) NrN | |

10	1	10	11	0	0	10	66 [3 × 22]	178	2/4 50(%) NrN
8	0	8	8	0	0	2	35	110 [5 × 22]	1/2 (50%) NrN
26	4	6	10	0	2	2	115 [5 × 23]	240 [10 × 24]	4/5 (80%) NrN
21	4	3	7	0	1	1	78 [3 × 26]	147	1/4 (25%) NrN
8	1	0	1	0	2	0	75 [5 × 15]	100 [10 × 10]	2/4 (50%) NrN
0	1	0	0	0	0	0	21	42 [3 × 14]	0/2 (0%) NrN

	Romans	1 Corinthians	2 Corinthians	1–2 Corinthians	Galatians	Ephesians	Philippians	Colossians	1 Thessalonians	2 Thessalonians
κύριον	4	6	6	12	0	1	1	3	2	0
τὸν κύριον	3	6	3	9	0	1	0	2	2	0
NrN	0/1 (0%)	1/3 (33%)	0/0	3/4 (75%) NrN	0/0	0/0	0/0	0/0	0/0	0/0
NrN Total	0/5 (0%) NrN	2/7 (29%) NrN	2/4 (50%) NrN	4/8 (50%) NrN	0/0	2/2 (100%) NrN	2/2 (100%) NrN	0/1 (0%) NrN	2/4 (50%) NrN	4/4 (100%) NrN

Table A.7 is continued above and should be read directly across with the top of page 275.

Table A.8. Pauline Letters: NrN for Singular Forms of θεός, κύριος, and πνεῦμα. Figures at 15 or above included in the NrN percentage count; columns and rows with NrN at 40–49 percent (gray), 50 percent (light gray), 51–99 percent (medium gray), and 100 percent (dark gray) colored.

	Romans	1 Corinthians	2 Corinthians	1–2 Corinthians	Galatians	Ephesians	Philippians	Colossians	1 Thessalonians
God, Lord, S/spirit (sg. forms)									
θεός (sg.)	153	103	79	182	30	31	23	21	36
ὁ θεός (sg.)	105	65	49	114	17	22	11	19	26
κύριος (sg.)	43	66 [3 × 22]	29	95	6	24	15	14	24
ὁ κύριος (sg.)	19	41	15	56 [4 × 14]	3	12	3	7	16
πνεῦμα (sg.)	34	37	17	54	18	14	5	2	5
τὸ πνεῦμα (sg.)	13	16	7	23	9	7	3	1	3
NrN	3/5 (60%)	1/6 (17%)	2/5 (40%)	2/6 (33%)	2/3 (67%)	2/3 (67%)	1/2 (50%)	0/2 (0%)	2/3 (67%)

Table A.8 is above should be read directly across with the bottom of page 275.

1–2 Thessalonians	1 Timothy	2 Timothy	1–2 Timothy	Titus	Philemon	Hebrews	Pauline Corpus	27-book New Testament	*NrN*
0	0	1	1	0	1	3	28 [2 × 14]	69 [3 × 23]	0/2 (0%) *NrN*
2	0	1	1	0	1	3	**22**	46 [2 × 23]	1/2 (50%) *NrN*
1/2 (50%) *NrN*	0/0	0/0	0/0	0/0	0/0	0/0	4/8 (50%) *NrN*	2/8 (25%) *NrN*	
1/6 (17%) *NrN*	0/0 (0%) *NrN*	2/2 (100%) *NrN*	2/4 (50%) *NrN*	0/0	0/0	0/2 (0%) *NrN*	5/12 (42%) *NrN*	5/12 (42%) *NrN*	

2 Thessalonians	1–2 Thessalonians	1 Timothy	2 Timothy	1–2 Timothy	Titus	Philemon	Hebrews	Pauline Corpus	*NrN*
18	**54**	**22**	12	**34**	13	2	**68**	611	7/15 (47%)
12	38	6	9	**15**	2	1	53	397	5/12 (42%)
22	46 [2 × 23]	6	**17**	23	0	5	16	287	6/13 (46%)
15	31	5	12	17	0	2	6	**156** [6 × 26]	4/9 (44%)
3	8	2	3	5	1	1	8	**150**	4/6 (67%)
1	4	0	1	1	0	1	4	**66**	1/3 (33%)
2/3 (67%)	1/4 (25%)	1/1 (100%)	1/1 (100%)	3/4 (75%)	-	-	1/3 (33%)	3/6 (50%)	

EXAMPLE 4: *NRN* AND *NRNR* IN THE CODICOLOGICAL-
CANONICAL DESIGN OF EARLY BIBLE CODICES

Highlighted Numerals

Name-related Numerals as well as multiples of the number 39 in the examples below are marked in boldface; multiples of the numbers 10, 13, 14,
and 18 as well as the two numbers 23 and 32, which are not categorized
as N*r*N, are written in italics (cf. the list of numerals in table 5.1 above).
Below, I shall refer to this latter group of six additional, but related numerals (23/32, 10, 13, 14, and 18), as N*r*N*r*.

Codex Sinaiticus

Codex Sinaiticus provides examples of N*r*N being used not only for purposes of canon shaping (**27 books** in the New Testament included, in
addition to two ecclesiastical writings, Epistle of Barnabas and Shepherd
of Hermas), but also for the more immediate codicological New Testament
design with **48 lines** [2 × 24] per column and **484 columns** [22 × 22]
making up the fourfold Gospel—thus arithmetically highlighting this
canonical subunit with the number 22 squared, the Hebrew alphabetical
number of completion. The remaining *23* (a N*r*N*r*) *New Testament books*—
the second main portion of the New Testament are allocated to altogether
578 columns [2 × 17 × 17], numerically highlighted by the numeral 2 and
the divine name number 17 squared. Within this second larger canonical
text-unit consisting of *23 books* and **578 columns** [2 × 17 × 17] we find
298 columns taken up by the Pauline Epistles, 147 columns by Acts, *64
columns [2 × 32]* by the seven Catholic Epistles, and *69 columns [3 × 23]*
by Revelation.

  As for some further details, we may note the following N*r*N/N*r*N*r*
numerical features in Sinaiticus for individual writings:

  John **27 pages, 104 columns** [4 × 26]; Luke **150 columns** [*10 × 15*];
Mark **22 pages**; Matthew *140 columns [10 × 14]*; the fourfold Gospel 121
pages [11 × 11] and **484 columns** [4 × 11 × 11 = 22 × 22].

  Romans *14 pages* (more precisely: 13.5 pages), **54 columns** [2 × 27];
1 Corinthians *13 pages*, **52 columns** [2 × 26], 2 Corinthians *36 columns*

[2 × 18]; 1–2 Corinthians **88 columns** [**4** × **22**]; Romans–2 Corinthians *36 pages [2 × 18]* (more precisely: 35.5 pages); Galatians **17 columns**; Philippians *13 columns*; Colossians *13 columns*; 1 Timothy *14 columns*; Romans–Colossians **51 pages** [**3** × **17**]; Romans–1 Thessalonians **54 pages** [**2** × **27**]; Romans–2 Thessalonians *56 pages [4* × *14]* (more precisely: 55.75 pages); Romans–Hebrews (i.e., letters addressed to communities, including Hebrews) **66 pages** [**3** × **22**]; Romans–Philemon **75 pages** [**5** × **15**].

Number of pages used for Gospels (121 pages [11 × 11] + one empty page at the end) and Pauline epistles (in Sinaiticus following directly after the Gospels; **75 pages** + one empty page at the end): *196 pages [14* × *14]*, alternatively (including the two empty pages) **198 pages** [**9** × **22**]; Matthew *140 columns [10* × *14]* (the first numerically distinct Gospels unit), Matthew (*140 columns*) + Mark (86 columns) + Luke (**150 columns** [**10** × **15**]) + John (**104 columns** [**4** × **26**]) = **484 columns** [**22** × **22**] (a second arithmetically distinct Gospels unit, in addition to Luke [**150 columns** [**10** × **15**]] and John [**108 columns** [**4** × **27**]]), that is, in Codex Sinaiticus, by means of NrN/NrNr, we can detect altogether four numerically demarcated textual subunits within the fourfold Gospel.

James *14 columns*, 1 Peter **15 columns**, 1–2 John *18 columns*; Catholic Epistles *64 columns [2* × *23]*;

Praxapostolos (211 columns) + Revelation (*69 columns [3* × *23]*) = *280 columns [7* × *40 = 20* × *14 = 2* × *10* × *14]*; Pauline Epistles (298 columns) + Praxapostolos (211 columns) + Revelation (*69 columns [3* × *23]*) = **578 columns** [**2** × **17** × **17**];

Luke (**150 columns** [**10** × **15**] + Acts (147 columns) = **297 columns** [**11** × **27**], that is, Luke and Acts are here arithmetically kept together as a literary unity by means of the two numerals 11 (potentially indicating fulfillment) and 27 (potentially indicating [alphabetical] fullness and completion);

Gospels (**484 columns** [**22** × **22**]) + Pauline Epistles (298 columns) + Acts (147 columns) + Catholic Epistles (*64 columns [2* × *32]*) + Revelation (*69 columns [3* × *23]*) = **484** [**22** × **22**] + **578** [**2** × **17** × **17**] = *1062 [59* × *18]* (59 is the seventeenth prime number; 18 is an NrNr). If we add the Epistle of Barnabas, which follows immediately after Revelation in Codex Sinaiticus on the same page where Revelation ends (this is not the case for Shepherd of Hermas, which starts on a new page after Barnabas) we get altogether *1062 columns [59 × 18]* + **54 columns [2 × 27]** = *1116 columns [2 × 31 × 18]*; 31 is the eleventh prime number, 18 is an NrNr.[34]

Codex Vaticanus

Now, as we move on to another significant megacodex, Codex Vaticanus, similar codicological NrN/NrNr patterns encounter the reader. Vaticanus includes *42 lines [3 × 14]* per column and embraces altogether (1) **572 columns [22 × 26]** allocated to the four Gospels + Acts (and *343 columns [7 × 7 × 7]* to the Synoptic Gospels), (2) **629 columns [37 × 17]** allocated to Gospels + Acts + Catholic Epistles, (3) **234 columns [6 × 39 = 9 × 26 = 3² × 26]** to the Pauline Epistles, (4) **78 pages [3 × 26]** to the Pauline Epistles (Romans to Hebrews), and (5) **288 pages [12 × 24]** to the Vaticanus corpus of New Testament writings (Matthew–Hebrews).[35]

Concerning further codicological design elements pertaining to NrN/ NrNr arithmetic in Vaticanus, we may note the following: Matthew *128 columns [4 × 32]*; Mark **78 columns [3 × 26]**; Synoptic Gospels 343 columns [7 × 7 × 7], *115 pages [5 × 23]*; fourfold Gospel 441 columns [3 × 3 × 7 × 7 = 3² × 7²]; and John *98 columns [7 × 14]*;

James *13 columns*, 1 Peter *13 columns*, 1–2 Peter **22 columns**, 1 John *14 columns*;

2 Corinthians *32 columns*; Ephesians **17 columns**; Hebrews *32 columns*; Pauline Corpus **234 columns [6 × 39 = 9 × 26 = 3² × 26]**;

Codex Alexandrinus

Codex Alexandrinus, too, demonstrates arithmetical features that can be linked to NrN/NrNr. Number of lines per column is *50 [5 × 10]* and for

---

34. For images of Codex Sinaiticus, see http://www.codex-sinaiticus.net/en/manuscript.aspx.

35. Heb 1:1–9:13 + later scribal addition for the remaining part of the text. For images of Codex Vaticanus, see https://digi.vatlib.it/view/MSS_Vat.gr.1209. There are potentially interesting canonical implications for the figures above pertaining to Pauline Corpus. Perhaps Vaticanus here provides an example of the early seven-church Pauline Corpus made up of ten letters (where Hebrews being included, as well, is addressed, not to a specific church but to the Hebrews).

the fourfold Gospel and Acts we can note the following: Matthew (vac. 1:1–25:6) 83 columns (my estimation); Mark **51 columns** [**3** × **17**]; Luke **88 columns** [**4** × **22**]; John **54 columns** [**2** × **27**]; Acts **81 columns** [**3** × **27**]; fourfold Gospel 276 *columns* [*12* × *23*] (my estimation); fourfold Gospel + Acts **357 columns** [**3** × **7** × **17**] (my estimation); Luke (**88 columns** [**4** × **22**]) + Acts (**81 columns** [**3** × **27**]) = *169 columns* [*13* × *13*, potentially indicating (divine) oneness];

Acts **81 columns** [**3** × **27**]; 1–2 Peter *14 columns*; Catholic Epistles 36 columns *[2* × *18]*, *18 pages*; Praxapostolos: Acts (**81 columns** [**3** × **27**]) + Catholic Epistles (*36 columns [2* × *18]*) = **117 columns** [**3** × **39**, potentially a threefold numerical indication of God's oneness];

Romans *30 columns [2* × *15]*; Hebrews **24 columns**, 1–2 Timothy **15 columns**; Pauline Corpus **170 columns** [**10** × **17**] (my estimation, based on 1–2 Corinthians embracing 49 columns; N.B. 2 Corinthians vac. 4:14–12:6).

Codex Washingtonianus

Our last codicological example, Codex Washingtonianus, includes similar arithmetical features, as the following figures indicate: **30 lines** [**2** × **15**] per column (one column per page); altogether **187 leaves** [**11** × **17**]; and **374 pages** [**17** × **22**]; Matthew *112 pages [8* × *14]*; John 82 pages (excluding two blank pages at the end of John)/*84 pages* (including two blank pages at the end of John) *[6* × *14]*; Matthew (*112 pages [8* × *14]*) + John (*84 pages [6* × *14]*) = *196 pages [14* × *14]*; Luke 116 pages; Matthew (*112 pages [8* × *14]*) + John (*84 pages [6* × *14]*) + Luke (116 pages) = **312 pages** [**13** × **24** =**12** × **26**]); Mark 62 pages; and, finally, the fourfold Gospel 372 pages (excluding the two blank pages)/**374 pages** [**17** × **22**] (including the two blank pages).[36]

---

36. For images, see https://www.csntm.org/manuscript/View/GA_032.

BIBLIOGRAPHY

Bauckham, Richard. "The 153 Fish and the Unity of the Fourth Gospel." *Neot* 36 (2002): 82–85.

Brown, Raymond E. *The Gospel According to John*, Anchor Bible Commentary 29. New Haven & London: Yale University Press, 2008 (1974).

Davies, W. D., and Dale C. Allison Jr. *A Critical and Exegetical Commentary on the Gospel according to Saint Matthew*. Vol. 1: *Introduction and Commentary on Matthew 1–7*. ICC. London: T&T Clark, 2004.

Labuschagne, Casper J. *Numerical Secrets of the Bible: Introduction to Biblical Arithmology*. Eugene, OR: Wipf & Stock, 2016.

PART D

CHRIST THE CENTER:
REGULA FIDEI AND
SCRIPTURAL THEOLOGY

11

THE EARLY RULE-OF-FAITH PATTERN AS EMERGENT BIBLICAL THEOLOGY

A major function of the early church's Rule of Faith (*regula fidei*), largely synonymous with the Rule of Truth or Ecclesiastical Rule,[1] was to guarantee that the faith community "read the Old Testament as the promise of the Gospel and the Gospel as the fulfilment of that promise."[2] As a key to such a reading of old and new Scriptures as a unified whole, the *regula fidei* was used as a summary of the faith,[3] or as the teaching foundation for Christian belief as revealed by Christ and handed down by the apostles.[4]

---

1. The three largely synonymous terms and their equivalents employed throughout the present chapter are 1) the Rule of Truth (χανὼν τῆς ἀληθείας/*regula veritatis*), Irenaeus's main term; 2) the Rule of Faith (χανὼν τῆς πίστεως/*regula fidei*), Tertullian's main term, and 3) the Ecclesiastical Rule (χανὼν ἐκκλησιαστικός), one of Clement of Alexandria's main terms (*Stromata* Book VI and VII). For a similar relationship between Scripture and Rule of Faith in Irenaeus, Tertullian and Clement, see Bengt Hägglund, "Die Bedeutung der 'regula fidei' als Grundlage theologischer Aussagen," *Studia Theologica* 12 (1958): 30–34, esp. 31. Translation of source texts are my own, unless indicated otherwise. In line with the early Christian (Greek) manuscript tradition, I have chosen to highlight in small caps the following words among the so-called *nomina sacra* demarcations (names of central figures of the faith abbreviated and supplied with an overbar): GOD, LORD, JESUS, CHRIST, FATHER, SON, SPIRIT, MAN and CROSS.

2. Mark Edwards, *Catholicity and Heresy in the Early Church* (Farnam, Surrey: Ashgate, 2009), 40.

3. Ellen Flesseman-van Leer, *Tradition and Scripture in the Early Church* (Leiden: Gorcum & Prakke, 1953), 165: "the regula is a summary, formulated according to the need of the moment, of the entire Christian faith;" Frances Young, "Christian teaching," in *The Cambridge History of Early Christian Literature*, eds. F. Young, L. Ayres and A. Louth (Cambridge: Cambridge University, 2004), 102. See Iren. *Epid.* 6 and Tert. *Praescr.* 13. Cf. also Tertullian's terminology in *Marc.* IV, 1: "Testaments," "Law" and "Gospel."

4. Clem. *Strom.* VI, 15.125.3; VII, 95.3. Cf. Philip Hefner ("Theological Methodology and St. Irenaeus," *The Journal of Religion* 44.4 (1964): 299), who argues that the Rule of Faith, and equivalent

Following an introduction to the early Christian notion of a *regula*
fidei, and a brief comment on a few passages in Irenaeus (*Haer.* I, 8.1–10.1;
III, 1.1–2; *Dem.* 6), this chapter explores certain practices integral to the
church's Rule of Faith, namely: Scripture interpretation (focussing on the
nomina sacra practice and the bipartite OT–NT arrangement), creedal
formulation, and the rite of initiation. It is argued that these basic textual[5], creedal[6] and ritual expressions[7] of early Christian existence shaped
common features of the majority church's emergent biblical theology.
"Biblical theology" is here understood in broad terms as the distinct
Christian theology held to be contained in the Jewish (OT) and specifically Christian Scriptures (NT) when perceived jointly as a textual unity.

Due to their defining qualities, Scripture and Rule of Faith emerged
within the faith community—to use the German theologian Karlmann
Beyschlag's phrasing—as "two sides of one and the same norm" (*zwei
Seiten einer Norm*).[8] As such, the *regula fidei* could even be seen as a
property of sacred Scripture, emphasising the arrangement of the Old
and New Testament texts into a whole, with special attention given to
reading biblical passages in their intra-scriptural context (Clem. *Strom.*
VI, 15.25.3; Iren. *Haer.* I, 8.1–10.1).[9] Alternatively, when associated more
with baptismal confession or apostolic tradition in the broader sense, the
regula could be viewed as a scripturally defined or aligned Rule.[10] Applied

---

terms used by Irenaeus, points to "an organic system or framework which constitutes the shape and
the meaning of God's revelation. Without the system, God's revelation is not intelligible." In this wider
discussion on the Rule, however, Hefner has not given due consideration to Irenaeus's remarks on
scriptural hermeneutics inherent in the scriptural account itself (cf., e.g., *Haer.* I, 8.1–10.1).

5. That is, scriptural.

6. That is, widely shared confessional formularies among Christians.

7. E.g., reception of the Rule of Faith through baptism.

8. Karlmann Beyschlag, *Grundriß der Dogmengeschichte*, vol. 1 (Darmstadt: Wissenschaftliche
Buchgesellschaft, 1982), 170.

9. See n. 14 below. This conclusion becomes particularly attractive in light of the special demarcation of so-called *nomina sacra* (see further below), such as FATHER, SON and SPIRIT in the Greek
Bible manuscripts, words that were specially emphasized, and, it seems, part of the early Rule-of-
Faith pattern. These three words are found in their *nomina sacra* forms, e.g., in papyrus P[46] and P[66],
both commonly dated to ca. AD 200 (cf. NA28, pp. 794–96).

10. In Tertullian's *Prescriptions against Heretics* 19, the Rule of Faith is presented as the hermeneutical key to Scripture reading: "For wherever it shall be manifest that the true Christian rule and
faith shall be, *there* will likewise be the true Scriptures and expositions thereof, and all the Christian

to various types of scriptural exegesis, this Rule of Faith, or Rule-of-Faith pattern of biblical reading, occurs around AD 200 in Irenaeus of Lyons,[11] Tertullian of Carthage and Clement of Alexandria, as well as in other early Christian writers.[12]

11.1 INTRODUCTORY REMARKS

11.1.1 *REGULA FIDEI* AND THE MOSAIC OF SCRIPTURE

Christ himself is said to be the originator of the Rule in Tertullian (ca. AD 160–220) and Clement of Alexandria (ca. AD 150–215/21).[13] Clement describes the Ecclesiastical Rule in a frequently quoted passage as "the agreement and unity of the Law and the Prophets with the Testament delivered at the coming of the Lord."[14] As such,[15] it provides the key hermeneutical guideline for his Scripture principle and biblical theology.[16] Clement's concern to relate the old Jewish and new Christian Scriptures to one another may here be concretely linked not only to the Ecclesiastical Rule, but also to the actual titles of the two major text corpora—"The Old"

---

traditions." (*Praescr.* 19 (ANF 3:251f.)). Clement of Alexandria as well as Irenaeus, place greater weight on Scripture's normative function than does Tertullian in this passage.

11. Irenaeus's *Demonstration of the Apostolic Preaching*, which attempts to integrate the Rule of Faith into the biblical expositon of the work (see *Epid.* 3, 6, 7, 98–100), is illustrative. Though I will deal briefly with Clement and Tertullian in this chapter, my main focus will be upon Irenaeus.

12. See, e.g., Hans Lietzmann, *A History of the Early Church*, vol. 1 (Cambridge: James Clarke & Co., 1951, 1993), 373–91.

13. Tert. *Praescr.* 13; 21; 37; *Apol.* 47; Clem. *Strom.* VII, 16.95.

14. "Κανὼν δὲ ἐκκλησιαστικός ἡ συνῳδία καὶ συμφωνία νόμου τε καὶ προφητῶν τῇ κατὰ τὴν τοῦ κυρίου παρουσίαν παραδιδομένῃ διαθήκῃ" (*Strom.* VI, 15.125.3). Clement of Alexandria's use of the Rule of Faith or Ecclesiastical Rule comes close to that of Irenaeus and Tertullian, especially in *Strom.* VI and VII. For Clement's broader use of the concept elsewhere, see Hägglund, *Sanningens regel—Regula veritatis. Trosregeln och den kristna traditionens struktur* (Skellefteå: Artos & Norma bokförlag, 2003) 27f.; and Heinz Ohme, *Kanon ekklesiastikos: Die Bedeutung des altkirchlichen Kanonbegriffs*, Arbeiten zur Kirchengeschichte, Bd. 67 (Berlin: Walter de Gruyter, 1998), 122ff.

15. I.e., as the Lord's/Christ's teaching. Cf. Christ as the beginning and principle of the teaching (ἀρχὴ τῆς διδασκαλίας) in Clement (*Strom.* VII, 95.3). Hägglund, *Sanningens regel*, 28.

16. Cf. *Strom.* VII, 16.96: "We obtain from the Scriptures themselves a perfect demonstration concerning the Scriptures"; and VII, 16.95: "For we have the LORD as the first principle of our teaching, leading us to knowledge, from beginning to end, in many and various ways through the Prophets, through the Gospel and through the blessed Apostles." See also Hägglund ("regula fidei," 33), who emphasizes that for Clement the Scripture is ultimately selfauthenticating (αὐτόπιστος). Cf. Iren. *Haer.* II, 27.1; II, 28.2. On the notion of "the covenants" in Clement, see Einar Molland, *The Conception of the Gospel in the Alexandrian Theology* (Oslo: Det Norske Videnskaps-Akademi, 1938), 69–75.

and "The New Testament"—introduced by Christian editors towards the
end of the second century.[17]

A couple of decades earlier, in Irenaeus of Lyons (ca. AD 125–202),
standard characteristics of his Scripture-linked Rule of Faith include
adherence to apostolic origins,[18] close association with defining monotheistic belief and other creedal material (*Haer.* I, 10.1), as well as with
baptismal teaching and confession (*Haer.* I, 9.4).[19]

However, in a manner similar to Clement of Alexandria, the bishop
of Lyons evinces a Rule that teaches the church to read the Scriptures as
a literary unity with a particular sequential ordering and textual arrangement (*Haer.* I, 8.1–10.1).[20] Irenaeus employs the classic hermeneutical rule
of the parts relating to the textual whole, and *vice versa*, in one of his
famous illustrations in *Against Heresies*. He likens the arrangement of
the biblical material to a beautiful mosaic of a king—in contradistinction
to an unappealing fox, where the textual bits and pieces of the artwork
have been misplaced, as in the Gnostic Valentinian Scripture interpretation (*Haer.* I, 9.4).[21]

11.1.2 SCHOLARLY VIEWS ON THE *REGULA FIDEI*

The *regula fidei* attained a multivalent function during the period we are
looking at, and could be equated with Scripture, baptismal confession,

---

17. Cf. David Trobisch, *The First Edition of the New Testament* (Oxford: Oxford University Press, 2000), 43–44. As for the use of the titles "Old" and "New Testament" in Clement of Alexandria (e.g., *Strom.* I, 5.28.2; ANF 2:305), see Wolfram Kinzig, "Καινὴ διαθήκη: The Title of the New Testament in the Second and Third Century," *JTS* 45.2 (1994): 529.

18. *Haer.* I, 10.1: "the apostles and their disciples"; and *Dem.* 3 (ACW 16): "the elders, the disciples of the apostles."

19. See further below; cf. Tomas Bokedal, "The Rule of Faith: Tracing Its Origins," *Journal of Theological Interpretation*, 7.2 (2013): 233–55.

20. Cf. Reinhold Seeberg's characterization of Irenaeus as a "biblical theologian," *Lehrbuch der Dogmengeschichte*, vol. 1 (Leipzig, 1908; 2nd ed.), 290 (quoted by John Lawson, *The Biblical Theology of St. Irenaeus* (London: Epworth Press, 1948), 2): "Irenäus ist Biblizist und er ist der erste grosse Vertreter des Biblizismus." The quotation in Seeberg, however, continues: "... Aber Iren. ist zugleich Traditionalist, nur im Sinne der kirchlichen Überlieferung darf die Bibel ausgelegt." The argument of the present chapter seeks to qualify the biblical theology of Irenaeus and others, without—as here in Seeberg—too quick recourse to tradition. See further Lawson, *The Biblical Theology of St. Irenaeus*, 97–118 and 292f.

21. See quote below, n. 50.

or apostolic tradition more broadly.[22] Thus, the tension posed between Scripture and unwritten Christian tradition in the Western churches since the Reformation and Counter-Reformation does not appear in the early Christian centuries, neither in the New Testament,[23] during the New Testament period, nor subsequently.

In 1 *Clement*, an epistle addressed to the Corinthian Christians towards the end of the first century, the author appeals to the church in Corinth to "conform to the renowned and holy rule of our tradition" (1 *Clem.* 7.2; τῆς παραδόσεως ἡμῶν κανόνα). As the equally renowned second-century *regula fidei* tradition became part of central Christian vocabulary as testified by Dionysius of Corinth (ca. AD 170), Irenaeus and Clement of Alexandria,[24] we shall seek to understand their precise intent concerning this novel expression.[25]

Notable scholars of the late nineteenth and twentieth centuries attempted to provide answers concerning the *regula's* profile. Theodor Zahn held the *regula fidei* to be "identical with the baptismal confession."[26] Adolf von Harnack, on the other hand, sought to broaden Zahn's understanding. He argued that the earliest *regula* should be defined in terms of

---

22. Hägglund, "regula fidei," 4.

23. So F. F. Bruce, "Scripture in Relation to Tradition and Reason," in *Scripture, Tradition and Reason: A Study in the Criteria of Christian Doctrine. Essays in Honour of Richard P. C. Hanson*, eds. Richard Bauckham and Benjamin Drewery (London: T&T Clark, 1998), 37. Bruce's claim seems to apply only to the New Testament material and tradition.

24. Dionysius refers to the *regula veritatis*/κανὼν τῆς ἀληθείας to counter Marcion; Eusebius, *Hist. Eccl.* IV, 23.4; LCL, vol. 153, trans. Kirsopp Lake (Cambridge, MA and London: Harvard University, 1926), 378. Somewhat earlier, Polycrates of Ephesus (ca. AD 130–96) appeals to the *regula fidei* in the Quartodeciman controversy. Cf. Ohme, *Kanon ekklesiastikos*, 249–53.

25. The first time the expression *regula fidei*/κανὼν τῆς πίστεως is used by early church writers, seems to be in Polycrates of Ephesus. For further details on the use of *regula veritatis* in Philo and elsewhere, see Ohme, *Kanon ekklesiastikos*, 21–58; and Bokedal, "The Rule of Faith: Tracing Its Origins," 236f.

26. Theodor Zahn, "Glaubensregel," in *Realencyklopädie für protestantische Theologie und Kirche* (ed. Albert Hauck; Leipzig: J. C. Hinrichs, 1899), 6:685; cf. Ferdinand Kattenbusch, *Das apostolische Symbol. Seine Entstehung, sein geschichtlicher Sinn, seine ursprüngliche Stellung im Kultus und in der Geschichte der Kirche. Ein Beitrag zur Symbolik und zur Dogmengeschichte*, vol. 1 (Leipzig: J. C. Hinrichs'sche Buchhandlung, 1894), 26–30; Jonathan J. Armstrong, "From the κανὼν τῆς ἀληθείας to the κανὼν τῶν γραφῶν: The Rule of Faith and the New Testament Canon," in *Tradition & the Rule of Faith in the Early Church: Essays in Honor of Joseph T. Lienhard. S.J.*, eds. Ronnie J. Rombs and Alexander Y. Hwang (Washington, D.C.: The Catholic University of America Press, 2010), 33.

the apostolic tradition rather than baptismal confession per se.[27] Harnack's position opened up for clearer association between the Rule of Faith and the Scriptures.[28] However, only with Johannes Kunze's monumental 1899 study *Glaubensregel, Heilige Schrift und Taufbekenntnis*[29] is the scholarly horizon helpfully broadened, and a clearly positive relationship between Christian Scripture and Rule of Faith posited.[30]

Key aspects of Kunze's approach have been discussed afresh by the Swedish theologian Bengt Hägglund.[31] With his distinctive emphasis, Hägglund affirms the early Christian notion of Rule of Faith as referring ultimately to the revelatory events themselves, stemming from God and Christ and passed on by the apostles.[32] In the first and second centuries, these events were held to be codified primarily in Scripture, apostolic tradition and baptismal confession. The rather abstract and flexible definition of the *regula fidei* that Hägglund suggests fits well with our main source texts discussing the early Rule of Faith.[33] Concerning the *regula* in Irenaeus, Tertullian and Clement, Hägglund writes: "Baptismal confession (as a brief summary of the contents of revelation), sacred Scripture,

---

27. Armstrong, "The Rule of Faith and the New Testament Canon," 34. Adolf von Harnack, *Lehrbuch der Dogmengeschichte*, vol. 1, *Die Entstehung des kirchlichen Dogmas* (Freiburg: Mohr, 1886, 1st ed.), 257; ibid (1909, 3rd ed.), 355ff. For a different emphasis on Harnack's contribution, see ibid., 361, and Hägglund, "regula fidei," 3.

28. Armstrong, "The Rule of Faith and the New Testament Canon," 34.

29. Johannes Kunze, *Glaubensregel, Heilige Schrift und Taufbekenntnis: Untersuchungen über die dogmatische Autorität, ihr Werden und ihre Geschichte, vornehmlich in der alten Kirche* (Leipzig: Dörffling & Franke, 1899).

30. As Armstrong points out ("The Rule of Faith and the New Testament Canon," 37), Kunze embraces Harnack's "insightful maxim:" "'Canon' was originally the rule of faith; the Scripture had in truth intervened." But, as Kunze indicates, Harnack's view on the relation between Scripture and Rule of Faith is rather ambiguous.

31. Hägglund, "regula fidei," 12f., 24, 27, and 33. For a similar approach to the question of Scripure and tradition in the early church, see also Flesseman-van Leer, *Tradition and Scripture*.

32. Iren. *Haer.* III, 3.4; 4.1. Hägglund, *Sanningens regel*, 11n9. Hefner ("Theological Methodology," 295) describes Hägglund's understanding of the *regula veritatis/fidei* in Irenaeus in the following wording: "Bengt Haegglund understands Irenaeus' chief concern as establishing the regula fidei or regula veritatis, by which Irenaeus refers to the original, immutable truth which the church holds, the Faith itself which is revealed in Scripture, in the kerygma of Christ and the apostles, and which is passed on to the believer in baptism. This truth is absolute truth; it is the revelation which lies behind the creed, the content of Scripture, and the proclamation of the tradition of the presbyterial succession; it constitutes the right knowledge of God and his redemptive action in the divine economy."

33. For various scholarly interpretations of the *regula fidei*, see, e.g., Hefner, "Theological Methodology;" and Ohme, *Kanon ekklesiastikos*.

apostolic tradition—all is comprised by the *regula fidei* or *regula veritatis*. Thus, this *regula* can be equated with one or the other property, however with neither of them being fully identical."[34]

Some more recent scholarship has continued to emphasize the close relationship between Scripture and *regula fidei*. Karl-Heinz Ohlig, when reflecting on the canon-formation process, holds the view that "the Rule of Faith is not an independent principle and norma normans beside Scripture," but the usage "of that which one already recognized through the appropriated Scriptures, as applied to what was still disputed."[35] Paul Blowers, who understands the connection between *regula* and Scripture in yet stronger terms, writes: "For Irenaeus and Tertullian alike it is imperative to identify the Canon of Truth or Rule of Faith as Scripture's own intrinsic story-line."[36]

The focus of the present chapter is the *regula fidei* as incipient biblical theology. I thus discuss the Rule of Faith (or Rule-of-Faith pattern of biblical reading) as a normative hermeneutical tool—implemented through Scripture, catechesis and baptism—that promotes the textual and theological unity of the corpus of Old and New Testament Scriptures.

11.2 SCRIPTURE AND *REGULA*: *HAER.* I, 8.1–10.1, III, 1.1–2, AND *DEM.* 6

To illustrate my primary assertion—that the *regula fidei*[37] is intimately linked to the (emerging) biblical theology of some major early church

---

34. Hägglund, "regula fidei," 4. Cf. also idem, *Sanningens regel*, 10. With regard to Tertullian, similarly Flesseman-van Leer, *Tradition and* Scripture, 165–66; and L. Wm. Countryman, "Tertullian and the Regula Fidei," *Second Century* 2 (1982): 226.

35. Karl-Heinz Ohlig, *Die theologische Begründung des neutestamentlichen Kanons in der alten Kirche* (Düsseldorf: Patmos-Verlag, 1972), 174.

36. Paul M. Blowers, "The *Regula Fidei* and the Narrative Character of Early Christian Faith," *Pro Ecclesia* 6 (1997): 212. Cf. ibid., 202: "The Rule of Faith served the primitive Christian hope of articulating and authenticating a world-encompassing story or metanarrative of creation, incarnation, redemption and consummation." See also Bokedal, "The Rule of Faith: Tracing Its Origins," 248–54.

37. *Regula veritatis* as a major Latin expression used to render the Greek equivalent κανὼν τῆς ἀληθείας (in *Against Heresies*) is complemented by the synonymous phrasing *regula fidei* (in *Demonstration of the Apostolic Preaching*). However, one term can still be preferred over the other, as Eric Osborn helpfully points out (*Irenaeus of Lyons* (Cambridge: Cambridge University, 2001), 145n17): "Generally the latter term [*regula fidei*] was preferred for internal use within the church and

writers[38]—I shall appropriate the following representative formulation of the Rule of Faith (here referred to as "the faith") as phrased by Irenaeus in his First Book *Against Heresies*:

> The church, though spread throughout the whole world, ... received (παραλαμβάνειν) from the apostles and their disciples the faith (πίστις) in one GOD the FATHER Almighty, who made the heaven and the earth, the sea and all that is in them; and in one CHRIST JESUS, the Son of God, who became flesh for our salvation; and in the Holy SPIRIT, who through the prophets proclaimed the economies (οἰκονομία), and the coming and birth from the Virgin, and the passion, and the resurrection from the dead, and the ascension of the beloved CHRIST JESUS our LORD in the flesh into the heavens, and his coming from the heavens in the glory of the FATHER to recapitulate all things and to raise up all flesh of the whole human race. (*Haer.* I, 10.1)[39]

As a summary statement of the faith and the baptismal teaching, the Rule is directly linked to Scripture and its exposition. First, our passage's immediate textual context in *Against Heresies* treats the Rule of Faith as part of a discussion on scriptural hermeneutics (*Haer.* I, 8.1–10.1).

Secondly, the faith "received from the apostles and their disciples" (I, 10.1) could be taken to refer to the revelatory events themselves (Hägglund) or a summary statement of that faith which was transmitted orally and then in written form. We recall the bishop's description of the transmission of the oral and written gospel in the introduction to Book Three of *Against Heresies*: This gospel, he states, was "handed down to us in the Scriptures, so that *that* would be the foundation and pillar of our faith." (*Haer.* III, 1.1) In the following section, Irenaeus connects these apostolic texts (the four Gospels) directly with the Rule-of-Faith pattern in its binitarian form: "These [the Gospel writers] have all declared to us that there is one GOD, Creator of heaven and earth, announced by the

---

the former term [*regula veritatis*] was preferred when argument was directed to heretics." For text critcal issues involved, see Ohme, *Kanon ekklesiastikos*, 61.

38. Cf. esp. Clem. *Strom.* VI, 15.125.3, cited in n. 14 above; and Iren. *Haer.* I, 8.1–10.1.

39. On Irenaeus's and the early church's use of *nomina sacra*, here in small caps, see below.

Law and the Prophets; and one CHRIST, the SON of GOD." (*Haer.* III, 1.2) Thereby, he evinces the close connection between Rule of Faith (binitarian summary of the faith), Jewish Scripture (the Law and the Prophets), and New Testament text (the fourfold Gospel). The intimate connection between Scripture and *regula* in *Haer.* (I, 10.1; III, 1.2) and *Epid.* (6ff.) lends support as well to a narrative approach, along the lines suggested by Paul Blowers: "The Rule of Faith served the primitive Christian hope of articulating and authenticating a world-encompassing story or metanarrative of creation, incarnation, redemption and consummation."[40] Irenaeus's catechetical piece, *Demonstration of the Apostolic Preaching (Epid. 1–100)*, renders such joint metanarrative employment of Scripture and Rule into one of our earliest "proto-orthodox" biblical-theological contributions, focusing on "the revelatory events themselves." (cf. *Haer.* II, 28.1; n. 52 below)."

Thirdly, as indicated in these passages from Book I and III of *Against Heresies* (I, 10.1 and III, 1.2) and in *Demonstration of the Apostolic Preaching* (6), the Jewish Scriptures are repeatedly referred to as an integrated part of the *regula fidei* formularies (cf. 1 Cor 15:3f.).[41] Phrasings like "[proclaimed] through the prophets," (*Haer.* I, 10.1) "announced by the Law and the Prophets," (III, 1.2) and "shown forth by the prophets according to the design of their prophecy" (*Epid.* 6) also serve to connect the old Scriptures (OT) with key events in the new (NT).[42] Irenaeus closely affiliates the fourfold Gospel discussed in *Against Heresies* (III, 1.1 and 11.8) with the Rule "announced by the Law and the Prophets." (III, 1.2)[43] And in *Demonstration of the Apostolic Preaching*, in Oskar Skarsaune's phrasing, Irenaeus devotes himself to

---

40. Blowers, "The *Regula Fidei* and the Narrative Character of Early Christian Faith," 202."

41. As in 1 Cor 15:3–4, the reference to the Scriptures is usually part of a christology section (cf. *Haer.* I, 10.1 (where the christology is part of the third article) and *Epid.* 6). In the heavily abbreviated binitarian form in *Haer.* III, 1.2, the reference to Scripture is retained as central, but as part of the first article of faith.

42. In *Epid.* 6, reference to the prophets is made in both the second and the third article of faith.

43. Cf. Hägglund, *Sanningens regel*, 17: Even if the Rule may refer to individual books of the Bible (*Haer.* III, 15.1), it still tends to focus on the scriptural contents, the basic doctrines of Scripture, rather than the biblical books as such; and ibid., 16: "As a matter of fact, the 'regula' always refers to Scripture, because through Holy Scripture—i.e. through the prophetic and apostolic message—and only through it [Scripture], truth has been revealed and handed down to us." See also Kunze, *Glaubensregel*, 100–27.

an Old Testament proof of the main points in the Rule of Faith, mainly its Christological part. ...The extensive summary of biblical history in chs. 11–42a clearly demonstrates the catechetical nature of Irenaeus' treatise ... this biblical history is the very content of the apostolic preaching and the Rule of Faith ... It is, so to speak, a fleshing out of the three articles of the "creed" comprised in short format in the Rule of Faith.[44]

Fourthly, the so-called *nomina sacra* word group, most likely marked off in Irenaeus's Scriptures (in small caps below),[45] provides a common textual pattern for Christian Scripture and the Rule of Faith; that is, the special demarcation by abbreviation (contraction or suspension with a horizontal stroke drawn above the abbreviation) of the Greek words for God (θεός; ΘΣ), Lord (κύριος; ΚΣ), Jesus (Ἰησοῦς; ΙΗ, ΙΗC, ΙΣ), Christ (χριστός; ΧΡ, ΧΡC, ΧΣ), Father (πατήρ; ΠΗΡ), Son (υἱός; ΥΣ) and Spirit (πνεῦμα; ΠΝΑ). These, and few additional specially written Greek short forms,[46] are found in contemporary OT manuscripts, e.g. P. Chester Beatty VI (second/third century AD),[47] and NT manuscripts, such as P[46] and P[66] (both ca. AD 200).[48] We also know that Irenaeus himself (or his scribe) most likely made use of these "sacred names," or *nomina-sacra* demarcations, in his own works, in line with Christian writing practice of the day (see P. Oxy. 405).[49]

---

44. Skarsaune, "The Development of Scriptural Interpretation in the Second and Third Centuries," 423–24.

45. Scribal *nomina sacra* demarcations—present in basically all extant Christian Greek Bible manuscripts—were arguably introduced into the biblical manuscript tradition no later than the first century (Larry W. Hurtado, "The Origin of the Nomina Sacra: A Proposal," *JBL* 117.4 (1998): 660). The palaeographer C. H. Roberts opts for a pre-70 dating (*Manuscript, Society and Belief in Early Christian Egypt, Schweich Lectures 1977* (London: Oxford University Press, published for the British Academy, 1979)). See also Martin Hengel, *The Septuagint as Christian Scripture: Its Prehistory and the Problem of Its Canon*, trans. Biddle (London and New York: T&T Clark, 2002), 41.

46. See below for a more complete list of early Greek *nomina sacra*.

47. The Center for the Study of New Testament Manuscripts lists P. Chester Beatty VI (Ralphs 963) among second-century manuscripts; see http://www.csntm.org/manuscript [accessed 28/02/2015].

48. Cf. n. 9 above. *Nomina sacra* in P[46] and P[66] include GOD, LORD, JESUS, CHRIST, SPIRIT, FATHER, SON, MAN and CROSS/CRUCIFY.

49. P.Oxy. 405, which makes use of *nomina sacra*, contains portions of *Haer.* III, 9.2–3 and was produced in the late second or early third century, just a few years after Irenaeus wrote his *Against Heresies*. See Irénée de Lyon, *Contre les heresies* 3, Sources chrétiennes 210 and 211, edited

Both the *nomina sacra* convention and the *regula fidei* pattern place a limited number of theologically significant names and words centre stage: GOD, FATHER, LORD, JESUS and CHRIST (cf. 1 Cor 8:6; John 20:28); GOD/FATHER, JESUS/SON/CHRIST/LORD and SPIRIT (cf. Matt 3:16–17; 28:19; 1 Cor 12:4–6; *1 Clem.* 46.6); JESUS, CHRIST and SON OF GOD (cf. Matt 16:16; John 20:31). As we will see below, the resemblance between these (dyadic/triadic) *nomina sacra* demarcations and the major names being part of the (dyadic/triadic) *regula fidei* formulary in *Against Heresies* I, 10.1 (one GOD the FATHER, one CHRIST JESUS; FATHER, SON and SPIRIT; the beloved CHRIST JESUS our LORD) is conspicuous.

In the following, I shall attempt to demonstrate the close link between certain features of Irenaeus's classic formulation of the Rule of Faith (*Against Heresies* I, 8.1–10.1 and elsewhere)[50] and an emergent biblical theology. I will discuss in brief: 1) the catechetical and ritual context of the *regula fidei*; 2) the creedal context of the *regula fidei*; and 3) the *regula's* textual–scriptural contextualization associated with the scribal *nomina sacra* demarcations.

11.3 CATECHETICAL AND RITUAL CONTEXT: THE RULE OF FAITH RECEIVED THROUGH BAPTISM

The close link between Scripture and *regula* can be seen in Irenaeus's critique of the Gnostic Valentinian reading of individual Bible passages, which were taken out of their original literary framework (*Against Heresies* I, 9.4). The bishop of Lyons complains, describing their exegetical method in rather derogatory terms:

---

and translated by Adelin Rousseau and Louis Doutreleau (Paris, 1974), Book 3/1, 126–30; Book 3/2, 104–08. In the transcription by Grenfell/Hunt of the fragments making up P.Oxy. 405 (reproduced in Book 3/1, 131), the following names are contracted as *nomina sacra*: "Christ" (x̄c̄), "Jesus" (īn̄) and "God" (θ̄ȳ). As part of the reconstructed section of the text of which the fragment was part, Grenfell/ Hunt also included *nomina sacra* demarcations for "Lord" (k̄c̄), "Spirit" (π̄n̄ā) and "Son" (ȳc̄). See also Andreas Schmidt, "Der mögliche Text von P.Oxy. III 405, Z. 39–45," NTS 37 (1991): 160.

50. Passages in Irenaeus mentioning the Rule of Truth/Faith include *Haer.* I, 9.4; I, 22.1; II, 27.1; III, 2.1; III, 11.1; III, 12.6; III, 15.1; IV, 35.4; and *Epid.* 3.

After having entirely fabricated their own system, they [the Valentinians] gather together sayings and names from scattered places and transfer them, as we have already said, from their natural meaning to an unnatural one. They act like those who would propose themes which they chance upon and then try to put them to verse from Homeric poems, so that the inexperienced think that Homer composed the poems with that theme, which in reality are of recent composition. … In the same way, anyone who keeps unswervingly in himself the Rule of Truth received through baptism will recognize the names and sayings and parables from the Scriptures, but this blasphemous theme of theirs he will not recognize. For even if he recognizes the jewels, he will not accept the fox for the image of the king. He will restore each one of the passages to its proper order and, having fit it into the body of the Truth, he will lay bare their fabrication and show that it is without support. (*Haer.* I, 9.4)[51]

Irenaeus's way of countering Valentinian text interpretation, as he presents it here, is by appeal to the Rule of Truth (*regula veritatis*). A correct reading of the Scriptures, he insists, must be pursued according to the *regula veritatis* pattern: "Anyone who keeps unswervingly (ἀκλινής) in himself the Rule of Truth received through baptism (διὰ τοῦ βαπτίσματος) will recognize the names and sayings and parables from the Scriptures." (*Haer.* I, 9.4; cf. *Epid.* 3) Baptism, Rule of Truth and Bible reading are here closely linked. True appropriation of Scripture—including an understanding of its names, sayings and parables—takes place in those who adhere to the Rule of Truth. Such is in contradistinction to Gnostic Valentinians and others who have abandoned the Christian *regula*—or "Truth itself" (*Haer.* II, 28.1)[52]—and the pattern of scriptural reading closely associated with it.

---

51. *St. Irenaeus of Lyons against the Heresies*, vol. 1, ACW 55, translated and annotated by Dominic J. Unger with further revisions by John J. Dillon (New York, N.Y./Mahwah, N.J.: The Newman Press), 47, modified. As for the expression "body of the Truth," see Hägglund, *Sanningens regel*, 12f.

52. *Haer.* II, 28.1: "And so, we have the truth itself as rule" (*habentes itaque regulam ipsam veritatem*). In this connection we note that Hägglund ("regula fidei," 5) and others take the expression *regula veritatis* to be an epexegetical genitive: it is Truth itself that is the rule or norm. For a different rendering of *Haer.* II, 28.1 (based on *regulam...veritat(is)*, rather than *regulam...veritatem*), see ACW

However, what, more precisely, should we presume the baptizand to have received "through baptism"? The Rule of Truth, to be sure. But what would that have entailed in the Irenaean church setting?

We shall consider a couple of things that may have crossed Irenaeus's mind. First, the claim that the Rule is "received through baptism" most certainly refers to the whole process of baptismal teaching.[53] This includes catechetical instruction to literate as well as illiterate catechumens (*Haer.* III, 4.1–2), and externally transmitted (i.e. teaching) as well as internally appropriated dimensions (i.e. reception) of the *regula*. Irenaeus appears to be summarizing the faith received at baptism (*Epid.* 7; *Haer.* I, 21.1). He does that by using dyadic/binitarian or triadic/Trinitarian short forms for the received faith, linked with scriptural exposition (cf. *Haer.* III, 1.2; *Epid.* 1–100, esp. 1, 3, 7, 98–100). J. N. D. Kelly emphasizes, "the catechetical preparation was dominated by those features of the impending sacrament which constituted its essence, the threefold interrogation with the threefold assent, and the threefold immersion."[54]

Secondly, the bishop of Lyons can still maintain a dual emphasis, on the binitarian/Trinitarian faith in which the catechumens have been instructed (cf., e.g., *Haer.* I, 10.1; III, 4.1–2; 11.1; 16.6; IV, 33.7), and on the formal reception of that faith through immersion in the name of the Triune God (*Haer.* I, 9.4; *Epid.* 3 and 7; cf. *Just.* 1 *Apol.* 61). In this connection, Alistair Stewart has recently argued that a christological profession of faith may have been recited just before the actual baptism, whereas the binitarian or Trinitarian Rule may have been part of the pre-baptismal instruction.[55] In line with such christological formulary, we notice the wording of what is probably the earliest profession of faith linked to baptism that we know of, namely the Western text of Acts 8.

65: 87, where Dominic J. Unger translates the opening line of the passage as follows: "Since, then, we possess the Rule of Truth itself and the manifest testimony about God."

53. Cf. *Haer.* I, 21.1; V praef.; and *Dem.* 3 and 7. Cf. J. N. D. Kelly, *Early Christian Creeds* (New York: Longman, 3rd rev. ed., 1972), 51f.

54. Ibid.

55. Alistair Stewart, "'The Rule of Truth ... which He Received through Baptism' (*Haer.* I, 9.4): Catechesis, Ritual, and Exegesis in Irenaeus's Gaul," in *Irenaeus: Life, Scripture, Legacy*, eds. Paul Foster and Sara Parvis (Minneapolis: Fortress, 2012), 153f. Cf. Kelly in footnote above.

At the baptism scene in Acts 8:36–37, as the Ethiopian eunuch is baptized, the following dialogue is presented: "What is to prevent my being baptized?" (8:36). "And Philip said, 'If you believe with all your heart, you may.' And he replied, 'I believe that JESUS CHRIST is the SON of GOD.' " (8:37, inserted)[56] In fact, Christ-confession, in one form or another, appears to have been associated with baptism from the beginning (cf. Heb 4:14; 1 John 4:15; 5:5; Mark 3:11; 5:7).[57]

If we assume that Stewart is right about a christological profession immediately prior to baptism, Irenaeus may have chosen to combine various confessional formularies in *Against Heresies* I, 10.1: pre-baptismal dyadic and triadic, and the older christological, confession.

On a general note, different formulas seem to have been used for the catechetical preparation (pre-baptismal teaching), and for liturgical profession of faith and the threefold interrogation at baptism.[58]

11.3.1 FIRST- TO FOURTH-CENTURY BAPTISMAL ACCOUNTS

Now, more light may be shed on Irenaeus's talk of the Rule being "received," as we study later baptismal accounts, such as Egeria's *Diary of a Pilgrimage* (46).[59] Egeria describes her impressions of catechesis and baptism from the Jerusalem church in the years AD 381–84.[60] Egeria's notes from her Jerusalem visit may be instructive when discerning what Irenaeus meant by the Rule being "received through baptism":

---

56. Cf. Paul F. Bradshaw, *Reconstructing Early Christian Worship* (London: SPCK, 2009), 69–70. *Nomina sacra*, here marked off in small caps, corresponding to the tenth-century miniscule 1739. For the general occurrence of *nomina sacra* in Christian Bible manuscripts from the second century on, see e.g. Hurtado, *Artifacts*, 95–134.

57. See Kelly (*Early Christian Creeds*, 14–19) for additional one-clause christologies, such as Acts 8:16, 19:5 and 1 Cor 6:11; and 1 Cor 12:3, Rom 10:9 and Phil 2:11.

58. Cf. Bradshaw, Reconstructing Early Christian Worship, 69.

59. Cf. also Augustine, *De Symbolo Ad Catechumenos* 1 (NPNF I 3:1): "Receive, my children, the Rule of Faith, which is called the Symbol (or Creed). And when ye have received it, write it in your heart, and be daily saying it to yourself." For connections between the Jerusalem rite as testified by Egeria and Western rites, see Bradshaw, *Reconstructing Early Christian Worship*, 73; cf. ibid., 60. See also Skarsaune (*Troens ord*, 38–76) for an historical overview of various aspects of the Creed in various parts of the early church, with focus on the Apostles' Creed. Skarsaune notes that the *redditio symboli*, that we encounter in Egeria's account, is not present in early third-century accounts, e.g. in Tertullian.

60. See Oskar Skarsaune, *Troens ord: de tre oldkirkelige bekjennelsene* (Oslo: Luther Forlag, 1997), 45f. For a brief historical introduction, see also Kelly, *Early Christian Creeds*, 30–33.

It is the custom here [in Jerusalem], throughout the forty days on which there is fasting, for those who are preparing for baptism to be exorcised by the clergy early in the morning, ... Beginning with Genesis he [the bishop] goes through the whole of Scripture during these forty days, expounding first its literal meaning and then explaining the spiritual meaning. In the course of these days everything is taught not only about the Resurrection but concerning the body of faith. This is called catechetics.

When five weeks of instruction have been completed, they then receive the Creed. He explains the meaning of each of the phrases of the Creed in the same way he explained Holy Scripture, expounding first the literal and then the spiritual sense. In this fashion the Creed is taught. ... Now when seven weeks have gone by and there remains only Holy Week ... each one recites the Creed back to the bishop. (*Itinerarium Egeriae 46*)[61]

The intimate connection that we meet—e.g. in Irenaeus's *Demonstration of the Apostolic Preaching*—between Scripture and *regula*/creedal material also encounters the reader of Egeria's rendering.[62] According to her diary notes, Scripture is read within a creedal and ritual framing. Just as in Irenaeus (*Haer.* I, 9.4), the Creed (or creedal sequences of the *regula*) is "received" during the course of pre-baptismal instruction (the so-called *traditio symboli*). In Holy Week each of the catechumens are then expected to "[recite] the Creed back to the bishop" (the so-called *redditio symboli*).[63]

---

61. *Egeria: Diary of a Pilgrimage*, translated and annotated by George E. Gingras, ACW 38 (New York, N.Y./Mahwah, N.J.: The Newman Press, 1970), 123–24. As for continuities and discontinuities between Rule of Faith, baptismal interrogations and the content of the later declaratory creeds, see Kelly, *Early Christian Creeds*, 40–52; and Liuwe H. Westra, *The Apostles' Creed. Origin, History, and some early Commentaries* (Turnhout: Brepols, 2002), 56–60, 37–43.

62. Cf. Skarsaune, "The Development of Scriptural Interpretation in the Second and Third Centuries," 423–24 (cf. quote above, n. 44)."

63. See Skarsaune, *Troens ord*, 45. Ibid. 46: In Rome, the *redditio symboli* takes place before the whole congregation. Cf. Rufinus, *A Commentary on the Apostles' Creed* 3; ACW 20, trans. J. N. D. Kelly (New York and Mahwah, N.J.: Newman Press, 1954), 31: "[In Rome] the ancient custom is maintained ... whereby candidates who are on the point of receiving the grace of baptism deliver the creed publicly, in the hearing of the congregation of the faithful."

A difference between baptismal teaching in the fourth as compared to the late second century is that the fixed Creed and the *redditio* symboli had not yet seen the day at the time of Irenaeus and Tertullian. Yet, at the highpoint of the Catechumenate, baptism in the Triune name seems to unite several authors, even at the early period we are concentrating on here: Matthew (28:19), Didache (7.1), Justin (1 *Apol.* 61), Irenaeus (*Epid.* 7), Clement of Alexandria (*Strom.* II, 11.2; V, 73.2; *Paed.* I, 42.1) and Tertullian (*Bapt.* 6.1; *Prax.* 26).[64] In Irenaeus's catechetical treatise we thus read:

> Now, this is what faith does for us, ... it admonishes us to remember that we have received baptism for remission of sins in the name of GOD the FATHER, and in the name of JESUS CHRIST, the SON of GOD, who became incarnate and died and was raised, and in the Holy SPIRIT of GOD; and that this baptism is the seal of eternal life and is rebirth unto God. (*Epid.* 3)[65]

Forceful additional testimony to an emerging Christian Trinitarianism and the benefits of the new birth is found in 1 *Clement* (ca. AD 96),[66] referring to "one GOD and one CHRIST and one SPIRIT of grace that was poured out upon us" (1 *Clem.* 46.6; cf. 58.2).[67]

From the above considerations of first- to fourth-century writings, we note the following overall implication for biblical theology: Scripture is read, taught, interpreted, and edited (bipartite OT–NT structure; use of the dyadic/triadic system of *nomina sacra*) within a christological and binitarian/Trinitarian *regula fidei* framework, closely tied to baptism in the Triune name (cf. *Epid.* 1–100).[68]

---

64. The references are listed in Eric Osborn, *The Emergence of Christian Theology* (Cambridge: Cambridge University Press, 1993), 181.

65. ACW 16:49, modified.

66. "Trinitarianism" is here used in a non-technical sense.

67. Codex Alexandrinus demarcates GOD, CHRIST and SPIRIT in 1 *Clem.* 46.6 as *nomina sacra*.

68. Triadic first- and second-century formularies (related to baptism) commonly appear either as GOD, JESUS/CHRIST/LORD, and SPIRIT (1 Cor 12:4–6; 1 *Clem.* 46.6; Just. 1 *Apol.* 61); or as GOD/FATHER, JESUS/CHRIST/SON, and SPIRIT (Matt 28:19; *Did.* 7.1; Just. 1 *Apol.* 61; Iren. *Epid.* 7). *Nomina sacra* demarcations highlighting the former are present, e.g., in P[46] (1 Cor 12:4–6) and Codex Alexandrinus (1 *Clem.* 46.6), and the latter, e.g., in Codex Alexandrinus and the Majority Text (Matt 28:19). See further Bokedal, "The Rule of Faith: Tracing Its Origins," 284.

11.4 CREEDAL CONTEXT: RULE OF FAITH
AND CHRISTOLOGICAL MONOTHEISM

Regula fidei's broad appeal to core textual,[69] ritual[70] and interpretative elements[71] of Christian faith placed this condensed theology of the early church on the same level of earnestness as that attained by the Jewish confession expressed in *The Shema* (Deut 6:4–9). In the Roman context, this confession had immediate political and religious implications embodied in the Jewish exemption from imperial cultic worship.

With regard to phrasing, bishop Irenaeus demonstrates a striking parallel between the Jewish *Shema* and his own formulation of the Rule of Faith in *Against Heresies* III, 1.2 and elsewhere.[72] Having told his readers how the gospel had first been preached orally, but later "by GOD's will," had been "handed down [*tradiderunt*] to us in the Scriptures," (*Haer.* III, 1.1)[73] he goes on to account for the authorship of the texts of the four Evangelists. Following on this brief report, Irenaeus makes an interesting claim pertaining to the Rule of Truth (*regula veritatis*): "These [the four Gospel writers] have all declared to us that there is one GOD, Creator of heaven and earth, announced by the Law and the Prophets; and one CHRIST, the SON of GOD" (*Haer.* III, 1.2; also quoted above).

We see here a second-century phrasing of Christian monotheistic faith that in various forms had first been formulated in the previous century, during the apostolic period. This had amounted to a "reconfiguring of Jewish monotheistic practice and thought" to accommodate Jesus with God as rightful recipient of devotion.[74] The characteristic binitarian structuring of early Christian faith, as found already in Paul (1 Cor 8:5–6; cf. 1 Tim 2:5 and Phil 2:9–11) and John (John 1:1), was thus shaped in a profound way by Early Jewish monotheism.[75] As the New Testament scholar

---

69. E.g., the system of *nomina sacra* and some key texts, such as 1 Cor 8:6 and Matt 28:19f.

70. In particular baptism; Iren. *Haer.* I, 9.4; Tert. *De Corona* 3; Hippol. *Traditio Apostolica* 21.9–18.

71. For example, pre-baptismal teaching; Iren. *Epid.*

72. Similarly *Haer.* I, 10.1; 22.1; III, 11.1; *Epid.* 6; and Tert. *Praescr.* 13; 36; *Virg.* 1; *Prax.* 2.

73. The quote continues: "so that *that* would be *the foundation and pillar of our faith*". Cf. 1 Tim 3:15; 2 Tim 2:15, 19.

74. Larry W. Hurtado, *Lord Jesus Christ: Devotion to Jesus in Earliest Christianity* (Grand Rapids: Eerdmans, 2003), 33.

75. Ibid., 29.

Larry W. Hurtado underlines, "What became 'Christianity' began as a movement within the Jewish religious tradition of the Roman period, and the chief characteristic of Jewish religion in this period was its defiantly monotheistic stance."[76]

Emphasis on monotheistic belief—found as a standard component of the *regula fidei* in the late second century—was an essential part of the Christian movement from the beginning. Not unsurprisingly, only in the New Testament we find the theme of God's oneness addressed some 49 times.[77] Paul and the Gospel writers assume the Jewish confession of God as one. For our purposes, it is particularly worth noticing that the confession of the God of Israel as the only God becomes a defining boundary marker; this is indicated by the early Jewish adoption of *The Shema* as a daily prayer (perhaps alluded to already in the NT; cf. Matt 22:37; Mark 12:29–30, 32; Luke 10:27; John 10:30; Rom 3:28–30; 1 Cor 8:6; Gal 3:20; 1 Tim 2:5; Jas 2:19).[78] Several Early Jewish authors testify to the central place attained by monotheistic belief and confession (*Let. Aris.* 131–32; *Jub.* 12:19–20; Jos., AJ 4:201).[79]

Also in Christian circles, the oneness and uniqueness of God is emphasised from the New Testament period onwards. As pointed out by the late Jaroslav Pelikan, in a discussion on "Creeds in Scripture,"

> [I]n response to a challenge, Jesus recites the primal creed of *The Shema*: "Hear, O Israel: the Lord our God, the Lord is one." In response to another challenge, the apostle Paul also recites *The Shema*, in order then to be able to say that for him and his fellow believers (employing a formula that does sound as though it might itself have come from an earlier Christian creed or hymn), "there

---

76. Ibid.

77. Darina Staudt, *Der eine und einzige Gott: Monotheistische Formeln im Urchristentum und ihre Vorgeschichte bei Griechen und Juden* (Göttingen and Oakville, CT: Vandenhoeck & Ruprecht, 2012), 286–89.

78. See Reinhard Feldmeier and Hermann Spieckermann, *God of the Living: A Biblical Theology* (Waco, TX: Baylor University Press, 2011), 106; Richard Bauckham, *Jesus and the God of Israel: God Crucified and Other Studies on the New Testament's Christology of Divine Identity* (Milton Keynes, UK: Paternoster, 2008), 94–106; and Larry W. Hurtado, "Monotheism," in The Eerdmans Dictionary of Early Judaism, ed. J. J. Collins and D. C. Harlow (Grand Rapids: Eerdmans, 2010), 963.

79. Feldmeier and Spieckermann, *God of the Living*, 107–8.

is one God, the Father, from whom are all things and for whom we exist, and one Lord, Jesus Christ, through whom are all things and through whom we exist." The profession of faith of the first ecumenical council of the church, convoked at Nicaea in 325 likewise in response to a challenge, opens not with a passage from the Gospels or from any other portion of the New Testament but with a Christian version of the same primal creed of Israel, which preceded the New Testament: "We believe in one God." And it does so as the foundation for everything that it then goes on to say about the Son of God as "consubstantial with the Father" [*homōousios tōi patri*].[80]

The Shema is here presented as a key element of Jewish (Jesus) and Christian faith (Paul and subsequent Christians), which, in its own particular way, unifies the Jewish and Christian Scriptures. Pelikan further notes that *The Shema* actually "dictates the language" for the opening lines of a broad spectrum of confessions, Orthodox, Catholic and Protestant.[81]

The *regula fidei* pattern in *Haer.* I, 10.1 that we have been considering above, complies with the creedal matrix laid out by Pelikan. The inclusion of "one" (εἶς) as part of the first and second articles ("in *one* GOD the FATHER" and "in *one* CHRIST JESUS ... our LORD," *Haer.* I, 10.1), but not of the third ("in the Holy SPIRIT"), highlights the similarities between Irenaeus's second-century *regula* and later Eastern creeds, such as the fourth-century Niceno-Constantinopolitan Creed.[82] On this feature Tyrannius Rufinus (ca. AD 345–410) maintains that almost without exception the Eastern churches give the creed in this form, stressing the *oneness* of God the Father and of the Lord Jesus Christ (*A Commentary on the Apostles' Creed* 4). Rufinus here gives credit to the Pauline influence

---

80. Jaroslav Pelikan, *Credo: Historical and Theological Guide to Creeds and Confessions of Faith in the Christian Tradition* (New Haven and London: Yale University Press, 2003), 130–31.

81. Pelikan, *Credo*, 131–32.

82. Jaroslaw Pelikan and Valerie Hotchkiss (eds.), *Creeds & Confessions of Faith in the Christian Tradition*, vol. 1 (New Haven and London: Yale University, 2003), 162.

(1 Cor 8:6):[83] "They confess, you see, ONE GOD and ONE LORD, in deference to the Apostle Paul."[84]

With its stark christological monotheistic emphasis, the *regula fidei* contributes to biblical theology by unifying the monotheistic *a priori* in the Old as well as the New Testament, placing confession in the *one* God and the *one* Christ at the heart of scriptural reading and application (cf. Deut 6:4; Isa 44:6; 45:22–23; 48:12; 1 Cor 8:6; Phil 2:5–11; 1 Tim 2:5; Rev 1:8, 17; 2:8; 21:6; 22:13).[85] Christological monotheism is at the heart also of our third practice (in addition to creedal formulation and the rite of initiation) integral to the church's Rule of Faith, namely the employment of *nomina sacra* as a scriptural supra-text.

11.5 TEXTUAL–SCRIPTURAL CONTEXT: RULE OF FAITH AND *NOMINA SACRA*

The scribal system of *nomina* sacra, introduced above, consists of some four to fifteen specially abbreviated words in Christian Bible manuscripts[86] supplied with a horizontal overbar (God, θϲ; Lord, κϲ, Jesus, ιη, ιηϲ, ιϲ; Christ, χρ, χρϲ, χϲ; Spirit, πνα; cross, ϲτροϲ; Father, πηρ; Son, υϲ; man/human being, ανοϲ; Jerusalem, ιηλμ; Israel, ιηλ; heaven, ουνοϲ; mother, μηρ; David, δαδ; Saviour, ϲηρ).[87]

---

83. Cf. 1 Tim 2:5, Eph 5:5–6 and Gal 3:20.

84. ACW 20:33.

85. Richard Bauckham helpfully comments ("Monotheism and Christology in the Gospel of John," in *Contours of Christology in the New Testament*, ed. Richard N. Longenecker [Grand Rapids, MI and Cambridge, UK: Eerdmans, 2005], 148): "For many scholars the christology of the Fourth Gospel is the 'highest' in the New Testament. In my view, this is a mistake—not in the sense of exaggerating the extent to which true and full divinity is attributed to Jesus in the Fourth Gospel, but in failing to recognize the extent to which this is also the case in most other parts of the New Testament. In my view, a 'christology of divine identity,' in which Jesus is understood to be included in the unique divine identity of the one and only God, the God of Israel, is pervasive in the New Testament writings." See also Martin Hengel, "Christology and New Testament Chronology," in idem, *Between Jesus and Paul: Studies in the Earliest History of Christianity* (Eugene, OR: Wipf & Stock, 1983, 2003), 30–47.

86. *Nomina sacra* are also used in other early Christian writings and elsewhere.

87. For an overview of *nomina sacra*, see Larry W. Hurtado, *The Earliest Christian Artifacts: Manuscripts and Christian Origins* (Grand Rapids: Eerdmans, 2006), 95–134. Substantial criticism of C. M. Tuckett's critique ("'Nomina Sacra:' Yes and No?" in *The Biblical Canons*, eds. J.-M. Auwers and H. J. de Jonge (Leuven: Leuven University Press, 2003), 431–58) of the scholarly majority view concerning the significance of the *nomina sacra* is provided by Hurtado, *Artifacts*, 122–34, and Jane Heath ("Nomina Sacra and Sacra Memoria Before the Monastic Age," *JTS* 61.2 (2010): 518–23).

The fourth-century Codex Vaticanus usually only makes use of the first four of these (GOD, LORD, JESUS, CHRIST),[88] whereas in Codex Sinaiticus, the five first normally are rendered in their *nomina-sacra* forms (GOD, LORD, JESUS, CHRIST, SPIRIT). However, Codex Sinaiticus (fourth century) and also Codex Alexandrinus (fifth century) make use of the whole system of Greek *nomina sacra* (ca. fifteen words), which causes some scholars to interpret the scribal phenomenon in terms of an "embryonic creed" engrafted into the text.[89]

Already in the second and third centuries, these (originally) Greek short forms were present in basically all Christian Bible manuscripts. Their frequent occurrence on a typical Old or New Testament page makes the text not only specifically Christian, but their presence—as a form of supra-textual markers—also helps weaving the Old and New Testament texts into a coherent whole. Furthermore, these four to fifteen words indicate a textual centre: 1) by consistently highlighting a strictly delimited number of names and words (the scribes of Codex Sinaiticus marked off the five standard *nomina sacra*, GOD, LORD, JESUS, CHRIST and SPIRIT in nearly every case), 2) by highlighting the connection between the variously rendered Tetragrammaton (the divine Name) and the *nomina sacra* (cf. esp. the binitarian *nomina sacra* configuration in 1 Cor 8:6: GOD, FATHER, LORD, JESUS, CHRIST),[90] and 3) key terms from the *nomina sacra* word-group (here in small caps)[91] are commonly constituting the main

---

88. Occasionally (some 3 percent of the occurences of the term) the Greek word for "Spirit" (ΠΝΑ) is rendered in its *nomen sacrum* form in the NT portion of Vaticanus.

89. The renowned palaeographer C. H. Roberts (*Manuscript*, 46) famously proposed that the *nomina sacra* "may be plausibly viewed as the creation of the primitive Christian community, representing what might be regarded as the embryonic creed of the first Church." The second-/ third- century NT manuscripts P[45], P[46], P[66] and P[75] contain eight to eleven words frequently written in their *nomina sacra* forms. See further Tomas Bokedal, "Notes on the *Nomina Sacra* and Biblical Interpretation," in *Beyond Biblical Theologies*, eds. H. Assel, S. Beyerle and C. Böttrich (WUNT 295; Tübingen: Mohr Siebeck, 2012), 277–81. (Reprinted as ch. 12 below.)

90. Cf. C. H. Roberts, *Manuscript*, 28.f., and Hurtado, *Artifacts*, 106: "although there is at least a certain broad phenomenological similarity between the *nomina sacra* and Jewish reverential treatment of the divine name, it seems most likely that the specific *nomina sacra* scribal practice represents something distinctive."

91. As for Irenaeus's or his scribe's likely use of *nomina sacra*, see 47 above; cf. also nn. 45-48 and 89.

building blocks of the *regula fidei* formularies, demarcating the three articles of faith, for example in *Demonstration of the Apostolic Preaching* (6):

> And this is the drawing-up of our faith, the foundation of the build-
> ing, and the consolidation of a way of life. GOD, the FATHER, uncre-
> ated, beyond grasp, invisible, one GOD the maker of all; this is **the
> first** and foremost **article of our faith**. But **the second article** is
> the Word of GOD, the SON of GOD, CHRIST JESUS our LORD, who
> was shown forth by the prophets ... and through Him were made
> all things whatsoever. He also, *in the end of times*, for the recapitu-
> lation of all things, is become a MAN among MEN, visible and tan-
> gible, in order to abolish death and bring to light life, and bring
> about the communion of GOD and MAN. And **the third article**
> is the Holy SPIRIT, through whom the prophets prophesied and
> the patriarchs were taught about GOD and the just were led in the
> path of justice, and who *in the end of times* has been poured forth
> in a new manner upon humanity over all the earth renewing MAN
> to GOD. (Iren. *Epid.* 6)[92]

We note the individual *nomina sacra* that may be associated with the three
articles of faith mentioned by Irenaeus: the first article (GOD, FATHER),
the second article (GOD, SON, CHRIST, JESUS, LORD, MAN), and the third
article (SPIRIT, MAN).

We are now in a position to make the present chapter's discussion
of the *regula fidei* somewhat more concrete. As our focus is the *regula*
as emergent biblical theology, we approach the Rule of Faith (or Rule-
of-Faith pattern of biblical reading) as a normative hermeneutical tool
that promotes the textual OT–NT dynamics and the theological unity of
Christian Scripture. In terms of function, this Rule may to some degree
even be equated with the two discussed editorial devices: the creedal pattern expressed through the *nomina sacra* in their intra-scriptural context,
and the particular arrangement of the Scriptures provided by the titles
"Old" and "New Testament." The creedal and hermeneutical concern of
the *regula fidei* is expressed also through these parallel editorial aids to

---

92. ACW 16:51, modified.

Scripture reading. In this sense, the two titles and the *nomina sacra*—being inscribed into the biblical manuscript tradition from the second century onwards—make the Rule-of-Faith pattern visible on the Old and New Testament page.

11.5.1 *NOMINA SACRA* AND BIBLICAL INTERPRETATION

The four earliest *nomina sacra* introduced into Christian Bible manuscripts were the Greek abbreviations for "God" (ΘС), "Lord" (ΚС), "Jesus" (ΙΗ, ΙΗС, ΙС) and "Christ" (ΧΡ, ΧΡС, ΧС). The special demarcation of these within the New Testament context is particularly conspicuous in passages such as 1 Cor 8:6, which highlights the *nomina sacra* short forms, while keeping the plural forms "gods" and "lords" written in full (8:5). Most of the ca. 50 Greek manuscripts containing 1 Cor 8:4–6 mentioned by Reuben Swanson in his *New Testament Greek Manuscripts* make this distinction between the singular (marked off as *nomina sacra*) and plural forms (written in full). To the same effect, in Codices Vaticanus and Sinaiticus, the use of "god" in the plural, θεοί (written in full),[93] is found eight times in the New Testament (John 10:34, 35; 1 Cor 8:5 (twice); Gal 4:8; Acts 7:40; 14:11 and 19:26).[94] In all eight cases the meaning is non-sacral. All other New Testament occurrences of the sacral word "God" are rendered in their contracted forms (ΘС).[95]

Forceful *nomina sacra* constellations involved in Scripture exposition concern Jesus and his cross. In our earliest NT manuscripts, these words are written in their *nomina sacra* forms ca. 100 and 95 per cent, respective-ly.[96] Our earliest example, however, comes from the *Epistle of Barnabas* and concerns a discussion of an OT manuscript—containing a *nomen sacrum* abbreviation for Jesus and the letter T, symbolizing the cross. The passage in *Barn.* 9 consists of a play with numbers, where the symbolic

---

93. Reuben Swanson (ed.), *New Testament Greek Manuscripts: Variant Readings Arranged in Horizontal Lines Against Codex Vaticanus. 1 Corinthians* (Wheaton, IL: Tyndale House Publishers, and Pasadena, CA: William Carey International University Press, 2003), 113f.

94. Similarly John 10:34–35 in P[66] and P[75], where the plural forms of "god" are written *plene*.

95. Bokedal, "Notes on the *Nomina Sacra*," 263–95, esp. 283–84 (reprinted as ch. 12 below).

96. Ibid., 273–76; the calculation is based on 74 second- to fourth-century NT manuscripts. For cross as a *nomen sacrum* occasionally containing the staurogram, see Hurtado, *Artifacts*, 134 and 135–54.

meaning of Abraham's 318 (written with the Greek letters TIH) servants in Genesis 14:14 is pondered:

> The number eighteen [in Greek] consists of an Iota [I], 10, and an Eta [H], 8. There you have Jesus. And because the cross was about to have grace in the letter Tau [T], he next gives the three hundred, Tau. And so he shows the name Jesus by the first two letters, and the cross by the other. For the one who has placed the implanted gift of his covenant in us knew these things. No one has learned a more reliable lesson from me. But I know that you are worthy. (*Barn.* 9.8f.)[97]

The central place of Christ and his cross is found not only in the *Epistle of Barnabas*, or in Paul (1 Cor 1:17; Gal 6:14), but also in other early Christian writers like Ignatius of Antioch. The latter makes some interesting comments on this theme when discussing Christ in the Scriptures: "For me, JESUS CHRIST is the ancient records [the Jewish Scriptures]; the sacred ancient records are his CROSS and death, and his resurrection, and the faith that comes through him."[98]

Similarly in Irenaeus, a hermeneutically revealing passage is found in *Against Heresies*:

> For if anyone reads the Scriptures with attention, he will find in them an account of CHRIST ... for CHRIST is the treasure which was hid in the field ... And, for this reason, indeed, when at this present time the law is read to the Jews, it is like a fable; for they do not possess the explanation of all things pertaining to the advent of the SON of GOD, which took place in human nature; but when it is read by the Christians, it is a treasure, hid indeed in a field, but brought to light by the CROSS of CHRIST. ... (*Haer.* IV, 26.1)[99]

As the scribal system of *nomina sacra* soon included additional words beyond the initial four (GOD, LORD, JESUS, CHRIST), such as CROSS,

---

97. *The Apostolic Fathers*, ed. Bart D. Ehrman, 2 vols., LCL 25 (Cambridge, MA: Harvard University Press, 2003), 2:45–47, modified.

98. *The Apostolic Fathers*, LCL 25, 291f., modified.

99. ANF 1:496, modified.

SPIRIT, FATHER and SON, the appearance of the biblical text was affected. A passage like Matthew 28:19, which seems to have influenced baptismal and creedal formularies,[100] thus attained more prominence also in terms of its *nomina sacra* demarcations. Editorial variations of this Matthean passage can be seen, from no words marked off as *nomina sacra* in Codex Vaticanus, to one in Bezae (SPIRIT), two in Sinaiticus and Washingtonianus (FATHER and SPIRIT), and three in Alexandrinus and the Majority Text: "in the name of the FATHER and of the SON and of the Holy SPIRIT" (Matt 28:19). For comparison, we may consider also the scene of Jesus' baptism in Matt 3:16–17. Words highlighted as *nomina sacra* in this passage are: JESUS, SPIRIT and GOD in Codex Vaticanus and Codex Washingtonianus (fourth/fifth century), and JESUS, SPIRIT, GOD, HEAVEN, and SON in Codex Sinaiticus.

From the above discussion of the scribal *nomina sacra* convention, the following themes may be considered when commenting and elaborating on the early faith community's biblical theology:

1. The centrality of the cross of Christ: The theme of JESUS CHRIST and the CROSS appear in several key texts from the first to early third century AD (cf. 1 Cor 1:17f.; Gal 3:1; *Barn.* 9, 11–12; Ign. *Phld.* 8.2; Just. *1 Apol.* 55; Iren. *Haer.* IV, 26.1; Tert. *Marc.* III, 22). "Cross" and "crucify" are highlighted as *nomina sacra* in second-/third-century NT papyri P[45], P[46], P[66] and P[75]. We note that reference to Jesus being nailed to the cross (*cruci fixum*) is part of Tertullian's account of the *regula fidei* in *Praescr.* 13.

2. The early binitarian structure (christological monotheism): The common binitarian pattern "one GOD, the FATHER ... and one CHRIST JESUS ... our LORD," found, e.g., in *Haer.* I,

100. See, e.g., Wolfram Kinzig and Markus Vinzent, "Recent Research on the Origin of the Creed," *JTS* 50 (1999): 535–59, 554–55; cf. Kelly, *Early Christian Creeds*, 12: "The Trinitarianism of the New Testament is rarely explicit; but the frequency with which the triadic schema recurs ... suggests that this pattern was implicit in Christian theology from the start." For the relationship between baptismal interrogations, *regula fidei* and the content of the later declaratory creeds, see ibid., 40–52; and Liuwe H. Westra, *The Apostles' Creed. Origin, History, and some early Commentaries* (Turnhout: Brepols, 2002), 56–60, 37–43.

10.1, highlights the same words that are emphasized through *nomina sacra* demarcations in 1 Cor 8:6 (P⁴⁶).

3. The standard triadic structure (non-technical Trinitarianism): The triadic pattern "GOD the FATHER … CHRIST JESUS, SON of GOD/LORD … and the Holy SPIRIT," present in *Haer.* I, 10.1 and *Epid.* 6, seems to share a similar textual–creedal emphasis as that inherent in the *nomina sacra* found in Matt 28:19 (Codex Alexandrinus and the Majority Text), Matt 3:16–17 (Codex Vaticanus), 1 *Clem.* 46.6 (Codex Alexandrinus), and 1 Cor 12:4–6 (P⁴⁶).

4. The prominence of christological titles and sequences: The frequently occurring Christ-sequences "SON of GOD … CHRIST JESUS our LORD" have the same words emphasized as those written as *nomina sacra* in central New Testament christologies (Rom 1:4 (Codex Alexandrinus); 1 Cor 1:9 (P⁴⁶); Matt 16:16 (Codex Sinaiticus); John 11:27 (Codex Sinaiticus) and 20:31 (Codex Sinaiticus).

11.6 THE EARLY RULE-OF-FAITH PATTERN AS EMERGENT BIBLICAL THEOLOGY: A PROPOSAL

By the late first century, the *nomina sacra*—highlighting a selection of particularly sacred figures of Christian faith—had been introduced into the Scriptures, providing implicit guide lines for Bible reading and exposition (cf. *Barn.* 9.8; *Clem. Strom.* VI, 2.84.3–4). A century later, when the Rule of Faith attained pride of place in Christian discourse, the titles "Old" and "New Testament" were coined for the main sections of the Christian Bible.[101]

---

101. According to Eusebius (*Hist. Eccl.* III, 3.1), Melito of Sardis (ca. AD 175) employs the term "Old Testament" as a title for the collection of the Jewish Scriptures (the Old Testament). A couple of decades later, Clement of Alexandria and Tertullian use the newly introduced term "New Testament" (*Strom.* I, 5.28.2: ἡ καινὴ διαθήκη; *Marc.* IV, 1: Tertullian uses the Latin terms *Testamentum* or *Instrumentum* to designate the main sections of the bipartite Christian Bible).

I propose that both these editorial devices could be understood as deliberate attempts by the early church to closely link Christian Scripture to the emerging "apostolic" *regula fidei* pattern.

By way of summary, within a Christian Scripture-based, creedal-monotheistic and ritual setting, a major function of the dyadic/triadic Rule-of-Faith pattern of scriptural reading was biblical-theological: To guarantee that the faith community "read the Old Testament as the promise of the Gospel and the Gospel as the fulfilment of that promise."[102] To this effect the *regula fidei* functioned as a normative hermeneutical tool, promoting the textual and theological unity of, as well as the distinction between, the corpus of Old and New Testament Scriptures (Iren. *Haer.* I, 8.1–10.1; Clem. *Strom.* VI, 15.125.3).

The ancient readers' decision to introduce the system of *nomina sacra* (probably first century AD) into their communal literature,[103] and to designate the two main sections of their Scriptures by the labels "The Old" and "The New Testament" (probably late second century AD),[104] effectively helped to accomplish this task.[105] [106]

BIBLIOGRAPHY

Augustine. *De Symbolo Ad Catechumenos* 1. Edited by Alexander Roberts, James Donaldson, Philip Schaff and Henry Wace. Second edition. NPNF I, 3:1; Hendrickson, 1996.

Bauckham, Richard. *Jesus and the God of Israel: God Crucified and Other Studies on the New Testament's Christology of Divine Identity.* Milton Keynes, UK: Paternoster, 2008.

---

102. Edwards, *Catholicity and Heresy*, 40.

103. See n. 45 above.

104. Earliest use of "Old Testament" in this sense is documented in Melito of Sardis (Euseb. *Hist. Eccl.* IV, 26.12–14); and of "New Testament" in Clement of Alexandria (*Strom.* I, 5.28.2) and Tertullian (*Marc.* IV, 1). See Trobisch, *The First Edition of the New Testament*, 43–44.

105. Scholars who have based their biblical theology/hermeneutics on the *regula fidei* include Peter Stuhlmacher (*How To Do Biblical Theology*, Princeton Theological Monograph Series, 38 (Eugene, OR: Pickwick Publications, 1995), 61–3) and Robert W. Jenson ("Hermeneutics and the Life of the Church," in *Reclaiming the Bible for the Church*, eds. Jenson and Braaten (Grand Rapids: Eerdmans, 1995), 96–98).

106. I would like to thank Chance M. Gorman for proofreading and commenting on the manuscript, and the two reviewers of this journal for valuable feedback.

————. "Monotheism and Christology in the Gospel of John." Pages 148–66 in *Contours of Christology in the New Testament*. Edited by Richard N. Longenecker. Grand Rapids, MI and Cambridge, UK: Eerdmans, 2005.

Beyschlag, Karlmann. *Grundriß der Dogmengeschichte*. Vol. 1. Darmstadt: Wissenschaftliche Buchgesellschaft, 1982.

Blowers, Paul M. "The *Regula Fidei* and the Narrative Character of Early Christian Faith." *Pro Ecclesia* 6 (1997): 199–228.

Bokedal, Tomas. "Notes on the *Nomina Sacra* and Biblical Interpretation." Pages 277–81 in Beyond Biblical Theologies. Edited by H. Assel, S. Beyerle and C. Böttrich. WUNT 295; Tübingen: Mohr Siebeck, 2012.

————. "The Rule of Faith: Tracing Its Origins." *Journal of Theological Interpretation*, 7.2 (2013): 233–55.

Bradshaw, Paul F. *Reconstructing Early Christian Worship*. London: SPCK, 2009.

Bruce, F. F. "Scripture in Relation to Tradition and Reason." Pages 35–64 in *Scripture, Tradition and Reason: A Study in the Criteria of Christian Doctrine. Essays in Honour of Richard P. C. Hanson*. Edited by Richard Bauckham and Benjamin Drewery. London: T&T Clark, 1998.

Countryman, L. Wm. "Tertullian and the Regula Fidei." *Second Century* 2 (1982): 208–27.

Edwards, Mark. *Catholicity and Heresy in the Early Church*. Farnam, Surrey: Ashgate, 2009.

Egeria: Diary of a Pilgrimage. Translated and annotated by George E. Gingras. ACW 38. New York, N.Y./Mahwah, N.J.: The Newman Press, 1970.

Eusebius. *Historia Ecclesiastica* IV, 23.4. LCL, Vol. 153. Translated by Kirsopp Lake; Cambridge, MA and London: Harvard University, 1926.

Feldmeier, Reinhard, and Hermann Spieckermann. *God of the Living: A Biblical Theology*. Waco, TX: Baylor University Press, 2011.

Flesseman-van Leer, Ellen. *Tradition and Scripture in the Early Church.* Leiden: Gorcum & Prakke, 1953.

Hägglund, Bengt. "Die Bedeutung der 'regula fidei' als Grundlage theologischer Aussagen," *Studia Theologica* 12.1 (1958): 1–44.

———. *Sanningens regel—Regula veritatis. Trosregeln och den kristna traditionens struktur.* Skellefteå: Artos & Norma bokförlag, 2003.

Harnack, Adolf von. *Lehrbuch der Dogmengeschichte, vol. 1, Die Entstehung des kirchlichen Dogmas.* First edition. Freiburg: Mohr, 1886.

Heath, Jane. "Nomina Sacra and Sacra Memoria Before the Monastic Age." *JTS* 61.2 (2010): 516-49.

Hefner, Philip. "Theological Methodology and St. Irenaeus." *The Journal of Religion* 44.4 (1964), 294–309.

Hengel, Martin. "Christology and New Testament Chronology." Pages 30–47 in *Between Jesus and Paul: Studies in the Earliest History of Christianity.* Eugene, OR: Wipf & Stock, 1983, 2003.

———. *The Septuagint as Christian Scripture: Its Prehistory and the Problem of Its Canon.* Translated by Biddle. London and New York: T&T Clark, 2002.

Hurtado, Larry W. *The Earliest Christian Artifacts: Manuscripts and Christian Origins.* Grand Rapids: Eerdmans, 2006.

———. *Lord Jesus Christ: Devotion to Jesus in Earliest Christianity.* Grand Rapids: Eerdmans, 2003.

———. "Monotheism." Pages 961–64 in The Eerdmans Dictionary of Early Judaism. Edited by J. J. Collins and D. C. Harlow. Grand Rapids: Eerdmans, 2010.

———. "The Origin of the Nomina Sacra: A Proposal." *JBL* 117.4 (1998): 655–73.

St. Irenaeus of Lyons. *Against the Heresies.* Vol. 1. ACW 55. Translated and annotated by Dominic J. Unger with further revisions by John J. Dillon. New York, N.Y./Mahwah, N.J.: The Newman Press, 1992.

————. *Against the Heresies*. Vol. 2. ACW 65. Translated and annotated by Dominic J. Unger with further revisions by John J. Dillon New York, N.Y./Mahwah, N.J.: The Newman Press, 2012.

————. *Proof of the Apostolic Preaching*. ACW 16. Translated by Joseph P. Smith; New York: Newman Press, 1952.

————. *Contre les heresies 3*. Sources chrétiennes 210 and 211, Book 3/1 and 3/2. Edited and translated by Adelin Rousseau and Louis Doutreleau. Paris, 1974.

Jenson, Robert W. "Hermeneutics and the Life of the Church." Pages 89–105 in *Reclaiming the Bible for the Church*. Edited by Jenson and Braaten. Grand Rapids: Eerdmans, 1995.

Kattenbusch, Ferdinand. *Das apostolische Symbol. Seine Entstehung, sein geschichtlicher Sinn, seine ursprüngliche Stellung im Kultus und in der Geschichte der Kirche. Ein Beitrag zur Symbolik und zur Dogmengeschichte*. Vol. 1. Leipzig: J. C. Hinrichs'sche Buchhandlung, 1894.

Kelly, J. N. D. *Early Christian Creeds*. Third edition. New York: Longman, 1972.

Kinzig, Wolfram. "Καινὴ διαθήκη: The Title of the New Testament in the Second and Third Century." *JTS* 45.2 (1994): 519–44.

Wolfram Kinzig and Markus Vinzent. "Recent Research on the Origin of the Creed," *JTS* 50 (1999): 535–59.

Kunze, Johannes. *Glaubensregel, Heilige Schrift und Taufbekenntnis: Untersuchungen über die dogmatische Autorität, ihr Werden und ihre Geschichte, vornehmlich in der alten Kirche*. Leipzig: Dörffling & Franke, 1899.

Lawson, John. *The Biblical Theology of St. Irenaeus*. London: Epworth Press, 1948.

Lietzmann, Hans. *A History of the Early Church*. Vol. 1. Cambridge: James Clarke & Co., 1951, 1993.

Molland, Einar. *The Conception of the Gospel in the Alexandrian*. Oslo: Det Norske Videnskaps-Akademi, 1938.

Ohlig, Karl-Heinz. *Die theologische Begründung des neutestamentlichen Kanons in der alten Kirche*. Düsseldorf: Patmos-Verlag, 1972.

Ohme, Heinz. *Kanon ekklesiastikos: Die Bedeutung des altkirchlichen Kanonbegriffs.* Arbeiten zur Kirchengeschichte, Bd. 67. Berlin: Walter de Gruyter, 1998.

Osborn, Eric. *The Emergence of Christian Theology.* Cambridge: Cambridge University Press, 1993.

———. *Irenaeus of Lyons.* Cambridge: Cambridge University, 2001.

Pelikan, Jaroslav. *Credo: Historical and Theological Guide to Creeds and Confessions of Faith in the Christian Tradition.* New Haven and London: Yale University Press, 2003.

Pelikan, Jaroslaw and Valerie Hotchkiss, eds. *Creeds & Confessions of Faith in the Christian Tradition.* Vol. 1. New Haven and London: Yale University, 2003.

Roberts, Colin H. *Manuscript, Society and Belief in Early Christian Egypt, Schweich Lectures 1977.* London: Oxford University Press, published for the British Academy, 1979.

Rufinus. *A Commentary on the Apostles' Creed 3.* ACW 20. Translated by J. N. D. Kelly. New York and Mahwah, N.J.: Newman Press, 1954.

Schmidt, Andreas. "Der mögliche Text von P.Oxy. III 405, Z. 39–45." *NTS* 37 (1991): 160.

Seeberg, Reinhold. *Lehrbuch der Dogmengeschichte.* Vol. 1. Second Edition. Leipzig, 1908.

Skarsaune, Oskar. "The Development of Scriptural Interpretation in the Second and Third Centuries – except Clement and Origen." Pages 373–442 in *Hebrew Bible/Old Testament: The History of Its Interpretation.* Vol. 1. Edited by M. Sæbø. Göttingen: Vandenhoeck & Ruprecht, 1996.

———. *Troens ord: de tre oldkirkelige bekjennelsene.* Oslo: Luther Forlag, 1997.

Staudt, Darina. *Der eine und einzige Gott: Monotheistische Formeln im Urchristentum und ihre Vorgeschichte bei Griechen und Juden.* Göttingen and Oakville, CT: Vandenhoeck & Ruprecht, 2012.

Stewart, Alistair. "'The Rule of Truth . . . which He Received through Baptism' (*Haer.* I, 9.4): Catechesis, Ritual, and Exegesis in

Irenaeus's Gaul." Pages 151–58 in *Irenaeus: Life, Scripture, Legacy*.
    Edited by Paul Foster and Sara Parvis. Minneapolis: Fortress,
    2012.
Stuhlmacher, Peter. *How To Do Biblical Theology*. Princeton Theological
    Monograph Series, 38. Eugene, OR: Pickwick Publications, 1995.
Swanson, Reuben ed. *New Testament Greek Manuscripts: Variant
    Readings Arranged in Horizontal Lines Against Codex Vaticanus.
    1 Corinthians.* Wheaton, IL: Tyndale House Publishers, and
    Pasadena, CA: William Carey International University Press,
    2003.
Trobisch, David. *The First Edition of the New Testament*. Oxford: Oxford
    University Press, 2000.
Tuckett's, C. M.. "'Nomina Sacra:' Yes and No?" Pages 431–58 in *The
    Biblical Canons*. Edited by J.-M. Auwers and H. J. de Jonge.
    Leuven: Leuven University Press, 2003.
Westra, Liuwe H. *The Apostles' Creed. Origin, History, and some early
    Commentaries.* Turnhout: Brepols, 2002.
Young, Frances. "Christian teaching." Pages 91–104 in *The Cambridge
    History of Early Christian Literature*. Edited by F. Young, L. Ayres
    and A. Louth. Cambridge: Cambridge University, 2004.
Zahn, Theodor. "Glaubensregel." Page 6:685 in *Realencyklopädie für
    protestantische Theologie und Kirche*. Edited by Albert Hauck;
    Leipzig: J. C. Hinrichs, 1899.

PART E

CHRIST THE CENTER:
NOMINA SACRA AND
BIBLICAL INTERPRETATION

12

NOTES ON THE *NOMINA SACRA* AND BIBLICAL INTERPRETATION

12.1 INTRODUCTION

A historic discovery. A waste-paper site of letters, books, contracts—secular and religious—written on papyrus from about 300 BC to AD 700, all relatively well-preserved under the Egyptian desert sand. Oxyrhynchus, 160 kilometers South-West of Cairo—an El Dorado for papyrologists and scholars of various disciplines. Between 1896 and 1907 the British archaeologists Bernard Grenfell and Arthur Hunt uncover half a million writings or fragments; one hundred years later, only just over one percent of them—6,000 texts—have been analysed and published,[1] while collections of unpublished papyri are held at several universities.[2] The sheer quantity and range of the material poses a real question to researchers: How can scholars find texts relevant to their particular areas of interest? For instance, a biblical scholar may want to know if a fragment is Christian. It would, of course, be very helpful if there were some kind of a marker, a *signum*, immediately indicating if a document is of Christian provenance.

Here a peculiar Christian scribal feature comes to our aid—a textual code providing quick visual access to some central Christian keywords.

---

1. See http://www.ees.ac.uk/research/Oxyrhynchus%20Papyri.html [accessed 01/05/10].

2. Owned by the Egypt Exploration Society, the bulk of the papyri is today housed for the Society by the University of Oxford in the Sackler Library.

Apparently already from the 1ˢᵗ (or perhaps the early 2ⁿᵈ) century, scribes
serving the Christian communities used a special device to textually mark
off the divine name and a few other sacred, or religiously important, Greek
names and their inflection forms.[3] They did this by contraction or suspension or a combination of both, according to a particular pattern—
usually by writing the first and last letters of the word—and by adding
a supralinear line above the abbreviation.[4] As one of their characteristic editorial features, the Greek Christian scriptures typically contained
these special markings of the names "God," "Lord," "Jesus," "Christ" and
"Spirit"—ΘΕΟC (ΘΥ), ΚΥΡΙΟC (ΚΣ), ΙΗCΟΥC (ΙΣ, ΙΗ, ΙΗC), ΧΡΙCΤΟC
(ΧC, ΧΡ, ΧΡC) and ΠΝΕΥΜΑ (ΠΝΑ) (the abbreviations in parenthe-
ses; the unaccented majuscule Greek characters and the open sigma are
characteristic of the early Greek papyri and parchments). In the 4ᵗʰ century Codex Sinaiticus these five names are abbreviated in almost every
case throughout the Old and New Testaments,[5] and the same tendency is
seen already in the 2ⁿᵈ- to early-4ᵗʰ-century manuscripts.[6] In Greek palaeography and biblical studies these intrinsically or contextually religious
terms—emphasized by abbreviation with an overbar drawn across the
word—are usually called *nomina sacra*—"sacred names."[7]

This scribal pattern is consistently carried out also in other early
Christian sources, so the scholars working with the papyri from
Oxyrhynchus can often use it to quickly find out if a text is of Christian
provenance. Paul Schubert in the recently published *Oxford Handbook of*

---

3. On dating, see Larry W. Hurtado, "The Origin of the *Nomina Sacra*: A Proposal", *Journal of Biblical Literature* 117 (1998): 660: "Allowing even minimal time for the practice to gain sufficient recognition and standardization would require an origin no later than the first century". The British palaeographer Colin H. Roberts (*Manuscript, Society and Belief in Early Christian Egypt*, Schweich Lectures 1977 (London: Oxford University Press, published for the British Academy, 1979)), has suggested a pre-70 dating for the introduction of *nomina sacra* in the Christian manuscript tradition.

4. Suspension, contraction, and a combination of both, respectively for the name ΙΗCΟΥC written in the nominative case: ΙΣ, ΙΗ, ΙΗC.

5. Dirk Jongkind, *Scribal Habits of Codex Sinaiticus* (Piscataway, N.J.: Gorgias Press, 2007), 64–7, based on an analysis of 175.4 folios.

6. For statistics on ΠΝΕΥΜΑ as a *nomen sacrum*, see 12.3.1–2 below.

7. The centred *linea superscripta* is typically drawn across all letters of the abbreviation (suspen-sion, contraction or conflation), though not always covering the whole word, but sometimes only half to three quarters of the space above the abbreviation (see e.g. the online display of Codex Sinaiticus, http://www.codex-sinaiticus.net/en).

Papyrology therefore can say that these names,[8] or rather combinations of names, "immediately indicate a Christian context."[9]

Beside the five above listed names, though usually not as consistently rendered in the Greek manuscript tradition, some ten other words are often marked off in this way.[10] The most important, occurring in the earliest New Testament manuscripts (2nd to early 4th century), are CTΑΥΡΟC/CTΑΥΡΟW (C̄T̄Ρ̄Ο̄C̄, C̄Ρ̄C̄, "cross/crucify"),[11] ΑΝΘΡW-ΠΟC (ᾹΝ̄Ο̄C̄, "man/human," including references to Jesus, e.g. "Son of Man"), ΠΑΤΗΡ (Π̄Ρ̄, Π̄Η̄Ρ̄, "Father," including references to God as Father), and ΥΙΟC (Ȳ̄C̄, "Son," including references to Jesus as Son).[12] Two further words, ΙΕΡΟΥCΑΛΗΜ (Ῑ̄Λ̄Η̄Μ̄, "Jerusalem") and ΙCΡΑΗΛ (Ῑ̄Η̄Λ̄, "Israel"), also occur as contractions with relative high frequency. The remaining four of the standard fifteen *nomina sacra*, arguably entering the list a little later (perhaps 3rd to 4th century), are not as consistently abbreviated.[13] They include: ΟΥΡΑΝΟC (Ο̄ῩΝ̄Ο̄C̄, "heaven"),

---

8. Arguments for a possible Jewish origin of the *nomina sacra*, advanced first by Ludwig Traube in 1907, have recently been made by James R. Edwards for the occurrence of ΘΕΟC written as a *nomen sacrum* in the Sardis Synagogue, "A Nomen Sacrum in the Sardis Synagogue", *JBL* 128, 4 (2009): 813–821. For a wider discussion on the possible Jewish origin of the practice, see Kurt Treu, "Die Bedeutung des Griechischen für die Juden im römischen Reich," *Kairos* 15 (1973): 123–44; English translation by Adler and Kraft can be found at http://eawc.evansville.edu/essays/nepage.htm [accessed 15/05/10]. See section 12.2 below.

9. Paul Schubert, "Editing a Papyrus", in Roger Bagnall (ed.), *The Oxford Handbook of Papyrology* (Oxord and New York: Oxford University Press, 2009), 200: Cf. Larry W. Hurtado, *The Earliest Christian Artifacts: Manuscripts and Christian Origins* (Grand Rapids, MI and Cambridge, UK: Eerdmans, 2006), 96: "The *nomina sacra* are so familiar a feature of Christian manuscripts that papyrologists often take the presence of these forms as sufficient to identify even a fragment of a manuscript as indicating its probable Christian provenance." Presence of *nomina sacra* is a relatively useful, but not, however, an absolute criterion of Christian provenance; cf. Christopher M. Tuckett, "'Nomina Sacra'—Yes and No?", Auwers and Jonge (eds.), *The Biblical Canons* (163; Belgium: Leuven University Press, Uitgeverij Peeters, 2003), 433. See also Kurt and Barbara Aland, *The Text of the New Testament: An Introduction to the Critical Editions and to the Theory and Practice of Modern Textual Criticism* (2nd edition; translated by Erroll F. Rhodes; Grand Rapids, MI: Eerdmans, 1989), 76.

10. For cccasional other names treated as *nomina sacra*, see below.

11. In the 2nd- to early-4th-century manuscripts CTΑΥΡΟC, but not CTΑΥΡΟW, is as consistently contracted as ΠΝΕΥΜΑ (see 3.1 below).

12. Besides the five regularly demarcated *nomina sacra* these additional four words occur contracted, e.g., in the important 2nd/early-3rd-century P[46] and in P[66], usually dated to ca. AD 200. In the early-3rd-century P[45], these same *nomina sacra* occur, except for ΑΝΘΡWΠΟC (in one instance ΧΡΙCΤΙΑΝΟΙ and in another ΥΨΟW are written as *nomina sacra* in P[45]). Similarly in P[47] (from the second half of the 3rd century), however with the exception for ΥΙΟC and CTΑΥΡΟC/CTΑΥΡΟW.

13. However, cf. 12.6.1 below.

MHTHP (M̄H̄P̄, "mother," including references to Jesus' mother), ⲆⲀⲨⲒⲆ (ⲆⲀⲆ, "David"), and CⲰTHP (C̄H̄P̄, C̄Ⲱ̄P̄), "saviour").[14] Beyond these, in a few instances words like MⲰYCHC (M̄Ⲱ̄, "Moses") in the Egerton fragments and ⲀⲒMⲀ (Ā̄Ī̄M̄Ā̄, "blood," as part of the phrase "the blood of Christ," Heb 9:14) in P[46] may also be marked off.[15] However, these latter two together with some other very rare occurrences of similar demarcations (by abbreviation or by the word written in full with a supralinear line) are to be treated as exceptions to the rule of the rather strictly limited number of words highlighted as *nomina sacra*. So, apart from such exceptions, the number tends to be limited to four or five (P[13]; the NT portion of Codex Vaticanus; the Latin text of Codex Bezae),[16] eight (P[45]; Codex Bezae),[17] nine (P[46]; P[66]),[18] eleven (P[75]),[19] thirteen (Codex Washingtonianus),[20] or some fifteen Christian keywords in the more devel-

---

14. Cf. 12.4.4 below. In the above enumeration and comments of the individual *nomina sacra* I am indebted to the similar list in Hurtado, *Artifacts*, 97f.

15. In P[15] KOCMOC is written similarly with a stroke over the word. In P[72] (P. Bodmer VII and VIII) the following words are written with a suprascript line: ⲆYNⲀMIC (abbreviated), NⲰⲈ, ⲀBPⲀⲀM, CⲀPPⲀ, MIXⲀHⲀ and ⲈNⲰX.

16. See also 12.4.1, below. On *nomina sacra* in Codex Bezae, see David C. Parker, *Codex Bezae: An Early Christian Manuscript and Its Text* (Cambridge: Cambridge University), 97–106. In the 2008 Accordance edition of the New Testament of Codex Vaticanus, based on the Tischendorf transcription, 2.9 percent of the occurrences of "Spirit" are contracted (10 occurrences in Matt 1:8, 20; 3:11, 16; 4:1; 22:43; Mark 1:8; 12:36; Acts 10:38; Phil 4:23), whereas "Father" (Matt 10:32) and "Israel" (Rom 11:2) are only contracted once each (0.3% and 1.6% respectively). In the Book of Jeremiah in Vaticanus, as a comparison, ⲠNⲈYMⲀ is abbreviated as a *nomen sacrum* 5 out of 6 times (83.3%), all of which are non-sacral (Jer 4:11, 12; 10:14; 28:11, 17); see Georg A. Walser, *Jeremiah: A Commentary Based on Ieremias in Codex Vaticanus* (Septuagint Commentary Series; Leiden: Brill, 2012).

17. The following eight *nomina sacra* are found in P[45] (early 3rd century) and Codex Bezae Cantabrigiensis (5th century): "Jesus," "Christ" (including one instance of "Christian" in P[45]), "Lord," "God," "Spirit," "Father," "Son" and "cross" (including "crucify" in Codex Bezae).

18. P[46] (2nd/early 3rd century) and P[66] (ca. 200) contain the same eight *nomina sacra* as Codex Bezae with the addition of anqrwpos. In P[46] ⲀⲒMⲀ is once written in full with a crossbar above the word. All other 29 occasions of ⲀⲒMⲀ in P[46] are written in full without a stroke.

19. P[75] contains the following *nomina sacra*: "Jesus," "Christ," "Lord," God," "Spirit," "Father," "Son," "man," "cross," "Israel" and "Jerusalem." The only occurrence of "saviour" (John 4:42) is written in full, as are all occurrences of "mother," "heaven" and "David."

20. Codex W does not include "Jerusalem" and "cross/crucify" among the *nomina sacra*. "Saviour" is abbreviated once. See the 2008 Accordance Electronic edition by OakTree Software, based on the New Testament Manuscripts in the Freer Collection, Part I: The Washington Manuscript of the Four Gospels, by Henry A. Sanders. New York: Macmillan, 1912.

oped 4ᵗʰ- and 5ᵗʰ-century system (Codex Sinaiticus; Codex Alexandrinus; see 12.4.1–3 below).[21]

The *nomina sacra* occur in practically all Greek New Testament and Christian Septuagint manuscripts. Obviously, this set of words is Christian or Jewish-Christian, the early core of which—"God," "Lord," "Jesus," "Christ"—appears to be divine names, *nomina divina*, or names intimately associated with the divine name.[22] With a few exceptions, scholars generally agree that the 3ʳᵈ- and 4ᵗʰ-century system of *nomina sacra* is appropriately described by this name.[23] Reflecting on their potential meaning, Larry Hurtado has argued that the *nomina sacra* should be looked at as a particular instance of early Christian interest in "visualizing" forms of piety, not only for scribes and readers, but perhaps also for a wider public of occasional onlookers.[24] C. H. Roberts has famously suggested that the *nomina sacra* "may be plausibly viewed as the creation of the primitive Christian community, representing what might be regarded as the embryonic creed of the first Church."[25] To Christopher M. Tuckett *nomina sacra* may have been introduced as reading aids in Christian manuscripts,[26] whereas for Jane Heath, focusing on function, it is not their use

---

21. In P⁷² (3ʳᵈ/early 4ᵗʰ century) "Jesus," "Christ," "Lord," "God," "Spirit" and "Father" are regularly abbreviated as *nomina sacra* with a stroke over the word. ΜΙΧΑΗΛ, ΑΒΡΑΑΜ, ϹΑΡΡΑ and ΕΝΩΧ written in full, each occurs once, and ΝΩΕ twice, all similarly demarcated with a *linea superscripta*. ΛΝΘΡΩΠΟϹ is normally written in full, but once abbreviated as a *nomen sacrum*.

22. Hurtado, *Artifacts*, 99; and Schuyler Brown, "Concerning the Origin of the *Nomina Sacra*", *Studia Papyrologica* 9 (1970): 7–19. Ludwig Traube, *Nomina Sacra: Versuch einer Geschichte der christlichen Kürzung* (Munich: Beck, 1907), 6, 17f., 33. Traube introduced the Latin designation *nomina sacra*. Earlier terminology that influenced Traube's is: E. M. Thompson's expression "sacred and liturgical contractions," H. Omont's designation *mots consacrés* and Christian von Stavelot's designation *nomina dei*. Later, Brown ("Concerning the Origin", 7–19) used the designation *nomina divina*.

23. Jane Heath ("*Nomina Sacra* and *Sacra Memoria* Before the Monastic Age", *JTS* 2010 (doi: 10.1093/jts/flq077): 21) comments: "the names in question *are* 'sacred,' inasmuch as they highlight the sacred figures of the Christian faith." According to Peter Head (http://evangelicaltextualcriticism. blogspot.com/2006/02/nomina-sacra.html [accessed 10.05.10]), Christopher Tuckett, who has been critical as to the correctness of ascribing sacredness to these words, similarly admits at a Cambridge seminar, that "by the 3rd/4th century *nomina sacra* did *function* in a 'religious' manner (i.e. it reflects a religious attitude to the names)."

24. Hurtado, *Artifacts*, 133: "[T]he visual encounter with the *nomina sacra* may have been experienced much more widely than the circle of those able to read aloud the text in which they occur." The later regular use of *nomina sacra* on icons and other Christian artwork may be indications of such wider usage from early on.

25. Roberts, *Manuscript*, 46.

26. Tuckett, "Yes and No?".

in the individual sentences or their semantic role within a sentence that matters, but "their collective presence on the page, highlighting to the eye the focus of meditation for the *whole act of reading*, while the reader works through the individual sentences. This facilitates recitation of the divine name as a pattern of prayer that is continual."[27] This attentiveness to the name brings us back to how most scholars view the early use of *nomina sacra*, namely by associating it with the special reverence accorded the Tetragrammaton, or at least "a certain broad phenomenological similarity between the *nomina sacra* and Jewish reverential treatment of the divine name."[28]

The two questions raised in this contribution are, first, to what extent the various *nomina sacra* occur in the early New Testament manuscripts, and, second, whether these words are significant for reading Christian biblical texts. I shall answer the latter in the affirmative, arguing that the *nomina sacra* found in the manuscripts may be helpful for understanding Christian biblical texts on the level of individual phrases (section 6) as well as on the level of the Christian canon (sections 6 and 7). First, however, I shall comment on the development and grouping of the abbreviation system (sections 2, 3 and 5) and the varied delimitation of the number of these words (section 4) in some early manuscripts.

12.2 THE DEVELOPMENT OF
THE SYSTEM OF *NOMINA SACRA*

Since Ludwig Traube's monumental study *Nomina Sacra: Versuch einer Geschichte der christlichen Kürzung* in 1907, much has been written on the origin and development of this characteristic scribal practice as part of the Christian manuscript tradition.[29] Advancements on Traube's posthumously published monograph have been made by, *inter alios*, A. H. R. E.

---

27. Heath, "*Sacra Memoria*", 23.
28. Hurtado, *Artifacts*, 106.
29. Traube, *Nomina Sacra*.

Paap,[30] Schuyler Brown,[31] José O'Callaghan,[32] Kurt Treu,[33] Colin H. Roberts,[34] David Trobisch,[35] and Larry W. Hurtado.[36] Christopher Tuckett's understanding of *nomina sacra* as reading aids and his questioning of the consensus view on the origins of the *nomina sacra*—that a strictly limited number of Christian keywords for devotional reasons[37] were being consistently marked off in biblical manuscripts—have been criticised from different vantage points by Hurtado and Heath.[38]

As regards the likely development of the system of *nomina sacra*, some different stages may be distinguished. I shall briefly comment on this below (points a-e), assuming with Hurtado and others that devotional reasons, including special treatment in writing of the divine name, were the driving force behind the practice and that its purpose was neither to save space nor the scribe's time:[39]

a) Following Roberts and Hurtado, I take IHCOYC to be the earliest *nomen sacrum*, which may have first been written as I̅H̅.[40] Early witnesses to this practice are the *Epistle of Barnabas* 9.7-9 (ca. 70-135 AD), the Egerton fragments (P. Lond. Christ. 1) and the Chester Beatty

---

30. A. H. R. E. Paap, *Greek Papyri of the First Five Centuries A.D.: The Sources and Some Deductions*, Papyrologica Lugduno-Batava 8 (Leiden: Brill, 1959).

31. Brown, "Concerning the Origin", 7-19.

32. José O'Callaghan, *Nomina Sacra in Papyrus Graecis Saeculi III Neotestamentariis* (Rome: Biblical Institute Press, 1970); O'Callaghan, "'Nominum sacrorum' elenchus in Graecis Novi Testamenti papyris a saeculo IV usque ad VIII", *Studia Papyrologica* 10 (1971), 99-122.

33. Treu, "Bedeutung".

34. Roberts, *Manuscript*.

35. David Trobisch, *Die Endredaktion des Neuen Testaments* (Göttingen: Vandenhoeck & Ruprecht, 1996). English translation: *The First Edition of the New Testament* (Oxford: Oxford University Press, 2000).

36. For an updated bibliography, see Hurtado, *Artifacts*; and Hurtado, "Origin". See also Heath, "*Sacra Memoria*"; Philip Comfort, *Encountering the Manuscripts: An Introduction to New Testament Paleography & Textual Criticism* (Nashville, TN: Broadman and Holman, 2005; Tomas Bokedal, *The Scriptures and the Lord: Formation and Significance of the Christian Biblical Canon. A Study in Text, Ritual and Interpretation* (PhD Diss., Lund University, 2005), 97-127; and Tuckett, "Yes and No?".

37. Primarily Jesus devotion and these words' association with the Tetragrammaton.

38. Tuckett, "Yes and No?", 431-58. Hurtado, *Artifacts*, 122-34. Heath, "*Sacra Memoria*", 4-8.

39. Cf. Roberts, *Manuscript*, 26. Hurtado, *Artifacts*, 100.

40. So Hurtado, "Origin", 664-71; Hurtado, *Artifacts*, 111-20.

papyrus P⁴⁵ (P. Chester Beatty II).⁴¹ Being the central name of earliest
Christianity,⁴² IHCOYC seems to have been around longer as a typical
Christian abbreviation than, e.g., KYPIOC or ΘEOC, both of which have
also been suggested as the earliest words to be abbreviated as *nomina
sacra*.⁴³ The greater variety in the way "Jesus" is written points, in my
view, in this direction. Whereas KYPIOC is practically always contracted
as K̄C̄, IHCOYC is written variously (by suspension, conflation or contraction) as I̅H̅, I̅H̅C̅ or I̅C̅. XPICTOC as a *nomen sacrum* demonstrates
the same variations (X̅P̅, X̅P̅C̅ and X̅C̅), and may thus also be early.⁴⁴

b) Equally important as deciding which of the primary four names—
"Jesus," "Christ," "Lord" or "God"—was first abbreviated in this characteristic way is their combination into a system of specially written words.
This seems to be the crucial moment, when the early core group of four
names are treated graphically in the same way—i.e. when: i) the divine
name is rendered as Θ̄C̄ or K̄C̄ and ii) "Jesus" and "Christ" are written respectively as I̅H̅, I̅H̅C̅ or I̅C̅, and as X̅P̅, X̅P̅C̅ or X̅C̅. Graphically,
"Jesus" and "God" are here treated alike (special abbreviation with
an overbar). In terms of christological background to the emerging
system of *nomina sacra*, in the New Testament Jesus is being revered
and confessed as X̅P̅C̅ and K̄C̄; in Johannine spirituality he is one with

---

41. Hurtado, *Artifacts*, 113, who also refers to P¹⁸ and P.Oxy. 1224 as containing this early suspension; Reidar Hvalvik, "Barnabas 9.7–9 and the Author's Supposed Use of Gematria", *NTS* 33 (1987),
276–82. See also Bokedal, *Scriptures*, 113–114.

42. Roberts, *Manuscript*, 35–48; Hurtado, "Origin", 664–71.

43. Explaining the origins of the system Ludwig Traube (*Nomina Sacra*) in 1907 opted for "God"
as the first *nomen sacrum* within the Greek Jewish community. Later on other words were treated
in the same way. Still later, the Christian community took over the convention and added yet other
words. Paap ("Greek Papyri"), who largely followed Traube, suggested "God" as the first *nomen
sacrum* used in the Greek Jewish communities. Christians took over this Jewish convention adding
other *nomina sacra* to the original Θ̄C̄. Brown ("Concerning the Origin") was of the opinion that
Kurios, as a Greek rendering of the *Tetragrammaton* and as the first *nomen sacrum*, was originally
used by the Christians. Treu ("Bedeutung") has argued that *Theos* as well as *Kurios* were both used as
the Greek rendering of the Tetragrammaton within a Jewish setting. Christian scribes took over this
convention adding yet other *nomina sacra*. Kristin De Troyer ("The Pronunication of the Names of
God", in *Gott Nennen: Gottes Namen und Gott als Name* (RPT 35; Tübingen: Mohr/Siebeck, 159–63)
argues that *Theos* treated as a *nomen sacrum* by the Jewish community provides the origin of the
system. See further Hurtado, "Origin", 664–71.

44. Contra De Troyer (see fn. 43 above)..

O ΠΑΤΗΡ (ΠΡ), and for Paul in 1 Cor 8:6 Jesus is being closely associated with God, and vice versa, in adapted language from Deuteronomy 6:4: ЄΙϹ ΘϹ ΚΑΙ Ο ΠΡ and [ЄΙϹ] ΚϹ ΙΗϹ ΧΡϹ (according to the reading in P[46]).[45] Beginning already in pre-Pauline circles, ΚΥΡΙΟϹ appears to be deliberately used ambiguously when applied to Jesus, referring both to the God of Israel and to Jesus Christ.[46] Interestingly, Schuyler Brown has argued that the reverential contraction of ΚΥΡΙΟϹ, which he takes as the first *nomen sacrum*, soon was extended "in one direction to ΘЄΟϹ and in the other direction to ΙΗϹΟΥϹ and ΧΡΙϹΤΟϹ."[47] Connections like these between the first few words rendered as *nomina sacra* are important for understanding the development and significance of the system, regardless of which name or names—ΚΥΡΙΟϹ (Brown), ΘЄΟϹ (Traube, Paap, De Troyer), ΚΥΡΙΟϹ and ΘЄΟϹ (Treu), ΙΗϹΟΥϹ (Roberts, Hurtado), or ΙΗϹΟΥϹ and ΧΡΙϹΤΟϹ—that was/were initially treated in this way.

In the 2nd/3rd-century manuscript P[46] and in Codex Bezae the preferred way of writing the primary four names is as ΙΗϹ, ΧΡϹ, ΘϹ and ΚϹ,[48] with their inflection forms, whereas in P[66] and in the New Testament portions

45. See, e.g., Larry W. Hurtado, *Lord Jesus Christ: Devotion to Jesus in Earliest Christianity* (Grand Rapids, MI and Cambridge, UK: Eerdmans, 2003), 114. For a different reading, see James D. G. Dunn, *Did the First Christians Worship Jesus: The New Testament Evidence* (London: SPCK and Louisville, KY: WJK, 2010), 107–10.

46. Cf. Hurtado, *Lord Jesus Christ*, 108–14; David B. Capes, *Old Testament Yahweh Texts in Paul's Christology* (WUNT 2/47; Tübingen: Mohr/Siebeck, 1992). See also C. Kavin Rowe, *Early Narrative Christology: The Lord in the Gospel of Luke* (Grand Rapids, MI: Baker Academic, 2006), 197–218: For Luke "[t]he visitation or coming of the God of Israel is thus so concentrated in the figure of Jesus that they can share an identity as κύριος. Yet, for Luke this unity in no way approaches a *Vermischung*, as Luke 2:11 and the use of Ps 110:1 in Luke 20:41–44 make particularly clear"; and Johansson Daniel, "*Kyrios* in the Gospel of Mark", *JSNT* 33.1 (2010): 101–24.

47. Brown, "Concerning the Origin", 18.

48. When rendered in their *nomina sacra* forms in P[46], ΚΥΡΙΟϹ and ΘЄΟϹ occur as two-letter contractions throughout. Whereas ΙΗϹΟΥϹ is consistently abbreviated using three letters in P[46], ΧΡΙϹΤΟϹ is rendered alternatively as a three-letter conflation (ΧΡϹ is preferred by the scribe) and a two-letter contraction (which may be the beginning of a scribal development towards writing ΧΡΙϹΤΟϹ as a two-letter contraction, the way "Lord" and "God" are written using only two letters). Regarding ΙΗϹΟΥϹ in P[45], the suspension form ΙΗ is preferred (possibly reflecting the earliest scribal convention of abbreviating "Jesus"), however with a few occurrences of ΙΗϹ as well as of ΙϹ. In P[75] (possibly reflecting a somewhat later stage in the way "Jesus" and "Christ" are abbreviated), the contraction ΙϹ is clearly preferred, with a few instances of ΙΗϹ occurring as well. The contraction form of ΧΡΙϹΤΟϹ, ΧϹ, is used throughout in this manuscript. In P[66] the contractions ΙϹ and ΧϹ are used throughout, as in the 4th-century Vaticanus and Sinaiticus (see fn. below).

of the 4th-century codices Vaticanus and Sinaiticus the four names are all contracted by using first and last letters only, $\overline{IC}$, $\overline{XC}$, $\overline{\Theta C}$ and $\overline{KC}$.[49]

c) Reasons for holding these four names to be the early core group of nomina sacra to which other words were later added are: i) these are the words most consistently (ca. 97-100 percent) written as nomina sacra in the extant early Greek NT manuscripts; ii) precisely these four names were the ones most consistently treated as nomina sacra in the early Christian Latin Bible translations;[50] iii) some of the fifteen words usually included among the nomina sacra, such as "mother," "saviour" and "David," seem to be late additions to the core group of four words (as well as to the standard 2nd/3rd-century list of some 5-11 words; see further sections 1 and 4). In other words, starting off with these four names as the earliest nomina sacra, we can be rather confident that to some degree we are dealing here with an expansion of the system up to the 4th century (see section 12.4 below).

d) It is, however, difficult to discern in detail how, when, and in what order the standard 2nd/3rd-century list developed. One possibility is that i) a gradual development took place between the late 1st/early 2nd and the early 4th century, after the core group had been introduced and standardised as part of the manuscript tradition. Another option would be ii) to assume some local or regional scribal variation beginning in the 1st and 2nd century in the way nomina sacra were used, including also the number of words incorporated. Arguably in response to such development or variation (i and ii) a conservative reaction can be observed in some early manuscripts, delimiting the number of words embraced by the practice. Such delimitation is probably what we find, e.g., in the NT of Codex Vaticanus (tending towards four or five words rendered as nomina sacra).

---

49. The following exceptions to the consistently used two-letter contractions in the NT of Vaticanus and Sinaiticus are found: In the NT of Vaticanus the following occurrences of IHCOYC are written in full: Matt 1:21; Mark 1:24; Luke 3:29 and Col 4:11; the two instances of XPICTOC written in full in 1 Pet 1:11 and 2 Cor 10:7a are arguably scribal mistakes. In the NT of Sinaiticus the following three instances of IHCOYC are written in full: Mark 16:6; Luke 3:29 and Col 4:11. In Rev 22:20 the conflation form $\overline{IHY}$ is used. In Rev 12:10 XPICTOC is written in full, and in Rom 7:4 the conflated genitive form $\overline{XPY}$ is used.

50. C. H. Turner, "The Nomina Sacra in Early Latin Christian MSS.", Studi e Testi 40 (1924): 62–74; cf. Traube, Nomina Sacra, 131ff.

e) After ΠΝЄΥΜΔ has been added to the early core group of four *nomina sacra*, soon a few more words are treated in a similar way, as witnessed by our 2nd- to early-4th-century Greek NT manuscripts. It may surprise us that "cross" is contracted in more than 90 percent of the occurrences in these NT manuscripts. Moreover, "Father" occurs as a *nomen sacrum* with relatively high frequency, whereas abbreviations of "man" and "Son" are less frequent. Contractions of "Israel" and "Jerusalem" are also attested in these early manuscripts. "Heaven" occurs abbreviated in P[115], and ΜΗΤΗΡ is contracted only once in the late 2nd/3rd-century P[121] (John 19:26 in P.Oxy. 4805). The words "David" and "saviour" seem to have entered the list later. ΔΔΥΙΔ and ϹΩΤΗΡ are never written as *nomina sacra* in the earliest NT papyri or parchments. In other words, like ΜΗΤΗΡ, ΔΔΥΙΔ (which is not contracted e.g. in the 3rd/4th-century P[1]) and ϹΩΤΗΡ seem to be late additions to the list of *nomina sacra* used for New Testament texts (see 12.3.1 below).

In the discussion below I will assume that there is some correlation between the frequency of *nomina sacra* in the earliest New Testament manuscripts (section 3) and the chronological development of the abbreviation system (section 2). The four words in the primary group, for example, almost always occur in their *nomina sacra* forms (97-100%) and are thus arguably introduced earlier in the list than, e.g. ΥΙΟϹ (ca. 36%) or ΜΗΤΗΡ (ca. 3%), which are not as frequently abbreviated in the earliest manuscripts.[51]

12.3 GROUPS OF *NOMINA SACRA* SORTED ACCORDING TO FREQUENCY

Hurtado, following Roberts, organises his list of fifteen *nomina sacra* into three groups. Based on the development of the scribal practice and the consistency with which individual *nomina sacra* are demarcated in the early New Testament manuscript tradition, he suggests that the primary four and earliest words being consistently marked off in more or less all

---

51. For a fuller picture of the likely development of the *nomina sacra* convention between the 1st and 4th centuries, early Greek Old Testament manuscripts need to be taken into account as well. This is not the focus here; however, several of the scholars referred to in this paper have included OT material as well in their analyses.

manuscripts are: "Jesus," "Christ," "Lord" and "God." Secondary *nomina sacra*, not as consistently demarcated, but also occurring from rather early on are: "Spirit," "cross/crucify" and "man/human being." The rest of the fifteen words, according to Hurtado joining the list latest, are categorised as tertiary.

However, with regard to details in Roberts' and Hurtado's organisation of the words, alternative views of the emergence of the *nomina sacra* have been offered by a few scholars. Since "Spirit" is consistently rendered as a *nomen sacrum* beside the earliest four, Dirk Jongkind, in his analysis of Codex Sinaiticus, has preferred to discuss five primary words, as has also Philip Comfort when analysing the earliest NT manuscripts.[52] From this, a good case could be made for including "Spirit" among the primary words, added from early on to the core group of four initial *nomina sacra*. However, here I will treat ΠΝΕΥΜΑ together with ϹΤΑΥΡΟϹ as a separate secondary group, both of which are contracted in about 90 percent of the occurrences of these two words in the earliest NT manuscripts. Based on these early manuscripts I will suggest some further modifications to Roberts' and Hurtado's lists.

Another reason for slightly modifying the common organisation of the list of *nomina sacra* into three groups is the seemingly late addition (probably 3rd/4th century) of ϹШΤΗΡ and ΔΑΥΙΔ (the respective contractions of which are absent from the earliest NT manuscripts) and perhaps of ΜΗΤΗΡ (occurring once in P[121]) and ΟΥΡΑΝΟϹ (present only in P[115]), which thus could make up two groups of their own (see 12.3.1, groups 6 and 7).[53] And, as we will see below, there are other reasons as well for grouping these words differently.

---

52. Jongkind, *Scribal Habits*. Comfort, *Encountering the Manuscripts*, 231. Cf. also J. Bruce Prior, "The Use and Nonuse of Nomina Sacra in the Freer Gospel of Matthew", in *The Freer Biblical Manuscripts: Fresh Studies of an American Treasure Trove*, Larry W. Hurtado (ed.) (Atlanta: Society of Biblical Literature), 147–66.

53. ϹШΤΗΡ occurs 9 times, ΔΑΥΙΔ 20 times, and ΜΗΤΗΡ 38 times—all written in full—in the 74 early NT manuscripts included here. I have counted the occurrences of these words where at least one letter of the word is visible in the manuscript (largely based on the transcription in Comfort/Barrett; see fn. 62 below).

12.3.1 APPROXIMATE NUMBER OF
NOMINA SACRA IN 74 EARLY NT MANUSCRIPTS

My suggestion for grouping the *nomina sacra* is based on the frequency of each word in the 2009 Accordance version of *The Text of the Earliest New Testament Manuscripts*, edited by Philip Comfort and David Barrett.[54] For the purposes of the present chapter this electronic publication (which is a corrected and enlarged version of the 2001 edition of the book) gives quick access to the approximate number of *nomina sacra* in 74 early NT manuscripts (roughly 2nd to early 4th century) up to and including P[123]. Based on the frequency of the *nomina sacra* occurrences in this edition, the groups below differ somewhat from Roberts' and Hurtado's organization of the words (*NS=nomina sacra* in the table below):[55]

1. Primary group: IHCOYC, XPICTOC, ΘEOC, KYPIOC (97-100% *NS*)[56]

2. Secondary group: CTAYPOC, ΠNEYMA (89-95% *NS*)[57]

3. Tertiary group: ΠATHP, CTAYPOW, ANΘPWΠOC (ca. 45-62% *NS*)[58]

4. Quarternary group: YIOC (ca. 36% *NS*)

---

54. Philip W. Comfort and David P. Barrett, eds., *The Text of the Earliest New Testament Greek Manuscripts* (Corrected and enlarged, Accordance electronic ed.; Wheaton: Tyndale House Publishers, 2001), November 2009.

55. Roberts' and Hurtado's three groups of *nomina sacra* include: primary group: IHCOYC, XPICTOC, KYPIOC, ΘEOC; secondary group: ΠNEYMA, ANΘPWΠOC, CTAYPOC; tertiary group: ΠATHP, YIOC, ICPAHΛ, IEPOYCAΛHM, OYPANOC, MHTHP, ΔAYIΔ, CWTHP. Roberts, *Manuscript*, 27; Hurtado, "Origin", 655f.

56. 99–100 percent of the words in the primary group are *nomina sacra* abbreviations when plural forms (never written as *nomina sacra*) of ΘEOC and KYPIOC are omitted. Similar results as the ones here listed can be found as well in Benjamin Overcash, "Σταυρος as a Nomen Sacrum: A Suggestion," unpublished conference paper presented at the SBL Papyrology and Early Christian Backgrounds Group, San Antonio, TX, 22 Nov 2016.

57. 96.1 percent of the instances of ΠNEYMA are either *nomina sacra* forms (89.2%) or usages of the word written in full not referring to the Holy Spirit (6.9%).

58. Approximately 74 percent of the occurrences of ΠATHP are either *nomina sacra* forms (53%) or non-sacred usages of the word written in full (21%).

5. Quinary group: ΙΕΡΟΥϹΑΛΗΜ, ΙϹΡΑΗΛ, ΠΝΕΥΜΑΤΙΚΟϹ (ca. 22-44% NS)[59]

6. Senary group: ΟΥΡΑΝΟϹ, ΜΗΤΗΡ (ca. 2-5% NS)

7. Septenary group: ΔΑΥΙΔ, ϹΩΤΗΡ (no NS)[60]

A preliminary conclusion that can be drawn from this list is the possibility of excluding the septenary and maybe the senary group from the earliest *nomina sacra* (used perhaps before the early 3rd century). This would be in line with the apparent attempt at delimitating the number of *nomina sacra* to 11 in the important early-3rd-century P[75], the extant NT text of which is basically identical to that of the 150 years later Vaticanus (in which the number of regularly contracted *nomina sacra* has been limited to 4 or 5).[61]

The first group containing what scholars consider to be the four earliest and most consistently rendered abbreviations is generally regarded as the core group of *nomina sacra*. In the 74 NT manuscripts I am here analysing, all occurrences (592, or so) of ΙΗϹΟΥϹ are written as *nomina sacra*, except for Luke 3:29 in P[4], where the word is referring to Joshua and is written in full. Similarly, ΧΡΙϹΤΟϹ, occurring ca. 364 times, is marked off as a *nomen sacrum* with perfect consistency throughout.[62] All 752, or thereabout, occurrences of ΘΕΟϹ written in the singular are *nomina sacra*.[63] The nine plural forms are all written in full (John 10:34, 35 in P[45], P[66] and P[75]; 1 Cor 8:5 (twice) and Gal 4:8 in P[46]). As expected, also

---

59. The arrangement of the quarternary and quinary groups could have been slightly differently made. I have chosen to treat ΥΙΟϹ separately, although the contraction of ΙΕΡΟΥϹΑΛΗΜ (provided that all occurrences of the Hellenistic form ΙΕΡΟϹΟΛΥΜΑ—which are always written *plene*—are excluded) is more frequent.

60. See fn. 53 above.

61. Aland and Aland, *Text*, 14. The delimitation of the number of *nomina sacra* in P[46] and P[66] could also work to support the probable absence of the words in the senary and septenary groups from 2nd-and early-3rd-century manuscripts (see 12.4.2 below).

62. The number of words counted for ΙΗϹΟΥϹ, ΧΡΙϹΤΟϹ, ΘΕΟϹ, and ΚΥΡΙΟϹ does not include conjectures in brackets in Comfort and Barrett, *Earliest New Testament Greek Manuscripts*. All words (*nomina sacra* forms and words written in full) in the 74 NT manuscripts I am analysing are included in the statistics only if at least one letter of the word is visible in the manuscript. See further fn. 65.

63. The one exception in Comfort and Barrett (*Earliest New Testament Greek Manuscripts*)—John 11:22 in P[66]—is an erratic transcription.

ΚΥΡΙΟC and its inflections, altogether ca. 389 occurrences, are regularly rendered in their *nomina sacra* forms.[64] Of the eleven times the word is written in full (ca. 2.8% of the total occurrences of the word), eight are plural (Acts 16:16, 19 in P⁴⁵; 1 Cor 8:5; Eph 6:5, 9; Col 3:22 and 4:1 in P⁴⁶; Luke 16:13 in P⁷⁵), one is singular with a non-sacral meaning (Luke 16:3 in P⁷⁵), and two are singular with a sacral meaning (1 Pet 3:12b and 2 Pet 2:9 in P⁷²). Thus, when written in the singular, ΚΥΡΙΟC is rendered as a *nomen sacrum* in approximately 99.2 percent of the occurrences of the word (ca. 378 out of 381).

All in all, in the 74 early NT manuscripts here analysed, ca. 2102 (591+364+761+389) occurrences of the names making up the primary group are written in their *nomina sacra* forms. Of the few instances of the four primary words written in full, two instances of ΚΥΡΙΟC with a sacred meaning are found (in P⁷²); and a few occurrences of ΘΕΟC (9 instances), ΚΥΡΙΟC (10 instances) and ΙΗCΟΥC (1 instance) with the word either in the plural or with a non-sacral meaning. Thus, if we omit the plural forms of ΘΕΟC (9 instances) and ΚΥΡΙΟC (8 instances) from the above figures, as these are never contracted, 99-100 percent of the words in the primary group are rendered as *nomina sacra* ("Jesus": 99.8%; "Christ": 100%; "God": 100%; and "Lord": 99.2%).

In the secondary group, CΤΑΥΡΟC is written as a *nomen sacrum* on 18 out of 19 occasions (written in full once in P¹³; contracted 18 times in P⁴⁵, P⁴⁶, P⁶⁶ and P⁷⁵), i.e., 94.7 percent are contractions. ΠΝΕΥΜΑ is rendered as a *nomen sacrum* 207 times out of 232, that is, 89.2 percent of the occurrences of the word. Of the 25 instances of ΠΝΕΥΜΑ written in full— several of which are found in P⁴⁶—I take 9 to refer to the Holy Spirit, that is, 3.9 percent. Thus, 96.1 percent are either *nomina sacra* forms (89.2%) or usages of the word written in full not referring to the Holy Spirit (6.9%).[65]

---

64. 2 Pet. in P⁷² has the genitive singular of ΚΥΡΙΟC written *plene* with a crossbar over the whole word, marking the word off in this way as a *nomen sacrum*.

65. 207 occasions of ΠΝΕΥΜΑ are written in their *nomina sacra* forms (the following occurrences of the contraction for ΠΝΕΥΜΑ are not visible and thus not included: 1 Cor 14:15 in P⁴⁶; John 19:30 in P⁶⁶; Luke 4:36, 9:39 and John 6:63 in P⁷⁵; Matt 3:16 in P¹⁰¹ and John 1:32 in P¹⁰⁶), whereas 25 are written in full. Of the latter, 8 are non-sacral (Luke 10:20 in P⁷⁵, Acts 5:16 in 0189; Rom 11:8, 1 Cor 14:14. 32, 2 Cor 7:13, 11:4 and Heb 12:23 in P⁴⁶), 9 sacral, referring to the Holy Spirit (John 3:34 in P⁸⁰; Rom 8:23, 15:13. 16, 1 Cor 2:10 (twice), 2 Cor 3:6, 13:13 and Heb 9:14 in P⁴⁶; and 8 neither clearly

Occurring with slightly less frequency, the first word in the tertiary group is ΠΑΤΗΡ, written as a *nomen sacrum* ca. 189 out of ca. 355 times (53%). In the case of ΠΑΤΗΡ it can be noted, however, that approximately 74 percent are either *nomina sacra* forms (53%) or non-sacred usages of the word written in full (21%), which gives us ca. 26 percent of the occurrences of ΠΑΤΗΡ written *plene* with a sacral meaning.[66] The next word in this group, the verb CTΑYPOW is contracted as a *nomen* (or *verbum*) *sacrum* 15 out of 24 times (62%),[67] and the third word, ΑΝΘΡWΠΟC, ca. 152 out of 340 times (about 45%).

In the quarternary group, YIOC is written as a *nomen sacrum* about 89 out of 246 times (ca. 36%).

In the quinary group, IEPOYCΑΛΗΜ is found contracted 17 out of 39 times (44%). The Hellenistic form of the word, IEPOCOΛYMΑ (38 occurrences), is always written in full. ICPΑΗΛ is contracted on 9 out of 37 occasions (24%) and ΠΝΕYMΑTIKOC 5 out of 22 times (22.7%) in two manuscripts (P[46] and P[72]).[68]

In the senary group, OYPΑΝΟC is contracted 7 out of 147 times (4.8%; only in P[115]) and MHTHP 1 of 39 times (2.6% of the occurrences in altogether 10 manuscripts; contracted only in P[121]).

There are no occurrences of *nomina sacra* forms in our early NT manuscripts (2nd to early 4th century) for the two words in the seventh and last group: ΔΑYIΔ and CWTHP.

---

sacred nor referring to the Holy Spirit (Rom 8:15, 1 Cor 6:17, 14:12, Phil 3:3 and Heb 12:9 in P[46]; John 3:6 in P[66]; Heb 12:9 in P[13] and Rev 1:4 in P[18]). I have counted no conjectures, only those occurrences of the word where at least one letter is visible (including a few instances of barely distinguishable letters with a dot beneath the transcription) and transcribed in the 2009 Accordance version of Comfort and Barrett, *Earliest New Testament Greek Manuscripts*. In some cases I have followed the printed 2001 edition of the book due to a mistake in the electronic version (e.g., Acts 19:1 in P[38], where the word ΠΝΑ should not be visible).

66. The distinction between sacred and non-sacred use of ΑΝΘΡWΠΟC and YIOC written *plene* is not as easily pursued as for ΠΑΤΗΡ (cf., e.g., the use of "son" in Heb 12:5–8); only the visible *nomina sacra* forms are here analysed for the former two words.

67. I choose here to distinguish CTΑYPOW from the noun CTΑYPOC due to the difference in frequency with which the verb and the noun occur in their *nomina sacra* forms in our 74 NT manuscripts, 62 and 95 percent respectively.

68. ΠΝΕYMΑTIKOC is not always regarded as a separate contraction by scholars, but treated together with ΠΝΕYMΑ.

12.3.2 COMPARISON BETWEEN 2ND/3RD- AND
4TH/5TH-CENTURY MANUSCRIPTS

When we compare the results above for our 74 early, or earliest, NT manuscripts (organised according to frequency) with what we find in the New Testament portion of the 4ᵗʰ- and 5ᵗʰ-century codices Vaticanus, Sinaiticus, Bezae and Washingtonianus,[69] the outcome for the primary four *nomina sacra* is roughly the same; that is, IHCOYC, XPICTOC, ΘΕOC and KYPIOC are as consistently contracted also in these later manuscripts. In Sinaiticus and Washingtonianus, ΠNEYMA, as well, is as regularly abbreviated as the words in the core group of four *nomina sacra*. In Bezae, however, ΠNEYMA is contracted slightly less, ca. 82 percent (129 occurrences of *nomina sacra* forms out of 157); of the 28 occurrences (17.8%) of ΠNEYMA written *plene*, 10 (6.4%) refer to the Holy Spirit,[70] which gives us 93.6 percent of the instances of ΠNEYMA written either in their *nomina sacra* forms or *plene* with a non-sacral meaning. In the NT portion of Vaticanus ΠNEYMA is written as a *nomen sacrum* in only about 2.9 percent of the occasions. A further difference between these later codices and the earliest manuscript tradition is the removal (or relative absence) of CTAYPOC as a *nomen sacrum* in Vaticanus, Sinaiticus and Washingtonianus, and the introduction of new *nomina sacra* contractions, e.g., ΔAYIΔ and CWTHP, in Sinaiticus. Some of the *nomina sacra* forms, including those for ANΘPWΠOC, ΠATHP and YIOC, are often difficult to determine in terms of their (intrinsic or contextual) sacredness. To some extent this difficulty is probably reflected in the frequency of *nomina sacra* abbreviations for these words. The frequency of contracted forms of YIOC is 36 percent in our 74 early NT manuscripts, 47 percent in the NT portion of Sinaiticus (47% in Jongkind, including OT and NT),[71] 11 percent in Washingtonianus, and 0 percent in both Bezae and the NT portion of Vaticanus. Corresponding statistics for ANΘPWΠOC is: 45 percent in

69. For alternative dating of Codex W, see Larry Hurtado's introduction in Hurtado (ed.), *The Freer Biblical Manuscripts: Fresh Studies of an American Treasure Trove* (Atlanta: Society of Biblical Literature), 15. I largely make use of updated Accordance modules for statistics on the *nomina sacra* in the NT texts of Vaticanus, Sinaiticus, Bezae and Washingtonianus.

70. In Codex Bezae ΠNEYMA is written in full—referring to the Holy Spirit—in John 4:24; 20:22; Luke 1:15. 35. 67; 3:16. 22; 4:1b; 10:21; and Acts 6:5.

71. Jongkind, *Scribal Habits*, 67.

the 74 early NT manuscripts, 29.5 percent in the NT portion of Sinaiticus (29% in Jongkind, OT and NT), 67 percent in Washingtonianus and again 0 percent in Bezae and the NT of Vaticanus. For ΠΑΤΗΡ the corresponding figures are: 53 percent contracted in the 74 early NT manuscripts, 24 percent in the NT portion of Sinaiticus (29% in Jongkind, OT and NT), 84 percent in Washingtonianus, 8 percent in Bezae and 0.3 percent in the NT portion of Vaticanus.

In sum, when the *nomina sacra* in Vaticanus, Sinaiticus, Bezae and Washingtonianus are compared to the frequency of abbreviated *nomina sacra* forms in our early 74 NT manuscripts for ΥΙΟC, ΑΝΘΡΩΠΟC and ΠΑΤΗΡ, we see both an increase and a decrease in the number of contractions for these words. The most important differences are the absence of basically all three *nomina sacra* forms for these words in Vaticanus, and in Bezae for ΑΝΘΡΩΠΟC and ΥΙΟC. Another significant difference is the increase of the use of both ΑΝΘΡΩΠΟC and ΠΑΤΗΡ as contractions in Codex Washingtonianus. Interestingly, ΥΙΟC is only contracted in 11 percent of the occurrences of the word in Washingtonianus, and not at all in Bezae and the NT of Vaticanus.

We see here some development among scribes in their use of *nomina sacra*, either by additions of words (e.g., ΔΑΥΙΔ and CΩΤΗΡ in Sinaiticus), by increased or decreased use of individual contractions (e.g., increase of ΠΑΤΗΡ and decrease of ΥΙΟC as contractions in Washingtonianus), or by delimitation of the number of *nomina sacra* used, which is the general tendency in the NT of Vaticanus. This, too, may be regarded as a development to some extent, as the four or five contractions used by the scribes of Codex Vaticanus receive a somewhat different emphasis precisely by their relative scarcity.

Having organized the different *nomina sacra* according to frequency in 74 early NT manuscripts and compared the results with some later manuscripts, we now turn again to the related issue of scribal delimitation or regulation of the number of *nomina sacra* in some individual manuscripts.

12.4 DELIMITATION OF THE
NUMBER OF *NOMINA SACRA* USED
IN INDIVIDUAL MANUSCRIPTS

12.4.1 FOUR OR FIVE WORDS

Preference for the primary four *nomina sacra* are found in the NT portion of Vaticanus as well as in some of the early Latin translations,[72] which treat as *nomina sacra* either the core group of four or the primary/secondary group of five (including ΠΝΕΥΜΑ but not ϹΤΑΥΡΟϹ). Also the 3rd-century P[13] sticks only to these five contractions,[73] and the scribal inclusion of ΠΝΕΥΜΑ as a standard contraction seems to be the common pattern among the manuscripts, 89.2% in the 74 early Greek NT manuscripts, 83.4% in the Latin and 84.8% in the Greek text of Codex Bezae,[74] ca. 99% in Codex Sinaiticus,[75] and 91.3% in the NT of Codex Washingtonianus (with the nine occurrences written in full being non-sacred uses of ΠΝΕΥΜΑ). Thus, as regards the Greek manuscript tradition, in 1924 C. H. Turner could write that of all our Greek manuscripts one hand of Vaticanus provides the only exception to the universal usage of abbreviating ΠΝΕΥΜΑ as a *nomen sacrum*.[76] Nonetheless, we can still trace the early stages of development (e.g., in the NT of Vaticanus, with only 2.9% of the occurrences of ΠΝΕΥΜΑ contracted, and in the Latin manuscripts *a*, *d* and *e* with *spiritus* partly written in full) when only the primary four were being preferred.[77] Perhaps one implication to be drawn from the limited number of words contracted in the NT portion of Vaticanus may be a very early dating of the exemplars used by the scribes, containing a rather primitive form of the *nomina sacra* system. However—and this

---

72. See Turner, "Early Latin Christian Mss.", 66–9.

73. Whereas "Jesus," "Christ," "God," "Lord" and "Spirit" are treated as *nomina sacra* in P[13], "Father," "Son," "man," "cross" and "David" are written in full.

74. Parker, *Codex Bezae*, 104.

75. Jongkind, *Scribal Habits*, 67.

76. Turner, "Early Latin Christian Mss.", 65.

77. On the Latin manuscript tradition, see Turner, "Early Latin Christian Mss.", 67; and Bernhard Bischoff, *Latin Palaeography: Antiquity and the Middle Ages* (translated by Dáibhí ó Cróinín and David Ganz; Cambridge: Cambridge University Press, in association with the Medieval Academy of Ireland, 1990), 87, 152–5.

is more likely (since, e.g., "Father" and "Israel" are found abbreviated; cf. fn. 16 above)—the conservative use of contractions in Vaticanus may also largely be explained by deliberate choices of delimiting the number of words handled in this way by the 4th-century scribes.

12.4.2 EIGHT, NINE OR ELEVEN WORDS

P[45] and the Greek text of Codex Bezae both contain the four primary and two secondary *nomina sacra* ("cross" and "crucify" counted together as one word), and in addition the words "Father" and "Son" from the tertiary and quarternary groups. In P[46] and P[66] we find, in addition to these eight *nomina sacra*, ΑΝΘΡѠΠΟC from the tertiary group treated in the same way. The important early-3rd-century P[75], containing all in all eleven *nomina sacra*, adds yet another two, ΙΕΡΟΥCΑΛΗΜ and ΙCΡΑΗΛ, in addition to the nine above.

12.4.3 THIRTEEN AND FIFTEEN WORDS

Codex Washingtonianus has thirteen words contracted as *nomina sacra* (CTΑΥΡΟC/CTΑΥΡΟѠ and ΙΕΡΟΥCΑΛΗΜ not included), and the whole list of fifteen words is present in Sinaiticus and in Codex Alexandrinus (ΠΝΕΥΜΑ and ΠΝΕΥΜΑΤΙΚΟC counted together as one word, and CTΑΥΡΟC/CTΑΥΡΟѠ occurring only rarely as contractions).[78]

The various delimitations of the number of *nomina sacra* in individual manuscripts indicate that the scholarly *nomina sacra* discussion need to take into account the seemingly deliberate choices by individual scribes to work with a rather well-defined selection of words.

12.4.4 LATE ADDITIONS

In the 4th-century Codex Sinaiticus there is a tendency to write ΟΥΡΑ-ΝΟC in full. Overall, in the 175 folios analysed by Jongkind, 25 percent of the occurrences of ΟΥΡΑΝΟC are contracted. However, in 1 Chr, Jdt., 4 Macc., Pss., XII Prophets and the Pauline Corpus, the word is always

---

78. Traube, *Nomina Sacra*, 73; Jongkind, *Scribal Habits*, 67f., 64;

written in full.[79] These figures provide some support to the general impression we get from the early NT papyri listed in Comfort's and Barrett's *The Text of the Earliest New Testament Greek Manuscripts*, where OYPΑNOC is contracted as a *nomen sacrum* only in P[115] containing the Apocalypse (mid- to late- 3rd century).[80] All seven occurrences of OYPΑNOC in P[115] are contracted. Interestingly, in the Book of Revelation in Codex Sinaiticus 78 percent (40 out of 51) of the occurrences of OYPΑNOC are marked off as *nomina sacra*.[81] Could this possibly be an indication of the word's inclusion among the *nomina sacra* by 3rd-century scribes, with the Book of Revelation playing a central role? Perhaps. In any case, from our extant early NT manuscripts (which, of course, are still rather fragmentary) OYPΑNOC appears to have entered the list only after the latter half of the 3rd century. Another late word—it occurs contracted only once in the early NT papyri—is MHTHP (see above). ΔΑΥΙΔ as a *nomen sacrum* also seems to have been added late, but is nonetheless contracted rather consistently in Sinaiticus (ca. 69 percent of the occurrences of the word).[82] However, none of these three words, OYPΑNOC, ΔΑΥΙΔ and MHTHP, are contracted in the NT portion of Vaticanus or in Codex Bezae. When the number of *nomina sacra* was still growing in the 2nd and 3rd centuries, some further additions, such as CTΑΥPOW[83] or ΠNEYMΑTIKOC (which is contracted in Sinaiticus with perfect consistency),[84] appear to have been added by association with previous words already included (here, CTΑΥPOC and ΠNEYMΑ).

12.5 PRESERVATION, ASSOCIATION, EXTENSION AND DELIMITATION

After the introduction of the earliest *nomina sacra* the system seems to have been employed using various scribal strategies, the most important of which was the scribal *preservation* of the primary group words in

---

79. Ibid., 67, 72f.

80. Comfort and Barrett, *Earliest New Testament Greek Manuscripts*.

81. 80, rather than 78, percent in Jongkind, *Scribal Habits*, 73.

82. Ibid., 68.

83. I take the contraction of CTΑΥPOW to be later than that of CTΑΥPOC; cf. 12.3.1 above.

84. 100 percent in Jongkind's analysis, *Scribal Habits*, 67.

practically all Christian Bible manuscripts (on the potential existence of early Christian scriptoria, see 12.7.2 below).

Many of the words in the secondary to septenary groups, but also in the primary group (see above), appear to have been introduced to the list by *association* to one or more previously included words, such as CTΑΥΡΟШ and ΠΝΕΥΜΑΤΙΚΟC (see 12.4.4 above). ΚΥΡΙΟC seems to have been associated with both Jesus and God, ΧΡΙCΤΟC with ΙΗCΟΥC, both being used as proper names already in the Pauline Corpus (cf. section 12.2, under b, above). Within a binitarian devotional framework, ΙΗCΟΥC, ΧΡΙCΤΟC, ΚΥΡΙΟC and ΘΕΟC seem to have been mutually associated with one another graphically, constituting the heart of the system.[85] As the scribal practice developed, CTΑΥΡΟC was associated with ΙΗCΟΥC (already in Barn. 9.7-9; see below), and ΠΝΕΥΜΑ arguably with ΚΥΡΙΟC ΙΗCΟΥC ΧΡΙCΤΟC and ΘΕΟC Ο ΠΑΤΗΡ within an emerging triadic/Trinitarian framing. At a later stage, and arguably within a slightly more developed Trinitarian framing, ΥΙΟC appears to have been added, probably being associated not only with ΠΑΤΗΡ and ΠΝΕΥΜΑ (e.g. Matt 28:19),[86] but with other *nomina sacra* as well, such as ΙΗCΟΥC, ΘΕΟC and ΑΝΘΡШΠΟC (e.g., Mark 1:1; "Son of God"; "Son of Man").[87] ΑΝΘΡШΠΟC may also have been associated with ΙΗCΟΥC.[88]

From relatively early on in the manuscript tradition, contractions of ΑΝΘΡШΠΟC, ΙΗCΟΥC and ΠΝΕΥΜΑ appear to have been used by *extension* also in non-sacral phrases, such as in references to Joshua in Old Testament texts among the Chester Beatty papyri (read typologically by

---

85. On the "binitarian nature" of early Christian worship, and for further references, see, e.g., Larry W. Hurtado, *At the Origins of Christian Worship: The Context and Character of Earliest Christian Devotion* (Grand Rapids: MI and Cambridge, UK: Eerdmans, 1999), 95–7.

86. For further comments on Matt 28:19, see 12.6.3 below.

87. Cf. Jongkind (*Scribal Habits*, 71–2) for the phrase ΥΙΟC ΤΟΥ ΑΝΘΡШΠΟΥ in Sinaiticus: "In summary, it seems that the phrase ΥΙΟC ΤΟΥ ΑΝΘΡШΠΟΥ has some influence on the use of *nomina sacra*, though the influence is not present in each Gospel, nor is the influence similar in each Gospel. The phrase contains proportionally more contracted forms of ΥΙΟC in Matthew and Luke than in other contexts and relatively fewer contracted forms of ΑΝΘΡШΠΟC in Mark, but in John it contains all of the contracted forms of ΑΝΘΡШΠΟC."

88. For a different understanding of ΑΝΘΡШΠΟC as *nomen sacrum*, see O'Callaghan, *Papyrus Graecis*, 29.

early Christians), or in profane uses of ΠΝΕΥΜΑ in the Book of Jeremiah in Vaticanus (see fn. 16 above).

Besides scribal employment of preservation, association and extension with regard to the *nomina sacra* convention, *delimitation* of the number of contractions used can also be observed, most noteworthily, as already pointed out, in Vaticanus, where the number of contractions is significantly smaller than in slightly earlier manuscripts. Perhaps deliberately, the reduced number of *nomina sacra* accentuates the impact of the maintained four (or five) primary contractions. In addition to the reduced number of sacred names in Vaticanus, we might note the much later example of Martin Luther, who kept three of the *nomina sacra* in his 1534 German Bible translation (see 12.7.3 below).

12.6 NOMINA SACRA AFFECTING INTERPRETATION?

When studying early Christian Bible manuscripts, some examples of individual occurrences of *nomina sacra* stand out with regard to their potential contribution to exegesis of the text or passage in question. I will discuss a couple of examples of this below.

12.6.1 "DAVID" IN MATTHEW 1:6 IN CODEX SINAITICUS

Of the 59 occurrences of ΔΑΥΙΔ in the New Testament portion of Codex Sinaiticus, 55 are written as *nomina sacra* (ΔΑΔ).[89] Of the 39 occurrences of ΔΑΥΙΔ contained in the four Gospels, all save one are rendered as *nomina sacra*.[90] Interestingly, the one exception is found in Matt 1:6. The name ΔΑΥΙΔ occurs 3 times in Matt 1:1 and 1:6:

> The book of the genealogy of JESUS CHRIST, the son of DAVID (ΔΑΔ), the son of Abraham. ... and Jesse the father of DAVID

---

90. Jongkind, *Scribal Habits*, 257–259, however, lists two instances where the word is written in full (one in Matthew and one in Luke). Scribe A is responsible for 37 of the 39 occurrences of the word and scribe D for two (in Luke); ibid., 257, 259.

(ΔΛΔ) the king. And David (ΔΛΥΕΙΔ) was the father of Solomon by the wife of Uriah.[91]

Together with "Jesus" and "Christ" the two first occurrences of "David" are rendered as *nomina sacra*, whereas the third mention of "David" (1:6b) not only lacks the *nomen sacrum* form, it also indicates a shift in the genealogy with the decline of Israel beginning in Matt 1:6b (adultery and assassination accomplished by David). This is the only time "David" is written in full in the four Gospels in Sinaiticus.[92] This scribal choice does not seem to be a coincidence.[93] To the contrary, we may suspect an intended connection between the way "David" is written in Matt 1:6b as compared to the rest of the Gospel(s) and the thoughts the scribe had about the exegesis of the text, or at least about the largely negative function of "David" in 1:6b.[94] Compared to the NT text in Codex Vaticanus and to Codex Bezae, in which ΔΛΥΙΔ is never demarcated as a *nomen sacrum*, the scribal practice in Sinaiticus can be seen as either a scribal preference or as a development in the consistency with which the name "David" is written (or, less likely, as a scribal mistake right at the beginning of the First Gospel). In Codex Washingtonianus most occurrences of "David" are written in full, except for one in Matthew 12:23, the two instances of the name in John 7:42, and five out of six occurrences in Mark.[95] Since there are no examples of ΔΛΥΙΔ written as a *nomen sacrum* in our extant papyri of the 2nd and 3rd centuries,[96] nor in the conservative Vaticanus or in the Greek text of Bezae, a qualified guess is that ΔΛΥΙΔ as a *nomen sacrum* was introduced perhaps around the late 3rd or early 4th century and from then on was often used rather consistently, as in the Gospels of Sinaiticus. Codex Alexandrinus, too, has all instances of "David" in the

---

91. RSV, modified.

92. See fn. 94 below.

93. See fn. 90 on the division of labour between Scribe A and D.

94. For a recent treatment of the significance of verse 1:6 in this regard, see Joel Kennedy, *The Recapitulation of Israel: Use of Israel's History in Matthew 1:1–4:11* (WUNT 2/257; Tübingen: Mohr/ Siebeck, 2008), 83–97, esp. 96: Drawing on 2 Samuel 11 and 12 Kennedy comments on Matt 1:6: "From Abraham to David there was an ascent, but from David to Exile, there is descent, in which the initial descent *toward* exile began with David himself."

95. The Gospels here follow the Western order: Matthew, John, Luke, Mark.

96. Comfort and Barrett, *Earliest New Testament Greek Manuscripts*.

Gospels contracted, save one (the genealogy in Luke 3:31). The Majority Text here largely follows Sinaiticus and Alexandrinus.

12.6.2 "GOD" AND "GODS" IN VATICANUS AND SINAITICUS

The use of ΘΕΟC in the plural is found 8 times in the New Testament in both Sinaiticus and Vaticanus (John 10:34, 35; 1 Cor 8:5 (twice); Gal 4:8; Acts 7:40; 14:11 and 19:26). In all cases the meaning is non-sacral. The distinction between reference to the one God (Θ̄C̄, always written as *nomen sacrum* contraction) and the gods (ΘΕΟΙ, always written in full) is here underlined by this non-usage of the *nomen sacrum* form each time ΘΕΟC occurs in the plural. The consistency with which this scribal practice is pursued is arguably related to an early scribal emphasis on Christian monotheistic belief.

12.6.3 MATT 28:19 IN FIVE EARLY MANUSCRIPTS

The so-called Great Commission in Matt 28:19 is variously rendered with regard to the use of *nomina sacra* in some early manuscripts. Vaticanus, using no *nomina sacra*, has: ΕΙC ΤΟ ΟΝΟΜΑ ΤΟΥ ΠΑΤΡΟC ΚΑΙ ΤΟΥ ΥΙΟΥ ΚΑΙ ΤΟΥ ΑΓΙΟΥ ΠΝΕΥΜΑΤΟC. Demarcating "Spirit" as a *nomen sacrum*, and leaving out the article before "Son," Bezae reads: ΕΙC ΤΟ ΟΝΟΜΑ ΤΟΥ ΠΑΤΡΟC ΚΑΙ ΥΙΟΥ ΚΑΙ ΤΟΥ ΑΓΙΟΥ Π̄Ν̄C̄. Sinaiticus and Washingtonianus use the abbreviated form for "Father" and the article before "Son": ΕΙC ΤΟ ΟΝΟΜΑ ΤΟΥ Π̄Ρ̄C̄ ΚΑΙ ΤΟΥ ΥΙΟΥ ΚΑΙ ΤΟΥ ΑΓΙΟΥ Π̄Ν̄C̄. Further development is found in Alexandrinus (followed by the Majority Text) with its triadic *nomina sacra* structure: ΕΙC ΤΟ ΟΝΟΜΑ ΤΟΥ Π̄Ρ̄C̄ ΚΑΙ ΤΟΥ Ȳ Ȳ ΚΑΙ ΤΟΥ ΑΓΙΟΥ Π̄Ν̄C̄. Two implications to be drawn from these differences are, first, the apparent development of the employment of *nomina sacra* in this passage, and, second, the probable deliberate use of *nomina sacra* as the passage became increasingly important not least for baptismal practice, which is arguably visible in the Byzantine text tradition. Moreover, "Spirit" belongs to the secondary group of *nomina sacra*, "Father" to the tertiary, and "Son" to the quarternary (see 12.3.1 above), which may partly account for the textual differences in Matt 28:19—including as well a chronological component—between these five manuscripts. Also, due to the discrepancy in *nomina sacra* usage, e.g., between Vaticanus and Alexandrinus, a potential difference in the interpretation of the two texts may be anticipated. While an "intra-Gospel understanding" of the former is quite possible,[97] the latter's employment of the triadic *nomina sacra* configuration more easily relates it to early Trinitarianism. Sinaiticus and Washingtonianus, on the other hand, here seem to be good representatives of the early *nomina sacra* practice including words mainly from the primary and secondary groups.

12.6.4 "JESUS" AND "CROSS" IN GENESIS 14:14[98]

The oldest witness to the *nomina sacra* convention that we know of is found in the *Epistle of Barnabas* (AD 70-135).[99] In *Barnabas* 9.7-9 the author presents an allegorical reading of the circumcision of Abraham's household in Gen 14 by elaborating on the number of persons circumcised, 318 servants, in the source rendered by the Greek letters TJE (T̅I̅H̅) with a crossbar over the letters. The rendering of the number 318 in Gen 14 is found also in other contemporary early Christian manuscripts (e.g. the 4th-century Chester Beatty Genesis manuscript and most probably also in the 2nd/3rd-century P. Yale 1).[100] This indicates that the author of Barnabas had a Christian copy of Gen 14:14 (something resembling the Genesis text in P. Chester Beatty IV) before him. The text in *Barnabas* 9 focusing on the name of Jesus and the cross reads:

97. See, e.g., John Nolland, "'In Such a Manner it is Fitting for Us to Fulfil All Righteousness': Reflections on the Place of Baptism in the Gospel of Matthew," in Stanley E. Porter and Anthony R. Cross (eds.), *Baptism, the New Testament and the Church: Historical and Contemporary Studies in Honour of R.E.O. White.* Journal for the Study of the New Testament Supplement Series 171 (Sheffield: Sheffield Academic Press, 1999), 75–80.

98. Modified versions of sections 12.6.4 and 12.6.6 have been previously published as part of Bokedal, "Scripture in the Second Century". In Michael F. Bird & Michael W. Pahl (eds.), *The Sacred Text: Excavating the Texts, Exploring the Interpretations, and Engaging the Theologies of the Christian Scriptures*, Piscataway, N.J.: Gorgias, 2010, and are reused here with permission from Gorgias Press (republished as ch. 2 above)..

99. Reidar Hvalvik, *The Struggle for Scripture and Covenant: the purpose of the epistle of Barnabas and Jewish-Christian competition in the second century* (Tübingen: Mohr/Siebeck, 1996), 23; and idem, "Barnabas 9.7-9 and the Author's Supposed Use of Gematria", NTS 33 (1987), 276–82.

100. For references, see Hurtado, *Artifacts*, 146f.

For Abraham, the first to perform circumcision, was looking ahead in the Spirit to Jesus when he circumcised. For he received the firm teachings of the three letters. For it says, "Abraham circumcised eighteen and three hundred men from his household." What knowledge, then, was given to him? Notice that first he mentions the eighteen and then, after a pause, the three hundred. The number eighteen [in Greek] consists of an Iota [J], 10, and an Eta [E], 8. There you have Jesus. And because the cross was about to have grace in the letter Tau [T], he next gives the three hundred, Tau. And so he shows the name Jesus by the first two letters, and the cross by the other. For the one who has placed the implanted gift of his covenant in us knew these things. No one has learned a more reliable lesson from me. But I know that you are worthy.[101]

Here an explicit reference to the *nomen sacrum* for Jesus represented by JE (=18) meets for the first time in our sources together with the symbol of the cross represented by the Greek letter *Tau* (=300).[102] The symbol of the cross is said to signify grace. The theme of the cross is further developed in the *Epistle of Barnabas* 11 and 12, there in connection with Christian baptism and the serpent raised by Moses in the desert. That the symbolic interpretation of the number 318 was known in Christian circles is further confirmed by Clement of Alexandria (ca. AD 150–215) in his reading of Gen 14:14. However, for Clement this interpretation seems to be past tradition rather than part of his own exegetical practice. Clement comments: "For it is said that the character for 300 is by its shape a symbol of the cross of the Lord."[103] On the whole, 2nd-century reading of the Scriptures is abounding in references to the sign of the cross, not least in the writings of Justin Martyr.

---

101. *The Apostolic Fathers* (ed. Bart D. Ehrman; 2 vols.; LCL 25; Cambridge, Mass.: Harvard University Press, 2003), 2:45–47. Note the reversed order of the numbers 300 and 18.

102. The number 18 (IH) referring to the name Jesus is found also in Irenaeus, *Against Heresies* 1, 3.3 and Hippolytus, *Commentary on Daniel* 2.27. See also Hvalvik, "Barnabas 9.7–9", 279, 282 fn. 27. See also Heath, "*Sacra Memoria*", 23–32.

103. *Stromateis* VI.2.84, 3–4, ANF, vol. 2.

12.6.5 "CROSS" AND "CRUCIFY" IN P[66],
JUSTIN AND TERTULLIAN

The great emphasis put on certain central names and words in the early Christian discourse, such as "Jesus" and "cross," is reflected in the way Christian scribes came to mark these words off in the manuscripts. For example, of the 19 occurrences of the word CTΑΥΡΟC in our extant 2nd- to early-4th-century NT manuscripts (see 12.3.1, above) 18 (95%) are written as *nomina sacra*. P[66] (Papyrus Bodmer II) in particular, usually dated to around AD 200, is an important witness to this type of cross piety. It contains three instances of "cross" written as *nomina sacra*, however with the typical Christian *tau-rho* sign (a compendium of the two Greek letters *tau* and *rho*) used as part of the abbreviation for CTΑΥΡΟC. Similarly the verb form CTΑΥΡΟW ("crucify") is used at least seven times with the *tau-rho* compendium, and as Hurtado points out, "[i]n each case the statement in which the noun or verb appears refers to 'Jesus' cross/crucifixion."[104] Being the earliest Christian use of the *tau-rho* monogram as part of a Christian keyword, and not as later "a freestanding symbol and general reference to Christ," it here functions as part of the abbreviations for "cross" and "crucify."[105] A representative Church teacher from roughly the period when these early manuscripts were produced is Justin Martyr (d. ca. 165), who in company with other early Church writers occupies himself much with Christian cross-symbolism.[106] Not only was the Greek letter *tau* used as part of the *tau-rho* monogram (preceding the later *chi-rho* monogram), in Justin, the letter *tau* is also itself a visual symbol of the cross. Hurtado points us to a vivid treatment in Justin, where the symbol of the cross is literally connected to all and everything:

---

104. Hurtado, *Artifacts*, 140.

105. Ibid., 136. See also idem, "The Earliest Evidence of an Emerging Christian Material and Visual Culture: The Codex, the *Nomina Sacra* and the Staurogram." In Stephen G. Wilson and Michel Desjardins (eds.), *Text and Artifact in the Religions of Mediterranean Antiquity: Essays in Honour of Peter Richardson* (Waterloo, Ont.: Wilfrid Lurier University Press, 2000), 271–88; Erich Dinkler, *Signum Crucis* (Tübingen: Mohr/Siebeck, 1967); Kurt Aland, "Neue Neutestamentliche Papyri II," *NTS* 10 (1963–64): 62–79; and idem, "Neue Neutestamentlich Papyri II," *NTS* 11 (1964–65): 1–21.

106. See further G.Q. Reijners, *The Terminology of the Holy Cross in Early Christian Literature: As Based upon Old Testament Typology* (Nijmegen-Utrecht: Dekker & Van de Vegt N.V., 1965).

Justin Martyr (*1 Apol.* 55) indicates that second-century Christians could see visual allusions to Jesus' cross in practically any object with even the remote shape of a T (e.g., a sailing mast with cross-beam, a plow or other tools with a crosspiece of any kind, the erect human form with arms extended, even the face with the nose extending at a right angle to the eyes).[107]

In Tertullian this exegetical tradition has been transferred to Latin speakers: "Now the Greek letter *Tau* and our own [Latin] letter T is the very form of the cross, which He [God] predicted would be the sign on our foreheads in the true Catholic Jerusalem."[108] Similar to Justin, who expounds, e.g., on Num 21:8-9 in this connection, Tertullian here comments on Ez 9:4. A still earlier tradition on this theme, referred to above, is found in *Barnabas* 9, where the symbol of the cross is said to express grace. These exegetical traditions focusing on one particular sign, letter or word ("cross" and the letter *tau*) are arguably closely related to the *nomina sacra* convention of reverentially marking off the Greek word for "cross." Hurtado has emphasised the strong *visual* association of the Greek leter *tau* with Jesus' cross and points out that "this certainly also fits with the fact that the earliest known Christian uses of the *tau-rho* device are in the special *nomina sacra* writing of the words for 'cross' and 'crucify.' "[109]

12.6.6 JESUS AND HIS CROSS AS MID-POINT— TOWARDS A CANONICAL READING[110]

In the early 2nd century the teaching of and about Christ—the gospel— whether in oral, written or re-oralised form, was often prioritised, it seems, even over against the Jewish Scriptures, which were now believed to being fulfilled. Christian Judaists in the early 2nd century, however, could still tend to regard Jewish Scripture as the ultimate authority. Ignatius of Antioch tells us about such different expectations of authority associated with the old Scriptures in his *Letter to the Philadelphians* (*Phld.* 8.2):

---

107. Hurtado, *Artifacts*, 147.
108. Quoted from ibid., 148, who cites from the ANF 3:340–41.
109. Hurtado, *Artifacts*, 148.
110. See footnote 98 above.

But I urge you to do nothing in a contentious way, but in accordance with the teaching of Christ. For I heard some saying: "If I do not find it in the ancient records [Gr. *archaiois* = the Jewish Scriptures], I do not believe in the Gospel." And when I said to them, "It is written," they replied to me, "That is just the question." But for me, Jesus Christ is the ancient records; the sacred ancient records are his cross and death, and his resurrection, and the faith that comes through him—by which things I long to be made righteous by your prayer.[111]

It is natural to take Ignatius's use of the Greek *archaios*, "ancient record," and his phrasing "it is written" in this quote to refer to the Jewish Scriptures.[112] However, the point he seems to be making implies a broader meaning, which involves an overall textual conception embracing the Jewish Scriptures, the Gospel and their christological interpretation. Or should we rather say that Ignatius and his Judaizing Christian dialogue partners are exhibiting a problem: whether the old Scriptures and the Gospel are communicating the same Christian message, or whether the credibility of Christian claims necessarily had to be grounded in the Jewish Scriptures? As the Antiochian bishop on his journey under armed guard to martyrdom in Rome sees things, the old Scriptures and the Gospel (in oral or written form) speak of Jesus Christ, "his cross and death and his resurrection and the faith which comes through him." Ignatius here appears to emphasise his understanding of what we may call a creedal-like centre of the Scriptures, consisting of a Christian narrative reading embracing this set of keywords. Jesus Christ, his cross, death and resurrection are identified with the very text of Ignatius' Scriptures. It is interesting to note that the reverentially abbreviated *nomina sacra* introduced universally in the Christian biblical manuscript tradition from at least the late 1st century on,[113] could quite possibly have been a means of

---

111. Ehrman, *The Apostolic Fathers*, vol. 1, LCL, 291f., modified.

112. For the unparalleled use of *archaios* referring to the Jewish Scriptures, see William R. Schoedel, "Ignatius and the Archives", in *HTR* 71 (1978): 97–106. Schoedel also indicates parallel passages in Josephus and Philo.

113. On dating the introduction of *nomina sacra* in Christian biblical manuscripts, see fn. 3 above.

bridging the creedal function that Ignatius here addresses with Scripture. Along these lines the British papyrologist C. H. Roberts has referred to the system of *nomina sacra* in the biblical manuscripts as an "embryonic creed of the first Church."[114] And Ignatius' christological reading in *Phld.* 8.2 perhaps also has the *nomina sacra* convention in mind: "But for me, Jesus Christ is the ancient records; the sacred ancient records are his cross and death, and his resurrection." In any case, as in *Barnabas* 9.7-9, Jesus and his cross are here made the mid-point in biblical interpretation. And as Roberts indicates, the choice of Christian keywords embraced by the scribal *nomina sacra* practice seems to parallel early creedal language. The *nomina sacra* convention probably could have supported Ignatius in his argumentation. And not only Ignatius but other Church writers as well. It is the more puzzling that these special Christian abbreviations are never directly referred to in the literature—with the exception of *Barnabas* 9— until the 9th-century grammarian Christian of Stavelot enquires about their meaning.[115]

12.7 NOMINA SACRA, TEXT AND CANON

Although the *nomina sacra* convention generally is not mentioned by early Church writers (the *Epistle of Barnabas* and Clement of Alexandria being noteworthy exceptions), we may nevertheless suspect that these demarcations—found on basically every page in the New Testament—were important for the early Christian communities. The Pauline letter openings, for example, often contain two or three contractions per verse (e.g., 1 Cor 1:1–9),[116] and David Trobisch has convincingly argued that the system of *nomina sacra* was one of the characteristic editorial features of the earliest Greek New Testament.[117] But why—beyond sheer ornamental considerations—were the *nomina sacra* important?

---

114. Roberts, *Manuscript*, 46. Also referred to above.

115. Traube, *Nomina Sacra*, 6–33.

116. In P[46] 1 Cor 1:1–18 has "Jesus" as nomen sacrum occurring 9 times, "Christ" 13, "Lord" 6, "God" 7, "Father" 1, "Son" 1, and "cross/crucify" 2 times; that is, 39 *nomina sacra* in these verses. Cf. fn. 128 below.

117. Trobisch, *The First Edition*.

I will conclude by referring to a few of the already discussed issues, focusing on aspects pertaining to canonicity, the system of *nomina sacra* as an early editorial feature of Christian Scripture, and, finally, the usage of *nomina sacra* by some comparatively recent theologians and Bible translators.

Nomina sacra potentially affect the identity of the biblical text and canon, and they do so in various ways relating not least to questions of scriptural unity, textuality and interpretation. And, as we shall see, there seems to be a close connection between the *nomina sacra* convention and the emerging Christian biblical canon formation.

12.7.1 CANONICAL SIGNIFICANCE

A few simple scribal rules for the use of *nomina sacra* seem to have been laid down from early on, such as the consistent treatment of the names "Jesus" and "Christ" as *nomina sacra*, which at least in some cases include also the Old Testament figure "Joshua" (IHCOYC in Greek).[118] A clear distinction is made between, on the one hand, "God" or "Lord" as sacred words (abbreviated as *nomina sacra*), and, on the other hand, these words as profane words in the plural ("gods" and "lords," written in full). Almost all 50 or so Greek manuscripts containing 1 Cor 8:4-6 treated by Reuben Swanson in his *New Testament Greek Manuscripts* make this distinction.[119] Pertaining to early Christian binitarian devotion, "Jesus," "Christ," "Lord" and "God" are consistently treated as *nomina sacra* in the earliest extant New Testament manuscripts (97–100%; 99–100%, when plural forms are excluded).

In terms of their significance on a canonical level, the following points can be made (a-f):[120]

a) The Jewish reverence for the Name, especially the Jewish practice of marking off the divine name reverentially in written form probably

---

118. In the 74 early NT manuscripts analysed above, the only time IHCOYC refers to Joshua in Luke 3:29 in P⁴ it is written in full.

119. Reuben Swanson (ed.), *New Testament Greek Manuscripts: Variant Readings Arranged in Horizontal Lines Against Codex Vaticanus. 1 Corinthians* (Wheaton, IL: Tyndale House Publishers and Pasadena, CA: William Carey International University Press, 2003), 113f.

120. The points below have largely been treated in Bokedal, *The Scriptures*, 97–127.

provides us with the key element in the religious background that primitive Christianity adapted in accordance with its own religious convictions and expressed in these early *nomina sacra*.[121] A major aim—relating to the early canonical process—of introducing the primary group of *nomina sacra* into the Christian scriptures, was arguably to graphically identify the Tetragrammaton (in Greek rendered as ΘΕΟC and ΚΥΡΙΟC) with the Greek names for "Jesus," "Christ," "Lord" and "God."[122] Just as in the contemporary Jewish setting, special treatment of the divine name was an essential dimension of Sacred Scripture.[123] We see a "Christianisation" of the Jewish Scriptures both when the codex is employed as the new book format and when the *nomina sacra* convention is systematically introduced.[124]

b) As "Jesus" and "God" are graphically treated in the same way, a binitarian pattern of devotion seems to lie behind the introduction of the earliest four *nomina sacra* (or *divina*) in the manuscript tradition (Hurtado). With the addition of "Spirit"—perhaps in the late 1st century, or earlier—the triadic *nomina sacra* arrangement found on basically every page of the biblical writings indicates a new textual centre or focus, a text in the text, communicating to the reader something essential about how to read and interpret the texts. These four or five primary words make up the core of the system; when new words are added, such as "Father," "Son," "man/human being," "Israel" and "Saviour," they are arguably linked (e.g., by creedal association) to the primary four or five (cf. sections 12.2 and 12.5 above). Significant in this connection is the tendency to regulate the number of *nomina sacra* in individual NT manuscripts—four or five (P¹³; Codex Vaticanus), eight (P⁴⁵; Codex Bezae), nine (P⁴⁶; P⁶⁶), eleven (P⁷⁵), thirteen (Codex Washingtonianus), or fifteen (Sinaiticus; see 12.4.1-3 above). Therefore it seems suitable to study the graphical, textual or theological function of the *nomina sacra* also for one manuscript at a time.

---

121. Hurtado, "Origin", 662–63. Cf. fn. 28, above.

122. The primary four words are often referred to as *nomina divina*; see above.

123. Cf. Bokedal, *The Scriptures*, 102, fn. 19.

124. An example of this is when *nomina sacra* such as "Spirit" and "Jesus"—arguably first marked off in the New Testament—are introduced into the Jewish Scriptures as well (attaining non-sacral meanings; e.g., when referring to Joshua). Cf. ibid., 123f.

c) Due to the consistent treatment of the words "Jesus," "Christ," "Lord," "God" (next to perfect consistency) and "Spirit" (next to perfect consistency, e.g., in Sinaiticus; ca. 90% consistency in the earliest NT manuscripts) as *nomina sacra* throughout the manuscript tradition, the divine name as related to the name of Jesus receives continuous attention. "Jesus" is directly associated with the divine name, and vice versa (with "Jesus" arguably being the first and most important *nomen sacrum*; see sections 12.1–3 above). As the *nomina sacra* are universally present in Christian biblical manuscripts—as far as we can see, already from the 1st century—their presence indicates that these texts were seen as both special and as forming a unity among themselves (e.g., editorial unity among individual NT texts, OT and NT texts, as well as the whole Christian biblical manuscript tradition over time—in Greek as well as in translations).[125] Also, the presence of *nomina sacra* potentially affects interpretation; a noteworthy example is the strong emphasis in some 2nd-century texts on "Jesus" and his "cross" (see 12.6.4–6 above).

d) The *nomina sacra* helped modifying the identity of the Scriptures as Scriptures over against the synagogue, making them specifically Christian (cf. section 12.1 above). They also facilitated the juxtaposition of the Jewish Scriptures and the new Christian (NT) writings—used for worship, missionary preaching, catechetical instruction, argumentation and devotion.[126]

e) In their capacity as supratextual markers, the *nomina sacra* constitute a text in the text—an early creedal structure engrafted into the textuality of the Scriptures (Roberts),[127] a focus of meditation for the *whole act of reading* (Heath) representing visualizing forms of Christian piety (Hurtado). Whichever perspective we choose when approaching this characteristic scribal practice, the following two components seem to be involved:

i) special textual treatment of the divine name, understood against the backdrop of early Jesus devotion (most likely related to a Christian "name theology"; cf., e.g., Phil 2:5–11);[128]

---

125. On the canon as text and further textual aspects of the Scriptures, see ibid., 95–270.

126. See ibid., 114–19.

127. Cf. ibid., 102, 119–23, 124–26.

128. Phil 2:5–11 interestingly contains potentially 14 *nomina sacra*—10 in Vaticanus, 11 in Sinaiticus and probably originally 12 in P[46] (all three with ΑΝΘΡѠΠΟC written in full); these late verses by

ii) a set of textually highlighted Christian keywords—such as "God," "Jesus," "Spirit," "cross" and "Jerusalem"—relating to early creedal formulations,[129] with the Church's earliest christology at the heart of the practice (also including a chronological component, as the system arguably develops up until the early 4th century).[130]

f) The function of the *linea superscripta* drawn across the *nomina sacra* contractions appears to be crucial. When the scribes in a few instances have chosen (deliberately or by mistake) not to abbreviate a particular *nomen sacrum*, sometimes the crossbar is still drawn above the word written in full, such as in the case of $\overline{\text{ΛΙΜΛ}}$ in P[46] or $\overline{\text{ΚΥΡΙΟϹ}}$ in P[72]. The crossbar is as important as the contraction. Usually, the function of the abbreviation together with the supracript line seems to be i) to draw the reader's attention—a warning that the word could not be pronounced as written, ii) to refer to the system of *nomina sacra* as a whole (within a particular manuscript), iii) to function as a graphic emphasis marking out a narrative or meta-textual centre, and iv) to editorially connect and unify different parts of the text with one another.

12.7.2 EDITORIAL FEATURES OF CHRISTIAN SCRIPTURE: SCRIPTORIA, CODEX FORMAT AND *NOMINA SACRA*

When we try to get a grasp of the early Christian Scriptures seen as a textual whole, e.g., as they appear physically in the big Old and New Testament codices, some editorial features of the text immediately strike the reader. The changed order of OT books, addition of new scriptures (NT writings) and the codex as the new book format were typical features of the Christian Scriptures. Compared to the Scriptures of Judaism,

the hand of Paul may even potentially provide us with an early key for understanding the *nomina sacra* system and the logic behind it. The roots of the system may very well be pre-Pauline and located to Jerusalem or Antioch, as has been previously suggested; see ibid., 137–46. Early traces of the practice may perhaps be found already in Gal 3:1; cf. Heath, "*Sacra Memoria*", 23–32. Cf. fn. 116 above and fn. 137 below.

129. See Bokedal, "Scripture in the Second Century"; and idem., *The Scriptures*, 120–22. Cf. 12.6.6 above.

130. The arguably strong connection between the *nomina sacra* practice and early creedal patterns has so far received only minor scholarly attention.

the 1st-and 2nd-century introduction of *nomina sacra* in Christian bibles
also set Christian Scripture apart as markedly different. Is it perhaps early
such usage of *nomina sacra* that is being partly referred to by the rabbis
when they prescribe the particular rulings on the legitimacy of destroying
heretical (especially Christian) scriptures "with their names"?[131] Maybe.
In any case, with David Trobisch we can view these demarcations of
Christian keywords as a characteristic editorial feature of not only the
New Testament writings, but of the Old Testament as well.[132] Introducing a
special Christian (or Jewish-Christian) manner of writing the divine name
throughout the Jewish Scriptures—including likely early use of Christian
"testimony sources" containing scriptural proof-texts[133]—probably also
aimed at demonstrating that the Scriptures "belong" to the Church.[134]

As the scribal *nomina sacra* practice was not only unique, but also
rather uniform and universally spread among the early churches, there
are reasons to presuppose the existence of Christian scribes working "relatively independent of the rest of the literary world"[135] and as a purposefully
organised community. Martin Hengel, discussing typical Christian scribal
customs (use of the codex format, *nomina sacra*, titles of the Gospels
and the beginnings of letters), is probably right when assuming that it is
"highly improbable that Christians in the early period had their 'sectarian
literature' copied in pagan scriptoria. Here they must rapidly have built
up their own 'codex production' also for the LXX text."[136] Pursuing this
argumentation, some of the scribal freedom in the use and non-use of
nomina sacra may be better explained, especially the probable expansion

131. Shabbat 116a, t. Shabbat 13:5, t. Yadaim 2:13; referred to by John Barton, *The Spirit and the Letter: Studies in the Biblical Canon* (London: SPCK, 1997), 118, 186.

132. Trobisch, *The First Edition*.

133. For use of Christian "testimony sources" or proof-texts from the Scriptures, e.g. in Justin Martyr, see Oskar Skarsaune, "Justin and His Bible". In Sara Parvis and Paul Foster (eds.), *Justin Martyr and His Worlds* (Minneapolis: Fortress, 2007), 56.

134. Cf. Reidar Hvalvik, *The Struggle for Scripture and Covenant: the Purpose of the Epistle of Barnabas and Jewish-Christian Competition in the Second Century* (WUNT 2/82; Tübingen: Mohr/ Siebeck, 1996); cf. fn. 126.

135. Martin Hengel, *The Four Gospels and the One Gospel of Jesus Christ* (Harrisburg, PA, Trinity Press International), 28

136. Ibid., 28. As Hengel points out, confident scribal witnesses already in the New Testament writings (Rom 16:22, 1 Peter 5:12) also point in this direction.

of the practice from "cross" to "crucify," from "Spirit" to "spiritual" or from
the core group of four *nomina sacra* to the addition of the words in the
secondary group, "Spirit" and "cross."

The possible early existence of Christian scriptoria, or scriptoria-like
milieus, in the major communities like Rome, Ephesus or Antioch helps
explaining the universality of some of the typical features of the Christian
Scriptures. On the codex and the *nomina sacra* as potentially serving as
two programs of standarisation with an impact on the organisation of the
early Church, T. C. Skeat comments:

> The significant fact is that the introduction of the *nomina sacra*
> seems to parallel very closely the adoption of the papyrus codex;
> and it is remarkable that those developments should have taken
> place at almost the same time as the great outburst of activity
> among Jewish scholars which led to the standardisation of the
> Hebrew Bible. It is no less remarkable that they seem to indicate a
> degree of organisation, of conscious planning, and uniformity of
> practice among the Christian communities which we have hith-
> erto had little reason to suspect, and which throw a new light on
> the early history of the Church.[137]

12.7.3 ACKNOWLEDGING THE *NOMINA SACRA*— LUTHER, NEWMAN AND BONHOEFFER

The *nomina sacra* are present in all, or nearly all, extant Greek and Latin
Christian manuscripts until the 15th century. From the 16th century on,
printed editions of the Bible began to replace the handwritten manuscripts.
Many printed versions preserved some of the features characteristic of the
nomina sacra, e.g., the Luther Bible of 1534, where the names "God," "Lord"
and "Jesus" are marked off—three of the words in the primary group (rendered in German as "GOtt," "HERR"/"HErr" and "JEsus"). In the Swedish
Bible edition of 1703 (the Bible of Charles XII) the Tetragrammaton is
similarly rendered by the Swedish names for "Lord" and "Jesus": "HERren"

---

137. *The Cambridge History of the Bible*, vol. 2, 72f.; cited in C. H. Roberts and T. C. Skeat, *The Birth of the Codex* (London: Oxford University Press, 1983), 57.

and "JEsus." Swedish Bibles used these *nomina sacra* until late in the 19th century. The editors of the King James Bible, on the other hand, chose to treat only the Tetragrammaton, rendered as "Lord," in the Old Testament as a *nomen sacrum*.

In the Anglo-Saxon context, the recognition of *nomina sacra* seems to have been less emphasised than in the German-speaking and Scandinavian countries. However, interestingly the British theologian, and later cardinal, John Henry Newman uses the system of *nomina sacra* in his writings. He kept to the convention of marking off the divine name reverentially in the 1830s and 40s. In his well-known tractates from this period, *nomina sacra* are used even in Newman's own text, that is, not only in direct Scripture citations. In line with early Church practice he marks off (using capital letters) the names "God," "Lord," "Jesus," "Christ" and "Spirit," but also the word "Saviour."[138]

In Germany a century later, another influential theologian and Church leader, Dietrich Bonhoeffer, also recognises the *nomina sacra* practice. Coming across old biblical manuscripts can be a thought-provoking experience. Reflecting on the differences between the handwritten biblical manuscripts and their printed successors, our modern bibles, Bonhoeffer comments:

> It is good, now and then, to remind oneself of the times of the handwritten and illustrated bibles, in which the name of Jesus was rendered with special reverence and beauty. By printing the Bible, it has perhaps become a rather despised book [lit.: precisely such a despised book].[139]

Bonhoeffer here notes some interesting discrepancies between old manuscripts and modern bibles. His implicit question may also be our own:

---

138. See, e.g., Rune Imberg, *Tracts for the Times: A Complete Survey of All the Editions.* Bibliotheca Historico-Ecclesiastica Lundensis 17 (Lund: Lund University Press, 1987), 143–64.

139. DBW 14 (Gütersloh: Gütersloher Verlagshaus, 1996), 510: "Es ist gut, sich hin und wieder an die Zeit der handgeschriebenen und gemalten Bibeln zu erinnern, wo der Name Jesu mit besonderer Andacht und Schönheit gezeichnet wurde. Durch das Drucken der Bibel ist sie vielleicht grade ein so verachtetes Buch geworden."; my translation; Dr. Jutta Leonhardt-Balzer helped with the literal translation in brackets. I am indebted to Dr. Rune Imberg for providing this reference.

Do these differences between the manuscript tradition and the printed Bible make a difference for reading New Testament (and biblical) texts?[140]

BIBLIOGRAPHY

Aland, Kurt. "Neue Neutestamentliche Papyri II." *NTS* 10 (1963–64): 62–79.

———. "Neue Neutestamentlich Papyri II." *NTS* 11 (1964–65): 1–21.

Aland, Kurt and Barbara. *The Text of the New Testament: An Introduction to the Critical Editions and to the Theory and Practice of Modern Textual Criticism.* Second edition. Translated by Erroll F. Rhodes; Grand Rapids, MI: Eerdmans, 1989.

The Apostolic Fathers. Edited by Bart D. Ehrman 2 vols.; LCL 25; Cambridge, MA: Harvard University Press, 2003.

Barton, John. *The Spirit and the Letter: Studies in the Biblical Canon.* London: SPCK, 1997.

Bischoff, Bernhard. *Latin Palaeography: Antiquity and the Middle Ages.* Translated by Dáibhí ó Cróinín and David Ganz; Cambridge: Cambridge University Press, in association with the Medieval Academy of Ireland, 1990.

Bokedal, Tomas. "The Scriptures and the LORD: Formation and Significance of the Christian Biblical Canon. A Study in Text, Ritual and Interpretation." PhD Diss., Lund University, 2005.

Bonhoeffer, Dietrich. *Dietrich Bonhoeffer Werke,* 14. Gütersloh: Gütersloher Verlagshaus, 1996.

Brown, Schuyler. "Concerning the Origin of the *Nomina Sacra.*" *Studia Papyrologica* 9 (1970): 7–19.

Capes, David B. *Old Testament Yahweh Texts in Paul's Christology.* WUNT 2/47; Tübingen: Mohr/Siebeck, 1992.

140. I want to thank Dr. Donald Wood, Dr. Dirk Jongkind and my wife Anna Bokedal for reading and commenting on an earlier draft of this chapter. Thanks also go to Philip Comfort and David Barrett and the staff at Accordance, Rex A. Koivisto, Matthew T. Williams and Rick Bennett, who helped providing electronic data on which this contribution rests. Invaluable online images for the project were provided by the Center for the Study of New Testament Manuscripts (http://www.csntm.org/manuscript).

Comfort, Philip. *Encountering the Manuscripts: An Introduction to New Testament Paleography & Textual Criticism*. Nashville, TN: Broadman and Holman, 2005.

Comfort, Philip W. and David P. Barrett, eds. *The Text of the Earliest New Testament Greek Manuscripts*. Corrected and enlarged, Accordance electronic ed. November 2009; Wheaton: Tyndale House Publishers, 2001.

Dinkler, Erich. *Signum Crucis*. Tübingen: Mohr/Siebeck, 1967.

Dunn, James D. G. *Did the First Christians Worship Jesus: The New Testament Evidence*. London: SPCK and Louisville, KY: WJK, 2010.

Heath, Jane. "*Nomina Sacra* and *Sacra Memoria* Before the Monastic Age." *JTS* 61.2 (2010): 516–49.

Hengel, Martin. *The Four Gospels and the One Gospel of Jesus Christ*. Harrisburg, PA: Trinity Press International, 2000.

Hurtado, Larry W. *At the Origins of Christian Worship: The Context and Character of Earliest Christian Devotion*. Grand Rapids: MI and Cambridge, UK: Eerdmans, 1999.

———. *The Earliest Christian Artifacts: Manuscripts and Christian Origins*. Grand Rapids, MI and Cambridge, UK: Eerdmans, 2006.

———. "The Earliest Evidence of an Emerging Christian Material and Visual Culture: The Codex, the *Nomina Sacra* and the Staurogram." Pages 271-88 in *Text and Artifact in the Religions of Mediterranean Antiquity: Essays in Honour of Peter Richardson*. Edited by Stephen G. Wilson and Michel Desjardins. Waterloo, Ont.: Wilfrid Lurier University Press, 2000.

———. "Introduction." Pages 1–16 in *The Freer Biblical Manuscripts: Fresh Studies of an American Treasure Trove*. Edited by Larry Hurtado. Atlanta: Society of Biblical Literature, 2006.

———. *Lord Jesus Christ: Devotion to Jesus in Earliest Christianity*. Grand Rapids, MI and Cambridge, UK: Eerdmans, 2003.

———. "The Origin of the *Nomina Sacra*: A Proposal." *Journal of Biblical Literature* 117 (1998): 655–73.

Hvalvik, Reidar. "Barnabas 9.7–9 and the Author's Supposed Use of Gematria." *NTS* 33 (1987): 276–82.

———. The Struggle for Scripture and Covenant: the purpose of the epistle of Barnabas and Jewish-Christian competition in the second century. WUNT 2/82; Tübingen: Mohr/Siebeck, 1996.

Imberg, Rune. *Tracts for the Times: A Complete Survey of All the Editions.* Bibliotheca Historico-Ecclesiastica Lundensis 17. Lund: Lund University Press, 1987.

Johansson, Daniel. "*Kyrios* in the Gospel of Mark." *JSNT* 33.1 (2010): 101–24.

Jongkind, Dirk. *Scribal Habits of Codex Sinaiticus.* Piscataway, N.J.: Gorgias Press, 2007.

Edwards, James R. "A Nomen Sacrum in the Sardis Synagogue." *JBL* 128, 4 (2009): 813–821.

Kennedy, Joel. The Recapitulation of Israel: Use of Israel's History in Matthew 1:1–4:11. WUNT 2/257. Tübingen: Mohr/Siebeck, 2008.

Nolland, John. "'In Such a Manner it is Fitting for Us to Fulfil All Righteousness': Reflections on the Place of Baptism in the Gospel of Matthew." Pages 63–80 in *Baptism, the New Testament and the Church: Historical and Contemporary Studies in Honour of R.E.O. White.* Edited by Stanley E. Porter and Anthony R. Cross. Journal for the Study of the New Testament Supplement Series 171. Sheffield: Sheffield Academic, 1999.

O'Callaghan, José. *Nomina Sacra in Papyrus Graecis Saeculi III Neotestamentariis.* Rome: Biblical Institute Press, 1970.

———. "'Nominum sacrorum' elenchus in Graecis Novi Testamenti papyris a saeculo IV usque ad VIII." *Studia Papyrologica* 10 (1971): 99–122.

Overcash, Benjamin. "Σταυρος as a *Nomen Sacrum*: A Suggestion." Unpublished conference paper presented at the SBL Papyrology and Early Christian Backgrounds Group, San Antonio, TX, 22 Nov 2016.

Paap, A. H. R. E. *Greek Papyri of the First Five Centuries A.D.: The Sources and Some Deductions.* Papyrologica Lugduno-Batava 8. Leiden: Brill, 1959.

Paget, James Carleton. "The Interpretation of the Bible in the Second Century." In *The New Cambridge History of the Bible.* Edited by Joachim Schaper and James Carleton Paget. Cambridge: Cambridge University Press, 2013.

Parker, David C. *Codex Bezae: An Early Christian Manuscript and Its Text.* Cambridge: Cambridge University, 1992.

Prior, J. Bruce. "The Use and Nonuse of Nomina Sacra in the Freer Gospel of Matthew." Pages 147–66 in *The Freer Biblical Manuscripts: Fresh Studies of an American Treasure Trove.* Edited by Larry W. Hurtado. Atlanta: Society of Biblical Literature, 2006.

Reijners, G. Q. *The Terminology of the Holy Cross in Early Christian Literature: As Based upon Old Testament Typology.* Nijmegen-Utrecht: Dekker & Van de Vegt N.V., 1965.

Roberts, Colin H. *Manuscript, Society and Belief in Early Christian Egypt.* Schweich Lectures 1977. London: Oxford University Press, published for the British Academy, 1979.

Roberts Colin H. and T. C. Skeat. *The Birth of the Codex.* London: Oxford University Press, 1983.

Rowe, C. Kavin. *Early Narrative Christology: The Lord in the Gospel of Luke.* Grand Rapids, MI: Baker Academic, 2006.

Schubert, Paul. "Editing a Papyrus." Pages 197–215 in *The Oxford Handbook of Papyrology.* Edited by Roger Bagnall. Oxord and New York: Oxford University Press, 2009.

Schoedel, William R. "Ignatius and the Archives." *HTR* 71 (1978): 97–106.

Skarsaune, Oskar. "Justin and His Bible." Pages 53–76 in *Justin Martyr and His Worlds.* Edited by Sara Parvis and Paul Foster. Minneapolis: Fortress, 2007.

Swanson, Reuben, ed. *New Testament Greek Manuscripts: Variant Readings Arranged in Horizontal Lines Against Codex Vaticanus. 1 Corinthians.* Wheaton, IL: Tyndale House Publishers and Pasadena, CA: William Carey International University Press, 2003.

Traube, Ludwig. *Nomina Sacra: Versuch einer Geschichte der christlichen Kürzung.* Munich: Beck, 1907.

Treu, Kurt. "Die Bedeutung des Griechischen für die Juden im römischen Reich", *Kairos* 15 (1973), 123–44. Translated by Adler and Kraft. http://eawc.evansville.edu/essays/nepage.htm [accessed 15/05/10]).

Trobisch, David. *Die Endredaktion des Neuen Testaments.* Göttingen: Vandenhoeck & Ruprecht, 1996. English translation: *The First Edition of the New Testament.* Oxford: Oxford University Press, 2000.

Troyer, Kristin De. "The Pronunication of the Names of God." Pages 159–63 in *Gott Nennen: Gottes Namen und Gott als Name.* RPT 35; Tübingen: Mohr/Siebeck, 2008.

Tuckett, Christopher M. "'Nomina Sacra' – Yes and No?" In *The Biblical Canons.* Edited by Auwers and Jonge. Belgium: Leuven University Press, Uitgeverij Peeters, 2003.

Turner, C. H. "The *Nomina Sacra* in Early Latin Christian MSS." *Studi e Testi* 40 (1924): 62–74.

Walser, Georg A. *Jeremiah: A Commentary Based on Ieremias in Codex Vaticanus.* Septuagint Commentary Series. Leiden: Brill, 2012.

PART F

CONCLUDING REFLECTIONS

13

CHRISTOLOGICAL TEXTUAL STRUCTURING OF THE NEW TESTAMENT CANON: HERMENEUTICAL REFLECTION ON THE PARTS AND THE WHOLE

13.1 MEANS OF TEXTUAL STRUCTURING: FAITH SUMMARIES AND CREEDAL CONNECTORS

This study opened with a brief overview of symbols and acronyms that the early Christians endorsed as summaries of their faith (ch. 1). One of the symbols, the equally popular and dramatic sign of the cross, had already been embraced within apocalyptic Jewish circles, as an emblem of divine election and belonging.[1] We saw that, among the early Christians, not only the cross, represented by the *nomen sacrum* CROSS (C̄T̄P̄O̅C̄) and the staurogram, ⳨ (cf. C̄⳨O̅Y̅ in P⁶⁶, John 19:19; chs. 1 and 12), but also other key symbols of recognition, such as the acronym ICHTHYS (ΙΧΘΥΣ), could be related to the biblical editorial system of *nomina sacra* ("sacred names," hereafter NS), offering a condensed visual expression of the new faith (chs. 1–13).[2] *Nomina Sacra* became a standard ingredient in Old and

---

1. Erich Dinkler, "Kreuzzeichen und Kreuz: Tav, Chi und Stauros," in *Signum Crucis: Aufsätze zum Neuen Testament und zur christlichen Archäologie* (Tübingen: Mohr, 1967), 32.

2. Cf. Col 1:20: "and through him GOD was pleased to reconcile to himself all things, whether on earth or in heaven, by making peace through the blood of his CROSS." (NRSV, modified); cf. also the reference to the cross in the Second Council of Nicaea (AD 787): "the honor we show to the

New Testament texts and other Christian literature and artistry—mosaics, graffiti, icons, and so on. As specially demarcated devotional and creedal terms, they helped connect the biblical (and other Christian) texts with kerygmatic/creedal summary accounts, by highlighting the central figures of the faith along with essential Christian vocabulary—GOD the FATHER, the SON LORD JESUS CHRIST, MAN/HUMAN BEING, CROSS/CRUCIFY, and the Holy SPIRIT (chs. 11 and 12). This connective function of the NS was both an innerbiblical phenomenon (continuous textual references to the kerygmatic/creedal aspect of the supratextual NS matrix itself) and an embedded drive toward mutually linking the biblical texts and extra-textual kerygmatic/creedal materials (e.g., through production, copying, reading, and interpretation of Scripture containing NS; and Scripture-based preaching, teaching, and liturgy/ritual). The NS here appear to have served as kerygmatic/creedal connectors even beyond their sheer visibility on the page, by inclusion, for example, also of associated arith-metical textual elements (chs. 5–10).[3] The term "creedal" or "creed," as used here, pertains to the Latin word *symbolum* (= "creed") and is employed in the sense Augustine understands the term (*Sermo* 213):

> So the *symbolum* [creed] is a briefly compiled rule of faith, intended to instruct the mind without overburdening the memory; to be said in a few words, from which much is to be gained. Thus, it is called a *symbolum* because it is something by which Christians can

---

form of the precious and life-giving cross, and the holy Gospels, and the other sacred objects we set up for devotion." Quoted from Michael Straus, "The Word as Word: A Canonical-Hermeneutical Approach to Translation with Paul's Letter to the Colossians as a Test Case" (PhD diss., University of Aberdeen, 2021), 158. The acronym ΙΧΘΥΣ represents the (first Greek letters of the) words "Jesus" (Ἰησοῦς), "Christ" (Χριστός), "God's" (Θεοῦ), "Son" (Υἱός) and "Savior" (Σωτήρ). Another symbol to mention in this connection is the Christogram, which was often supplied with an alpha-omega siglum.

3. More or less all key kerygmatic/creedal structures that include NS in Irenaeus's presentation of the Rule of Faith in *Haer.* 1.10.1 (discussed in ch. 11) were identified as *Name-Related Numerals* (*NrN*) in the corresponding structures in the biblical material (chs. 5–10). We can note in particular, that Irenaeus's pairing of terms from the NS word-group are all among the arithmetically highlighted ones listed in §9.1 above (being numerically associated with the Tetragrammaton): §§9.1.30 (θεός <AND> πατήρ), 9.1.33 (θεός <AND> λόγος), 9.1.25 (θεός <AND> υἱός), 9.1.38–39 (Ἰησοῦς <AND> χριστός; ιησ* <AND> χρι*), 9.1.40 (κύριος <AND> χριστὸς Ἰησοῦς), 9.1.82 (ἄνθρωπος <AND> ἄνθρωπος), 9.1.81 (θεός <AND> ἄνθρωπος) and 9.1.45 (πνεῦμα <AND> ἅγιος). These word combinations are represen-tative of the Rule-of-Faith pattern and characteristic of both typical *regula fidei* formularies and key scriptural NS configurations.

recognize each other (*Symbolum est ergo breviter complexa regula fidei, ut mentem instruat nec oneret memoriam; paucis verbis dicatur, unde multum acquiratur. Symbolum ergo dicitur, in quo se agnoscant Christiani*).[4]

13.2 HOW THE *RULE OF FAITH*, THE *NOMINA SACRA*, AND NUMERICAL PATTERNS SHAPE THE CANON

The overall theme of the present study—how the Rule of Faith, the *NS*, and numerical patterns shape the canon—was treated in chapters 1–12, in the first place with reference to Jesus Christ and the divine name as the center of Christian discourse. We saw that Bible reading in late second-century teachers commonly meant Christ-centered Triune exegesis of the Scriptures (§2.4.2 and ch. 11). A soteriological emphasis was added by directing readerly attention to Christ and his cross (§§1.1; 2.3; 2.4.1; 4.4.1; 11.5.1; 12.2e; 12.6.4–6; 12.7.1e; 13.1, 4). Thus, in the early Christian period, theology, Christology, and soteriology arguably went hand in hand (cf. 1 Thess 5:9–10; and Irenaeus *Epid.* 3), including Triune soteriological words of encouragement (cf. 2 Thess 2:13; Irenaeus *Epid.* 6–7).[5]

Chapters 2–4 explored the Christian canon formation process, more specifically, with attention directed to the relationship between the

---

4. Quoted from Michael Straus, "Word as Word," 101n361. Cf. Wolfram Kinzig, *Faith in Formulae: A Collection of Early Christian Creeds and Creed-Related Texts*, vol. 2, Oxford Early Christian Texts (Oxford: Oxford University Press, 2017), §316e. For a discussion of the notion of *symbolum*, see further J. N. D. Kelly, *Early Christian Creeds*, 3rd ed. (London: Continuum, 2006), 52–61: "Whatever the ultimate reasons for the selection of this word [symbol/*symbolum*], there can be no doubt that as used in the third century it denoted the baptismal questions and answers. Later it became the regular title of the declaratory creed. How this change came about, and at what precise date, we cannot now determine with certainty. The transference, however, was a natural and easy one, for the kinship between declaratory creeds and the baptismal interrogations was extremely close: it probably coincided with the introduction of declaratory creeds into the ceremonial preparation for baptism. It was fully established by the middle of the fourth century, as we can infer from the allusions of Rufinus, St Augustine and others to the tradition and reddition of the creed. ... The grand discovery to which our lengthy discussion has led is that the classical name for baptismal creeds was itself in origin bound up in the most intimate way with the primitive structure of the baptismal rite" (60–61).

5. Correspondingly, in the Synoptics Jesus came to "proclaim and inaugurate the kingdom of God" and in John "to bring eternal life" (Richard J. Bauckham, "Christology," in *Dictionary of Jesus and the Gospels*, ed. Joel B. Green, Jeannine K. Brown, and Nicholas Perrin, 2nd ed. [Downers Grove, IL: IVP Academic, 2013], 126).

emergent biblical canon, the *regula fidei,* and the editorial-scribal NS practice. Chapters 3 and 4 stressed the close relationship between Scripture
and canon, with canon presented as a property of sacred Scripture.
It was claimed that Scripture and the Rule of Faith functioned in the
faith communities as "two sides of one and the same norm" (*zwei Seiten
einer Norm*).[6] The Rule of Faith took on a structuring function vis-à-
vis the Scriptures—to guarantee that the faith community "read the Old
Testament as the promise of the Gospel and the Gospel as the fulfilment
of that promise."[7] The *regula fidei* here functioned as a normative hermeneutical tool, promoting not only the textual and theological unity of,
but also the distinction between, the corpus of Old and New Testament
Scriptures (ch. 11; Irenaeus *Haer.* 1.8.1–10.1; Clement *Strom.* 6.15.125.3).

In chapters 5–10, Triune structures like the one found in 2 Thess 2:13—
containing the words θεός, κύριος, and πνεῦμα—were noted as inherently
Triune, in the Pauline writings, in at least three ways: (1) by the inclusion
of the Triune structure θεός <AND> κύριος <AND> πνεῦμα in a number
of Pauline verses (Rom 1:4; 15:30; 1 Cor 6:11; 12:3; 2 Cor 13:13; Eph 1:17;
1 Thess 5:23; 2 Thess 2:13; search in Accordance), (2) by triadic textual
demarcation of the three included terms as NS, "sacred names" (contraction of a selection of sacred Greek words, supplied with an overbar), and
(3) by the potential arithmetical allusion to the Tetragrammaton (YHWH
= 26; cf. table 5.1, ch. 5 above) by means of the terms included in the Triune
Name-related configuration θεός <AND> κύριος <AND> πνεῦμα appearing
altogether **twenty-six times** in Pauline Corpus (each word counted separately; THGNT, NA28, ℵ, TR, TF 35; textual scope: verse; alternatively
170 times [10 x 17] for THGNT paragraph as textual scope). Similar
Triune numerological shaping of subcanonical text-units were further
observed as linked to the NS terms included in the Triune structure θεός
<AND> Ἰησοῦς χριστός <AND> πνεῦμα, appearing all in all **twenty-six
times** in the full New Testament (each word/expression counted separately; THGNT, NA28, ℵ; textual scope: verse; alternatively **182 times [7**

---

6. Karlmann Beyschlag, *Gott und Welt,* vol. 1 of *Grundriß der Dogmengeschichte* (Darmstadt: Wissenschaftliche Buchgesellschaft, 1982), 170 (author's translation); ch. 11.

7. Mark Edwards, *Catholicity and Heresy in the Early Church* (Farnham: Ashgate, 2009), 40.

x 26] for THGNT paragraph as textual scope).[8] Using the same method, we noted as well the altogether **twenty-six occurrences** in the full New Testament of the three words θεός, υἱός, and πνεῦμα (allocated to eight New Testament passages) when appearing together in the same verse (each word counted separately; THGNT, NA28, ℵ, TR, TF 35).[9] Triune numerological textual patterning, involving two different arithmetic search methods, was found in the canonical subunits that compose the New Testament (chs. 6–10). Similar Triune structures were further detected in Ignatius of Antioch, Eusebius, Basil the Great, and Athanasius. In chapter 7, we continued our reflection on word-frequencies aligning with *Name-related Numerals* (*NrN*) and their link to innertextual canonical shaping.

Chapter 12, which described the inauguration and significance of the NS, proposed that a major aim—pertaining to the early canonical process—of introducing the core group of *nomina sacra* into the Christian scriptures, was to graphically identify the Tetragrammaton (in Greek rendered as ΘЄOC and ΚΥΡΙOC) with the Greek names for "Jesus," "Christ," "Lord" and "God."[10] With parallels in contemporary Judaism, special early Christian treatment of the divine name seems to have been an essential dimension of Holy Writ; and a "Christianization" of the Jewish Scriptures took place not only by means of Christian employment of the codex as the new book format but, more importantly, with NS being systematically introduced into the Scriptures. As textual/supratextual markers, the NS helped identify Christian Scripture as Scripture. This took place (1) by textually/graphically treating the words "Jesus" and "God" in the same way, (2) by including the triadic NS at more or less every page of the emerging New Testament, thus indicating a Christian textual center, (3) and by editorially employing the NS as a form of kerygmatic creedal structure

---

8. The following eight verses are included in the count: Rom 1:4; 15:30; 1 Cor 6:11; 2 Cor 13:13; Eph 1:17; 1 Thess 5:23; 1 Pet 1:2; and 1 John 4:2.

9. Mark 3:11; Luke 1:35; Acts 2:17; Rom 1:4, 9; 8:14; Gal 4:6; and Heb 10:29; corresponding result for Pauline Corpus is **17 occurrences** (textual scope: verse)/ **132 occurrences [6 x 22]** (textual scope: THGNT paragraph).

10. The primary four words are often referred to as *nomina divina*.

engrafted into the textuality of the Christian Scriptures, "representing what might be regarded as the embryonic creed of the first Church."[11]

13.3 MEANS OF TEXTUAL STRUCTURING: *INCLUSIOS* AND MARKERS OF TEXTUAL WHOLES

Arguably the most popular combination of NS, both as part of artistic representations and in the New Testament, was the christological expression JESUS CHRIST (ι̅c̅ x̅c̅; figures below from THGNT, unless otherwise indicated), featuring 88 times [4 × 22] in the Pauline Corpus, 44 times [2 × 22] in the Praxapostolos (Acts + Catholic Epistles), and 140 times [10 × 14] in the full New Testament.[12] As argued in chapter 5, a numerical reference to the textual whole—by means of multiples of the Hebrew alphabetical fullness number 22—may here be intentional on the part of the authors/editors of the Pauline Corpus and the Praxapostolos, with 88 [4 × 22] and 44 [2 × 22] appearances, respectively, of the phrase JESUS CHRIST (ι̅c̅ x̅c̅) in these canonical subunits.[13]

---

11. C. H. Roberts, *Manuscript, Society and Belief in Early Christianity*, Schweich Lectures 1977 (Oxford: Oxford University Press, 1979), 46.

12. Corresponding figures for CHRIST JESUS (x̅c̅ ι̅c̅) are: Pauline Corpus 83 occurrences, Praxapostolos 6 occurrences, and the full New Testament 89 occurrences. For corresponding figures in NA28, see note 13 below.

13. Both 88 [4 × 22] and 44 [2 × 22] are NrN, as defined in ch. 5 (i.e., multiples of 22, 24, and 27, on the one hand, and 15, 17, and 26, on the other). The number of appearances of the phrase in the genitive, too, occur as NrN, namely 34 appearances [2 × 17] of Ἰησοῦ χριστοῦ in Praxapostolos and 72 [3 × 24] in Pauline Corpus (THGNT). In Codex Sinaiticus (א), the following NrN feature for the genitive forms ι̅υ̅ x̅υ̅: Pauline Corpus 78 times [3 × 26], Romans 17 times, 1–2 Corinthians 15 times, Catholic Epistles 27 times, 1–2 Peter 17 times, and the full New Testament 120 times [5 × 24]. x̅υ̅ ι̅υ̅, moreover, occurs 24 times in Pauline Corpus (א). In NA28, the expression JESUS CHRIST (ι̅c̅ x̅c̅) is allocated as follows: the twenty-seven-book New Testament 135 times [5 × 27], the Pauline Corpus 83 times, and Praxapostolos 44 times [2 × 22]. In the Byzantine text form, the expression JESUS CHRIST (ι̅c̅ x̅c̅) is allocated as follows: the twenty-seven-book New Testament 119 times [7 × 17], Romans 22 times, 1–2 Corinthians 26 times, and 1–2 Thessalonians 17 times (all of which are NrN; see further ch. 5). JESUS CHRIST (ι̅c̅ x̅c̅) further appears 108 times [4 × 27] in the Ignatian letter corpus (in Michael Holmes, *Apostolic Fathers: Greek Texts and English Translations of Their Writings*, 3rd ed. [Grand Rapids: Baker Academic, 2007]) and 22 times in Justin's *Dialogue with Trypho* (Migne). In line with the arithmetical argument presented in ch. 5, the following New Testament figures may be deliberate on the part of the authors and editorial/scribal team producing the texts: JESUS CHRIST (ι̅c̅ x̅c̅) appearing 8 times (with potential reference to the resurrection and new creation) in Galatians, Ephesians, and 1 Peter, respectively (see discussion below); Ἰησοῦς <AND> χριστός featuring altogether 22 times in the four Gospels, 352 times [2 × 8 × 22] in Pauline Corpus, 60 times [4 × 15] in Romans, 14 times in 1 Thessalonians (with potential numerological allusion to the Davidic

As for the textual parts in Galatians contributing to this canonical whole, we may note the key role obtained for JESUS CHRIST (ι̅c̅ x̅c̅) in the opening verse (Gal 1:1), forming an *inclusio* with the final line in Gal 6:18.[14] The phrase ι̅c̅ x̅c̅ occurs altogether eight times in the epistle.[15] The same pattern can be noted for Ephesians, with its eight occurrences of JESUS CHRIST (ι̅c̅ x̅c̅), the first of which appears in Eph 1:1, which analogously forms an *inclusio* with the last verse in Eph 6:24.[16] Interestingly, exactly the same structure is found in 2 Peter, similarly with altogether eight occurrences of the phrase, with the opening and concluding ι̅c̅ x̅c̅ in 2 Pet 1:1 and 3:18 providing an *inclusio* for the letter as a whole.[17]

---

number 14; see table 5.1 above), 26 times in 2 Timothy, 54 times [2 × 27] in 1–2 Timothy, 34 times [2 × 17] in 1-2 Peter (1-2 Peter textual scope: verse; see further table 5.1 for potential significance of 15-, 17-, 22-, and 27-multiples).

14. Craig S. Keener (*Galatians: A Commentary* [Grand Rapids: Baker Academic, 2019], 50) comments on Gal 1:1: "That Paul did not receive his commission *from mere human beings* (lit., from a human) but *through Jesus Christ and God the Father* (1:1) suggests that Paul understands Jesus as more than human (though Paul does not deny Jesus's humanity; 4:4). (Both earlier and more recent commentators offer this observation)" (emphasis original).

15. The expression CHRIST JESUS (x̅c̅ ι̅c̅), too, occurs eight times in Galatians. The altogether sixteen [4 × 4] appearances of JESUS CHRIST and CHRIST JESUS in Galatians may be a numerical allusion to the universality emphasis in the letter (cf. Gal 3:28–29: "πλ̅ντεc ͞γλρ ͞γμειc ειc εcτε εν x̅ω̅ ι̅γ̅," Codex Vaticanus [B]; see further table 5.1 in ch. 5 for potential significance of the number 4).

16. "ἀπὸ θεοῦ πατρὸς ... καὶ κυρίου Ἰησοῦ χριστοῦ," in Eph 1:2 further forms an *inclusio* with Eph 6:23; and κύριος <AND> Ἰησοῦς <AND> χριστός, appearing in Eph 1:2 and 1:3 likewise forms an *inclusio* with Eph 6:23 and 6:24. All in all, the three words involved in the Accordance search κύριος <AND> Ἰησοῦς <AND> χριστός appear twenty-two times in Ephesians (each word counted separately). We may here note, as well, the twenty-two occurrences of χριστὸς Ἰησοῦ and the twenty-seven for Ἰησοῦς χριστός + χριστὸς Ἰησοῦ in 1–2 Timothy (cf. table 5.1, for potential significance of 22 and 27). Philemon demonstrates similar features regarding χριστός, appearing eight times in the letter, and where χριστός in Phlm 1 and 25 forms an *inclusio* for the letter as a whole; similarly, Ἰησοῦς χριστός in Phlm 3 and 25, χριστὸς Ἰησοῦς in Phlm 1 and 23, χριστὸς Ἰησοῦς (x̅γ̅ ι̅γ̅) in Phlm 1 with Ἰησοῦς χριστός (ι̅γ̅ x̅γ̅) in Phlm 25, and χάρις ... κύριος ... Ἰησοῦς χριστός in Phlm 3 and 25. In 1 Corinthians, ἐν χριστῷ Ἰησοῦ in 1 Cor 1:2, further forms an *inclusio* with the final verse, 16:24. In 2 Corinthians, κυρίου Ἰησοῦ χριστοῦ in 2 Cor 1:2 forms an *inclusio* with the final verse in 2 Cor 13:13. A similar *inclusio* pattern features also for χριστὸς Ἰησοῦς in Colossians (1:1 and 4:12), for χριστὸς Ἰησοῦς (x̅γ̅ ι̅γ̅) in Phil 1:1, and Ἰησοῦς χριστός (ι̅γ̅ x̅γ̅) in Phil 4:23; and for the fourteen appearances of Ἰησοῦς in Revelation (1:1 and 22:21); 14 may here be a numerological messianic allusion to Jesus as son of David; cf. table 5.1; fourteen appearances of the *nomen sacrum* JESUS are found also in 1 Timothy and in Hebrews (see further appendix above). As for the Pauline Corpus as a whole, we can further note the twenty-two occurrences of Ἰησοῦς (nom.) and the twenty-seven of Ἰησοῦν (acc.; for the alphabetical numbers 22 and 27, see table 5.1 above).

17. The number eight may here be an arithmetical allusion to the notion of resurrection and new creation (see table 5.1; cf. also the eight occurrences of Νῶε, "Noah," in the New Testament and the association of Noah with the number eight in 1 Pet 3:20 ["eight lives were saved by water"] and 2 Pet 2:5 ["saved Noah the eighth person"]).

At the next canonical subunit level, both the Pauline Corpus and the Catholic Epistles begin and end with ιϲ χϲ as an *inclusio*, demarcated in Rom 1:1 and Phlm 25 (ιυ χυ in the first and last verse in Pauline Corpus in א and A) and in Jas 1:1 and Jude 25 (ιυ χυ in the first and last verse in the Catholic Epistles in א, B, and A).[18] The four Gospels and Acts, too, incorporate this *nomina sacra inclusio*, with ιυ χυ featuring in Matt 1:1, the opening verse of Matthew, and Acts 28:31, the closing verse of Acts. We thus come across altogether three potential *inclusios* involving the genitive forms ιυ χυ for three of the major canonical subunits, highlighting as literary/canonical subunits Matt 1:1–Acts 28:31, Jas 1:1–Jude 25, and Rom 1:1–Phlm 25.[19]

Another series of both obvious and, at the same time, perhaps less obvious potential *inclusios*, involving the name JESUS (ιϲ), is the enclosure of the key *nomen sacrum* JESUS (ιϲ) in (1) the first (Matt 1:1) and last verse (John 21:25) of the fourfold Gospel, (2) the first (Matt 1:1) and last verse (Acts 28:31) of Gospels + Acts, (3) the first (Acts 1:1) and last verse (Jude 25) of Praxapostolos (as exemplified, e.g., by manuscripts B and A), (4) the first (Jas 1:1) and last verse (Jude 25) of the Catholic Epistles, (5) the first (Rom 1:1) and last verse (Phlm 25) of Pauline Corpus (as exemplified, e.g., by Pauline Corpus in א and A), (6) the first (Rev 1:1) and last verse (Rev 22:21) of Revelation, and (7) the first (Matt 1:1) and last verse (Rev 22:21) of the standard twenty-seven-book New Testaments (first and last verse in the twenty-seven-book New Testament in א).[20] That is,

---

18. For the Catholic Epistles the *inclusio* involves also κύριος: κϲ ιϲ χϲ in Jas 1:1 and ιϲ χϲ ... κϲ in Jude 25.

19. We may note, as well, the potential *inclusios* for several canonical subunits regarding the pairing of words—in the same verse/passage—beginning with either the Greek letter *iota* (as in Ἰησοῦς) or the letter *chi* (as in χριστός). Accordingly, ι* <AND> χ*occur as follows: Matt 1:1/Mark 1:1 and John 21:25 (first and last verse of the fourfold Gospel), Matt 1:1/Mark 1:1 and Acts 28:31 (first and last verse of Gospels + Acts), Jas 1:1 and Jude 25 (first and last verse of the Catholic Epistles), Rom 1:1 and Phlm 25 (first and last verse of Pauline Corpus), Rev 1:1 and 22:21 (first and last verse of Book of Revelation), and Matt 1:1 and Rev 22:21 (first and last verse of the standard canonical New Testament). For further observations regarding ι* <AND> χ*, see Tomas Bokedal, "'But for Me, the Scriptures Are Jesus Christ' (ιϲ χϲ; Ign. *Phld.* 8:2): Creedal Text-Coding and the Early Scribal System of Nomina Sacra," in *Studies on the Paratextual Features of Early New Testament Manuscripts*, ed Stanley E. Porter, David I. Yoon, and Chris S. Stevens, TENTS (Leiden: Brill, forthcoming).

20. Regarding *inclusios*, Adela Yarbro Collins (*Mark: A Commentary*, ed. Harold W. Attridge, Hermeneia [Minneapolis: Fortress, 2007], 89) comments: "A number of scholars have argued, or proceeded on the assumption, that these devices [*inclusios*; or ring compositions], originally designed

all these seven major canonical subunits seem to be highlighted, innerbib-lically, through these seven *inclusios*.[21] Though with less consistency we may also note the similar potential *inclusios* regarding the *nomen sacrum* κ̄ς̄, LORD, that we find in Mark 1:3 and Mark 16:20 (potential *inclusio* for Mark); Luke 1:6 and Acts 28:31 (potential *inclusio* for Luke-Acts); Jas 1:1 and Jude 25 (*inclusio* involving the first and last verse of the Catholic Epistles); Rom 1:4 and Phlm 25 (potential *inclusio* for the Pauline Corpus); Matt 1:20/Mark 1:3/Luke 1:6 and Rev 22:21 (potential *inclusio* for the full twenty-seven-book New Testament).[22] In addition to the aforementioned comments on JESUS and LORD, these two key NS—JESUS (ῑς̄) and LORD (κ̄ς̄)—may here be viewed also together in their respective textual *inclusio* functions outlined above.

A similar potential macrocanonical *inclusio*, involving Matthew and Revelation, can be noted, as well, for the first and last instances, in Matt 1:1 and Rev 22:16, of the twenty-four New Testament appearances of Ἰησοῦς <AND> Δαυίδ (the NS JESUS and DAVID occurring together in the same verse/passage altogether **twenty-four times** in eleven New Testament verses, as the two words are counted separately; alternatively **72 times** [**3 x 24**], when the THGNT paragraph is used as textual scope).[23] This may be understood as a double reference to the textual/canonical whole,

---

for use on the level of the sentence or small section [repetition of a word or a phrase at the beginning and end to delimit a textual unit] of a work, came to be used in larger contexts, even to structure an entire work." I owe this observation regarding Matt 1:1 and John 21:25 to a discussion with Zachary Bradley (see also note below).

21. In addition, we may note potential *inclusios*, involving the name JESUS (ῑς̄), also for (8) Acts, with JESUS (ῑς̄) occurring in Acts 1:1 and Acts 28:31; for (9) 1 Peter, (10) 2 Peter, and (11) 1–2 Peter, with JESUS (ῑς̄) occurring in 1 Pet 1:1 and 1 Pet 4:11, in 2 Pet 1:1 and 2 Pet 3:18, and in 1 Pet 1:1 and 2 Pet 3:18; for (12) Jude, with JESUS (ῑς̄) occurring in Jude 1 and Jude 25; for (13) Romans, with JESUS (ῑς̄) occurring in Rom 1:1 and Rom 16: 27; for (14) 1 Corinthians, (15) 2 Corinthians, and (16) 1–2 Corinthians, with JESUS (ῑς̄) occurring in 1 Cor 1:1 and 1 Cor 16:23, 2 Cor 1:1 and 2 Cor 13:13, and 1 Cor 1:1 and 2 Cor 13:13; for (17) Galatians, with JESUS (ῑς̄) occurring in Gal 1:1 and Gal 6:18; for (18) Ephesians, with JESUS (ῑς̄) occurring in Eph 1:1 and Eph 6:24; for (19) Philippians, with JESUS (ῑς̄) occurring in Phil 1:1 and Phil 4:23; for (20) 1 Thessalonians, (21) 2 Thessalonians and (22) 1–2 Thessalonians, with JESUS (ῑς̄) occurring in 1 Thess 1:1 and 1 Thess 5:28, in 2 Thess 1:1 and 2 Thess 3:18, and in 1 Thess 1:1 and 2 Thess 3:18; and for (23) Philemon, with JESUS (ῑς̄) occurring in Phlm 1:1 and Phlm 25.

22. Cf. note 3, ch. 1, on the number of NS in the twenty-three opening verses in the New Testament.

23. Cf. also the *inclusios* Ἰησοῦς <AND> βιβλ*, spanning Matt 1:1 and John 21:25 (that is, the four-fold Gospel), βίβλος for Matt 1:1 and Rev 20:15 and βιβλ* for Matt 1:1 and Rev 22:19 (with the latter two spanning the twenty-seven-book New Testament of standard New Testaments, from Matthew

by means of (1) a Davidic–messianic *inclusio*, spanning the text between Matt 1:1 and the end of Revelation (Rev 22:16), and (2) an arithmetic reference within the same textual scope by means of a Greek alphabetical fullness marker (the twenty-four letters in the Hellenistic Greek alphabet), namely the altogether twenty-four New Testament appearances of the two words JESUS and DAVID, when occurring together.[24]

To sum up the above, textual and text-related wholes, made up of their respective parts, may be variously indicated, for example, by symbols (e.g., the acronym ICHTHYS), numerical signposts (e.g., word-frequency multiples of alphabetical fullness numbers), literary *inclusios* (e.g., by means of *NS*), or macrotextual structures (e.g., the editorial-scribal system of *NS*). The whole, as the basic hermeneutical rule tells us, is here more than the sum of its parts—a fuller expression with regard to meaning than the mere addition of the parts constituting the whole (e.g., the *NS* system merging with the Scriptures). However, it may also be the case that a particular part not only connects or contributes to this whole, but is also itself in a position to represent the whole, such as the identifying messianic *NS* compounds ι̅ϲ̅ χ̅ϲ̅, JESUS CHRIST, in Eph 1:1, being both part of and representative of the Eph 1:1–6:24 *inclusio*. A similar function of textual parts, potentially representing the whole, arguably applies as well to other *NS* combinations, featuring as brief statements of the faith in John 20:31; 1 Cor 1:3; 2 Cor 13:13, and elsewhere.

---

to Revelation). In addition, we may note, as well, the potential fullness reference, intended for the forty-eight New Testament occurrences [2 × 24] of βιβ* (see table 5.1 for the alphabetical number 24).

24. Ἰησοῦς <AND> Δαυίδ feature in the following 11 New Testament verses/passages: Matt 1:1; 9:27; 20:30; Mark 10:47; 12:35; Luke 6:3; 18:38; Acts 1:16; 7:45; 2 Tim 2:8; and Rev 22:16; for potential significance of the number 11 as a reference to prophetical fulfilment, see table 5.1. The corresponding figure for Codex Sinaiticus (א) is: 26 New Testament appearances, featuring in 12 verses (see table 5.1 for 26 as a NrN). We may further note the following related *NS* configurations in Codex Sinaiticus (א): Ἰησοῦς <AND> υἱός <AND> Δαυίδ Synoptic Gospels/New Testament 24 appearances, involving the following 7 verses: Matt 1:1; 9:27; 20:30; Mark 10:47; 12:35; Luke 18:38–39; and Ἰησοῦς <AND> ὁ <AND> υἱός <AND> Δαυίδ: Synoptic Gospels/New Testament 26 appearances, involving the following 5 verses: Matt 9:27; 20:30; Mark 10:47; 12:35; Luke 18:39. As for the macrocanonical *inclusio* mentioned above—the name JESUS (ι̅ϲ̅) in Matt 1:1 and Rev 22:21—we may add the further observation that JESUS (ι̅ϲ̅) features altogether 912 times [38 × 24] in the New Testament (THGNT), which, again, is an alphabetical 24-multiple, potentially indicating fullness and completeness. The *nomen sacrum* DAVID, moreover, is allocated as follows: Matthew 17 times, Matthew–Mark 24 times, four Gospels 39 times (see table 5.1, for potential significance of these figures); see further appendix for figures involving Δαυίδ and υἱὸς Δαυίδ (γ̅ϲ̅ λ̅λ̅λ̅).

13.4 MEANS OF TEXTUAL STRUCTURING: INDICATING THE BEGINNING, MIDDLE, AND END

As for the wider structural importance of the NS sequence JESUS CHRIST (ῑϲ̄ χϲ̄), a visible New Testament link between textual parts and textual whole can further be detected for the Synoptic Gospels. Mark, for example, opens with the well-known words ἀρχη τογ ϵγαγγελιογ ῑγ̄ χγ̄ γγ̄ θγ̄ (א͎ᶜ), "The beginning of the Gospel of JESUS CHRIST, the SON of GOD," which includes JESUS CHRIST (ῑγ̄ χγ̄) and two additional NS (γγ̄ θγ̄).²⁵ These four specially highlighted words appear together in altogether nine New Testament verses/passages, and their appearance in Mark 1:1 turns out to be paramount for the Gospel as a whole, as JESUS, being identified as the SON of GOD, is key to the framing of Mark's Gospel (NS as in א): at the beginning (Mark 1:11: "You are my SON [γϲ̄], the Beloved"), the middle (9:7: "This is my SON [γϲ̄], the Beloved"), and the end (15:39: "Truly this man was GOD's son" [γϊοϲ²⁶ θγ̄]).²⁷ The narrative christological

---

25. Thirty-nine times (THGNT, NA28; involving the following nine verses: Matt 26:63; Mark 1:1; John 20:31; Rom 1:4; 1 Cor 1:9; 2 Cor 1:19; Gal 3:26; 1 John 5:20; 2 John 3. Corresponding figure for א is thirty-four times [2 × 17]. See table 5.1, ch. 5, above, for potential significance of the number 39). ἀρχη τογ ϵγαγγελιογ ῑγ̄ χγ̄ in א*. See further Tommy Wasserman, "The 'Son of God' Was in the Beginning (Mark 1:1)," *JTS* 62 (2011): 20–50; and Wasserman, "Historical and Philological Correlations and the CBGM as Applied to Mark 1:1," *TC: A Journal of Biblical Textual Criticism* 20 (2015): 1–11. As the earliest written Synoptic Gospel, Mark 1:1 (ϵγαγγελιογ ῑγ̄ χγ̄ γγ̄ θγ̄ ; א͎ᶜ) may be said to form an *inclusio* with the closing paragraphs of the Gospel, John 20:31 (ῑϲ̄ ϵϲτιν ο χϲ̄ ο γϲ̄ τογ θγ̄; א*).

26. γϲ̄ in Codices Alexandrinus (A), Ephraemi Rescriptus (C), and Washingtonianus (W).

27. The four narratively, kerygmatically, and creedally central words occur together in the same verse in Matt 26:63; Mark 1:1; John 20:31; Rom 1:4; 1 Cor 1:9; 2 Cor 1:19; Gal 3:26; 1 John 5:20; and 2 John 3 (THGNT, NA28, TF 35/Majority Text). In these nine verses, when counted separately, the four words appear altogether thirty-nine times (see table 5.1, for potential significance of the number 39: "YHWH is one"; search in Accordance: Ἰησοῦς <AND> χριστός <AND> υἱός <AND> θεός [each word counted separately]). The corresponding figure for א is thirty-four times [2 × 17] (see table 5.1, for potential significance of the number 17). Cf. F. F. Bruce, *The Spreading Flame: The Rise and Progress of Christianity from Its First Beginnings to Eighth-Century England* (Nashville: Kingsley, 1981), Kindle location 5541–48: "the ... title 'Son of God' ... used of Jesus, ... also had a special significance. The words of Psalm 2:7, in which the God of Israel addresses His anointed one (His Messiah) with the words 'Thou art my son,' were applied to Jesus by the Heavenly Voice which addressed Him at His baptism. But to Him the title 'Son of God' was no merely official messianic designation. It expressed His own awareness of the unique filial relationship which He constantly enjoyed with His Father. This awareness finds supreme expression in the oracle of Matthew 11:27 and Luke 10:22." Cf. Aristotle (*Poetics*, Part 7; trans. S. H. Butcher), commenting on the beginning, middle, and end in tragedy/poetical composition: "Now, according to our definition Tragedy is an imitation of an action that is complete, and whole, and of a certain magnitude; for there may be a whole that is wanting in

highpoints in the two middle chapters of Mark—in Mark 8:29 and 9:7, portraying JESUS as the CHRIST (o x̄c̄) and SON of GOD (o ȳc̄ ΜΟΥ Ο ΔΓΑΠΗΤΟC)—thus connect back to the opening line of Mark 1:1 (ΤΟΥ ΕΥΑΓΓΕΛΙΟΥ ιȳ x̄ȳ ȳȳ θȳ) and 1:11 (CΥ ΕΙ Ο ȳc̄ ΜΟΥ Ο ΔΓΑΠΗΤΟC), as well as to the passion at the end of the Gospel (Mark 14:61 [o x̄c̄ o ȳc̄ ΤΟΥ θȳ]; 15:32 [o x̄c̄ o ΒΑCΙΛΕΥC ιCΡΑΗΛ]; and 15:39 [ΑΛΗΘѠC ΟΥΤΟC Ο ΑΝΘΡѠΠΟC ΥιΟC²⁸ θȳ ΗΝ]).

In all four canonical Gospels, JESUS-as-the-CHRIST/-SON-of-GOD pattern is crucial, and appears, toward the end of the Gospel of John, as a précis of the whole Gospel: ΤΑΥΤΑ ΔΕ ΓΕΓΡΑΠΤΑΙ ιΝΑ ΠΙCΤΕΥCΗΤΕ ΟΤΙ ιc̄ ΕCΤΙΝ Ο x̄c̄ Ο ȳc̄ ΤΟΥ θȳ (John 20:31; ℵ). Moreover, as pointed out by Martin Hengel and others, this Johannine verse functions canonically as a summary account for all four Gospels:²⁹ "These are written so that you may come to believe that JESUS is the CHRIST the SON of GOD, and that by believing you may have life in his Name" (John 20:31).³⁰

---

magnitude. A whole is that which has a beginning, a middle, and an end. A beginning is that which does not itself follow anything by causal necessity, but after which something naturally is or comes to be. An end, on the contrary, is that which itself naturally follows some other thing, either by necessity, or as a rule, but has nothing following it. A middle is that which follows something as some other thing follows it. A well-constructed plot, therefore, must neither begin nor end at haphazard, but conform to these principles."

28. ȳc̄ in Codices Alexandrinus (A), Ephraemi Rescriptus (C), and Washingtonianus (W).

29. Hengel, *The Four Gospels and the One Gospel of Jesus Christ: An Investigation of the Collection and Origin of the Canonical Gospels*, trans. John Bowden (London: SCM, 2000), 95: "Despite all the major differences, indeed oppositions, Mark's work already has basically the same aim as the Fourth Gospel, which is quite different in kind but ultimately related in its theological concern: 'But this is written that you may believe that Jesus is the Christ, the Son of God, and that believing you may have life in his name' (20.31)."

30. As for potential numerological indication by NrN (see further chs. 5–10 and table 5.1 above; NrN in boldface below), involving the four NS discussed above, we may note the following: Ἰησοῦς <AND> χριστός <AND> υἱός <AND> ὁ <AND> θεός: New Testament **68 times** [4 × 17], Matthew–Mark/Synoptic Gospels **17 times**; Ἰησοῦς <AND> χριστός <AND> υἱός <AND> θεός: New Testament **39 times**; χριστός <AND> υἱός <AND> ὁ <AND> θεός: New Testament **108 times** [4 × 27], Matthew–Mark **22 times**, Pauline Corpus **39 times**, John **15 times**, 2 John **15 times**, 1–2 John/Praxapostolos **26 times**; χριστός <AND> υἱός <AND> θεός: New Testament **48 times** [2 × 24]; ὁ Χριστός: New Testament **150 times** [10 × 15], Matthew–Mark **15 times**, Luke–Mark **15 times**, Gospels + Acts **48 times** [2 × 24], 2 Corinthians **15 times**; Ἰησοῦς <AND> ὁ χριστός: New Testament **30 times** [2 × 15]; ὁ Ἰησοῦς <AND> ὁ υἱός: four Gospels **39 times**, Matthew **14 times**; Ἰησοῦς χριστός <AND> υἱός: New Testament **22 times**; Ἰησοῦς χριστός <AND> ὁ <AND> υἱός: New Testament **45 times** [3 × 15], Pauline Corpus **14 times**, 1–2 John/Catholic Epistles **24 times**; Ἰησοῦς <AND> ὁ <AND> υἱός: four Gospels **289 times** [17 × 17], Matthew–Mark **132 times** [6 × 22], Synoptic Gospels **182 times** [7 × 26], Luke–Acts **66 times** [3 × 22], Catholic Epistles **52 times** [2 × 26], 1 John **48 times** [2 × 24], 1–2 John **52 times**

In connection with this passage in the concluding chapters of John, it is interesting to dwell, for a moment, on C. H. Roberts's and Larry Hurtado's claim that the Johannine phrase "that by believing you may have life in his Name" (John 20:31) includes a reference to the numerical value 18 of the Hebrew word for life, *khai* (18 = חי), as they point out that this is equivalent to the numerical value of the early *nomen sacrum* form for Ἰησοῦς, ιη (= 18).[31] Roberts and Hurtado explain the Johannine phrase, "to have life (18 = חי) in his Name (ιη = 18])" (John 20:31), with reference to such a Jewish-Christian *gematria*.[32] If this interpretation of John 20:31 is correct—"these are written so that you may come to believe that JESUS [ιη/ιc] is the CHRIST [χρ/χc], the SON of GOD [yc τογ θγ], and that through believing you may have life in his Name"—it is possible, or even likely, that these (early forms of) NS demarcations were employed also by the author(s) and/or early editor(s) of John's Gospel.[33]

[2 × 26]; Ἰησοῦς <AND> υἱός <AND> θεός: Matthew–Mark 14 times, Gospels + Acts **34 times** [2 × 17], Pauline Corpus **15 times**, Praxapostolos **22 times**; Ἰησοῦς <AND> ὁ υἱός <AND> θεός: New Testament 39 times; Ἰησοῦς <AND> ὁ <AND> υἱός <AND> ὁ <AND> θεός: New Testament **135 times** [5 × 27], Matthew–Mark **30 times** [2 × 15], Luke–John **30 times** [2 × 15], four Gospels **60 times** [4 × 15], Acts 14 times, Pauline Corpus 28 times [2 × 14], 1 John 28 times [2 × 14]; ὁ <AND> υἱός <AND> ὁ <AND> θεός: Matthew–Mark **78 times** [3 × 26], Luke **60 times** [4 × 15], John **105 times** [7 × 15], Luke–John **165 times** [11 × 15], four Gospels **243 times** [9 × 27], Acts **54 times** [2 × 27], Gospels + Acts **297 times** [11 × 27], 1–2 Corinthians **17 times**, Pauline Corpus **135 times** [5 × 27], 1 John **96 times** [4 × 24], Praxapostolos **168 times** [7 × 24]; υἱός <AND> θεός: New Testament **204 times** [12 × 17], Matthew **24 times**, John **34 times** [2 × 17], Gospels + Acts **108 times** [4 × 27], Pauline Corpus **52 times** [2 × 26], Romans **15 times**, and Praxapostolos **54 times** [2 × 27].

31. Roberts, *Manuscript, Society and Belief in Early Christianity*, 35–48; Hurtado, "The Origin of the Nomina Sacra: A Proposal," *JBL* 117 (1998): 664–71.

32. *Khet* = 8; *yod* = 10. We may further note that חי (life; living; family, life) occurs 396 times [18 × 22] in the MT, 104 times [4 × 26] in the Pentateuch, 98 times [7 × 14] in the Former Prophets, 68 times [4 × 17] in the Latter Prophets, 126 times [7 × 18] in the Writings, 24 times in Leviticus, 46 times [2 × 23] in 1–2 Samuel and 1–2 Kings, respectively, 26 times in 1 Kings, 26 times in Ezekiel, 39 times in Psalms (perhaps numerically somehow related, we can note the 39 occurrences of the Greek word ΖΩΗ, "life," in Pauline Corpus [THGNT, NA28, Textus Receptus, א]), 34 times [2 × 17] in Proverbs, and 22 times in Ecclesiastes. For potential significance of the numerals 4, 7, 14, 17, 18, 22, 23, 26, and 39, see table 5.1 above. Possibly arithmetically related to the above, we may note, as well, the number of occurrences of the two words נביא, "prophet," and קום, "raise up," when occurring together in the same verse/passage (נביא <AND> קום), the total appearances of which are 18 in the MT, with potential allusion to Deut 18:18.

33. Hurtado, "Origin," 665–69; and Hurtado, *The Earliest Christian Artifacts: Manuscripts and Christian Origins* (Grand Rapids: Eerdmans, 2006), 114–20. Codex Vaticanus (B) includes ιc, χc, and θγ in John 20:31. For an argument of a yet earlier inauguration in New Testament manuscripts of the NS, already in the Pauline Corpus, see Bokedal, "'But for Me.'"

Now, if we choose to take this argument one step further, combining it with observations pertaining to the *Name-Related Numeral(s)* (*NrN*; in boldface below) involved (discussed in ch. 5), the following interesting figures emerge: For John's Gospel, the following 4 *NS* word-frequencies, and their sum, feature (cf. the 4 *NS* in John 20:31): Ἰησοῦς (**240 occurrences** [**10 × 24**]) + χριστός (19 occurrences) + θεός (**81 occurrences** [**3 × 27**]) + υἱός (56 occurrences [**4 × 14**]) = **396 occurrences** [**18 × 22**], arguably indicating, arithmetically, the significance of the number 18 (= life [חי] in Jesus's [ιη] Name)—here aligned with the factor **22**, which is a *NrN*, signifying alphabetical fullness (cf. the 22 radicals of the Hebrew alphabet).[34] The corresponding sum for 1 John, moreover, is **104 occurrences** [**4 × 26**], in other words, the sum of appearances of these same four *NS*: Ἰησοῦς (12 occurrences) + χριστός (8 occurrences) + θεός (62 occurrences) + υἱός (**22 occurrences**) = **104 occurrences** [**4 × 26**] (with a possible allusion to the numerical value of the Tetragrammaton, which is **26**; here together with the factor **4**, which may serve as a reference to universality: YHWH for everyone; cf. table 5.1, ch. 5). In other words, it appears that in both John and 1 John, Jesus as Christ and Son of God emerges as a potential textual center also in this numerological sense— with reference to the Tetragrammaton (see further ch. 5 above for similar examples, involving christological and Triune configurations). As we noted in chapters 3–5, *NrN* feature as well in the arrangement of the biblical canon: **22/24** (or 39) **Old Testament books, 27 New Testament books, 66 writings** [**3 × 22**] in the standard Protestant canon; and **260 chapters** [**10 × 26**] in the standard New Testament.

---

34. The sum of the occurrences of the four Johannine terms appears as *NrN* in THGNT, Codex Sinaiticus, and TR; Ἰησοῦς (**240 times** [**10 × 24**]) + χριστός (19 times) + θεός (**81 times** [**3 × 27**]) + υἱός (56 times) = **396 times** [**18 × 22**] in THGNT (as for the sum 396 pertaining to "life," חי, cf. also note above); Ἰησοῦς (237 times) + χριστός (18 times) + θεός (82 times) + υἱός (53 times) = **390 times** [**10 × 39 = 15 × 26**] in ℵ; Ἰησοῦς (254 times) + χριστός (21 times) + θεός (84 times) + υἱός (57 times) = **416 times** [**16 × 26**] in Textus Receptus. See table 5.1, ch. 5, for potential significance of the numbers 10 and 39. Corresponding figure in ℵ for 1 John is: Ἰησοῦς (11 times) + χριστός (8 times) + θεός (64 times) + υἱός (**22 times**) = **105 times** [**7 × 15**]. We may also note the following parallel in the Hebrew Bible: By specifying the **396 occurrences** [**18 × 22**] of חי, "life; living" in the MT, these 396 occurrences in the twenty-four-book Hebrew Bible may here be intentionally linked to the sum in John of the occurrences of Ἰησοῦς (**240 times** [**10 × 24**]) + χριστός (19 times) + θεός (**81 times** [**3 × 27**]) + υἱός (56 times) = **396 times** [**18 × 22**]; cf. also the **396 occurrences** [**18 × 22**] of YHWH in the book of Numbers.

Interestingly, as a literary midpoint also in the First Gospel, the bringing together of the two christological titles— CHRIST/MESSIAH (x̄c̄) and SON of GOD (ȳc̄ τoy θ̄ȳ)—is managed somewhat differently, namely by extending Peter's confession in Mark 8:29 to include, as well, an explicit reference to Jesus's sonship. This is done by placing the confession in Matt 16:16 (cy ei o x̄c̄ o ȳc̄ τoy θ̄ȳ τoy zωntoc [א], "You are the CHRIST, the SON of the living GOD") in the narrative middle. Early Christian scriptoria decided to place this particular verse right at the center of Matthew, namely as the middle, 203rd, paragraph (out of Matthew's altogether 405 paragraphs, in line with the ancient paragraph division, adopted by THGNT).

Other New Testament attempts at presenting the core, key structure, or the sum, of the gospel can also be found elsewhere in the Gospels, and beyond. The presentation of Jesus's opening of his ministry at the outset of the Galilean ministry (Mark 1:15 par.) amounts to precisely that.[35] Luke, too, seeks to convey the central gospel preaching in the book of Acts (Acts 2:14–40; and 10:34–43).[36] In Paul, moreover, we encounter brief kerygmatic statements: in Rom 10:9–13, the *homologia*/confession "JESUS is LORD" (κ̄c̄ ῑc̄) coupled with the belief that "GOD [θ̄c̄] raised him from the dead," and in 1 Cor 1:17/Phil 3:18 with reference to the "CROSS of CHRIST" (c̄τρoc̄ τoy x̄ρȳ; c̄τρoy τoy x̄ρȳ; P[46]; cf. §5.10 above, for related arithmetical–kerygmatic NS configurations). In the modern period, we may also notice Martin Kähler's portrayal of the literary structure of the Gospels as passion narratives supplied with introductions (cf. §1.4 above).

---

35. Cf. Hengel's (*Four Gospels and the One Gospel*, 95) comment on Mark 1:15: "The εὐαγγέλιον τοῦ θεοῦ of the dawn of the rule of God preached by Jesus on his public appearance (1.15), which is a thematic summary of the beginnings of his message, extends throughout Jesus' words and actions, passion and resurrection to become the comprehensive εὐαγγέλιον Ἰησοῦ χριστοῦ υἱοῦ θεοῦ at the beginning (1.1), which gives the work its title. Even Jesus' exaltation to the right hand of God and his Parousia are addressed here by way of anticipation; indeed one can ask whether hints like 1.2; 12.6 and 37 do not even cautiously indicate the pre-existence of Christ."

36. Cf. Craig S. Keener, *Acts: An Exegetical Commentary*, vol 1: *Introduction and 1:1–2:47* (Grand Rapids: Baker Academic, 2012), 862–990.

13.5 THE IMPORTANCE OF
STRUCTURE FOR LEARNING

On a more general, didactic, note, we may here recall the benefits for learning that *structure* may provide for the things to be learned. When, in this book, we have discussed Christ as center, canonical arrangement, *regula fidei* as Triune-christological summary and the related NS as supra-textual matrix, Jerome Bruner's classic work, *The Process of Education*, is of interest for our argument. Bruner writes:

> Grasping the structure of a subject is understanding it in a way that permits many other things to be related to it meaningfully. To learn structure, in short, is to learn how things are related. ... The teaching and learning of structure, rather than simply the mastery of facts and techniques, is at the center of the classic problem of transfer. ... Learning should not only take us somewhere; it should allow us later to go further more easily.[37]

The organizing textual and doctrinal function ascribed to the Rule of Faith, in the early church, may, indeed, be a good illustration of Bruner's didactic emphasis on the importance of structure—the Rule as it articulates the faith, relating as well to the shaping of church dogmatics, the scriptural NS system, and the canonical scope and arrangement of the Old and New Testaments.[38] As we saw in chapter 11, Irenaeus, too, appeals to the *regula*

---

37. Jerome S. Bruner, *The Process of Education*, rev. ed., Kindle ed. (Cambridge: Harvard University Press, 1977), Kindle locations 249–50, 291–92, 336, respectively. Cf. also Kindle locations 339–43: "Learning in school undoubtedly creates skills of a kind that transfers to activities encountered later, either in school or after. A second way in which earlier learning renders later performance more efficient is through what is conveniently called nonspecific transfer or, more accurately, the transfer of principles and attitudes. In essence, it consists of learning initially not a skill but a general idea, which can then be used as a basis for recognizing subsequent problems as special cases of the idea originally mastered. This type of transfer is at the heart of the educational process—the continual broadening and deepening of knowledge in terms of basic and general ideas." I am grateful to Michael Hedrick for directing me to Bruner's work.

38. Cf. Ben Myers, *The Apostles' Creed: A Guide to the Ancient Catechism*, Christian Essentials (Bellingham, WA: Lexham Press, 2018), 4: "The rule of faith had two functions. First, it was educational. It formed the basis of catechesis for new believers. ... The threefold confession of faith was to be written on the heart so that it could never be lost or forgotten. ... Second, the rule of faith was sacramental. It was not only used as a catechism in preparation for baptism but was also part of the baptismal rite itself. A person becomes a disciple of Jesus and a member of his community by making the threefold pledge of allegiance. Baptism is a threefold immersion into the life of God. The baptism

fidei matrix when presenting the Christian faith and the basic interpretative pattern he associates with Christian Scripture reading.

13.6 LEARNING THE RULE OF FAITH

On a preconclusionary note, we may thus, again, bring to mind Irenaeus's rich account of the interpretative principle of the *regula fidei/veritatis*—embraced by catechized and baptized Christians—by means of three examples: (1) pertaining to the Gospels: "These [the four Gospel writers] have all declared to us that there is one GOD, Creator of heaven and earth, announced by the Law and the Prophets; and one CHRIST, the SON of GOD" (*Haer.* 3.1.2); (2) pertaining to the christological inner structuring of Old Testament Scripture: "For if anyone reads the [Jewish] Scriptures with attention, they will find in them an account of Christ ... for Christ is the treasure which was hid in the field" (*Haer.* 4.26.1; see further chs. 2 and 6 above);[39] and (3) pertaining to the Rule of Faith received by the catechumens and passed on in the church, as phrased in *Demonstration of the Apostolic Preaching*:

And this is the drawing-up of our faith, the foundation of the building, and the consolidation of a way of life. GOD, the FATHER, uncreated, beyond grasp, invisible, one GOD the maker of all; this is the first and foremost article of our faith. But the second article is the Word of GOD, the SON of GOD, CHRIST JESUS our LORD, who was shown forth by the prophets according to the design of their prophecy and according to the manner in which the FATHER disposed; and through Him were made all things whatsoever. He also, *in the end of times* [cf. Dan 11:13], for the recapitulation of all things, is become a MAN among MEN, visible and tangible, in order to abolish death and bring to light life, and bring about the communion of GOD and MAN. And the third article is the Holy SPIRIT,

---

of our regeneration takes place through these three articles, granting us regeneration unto God the Father through his Son by the Holy Spirit.' [reference to Irenaeus, *Epid.* 7]."

39. Similarly Clement of Alexandria, and Origen: "All the Scriptures are one book because all the teaching [λόγου] that has come to us about Christ is recapitulated in one single whole" (*Comm. Jo.* 5.6)"; also quoted in §§1.2 and 2.3 above.

through whom the prophets prophesied and the patriarchs were taught about GOD and the just were led in the path of justice, and who *in the end of times* has been poured forth in a new manner upon humanity over all the earth renewing MAN to GOD (Iren. *Epid.* 6).[40]

By the Rule, Irenaeus here ultimately refers to truth itself, which has been revealed—the divine, and the revelatory events themselves—or the faith that rests on this revelation, that is, on the facts of salvation history.[41]

An additional didactic *regula fidei* dimension is articulated through the Lyons bishop's confidence that those among the gentiles who cannot read the Scriptures, nonetheless may acquire knowledge of the corresponding faith content conveyed through the Rule (cf. *Haer.* 3.4.1–2). And, to those who want to proceed further in knowledge and faith, Irenaeus commends the firm *regula fidei* pattern also for future exploration of the Scriptures: "Whoever keeps the Rule of Truth, which they received through baptism, unchanged in their heart, will know … [the things taught] from the Scriptures. (*Haer.* 3.4.1).[42] Tertullian boldly expresses a similar thought: "To know nothing against the Rule, is to know everything" (*Adversus regulam nihil scire, omnia scire est; Praescr.* 14.5).

Clement of Alexandria, as we saw (ch. 11), further notes a related structural element that the Rule of Faith/ecclesiastical canon provides for continuous Scripture reading in the following dense phrasing: "The Canon of the Church is the agreement and unity of the Law and the Prophets with the Testament delivered at the coming of the Lord" (*Strom.* 6.125.2). The point Clement is making regarding this scriptural balancing—or inner coordinating of the Jewish Scriptures directed toward their fulfillment at the coming of the Lord Jesus—is related to what Irenaeus is doing when displaying the major Christology portion of the Rule, as part of the third article about the Spirit of prophecy (*Haer.* 1.10.1); or when relating the

---

40. Irenaeus, *Proof of the Apostolic Preaching*, trans. Joseph P. Smith, ACW 16 (New York: Newman, 1952), 51 (emphasis added).

41. Bengt Hägglund, *Sanningens regel, Regula Veritatis: Trosregeln och den kristna traditionens struktur* (Skellefteå: Artos, 2003), 16.

42. Similarly in the first book of *Adversus Haereses*: "Anyone who keeps unchangeable in himself the Rule of the Truth received through baptism will recognize the names and sayings and parables from the Scriptures" (*Haer.* 1.9.4).

Rule to the sequential ordering of the Scriptures (1.8–9) and to the one and only God being scripturally disclosed (*Haer.* 3.1.2 and *Epid.* 6; quoted above). Overall, the Rule implements a two-testament structure to the canonically unified Scriptures, a Triune christological reading, and a deep canonical appreciation for the Old Testament texts also in their own right (*Haer.* 1.8.1–10.1).[43]

As part of a broad discussion of the *regula fidei*, it is important to keep in mind also its universality feature: the *regula fidei* (the faith) as one and the same Rule of Faith (faith) for everyone—ecumenically safeguarding a common Christian teaching and identity. In Irenaeus's phrasing:

> The church, indeed, though disseminated throughout the world, even to the ends of the earth, received from the apostles and their disciples the faith in one GOD the FATHER. ... For, though the languages throughout the world are dissimilar, nevertheless the content/substance/power of the tradition [ἡ δύναμις τῆς παραδόσεως] is one and the same. To explain, the churches which have been founded in Germany do not believe or hand down anything else; neither do those founded in Spain or Gaul or Libya or in the central regions of the world. But just as the sun, GOD's creation, is one and the same throughout the world, so too the light, preaching of the truth, shines everywhere and enlightens all men who wish to come to the knowledge of the truth. ... For, since the faith is one and the same, neither they who can discourse at length about it add to it, nor they who can say only a little substract from it (*Haer.* 1.10.1–2).

---

43. For a more detailed account of the relationship between the Rule of Faith and the canon formation process, see Tomas Bokedal, "The Rule-of-Faith Pattern and the Formation of Canonical Sub-Units—A Proposal," in *The New Testament Canon in Contemporary Research*, ed. Benjamin P. Laird and Stanley E. Porter, TENTS (Leiden: Brill, forthcoming). Hägglund, *Regula Veritatis*, 44 (my translation): "The content of the Old Testament does not only consist of the historical background to the Christian religion, but belongs to the plan of salvation, which in Jesus Christ has achieved its completion and final explanation. It is not only the case that the Old Testament types and promises are interpreted from the viewpoint of fulfillment and from the facts to which the Gospels testify; but also in the sense that the series of events in the new covenant are interpreted so that they correspond with the Old Testament revelation, and thus together form a unified order of salvation history."

13.7 ROYAL IMAGERY

Coming to a close, we will end, as we began, with Irenaeus's mosaic of the "beautiful image of a king, carefully made out of precious stones" (*Haer.* 1.8.1), directing us to a vision of the whole—how the bits and pieces relate to the finished work (see introduction). Irenaeus puts emphasis on the different assertions made in the Scriptures as part of a totality, a scriptural (theological) whole. The three early Christian text-regulative strategies of canon, Rule of Faith, and *nomina sacra*—as argued in the present study—provided the church with its key hermeneutical principles, aligned with the anticipation of the fuller picture, the textual whole. The canon and its textual subunits set a limit for the text and helped define an agenda for normative reading in close affiliation with the *regula fidei* (chs. 2–5); the Rule of Faith provided a firm set of principles for basic Christian text hermeneutics and theological reading (ch. 11); and the canonical Triune-christological *NS* assisted in the textual and theological connection of the two—Scripture with *regula*, *regula* with Scripture (chs. 5–12).[44]

It is not difficult to see here the hard-edged contrast between this Rule-of-Faith pattern of scriptural interpretation and Ulrich Luz' portrayal of historical-critical method in biblical studies, mentioned in the opening sections of this study (see §1.2 above):

The interpretations of the ancient church, the Middle Ages, and the early modern period before the Enlightenment are of abiding importance, because they always connect an individual biblical

---

44. As for NrN, discussed in chs. 5–10 above, we may note the following (in boldface) for the sum in the New Testament writings of the word-frequencies of the two Greek words that make up the expression "Holy Scripture," ἁγία γραφή, used by Justin Martyr, Theophilus of Antioch, and others: ἅγιος + γραφή (THGNT) Matthew 14 times, Matthew–Mark **24 times**, Luke **24 times**, Synoptic Gospels **48 times** [2 × 24], John 17 times, four Gospels **66 times** [3 × 22], Luke-Acts **85 times** [5 × 17], Romans 27 times, 1–2 Corinthians **22 times**, Catholic Epistles **24 times**, Praxapostolos **85 times** [5 × 17], New Testament **286 times** [11 × 26 = 13 × 22] (cf. table 5.1 above). These NrN figures may indicate an awareness among those responsible for composing and editing the New Testament writings of producing holy writ, alongside the Jewish Scriptures (cf. also the following figures for *BHS*: כתב (unpointed), "to write; writing," MT **260 times** [10 × 26], Deuteronomy 22 times, 2 Kings **30 times** [2 × 15], Esther 26 times, the Prophets (Former and Latter) 105 times [7 × 15], the Writings 117 times [3 × 39]; כְּתָב, "writing," MT **17 times**; and for the New Testament (THGNT): γραφ*, "writ-," twenty-seven-book New Testament **240 times** [10 × 24], Matthew–Mark 27 times, Luke **24 times**, Synoptic Gospels **51 times** [3 × 17], Pauline Corpus **78 times** [3 × 26], 1–2 Corinthians **30 times** [2 × 15], Catholic Epistles **30 times** [2 × 15], and 1–2 John **15 times**.

text to the entirety and the center of faith, whether that be the two-natures doctrine, the *regula fidei*, gnostic enlightenment, church dogma, or the Reformation's justification by faith. By contrast, historical-critical scholarship distances the text to be interpreted not only from the interpreters, their faith convictions, and the church's belief; it also, by emphasizing its distinctiveness, distances the text from the entirety of the biblical witness.[45]

Over the past two centuries, in historical-critical engagement with Old and New Testament texts, none of the four domains stressed in the present study (Christ as textual center, a broad canonical approach to the text, the Rule-of-Faith pattern, and the closely aligned system of NS as vital to Old Testament/New Testament exegesis and devotional-creedal shaping of the canon) obtained any significant role, if at all noticed.[46] However,

---

45. Ulrich Luz, *Matthew 1–7: A Commentary*, rev. ed., Hermeneia (Minneapolis: Fortress, 2007), 64. Cf. Peter Stuhlmacher, *Historical Criticism and Theological Interpretation of Scripture: Toward a Hermeneutic of Consent* (London: SPCK, 1977), 62: "Historical criticism detaches from the present the historical phenomena which it examines, and despite all tradition and the history of their effects, describes them at a historical distance. Historical criticism of the traditional variety thus distances history from the present and achieves no union of the then and the now. This distancing effect is welcome and tolerable only so long as the goal of historical research is the intellectual mastery of history and the emancipation from all inhibiting tradition. But as such this cannot be the aim of a church whose very identity stands or falls by its connection with Holy Scripture."

46. Cf. Straus's ("Word as Word," 7) cautious use of historical-critical method, while, at the same time, drawing on reception-historical, theological, and other dimensions in translation into English of the Greek New Testament text: "And while it [Straus's thesis on method in translating the New Testament] credits the importance of historical-critical research into the 'world behind the text,' it neither limits textual meaning to what is 'imagin[ed]' to be present in the minds of ancient writers [references to Antonio Piñero and Jesús Peláez, *The Study of the New Testament: A Comprehensive Introduction*, Tools for Biblical Study 3 (Leiden: Deo, 2003), 345; and Donald A. Hagner and Stephen E. Young, "The Historical-Critical Method and the Gospel of Matthew," in *Methods for Matthew*, ed. Mark Allan Powell, Methods in Biblical Interpretation (Cambridge: Cambridge University Press, 2009), 15], nor translates with the goal of 'reproduc[ing]' the same in the minds of modern readers [reference to Eugene Nida and Charles R. Taber, *The Theory and Practice of Translation*, Helps for Translators 8 (Leiden: Brill, 1969), 200]." Cf. Tomas Bokedal, *The Formation and Significance of the Christian Biblical Canon: A Study in Text, Ritual and Interpretation* (London: Bloomsbury T&T Clark, 2014), 51, applying aspects of Hans-Georg Gadamer's notion of the classic to the biblical canon: "understanding ... the church's canon implies an historical and a normative aspect, both of which ask for contextualization in the present situation. Precisely as classic, then, the canon has the potential of surviving the contingencies of history, as well as historical reflection. In Gadamer's phrasing: 'the classical is something that resists historical criticism because its historical dominion, the binding power of the validity that is preserved and handed down, precedes all historical reflection and continues in it.' Inasmuch as it functions as classic for the present, Gadamer puts forth the classical as a 'truly historical category, precisely because it is more than a concept of a period or of a historical

glimpses of a change of attitude and methodology among biblical exegetes can be seen in scholars such as Brevard S. Childs, Markus Bockmuehl, and others.[47]

Yet, as we have seen throughout our discussion, to earlier informed minds, such as Irenaeus (ca. 125–202 AD) on the *regula fidei*, and Augustine (354–430 AD) and Martin Luther (1483–1564) on the related *symbolum/* creed, the Rule-of-Faith pattern was vital for Christian canonical reading, biblical theology, doctrinal structuring, faith, and identity. Further, to them, the Old Testament, the New Testament and dogmatics were not separate disciplines/areas of study, but could, and needed to, be studied together.

Accordingly, Irenaeus helps us to further reflect on the transmission of Christian faith in the introductory lines of his *Demonstration of the Apostolic Preaching (Epideixis).*[48] The theme as well as the literary structure of this early catechetical work from around AD 202, addressed to Marcianus, concern the *regula fidei*, here referred to simply as the faith:

> Knowing, my dear Marcianus, your inclination to walk the path of GOD's service (which alone brings man to eternal life), I both congratulate you, and pray that you may keep the faith in its purity and so be well-pleasing to GOD your Maker. Would it were possible for us to be always together, to help each other, and to relieve

---

style.' " Cf. also Hans-Georg Gadamer, *The Relevance of the Beautiful and Other Essays*, ed. with an introduction by Robert Bernasconi, trans. Nicholas Walker (Cambridge: Cambridge University Press, 1986), 142: "What speaks to us in Holy Scripture certainly does not rest primarily upon the art of writing, but upon the authority of the one who speaks to us in the Church."

47. See, e.g., Childs, *Biblical Theology of the Old and New Testaments: Theological Reflection on the Christian Bible* (London, SCM, 1992), 87: "It also seems to me true that after the task of biblical theological reflection has begun in which the original integrity of both testaments has been respected, there is an important function of hearing the whole of Christian scripture in the light of the full reality of God in Jesus Christ" (cf. also §1.2 above); and Bockmuehl, *Seeing the Word: Refocusing New Testament Study*, Studies in Theological Interpretation, Kindle ed. (Grand Rapids: Baker Academic, 2006), Kindle location 1414–18: "There is in fact a strong case that the New Testament text itself begs to be read systematically, whether as a canonical whole or in its constituent parts. This is not inherently a novel idea: among recent writers on New Testament theology, Peter Stuhlmacher (esp. 1992–99, including his summary: 2.309–11), Ferdinand Hahn (2002), and others (e.g., I. H. Marshall 2004 and Matera 2005) stress such coherent diversity. Here it seems worth reiterating this concern as something to which the New Testament itself points as its implied reading. This is in a sense a corollary to the argument we developed ... [above]: not only does the New Testament imply a certain kind of reader, but in fact the shape of its own text elicits at least the outline of a certain kind of reading."

48. Irenaeus, *Proof of the Apostolic Preaching*, 47–50.

the preoccupations of earthly life by daily conference on profit-
able themes. As it is, since we are at the present time distant in
body from each other, we have not delayed, so far as may be, to
commune with you a little in writing, and to set forth in brief the
preaching of the truth, to confirm your faith. What we are sending
you is in the form of notes on the main points, so that you may find
much matter in short space, comprehending in a few details all the
members of the body of truth, and receiving in brief the proof of
the things of GOD. (*Epid.* 1, modified)

Piety is clouded and loses its luster by contamination, by impu-
rity of body, and is broken and stained and loses its integrity when
falsehood enters the soul but it will be preserved in beauty and
measure by the constant abiding of truth in the mind and of holiness in the body. For what is the use of knowing the truth in word,
while defiling the body and accomplishing the works of evil? Or
what real good at all can bodily holiness do, if truth be not in the
soul? For these two rejoice in each other's company, and agree
together and fight side by side to set man in the presence of GOD.
(*Epid.* 2, modified)

So, ... we must keep strictly, without deviation, the Rule of
Faith, and carry out the commands of GOD, believing in GOD,
and fearing him, because he is LORD, and loving him, because he
is FATHER. Action, then, is preserved by faith, because *unless you
believe*, says Isaias, *you shall not continue*; and faith is given by truth,
since faith rests upon reality: for we shall believe what really is, as
it is, and, believing what really is, as it is forever, keep a firm hold
on our assent to it. Since, then, it is faith that maintains our salvation, one must take great care of this sustenance, to have a true
perception of reality.

Now, this is what faith does for us, as the elders, the disciples of
the apostles, have handed down to us. First of all, it admonishes us
to remember that we have received baptism for remission of sins in
the name of GOD the FATHER, and in the name of JESUS CHRIST,
the SON of GOD, who became incarnate and died and was raised,

and in the Holy SPIRIT of GOD; and that this baptism is the seal of
eternal life and is rebirth unto GOD, that we be no more children
of mortal men, but of the eternal and everlasting GOD; and that
the eternal and everlasting One *is* God, and is above all creatures,
and that all things whatsoever are subject to him; and that what is
subject to him was all made by him, so that GOD is not ruler and
LORD of what is another's, but of his own, and all things are GOD'S;
that GOD, therefore, is the Almighty, and all things whatsoever are
from GOD. (*Epid.* 3, modified)

Augustine, as we saw, identified the Apostles' Creed "as a briefly compiled
rule of faith" (*Sermo* 213).[49] This understanding of the Rule continued in
the church. For Martin Luther, too, the Apostles' Creed seems to have
functioned as a condensed rule of faith.[50] Luther, who regularly recited
the Apostles' Creed at least eight times per day (morning and evening,
before and after meals), warmly embraces the Creed, emphasizing both
the subjective and objective side of faith:[51]

---

49. Cf. also Augustine, *Symb.* 1 (*NPNF* 1/3.1:369): "Receive, my children, the Rule of Faith, which
is called the Symbol (or Creed). And when ye have received it, write it in your heart, and be daily
saying it to yourself." As noted by Kelly (*Early Christian Creeds*, 40–52, 60–61), Andrew Louth
(*Discerning the Mystery: An Essay on the Nature on Theology* [Oxford: Clarendon, 1983], 84), and
Anthony Thiselton (*New Horizons in Hermeneutics: The Theory and Practice of Transforming Biblical
Reading* [Grand Rapids: Zondervan, 1992]), Irenaeus's understanding of the actual content of the
regula fidei "comes extremely close in verbal form to the wording of the Apostles' Creed" (Thiselton,
New Horizons in Hermeneutics, 156). See further Liuwe H. Westra, *The Apostles' Creed: Origin, History,
and Some Early Commentaries,* Instrumenta Patristica 43 (Turnhout: Brepols, 2002), 56–60; 37–43;
over against alternative theories (Wolfram Kinzig et al.), Westra offers support to Kelly's view of
the close continuity between the early *regula fidei* pattern, in particular as expressed through the
early triadic baptismal interrogation practice: "Kelly considers baptismal questions ('interrogatory
creeds') and declaratory summaries of faith ('creeds in the strict sense of the term') as more or less
interchangeable manifestations of the same phenomenon, of which the baptismal questions came
first. ... One may well wonder whether Kelly's point of view, according to which the baptismal questions are nothing more than the Creed in interrogatory form, may not come near the truth after all.
This hypothesis is strengthened by a number of sources" (56, 58). See also note on Kelly's view above.

50. See Todd R. Hains ("Martin Luther and the Analogy of Faith" [PhD diss., Trinity Evangelical
Divinity School, 2019], 17, 14–15) for helpful comments on the relationship between the Apostles'
Creed, the analogy of faith (*analogia fidei*), the analogy of Scripture (*analogia scripturae*), and the
rule of faith (*regula fidei*).

51. Cf. Hains, "Martin Luther and the Analogy of Faith," 11n44, referring to Bengt Hägglund ("Die
Bedeutung der Regula fidei als Grundlage theologischer Aussagen," *ST* 12 [1958]: 1–44): "Modern
theologians tend to restrict faith to its subjective sense only (*fides qua creditur*). He [Hägglund] states
that the rule of faith embodies 'the entire teaching of the church, the teaching that was proclaimed

I believe the words of the Apostles' Creed to be the work of the Holy Ghost; the Holy Spirit alone could have enunciated things so grand, in terms so precise, so expressive, so powerful. No human creature could have done it, nor all the human creatures of ten thousand worlds. This Creed, then, should be the constant object of our most serious attention. For myself, I cannot too highly admire or venerate it.[52]

BIBLIOGRAPHY

Augustine. *De symbolo ad catechumenos 1*. NPNF 1/3.1:369–75.

Bauckham, Richard J. "Christology." Pages 125–34 in *Dictionary of Jesus and the Gospels*. Edited by Joel B. Green, Jeannine K. Brown, and Nicholas Perrin. 2nd ed. Downers Grove, IL: IVP Academic, 2013.

Beyschlag, Karlmann. *Grundriß der Dogmengeschichte*. Vol. 1: *Gott und Welt*. Darmstadt: Wissenschaftliche Buchgesellschaft, 1982.

Bockmuehl, Markus. *Seeing the Word: Refocusing New Testament Study*. Studies in Theological Interpretation. Kindle ed. Grand Rapids: Baker Academic, 2006.

Bokedal, Tomas. "'But for Me, the Scriptures Are Jesus Christ' ($\overline{IC}$ $\overline{XC}$; Ign. *Phld*. 8:2): Creedal Text-Coding and the Early Scribal System of Nomina Sacra." In *Studies on the Paratextual Features of Early New Testament Manuscripts*. Edited by Stanley E. Porter, David I. Yoon, and Chris S. Stevens. TENTS. Leiden: Brill, 2023.

---

by the apostles and prophets and that is grounded in Scripture' (3–4, quoting p. 4); '*die ganze Lehre der Kirche, die Lehre die von den Aposteln und Propheten verkündigt worden und in der heiligen Schrift niedergelegt ist.*' Therefore, development is an inappropriate term for talking about Christian doctrine; the substance of Christian faith remains unchanged, though applied through new leaders and expositors to new situations and cultures (37). Hägglund calls theologians and exegetes to judge new methodologies by their interpretive fruits: do they fit with the faith (40)?"

52. Martin Luther, *Table Talk*, §cclxiv, https://ccel.org/ccel/luther/tabletalk/tabletalk.v.ix.html; for further reading, see, e.g., Myers, *Apostles' Creed*. John Calvin somewhere expresses a similar view: "What is noteworthy regarding the creed is this: We have in this a summary of our faith, perfect and complete in all details; and it contains nothing which does not have its foundation in the pure Word of God."

———. *The Formation and Significance of the Christian Biblical Canon: A Study in Text, Ritual and Interpretation*. London: T&T Clark, 2014.

———. "The Rule-of-Faith Pattern and the Formation of Canonical Sub-Units." In *The New Testament Canon in Contemporary Research*. Edited by Benjamin P. Laird and Stanley E. Porter. TENTS. Leiden: Brill, forthcoming.

Bruner, Jerome S. *The Process of Education*. Rev. ed. Kindle ed. Cambridge: Harvard University Press, 1977.

Butcher, S. H. *Aristotle's Theory of Poetry and Fine Art, with a Critical Text and Translation of the Poetics*. London: Macmillan, 1895.

Childs, Brevard S. *Biblical Theology of the Old and New Testaments: Theological Reflection on the Christian Bible*. London: SCM, 1992.

Collins, Adela Yarbro. *Mark: A Commentary*. Edited by Harold W. Attridge. Hermeneia. Minneapolis: Fortress, 2007.

Dinkler, Erich. "Kreuzzeichen und Kreuz: Tav, Chi und Stauros." Pages 1–25 in *Signum Crucis: Aufsätze zum Neuen Testament und zur christlichen Archäologie*. Tübingen: Mohr, 1967.

Edwards, Mark. *Catholicity and Heresy in the Early Church*. Farnham: Ashgate, 2009.

Gadamer, Hans-Georg. *The Relevance of the Beautiful and Other Essays*. Edited with an introduction by Robert Bernasconi. Translated by Nicholas Walker. Cambridge: Cambridge University Press, 1986.

Hägglund, Bengt. "Die Bedeutung der Regula fidei als Grundlage theologischer Aussagen." *ST* 12 (1958): 1–44.

———. *Sanningens regel—Regula Veritatis: Trosregeln och den kristna traditionens struktur*. Skellefteå: Artos, 2003.

Hagner, Donald A., and Stephen E. Young. "The Historical-Critical Method and the Gospel of Matthew." Pages 11–43 in *Methods for Matthew*. Edited by Mark Allan Powell. Methods in Biblical Interpretation. Cambridge: Cambridge University Press, 2009.

Hahn, Ferdinand, *Theologie des Neuen Testaments*, 2 vols. Tübingen: Mohr Siebeck, 2002.

Hains, Todd R. "Martin Luther and the Analogy of Faith." PhD diss., Trinity Evangelical Divinity School, 2019.

Hengel, Martin. *The Four Gospels and the One Gospel of Jesus Christ: An Investigation of the Collection and Origin of the Canonical Gospels.* Translated by John Bowden. London: SCM, 2000.

Holmes, Michael. *Apostolic Fathers: Greek Texts and English Translations of Their Writings.* 3rd ed. Grand Rapids: Baker Academic, 2007.

Hurtado, Larry W. *The Earliest Christian Artifacts: Manuscripts and Christian Origins.* Grand Rapids: Eerdmans, 2006.

———. "The Origin of the Nomina Sacra: A Proposal." *JBL* 117 (1998): 655–73.

Irenaeus. *Proof of the Apostolic Preaching.* Translated by Joseph P. Smith. ACW 16. New York: Newman, 1952.

Keener, Craig S. *Acts: An Exegetical Commentary.* Vol. 1: *Introduction and 1:1–2:47.* Grand Rapids: Baker Academic, 2012.

———. *Galatians: A Commentary.* Grand Rapids: Baker Academic, 2019.

Kelly, J. N. D. *Early Christian Creeds.* 3rd ed. London: Continuum, 2006.

Kinzig, Wolfram. *Faith in Formulae: A Collection of Early Christian Creeds and Creed-Related Texts.* 4 vols. Oxford Early Christian Texts. Oxford: Oxford University Press, 2017.

Louth, Andrew. *Discerning the Mystery: An Essay on the Nature on Theology.* Oxford: Clarendon, 1983.

Luz, Ulrich. *Matthew 1–7: A Commentary.* Rev. ed. Hermeneia. Minneapolis: Fortress, 2007.

Marshall, I. Howard. *New Testament Theology: Many Witnesses, One Gospel.* Downers Grove, IL: IVP & Leicester, England: Apollos, 2004.

Matera, Frank J., *New Testament Theology: Exploring Diversity and Unity.* Louisville & London: Westminster John Knox Press, 2007.

Myers, Ben. *The Apostles' Creed: A Guide to the Ancient Catechism.* Christian Essentials. Bellingham, WA: Lexham Press, 2018.

Nida, Eugene A., and Charles R. Taber. *The Theory and Practice of Translation.* Helps for Translators 8. Leiden: Brill, 1969.

Piñero, Antonio, and Jesús Peláez. *The Study of the New Testament: A Comprehensive Introduction.* Tools for Biblical Study 3. Leiden: Deo, 2003.

Roberts, C. H. *Manuscript, Society and Belief in Early Christianity.* Schweich Lectures 1977. Oxford: Oxford University Press, 1979.

Straus, Michael. "The Word as Word: A Canonical-Hermeneutical Approach to Translation with Paul's Letter to the Colossians as a Test Case." PhD diss., University of Aberdeen, 2021.

Stuhlmacher, Peter. *Biblische Theologie des Neuen Testaments: Grundlegung. Von Jesus zu Paulus,* vol. 1. Göttingen: Vandenhoeck & Ruprecht, 1992, 2005.

———. *Biblische Theologie des Neuen Testaments: Von der Paulusschule bis zur Johannesoffenbarung Der Kanon und seine Auslegung,* vol. 2. Göttingen: Vandenhoeck & Ruprecht, 1999.

———. *Historical Criticism and Theological Interpretation of Scripture: Toward a Hermeneutic of Consent.* London: SPCK, 1977.

Thiselton, Anthony C. *New Horizons in Hermeneutics: The Theory and Practice of Transforming Biblical Reading.* Grand Rapids: Zondervan, 1992.

Wasserman, Tommy. "Historical and Philological Correlations and the CBGM as Applied to Mark 1:1." *TC: A Journal of Biblical Textual Criticism* 20 (2015): 1–11.

———. "The 'Son of God' Was in the Beginning (Mark 1:1)." *JTS* 62 (2011): 20–50.

Westra, Liuwe H. *The Apostles' Creed: Origin, History, and Some Early Commentaries.* Instrumenta Patristica 43. Turnhout: Brepols, 2002.

SUBJECT AND NAME INDEX

GREEK AND HEBREW
TERMS INDEX

GREEK

HEBREW

COMBINED GREEK
SEARCHES INDEX

This index lists where some combined searches are found, both in the format "term <AND> term" and in the format "term + term" (see 6.1 and 6.2). As the type of search is not distinguished below, the index utilizes *and* in italics, as opposed to "AND" and "+".

MODERN AUTHORS INDEX

SCRIPTURE INDEX

OLD TESTAMENT

NEW TESTAMENT

OTHER ANCIENT
WITNESSES INDEX

EVERY PAGE IS THE
LONG STORY SHORT

The Evangelical Biblical Theology Commentary (EBTC) series locates each biblical
book within redemptive history and illuminates its unique theological contributions.
All EBTC volumes feature informed exegetical treatment of the biblical book and
thorough discussion of its most important theological themes in relation to the
canon—in a style that is useful and accessible to students of Scripture.

LexhamPress.com/EBTC